Java™ Programming: Advanced Topics

Third Edition

Joe Wigglesworth
IBM Toronto Software Lab
Paula McMillan
IBM Toronto Software Lab

THOMSON

COURSE TECHNOLOGY

Australia • Canada • Mexico • Singapore • Spain • United Kingdom • United States

Java Programming: Advanced Topics, Third Edition

is published by Course Technology.

Managing Editor:
Jennifer Muroff

Product Manager:
Alyssa Pratt

Associate Product Manager:
Janet Aras

Editorial Assistant:
Amanda Piantedosi

Production Editor:
Aimee Poirier

Developmental Editor:
Sydney Jones

Cover Designer:
Nancy Goulet

Disclaimer
Course Technology reserves the right to revise this publication and make changes from time to time in its content without notice.

The Web addresses in this book are subject to change from time to time as necessary without notice.

Sun is a registered trademark of Sun Microsystems. Java and JavaBeans are trademarks of Sun Microsystems. DB2 and WebSphere are registered trademarks of International Business Machines Corporation.

ISBN 0-619-15968-5

BRIEF
Contents

TABLE OF

Contents

CHAPTER ELEVEN
Network Programming   711

CHAPTER TWELVE
Security   749

CHAPTER THIRTEEN
Building Web Applications   811

Preface

Welcome to *Java Programming: Advanced Topics, Third Edition!* This book is written for programmers who want to expand their knowledge of Java and related technologies from a beginner or introductory level to the level of practical skill expected of a professional programmer. Read this book if you fit any of these criteria:

- You have completed a first course in Java programming and want to master the language fully.

- You have used another object-oriented language, such as C++, and want to transfer your skills to Java and related technology.

- After a few months learning Java informally on the job, you want to consolidate your Java skills on a sound foundation.

Much of this book focuses on *Java 2 Standard Edition* (J2SE), and its primary goal is to cover all aspects of J2SE that may not be covered by a first course in Java programming.

Such has been the success of the Java 2 platform that it is now often a component—one could argue an enabling foundation—for many technologies that cooperate and interoperate to support the Web-based environment embraced by much of the information technology industry. The Internet and XML-based applications are other enabling foundations for the Web-based paradigm. A professional Java programmer must be able not only to code Java in isolation, but also to develop Java programs that interoperate with the Internet, XML, and other technologies.

For this reason, the later chapters of this book shift the focus to *Java 2 Enterprise Edition* (J2EE) and XML. These chapters cover the key elements of Java in enterprise and Web environments to the level often required of entry-level programmers.

HOW TO USE THIS BOOK

This book assumes you have mastered the basics of Java programming and begins where many introductory courses end. Some topics, such as creating multithreaded programs or using the Swing classes to build a graphical user interface (GUI), may repeat what you have learned previously. However, this book provides more comprehensive discussions than a typical first text and tries to explain the related concepts in greater depth than most introductory courses can achieve. Some chapters, such as the chapter on Enterprise JavaBeans may even be a stretch for a second course. Therefore, the enterprise chapters aim to present high-level concepts and sufficient detail for you to evaluate whether you need to continue your studies by pursuing these topics in greater depth.

The topics in the following list are not covered in this book because you should already know about them. However, many are used freely in code examples. As well as being common in first Java courses, these basics are well described by many Java tutorials that are available online or in CD format. You can use the quiz and questions at the end of Chapter 1 to review and test your knowledge of these Java basics:

- Understanding the role of the Java Virtual Machine (JVM) and the services it provides, such as garbage collection and dynamic loading of classes
- Using the Software Development Kit (SDK) command-line tools to compile and start programs
- Building Java programs that consist of several classes
- Grouping classes in packages and using **import** statements to resolve names defined in other packages
- Applying correct syntax to declarations, statements, and comments
- Understanding that a block of statements delimited by braces (**{** and **}**) is a scope and that the scope of variables declared within a block is limited to the block
- Using all Java language keywords and operators
- Building arithmetic, **boolean**, and character expressions
- Using **String** and **StringBuffer** objects to work with strings
- Manipulating arrays
- Coding loops and conditional statements
- Passing variables of primitive and reference types as method arguments and receiving variables of primitive and reference types as return values
- Calling the methods of **Math**, **System**, and other classes in the **java.lang** package; performing I/O to the predefined objects **System.in**, **System.out**, and **System.err**
- Overloading methods, including defining multiple constructors for a class
- Creating class variables and class methods using the keyword **static**
- Initializing local, instance, and class variables, including using static initializer blocks
- Wrapping primitive types in wrapper classes, such as **Integer**, **Boolean**, and **Double**, to use primitive values as objects
- Recognizing when implicit casting occurs and when explicit casting is allowed or required

- Defining interface types; defining classes that implement interfaces; defining interfaces that extend other interfaces; defining classes that extend other classes as well as implement interfaces

- Identifying situations where an abstract superclass is more appropriate than an interface

- Creating inheritance hierarchies of subtypes and supertypes; constraining inheritance with the **abstract** and **final** qualifiers

- Inheriting and overriding methods; overriding methods **equals**, **toString**, and **hashtable** of the **Object** class

- Understanding how dynamic binding selects an inherited or overriding instance method when calling a method on an object in an inheritance hierarchy

- Chaining constructors using the object references **this** and **super**; accessing members of the current class and superclass using the object references **this** and **super**

- Using private, protected, and package scopes to encapsulate data and behavior in classes; setting the visibility of class members using the qualifiers **public**, **private**, and **protected**

- Handling exceptions in try, catch, and finally blocks; nesting try and catch blocks and rethrowing exceptions from inner catch blocks to outer catch blocks

- Recognizing when **Throwable** objects are *checked exceptions* that must be declared in the throws clause of a method declaration

- Defining application-level exception classes that extend **java.lang.Exception**; throwing and handling application-level exceptions

- Building simple GUIs using the classes in the **java.awt** package

- Creating applets and embedding applets in Web pages; testing applets with the **appletviewer** utility and running them from a Web browser

OVERVIEW OF THE CHAPTERS IN THIS BOOK

This book consists of 14 chapters and 2 appendices. Three chapters are accompanied by primers on the CD. These primers supply background knowledge on non-Java technology required to understand the chapter's content. For example a primer on relational databases and SQL is associated with the Chapter 9 on Java database connectivity. Some chapters are accompanied by tutorials on the CD. Tutorials walk the reader through using IBM WebSphere Studio Application Developer (Application Developer) to build or run the examples in this book.

A fast-paced fourteen-week course may attempt to cover this entire book, but another course may spend more time on some chapters and skip others completely. The exercises and examples in all chapters are independent of those in other chapters, so you can alter the order or omit a chapter. However, each chapter does assume you know the material in preceding chapters.

- Chapters 1 through 9 complete the discussion of the J2SE platform begun in your first course in Java. These chapters cover topics that are considered advanced for students learning the Java language, such as inner classes, object serialization, the collections framework, multithreading, the JFC and Swing, JavaBeans, and using databases.

- Chapters 10 through 12 branch out into topics that are of great interest in the IT industry and are topical at this stage in the evolution of Java-related technology. The topics covered provide the foundation that makes Java attractive to enterprises where applications may be distributed over networks and run in business-to-business (B2B) or business-to-customer (B2C) situations.

- Chapters 13 and 14 cover J2EE topics and show how Java is now used with the Internet and in distributed applications.

Chapter 1, "Introduction to Advanced Java Programming," describes the three editions of the Java 2 platform. It reviews how Java supports object-oriented concepts. Standard tools that come with the Java platform are described here, and a popular integrated development environment (IDE), IBM WebSphere Studio Application Developer, is introduced.

Chapter 2, "Classes and Objects," covers advanced aspects of defining classes and manipulating objects in Java. The specific topics include finalizer methods and garbage collection, cloning objects, Runtime Type Information and the Application Programming Interface (API) for reflection, nested types, and inner classes.

Chapter 3, "Input/Output and Serialization," gives a brief review of I/O for byte- and character-oriented streams before moving on to file I/O, including random access files, the new I/O (NIO) programming interface of the **java.nio** package, and object serialization.

Chapter 4, "A Wealth of Utilities," concentrates on the packages **java.util** and **java.text**. Topics include using the Java collection framework, regular expressions, resource bundles and properties files, locales, and formatting data of different types.

Chapter 5, "Multithreading," provides a comprehensive discussion of multithreading including interthread communication and thread groups.

Chapter 6, "Common Elements of Graphical User Interfaces," introduces the Java Foundation Classes (JFC). It explains the principles of programming GUIs and the relationship between the Abstract Windowing Toolkit (AWT) and Swing classes. This chapter covers layout managers, the AWT event model, and the Swing separable-model architecture.

Chapter 7, "Components and Facilities for Rich Graphical User Interfaces," provides a survey of the Swing classes with plentiful code samples. This chapter also covers the Java print service API.

Chapter 8, "JavaBeans," introduces the JavaBean component model and describes the JavaBean specification in detail. Learn how to define a class that is a bean, manipulate the bean properties, and handle bean events. Create customized editors and a companion

`BeanInfo` class. Explore the demonstration Bean Development Environment provided by Sun Microsystems.

Chapter 9, "Using Relational Databases," describes Java Database Connectivity and the API in the `java.sql` and `javax.sql` packages. Learn how to connect to databases, send SQL statements to relational database management systems, and manipulate data stored in databases from your Java programs.

Chapter 10, "XML," introduces the technology that is rapidly becoming the industry standard for data transfer and interprogram communication. Learn what XML is and why Internet, XML, and Java technologies together are having a revolutionary effect on the IT industry. This chapter discusses tools and APIs with which Java programmers can manipulate XML files.

Chapter 11, "Network Programming," discusses the fundamentals of JVM support for applications that are distributed over networks. It discusses the `java.net` package and how to work with URLs and sockets. This chapter also explains how a class in one JVM can call a method on a class running another JVM through Remote Method Invocation.

Chapter 12, "Security," discusses how Java APIs and a number of relatively new technologies can be used together to ensure privacy, data integrity, authorize access when applications are distributed over a network. This chapter introduces some of the established technologies in this quickly evolving field, including the Secure Socket Layer (SSL) network protocol, public key encryption (PKI), digital signatures, the Java Authentication and Authorization Service (JAAS) APIs and Java cryptography tools.

Chapter 13, "Web Applications," teaches how to build Web-enabled applications that deliver truly dynamic content over the Web. Learn how Web browsers, Web servers, Application servers, HyperText Transfer Protocol (HTTP), HyperText Markup Language (HTML) or XML HyperText Markup Language (XHTML), and Java work together. The chapter focuses on programming servlets and Java Server Pages (JSPs).

Chapter 14, "Enterprise JavaBeans," gives an overview of Enterprise JavaBean (EJB) technology, in the process describing many of the key features of the Java 2 Enterprise Edition platform. This chapter describes session, entity, and message-driven beans. It explains how EJBs are used as distributable, transaction-aware, and secure components in large-scale enterprise applications. Learn how to build EJBs using the tools of Application Developer.

Appendix A, "Java- and Web-Related Technology," gives brief descriptions of features of the Java platform standard edition not covered in the chapters and gives an overview of enterprise edition services. It then introduces some technologies that build upon the Java platform, most notably Web services. Finally it discusses CORBA and the relationship between the Java platform and CORBA.

Appendix B, "Resources on the Web," is an HTML document on the CD-ROM. Load the file `AppendixB.html` into your Web browser when you are online, and then follow the links to resources for technologies and topics discussed in this book.

xx   **Java Programming: Advanced Topics, Third Edition**

FEATURES

Java Programming: Advanced Topics is an exceptional book because it also includes the following features:

- **Code examples**: In addition to code examples printed in the book, source and executable classes are provided on the CD-ROM so that you do not need to type any of the examples that appear in the book.

- **Software**: All software required to run the examples in this book is included on CD-ROM: a trial version of IBM WebSphere Studio Application Developer version 5.0, IBM DB2 UDB Personal Edition version 8.1.2, Java 2 Platform Standard Edition version 1.4.1 Software Development Kit, and JavaBeans Development Kit version 1.1. The CD-ROM also contains a copy of jGrasp.

- **Primers**: Three primers on the CD-ROM provide background knowledge in non-Java topics to support specific chapters. The primers are "Relational Databases and Structured Query Language" for Chapter 9, "HTML and XHTML" for Chapter 13, and "Messaging Middleware and the Java Message Service" for Chapter 14.

- **Tutorials**: Several tutorials on the CD-ROM supplement the directions for running samples by giving step-by-step directions for building and running selected examples in Application Developer.

- **Warnings**: The Java platform is an evolving software technology. New features are added with every version, and other features are deprecated. To deprecate a language feature or API is to associate a warning with it, so developers know to avoid it. Deprecated features may not be included in future versions of the Java platform; often the same functionality is provided by new and improved features. Warnings in this book point out new features and deprecated features and give historical perspective on the feature being discussed.

- **Code**: All code appears as `int=3`.

- **Keywords**: Keywords appear as `int`.

- **Tool and filenames**: Program filenames appear as `AssertTester.java`.

- **New terms**: New terms appear in *italics*.

CT TEACHING TOOLS

All the teaching tools for this text are found in the Instructor's Resource Kit, which is available from the Course Technology Web site (`www.course.com`) and on CD-ROM.

- **Instructor's Manual**: The Instructor's Manual has been quality assurance tested. It is available on CD-ROM and through the Course Technology Faculty Online Companion on the World Wide Web. The Instructor's Manual contains the following items:

  - Answers to all the questions and solutions to all the exercises.

- Chapter Notes, which contain background information from the author about the instructional progression of the chapter.

- Technical Notes, which include troubleshooting tips as well as information on how to customize the readers' screens to closely emulate the screen shots in the book.

■ **ExamView®.** This textbook is accompanied by ExamView, a powerful testing software package that allows instructors to create and administer printed, computer (LAN-based), and Internet exams. ExamView includes hundreds of questions that correspond to the topics covered in this text, enabling students to generate detailed study guides that include page references for further review. These computer-based and Internet testing components allow students to take exams at their computers, and save the instructor time because each exam is graded automatically.

■ **Solution files**: Solution files contain possible solutions to all the problems students are asked to create or modify in the end-of-chapter exercises. (Due to the nature of software development, student solutions might differ from these solutions and still be correct.)

■ **Data files**: Data files, containing all data that readers will use for the chapters and exercises in this textbook, are provided through Course Technology's Online Companion on the Instructor's Resource Kit CD-ROM and on the Student Resource Kit CD-ROM. A Help file includes technical tips for lab management.

ACKNOWLEDGMENTS

Joe Wigglesworth thanks his parents for their support through the years and thanks his wonderful wife, Maria, and their children, Darius and Iona, for their patience and understanding. Without support from Maria and smiles and laughter from Darius and Iona, this book would not have been possible.

Paula McMillan expresses gratitude to the Toronto practice of the WebSphere Training and Technical Enablement group for granting some time away from IBM to write this book, and to her adult children Joy, Alison, and Thomas Lumby for tolerating a distracted and over-busy mother during the writing period. Also family friend Sarah Sackrule made a significant contribution with moral support and 3:00 a.m. cups of tea.

We would like to thank the following reviewers: Alla Grinberg, Montgomery College; Craig Murray, Indiana University—Purdue University, Indianapolis; Erica Wilson, Northlake College; Anne B. Horton, AT&T Laboratories; Mahmood Doroodchi, Milwaukee Area Technical College; Scott Mutchler, Virginia Western Community College

Read This Before You Begin

To the Reader

Using the CD that Accompanies This Book

This book comes with two CDs. On these CDs you find all software required to work through the book and run all code examples, three primers, eight tutorials, and an Appendix B, as explained earlier in this preface. Tutorials are gathered into the folder `Tutorials` and primers into the `Primers` folder, both on the root folder of the CD-ROM. For more details on finding files and installing the software, refer to the `ReadMe.html` file in the root folder of the CD-ROM. You can view the `ReadMe.html` file using an HTML editor or a Web browser.

All code samples that appear in this book are stored in folder `Data\examples`, inside `Data\examples`, there is folder for each chapter. For example, you can find the sample programs for Chapter 5 in `X:\Data\examples\threads`, where `X` is the drive letter of your CD. Source code for selected end-of-chapter questions is stored in the folder `X:\Data\questions\c1` for Chapter 1, `X:\Data\questions\c2` for Chapter 2, and so on. You can copy the `data` folder to your hard drive. Alternatively, you can run most of the samples directly from the CD by adding `X:\Data` to your `CLASSPATH` environment variable, as described in the section, "How the Launcher Finds Classes," in Chapter 1. For instruction on running the examples in Application Developer, follow Tutorial A on the CD-ROM.

The Java 2 Platform Standard Edition Software Developer Kit (J2SDK) contains the JVM, Java compiler, and other command-line tools you can use to compile and run programs. Version 1.4.1 of the J2SDK is included on the CD. Most serious professional developers prefer an integrated development environment (IDE) and benefit enormously from the productivity tools most IDEs provide. This book uses the command-line tools where they are sufficient but also introduces the IBM WebSphere Studio Application Developer (Application Developer) product, a powerful IDE from IBM. In later chapters, where an application server is required, samples are based on the WebSphere test environment built into Application Developer. The CD-ROM that accompanies this book contains an installable copy of Application Developer version 5.0.

Some chapters require additional software: The samples in Chapter 9 access a relational database manager and a version of IBM DB2 UDB is on the CD. Chapter 8 uses the Beans Development Kit from Sun, and it is also included on the CD.

Using Your Own Computer

If you are going to work through this book using your own computer, you need:

- **Computer System**: Microsoft Windows XP or Microsoft Windows 2000 service pack 3 (or later), and the Java 2 Platform Software Development Kit (J2SDK), Standard Edition version 1.4 must be installed on your computer.

Visit Our World Wide Web Site

Additional materials designed especially for users of *Java Programming: Advanced Topics, Third Edition* and other Course Technology products are available on the World Wide Web. Go to www.course.com.

To the Instructor

The Java source and compiled code for all the example programs in this book are provided on the book's companion CD-ROM. You can also download these files over the Internet. See the inside front cover of this book for more details.

Course Technology Data Files

You are granted a license to copy the data files to any computer or computer network used by readers who have purchased this book.

1

INTRODUCTION TO ADVANCED JAVA PROGRAMMING

In this chapter you will:

♦ Review what Java is and differences between the three editions of the Java 2 platform: J2SE, J2EE, and J2ME

♦ Explore the context in which Java and related technologies are evolving

♦ See how Java supports object-oriented programming and look at some popular design patterns

♦ Learn how to use the basic tools that version 1.4 of Java 2 Software Development Kit provides, especially `javac`, `java`, `javadoc`, and `jar`

♦ Enter, compile, and run a sample program using IBM WebSphere Studio Application Developer

♦ Find out what is new in the 1.4 version of the standard Java platform

OVERVIEW OF THE JAVA PLATFORM

The appeal of Java is that it is more than just a programming language; it is also a platform. Most programming languages have no features for multithreading, GUI-building, or networking. They force you to use a hardware- or operating system–dependent API that binds programs to a specific hardware architecture or operating system. The Java platform is the first technology to fully integrate a programming language with operations usually performed by the native operating system in a way that lets you build programs that can run on a wide range of hardware architectures and host native operating systems.

When you install the current version of Java, you load the Java 2 platform on your system. The J2SDK provides a set of tools for developing and running Java programs, including the JVM, a compiler, and many other utilities. The SDK also includes documentation and compiled versions of all classes that make up the API provided by the Java platform. These classes are called the core classes and are grouped into packages.

The Java platform has become a leading standard for the IT industry, and even the most traditional environments are conforming to Java standards. Descriptions commonly applied to Java include:

■ The Java language is *object-oriented*. See the section "Object-Oriented Programming in Java" for an elaboration of this claim.

- Java code is *architecture-neutral* and *portable*. The JVM provides a standard for data storage, compiled bytecode, and interfaces to the native environment. Compiled classes run with consistent results on any implementation of a JVM.

- Java is not only *network-savvy* but also designed for use with the Internet and other TCP/IP-based networks.

- Many features of the Java language and API lend themselves to creating *robust* programs. For example, the JVM automatically performs memory management tasks that are notorious sources of problems in languages such as C and C++.

- Java programs are *secure*. Security is a complex issue for which there are problems and solutions at many levels. Security features of the JVM and security standards for Java, XML, and Web technologies are constantly developing to keep pace with emerging new uses for Java. Chapter 12 looks at some Java-related technologies for security.

- Java is *high performance*. Originally, the IT industry expressed concern that Java performance could not match compiled native code. However, just-in-time (JIT) compilers, improved garbage collection and multithreading algorithms, and other enhancements have narrowed the gap between Java code and native code to a virtual nonissue.

- Java programs *scale* from classes that perform simple utilities to sets of components that compose the IT infrastructure for large enterprises. Performance enhancements, new developments in security, and sound object-oriented design principles can be combined in Java to allow for the creation of robust applications that can handle huge numbers of simultaneous transactions.

- The claim that Java is *simple* is debatable. The early versions of Java were indeed easier to learn and use than the most popular languages of the 1990s. Java syntax is based upon C and C++, but omits the most difficult or error-prone constructs. The JVM removed the need to learn a programming language and details of the host operating system. However, the key to becoming proficient and then expert in Java is becoming familiar with the core API and the ever-expanding set of Java-related technologies. Some Java-based technologies, such as EJBs, are complex. How simple Java is depends largely on how much you include in the scope of your learning objectives. The strength and complexity of Java derive from the fact that the Java platform is dynamic and constantly adapting to demands of the IT industry.

- Java is *dynamic* in many ways. Every release adds support for industry standard technologies. Recent enhancements support XML for data interchange, Secure Socket Layer (SSL) for security, and much more. Well-designed classes are reusable, and application building is increasingly a matter of combining existing components, especially JavaBeans and Enterprise JavaBeans. The software development process itself has a dynamic quality. Java lends itself to *agile programming*, a methodology that adapts object-oriented techniques to maximize adaptability to changing circumstances and minimize overheads by eliminating rigidity and formality in the development process. For the key precepts of agile programming see `http://www.agilemanifesto.com`.

To run Java programs but not develop new ones, you need the Java 2 Java Runtime Environment (JRE). The SDK and JRE are downloadable for free from the `java.sun.com` Web site and are also included in many products created by independent vendors. For example, most Web browsers have or let you plug in a JRE to run applets. Many proprietary IDEs add productivity tools to the SDK and JRE.

Java Programs and Components

In this book, the term *program* is used loosely to refer to any executable Java code that could be one class, several cooperating classes and interfaces, or a large-scale enterprise application. Often the classes you build run only in the context of a wider application, to also use the term *application* loosely. Java programmers tend to think not so much in terms of programs, but rather in terms of classes, or even more generically, in terms of types that can be combined to form applications or used as components in multiple applications.

The safest approach is to think in terms of components that perform specific tasks and have well-defined interfaces through which client code calls upon their services. Java programmers create sets of cooperating types organized into packages far more often than they write entire programs driven by a single or main class. Indeed, the later approach runs contrary to the nature of object-oriented programming. Do not be misled by the fact that many examples in this book are single classes that stand alone and perform some specific task. These programs are small for the purpose of demonstrating a specific API or a point of Java grammar and are not examples of how to design object-oriented programs in Java.

Every Java class and interface you define has potential for reuse, either directly or by being extended through subtyping. All programs are collections of classes and interfaces. Moreover, applications often include non-Java elements—HTML documents in Web applications, XML files that carry data between components, or code in some other language such as a stored procedure in a database—that must run as part of the application you are building.

In Java, you can create the following types of programs or components:

- *Java applications* can be anything from large suites of software to simple utilities. Java applications run in the JVM, supplied by the JRE, installed on a native host platform. The entry point is the **main** method of the class specified in the SDK **java** command or launched in the IDE of your choice. You can create a simple command-line application or code a Java GUI using the API described in Chapters 6 and 7 of this book.

- *JavaBeans* are Java classes or program components that conform to strict programming conventions. Build beans to make your classes reusable or configurable software components. Professional programmers usually follow some of the JavaBean conventions in all classes as good programming practice. If you follow more of the conventions, you can use specialized development tools for JavaBeans to assemble programs visually by adding beans to a work surface and then connecting them. Many of the core classes, especially the visual components in the `java.awt` and `javax.swing` packages, are beans. Chapter 8 describes the JavaBeans standard and how to create and use beans.

- *Applets* are components that can be launched from HTML documents and run in the context of a Web browser or applet viewer utility. HTML is a tagging language understood by Web browsers, and HTML documents contain the text and graphics with tags to control the appearance of the page. Use HTML `<object>` and `<embed>` tags to add applets to Web pages. Applets tend to be small programs. Often they add visual or multimedia effects to Web pages, provide a richer user interface than HTML allows, or connect to applications running on the server to provide some distributed processing on the client side.

  The classes and interfaces used by an applet are downloaded from a Web server at the same time as the HTML page that contains the applet tags. One of the problems related to applets is the download time. Other forms of client-side processing, such as JavaScript, are popular alternatives to applets.

  The main class of an applet must extend `java.applet.Applet` or `javax.swing.JApplet`. Except for some specific programming considerations and a few APIs that only applets can access, writing an applet is much like writing any other class.

  This book does not cover applets because first courses in Java usually do that very well. Indeed, writing applets can be an excellent introduction to Java programming. You can also learn about applets by following the applet trail of the tutorial at `http://java.sun.com/docs/books/tutorial`.

- *Servlets*, like applets, are components that generate content for Web pages at runtime. Unlike applets, servlets run on application servers as part of a Web application in which Java processing occurs on the server side. One great advantage of servlets over applets is that the dynamic content is returned to the Web browser in ordinary HTML documents for display. As a result, you can create Web applications that display dynamic content but require minimal resources on the client workstations and minimize download time. A Web application that relies heavily on applets has what is called a *thick* or *fat client*. Moving processing to the server side creates a *thin client*.

  Typically, a servlet is used to process an HTML form submitted by a Web client and return an HTML response page. In a Web application, the user interface is the collection of HTML pages presented to the user. Servlets act as the bridge between HTML and Java. A servlet receives a user request and acts as the entry point into the server-side application code. The servlet can then return the response in HTML format.

Servlets are considered an enterprise feature of Java, and the servlet API is not included in the standard SDK. Chapter 13 of this book teaches how to build Web applications and program servlets.

■ A variation on servlets is *Java Server Pages* (JSPs). JSPs are written in HTML but contain Java code snippets enclosed in special tags. Application servers compile JSPs into servlets—a process called page compilation—and then run the resulting servlet on the server side. You can do the same job with a servlet or a JSP, and you can base the decision of which to use on the ratio of dynamic to static content or whether you prefer to work in HTML or Java. Think of a servlet as a Java class with embedded HTML and a JSP as an HTML document with embedded Java.

A popular practice is to use servlets to receive requests from HTML and JSPs to return the HTML responses. This scenario, as well as JSPs and servlet programming, is described in Chapter 13.

■ *Enterprise JavaBeans* (EJBs) are server-side components used in distributed enterprise environments. The EJB specification makes up a large part of the J2EE specification and defines the structure of EJBs and nature of Enterprise Java Servers (EJSs) in which EJBs run. The goal of the EJB architecture is to let programmers concentrate on the business logic performed by EJB methods and declare which services are required from the EJS. EJBs are always reusable components that can be used in many different applications, some of which can run simultaneously.

Separate XML files called deployment descriptors specify characteristics of the EJB, such as transactional requirements, security settings, and the names by which client programs find EJBs. Usually, a proprietary application server acts as an EJS by providing an EJB container. The container creates the runtime context for the EJB. EJB containers provide transactions, security, and other services.

Use EJBs to perform processing tasks at the core of an application. For example, process persistent data or complete business transactions. EJBs never include the user interface. To access an EJB and provide a user interface, create an EJB client. The client can be a simple Java application, a servlet in a Web application, or another EJB.

One EJB consists of several classes and interfaces, some of which are generated at installation time according to the characteristics declared in the deployment descriptor. EJBs bring considerable overhead and are usually used in large or sensitive business applications where quality-of-service requirements justify the complexity.

In practice, an EJB development environment is essential to build and deploy EJBs. Chapter 14 of this book discusses EJBs and uses Application Developer to build and test samples.

The Three Editions of the Java 2 Platform

The Java 2 platform comes in three editions—standard, enterprise, and micro—to meet the needs of different communities.

Java 2 Standard Edition.   J2SE is the Java platform that most students of Java learn first and with which programmers working in a personal computer environment are most familiar.

J2SE provides the tools and runtime for developing and running standalone Java applications, applets that run in a Web browser or applet viewer utility, and Java programs that are clients of distributed enterprise applications. The standard edition provides the complete Java language, and the core classes provide the API required by any program that runs in a single JVM. The Standard edition also contains the API that allows a set of Java programs running in different JVMs to communicate with each other in a client-server or peer-to-peer topology. Chapter 12 describes the classes that provide the Networking API.

J2SE is the basis for the other two editions, J2EE and J2ME. Sound knowledge of J2SE is required to use the other editions.

Java 2 Enterprise Edition.   J2EE is primarily designed for server-side Java components that participate in Web or enterprise applications. The J2EE specification defines the API used by Java components to interact with software that supports the J2EE infrastructure. J2EE components include servlets and JSPs used in Web applications and EJBs used in enterprise applications. Chapter 13 of this book discusses Web applications, and Chapter 14 introduces EJBs.

Unlike J2SE, J2EE is much more than a set of tools and APIs. The J2EE specification sets requirements for application servers, and much of the specification document is written for software vendors who build and market J2EE-compatible servers. The J2EE specification states that application servers provide *containers* in which JVMs run and lists services, such as security, transaction management, and database connection pooling, that containers must make available to Java components (see Figure 1-1). The J2EE specification does not describe in detail how these vendors implement the services in their proprietary products, but it defines the API through which Java components use the services. J2EE defines different kinds of containers, and each container has a JVM. For example, the Web browser provides the container for an applet. Servlets and JSPs run in Web containers and EJBs run in EJB containers. A J2EE-compliant application server provides Web and EJB containers and many services required by the J2EE specification. The J2EE services that fall outside the scope of this book are briefly described in Appendix A.

Unlike J2SE, J2EE is designed to support a specific application architecture. It is possible to create a J2EE application that does not conform, but J2EE strongly encourages a tiered architecture with three or more tiers as shown in Figure 1-1. The three basic tiers are as follows:

- The client tier contains presentation logic and the user interface. Often the client tier consists of Web pages running in a Web browser.

- The middle tier includes the application server and contains server-side code that interacts with the client tier. Application logic resides in the middle tier, but typically calls upon third and other tiers to perform specific business operations.

- Manipulation of permanent data stores, interaction with legacy systems, and the like make up the third or later tiers.

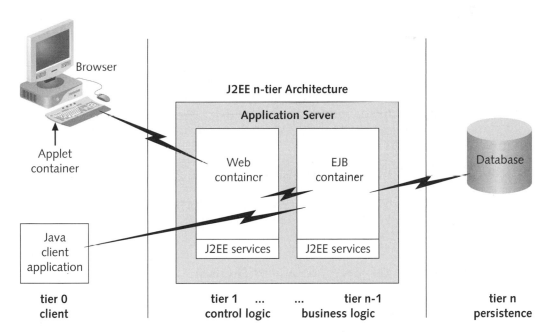

Figure 1-1   Containers in the n-tier J2EE architecture

J2EE also specifies how programs are packaged for distribution and installation into application servers. Although J2SE provides the `jar` utility and most Java programmers use jar files as a convenient way to distribute classes, J2EE defines additional types of archive files and mandates in detail how applications are packaged in the following archives:

- *Web archive* files (war files) contain all servlet classes, JSPs, HTML pages, and other resources that make up a Web application. War files also contain XML documents called deployment descriptors that specify runtime characteristics of the Web application, such as the published names and security settings.

- *EJB jar* files contain the EJB classes and interfaces that make up EJBs. These jars also contain deployment descriptors that specify runtime characteristics of the EJBs, such as which container services each EJB uses.

- Entire enterprise applications are packaged in *enterprise application archives* (ear files). Ear files typically contain war files, EJB jar files, and possibly client jars so that an enterprise application has a nested structure. The deployment descriptor of the top-level ear lists the Web and EJB modules contained in the enterprise application.

Due to the potential complexity of building and packaging Web and enterprise applications to conform to J2EE, developers usually choose a proprietary IDE and depend heavily on the tools provided by their choice of software vendor. It is possible to use a development environment and application server from different sources and even mix tools and servers in a heterogeneous environment.

Java 2 Micro Edition.   J2ME is designed for embedded devices and consumer products, such as PDAs, smart cards, and mobile phones. The JRE is highly optimized to allow for limited I/O capabilities, processing power, and memory space. The J2ME architecture allows for the creation of JVM configurations with minimal class libraries sufficient to provide required functionality for devices that have similar characteristics. Two configurations are Connected Limited Device Configuration (CLDC) and Connected Device Configuration (CDC).

A J2ME application is written once for a range of devices and then downloaded to the target devices. J2ME technologies include toolkits for wireless devices, database access, security, 3D graphics and multimedia, and much more. A rather specialized set of developers work with J2ME, and this book does not discuss it further.

A Brief History of the Java Platform

The history of Java is not very long. The story starts at the beginning of the 1990s when Sun Microsystems was working on consumer electronics. Unit price is of prime importance in consumer electronics, and developers use the cheapest chips available. If prices change so that a different chip set becomes cheaper, developers have to switch. Sun Microsystems was pursuing the goal of creating software that was portable so that it could be switched quickly to new or less expensive chips. Sun created an experimental, hand-held computer called the *7, which was intended for controlling home appliances. James Gosling was the technical leader of the project. The *7 never became a retail product, but the developers at Sun began to see that the computer language they developed for the *7 could be useful in other ways. For instance, the team could apply it to the Web, where compactness and simplicity are important requirements. Others envisioned it for embedded systems in electronic appliances, enterprise-wide applications, and network computing.

At first, the language was called Oak, supposedly in honor of a tree that grew outside Gosling's window. When the development team learned that there was already a computer language called Oak, they had to change the name and eventually settled on Java, perhaps in recognition of the role caffeine plays in software development. A pleasing side-effect is that, when it comes to coining derivative names, such as "beans," Java may have more potential than Oak.

The announcement of the Java programming language generated an unprecedented impact on the software-development world. The Java platform evolved rapidly and grew in popularity. A number of factors contributed to Java's stunning growth: the maturing of object-oriented methodology, emergence of the Internet as a vehicle for doing business, and increased user demand for user-friendly graphical interfaces.

Inevitably, the Java platform also grew in size and complexity as additional language features and core classes were added. New APIs are still being defined to meet the needs of companies and organizations adopting Java as their IT platform and to keep pace with advancements in the Web and related technology.

The official history is very short:

- Sun Microsystems made Java version 1.0 available to the IT community in 1995.

- Version 1.1 was released in 1997 and added significant features to the Java language, including inner classes and JavaBeans. At this point, the Java language stabilized, and the API grew from about 200 classes to near 500.

- The much-anticipated version 1.2 appeared in 1998. Version 1.2 is also known as the Java 2 platform. The Java 2 platform includes the Java Foundation Classes (JFC), and after its introduction the core APIs contained 1600 predefined types. The Swing API for GUI-building composes one part of the JFC. The introduction of Java 2 is generally considered the point at which Java technology matured into an industrial-strength platform.

- In June of 1999, Sun announced the three editions of the Java platform: J2SE, J2EE, and J2ME. This announcement signaled the success of Java in very different environments.

- Version 1.3 of J2SE appeared in 2001 and 1.4 followed in 2002. Version 1.4 is a major release that more than doubles the number of core classes and interfaces. See the section "Recent Additions to the Java 2 Platform" for highlights.

- Version 1.3 of J2EE became available in 2002. At the time of this writing, J2EE remains at version 1.3 and a beta of 1.4 is available. Therefore, the chapters of this book that focus on the Enterprise Edition are based on version 1.3 of J2EE. Many of the features new to J2EE in versions 1.3 and 1.4 fall outside the scope of this book.

In the beginning of Java history, the Java tools for developers were contained in one toolkit called the Java Development Kit (JDK). Sun Microsystems wisely made the JDK and JRE downloadable for free. From the release of version 1.2, the developer toolkit is renamed the Java 2 Software Developer Kit (J2SDK), although the J2SDK for Standard Edition is still often called the JDK.

Many early Java programmers learned Java by experimenting with the JDK, often using no tools other than the command-line utilities included in the JDK. A popular early use for Java was to write applets to add effects, such as multimedia, to Web pages. The language quickly proved its suitability for much more than glamorizing Web pages. As performance and security improved, Java was used increasingly for business applications and quickly spread from the client side to the server side of Web-enabled applications. At the same time, the original role of applets has increasingly given way to alternative client-side technologies, such as JavaScript and dynamic HTML.

Java is now the de facto standard for distributed and Web-oriented applications in non-Microsoft environments. With J2EE comes the infrastructure to support e-commerce and enterprise applications, especially in complex environments where rapidly evolving technology and distributed architectures require standardized interfaces between scalable, reusable, and secure application components.

One of the patterns in the evolution of the J2SE platform is that APIs first introduced as optional extensions to the core classes have become incorporated into later versions of J2SE. For example, the Java Database Connectivity (JDBC) APIs described in Chapter 9 are split into two packages: One contains the API that performs basic database access, and another was considered optional prior to J2SE version 1.3. Another example is Java Naming and Directory Interface (JNDI) that prior to version 1.3 was required only by J2EE. JNDI is described in Chapter 11.

New technologies build upon Web infrastructure and industry standards, such as XML for information interchange and Web Services for remote access to software services. The leading software vendors are starting to work together to ensure interoperability between Java 2 and Microsoft Windows and .NET platforms. This is particularly true in the case of Web Services. The Appendix of this book provides introductions to Web Services and some other advanced Java- and Web-related technologies.

In this book, comments about how API and language features have changed over the years are indicated in notes like this. Use these notes as warnings that old books or code may conform to a version of Java that is no longer current. Often such code still works because of a Java convention for easing the introduction of changes to the core API: New methods are added and old methods are retained but marked *deprecated*. Eventually deprecated methods are dropped, but for a considerable period the JRE continues to support them. The compiler outputs warnings if you compile classes that call deprecated methods. You should eliminate deprecated code from your programs, because there is no guarantee how long the code will work. Also consider that some methods are deprecated because of inherent flaws that became apparent after a version of the Java platform was released.

The Java Community Process

Sun Microsystems is the company that created Java, but a much wider organization determines how Java technology evolves. After developing Java, Sun Microsystems established the Java Community Process (JCP). The purpose of the JCP is to develop and revise specifications of Java-based technology, create reference implementations, and build test suites. Over the years, the JCP has become a formal and powerful organization. It ensures that Java technology evolves to meet the needs of the JCP's diverse membership.

The JCP updates Java technology by processing Java Specification Requests (JSRs). One or more members propose a new specification or revision to an existing specification by requesting that a new JSR be created. JSRs can relate to the J2SE, J2EE, or J2ME. Many of the core APIs began as JSRs proposed by a software vendor offering a proprietary solution to the entire Java community. A new JSR is assigned a number by which it can be tracked. For example, the Java API for XML parsing (JAXP) was JSR 5 prior to its final release in March of 2000.

A proposed API is likely to be changed during the JSR process as a group of experts produce drafts of the specification and a reference implementation. An executive committee reviews the specification to ensure it does not overlap or conflict with other APIs in the Java platform. JSR specifications are also published and available for public review. The JSR process can take several months, so Java developers and software vendors often have advance notice of new APIs and changes coming in the next version of the Java 2 platform. Anyone can join the JSR mailing list or view the online list of JSRs at `http:\\www.jcp.org`.

The JCP is an open organization, but members must sign an agreement with Sun and pay a small annual fee. Over 300 individuals and companies now belong to the JCP. At the time of this writing, the executive committee for J2SE and J2EE consist of representatives from Apache Software Foundation, Apple, BEA, Borland, Caldera Systems, Cisco Systems, Fujitsu Limited, Hewlett-Packard, IBM, IONA Technology, Macromedia, Nokia Network, Oracle, SAP, Sun Microsystems, and one individual member.

OBJECT-ORIENTED PROGRAMMING IN JAVA

Java is an object-oriented programming language, and the Java platform provides an architecture that lends itself to supporting object-oriented methodology. The purpose of this section is to ensure that you do not lose sight of the principles of *object-oriented analysis and design* (OOAD) as you work through this book and focus on the details of using the API provided by the Java 2 platform.

In *object-oriented programming* (OOP), a program is a collection of objects that send messages to each other. In Java, the objects are instances of classes. The methods of a class compose the protocol or API through which other classes send messages to the objects of the class. The flow in OOP is determined by the methods objects call on each other and the order in which the methods are called.

The first stage in OOAD is performing some object-oriented analysis of the problem domain (what the program models). The analysis stage identifies the real-life objects to be represented in code. The next stage, object-oriented design, identifies the classes to be implemented in code and the fields and methods the classes must contain to model the behavior of real-life objects. You should not start to write code until the design clarifies the responsibilities of each class and the protocol for using each class.

A standard OOAD technique is to build graphical representations of the objects, classes, and associations between them using the Unified Modeling Language (UML). UML defines a set of standard diagrams and is described at `http:\\www.uml.org`. This book does not cover UML, but does include a few UML diagrams, such as Figure 1-25. When you have a set of UML diagrams that communicates the design to all developers working on the project, implementing the program becomes a relatively straight-forward process of converting the types and associations represented in UML into Java classes and interfaces.

Object-Oriented Methodology

You must never omit the analysis and design stage when building a Java program. All programmers writing classes should understand the real-world objects that their classes model. Here are two OO rules of thumb for managing an application development project:

Model the Real World as Much as Possible

For example, if the business activity you are modeling is a courier service, you probably need classes that represent shipping orders, parcels, senders, recipients, destinations, carriers, schedules, invoices, payments, status checkers, and so on. Decide what the primary role of each class should be, and make sure that the tasks the class performs are consistent with that role. Instances of your class can represent real-world entities, such as parcels and destinations, or abstractions, such as a schedule managers and routing algorithms.

Consider how the real-world objects interact with each other. Design the protocol of each class accordingly. The *protocol* is the set of externally callable methods of a class and is the most important element of the design of any class. For example, the `Carrier` class may have methods `assignShippingOrder`, and `getShippingOrderStatus`. The protocol can be called the class interface, but this can be confused with the Java keyword `interface`.

You can always revise a class and improve its internal algorithms with minimal impact on the system as a whole. But changes that alter the responsibilities of a class or its protocol have a ripple effect and require that other code also be modified. In general, if redesigning a class brings it into closer alignment with the real world, the resulting refactoring exercise may be beneficial. *Refactoring* occurs when you modify a set of classes to implement a design change that affects more than one class. For example, to allow international delivery, you may create subclasses of `Destination`, and modify the `Invoice` class to add duty charges and convert currencies depending on the type of `Destination` of a `Parcel` object. Do not refactor to suit a programming convenience, a data structure, or a quirk of the user interface, because such changes may undermine the object-oriented design of the system.

Well-designed object-oriented software is likely to continue to work as requirements change and as functionality is added. The key benefits of object-oriented programming are code reuse, flexibility to respond to changing circumstances and requirements, and ease of maintenance.

Build a Large Application Incrementally

Object-oriented software projects of significant size should adopt an incremental and iterative approach to development. In large projects, functionality is typically added in stages and each identifiable stage is an *increment*. Start each increment by deciding what new functionality to include, based in part on a master plan and in part on user response and experiences from the previous increment. Phasing in functionality fits the modern reality that requirements change, often very quickly. If your development project has a two-year plan, chances are that a functional specification completed at the start of the two years does not meet user requirements two years later. If your master plan identifies four increments—for example, provide basic courier services in three months; add express and international delivery in six months; add short term storage with delayed delivery in a year; provide long term storage and warehousing services at the end of two years—let the specifications for later increments be less detailed than for the earlier increments.

An increment adds functionality and usually ends with the release of a new version of the software. Each increment contains analysis, design, coding, testing, and deployment stages. Far from being distinct milestones, these stages tend to overlap and blend in object-oriented methodology. For example, the testing stage can reveal design flaws that must be fixed by refactoring the classes.

The incremental process is cyclical. Testing and maintenance of one increment can merge with analysis and design for the next increment.

An *iteration* is a short-term development cycle within an increment. Many iterations may occur during one increment. Usually, only the development team is aware of the iterative cycle. For example, iterations may take the form of an informal daily plan-code-integrate-test routine. Rather than add new functionality, iterations improve the acceptability, scalability, or performance of an application. Over several iterations, the system becomes more robust as more what-if scenarios and exceptional circumstances are handled. Typically, the most critical requirements and expected behavior are coded in the first iterations of an increment. The less likely or less important scenarios are added toward the end of the increment.

Object-Oriented Features of Java

The previous section described some strategies that apply OO principles to the management of application development projects. The focus of this book is the implementation stage, when you realize the entities identified during object-oriented analysis and design by creating the classes that make up a Java program. How does Java support object-oriented programming?

Java supports the following fundamental features of all object-oriented languages:

- Abstract data types
- Encapsulation
- Inheritance
- Polymorphism

Abstract Data Types

Classes are abstract data types. Java programs are collections of classes, and all executable code must belong to a class. Thus, in Java you are forced to code a software system as a set of classes. If your classes are true to your application design, instances of classes model real-world objects or concepts. Every class is an abstraction for objects of some sort.

Many classes contain data, and their primary responsibility may be to maintain that data, set values, and return values when asked. Abstract data types are not just data structures like linked lists and arrays. They are any objects that have a *state* and own the responsibility for storing that state. Such objects can ensure that only valid settings are applied, that requests to change values meet security requirements, and that changes are allowed at the time of the request.

What is the state of an object? At any point of time during execution, the set of values of all instance fields defined in the class make up the state of the object. Similarly, the state of the program is the combined state of all objects in the program.

A companion concept to abstract data types is that of strict typing. In *strict typing*, the type of an expression or variable is fixed and there are strict rules about how objects or expressions of different types can be used. Java is a strictly typed language. For example, the statement

```
Dog fido = new Policy();
```

is illegal unless `Policy` is a subclass of `Dog`. The effect of strict typing is that you cannot treat a variable as though it has a different type.

Encapsulation

A key element of object orientation is that objects shield their internal state from all other code. They may provide methods that set and get values, but code that uses the class must call these methods and cannot directly change the internal state of objects. The great advantage is that an object retains control of its state and has sole responsibility for ensuring its validity.

Enforcing encapsulation is not automatic in Java. You must code it, and most programmers implement encapsulation by declaring fields with the qualifier **private** or **protected**.

Where appropriate, programmers implement get and set methods through which other classes access the state of an object. For example, a `BankAccount` class has a private instance field called `balance`, and this field stores the current balance of each `BankAccount` object. If other classes can ask what the balance is, the class defines a public method `getBalance`. Typically, a `BankAccount` class has public `deposit` and `withdraw` methods that client code can call. These methods affect the balance, but indirectly as the result of deposit or withdraw operations. Setting the balance directly is not allowed, so the `BankAccount` class does not have a public `setBalance` method.

The effect of encapsulation is that other classes do not know and should not care how abstract data types store information. The actual type and arrangement of fields, and even whether the values are stored in fields, calculated, or retrieved from databases on demand, are implementation details known only to the encapsulating class.

The benefit of encapsulation is robustness and ease of maintenance. One class is responsible for each piece of information. You don't have to code the same validity checks in multiple places, or update several parts of your program to change how one piece of information is stored.

Inheritance

Code reuse is one of the goals of object-oriented programming. One form of code reuse is loading the same class in different programs. Inheritance is another form that not only reuses classes, but also adapts them to new circumstances. Inheritance establishes *is-a* relationships between types of objects. For example, a truck is a vehicle. A car is also a vehicle. Inheritance relationships are based on generalization and specialization. When you have a class that models a generic type of object, such as vehicle, you can reuse the code that is common to all vehicles when creating the specialized types, such as truck, car, and bus.

With inheritance comes additional *abstraction*. For example, a ticket ordering system can sell tickets to concerts, plays, and baseball games. By introducing the abstraction of attraction, your system can sell tickets to objects of type `Attraction`, and subclasses of `Attraction` can be `Concert`, `Play`, and `BaseballGame`. Now you can code several common characteristics only once, in the `Attraction` class, and reuse that code with the different types of events. One benefit of inheritance is programmer efficiency, as less code needs to be written.

Another benefit is flexibility and adaptability as new requirements arise. For example, you can expand the ticket ordering system to handle new types of events by defining new subclasses of `Attraction`, without having to change the existing classes.

All object-oriented programming languages support inheritance. In Java, inheritance is implemented with superclasses and subclasses, and the keyword **extends** as in the following declarations:

```
class Car extends Vehicle { /* … */};
class Rodeo extends Attraction { /* … */};
class SportsCar extends Car { /* … */};
```

Some object-oriented languages allow multiple inheritance. In *multiple inheritance* a class has more than one parent class. For example, how do you categorize a musical production that is both a play and concert? In C++ you can define a class `Musical` that is derived from both `Play` and `Concert`. Multiple inheritance has inherent complexities, and the creators of Java wisely chose not to support it.

In Java you must do more analysis and decide which characteristics require an abstract data type and which are pure behavior. You may have to add a layer of abstraction. For example, if you consider that plays and concerts are both theatre attractions but have different behaviors, you can create Java interfaces for `Play` and `Concert`. Then the class `Musical` can extend `TheatreAttraction` and implement both `Play` and `Concert`. The declaration could be:

```
class Musical extends TheatreAttraction
    implements Play, Concert { /* … */}
```

This last example may seem a bit contrived, but it illustrates that Java interfaces are part of the inheritance mechanism. Time has proven that interfaces are not only effective solutions to the multiple inheritance problem, but also very useful constructs for abstracting behaviors. Java has the concept not only of superclass and subclass, but also of supertype and subtype, where a type can be a class or an interface.

Polymorphism

The true power of inheritance is realized in polymorphism. Many experts argue that a language is not truly object-oriented unless it supports polymorphism. Unfortunately, the word polymorphism means different things to different people. Very loosely, polymorphism allows the same code to have different effects at runtime, depending on the context in which the code is used. Sometimes polymorphism is defined broadly to include method overloading and templates as used in C++. A strict definition says that dynamic binding is the only true implementation of polymorphism.

Dynamic binding is the mechanism that makes method *overriding* work. Dynamic binding resolves at runtime which version of a method to call when a method is implemented by more than one class in an inheritance hierarchy. The JVM looks at the type of the object for which the call is made, not at the type of the object reference in the calling statement. The JVM then binds the call to the method implemented or inherited by the object. For example, if `attraction` is an object reference of type `Attraction`, the statement `attraction.reserveSeats` may result in a call to method `Concert.reserveSeats` or `BaseballGame.reserveSeats`, depending on the type of the specific object. The calling method may not know the type, but the JVM does because it keeps track of all object references and objects. As a result, you can write a very general method that operates on any kind of `Attraction` and trust the JVM to bind to the appropriate `reserveSeats` method.

Dynamic binding gives tremendous flexibility to Java classes. You can exploit inheritance relationships by writing code for the superclass that can work for all subclasses. In Java, you do not have to do any special coding to take advantage of dynamic binding, because it is automatic. However, you can exert some control over whether dynamic binding occurs with the keywords **abstract** and **final**.

Design Patterns and Frameworks

Understanding object-oriented methodology and mastering the Java language constructs that support object-oriented programming are two of the three essential skills for successful Java programming. The third skill is recognizing common problems and applying the appropriate design pattern to solve them. Like master chess players who see patterns in the arrangement of pieces on a chessboard and have a repertoire of strategies from which to select, experienced Java programmers are familiar with a number of well-established design patterns and know how to implement them.

A *design pattern* is a proposed solution to common design problems. Patterns can describe the architecture of software at a high level, specify in detail which classes and methods to define, or fall somewhere in between. All design patterns are guidelines for designing classes. You should become familiar with a number of well-known design patterns so you can reuse proven solutions instead of solve common problems from first principles. You gain from the wisdom and experience of others and probably produce more flexible and robust code.

Design patterns are abstractions you read about. In contrast, *frameworks* are collections of reusable classes. Often frameworks implement design patterns. Typically, you use frameworks by extending the provided types so that the subtypes are specific to your application. The SDK contains many frameworks. For example, the *observer design pattern* is implemented in the core API by the **Observer** interface and **Observable** class and is described in Chapter 4.

The study of design patterns is a large and ever growing subject that cannot be condensed into a book such as this. The goal of this section is to encourage you to think in terms of design patterns when designing your programs. A few of the most important or simple design patterns are introduced here.

Model-View-Controller Design Pattern

Application layering refers to creating an architecture that organizes sets of classes into layers so that each layer plays a specific role in processing the scenarios that application supports. Model-View-Controller (MVC) is a design pattern that separates user interface, control logic, and core business activities into distinct layers, as shown in Figure 1-2. MVC is widely accepted and is compatible with the n-tier application architecture of J2EE.

For an example of the opposite of MVC, consider a GUI control that triggers a business activity such as requesting a quote for a mortgage. Does the code that implements the button also calculate mortgage payments and display the results? If the core business activity code is mixed with the user interface, MVC is not being used.

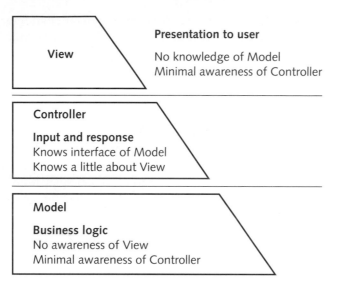

Figure 1-2 The MVC design pattern

The essential feature of MVC is complete separation of the model and view. A benefit is that you can radically change the user interface and not impact the algorithms and business rules modeled in the core of the application. Similarly, you can rework the model and maintain the same user interface. Changes to the protocols of view or model classes affect the controller layer.

The controller receives input from the view and uses the protocol of the model layer to submit requests that trigger business processes. The model returns information to the controller, which in turn passes the results back to the view. However, the view is responsible for transforming and displaying the results. The role of the controller layer is limited to middleman.

For another example of MVC, consider a financial planning package that displays the allocation of your investments in three views: a table of numbers, a pie chart, and a line graph. This program may let you alter your investment strategy by modifying the numbers in the table, shifting points on the graph, or changing the size of wedges in the pie. When you make a change in one view, the other views adjust to show the impact. How is this possible? The financial package must have one model containing financial data. But it has three views that display the numbers in different ways. The views have Java GUIs and are event driven. They can each send commands to the controller, which in turn calls methods of the model to change the allocation of investments. The model layer returns updated financial figures to the controller. In addition, a notification mechanism is set up, possibly using the observer design pattern so that the controller automatically notifies all three GUIs to update their displays.

As a design pattern, MVC is more a recommended approach to application architecture than a suggested coding pattern. It is mentioned again in various parts of this book, because MVC and model-view separation are implemented in many of the Java APIs.

Object Creation Patterns

Sometimes creating an instance of a class using the **new** operator is not appropriate. Thus, there are a number of design patterns related to object creation.

- *Singleton design pattern*: One common problem is how to ensure that only one instance is ever created. For example, a taxicab company has many taxis but only one dispatcher. The dispatcher must be available to many different parts of the application. If each piece of code that called a method on the dispatcher first created a dispatcher instance, there would be a multitude of dispatchers and the program would not model reality.

  A solution here is the singleton design pattern. To implement the singleton design pattern, declare the constructor of the **Dispatcher** class to be private, and define a private class variable for the single dispatcher object. Then write a method that returns an object reference to the dispatcher for other classes to use. The code can look like Figure 1-3.

```
public class Dispatcher {
   private Dispatcher dispatcher = null;
   private Dispatcher() {
      // initialize the dispatcher
   }
   public Dispatcher singleton () {
      if (dispatcher == null) {
         dispatcher = new Dispatcher();
      }
      return dispatcher;
   }
   // other methods
   }
```

Figure 1-3   A class implementing the singleton design pattern

- *Factory design pattern*: Another problem is how to create an instance of an object when you don't know which subclass to use or don't have all the information needed to initialize the object. Here you can use a factory design pattern. Create a factory class as a helper to the target class. Factory classes are classes that return objects of some other type, and whose main responsibility is to instantiate and initialize those objects.

  For example, you may be issuing insurance policies. There may be many types of policies implemented as subclasses of **Policy**. If deciding which type to issue to any one customer requires some processing, you can use a **PolicyFactory** object with a **createPolicy** method along the lines of Figure 1-4.

```
public interface PolicyFactory {
   Policy createPolicy();
}
public class PolicyBuilder implements PolicyFactory {
   Policy createPolicy() {
      Policy p = null;
      // determine type of policy
      if ( /* … */ ) {
         // …
         p = new HighRiskFloodPolicy();
      } else if ( /* … */ ) {
         // …
          p = SingleDwellingConentPolicy();
      } else {
         // …
      }
      return p;
      }
}
```

Figure 1-4   An implementation of the factory design pattern

Structural Patterns

Some design patterns remove difficulties you encounter when you try to use packages of classes from different sources in one program.

- *Adapter design pattern*: One solution is called the adapter pattern. A simple version of adapters can be implemented using Java interfaces. For example, suppose you have programs from different countries that find cooking recipes. One works in metric units (liters and kilograms) and the other uses Imperial (pounds and pints). You can define an interface that uses the unit you want and modify the classes that work in the different measuring systems to implement the interface of your measuring system.

  Another form of adapters is implemented in the **java.awt.event** package to help your program handle user events from Java GUIs. The SDK includes listener interfaces that have methods for different kinds of GUI events. For example, when the user closes the window of a running program, a **WindowEvent** occurs. The **WindowListener** interface defines methods for all possible window events. If you write a class that implements **WindowListener**, you must provide a handler method for all seven types of window events. The SDK also includes a **WindowAdapter** class that implements **WindowListener** and provides default (empty) handlers for the seven types of events. If your program can ignore all but the window closing event, you can write a class that extends **WindowAdapter** and overrides only the **windowClosing** method.

- *Façade design pattern*: When you want to use a set of classes that you cannot modify or extend, but do not find their protocol appropriate, you can implement the façade design pattern. To implement a façade, you create a class or set of classes that has the desired protocol. Client code calls methods of the façade classes. The façade classes perform any required mappings and call the methods of the original classes. Façades are useful in many circumstances. Often façade layers are included in applications to provide simplified, restricted, or secure access to existing code. You can use façades to provide a common protocol to disparate APIs.

  For example, your company may have a suite of classes for submitting business expense claims. The existing classes may work well but not be easy to use. Perhaps you must make six method calls to claim an allowable expense such a buying box of paper for the printer. You can write a façade class, such as `BusinessSuppliesPurchase`, that has a `submitClaim` method. The `submitClaim` method can receive the amount, date, and employee id information as arguments and perform the six complex method calls on the existing classes. The `BusinessSuppliesPurchase` class provides a façade that maps the `submitClaim` method onto a complex protocol and set of classes that the client never sees or uses directly.

The list of design patterns and categories of design patterns is endless. The observer design pattern mentioned briefly here is a behavioral design pattern.

STANDARD SDK TOOLS

The Java platform includes a tool set for developing Java programs. The J2SDK tools run only in a command-line window and provide basic functionality. Nevertheless, they are adequate for developing Java programs, and you can work through much of this book using them.

The following list contains the most frequently used SDK tools. The example commands apply to the Windows implementation of the Java platform. Most of the commands are cross-platform, but options and syntax may vary according to the file system and command-line processor of the native operating system. Complete documentation of all tools for specific implementations of the Java platform is included in the documentation for J2SDK. You can also type each command name on a command line to see a summary of the command syntax and options.

- `javac` is the Java compiler. This command compiles Java source into *bytecode*, the equivalent of assembly code for the JVM. Run `javac` for all types of source files, including applications, applets, and servlets. To use `javac`, you must supply as input a Java source file with the file extension `.java`. The output consists of one or more bytecode files with the file extension `.class`. You can include the absolute path to find the file; otherwise, the compiler assumes the filename is relative to the current folder. You must include the file extension `.java`. For example, to compile the file that contains the class `MyClass`, the command may be one of the following:

```
javac MyClass.java
javac D:\mywork\mypackage\MyClass.java
```

See the section "How the Compiler Finds Classes" for more details on the `javac` command.

- `java` launches a Java program. This command starts a Java runtime environment, loads the specified class, and then invokes the **main** method of that class. Enter the `java` command followed by the name of the class you want to run and any command-line arguments you want to pass to the program. Include the package name but not the file extension, because you are supplying a class name, not a filename. The class name is case-sensitive. For example, to run the class `MyClass` in package `mypackage`, the command is:

```
java mypackage.MyClass
```

In earlier releases of the SDK a separate launcher, the `jre` tool, was used for deployment. The `jre` tool is no longer provided, and you now use the `java` command to run a class in the SDK and JRE. See the section "How the Launcher Finds Classes" for more details on the `java` command.

- `javadoc` generates a web of HTML documents that make up online documentation for packages of classes. One popular, innovative feature of Java technology is the ability to generate online documentation for your classes automatically, by using `javadoc` and a unique format for comments in your code. Use `javadoc` to create documentation for other programmers who may use your classes, not for end-user documentation.

The "Doc Comments" section of this chapter describes how to insert comments for `javadoc` into your Java source code, how to run the `javadoc` tool, and how to use the output.

- `appletviewer` is a utility that runs applets outside a Web browser. The command-line arguments for **appletviewer** are one or more URLs for HTML documents. For a file that resides on the local file system, the URL is the same as the filename. Specify the path relative to the current folder. The `appletviewer` tool discards all text in the HTML document except `<object>`, `<embed>`, or `<applet>` tags. The tool then runs each applet in the viewer window. Unless you specify otherwise, the applet runs in the Java HotSpot Client VM.

For example, to view the applets used by Web page `mypage.html`, which is in a folder called **myweb**, you can enter the following from the folder that contains **myweb**:

```
appletviewer myweb\mypage.html
```

1

For the `appletviewer` command, whether filenames are case-sensitive depends on your browser and the native operating system. Be careful with filenames, because the tags in the HTML document give the location of the `.class` file for the applet relative to the current folder when you issue the `appletviewer` command.

- `jdb` is the Java debugger. This debugger has limited functionality; the proprietary Java application-development products have more sophisticated debuggers.

- The `jar` utility combines several files into a single *Java archive* (JAR or jar) file or expands a jar file. A jar file is a zip file with some extra options. You can open a jar with a zip or unzip utility. Use jar files to deploy and distribute programs. See the section "Packaging a Program for Distribution" later in this chapter for more details.

- The `extcheck` utility detects version conflicts of a specified jar file and optional packages installed in the J2SDK. Jar files holding optional packages contain a manifest file with headers that identify the specification title and version. This utility compares the headers with jars installed in the extension folder, `jre\lib\ext` by default, and returns 0 if no conflict is found.

Optional packages are packages of Java classes and associated native code that extend the functionality of the core Java platform. Optional packages are distributed as jar files. These jars should contain a manifest file that specifies information, such as the name, vendor, and version of the extension. The *Java Extension* mechanism is a feature of the Java platform that lets the JVM use optional packages the same way it uses core classes, so that they do not have to be put on the classpath, and makes it possible for optional classes to be retrieved from URLs if they are not already installed.

All jar files have the potential of becoming optional packages in either of following ways:

- A jar placed in the optional packages folder of the SDK, `jre\lib\ext`, and optional packages folder of the JRE, `lib\ext`, is an *installed optional package*.

- A jar referenced in the classpath header of the manifest file of the jar containing an applet or application is a *download optional package*. The extension mechanism does not install download optional packages into the SDK or JRE. Download optional packages cannot contain native code.

In earlier releases, optional packages were known as standard extensions or extensions. Version 1.3 of Java 2 expanded the set of attributes in the manifest file of a jar containing an applet to specify version and vendor information and download URLs for optional packages that the applet requires.

How the Launcher Finds Classes

The `java` command locates bytecode files by class name. Conforming to the file-naming conventions is important, because the launcher loads bytecode from the file with the extension `.class` and with the case-sensitive base filename that matches the class name. If the class is in a package, the package must be in a folder that has the same case-sensitive name as the package. You must specify the package name in the `java` command, but separate the package and class names with dots instead of the character your operating system uses to indicate subfolders. For example, if `TestClass` is a class in a package called `testing`, and `testing` is a subfolder of the current folder, the commands to compile and run `TestClass` on Windows-based platforms are:

```
javac testing\TestClass.java
java testing.TestClass
```

The launcher can dynamically load classes as required while a program is running. If it cannot find a `.class` file, the launcher terminates your program with an error message. It searches for and loads classes in the following order:

1. The bootstrap classes that make up the core API, which are in the `rt.jar` in subfolder `jre\lib` of the Java 2 install folder

2. The optional packages that extend the Java platform

3. User classes or any classes that do not use the Java Extension mechanism

In general, you need to specify only the location of user classes, because bootstrap and optional classes are found automatically. The three-step load order listed previously makes it difficult to accidentally hide or omit a bootstrap class.

To find user classes, the launcher refers to the user classpath. Use the `-classpath` or `-cp` option of the `java` command to specify folders, jars, or zip files that hold user-defined types. To search more than one location, specify several paths separated by semicolons. For example, if you are in any folder on any drive, the following command finds and runs the public class `MyClass`:

```
java -cp C:\jars\my.jar;D:\myJava MyClass
```

The locations are searched in the order that they appear in the classpath, so the preceding command looks in the jar file `my.jar` before finding `MyClass.class` in the `myJava` folder. On operating systems that have environment variables, you can set up an environment variable called `CLASSPATH` to hold the search list. On Windows platforms, open a command window and enter a `SET` command, such as the following:

```
SET CLASSPATH=C:\jars\my.jar;D:\myJava;%CLASSPATH%
```

To run most example programs in this book directly from the CD, enter the command

```
SET CLASSPATH=X:\Data;%CLASSPATH%
```

but substitute for `X` the drive letter of your CD. In this `SET` command, `%CLASSPATH%` represents the previous value of `CLASSPATH`, so the new locations are inserted at the beginning of the existing search path. If you set `CLASSPATH` in a command-line window, the settings hold for the duration of the command-line session. Use features of your operating system to set CLASSPATH permanently. The –classpath command option overrides the CLASSPATH environment variable.

How the Compiler Finds Classes

The Java platform has strict naming conventions for files and classes. If a class is declared with the qualifier **public**, it can be run as an application or used by other classes that are not in the same package. For public classes, the file that contains the source must have the same name as the class and every public class must be in a separate file. Names are case-sensitive in the Java platform, even on operating systems on which filenames are not case-sensitive, and filenames must match class names exactly, including uppercase and lowercase.

Use the –d option to tell the compiler to output the bytecode files to a different folder from the location of the source.

When the source the compiler is processing uses another class, the javac compiler, like the launcher, looks for the referenced class in the path specified by the –classpath option or CLASSPATH environment variable and by using the class name to identify the file. The javac command also has a –sourcepath option that you can use to specify the location of input source files when it is different from the location of the compiled classes. If you do not specify –sourcepath, the compiler searches the same locations for source and bytecode.

If there is no .class file but there is a .java file, or if there is a .class file but its modification timestamp is earlier than that of the .java file, the .java file is compiled to create an up-to-date .class file. If neither a .java file nor a .class file exists in the search path, the compiler reports an error.

By default, the javac compiler checks the validity of .class files automatically. A side-effect of this mechanism is that you can run javac against one class and the compiler can inform you of an error in another class in a different file. If you find these error messages annoying, try to make sure all referenced classes are compiled first.

javadoc COMMENTS

The javadoc tool is a utility for generating HTML documentation directly from comments in Java source code. The relevant comments have a special form and are called *doc comments*. Doc comments start with a slash and two asterisks (/**) and terminate with one asterisk and a slash (*/) so they look like ordinary block comments to the compiler. Here is an example:

```
/**
 * A sample doc comment.
 */
```

When run on a suite of packages, the `javadoc` tool creates a web of HTML pages. The web includes a page for each class that lists all methods and fields in the class. Other pages in the web show all classes in a hierarchy diagram, list all packages and all classes in each package, and provide an index of fields and methods in all classes.

Doc comments should include all information developers need to use your classes. A good example of `javadoc` output is the downloadable documentation for the J2SDK API. This standard documentation is generated from extensive doc comments in the core API. Including doc comments in all code that you write is an excellent practice. Most Java IDEs support doc comments and have a `javadoc` utility built in. Some generate skeleton doc comments for you.

You can insert descriptive text into your source code and have that text automatically included in the documentation produced by `javadoc`. Use doc comments to explain the purpose of a class, what methods do, what the arguments represent, what exceptions may be thrown, and the like.

Unlike the other kinds of comments, doc comments are meaningful only when placed before declarations. Misplaced doc comments are ignored. You can put doc comments before the declarations of classes and members, but not before executable statements within methods. Generally, you provide doc comments for the elements of Java code that are important to the programmers using the code. For example, you usually describe the arguments of a method and what the method returns. Doc comments can appear before the following kinds of declarations:

- *Class*: Doc comments should briefly state the purpose of a class and then can list the author, version, whether the class is deprecated, or when it was introduced, and provide links to related types.

- *Interface*: Doc comments should briefly state the purpose of an interface and then can list the author, version, whether the interface is deprecated, or when it was introduced, and provide links to related types.

- *Field*: Doc comments should briefly state the purpose of the field and then can state whether the field is serializable and provide links to related methods or fields.

- *Method*: Doc comments should briefly state the purpose of the method and then list parameters, the return value, unchecked exceptions listed in the throws clause, whether the method is deprecated, and provide links to related methods or fields.

The example programs in this book use doc comments. For example, the class `examples.intro.AssertTester` that appears later in this chapter has two doc comments, as shown in Figure 1-5.

```
package examples.intro;
/**
 * class to demonstrate assert facility of J2SDK v1.4
 */
public class AssertTester {
/**
 * main method of AssertTester prints program
 * arguments to <code>System.out</code>
 * @param args[] command line arguments
 * @throws java.lang.AssertionError
 * occurs if no arguments are supplied
 * or an argument has more than 3 characters
 */
      public static void main(String[] args) { /*…*/ }
}
```

Figure 1-5   Start of a class definition containing doc comments

Notice that the first line of each doc comment provides brief a description of the following program element. As a rule, you should start the doc comment for a class or method with a one-sentence overview of the class or method.

To parse a doc comment, javadoc looks at the characters that come after /** and before the matching */. It discards the * characters at the start of each line. For all but the first line, javadoc also ignores blanks and tabs preceding the initial * characters. The text that remains after the * characters and the white space are trimmed off is incorporated into the HTML documentation.

Because the text is inserted into HTML documents, you can include HTML markup. Avoid using HTML tags for headings, because the tool generates its own headings. You may have to experiment to find out which tags are safe. As a rule of thumb, HTML tags that change the font or highlight characters work well, but HTML tags that alter the structure of an HTML document may conflict with javadoc presentation. In the listing in Figure 1-5, the HTML tags <code> and </code> highlight the destination of the program output. This book does not teach HTML, but Chapter 13 gives an introduction to HTML and XHTML.

Using javadoc Tags

In addition to including HTML tags, you can include javadoc tags in your doc comments. Use them to generate subheadings such as "Parameters," "Returns," and "See Also" in the description of classes, interfaces, and members.

Syntax

`@tag`

Dissection

All `javadoc` tags start with an `@` character. Each tag must start a new line. Whether the tag is appropriate or not depends on what it precedes. Most of the `javadoc` tags and the headings that they produce are listed here, in the order that they usually appear in source code.

Tags

- To create a heading "Author," insert the following tag:

  `@author` *`author_name`*

  You can put this tag before a class or an interface. The name can be any string. This tag is ignored unless you include the `-author` option when you run `javadoc`.

- To create a heading "Version," insert the tag:

  `@version`

  You can put this tag before a class or an interface. Often, the version text follows a numerical pattern such as 1.1 or 3.0.2. This tag is ignored unless you include the `-version` option when you run `javadoc`.

- To include the value of a constant in the constant field values page, insert the following in the doc comment for a static final field, including the braces (**`{}`**):

  `{@value}`

- To create a heading "Parameters," insert the following tag:

  `@param` *`variable_name`*

  This tag goes before the definition of a method. It gives the name of one argument of a method followed by a description. If the method has more than one argument, provide a **`@param`** tag for each argument. Group these tags together.

- To create a heading "Returns," insert the following tag:

  `@return` *`description`*

  Put this tag before a method definition to describe the return value of a method.

- To create a heading "Throws," insert either of the following two synonymous tags:

  `@exception` *`fully_qualified_class_name description`*

  `@throws` *`fully_qualified_class_name description`*

  Put this tag before a method definition to list and describe an exception that the method can throw. The fully qualified class name is a hypertext link to the exception class. If the method can throw more than one type of exception, provide an **`@exception`** or **`@throws`** tag for each exception class. You should group these tags together.

- To create a heading "See Also," insert one of the following tags:

  @see *package.class_name*

  @see *package.class_name#field_name*

  @see *package.class_name#method_name(argument_list)*

  Use this tag in any doc comments to insert cross-references in the HTML documentation. This tag creates a hypertext link to another class or member. You can omit the package name for classes in the current package and the class name for other members of the same class. You can include any number of **@see** for one declaration.

- To generate an inline hypertext link, insert the following tag, including the braces (**{}**), anywhere in a doc comment:

  {@link *name label*}

  You can use this tag in any doc comment. Unlike other **javadoc** tags, a **{@link}** often appears in the middle of a sentence in a doc comment. For example, if the following appears in a doc comment in a class called **MyClass**:

  ```
  To do magic, use the {@link #myMethod(args) myMethod} method.
  ```

  the resulting HTML includes

  ```
  To do magic, use the <a href="MyClass.html#myMethod(args)">
  myMethod</a> method.
  ```

- Use the following tag to get a relative link to the root directory of the generated documentation web:

  {@docRoot}

  This is useful when you want to include a standard file, such as a copyright page or company logo, in all generated pages. The **javadoc** tool puts files in hierarchical directories, and without this tag the relative path to the target file can be different from page to page in the generated documentation web. The following generates a link from all pages in the web to a file called **install.html**:

  ```
  /**

   * See the <a href= "{docRoot}/install.html">Installation Notes.</a>

   */
  ```

- To create a heading "Since," insert the following tag:

  @since *text*

  You can use this tag in any doc comment. The text explains when the package, class, or member became available. In the Java platform API documentation, the text is usually "JDK 1.0," "JDK 1.1," or "JDK 1.2" reflecting the fact that the Java 2 SDK was previously called the Java Development Kit (JDK).

- To create a heading "Deprecated," insert the following tag:

  `@deprecated` *text*

  Typically, you use the **@deprecated** tag for a package, class, or method that is legacy code from an earlier version. If you cannot delete old code because others may still depend on it, this tag gives you an opportunity to inform developers that the class or method may not be available in the future. The text should include either `"Replaced by....."` or `"No replacement."`

- To say that a class is *serializable* means that objects of the class can be saved, usually by writing the object(s) to file, in a form suitable for restoring later. Object serialization is discussed in Chapter 3. You should indicate fields that are saved when the object is serialized using one of the following tags:

  `@serial` *field_description*

  `@serialField` *field_name field_type field_description*

  `@serialData` *data_description*

The compiler looks at doc comments as it is compiling a class and sets an attribute on the `.class` file for any deprecated class, method, or interface that it finds. Whenever a class is compiled, the `.class` file attributes of the classes, methods, and interfaces that the class uses are checked to see whether they are deprecated. The compiler prints a warning when asked to compile code that uses a deprecated class, interface, or method.

Creating HTML from `javadoc`

The only reason to include doc comments, rather than ordinary comments, in your code is to prepare to run the `javadoc` tool or the feature of your IDE that generates HTML documentation from source code. Usually, you run `javadoc` against the source for all classes in a package or suite of packages. The tool parses the doc comments in the input files. To get HTML output in the standard format, simply run the `javadoc` program.

You can customize the `javadoc` output by writing a doclet. A *doclet* is a plug-in program for the `javadoc` tool that formats and outputs the required documentation. By default, `javadoc` uses a standard doclet that comes with the Java platform. The `javadoc` tool preprocesses the doc comments into a data structure and delegates to a doclet the job of converting the data into output. A doclet could, for example, generate documentation that conforms to your company's style guidelines, generate XML or RTF files rather than HTML, recognize customized `javadoc` tags, or perform special tasks, such as detecting methods that have no doc comments. The classes in the package **com.sun.javadoc** provide the API used by doclets.

Regardless of whether you use the standard doclet or another doclet for customized output, you run the `javadoc` command to create the documentation.

1

Syntax

```
javadoc [options] package_or_class_names
```

Dissection

The most commonly used options of the `javadoc` tool are listed in the following section. After the options you can supply one or more class names or package names separated by spaces.

Options

- `-author`

  Specify the `author` option to tell `javadoc` to process `@author` tags, which are ignored by default.

- `-classpath path;path;`

  The `-classpath` option tells `javadoc` where to look for classes that are referenced in the definition of classes being documented. For example, the return type of a method may be a referenced class. Classes mentioned in doc comments are not referenced classes. The `javadoc` tool loads referenced classes while it is running and prints a message if it cannot find them.

- `-d folder_name`

  If you want to place the HTML output files in any folder other than the current folder, specify a destination with the `-d` option. The folder must already exist.

- `-doclet class`

  The `-doclet` option gives the name of the class that starts the doclet to be used by this run of `javadoc`. Omit this tag to use the standard doclet.

- `-nodeprecated`

  Specify `nodeprecated` to exclude sections marked with the `@deprecated` tag.

- `-noindex`

  Specify `noindex` to tell `javadoc` not to output the index page that `javadoc` creates by default.

- `-notree`

  Specify `notree` to tell `javadoc` not to output the class hierarchy page that `javadoc` creates by default.

- `-overview path\filename`

  If you want overview documentation, you must prepare a source file for the overview. The `overview` option gives the name of this file. Typically, you use a file named `overview.html` that resides in the same folder as the top-level package.

- -package

  Specify `package` to include all classes and members except those with private access. The default is `protected`.

- -private

  Specify `private` to include all classes and members. The default is `protected`.

- -protected

  Specify `protected` to include protected and public classes and members. This is the default.

- -public

  Specify `public` to include only public classes, interfaces, and members. The default is `protected`.

- -sourcepath *path;path;...*

  When `javadoc` is operating on packages, you can specify search paths for the packages with the `-sourcepath` option.

- -version

  Specify `version` to tell `javadoc` to process @`version` tags, which are ignored by default.

Code Example

```
javadoc -d docs -source 1.4 examples.intro
Loading source files for package examples.intro...
Constructing Javadoc information...
Standard Doclet version 1.4.1
Generating docs\constant-values.html...
Building tree for all the packages and classes...
Building index for all the packages and classes...
Generating docs\overview-tree.html...
Generating docs\index-all.html...
Generating docs\deprecated-list.html...
Building index for all classes...
Generating docs\allclasses-frame.html...
Generating docs\allclasses-noframe.html...
Generating docs\index.html...
Generating docs\packages.html...
Generating docs\examples\intro\package-frame.html...
Generating docs\examples\intro\package-summary.html...
Generating docs\examples\intro\package-tree.html...
Generating docs\examples\intro\AssertTester.html...
Generating docs\package-list...
Generating docs\help-doc.html...
Generating docs\stylesheet.css...
```

1

Code Dissection

This `javadoc` command generates documentation on the package containing example code for this chapter, `examples.intro`. The package directory resides in the current folder. This package contains just one class called `AssertTester`. Here, the compiler switch `-source 1.4` is needed because this particular class uses a language feature new to version 1.4. See the section "Recent Additions to the Java 2 Platform" for more details.

The resulting documentation is added to an existing subfolder of the current folder called `docs`. The output listed here appears on the console when you run `javadoc`. Of course, the output of interest is the set of HTML files that the console output says it is generating.

When documenting packages, the `javadoc` tool locates input files much like the `javac` compiler does:

- You can specify an input location other than the current folder by including the `-sourcepath` option.

- If you omit `-sourcepath`, `javadoc` uses the paths specified with the `-classpath` option for source and referenced classes.

- If you specify neither option, `javadoc` uses the paths set in the `CLASSPATH` environment variable.

- If `CLASSPATH` is not set, `javadoc` looks in the current folder.

To run `javadoc` on one or more classes, you must go to the folder that contains the classes or give the full path to the source files. The `-sourcepath` option applies only at the package level. For example, to generate documentation just for the `examples.intro.AssertTester` class when `examples` is a subfolder of folder `data` on the D: drive, issue the following command:

```
javadoc -d docs -source 1.4 D:\Data\examples\intro\AssertTester.java
```

Some of the HTML pages and subfolders created in the `docs` folder by this command are listed in Figure 1-6.

File or Subfolder Name	Description
`help-doc.html`	This file describes the structure of the generated documentation web.
`index.html`	The root of this documentation web is shown in Figure 1-7. This file defines a frameset that starts by showing `allclasses-frames.html` and `package-summary.html`. Versions without frames are also generated.
`allclasses-frames.html`	This file contains a list of all classes and interfaces in all packages.

Figure 1-6   Files created by the `javadoc` command

File or Subfolder Name	Description
`package-summary.html`	This file shows a summary of packages in the current documentation web when the `javadoc` command is run on one or more packages.
`constant-values.html`	This file lists all constants defined in all classes and interfaces.
`deprecated-list.html`	This file lists all deprecated types and members.
`overview-tree.html`	This file shows the package and class hierarchies.
`examples\intro`	This subfolder of `docs` contains pages for the types in package `examples.intro` plus pages such as package summary and hierarchy.
`examples\intro\AssertTester.html`	This page describes the class `AssertTester` in package `examples.intro` and is shown in Figure 1-8.

Figure 1-6   Files created by the `javadoc` command (continued)

The file `index.html` lists all the packages documented in this HTML web. To display this file, open it with your Web browser. It resides in the folder specified with the `-d` option when you ran the `javadoc` tool. Figure 1-7 shows the `index.html` generated when the `javadoc` tool is run on a single package that contains a single class. Use the links at the top of the page to navigate the documentation web.

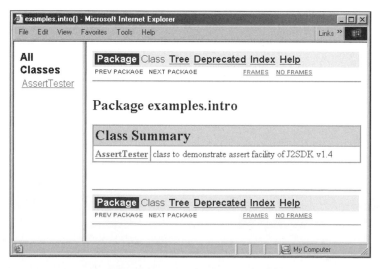

Figure 1-7   An `index.html` file generated by `javadoc`

If you click the `index` navigation link, you see a page that lists fields and methods in alphabetical order and provides links to each one. Click package `examples.intro` to bring up a list of the classes in the `examples.intro` package. Click `AssertTester` in that list to display the page partially shown in Figure 1-8.

In Figure 1-8, notice that the description method **main** uses the text from the doc comments in the source file. The **javadoc** output includes additional useful information, such as the class–relationship diagram near the top of the page.

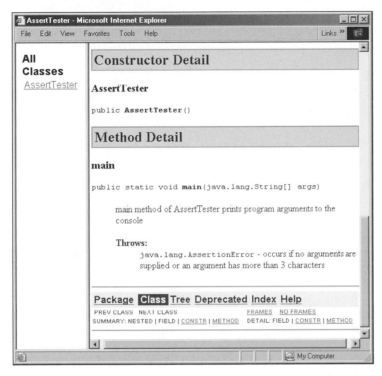

Figure 1-8   Part of the **javadoc** HTML page for the **AssertTester** class

PACKAGING PROGRAMS FOR DISTRIBUTION

A very important step in software development is packaging your code for distribution and ensuring that your users can install or deploy your classes. When you work in Java, you often end up with a large number of relatively small files containing classes, multimedia resources, data, and possibly your source and **javadoc** output. The standard way to distribute J2SE is to combine them into a Java archive file using the **jar** tool. Packaging for J2EE is more complex and is discussed in Chapters 13 and 14.

Before you run the **jar** tool, make sure your files reside in the proper folders on your file system. The resulting jar file contains a folder structure that mirrors the folders and subfolders you input to the **jar** command. You can list input files individually, but an easy and common practice is to specify folder names and let the tool automatically process all files and subfolders in the folders you specify.

Syntax

```
jar [options] [manifest] destination input-files
```

Dissection

The most commonly used forms of the `jar` command for building and extracting files from a jar file are listed here.

Options

To specify an option, include its letter to the option token. For example, to specify options `c`, `f`, and `v`, you specify option `cvf`. Note that option letters are case-sensitive. Some options are:

- c   Create a new or empty jar.

- t   Type a list of the contents of an existing jar.

- x   Extract files from an existing jar.

- f   The jar file is named in a `jar` command. If you do not supply this argument and a name for the jar file, the tool reads from or writes to the console.

- m   Include manifest information from the named manifest file.

- 0   (digit 0) Do not compress the contents of the jar. If you omit the `0` option when building a jar, the file is compressed using the same compression format as a zip file.

- M   Do not create a manifest file.

- u   Update an existing file by adding files or changing the manifest.

- v   Send verbose status output to the console.

Manifest

An optional manifest within the jar lists the files in the jar and information about the elements stored in those files. J2SE does not require a manifest for ordinary classes. However, you must specify that a class is a JavaBean in the manifest. Chapter 8 describes how to package JavaBeans. J2EE uses manifest files extensively.

If you have a manifest in a separate file, specify the manifest filename after the options on the command line. For example, to package the class that contains the **main** method of an application, you can prepare a manifest that identifies the **main** class, as in

```
Manifest-Version: 1.0
Main-Class: HelloWorld
```

Each line in a manifest file contains a name-value pair with a colon separating the name string from the value string. You can create a manifest with a text editor. If the previous two-line file is called `HelloManifest.MF`, you can include this manifest when you create a jar containing the `HelloWorld` class with the `jar` command:

```
jar -cfm HelloWorld.jar HelloManifest.MF HelloWorld.class
```

Destination

Specify the jar filename after the options and optional manifest file.

Input Files

List the input files, which may include the jar itself if you are working with an existing jar. You can use wildcards in filenames. For example, specify * to include all files in the current folder.

Code Example

```
jar 0cf myProg.jar myApp media
```

Code Dissection

The current folder has two subfolders: `myApp` contains the classes in a package called `myApp`, and `media` contains audio and image files used by the classes. With this command, you can package them all into one jar called `myProg`. The resulting jar is not compressed and has a default manifest.

Code Example

```
jar tf examples.jar
```

Code Dissection

The `jar` command lists the contents of `examples.jar`.

You can distribute packages of classes that are used by applications and applets in jar files. To deploy an application distributed in a jar file, make sure the jar file is listed on your `CLASSPATH`.

BUILDING A PROGRAM WITH APPLICATION DEVELOPER

Earlier, this chapter reviewed the command-line tools that come with the SDK. For most of this book, the SDK tools suffice, but using the command line can be awkward and these tools have very basic functionality. Instead, you can use any IDE that supports J2SDK version 1.4. This book introduces a very powerful IDE marketed by IBM: WebSphere Studio Application Developer, version 5. Part of the reason for this choice is that Application Developer has excellent productivity tools for creating J2EE applications, and using those tools makes it reasonable for this book to include working examples for the J2EE concepts introduced in later chapters.

Use this section as a first tutorial on using Application Developer. An installable version of the product is included on the CD, together with installation instructions. The program you develop here is simple—a variation on the `HelloWorld` program—but it serves to show the basics of application development in Application Developer. Just as the `HelloWorld` program uses only a tiny portion of the J2SE platform, this tutorial shows very little of Application Developer.

Application Developer is a complex tool with features for many aspects of application development. It is used by developers with different skills and areas of technical expertise. Like all good IDEs, it includes debug, test, and deployment tools. The test environment can be a complete installation of WebSphere Application Server or Apache Tomcat. With Application Developer, you can write Java programs, design your Swing or AWT GUI visually, create Web applications using a WYSIWYG editor for HTML and graphics design tools, develop EJBs and J2EE enterprise applications, connect to the enterprise through J2EE-compatible messaging, work with XML files and transforms, manipulate databases and data sources, create Web Services, profile running applications, connect to source code control systems for team development, and much more.

IBM WebSphere Studio is a family of products that includes the four products in the following list. All these Java IDEs are based on an open-source workbench technology called *Eclipse*, which is designed to be extendable, so different vendors can and do provide IDEs built for different purposes by plugging tools into the *Eclipse* framework. The WebSphere Studio products are *Eclipse*-based IDEs from IBM.

- *Site Developer* includes all development tools and a test environment for J2SE programs and Web applications. This edition is adequate if you are building Java or Web applications that use only servlets and JSPs from J2EE. Site Developer is adequate for all but Chapter 14 of this book.

- *Application Developer* is the flagship WebSphere Studio product. It has all the features of Site Developer and adds full support for J2EE applications. With Application Developer you can build EJBs and Web services.

- *Integration Edition* has all that Application Developer has and adds support for the Java 2 Connection Architecture for connecting to Enterprise Information Systems, and extensions to Web services tools for modeling long running business processes.

- *Enterprise Developer* packages many IBM products for development in large enterprise environments. Integration Edition is one of the included products.

A note of warning: Application Developer does require a fairly powerful install platform. If your computer is less than a Pentium 3 with 256M of RAM, you may find that Application Developer operates slowly. Application Developer runs on Windows and Linux platforms only, but creates files that can be deployed on a WebSphere Application Server or other J2EE-compliant servers running on a wide range of platforms.

Application Developer Tutorial

You can start Application Developer from the Windows Start menu, but may prefer to add a shortcut to your Windows desktop. The first window you see when the product comes up asks what workspace to use. The workspace is a folder on your disk in which the product stores all your work files. You can accept the default or enter any folder name. If you enter the name of a folder that does not exist, Application Developer initializes a new workspace in that location. Using this feature makes it easy to revert to the equivalent of a fresh install when starting a new project, or whenever you want.

When Application Developer opens, the IDE may look like Figure 1-9. To reduce image size, some of the screen area has been cut.

Figure 1-9   Application Developer open to the J2EE perspective

The Application Developer IDE is organized into windows called *perspectives*, and each perspective groups together a number of work and information areas called *views*. Each perspective is designed to suit the needs of a different type of developer. Perspectives and views are highly customizable, but this tutorial uses the default arrangement. Usually, Application Developer opens to the J2EE perspective where you build EJBs and enterprise applications. You can change the initial perspective during install, so you see a different perspective when the product opens.

Regardless of what perspective you are in, you'll find the following parts of the IDE:

- Under the title bar is the main menu and under it the main toolbar. If you pause with the mouse over any button, a ToolTip or flyover-help tells what the button does.

- Down the left is a perspectives toolbar, used to change perspectives quickly.

- Most perspectives show four areas by default:
  - A Navigation tree in the upper left groups program elements according to the nature of the work done in this perspective. This tree is a hierarchical view of your workspace but does not necessarily mirror the organization of folders on the disk.
  - The upper right is an Editor view where you perform much of your work. If a file is open, its name appears in a tab followed by an X on which you click to close the file.
  - An Outline view showing the structure of the document now open for editing may appear in the lower left as in Figure 1-9 or in the upper right as in Figure 1-10.
  - Most perspectives show status information in the lower right. A Tasks view lists unresolved problems identified by the product and tasks you have entered as reminders to yourself.

- Several views may occupy the same area, in which case you see tabs that bring different views to the front.

The first word in the title bar is the name of the current perspective. If this word is "Java," skip to Step 2 of the tutorial "Selecting version 1.4 of the JRE."

Step 1: Opening the Java perspective

To change perspective:

1. Click the **Open a Perspective** button, ⊞, in the perspectives toolbar.

2. A drop-down menu appears. Select **Java** or the name of the perspective you want. If the perspective name does not show, select **Other** to open the complete list. Then you can select the perspective by name and click **OK** to open the perspective.

3. After a brief pause, the Java perspective should appear. Note that **Java** is the first word in the title bar and the Java Perspective button, ⊞, has been added to the perspective menu. You can use buttons like this one to change perspective quickly.

   Figure 1-10 shows the Java perspective before development starts. By default, the Package Explorer view occupies the left side of the screen and the Outline view is on the right. The Package Explorer groups files by project, package, and class. Projects are artifacts of Application Developer. They group files that you use together. In Application Developer you always work in a project, and one development exercise may require several different kinds of projects.

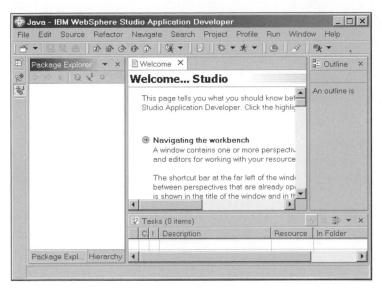

Figure 1-10   The Java perspective of Application Developer

Step 2: Selecting version 1.4 of the JRE

Because Application Developer is designed for building J2EE applications, it comes with version 1.3 of the JRE. If version 1.4 of the JRE is installed on your workstation, you can set Application Developer to use it—or any other installed JRE. The `HelloWorld` program works with SDK 1.3. However, if you are going to use Application Developer for all the examples in this book, you will need some 1.4-specific features eventually. Now is a good time to load the 1.4 JRE.

1. To set the JRE in Application Developer, you set a preference for your workspace. In the main menu select **Window** and then **Preferences**.

2. In the list on the left of the Preferences window, expand **Java** and then select **Installed JREs**. On the right you see the Standard VM installed with Application Developer. Click the **Add** button to add another to the list of JREs known to Application Developer.

3. Fill in the **Add JRE** dialog box as shown in Figure 1-11. Enter a name, such as **J2SE v1.4**, and click the **Browse** button to find the home folder of the version 1.4 J2SDK you installed. Note that the system library `rt.jar` is found automatically if you specify a valid J2SDK install folder. Leave **Use default system libraries** checked and click **OK**. Application Developer now knows where you installed the version 1.4 J2SDK on your workstation.

Figure 1-11   Loading the version 1.4 JRE into Application Developer

4. When you return to the Preferences dialog box, the new JRE is listed, but not yet selected as the default JRE. Check the box beside the JRE you just loaded, as shown in Figure 1-12, and click **OK**.

Now all programs you write are compiled and executed using the J2SDK that you installed. When you get to Chapters 13 and 14, return to the 1.3 version JRE by returning to the dialog box shown in Figure 1-12 and selecting **Standard VM Detected VM** from the list of installed JREs.

Step 3: Creating a Java project, package, and class

You must create a Java project to contain Java code. Then create a package and finally a class for the `HelloWorld` program. Using Application Developer wizards completes these tasks quickly and reduces opportunities for error.

1. Click the Create a Java Project toolbar button, 🔳. Fill in the Java Project dialog box as shown in Figure 1-13. Enter project name **WSADdemo**, leave the check box to **Use default** directory selected, and click **Finish**.

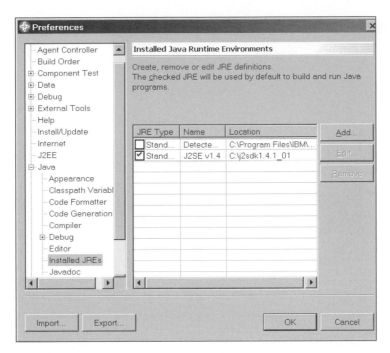

Figure 1-12   Selecting a default JRE for Application Developer

2. When the project appears in the Package Explorer view, make sure it is high-lighted and click the **Create a Java Package** toolbar button, 🔳, to add a Java package to the selected project. Fill in the dialog box as shown in Figure 1-14. Make sure the source folder is **WSADdemo**, enter package name **learning**, and click **Finish**.

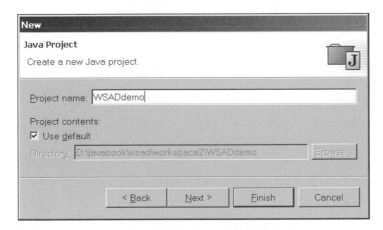

Figure 1-13   The Create Java Project Wizard

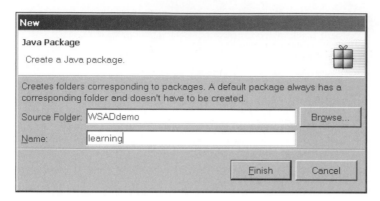

Figure 1-14   The Create a Java Package Wizard

3. When the package appears under the project in the Package Explorer view, make sure it is highlighted, and click the **Create a Java Class** toolbar button, , to add a Java class to the selected package. Fill in the dialog box as shown in Figure 1-15. Make sure the source folder is **WSADdemo** and package name is **learning**; enter a class name **HelloWorld** and select the modifier **public** if it is not already selected. Check all boxes to create method stubs and then click **Finish**.

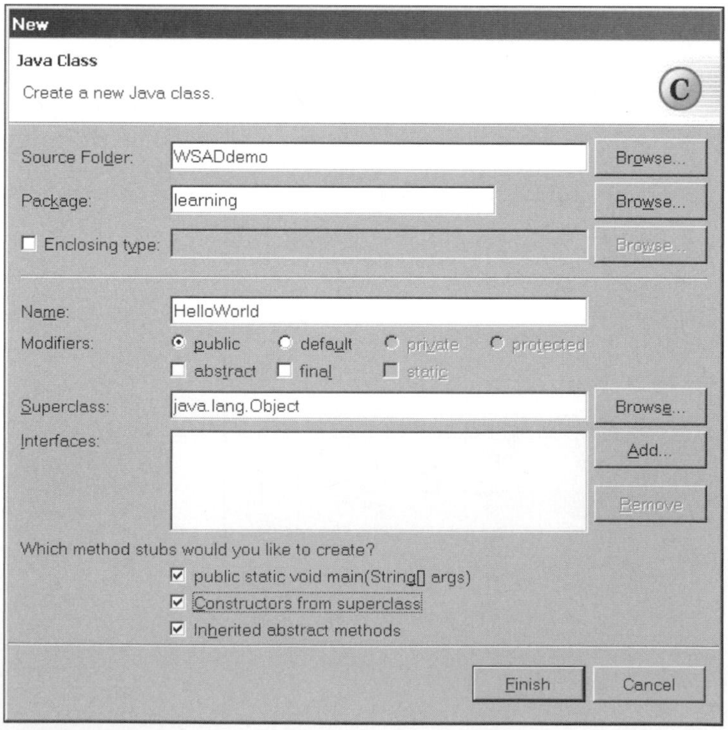

Figure 1-15   The Create a Java Class Wizard

The Java perspective should look similar to Figure 1-16. The wizard leaves the new class open in the Java editor. The Outline view on the left lists generated class members. Notice that initial doc comments have been generated.

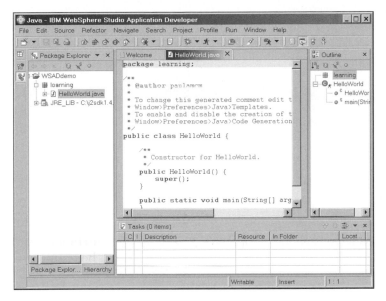

Figure 1-16   The Java perspective showing a generated class

Step 4: Entering the code for the `HelloWorld` class

   1. Before you start entering code, double-click the editor title bar to expand the editor area to fill the entire IDE window. At this point you can type in the rest of the code. You could simply copy-type from Figure 1-17. However, you gain more by exploring some of the features of the editor. Follow the remaining steps to try a few of the many assists built into the editor.

```
package learning;
import java.io.*;
/**
 * @author Java Student
 * A first program created with IBM
 * WebSphere Studio Application Developer version 5
 */
public class HelloWorld {
    String name = null;
    /**
     * Constructor for HelloWorld.
     */
```

Figure 1-17   Complete listing of a `HelloWorld` program

```
    public HelloWorld() {
        super();
    }
    /**
     * main method creates an object that says hello
     */
    public static void main(String[] args)
            throws IOException {
        HelloWorld hw = new HelloWorld();
        System.out.print("What is your name? ");
        BufferedReader br =
            new BufferedReader(new
                InputStreamReader(System.in));
        String name = br.readLine();
        hw.setName(name);
        hw.sayHello();
    }
    /**
     * sayHello method prints a greeting on the console
     */
    void sayHello() {
        System.out.println("Hello " + getName());
    }
    /**
     * Returns the name.
     * @return String
     */
    public String getName() {
        return name;
    }
    /**
     * Sets the name.
     * @param name The name to set
     */
    public void setName(String name) {
        this.name = name;
    }
}
```

Figure 1-17   Complete listing of a `HelloWorld` program (continued)

2. Start typing the code from the top. Stop typing before the call of method **readLine** and pretend you have forgotten this method. Position the cursor immediately after the **br.** and press **Ctrl+Space**. This opens the code assist as shown in Figure 1–18. A list of the methods in the **BufferedReader** class appears, and you can double-click to select the method you want.

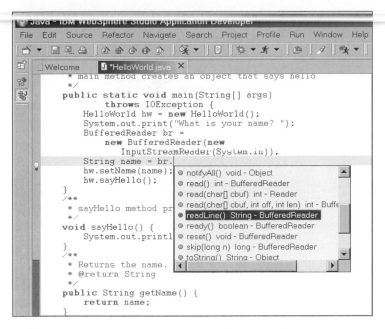

Figure 1-18   A code-assist feature of the Application Developer Java editor

3. Hover with the mouse over the method name **readLine** in your code and see a box pop up describing what the **BufferedReader.readLine** method does.

4. Continue entering code to the end of the **sayHello** method. Use a wizard to automatically generate a getter and setter method for the field **name**. Before you can do this, double-click the editor title bar to return to original size and make the Outline view visible.

5. Right-click the field **name** in the outline view and select **Generate Getter and Setter** from the pop-up menu, as shown in Figure 1-19. When the Generate Getter and Setter dialog box appears, make sure boxes to generate **getName** and **setName** methods are set. Then click **OK**.

6. Press **Ctrl+S** to save and compile, or right-click in the editor area and select **Save** from the pop-up menu.

7. Error symbols, ⊗ , appear at the start of lines with errors. The most likely reason for errors is typing mistakes. Fix all errors and save again until you get a clean compile. If you have a error on the line

```
public class HelloWorld {
```

make sure the class definition has a closing **}**.

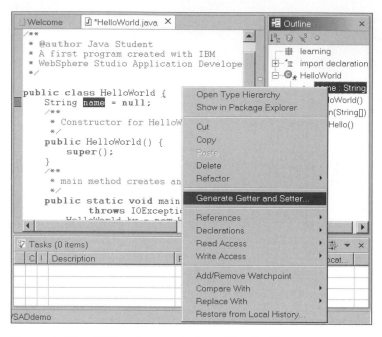

Figure 1-19   Editing Java code from the Outline view

8. As a final touch, right–click over any whitespace in the editor area and select **Format** from the pop-up menu, as shown in Figure 1-20. See how the code is neatly formatted. You can change the look of the editor's formatting para-meters, content of the default `javadoc` and the like, using the **Windows, Preferences** menu.

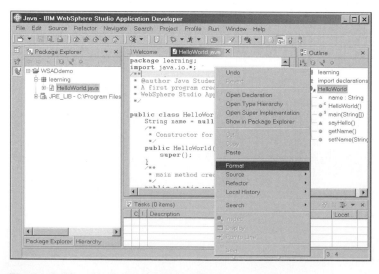

Figure 1-20   Features of Java editor

9, Click the **X** on the tab beside the class to close the editor. If a dialog box
asks whether to save changes, select **Yes**.

Step 5: Running the program

Application Developer can launch a program in a variety of ways. For example, it can install
and run Web applications on a test application server. To run a simple class in the JRE:

1. Make sure **HelloWorld.java** is selected in the Package Explorer view now
   visible on the left of the screen. Click the down arrow beside the **Run**, 🏃 ▾,
   toolbar button.

2. From the pop-up menu select **Run As** and then **Java Application**, as in
   Figure 1-21. When you want to enter command-line arguments or pass
   `javac` arguments to the compiler, select **Run** and complete the dialog boxes.

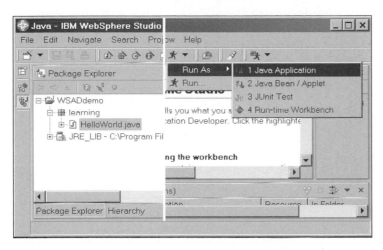

Figure 1-21   Running a Java application in Application Developer

The output should appear on the Console view, which should automatically replace the
Tasks view on the lower right of the IDE. Figure 1-22 shows the expected output.

Figure 1-22   Output from a Java application in the Application Developer Console view

Step 6: Exporting code and closing Application Developer

You can export an individual class, a package, or a project to individual files, or export
a jar file. Find out how to do so by asking the Help system:

1. To ask the IDE how to perform a task, click **Help** on the main menu and
   Help Contents from the drop-down menu.

2. In the **Search** box of the Help window, enter a phrase like **exporting files**. Depending on your query, building a search index may take a few moments.

3. Click a likely topic from the list of search results on the left of the Help menu. Follow the instructions that appear on the right. Hint: To use the Export Wizard, highlight the item you want to export and select **Export** from the **File** menu. Then you complete dialog boxes to specify exactly what to export, select how to package the exported code, and identify the destination.

4. When you are satisfied, you can close Application Developer by selecting **Exit** from the **File** menu or clicking the Windows **close box**.

5. The Help system built into Application Developer is excellent and includes a number of sample scenarios for you to follow. To really learn how to use Application Developer, select **Help Contents** from the **Help** menu, expand **Application developer information**, and then **Getting Started** in the navigation tree. Find and then select **Tutorial: Workbench basics**. Explanations and instructions telling you how to proceed appear on the right side of the Help window.

RECENT ADDITIONS TO THE JAVA 2 PLATFORM

Every new version of the Java platform includes some bug fixes and new APIs. In the process some old APIs can become deprecated. Sometimes the new APIs are minor enhancements, while others apply a new implementation architecture to existing classes. For example, in version 1.2, the Collections framework of classes was introduced and the implementations of the existing six collection classes were reworked to become compatible with the collections architecture. Chapter 4 discusses the collection classes in core package `java.util`. Sometimes the addition of a new API changes the status of an existing API from an optional extension to part of the core classes. For example, the `javax.sql` package is part of JDBC 3.0 and became part of J2SE in version 1.3. JDBC 3.0 is described in Chapter 9.

Less frequently in recent years, new tools have been added and the language itself enhanced. It is true to say that the Java language has been stable, but not frozen, since version 1.1 and the Java 2 platform since version 1.2 or Java 2. However, like any living language and platform, Java is still evolving. Version 1.4 brings one significant addition to the language, the `assert` keyword, one new tool, `Java Web Start`, and many new APIs.

To review all changes since the beginning of Java, or even all the changes between version 1.3 and 1.4, would not be productive at this point. Most changes are simply incorporated into the text of the relevant chapters of this book and, where significant, are marked with a caution note. The purpose of this section is to highlight the more interesting changes and discuss some new features that do not fit into any other chapter of this book.

Assertions

Version 1.4 of the Java language gives you the ability to verify that assumptions that your code depends upon are true. For example, you may want to check requirements or pre-conditions, such as verify that an object reference is not **null**, or verify intermediate results of an algorithm, such as determine that certain elements in a list that is partially sorted are indeed in order. Use the assertion facility during development and not in production, because the **assert** statement throws an exception if the test **boolean** expression evaluates to **false**.

Syntax

```
assert    boolean_expression;
assert    boolean_expression : errorcode;
```

Dissection

- An assertion statement can appear in any reachable place in the body of a method.

- When the Boolean expression does not evaluate to **true**, an assert statement throws a **java.lang.AssertionError**. The **AssertionError** class is a subtype of **java.lang.Error** and therefore a system exception. It terminates the running program.

- When the Boolean expression has the value **true**, the program continues to run.

- If you supply an errorcode expression of any type, its value is passed to the **AssertionError** object, typically to be available for inclusion in the error message.

Code Example

```
public static void main(String[] args) {
  assert args.length > 0;
  for ( int i = 0; i < args.length; i++ ) {
    assert args[i].length() < 4:
      "Argument " + i + " is too long";
    System.out.println( "Arg[" + i + "] = "
      + args[i] );
}
```

Code Dissection

For demonstration purposes, this **main** method stops with an **AssertionError** unless at least one command-line argument has been passed to the program. After the first assertion succeeds, the method checks that no command-line argument is longer than three characters. The second **AssertionError** contains the message **"Argument *i* is too long"**.

The keyword **assert** is new with version 1.4, and the compiler does not recognize it by default. The sample **main** method here is from a class called **examples. intro.AssertTester**. When compiling with the **javac** command, use the switch

-source 1.4, because the javac compiler defaults to version 1.3. To compile this class, copy the folder X:\Data\examples\intro from the CD to a folder on your hard drive. Open a command line window and issue the commands listed here. The first command assumes you copied X:\Data\examples\intro to folder C:\javaSamples:

```
cd javaSamples
javac -source 1.4 examples\intro\AssertTester.java
```

By default, assertions are not enabled in the JVM. Therefore you do not have to remove them from your code when you send the class to a production environment. Assertion statements are ignored unless you launch using the java command with the switch -enableassertions or -ea for short.

Figure 1-23 shows what happens when you run AssertTester with and without arguments, and with and without the -ea switch.

Java Command (on One Line)	Output of AssertTester
java examples.intro.AssertTester	*blank — no output*

java -ea
 examples.intro.AssertTester
	Exception in thread "main"
	    java.lang.AssertionError at
	    examples.intro.Assert
	    Tester.main
	    (AssertTester.java:15)

java examples.intro.AssertTester one two three	Arg[0] = one Arg[1] = two Arg [2] = three

java -ea
 examples.intro.AssertTester
 one two three
	Arg[0] = one
	
	Arg[1] = two
	Exception in thread "main"
	    java.lang.AssertionError:
	    Argument 2 is too long
	at examples.intro.AssertTester.main
	    (AssertTester.java:18)

Figure 1-23   The effect of assertions in the AssertTester class

Follow these instructions to run the AssertTester class and other programs that include assertions in Application Developer.

- To set the compiler option -source 1.4:
    1. From the **Window** menu, select **Preferences** to open the Preferences dialog.
    2. Expand the tree on the left by clicking the **+** beside **Java**.
    3. Click **Compiler** on the left and then the **JDK compliance** tab on the right of the Preferences dialog.

4. Select **1.4** from the Compiler compliance level drop-down list.

5. Click **OK** to accept the setting and close the Preferences dialog.

■ To set the launcher option **-enableassertions** or **-ea**:

1. In the Package Explorer of the Java perspective, click on the class you want to run so that is it highlighted.

2. Click the **Run** toolbar button to open its drop-down menu, and select **Run** from the menu.

3. When the Launch Configurations dialog opens, click the **Arguments** tab to open the Arguments dialog.

4. In the top text area, labeled "Program arguments," you can type command-line arguments exactly as you would enter them on a command line. For example you can enter **one two three** to test the `AssertTester` class. In the bottom text area, labeled "VM arguments," you can enter options for the `java` command. In the bottom area, enter **-enableassertions** or **-ea**.

5. Click **Apply** and then **Run**. The Launch Configuration menu closes automatically and the highlighted class runs. The VM options and command-line arguments remain set until you open the Launch Configurations dialog again to change them.

Java Web Start

`Java Web Start` is a deployment product bundled with J2SE starting with version 1.4. If you use a Windows platform, you may notice that `Java Web Start` is installed automatically with the J2SDK. By default on Windows, the J2SDK installation program adds the program `javaws.exe` to your `C:\Program Files` folder and adds a shortcut to your Windows desktop. You can use this tool to run applications that do not reside on your local computer. The version installed with the SDK comes with links to some sample programs on a Sun site preloaded into the `Java Web Start` user interface. The main purpose of the product is to provide a distribution mechanism so developers can make J2SE programs easily available over the Web to users.

To distribute a program, developers can build HTML pages containing links to access programs. Developers must package the programs and all required resources in jar files and make them available on a Web server. Then users can launch the applications from a Web browser by accessing the HTML page and clicking links. To the user, loading the target program is as simple as following a link to any URL. But the destination of the link is actually the launch file, and the browser launches the `Java Web Start` tool to download, cache, and run the requested program. Users can also run `Java Web Start` outside of a Web browser and even add shortcuts to remote programs to their local desktop.

`Java Web Start` first checks whether a version of the program is installed locally, and then whether the local version is up-to-date. If necessary, it downloads the program and launches it to run in a local JRE. Any J2SE program can be deployed through the tool. Java security is supported, and unsigned applications run in a restricted environment.

The technology behind `Java Web Start` is a product of the JSR process: the Java Network Launching Protocol (JNLP) and API. The `Java Web Start` tool is a reference implementation for JNLP. The JNLP specification is currently under development as JSR 056 and available to the public so that software developers can implement JNLP in their own products.

New APIs in the J2SDK

Figure 1-24 summarizes some of the APIs added to the core classes in version 1.4. The list is far from comprehensive; it mentions the features that are generally considered useful by the widest portion of the Java community, or have been available as extensions with earlier versions of the SDK. The value of some of the listed features and the great many other additions may become more apparent as you explore more advanced features of J2SE and J2EE.

Technology	Description	See Chapter
Java API for XML Processing (JAXP)	JAXP is already well known and has been a standard extension for some time. Classes that perform DOM and SAX parsing are in package `javax.xml.parsers`. You can also use classes in `javax.xml.transformations` to apply XSLT transforms.	10
New I/O (NIO) API	The `java.nio` package adds high performance I/O using a new architecture not based on the `java.io` types. Use the new `FileChannel` class to read and write files like a buffer in memory or lock files to prevent conflicts due to concurrent access by multiple users. `SocketChannel` objects can perform non-blocking, and therefore perform highly scalable, I/O to network connections.	3
Secure Sockets and HTTPS	The `javax.net.ssl` package supports the secure socket protocol so your programs can communicate over HTTPS.	12
Security	The Java Cryptography Architecture (JCA), Java Secure Socket Extension (JSSE), and Java Authorization and Authentication Service (JAAS) are core packages and no longer optional extensions.	12
Regular Expressions	The package `java.util.regex` contains classes for comparing, matching, and modifying strings based on patterns, as in the Perl language.	4

Figure 1-24   Some features new to J2SDK v 1.4

Technology	Description	See Chapter
Java Print Service	The `javax.print` package supports the new unified printing model and integrates 2D graphics.	7
Java Naming and Directory Interface	Typically, naming services are used to associate standard names with data and resources, and directory services give access to hierarchically organized data. Java programs can access naming and directory services provided by LDAP, COS Naming, RMI Registry, and DNS providers through the `javax.naming` packages. Previously JNDI worked with J2EE and was an extension to J2SE.	11

Figure 1-24   Some features new to J2SDK v 1.4 (continued)

CHAPTER SUMMARY

- ❏ Java is more than a language: It is a platform. The Java 2 platform comes in three versions: Java 2 Standard Edition (J2SE), Java 2 Enterprise Edition (J2EE), and Java2 Micro Edition (J2ME). This book deals mostly with J2SE but introduces J2EE.

- ❏ The Java platform has seen unprecedented growth in popularity and in capability since its introduction in 1995. It is now an industry standard for distributed applications that use the Web or run in distributed environments.

- ❏ The original claims that Java is platform neutral, portable, network-savvy, high performance, robust, and secure still apply, but the claim to simplicity is no longer accurate. Changes to the Java platform are the result of the Java Community Process, in which many leaders of the IT industry participate.

- ❏ You can write different kinds of programs in Java including standalone applications, applets, servlets and JSPs, JavaBeans and Enterprise JavaBeans (EJBs):

  - Applets run from Web pages in browsers.

  - Servlets and JSPs are server-side code used in Web applications and run on J2EE-compliant application servers.

  - EJBs are server-side components supported by J2EE and run in EJB containers provided by J2EE-compatible application servers.

- ❏ Java is an object-oriented language and lends itself to the creation of reusable components. JavaBeans and EJBs are component architectures.

- ❏ Java language conforms to the object-oriented requirements by supporting abstract data types, encapsulation, inheritance, and polymorphism. It also lends itself to iterative and incremental object-oriented development methodology and the implementation of design patterns for object-oriented languages.

❑ Model-View-Controller is a strongly recommended design pattern based on creating layered software architecture with clear separation between presentation (view) and business logic (model) layers. The controller layer passes requests and responses between the view and model.

❑ A variety of application development tools are available. The SDK includes command line tools for developers. This chapter describes the `javac` compiler, `java` launcher, `javadoc` documentation builder, and `jar` packaging utility.

❑ Most Java developers use a proprietary IDE that provides productivity tools for building, debugging, testing, and packaging Java programs. One powerful IDE is IBM WebSphere Studio Application Developer.

❑ At the time of this writing, the latest version of J2SE is 1.4 and of J2EE is 1.3. The J2SDK version 1.4 adds the **assert** keyword to the language and introduces the **Java Web Start** distribution tool. The core API has expanded greatly with version 1.4, but many of the new APIs were previously available as optional extensions or used with J2EE.

REVIEW QUESTIONS

These questions cover material in this chapter and review basic constructs of the Java language that you should know before reading this book.

1. If you issue the command `javac MyClass.java` and `MyClass` uses the public class `HerClass`, which, in turn, uses the public class `HisClass`, which of the following statements accurately describes what source files are compiled? Select the best answer.

   a. The files `MyClass.java`, `HerClass.java`, and `HisClass.java` are compiled immediately.

   b. The files `MyClass.java`, `HerClass.java`, and `HisClass.java` are compiled only if the modification timestamp is more recent than the `.class` bytecode file with the same base filename.

   c. The file `MyClass.java` is compiled immediately, but `HerClass.java` and `HisClass.java` are compiled only when a statement that uses them is executed, and only if the modification timestamp is more recent than the `.class` bytecode file with the same base filename.

   d. The files `MyClass.java` and `HerClass.java` are compiled if the modification timestamp is more recent than the `.class` bytecode file with the same base filename. The file `HisClass.java` is not compiled because `MyClass.java` does not have any direct dependency on it.

   e. The file `MyClass.java` is compiled immediately. `HerClass.java` is compiled if the modification timestamp is more recent than the `.class` bytecode file with the same base filename. The file `HisClass.java` is compiled if `HerClass.java` is compiled *and* if the `HisClass.java` modification timestamp is more recent than its `.class` bytecode file.

2. Which of the following are valid declarations of the main method of a class? Select all that apply.

   a. `public static int main( String[ ] args);`

   b. `public void main (String [ ] param);`

   c. `static public main( String param [ ]);`

   d. `static void main( String [ ] param );`

   e. `public static void main ( String args[ ] ) throws`
      `IOException;`

   f. `public static void main( String args);`

   g. `static public int ( String args[ ] ) throws IOException;`

3. Insert a sample comment with the content "this is a comment" as a single-line comment, a block comment, and a doc comment and insert each as close as possible to the identifier `Feline` in this statement:

   ```
   Animal cat = new Feline();
   ```

4. Which of the following are special tags recognized by the `javadoc` tool? Select all that apply.

   a. `@param`

   b. `@since`

   c. `@obsolete`

   d. `@returns`

   e. `@throws`

5. Which of the following are legal Java identifier names? Select all that apply.

   a. `counter1`

   b. `$index`

   c. `name-7`

   d. `Iterator.Class`

   e. `array`

6. Examine the following set of tokens:

   ```
   goto          unsigned          class
   switch        null              double
   label         transient         template
   ```

   Which of the following statements are true? Select all that apply.

   a. `template` and `unsigned` are not reserved words.

   b. All of the words in the list are reserved words.

   c. `label` is not a reserved word.

   d. `goto` is a reserved word, but its use is not allowed.

   e. `null` is a keyword.

7. Examine the following lines of code:

```
for ( a = 0; a < 3;   a++ ) {
    if ( a == 1 ) continue;
    for ( b = 0; b < 3; b++ ) {
        if ( b == 1 ) break;
        System.out.println( a + ", " + b );
    }
}
```

Which of the following lines are included in the output when the method that contains these lines is run? Select all that apply.

a. 0, 0

b. 0, 1

c. 0, 2

d. 1, 0

e. 1, 1

f. 1, 2

g. 2, 0

h. 2, 1

i. 2, 2

8. Examine the following code:

```
public class Quiz1_8 {
    public static void main( String[] args ) {
        String a = new String( "Hello" );
        String b = new String( "Hello" );
        System.out.println( a == b ? "true" : "false" );
    }
}
```

Which one of the following statements correctly describes the behavior when this program is compiled and run?

a. Compilation is successful and the output is `true`

b. Compilation is successful and there is no output.

c. Compilation is successful and the output is `false`

d. The compiler rejects the expression (a == b ? "true" : "false") because the C-style ternary ? : operator is not supported in Java.

e. Compilation is successful, but a `ClassCastException` occurs during execution.

9. Examine the following code:

```
public class Quiz1_9 {                              // 1
    public static void main( String[] args ) {      // 2
        Integer x = null;                            // 3
        if ( args.length >= 1 ) {                    // 4
            x = new Integer( args[0] );              // 5
        }                                            // 6
        if ( args.length >= 2 ) {                    // 7
            x = new Integer( args[1] );              // 8
        }                                            // 9
        System.out.println( x );                     // 10
        x = null;                                    // 11
    }                                                // 12
}                                                    // 13
```

What is the first line after which the object created on line 5 can be garbage collected?

a. line 6

b. line 8

c. line 9

d. line 11

e. line 13

10. Examine the following code:

```
public class Quiz1_10 {
    private static final double A = 5.6;
    private double b;
    Quiz1_10( double z1, double  z2 ) {
        b = z1 * z2;
    }
    Quiz1_10 ( double z ) {
        if ( z > 0.0 ) {
            this( z, 2.0 );
        } else {
            this( z, 1.0 );
        }
    }
    public static void main( String[] args ) {
        System.out.println( new Quiz1_10( 4.0, 3.0 ) );
    }
    public String toString() {
        return( "b = " + b );
    }
}
```

Which one of the following statements correctly describes the behavior when this program is compiled and run?

a. The compiler rejects the expression new Quiz1_10(4.0, 3.0) because it is not possible to create an object without a name.

b. Compilation is successful and the output is b = 12.0.

c. The compiler rejects the line this(z, 2.0); because it is not the first statement in the constructor.

d. The compiler rejects the second definition of the method Quiz1_10 because a constructor has already been defined.

11. Which of the following are valid qualifiers for defining members of a class? Select all that apply.

a. static

b. const

c. protected

d. package

e. abstract

12. Examine the following code:

```
public class Quiz1_12 {
    Boolean condition;
    public void testCondition() {
        if ( condition ) {
            System.out.println( "TRUE!" );
        } else {
            System.out.println( "FALSE!" );
        }
    }
    public static void main( String[] args ) {
        Quiz1_12 a = new Quiz1_12();
        a.testCondition();
    }
}
```

Which of the following statements are true? Select all that apply.

a. The compiler rejects the expression if (condition) because condition is used before it is initialized.

b. The value of the variable condition is null when it is tested in the first statement of testCondition.

c. Compilation is successful and the output is TRUE!

d. Compilation is successful and the output is FALSE!

e. The compiler rejects the statement (condition){ /*… */ } because condition is not a boolean expression.

13. Examine the following code taken from a single source file.

```
class Vehicle {
   protected void goSomewhere() {
      System.out.println( "travelling..." );
   }
}
public class Bicycle extends Vehicle {
   public void goSomewhere() {
      System.out.println( "pedalling..." );
   }
   public static void main( String[] args ) {
      Bicycle x = new Bicycle();
      x.goSomewhere();
   }
}
```

Which of the following statements are true when the code is compiled and run? Select all that apply.

a. The compiler rejects the definition of the class `Bicycle` because the keyword `extends` is not appropriate for a superclass and should be replaced by the keyword `implements`.

b. The compiler rejects the definition of `Bicycle.goSomewhere` because its access specifier does not match the access specifier of `Vehicle.goSomewhere`.

c. Compilation is successful and the output is `travelling...`

d. Compilation is successful and the output is `pedalling...`

e. It is optional for the class `Bicycle` to implement the method `goSomewhere`.

14. Examine the following code taken from a single source file:

```
abstract class Barbeque {
   public abstract void ignite();
   public void cook() {
      System.out.println( "put food on the "
                          +"grill and wait" );
   }
}
class GasBarbeque extends Barbeque {
   public void ignite() {
      System.out.println( "turn on gas and "
                          +"light match" );
   }
}
class CharcoalBarbeque extends Barbeque {
   public void ignite() {
      System.out.println( "pour on lighter "
                          +"fluid and light match" );
   }
}
```

```
public class Cookout {
   public static void makeDinner( Barbeque b ) {
      b.ignite();
      b.cook();
   }
   public static void main( String[] args ) {
      GasBarbeque gb = new GasBarbeque();
      CharcoalBarbeque cb = new CharcoalBarbeque();
      makeDinner( gb );
      makeDinner( cb );
   }
}
```

Which of the following statements are true when the code is compiled and run? Select all that apply.

a. The compiler rejects the definition of Cookout.makeDinner because it is not possible to instantiate the argument b of the abstract class Barbeque.

b. The compiler rejects the definition of the classes GasBarbeque and CharcoalBarbeque because they do not implement the method Barbeque.cook.

c. Compilation is successful and the output is:

```
turn on gas and light match
put food on the grill and wait
pour on lighter fluid and light match
put food on the grill and wait
```

d. The compiler rejects the statements makeDinner(gb); and makeDinner(cb); because the type of gb or cb does not match the input type of Barbeque.

15. Which of the following are valid class definitions? Assume X and Y are pubic interfaces and P and Q are concrete public classes? Select all that apply.

a. final class A { }

b. public class B implements X, Y { }

c. public class C extends P, Q { }

d. abstract class extends P, implements X { }

e. abstract final class E { }

16. Examine the following code taken from a single source file:

```
class A {
   protected double d = 3.14;
   public static void f() {}
   public void g() {}
}
class B {
   public void m() {}
```

```
    }
class C extends A {
    protected static void s() {}
    void t() {}
}
```

Which of the following methods have direct access to the field A.d? Select all that apply.

a. A.f()

b. A.g()

c. B.m()

d. C.s()

e. C.t()

17. When does the compiler reject a method because the declaration does not contain a throws clause?

18. Examine the following code:

```
class BinEmpty extends Exception { }
class StockBin {
    private int itemsInBin = 0;
    public StockBin( int initialCount ) {
        itemsInBin = initialCount;
    }
    public void removeFromBin() throws BinEmpty {
        if ( itemsInBin == 0 ) {
            throw new BinEmpty();
        } else {
            --itemsInBin;
        }
    }
}
public class Warehouse {
    public static void main( String[] args ) {
        try {
            StockBin b = new StockBin( 1 );
            b.removeFromBin();
            b.removeFromBin();
        }
        catch( BinEmpty be ) {
            System.out.println( "Oops, no more!" );
        }
        finally {
            System.out.println( "Cleaning up" );
        }
    }
}
```

Which of the following statements are true when the code is compiled and run? Select all that apply.

a. The compiler rejects the definition of the method `Warehouse.main` because it does not have a throws clause declaring the exception class `BinEmpty`.

b. The class `BinEmpty` defines a class of checked exceptions.

c. Compilation is successful and the output is:

```
Oops, no more!
Cleaning up
```

d. Compilation is successful and the output is:

```
Oops, no more!
```

19. Which method of the `JApplet` class is called when the applet is loaded? Select the best answer.

a. `init`

b. `start`

c. `begin`

d. `play`

e. `load`

20. Which methods of the `JApplet` class are called when the HTML page on which an applet is defined is removed from the browser's window and then brought back? Select the best answer.

a. `init`

b. `start`

c. `destroy`

d. `stop`

e. `load`

PROGRAMMING EXERCISES

To get the files required for the Debugging and Complete the Solution exercises, copy the folder `\Data\questions\c1` from the CD that accompanies this book to folder `questions\c1` on your hard drive. Work in the folder that contains questions. Make sure `questions` contains folder `c1`, and `c1` contains the original Java source files.

Debugging

1. Correct all the errors in the following program:

```java
package questions.c1;
public class Debug1_1 {
    public static void main( String[] args ) {
```

```
        Object[] stuff = new Obj      [ ];
        stuff[0] = "eggs";
        stuff[1] = new StringBuffer( "flour" );
        stuff[2] = 3.56;
        stuff[3] = 'c';
        stuff[4] = 123;
        for( int i = 0; i < stuff.length; i++ ) {
           System.out.println( stuff[i] );
        }
     }
  }
```

2. Correct the following program so that the output prints two lines:

```
    A wild dog is wild
    A pet cat is tame
```

```
package questions.c1;
public class Debug1_2{
   public static void main( String[] args ) {
      StringBuffer wild = "fox";
      StringBuffer tame = "dog";
      wild = tame;
      tame.setCharAt( 0, 'c' );
      tame.setCharAt( 1, 'a' );
      tame.setCharAt( 2, 't' );
      wild.insert( 1, "wild " );
      tame.insert( 1, "pet " );
      System.out.println( "A " + wild + " is wild" );
      System.out.println( "A " + tame + " is tame" );
   }
}
```

3. Correct all the errors in the following program:

```
package questions.c1;
class Tool {
   private String name = "";
   public void setName( String n ) {
      name = n;
   }
   public String getName() {
      return name;
   }
   String toString() {
      return name;
   }
}
public class Hammer extends Tool {
   private int weight;
   public void setWeight( int w ) {
```

```
        weight = w;
    }
    public int getWeight() {
        return weight;
    }
    String toString() {
        return Tool.toString() + " "
                + String.valueOf( weight );
    }
    public static void main( String[] args ) {
        Hammer sledge = new Hammer();
        sledge.setName( "sledgehammer" );
        sledge.setWeight( 10 );
        System.out.println( sledge );
    }
}
```

4. Correct all the errors in the following program:

```
package questions.c1;
interface RiceCereal {
    protected void snap();
    protected void crackle();
    protected void pop();
}
public class Krispies implements RiceCereal {
    protected void snap() {
        System.out.println( "Snap!" );
    }
    protected void crackle() {
        System.out.println( "Crackle!" );
    }
    public static void main( String[] args ) {
        Krispies k = new Krispies();
        k.snap();
    }
}
```

5. Correct all the errors in the following program without changing the definition of the interface:

```
package questions.c1;
interface IfaceDebug1_5{
    public void f( int input );
}
class OutOfRangeException extends Exception {
}
public class Debug1_5 implements IfaceDebug1_5 {
    public static final int MAX_X = 1000;
    public static final int MIN_X = 10;
    private int x;
```

```
public void f( int input ) {
    setX( input );
}
public int getX() {
    return x;
}
public void setX( int value ) {
    if ( value >= MIN_X && value <= MAX_X ) {
        x = value;
    } else {
        throw new OutOfRangeException();
    }
}
public static void main( String[] args ) {
    Debug1_5 a = new Debug1_5();
    a.f( 275 );
    System.out.println( a.getX() );
}
}
```

Complete the Solution

1. Add doc comments to the file `questions\c1\Complete1_1.java` before the definition of `class Complete1_1` and before the definition and all fields and methods. Run the `javadoc` tool on the class and then look at the generated web, starting by opening file `index. html` in a Web browser.

2. Modify the source for class `questions.c1.TabbyCat` in the file `questions\c1\TabbyCat.java`. Add the `Cat` interface definition with the methods `eat`, `sleep`, and `play` so that the class `TabbyCat` compiles successfully.

3. Modify the file `questions\c1\Constructors.java`. Complete the `Constructors` class definition by adding two more constructors to simulate the use of default values. The `int` default value for the first parameter is 0, and the `double` default value for the second parameter is 1.0. Both of the constructors you add should call the constructor provided.

4. Modify the file `questions\c1\Book.java`. Define class `Book` to extend the abstract class `questions.c1.ReadingMaterial` defined in this file. Because reading material comes in many forms, the content is the generic type `Object`. The `Book` class can use the `String` class as its content type.

5. Modify the file `questions\c1\SetOfCharacters.java`. Complete the `SetOfCharacters` class so that it throws an `AlreadyInSetException` if an attempt is made to add a character to a set for the second time. Define the exception class `AlreadyInSetException`. Take advantage of the exception class's superclass constructor to set a message that indicates which character is in error.

Discovery

1. Write a simple utility to calculate a person's body mass index (BMI) by applying the following formula:

   $BMI = weight\_in\_kilograms \ / \ height\_in\_meters^2$

   Stage 1: The user inputs his or her weight in kilograms and height in meters as command-line arguments. The program calculates and prints the BMI. To test the program, use the fact that a large person who is 2 meters tall and weighs 100 kg has a BMI of 25.

   Stage 2: Enhance the program to accept height input in Imperial or metric units. You can use the following conversion formula. Instead of command line arguments, prompt the user for height, units ("inches" or "meters"), weight, and units ("pounds" or "kilograms").

   1 kilogram = 2.2 pounds
   1 meter = 39.36 inches

   Stage 3: BMI values in the range 20 to 27 are considered compatible with good health, with 22 to 25 being the ideal range for average body types. If your program is correctly outputting BMI values, enhance it to print a message for the five possibilities:

   ❑ BMI is too low for optimum health.

   ❑ BMI is low but not a health risk.

   ❑ Congratulations for an ideal BMI.

   ❑ BMI high but not a health risk.

   ❑ BMI is too high for optimum health.

2. Implement the object model shown in Figure 1-25 to implement a small banking application. Create five classes: `Bank`, `BankAccount`, `SavingsAccount`, `CheckingAccount`, and `Customer`. `Bank` should be a singleton class. For simplicity, the bank stores bank accounts in one array and customers in another. All bank accounts are savings accounts or checking accounts, and any customer may have zero or one account of each type.

   The difference between the two accounts affects only the `withdraw` method. The `deposit` method simply increments the balance. The `withdraw` method decrements the balance, but cannot always do so. A customer can withdraw from a `SavingsAccount` only an amount less than or equal to the current balance. For a `CheckingAccount` the logic is:

   ❑ Withdraw the amount if less than or equal to the balance.

   ❑ If the customer has a `SavingsAccount`, and the `SavingsAccount` has enough money to cover the shortfall in the `CheckingAccount`, transfer enough money from savings to checking to cover the withdrawal. Then withdraw the money.

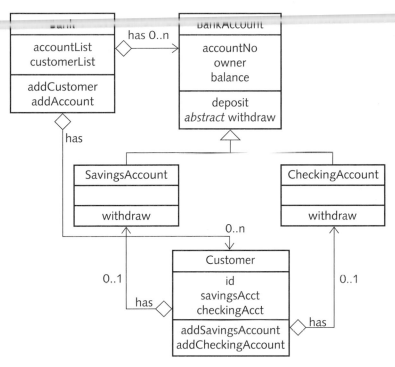

Figure 1-25   Object model for a banking application

❑ If the customer has no savings account, or the total of both accounts is less than the withdrawal amount, issue an **InsufficientFundsException** exception.

Add a **main** method to the **Bank** class to test. Create one customer and give that customer a savings account. Try a deposit and withdrawal. Give the customer a checking account and try another deposit. Try withdrawals that succeed without a transfer, that transfer funds from savings, and for which there are insufficient funds.

3. Create a class called **Inventory** that could maintain an in-memory record of items a store has in stock. The class holds the stock data in an array with elements of type **StockItem**. You can replace the array with a collection class if you are familiar with collection classes. The **StockItem** class is intended to be accessed only through **Inventory**, so should have package scope.

Create an interface **Identifiable** for objects that have a unique identifier stored as a **String**. (**Identifiable** must define method **getIdentifier** and method **setIdentifier** that can throw a **DuplicateIdentifierException**.) Each **StockItem** must be an **Identifiable** object and also store the quantity in stock as an **int** and the unit price as a **float**.

Define class `InventoryException` that is a checked exception and the super-class of `DuplicateIdentifierException`, and other exception types thrown by the methods in the following list. The constructor of `Inventory` must have one argument that specifies the maximum number of stock items. The `Inventory` class must have at least the following public methods and a **main** method to test them:

□ **public int** add(**String** id, **int** quantity, **float** price)

Adds a stock item. If an item with the specified ID already exists, the method throws a `DuplicateItemException`. Otherwise, the method creates a new `StockItem` object and adds it to the array. The return value is the number of items recorded in the array when the operation is complete.

□ **public int** remove (**String** id)

Removes a stock item. If no items match the specified ID, the method throws an `ItemNotFoundException`. The return value is the number of items recorded in the array when the operation is complete.

□ **public void** setQuantity(**String** id, **int** quantity)

Changes the recorded number in stock for the item that matches the specified ID. If no items match the specified ID, the method throws an `ItemNotFoundException`. If the quantity is less than 0, the method throws a `NegativeQuantityException`.

□ **public int** getQuantity(**String** id)

Returns the number in stock for the item that matches the specified ID. If no items match the specified ID, the method throws an `ItemNotFoundException`.

□ **public void** setPrice(**String** id, **float** price)

Changes the recorded price for the item that matches the specified ID to the specified price. If no items match the specified ID, the method throws an `ItemNotFoundException`. If the price is less than 0.0, the method throws a `NegativePriceException`.

□ **public float** getPrice(**String** id)

Returns the price for the item that matches the specified ID. If no items match the specified ID, the method throws an `ItemNotFoundException`.

□ **public void** stockReport()

Prints an inventory report that states how many stock items the store has in inventory and then prints the ID, quantity, and price of each item.

Add a test **main** method that exercises all the other methods. The **main** method should catch and recover from all `InventoryExceptions`.

2

CLASSES AND OBJECTS

INTRODUCTION

You cannot even begin to program in the Java programming language without defining at least one class because of the fundamental importance of class definitions in the language. You already have a basic knowledge of how to work with classes, and this chapter introduces you to advanced topics that build upon your existing knowledge. The chapter begins with an examination of the use of finalizer methods for handling the cleanup of objects, followed by cloning, or duplicating objects, and obtaining run-time type information (RTTI) about objects and classes. The package **java.lang** includes the classes and interfaces that support these two activities. Both involve programming techniques that operate on classes, rather than calls to methods of classes to achieve other ends. Learning about these topics can greatly increase your understanding of the nature of classes. To understand how cloning and RTTI work, you must have a solid understanding of Java types, classes, inheritance, and exception handling.

This chapter also covers nested classes and inner classes and adopts the terms introduced in this paragraph to differentiate between these two very different ways of enclosing classes inside other classes. A *nested class* is a class that is defined inside the definition of another class. A nested class may also be an *inner class*, depending upon how it is defined. The differences between the two relate mainly to scope and accessibility, and not to the nature of the class. Inner classes are very different in nature from other classes. An inner class can be a member of the class that encloses it or local to a block of code. This book uses the term *enclosed class* for any nested class that is an inner class and for a nested class that is not an inner class. A class in which a definition of the enclosed class appears is an *enclosing class*. For simplicity, this book applies the term nested class to an enclosed class that is not a member or local inner class. It uses the term inner class otherwise. Java programmers also use the terms top-level inner classes or static inner classes (for reasons that you will later see) for nested classes.

CLASSES AND OBJECT-ORIENTED PROGRAMMING

If you have programmed in an object-oriented (OO) language, such as C++ or Smalltalk, you should appreciate that it is not just a syntactic quirk of the Java programming language that forces you to put all your code into classes. Boiled down to its essence, implementing object-oriented programs means defining classes and reusing existing classes in such a way that the program is driven entirely by method calls between the classes.

In OOP, you no longer design a program based on the flow of control. Flowcharts are of little use. Instead you start by analyzing the real-life entities, relationships, and scenarios that your program is to model. Object-oriented analysis (OOA) focuses on the elements of the problem to be solved. The analysis leads to an object-oriented design (OOD) process in which you determine what classes or types of objects you need, what information or attributes objects of each type must hold, and what their behavior is or, in OO terms, what messages from other objects they can process. Then, at the implementation stage, you program classes in Java or another object-oriented programming language. In the Java programming language, attributes become fields of classes, and messages become methods of classes.

As an illustration, consider that a banking model is likely to include a type for bank accounts, with attributes such as account number and balance. Bank account objects should accept messages from account owners to perform deposits, withdrawals, and other transactions. The account owners are another type of object, with attributes such as owner name and address.

The bank or branch office is also a type. Unlike accounts and owners, you may impose a restriction that there can be only one bank object in your program, but the bank is still an object that has its own type. You may want to add a transaction log attribute to bank accounts for use when the bank sends monthly statements to account owners. Transaction log objects typically contain a collection of transaction objects. They accept

2

messages from accounts to add ... ... g ... ... record a
deposit—and from the bank to print or clear the log.

When designing classes, you should concentrate on the interface between classes before coding their internal workings. For example, determine which class provides the deposit method, and then determine which classes may call the deposit method. Do the same for all methods. Make sure all the scenarios you can think of are covered. In the process, draw up a list of attributes that each class must maintain. Eventually, you will arrive at a fairly accurate specification for the classes you need.

Another phenomenon occurs in object-oriented development: the analysis, design, implementation, test, and deployment stages tend to overlap and become cyclic as you iterate toward a solution. For example, testing can reveal a weakness that was overlooked during analysis and implementation and that should be addressed by a design change. Far from being a problem, this nonlinear process provides strength. You can build and deploy part of the solution to prove that key classes interact properly. Then, you can refine and expand the solution as you add classes. In addition, you can create a quick, simple implementation of classes for speedy deployment and then improve performance or robustness during subsequent iterations.

If the internal implementation and public interface of a class are clearly separated, you can completely rewrite one or more methods and no other class may need to be changed. The concept of *encapsulation* refers to the fact that fields and methods can be hidden from the outside world. Declare selected methods in a way that makes them visible to other classes and to those methods that make up the interface of the same class. It is a good practice to hide all attributes, or in Java terms, declare all fields private, and provide methods that other classes can call to get and set values. This approach enforces encapsulation of attributes and gives your class a chance to validate or filter requests to set values.

Object-oriented analysis and design is a science and art in its own right. Careers can be made designing object models, and the models can be independent of the programming language in which they are to be implemented. As a programmer, your starting point may be an object model that was created by an architect or object modeler. You may work on just a few of the classes in a project that requires dozens or hundreds of types of objects. The rest of this chapter focuses on advanced features of the Java programming language that relate to the definition and usage of classes and objects.

USING CONSTRUCTORS AND FINALIZERS

Constructors are methods that prepare newly created objects for use. *Finalizers* are methods that perform any actions, such as releasing memory buffers or closing network connections, that should be completed before the objects are discarded.

In the Java programming language, the most common way to invoke a constructor is through the **new** keyword. The **java.lang.Class.newInstance** method and the new `java.lang.reflect.Constructor.newInstance` method also invoke the constructor, but they are not commonly used.

 Version 1.1 of the Java platform introduced the method `java.lang.reflect.Constructor.newInstance` along with the entire package `java.lang.reflect`. This package supports run-time type information and is known as the Reflection API. `java.lang.reflect` defines the `Constructor` class.

All objects are stored on the program heap. When you are finished with an object, you are not responsible for freeing memory on the heap. Instead, the Java platform automatically performs garbage collection from time to time. Not explicitly destroying an object leaves a gap when performing specialized cleanup before throwing away an object. For example, how do you flush the contents of a buffer to an output file before you destroy the object that contains the buffer? Finalizers can perform this function.

Constructors

In your previous experience with the Java programming language, you saw that when you create an object with the **new** keyword, you call the constructor. The purpose of the constructor is to prepare the object to be used, and that typically involves initializing the fields of the object. You can include the arguments for the constructor as input to this initialization process if the default values for the fields are not appropriate. The syntax of invoking constructors requires that you must always include the parentheses, even if you are using a constructor that takes no arguments. The following statements construct objects:

```
File outputFile = new File( args[1] );
Fraction third = new Fraction( 1, 3 );
Whatever thing = new Whatever();
```

When you define your Java class, you define constructors much like you define other methods. The rules are as follows:

- Give the constructor the same name as the class name.

- Do not specify a return type, not even **void**. A constructor cannot return a value.

- You can specify as many arguments as you like. The arguments can have any defined type, including the class of the constructor.

The Java programming language provides default constructors if you do not define any constructors for a class. The compiler-generated default constructor takes no arguments. If you define your own constructor, the compiler no longer provides a default constructor. Therefore, if you define one constructor, you must define all the forms of constructors that your class needs.

For example, if you define one constructor that has at least one argument, your class will not have a constructor with no arguments unless you also explicitly define one.

Finalizers

Because the Java platform frees memory for you when objects are destroyed, you often do not need finalizers. Generally, you should use finalizers only for necessary cleanup tasks, such as releasing memory buffers allocated by the object or closing network connections, and even then, you should use them sparingly. A commonly used alternative to providing finalizers is to define a method called **close** or **dispose**, which has two advantages: It can be called explicitly as needed, and the timing of the method call is not in doubt. You should not build into your code dependency on the timing of activities of finalizers. If you do so, you are forced to run the finalizers explicitly before executing the dependent code.

The following sections present finalizer syntax and example usage. They also include a discussion of rules to keep in mind when writing code that uses finalizers.

Syntax of the Finalizer Method

```
protected void finalize() [throws Throwable]
        block
```

Finalizer Syntax Dissection and Usage Tips

- You should declare **finalize** with the access specifier **protected**. A finalizer cannot have private or package access because it overrides a protected method of **Object**. Public access is valid, but giving users of your class access to this method is very dangerous and not recommended because you lose control of when the method is used.

- The **finalize** method cannot take arguments or return a value. You can include any valid code you want.

- Although it is not strictly necessary, you should include the clause **throws Throwable** to allow for a subclass to include a finalizer that does throw an exception.

- The block is the body of the **finalize** method.

Finalizer Code Example

```
protected void finalize() throws Throwable {
    MyOutputStream.flush();
}
```

Code Dissection

This finalizer flushes any output that remains in a field that is the object reference for an output stream object.

The output of the finalizer consists of whatever data is left in the output stream when the finalizer is run, and the output stream determines the destination of the output.

In class inheritance hierarchies, there are additional considerations for finalizers in classes that have superclasses other than **Object**.

If the class of an object that is destroyed during garbage collection has a **finalize** method, the finalizer is run before the storage for the object is freed. Therefore, the automatic running of finalizers is tied to garbage collection. Do not rely on garbage collection to run finalizers because you cannot control when, or even whether, garbage collection occurs. The Java Virtual Machine (JVM) may never perform garbage collection if it does not run low on memory.

You should never call the **finalize** method directly. Let the JVM decide when the method needs to run. Following are details of the methods available to control the use of finalizer methods in an application.

Class

java.lang.System

Methods

- **void runFinalizersOnExit(boolean *b*)**
  If you call **runFinalizersOnExit** and supply an argument that evaluates to **true**, the JVM guarantees to run the finalizers for all objects some time before program termination. When the argument is **false** or the **runFinalizersOnExit** method is not called, finalizers may run, but there is no guarantee that they will run. This method has been deprecated in the Java 2 platform and is no longer recommended because it is inherently unsafe.

- **void runFinalization()**
  Call **runFinalization** to request that the JVM run finalizers for all objects that have been discarded, but for which finalizers have not yet run. There is no guarantee that finalizers will be run as a result of calling **runFinalization**.

You can call **runFinalization** any time. However, you should do so only when executing the code in the finalizers is imperative for your application to perform properly, because use of the **runFinalization** method may negatively impact the performance of your application. This method is most effective when used after calling the method **System.gc** to request that garbage collection take place.

 Version 1.1 of the Java platform introduced the method **runFinalizersOnExit**. Previously you had no way to force finalizers to run at the end of a program. Unfortunately, the method has proved to be inherently unsafe in the multithreaded environment of the JVM and has been deprecated in the Java 2 platform.

To make your programs more efficient and easier to maintain, let the JVM decide when to finalize objects. The technique of forcing finalization is inefficient.

Figure 2-1 describes a Java class, called FinalizerClass, that has a finalizer. Because FinalizerClass is a public class, it is found in a file called FinalizerClass.java. The structure of packages mirrors the file system, so you will find this file in the X:\Data\examples\classes directory on the CD. (Here X: is the drive letter of the CD.)

```
package examples.classes;
/** A Java class to demonstrate how a finalizer
 * method is defined and used
 */
public class FinalizerClass {
   private int a, b;
   /** Class default constructor method */
   public FinalizerClass() {
      a = 1;
      b = 2;
      System.out.println( "Constructing an object!" );
   }
   /** Class finalizer method
    * @exception Throwable Any exception at all
    */
   protected void finalize() throws Throwable {
      System.out.println( "Doing object cleanup!" );
   }
   /** Test method for the class
    * @param args Not used
    */
   public static void main( String[] args ) {
      FinalizerClass x = new FinalizerClass();
      FinalizerClass y = new FinalizerClass();
      x = null;
      y = null;
      System.gc();
      System.runFinalization();
   }
}
```

Figure 2-1 FinalizerClass: a class to demonstrate how a finalizer method is defined and used

To execute the FinalizerClass program from the CD, first add the directory X:\Data to the system environment variable, CLASSPATH, then invoke the following command:

```
java examples.classes.FinalizerClass
```

Possible output from executing this program is shown in Figure 2-2.

```
Constructing an object!
Constructing an object!
Doing object cleanup!
Doing object cleanup!
```

Figure 2-2　Possible output from executing the `FinalizerClass` program

The declaration of `FinalizerClass.finalize` includes a **throws** clause that allows any exception to be thrown. The **throws** clause is not required for this class, but including it gives subclasses the opportunity to throw exceptions in their finalizer methods in the event that some serious, unrecoverable error occurs.

There is an alternative to using finalizer methods to perform cleanup actions as a program terminates. The class **java.lang.Runtime** provides methods for you to specify a **Thread** object, known as a shutdown hook thread, that will be executed when the virtual machine begins its shutdown sequence. The advantage of using such a thread is that you can put all your cleanup code in one place, and you can be sure that it will be invoked as shutdown begins, regardless of what objects may exist at shutdown time. If you use more than one of these threads, you cannot specify the order in which these threads are started, and all these hook threads run concurrently—not sequentially. When all the hooks have finished, the virtual machine will then run all uninvoked finalizers if finalization-on-exit has been enabled. Details on how to define a **Thread** object are provided in Chapter 5.

Below are the details of the methods that you use to work with shutdown hook methods.

Class

java.lang.Runtime

Methods

- **void addShutdownHook(Thread** *hook* **)**
  Registers a shutdown hook to be started by the virtual machine when the virtual machine begins its shutdown sequence.

- **boolean removeShutdownHook(Thread** *hook* **)**
  Removes a previously registered hook from the list of hooks to be started when the virtual machine begins its shutdown sequence. The returned value will be **true** if the specified hook was previously registered and was removed from the list successfully.

The ability to add and remove shutdown hooks was added in version 1.3 of the Java 2 platform.

REFERENCE OBJECTS AND THE GARBAGE COLLECTOR

2

Developers using sophisticated techniques, such as object caches and flexible data-mapping schemes, may require finer control over the finalization process than finalizer methods provide. The set of classes in the package **java.lang.ref** provides a measure of interaction with the garbage collector. You can create a reference object by instantiating the classes **SoftReference**, **WeakReference**, or **PhantomReference** and passing an object reference to an object used by your program as an argument of the constructor. When the garbage collector operates on objects, it changes the reachability level of the object. You can use the reference classes to determine the status of an object and then perhaps perform specialized finalization actions. Reachability levels are described in Figure 2-3.

For an example of how these reference objects can be used effectively, refer to the discussion of the **WeakHashMap** collection class in Chapter 4.

Level	Description
Strong	An object is strongly reachable while your program is using object references for it.
Soft	When there are no more strong references, an object may still be reachable by a reference object of type **SoftReference**. If memory is low, the garbage collector may clear soft references.
Weak	The garbage collector can finalize objects that have only weak references.
Phantom	After an object has been finalized, it can have a reference object that is a **PhantomReference** occupied by unreachable objects that can be reclaimed by the JVM. These objects are not reachable by any sort of reference object.

Figure 2-3   Reachability levels of objects

The Java platform has matured since it was originally released and has proven to be flexible, reliable, and fast enough for use in mission-critical, large-scale projects. The package **java.lang.ref** was introduced in the Java 2 platform to meet the demands of developers whose Java programs test the size and other constraints of the computer or network upon which their programs run.

CLONING OBJECTS

Before long, you are bound to run into the deceptively simple-sounding problem of copying objects. For the primitive types, there is no problem: just use the assignment operator. However, using the assignment operator with object references changes only the references, not the objects referenced.

To copy objects of reference types, you must clone the objects. Cloning involves calling the method **clone**, which is available for all objects of reference types, including instances of classes and arrays.

Class

`java.lang.Object`

Purpose

The **Object** class defines methods that are available in all objects of reference types.

Method

- `Object clone()`
  The method **clone** creates a duplicate of the object for which the method is called and returns an object reference to the new object. The returned value must be cast for the actual type of the object.

The following lines show why using the assignment operator to copy objects may not have the desired effect:

```
Pair x = new Pair( 5, 6 );
Pair y = new Pair( 54, 40 );
x = y;
```

As shown in Figure 2-4, these lines produce two object references, x and y, for the same object, instead of two object references for separate but identical objects. Also, the object that x originally referred to may not be accessible through any object reference and thus becomes available for garbage collection.

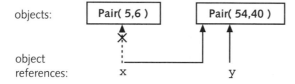

Figure 2-4   Assigning object references

Figure 2-5 shows what happens when this code fragment is rewritten to call **clone**, as follows:

```
Pair x = new Pair( 5, 6 );
Pair y = new Pair( 54, 40 );
x = ( Pair ) y.clone();
```

2

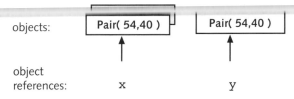

object
references: x   y

Figure 2-5   Calling `Object.clone`

Now **x** and **y** are object references for two different objects that are identical to each other.

You must cast the value returned from **clone** to an object reference for the correct type of object. If you feel this casting is unsafe, rest assured that the Java Virtual Machine (JVM) throws an exception of the type **ClassCastException** if the cast is inappropriate.

For the reference types, you usually want to make a deep copy rather than a shallow copy of an object. When you create a shallow copy, you duplicate the data members of an object, regardless of whether some members are object references. A shallow copy makes no attempt to make duplicates of the referenced objects. As a result, the copy and the original can contain object references for the same object. A deep copy duplicates the objects referred to by object references and inserts a new object reference for the duplicate object into the copy. Figure 2-6 illustrates a shallow and deep copy of an object **z** that contains an object reference for object **x**.

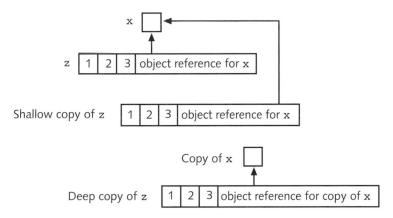

Figure 2-6   Shallow and deep copies

The method **Object.clone** performs a shallow copy. It copies all fields of the original object to the new object, regardless of whether the fields are primitive types or object references. This works for many, but not all, classes. If a class is mutable and has any fields that are object references to mutable objects of reference type, the class should provide an implementation of **clone** that returns a deep copy. Alternatively, you may want to prevent an object from being cloned. For example, if instances of a class cannot be duplicated in some safe and meaningful way, the class should not be cloneable.

Next comes the question of how to tell whether the classes of object references that are fields in the class also override the **clone** method. Often, whether your class is clone-able depends on whether all fields in the class are cloneable. The Java platform includes a core interface called **Cloneable** for the specific purpose of indicating whether objects are cloneable.

Making Objects Cloneable

One of the cornerstones of the philosophy of the Java programming language is that subclasses inherit no surprising behavior from superclasses. In the case of copying objects, whether cloning works depends upon whether the class is defined to implement the core interface **Cloneable**. If a class is declared to implement **Cloneable**, you can assume it is safe to call **clone** for instances of that class and use the objects produced by the **clone** method. If you call **clone** for a class that does not implement **Cloneable**, the exception **CloneNotSupportedException** is thrown. This may not be the behavior you want, but it is safer than and preferable to a default clone that gives no outward sign of error and creates a corrupt copy.

If you call **clone** for an instance of a class that uses the default method **Object.clone**, you must take one of the following actions:

- Wrap a **try** block around the call of **clone** and catch the possible **CloneNotSupportedException** exception.

- Add the **CloneNotSupportedException** exception to the **throws** clause for the method that calls **clone**.

The definition of **clone** in the **Object** class lists **CloneNotSupportedException** in its **throws** clause. When you override **Object.clone** in your class, you have the option of removing **CloneNotSupportedException** from the **throws** clause of your **clone** method.

The **Cloneable** interface is an example of a *marker interface*. Marker interfaces have no methods. Note, for example, that the interface **Cloneable** does not define the method **clone**. The sole purpose of a marker interface is to attach a piece of type information to a class. In this case, declaring a class with **implements Cloneable** means that the class supports the cloning of its objects. When you define a class, you can use **Cloneable** like an on-off switch. If you implement **Cloneable**, the class supports cloning. That is all you have to do to enable the inherited **clone** method. If you do not implement **Cloneable**, the **clone** method throws an exception. Pseudocode for **Object.clone** is essentially as follows:

```
if the object is an instance of Cloneable
    then make a shallow copy of the entire object
    else throw CloneNotSupportedException
end if
```

Figure 2-7 shows an example class called Pair. The class declares fields and they are integers. Therefore, the default **clone** method is adequate.

```
package examples.cloning;
/** An example class used to demonstrate how to
  * enable cloning for a class without fields that
  * contain object references.
  */
public class Pair implements Cloneable {
   private int a, b;
   /** Class constructor method
     * @param initA Initial value for the first field
     * @param initB Initial value for the second field
     */
   public Pair( int initA, int initB ) {
      a = initA;
      b = initB;
   }
   /** Convert object to String representation
     * @return The value of the array as a String
     */
   public String toString() {
      return "( " + a + ", " + b + " )";
   }
   /** The test method for the class
     * @param args Not used
     * @exception CloneNotSupportedException
     *                If clone not supported by
     *                inherited clone method
     */
   public static void main( String[] args )
         throws CloneNotSupportedException {
      Pair x = new Pair( 5, 6 );
      System.out.println( x );
      Pair y = ( Pair ) x.clone();
      System.out.println( y );
   }
}
```

Figure 2-7   **Pair:** an example of enabling cloning for a class without object reference fields

The output from running the program of Figure 2-7 is shown in Figure 2-8.

```
( 5, 6 )
( 5, 6 )
```

Figure 2-8   Output from the **Pair** program

The method **main** contains a **throws** clause because the class inherits **Object.clone**, which can throw the exception **CloneNotSupportedException**.

Overriding the Default Clone Method

For objects related by an inheritance hierarchy to be cloned correctly, each class in the hierarchy that has object reference fields must override **clone**. The reason is that the class at each level of the hierarchy is responsible for cloning the fields it defines and relies on the **clone** method of its superclass to copy the fields it inherits. Here are some guidelines for implementing **clone**:

- If classes outside the package, other than subclasses, are to be allowed to use your implementation of the **clone** method, declare your method with the access specifier **public**. The **Object.clone** method is a protected method.

- When you implement **clone**, it is not necessary to program it to deal with fields of the primitive types. You can leave them for the default **clone** method to handle.

- Define the **clone** method to copy objects for all fields that are reference objects. The only exceptions to this rule are object references for immutable objects. For example, objects of classes like **String** and the wrapper classes for the primitive types, such as **Integer**, **Character**, and **Double**, cannot be changed. Because the objects are immutable, clones that have references to the same object cannot cause problems. A different complication occurs when one or more fields are object references for classes that do not support cloning. When this happens, you must fall back on the "brute force" method of creating a new object of the class and then calling public methods to copy the fields one by one.

- To make sure every superclass in the hierarchy has a chance to copy the fields it defines, start your definition of **clone** with the following statement:

  ```
  super.clone();
  ```

  This statement calls the **clone** method of the superclass. You should repeat the statement in every superclass until **Object.clone** initiates the cloning process by making a shallow copy of the entire object. Then, as the call stack retreats, each class should call the **clone** methods for its object references to mutable objects. In the end, everything is cloned correctly.

Figure 2-9 is an example of a class that inappropriately uses the default **clone** method.

```
package examples.cloning;
/** An example class used to demonstrate what
 * happens when the default Object.clone method
 * is not overridden in a class with object
 * reference fields.
 */
public class IntArrayShared implements Cloneable {
   private int[] a;
   /** Class constructor method
     * @param size The maximum number of elements
     * @param initValue The initial value given
     */
   public IntArrayShared( int size, int initValue ) {
      a = new int[size];
      for( int i = 0; i < a.length; i++ ) {
         a[i] = initValue;
      }
   }
   /** Obtain the value of an array element
     * @param index the array index of interest
     * @return the value at the specified index
     */
   public int elementAt( int index ) {
      return a[index];
   }
   /** Set the value of an array element
     * @param index the array index to be updated
     * @param newValue the new value given
     */
   public void setValue( int index, int newValue ) {
      a[index] = newValue;
   }
   /** Converts the object into a String
     * @return The value of the array as a String
     */
   public String toString() {
      StringBuffer sb = new StringBuffer( "[ " );
      for( int i = 0; i < a.length; i++ ) {
         sb.append( a[i] + " " );
      }
      return sb.append( "]" ).toString();
   }
   /** The test method for the class
     * @param args Not used
     * @exception CloneNotSupportedException
     *            The inherited clone method may
     *            throw this exception
     */
```

Figure 2-9 `IntArrayShared`: an example of potential problems when the `clone` method isn't overridden

```
    public static void main( String[] args )
        throws CloneNotSupportedException {
      IntArrayShared x = new IntArrayShared( 5, 0 );
      IntArrayShared y = ( IntArrayShared ) x.clone();
      System.out.println( x );
      System.out.println( y );
      x.setValue( 2, 9999 );
      System.out.println( x );
      System.out.println( y );
    }
}
```

Figure 2-9   `IntArrayShared`: an example of potential problems when the `clone` method isn't overridden (continued)

The output from running the program shown in Figure 2-9 is given in Figure 2-10.

```
[ 0 0 0 0 0 ]
[ 0 0 0 0 0 ]
[ 0 0 9999 0 0 ]
[ 0 0 9999 0 0 ]
```

Figure 2-10   Output from the `IntArrayShared` program

The reference field defined in Figure 2-8, which is an array of integers, is not immutable. Therefore, the inherited **Object.clone** method does not properly clone the field. Notice from the output that the clones are not independent.

Figure 2-11 shows how the **clone** method should be written. This method is taken from the example class **examples.cloning.IntArray**. The class **IntArray** is identical to the previous example, **IntArrayShared**, except that **IntArray** overrides the **clone** method with the following method:

```
/** Provide a clone method specifically for the
  * IntArray class
  * @exception CloneNotSupportedException
  *               Superclass may throw this
  * @return A clone of the object
  */
public Object clone()
        throws CloneNotSupportedException {
    IntArray newObject = ( IntArray ) super.clone();
    newObject.a = ( int[]) a.clone();
    return newObject;
}
```

Figure 2-11   `IntArray`: an example of how to properly override the `clone` method

When you use this proper **clone** method, the output is shown in Figure 2-12.

```
[ 0 0 0 0 0 ]
[ 0 0 0 0 0 ]
[ 0 0 9999 0 0 ]
[ 0 0 0 0 0 ]
```

Figure 2-12   Output from the `IntArray` program

The proper **clone** method has a number of notable features:

- The return type is **Object** because it overrides **Object.clone**. Therefore, the returned object must be cast to type **IntArray**.

- It calls **super.clone** to clone the fields in the superclass. This statement could be omitted in this case because **Object** is the direct superclass of **IntArray**. However, including this statement is never an error and is always the safest approach.

- Next, **IntArray.clone** calls the **clone** method for the field a, which is an array. Like any reference object, this array has a **clone** method. The **clone** method used by arrays makes a shallow copy, which is adequate in this case. If the elements of the array are themselves reference objects, as in an array of arrays, you have no choice but to clone each element explicitly. Unfortunately, a way to override the **clone** method of an array does not exist.

Defining Cloneable Classes

The **Cloneable** interface gives the creator of the class the responsibility of deciding whether instances of the class are cloneable. Moreover, the decision affects not only the class being defined, but all subclasses that may extend the class in the future.

When you are deciding whether to implement the **Cloneable** interface, consider the impact on subclasses for which the class is the superclass, as well as on unrelated classes that use the class. Here are five possible approaches you can provide:

1. All objects of the class can be cloned. The simplest option is to support cloning fully, by

   - Defining the class with **implements Cloneable**.

   - Inheriting or overriding the default **clone** method. If you override the method, do not throw any exceptions in your implementation, but do include **CloneNotSupportedException** in the **throws** clause.

   This approach provides the most flexibility for any subclasses. A subclass that extends the class has the same options for implementing cloning as the class.

Example:

```
class SubClass extends SuperClass
                        implements Cloneable {
    // optionally implement clone
    public Object clone()
            throws CloneNotSupportedException {
        // do not throw CloneNotSupportedException
    }
}
```

2. Objects of the class are cloneable only if all contained objects are also cloneable. This is an attractive option for classes that do not have control over what they contain. Collection classes usually use this technique. To support cloning conditionally

- Define the class with **implements Cloneable**.

- Implement **clone**. For the fields of reference types, call the **clone** method of those classes. To give these contained objects an opportunity to throw an exception, include **CloneNotSupportedException** in the **throws** clause of the **clone** method.

A subclass that extends this class has the same options for implementing cloning as the class.

Example:

```
class SubClass extends SuperClass
                        implements Cloneable {
    OtherClass fieldName;
    // Implement clone if fields are object
    // references
    public Object clone()
            throws CloneNotSupportedException {
        fieldName = (OtherClass) fieldName.clone();
        // do not throw CloneNotSupportedException
    }
}
```

3. Objects of the class are not cloneable, but a subclass can extend the class in such a way that its objects are cloneable. To let subclasses support cloning, but not publicly support cloning in the class:

- Omit **implements Cloneable** from the class definition. Leave implementing the interface up to the subclass.

- Override or inherit the **clone** method. Even though the class is not cloneable, you should provide a **clone** method that correctly duplicates the fields defined in the class, for the sake of cloneable subclasses.

2

Although this class does not allow cloning, a subclass can implement
Cloneable, inherit or override the **clone** method, and become fully cloneable.

Example:

```
class SubClass extends class SuperClass {
   OtherClass fieldName;
   // implement clone if fields are object
   // references
   public Object clone()
           throws CloneNotSupportedException {
      fieldName = (OtherClass) fieldName.clone();
      // do not throw CloneNotSupportedException
   }
}
```

4. No object of the class or any class that extends the class can be cloned. Do
not support cloning if you are designing a class of objects in which the subclass objects must be unique. For example, it may be a design criterion of the
application that only one copy of an object is allowed. To prohibit cloning

- Omit **implements Cloneable** from the class definition.

- Implement a **clone** method that always throws a
  CloneNotSupportedException object.

Even if a subclass implements **Cloneable** and overrides **clone**, the exception
is thrown when the subclass calls **super.clone** for the fields it inherits from
your class. Therefore, you guarantee that no subclass can clone an object.

Example:

```
class SubClass extends SuperClass {
   // implement clone to throw an exception
   public Object clone()
           throws CloneNotSupportedException {
      throw new CloneNotSupportedException();
   }
}
```

5. The class is an abstract class and all subclasses are required to provide a
clone method that does not throw **CloneNotSupportedException**. To
force a subclass to support cloning

- Optionally add **implements Cloneable** for clarity.

- Define a **clone** method and declare it to be **abstract**.

- Omit **CloneNotSupportedException** from the **throws** clause of **clone**.

Example:

```
abstract class SubClass extends SuperClass {
   public abstract Object clone();
}
```

Run-Time Type Information

Some programming challenges arise from the environments supported by the Java platform and the very nature of programs that you write in the Java programming language. For example, many programs are driven by a graphical user interface (GUI) or run in a distributed environment. As a result, you may find that your class has to deal with objects for which the type is not known. These objects may be instances of classes created by different programmers and may even be instances of classes that did not exist when you wrote and tested your class. So the type information about the objects in use within a program cannot be known until the program is running. This information is collectively known as run-time type information (RTTI). An important use of RTTI is to access members of classes that you cannot know about when you develop your class. For example, your method may extract information from a database and need the flexibility to display records for which the structure is unknown at development time.

RTTI can also be helpful in debugging the code. For example, one effect of the dynamic binding inherent in object-oriented programming is that a method can receive a different type of object than it expects. The object received as an argument to a method can instantiate a subclass of the argument type. A good debugger can show you what is happening at runtime, or you can use RTTI to determine whether you are operating on the type of object for which the method was designed.

RTTI also helps to make up for the lack of parameterized types in the Java programming language. For example, in an argument list, you must specify the type of every argument of every method, and the only flexibility is that dynamic binding lets you specify a superclass when a subclass object may actually be passed. You can pass the most general type, `Object`, to a method and let the method use RTTI to determine how to use the object.

Determining the Type of Objects

Built into the Java programming language is an operator, `instanceof`, that you can use to ask whether an object is an instance of a particular class or any of its subclasses. This operator is useful in situations such as the following: You are writing a method that receives an object reference, of a type such as `BankAccount`. The superclass `BankAccount` may be extended by the classes `CheckingAccount` and `SavingsAccount`. If the method must handle the different kinds of `BankAccount` subclasses differently, you can use the `instanceof` operator.

Syntax

```
object_reference instanceof class_name
object_reference instanceof interface_name
```

2

Discussion

- The operator **instanceof** returns a **boolean** value. The result is **true** if the object on the left of the operator is an instance of the class or a subclass of the class on the right of the operator. The result is **false** otherwise.

- You can also use **instanceof** to ask whether the class of the object implements a particular interface. For example, you may want to know if an object is **Cloneable**.

- The **instanceof** operator does not work for the primitive types. The leftmost argument must be an object reference. If the value of the object reference is **null**, **instanceof** returns **false**, regardless of the type of the object reference.

- If the object is an instance of a class that extends the class or implements the interfaces specified by the rightmost argument, the value returned by **instanceof** is **true**.

Code Example

```
if ( account instanceof CheckingAccount ) {
    // process a checking account
}
else {
    // process all other account types
}
```

Code Dissection

If the account object is a **CheckingAccount**, it must also be a **BankAccount**. The operator is most useful when you know the supertype, or superclass, of an object, but you want to determine which subclass the object instantiates.

Accessing Information about Classes at Runtime

For every class and every instance of a class that a program uses, the JVM creates an object with the type **Class**. This object contains information about the class and is itself an instance of a class called **Class**. The Java platform creates the **Class** object automatically and stores in it several facts about the class, so that you can access the information at runtime.

You can call a method to get the **Class** object for a class or an instance of a class.

Class

java.lang.Object

Purpose

The **Object** class defines the methods that are available in all objects of reference types.

Methods

- `Class getClass()`

  The **getClass** method returns an object reference for a **Class** object.

You do not create **Class** objects, and no constructor for the class **Class** is available. Instead, use one of the following methods to access the **Class** object for a class or an object:

- Use the **Object.getClass** method for any object. All objects of reference type inherit this method. It is **public**, so you can always use it. Also, the method is **final** so that you cannot override it. For example, the following statement gets the class for an object called **account**:

  ```
  Class classAcc = account.getClass();
  ```

- If you know the name of a class or interface, you can use a class variable that the Java programming language adds to every class automatically. The name of the class variable is **class**, and it contains a reference to the corresponding **Class** object. For example, the following statement assigns an object reference for the **Class** object of the BankAccount class to classBankAcc:

  ```
  Class classBankAcc = BankAccount.class;
  ```

- If you know the full name of the class or interface, call the **class** method **Class.forName**, passing the fully qualified name of the class as a **String** argument. For example, the following statement assigns an object reference for the **Class** object of the BankAccount class to classBankAcc, if the BankAccount class is in the subpackage Banking of the package Financial:

  ```
  Class classBankAcc =
      Class.forName( "Financial.Banking.BankAccount" );
  ```

  If the named class is not loaded into the JVM, calling this method forces the JVM to load the class. The sample program in Figure 2-13 uses this method.

 The field **class** was added after the original version of the Java platform to simplify the process of accessing the **Class** object when the class name is known. This addition is one of many changes to enhance RTTI support in version 1.1 of the Java platform.

Support for RTTI changed very little between version 1.1 of the JDK and the Java 2 platform. One change of note in Java 2 is the introduction of an over-loaded **Class.forName** method with three arguments.

After you have a reference to a **Class** object, you can send messages to it to ask questions about the class that the object describes.

Class

java.lang.Class

Purpose

The **Class** class provides run-time information about Java classes.

Methods

■ Class forName(String classname)
  Class forName(String classname, boolean initialize,
  ClassLoader loader)

  The **forName** method returns the **Class** object for the given class name. If you use the form with three arguments and set the **boolean** argument to **false**, the class is not initialized. Otherwise the JVM performs initialization. You can also specify which loader to use by providing an object of type **java.lang. ClassLoader** as the third argument. By default, the JVM uses the bootstrap loader, but you can provide a nonstandard class loader to extend the way the JVM locates classes or to add security checks. You can specify **null** or **this.getClass().getClassLoader()** to use the default loader.

■ ClassLoader getClassLoader()

  All **Class** objects contain a reference to their loader. The returned object is of type **java.lang.ClassLoader** and represents the loader that loaded the class or interface into the JVM.

■ String getName()

  The **getName** method returns the fully qualified name of the class, interface, array, or primitive type.

■ Class getSuperclass()

  The **getSuperclass** method returns a reference to the **Class** object for the superclass of the class. If called for an instance of **Object**, or a type that is not a direct or indirect subclass of **Object**, the method returns **null**.

■ boolean isArray()

  The **isArray** method returns **true** if the **Class** object represents an array type, and **false** otherwise.

■ boolean isInstance(Object object)

  The **isInstance** method returns **true** if the specified object can cast to the type described by the **Class** object, and **false** otherwise. If the argument has the value **null**, this method returns **false**, regardless of the type of the argument.

- boolean isInterface()

  The **isInterface** method returns **true** if the **Class** object represents an interface, and **false** otherwise.

- Object newInstance()

  The **newInstance** method creates a new instance of the class and returns an object reference to the new object. You should cast the reference from type **Object** to the actual class of the object. If this method is used with the **Class** object of an interface or an abstract class, an **InstantiationException** exception is thrown. The constructor of the class without arguments is called to create the new instance. If such a constructor does not exist, the program terminates with a **NoSuchMethod** run-time error.

Figure 2-13 shows a sample program that exercises the **instanceof** operator and the **Class** class.

```
package examples.rtti;
/** A class used to demonstrate RTTI concepts
  */
public class CreateByName {
  /** Test method for the class
    * @param args names of classes to be
    *            instantiated
    */
  public static void main( String[] args ) {
     for ( int i = 0; i < args.length; i++ ) {
        try {
           Class x = Class.forName( args[i] );
           Object y;
        try {
           if ( x.isInterface() ) {
              System.out.println( "The class " +
                 x.getName() + " is an interface "
                 + "and can't be instantiated." );
           } else {
              y = x.newInstance();
              if ( y instanceof java.awt.Component ) {
                 System.out.println( "The GUI "
                    + "component class "
                    + x.getName() + " was specified." );
              } else {
```

Figure 2-13   CreateByName: a class to demonstrate RTTI concepts

```
                              + "component class "
                              + x.getName() + " was specified." );
                    }
               }
          } catch( InstantiationException ix ) {
               ix.printStackTrace();
          } catch( IllegalAccessException iax ) {
               iax.printStackTrace();
          } // end inner try
     } catch( ClassNotFoundException cnfx ) {
          System.err.println( "Sorry, the class "
          + args[i] + " could not be found." );
     } // end outer try
     } // end for
   } // end main
} // end CreateByName
```

Figure 2-13   `CreateByName`: a class to demonstrate RTTI concepts (continued)

Suppose that you run the program in Figure 2-13 using the command (on one line) shown in Figure 2-14, then you should expect to see the output shown in Figure 2-15.

```
java examples.rtti.CreateByName java.lang.String
     java.awt.Button java.lang.Gazoom java.lang.Cloneable
```

Figure 2-14   Sample command line invocation of the `CreateByName` program

The output is

```
The non-GUI component class java.lang.String was specified.
The GUI component class java.awt.Button was specified.
Sorry, the class java.lang.Gazoom could not be found.
The class java.lang.Cloneable is an interface and can't be instantiated.
```

Figure 2-15   Output from the `CreateByName` program

The **main** method receives the names as arguments. It obtains the **Class** object for each name supplied. The **main** method then tests whether the name represents an interface or a class. If it is an interface, **main** prints a message. Otherwise, **main** instantiates the class and then determines whether the object is a **Component**. The class **Component** is defined in the **java.awt** package, and **Button** is a subclass of **Component**. In all cases, **main** prints appropriate messages.

The use of `java.awt.Component` here is incidental. Any class would have served this purpose. The relevant parts of this code are the nested try blocks and the catch clauses. When run with the input class names shown in Figure 2-14, the only exception thrown and caught is a `ClassNotFoundException` exception.

CASTING BETWEEN TYPES

The operation of casting between types is essentially forcing an object or primitive type to behave as a different type of object or primitive type. It is usually necessitated because the return type of a method you are required to use doesn't match with the input type of another required method. Whenever you cast between types, the operation may not be safe. In this context, safe means that no information can be lost or corrupted as a result of the cast. The JVM ensures that only safe casts are performed. For example, casting from a type with a narrower range of values to a type with a wider range of values, such as from a `float` to a `double`, or from a subclass to its superclass class, is always safe. An unsafe cast can be from a wider type to a narrower type, or between classes that are not a direct or indirect subclass and superclass of each other. For example, casting from `long` to `short` or from `String` to `Exception` is unsafe.

In the case of primitive types, the compiler allows explicit casting as a way for you to indicate that you know a particular cast may not be safe and are aware of the potential problems. For example, you can convert from a `double` to a `float` if you cast explicitly. Even explicit casting has limits. For example, you cannot cast a `boolean` to an `int`.

For the reference types, deciding what is safe is not so easy. The compiler can detect casts between types that are not a subclass and superclass of each other, and some unsafe casts from superclass to subclass that force an object of the more generalized superclass to behave as a more specialized subclass object. When the compiler detects a cast that is definitely unsafe, it outputs an error message. When the compiler cannot tell whether a cast between classes is safe, it assumes the code is correct and leaves the JVM with the job of checking the cast at runtime.

Therefore, some unsafe casts can be attempted at runtime. When this happens, the JVM throws a `ClassCastException` exception. This exception can occur only in casts between subtypes and supertypes, because the compiler always detects other casts as errors.

The class `ClassCastException` extends `RunTimeException`. The reason is that casting exceptions are unpredictable. They can happen anywhere. If it were an `Exception`, you would have to list `ClassCastException` in the `throws` clause of every method that casts classes. You can still catch this exception, as the next sample program does.

In the sample program shown in Figure 2-16, the abstract class `Animal` is superclass to the classes `Reptile` and `Mammal`.

2

```
package examples.rtti;
/** Classes to demonstrate a run-time cast error
  */
public class BadCast {
   /** Test method for the class
     * @param args not used
     */
   public static void main( String[] args ) {
      Mammal horse = new Mammal( "horse" );
      Reptile snake = new Reptile( "snake" );
      Mammal mouse = new Mammal( "mouse" );
      horse.categorize();
      snake.categorize();
      mouse.categorize();
   }
}
/** A generic animal class
  */
class Animal {
   protected String name;

   public Animal( String name ) {
      this.name = name;
   }
   public void categorize() {
      try {
         if ( ( (Mammal) this ).isRodent() ) {
            System.out.println( "A " + name
                                + " is a rodent." );
         } else {
            System.out.println( "A " + name
                                + " is not a rodent." );
         }
      }

      catch ( ClassCastException ccx )  {
         ccx.printStackTrace();
      }
      try {
         int legs = ( (Reptile) this ).numLegs();
         System.out.println( "A " + name + " has "
                             + legs + " legs." );
      } catch ( ClassCastException ccx )  {
         ccx.printStackTrace();
      }
   }
}
```

Figure 2-16   BadCast: a program to demonstrate a run-time cast error

```
/** The class representing all mammals
   */
class Mammal extends Animal {
   private static String[] rodents
      = { "rat", "rabbit", "mouse", "beaver" };
   public Mammal( String name ) {
     super( name );
   }
   public boolean isRodent() {
      for ( int i = 0; i < rodents.length; i++ ) {
         if ( name.equals( rodents[i] ) ) {
            return true;
         }
      }
      return false;
   }
}
/** The class representing all reptiles
   */
class Reptile extends Animal {
   public Reptile( String name ) {
      super( name );
   }
   public int numLegs() {
      if ( name.equals( "snake" ) ) {
         return 0;
      } else {
         return 4;
      }
   }
}
```

Figure 2-16 `BadCast:` a program to demonstrate a run-time cast error (continued)

The output of Figure 2-16 is shown in Figure 2-17.

```
A horse is not a rodent.
java.lang.ClassCastException
        at examples.rtti.Animal.categorize(BadCast.java:42)
        at examples.rtti.BadCast.main(BadCast.java:13)
java.lang.ClassCastException
        at examples.rtti.Animal.categorize(BadCast.java:30)
        at examples.rtti.BadCast.main(BadCast.java:14)
A snake has 0 legs.
A mouse is a rodent.
java.lang.ClassCastException
        at examples.rtti.Animal.categorize(BadCast.java:42)
  at examples.rtti.BadCast.main(BadCast.java:15)
```

Figure 2-17 Output from running the `BadCast` program

2

The program in Figure 2-16 creates objects to represent different animals, each of which can be a `Mammal` or a `Reptile`. Both `Mammal` and `Reptile` classes extend the class `Animal`. The method `Animal.categorize` can receive any kind of animal as an argument. It casts the argument to a `Mammal` to call the `Mammal.isRodent` method and to a `Reptile` to call the `Reptile.numLegs` method. However, at runtime, the `Mammal` objects **horse** and **mouse** cannot be safely cast to `Reptile` objects, and the `Reptile` object **snake** cannot be safely cast to a `Mammal`. When these casts are attempted, the JVM throws the exception **ClassCastException**.

USING THE REFLECTION API

Sometimes you need to know much more about a type than the information provided by the **Class** class. For this purpose, you can use the classes in the package **java.lang.reflect**, otherwise known as the *Reflection API*. This set of classes increases the power and usefulness of the **Class** class.

The Reflection API supports an activity called *introspection*, which essentially asks a class to describe itself. JavaBeans technology depends on introspection. In Chapter 8, you learn that JavaBeans are classes that conform to a rigid coding standard, so that they can be used as input for JavaBeans-based development tools. The tools use introspection to analyze the JavaBeans and then give the developers ways, often through graphical interfaces, of building programs quickly from the JavaBeans.

The Reflection API became available in version 1.1 of the Java platform. The **Class** class, as defined in the original Java platform, proved to be very useful. Nevertheless, the **java.lang.reflect** package was added to satisfy requests that the **Class** class be extended.

One of the most important advances in Java technology since the first release of the Java platform is the formulation of a standard for JavaBeans. Many of the changes introduced in version 1.1 converted the core classes into JavaBeans. One very important use of the Reflection API is to support JavaBeans-based tools.

The Reflection API gives an object the ability to reflect upon itself and discover its contents. The package **java.lang.reflect** defines a number of classes that together give a complete description of an object. Three classes represent the building blocks of classes: **Constructor**, **Method**, and **Field**. The most commonly used methods of these classes are listed here.

Class

`java.lang.reflect.Constructor`

Purpose

Each instance of the **Constructor** class provides information about one constructor of a class, and provides a way for the calling program to create an object using the constructor.

Methods

- `Class[ ] getExceptionTypes()`

  The **getExceptionTypes** method returns an array of **Class** objects for the types of exceptions defined to be thrown by the constructor. Each element of the array is an object reference for the **Class** object of one argument. The returned array will have a length of zero if no exceptions are defined.

- `Class[ ] getParameterTypes()`

  The **getParameterTypes** method returns an array of **Class** objects for the arguments of the constructor. Each element of the array is an object reference for the **Class** object of one argument. The order of the elements reflects the order in which the arguments are listed in the definition of the constructor.

- `Object newInstance( Object[ ] args )`

  The **newInstance** method creates an instance of the class and returns an object reference for the new object. The elements in the array of type **Object** object are passed as arguments to the constructor.

Class

`java.lang.reflect.Method`

Purpose

Each instance of the **Method** class provides information about one method of a class, and provides a way for the calling program to call the method. The method may be a class method or an instance method, and may be abstract.

Methods

- `Class[ ] getExceptionTypes()`

  The **getExceptionTypes** method returns an array of **Class** objects for the types of exceptions defined to be thrown by the method. Each element of the array is an object reference for the **Class** object of one argument. The returned array will have a length of zero if no exceptions are defined.

■ Class[] getParameterTypes()

The **getParameterTypes** method returns an array of **Class** objects for the arguments of the method. Each element of the array is an object reference for the **Class** object of one argument. The order of the elements reflects the order in which the arguments are listed in the definition of the method.

■ Class getReturnType()

The **getReturnType** method returns an object reference for the **Class** object of the return type of the method.

■ Object invoke(Object object, Object[] args)

■ The **invoke** method invokes the method with the object specified in the first argument. For a class method, the first argument has the value **null**. The elements in the array of type **Object** are passed as arguments to the method.

Class

java.lang.reflect.Field

Purpose

Each instance of the **Field** class provides information about one field of a class and provides the calling program with a way to get and set the value of the field. The field may be a class variable or an instance variable.

Methods

■ Class getType()

The **getType** method returns an object reference for the **Class** object of the field.

■ Object get(Object object)

The **get** method returns the value of the field for the specified object. This class also has methods to return the value of a field as a value of any of the primitive types. For example, the **getBoolean** method returns the value of a static or instance **boolean** field, and the **getDouble** method returns the value of a static or instance **double** field, or of another primitive type convertible to type **double** via a widening conversion.

■ void set(Object object, Object value)

The **set** method sets the value of the field for the specified object to the specified value. This class also has methods to set the value of a field as a value of any of the primitive types. For example, the **setBoolean** method sets the value of a static or instance **boolean** field, and the **setDouble** method sets the value of a static or instance **double** field.

The type of most arguments and of many return values of the methods in the Reflection API classes is **Object**. Therefore, you can actually pass any type of object, and any type may be returned. But what about the primitive types? The Reflection API classes use the wrapper classes for the primitive types. Some of the methods in these classes, such as **Field.getType** and **Method.getReturnType**, return an object reference for a **Class** object. Use the methods in the **Class** class with these object references to get more information about the returned objects.

The classes **Constructor**, **Method**, and **Field** implement an interface called **Member**. Therefore, all three classes provide the methods defined in **Member**.

Interface

java.lang.reflect.Member

Purpose

The class that implements this interface provides identifying information about a member of a class.

Methods

- **Class getDeclaringClass()**

  The **getDeclaringClass** method returns an object reference for the **Class** object of the class in which the member is defined.

- **String getName()**

  The **getName** method returns the name of the member as a **String**.

- **int getModifiers()**

  The **getModifiers** method returns the Java programming language's access specifiers and qualifiers that apply to the member. The return value is encoded in an **int**. Use the **Modifier** class to decode the **int** value.

Two additional classes complete the suite of Reflection API classes: **Array** and **Modifier**.

Class

java.lang.reflect.Array

Purpose

The **Array** class provides methods to manipulate a **Field** object as an array. The **Field** class has only methods for getting and setting individual values. Use this class with the **Field** class when the field is an array. To determine whether a **Field** object is an array, call the **Class.isArray** method and pass the value returned by **Field.getType**.

2

Methods

- **Object get(Object object, int position)**

  The **get** method returns an object reference for the element at the specified position in the array. The **Array** class has methods that return the values of individual elements as values of the primitive types.

- **void set(Object object, int position)**

  The **set** method sets the value of the element at the specified position to the value of the first argument.

- **int getLength()**

  The **getLength** method returns the number of elements in the array.

- **Object newInstance(Class type, int length)**

  The **newInstance** method creates a new array to hold the specified number of elements of the specified type and returns an object reference for the new array.

- **Object newInstance(Class type, int[] dimensions)**

  The **newInstance** method creates a new multidimensional array to hold the specified number of elements of the specified type and returns an object reference for the new array.

Class

java.lang.reflect.Modifier

Purpose

The **Modifier** class contains a number of constants that represent the access specifiers and qualifiers that can be applied to members. It also provides class methods that return **true** if a member has a certain qualifier and **false** otherwise. For example, the method **isStatic(int value)** returns **true** only when called for a static member. The constant **STATIC** is an **int** representing the modifier **static**. Call the method **Member.getModifiers** to get the value to pass to the methods in this class.

How can you access the **Class** object for a primitive type when you cannot invoke a method such as **getClass** for a primitive type? Each wrapper class for a primitive type has a field called **TYPE** that is a reference to the **Class** object for its corresponding primitive type. Just like the field **class** of all reference types, the field **TYPE** of wrapper classes is a public, static, and final field. For example, **Integer.TYPE** is a reference to the **Class** object for **int**. Be careful not to confuse **Integer.TYPE** with **Integer.class**. The first refers to the **Class** object for primitive type **int**, and the second refers to the **Class** object for the wrapper class **Integer**.

What about methods that do not return a value and have return type **void**? The package **java.lang** contains a wrapper class named **Void** for the primitive type **void**.

 To provide run-time type information about **void**, the class **java.lang.Void** was added to the core classes at the same time as the Reflection API. The purpose of **Void** was to contain the **Void.TYPE** field.

Figure 2-18 is a sample program that uses the Reflection API to make a list of the methods in the **String** class.

```
package examples.rtti;
import java.lang.reflect.*;
/** A class used to demonstrate the use of the
  * Reflection API
  */
public class ListStringMethods {
   /** Test method for the class
     * @param args not used
     * @exception ClassNotFoundException
     *              Thrown if the class being
     *              investigated isn't found
     */
   public static void main( String[] args )
       throws ClassNotFoundException {
      Method[] ma
        = String.class.getMethods();
      for ( int i = 0; i < ma.length; i++ ) {
         System.out.println( ma[i] );
      }
   }
}
```

Figure 2-18   `ListStringMethods`: an example class that uses the Reflection API

The output is a complete list of the methods in the **String** class and is too long to include here. The first three lines are shown in Figure 2-19.

```
public int java.lang.String.hashCode()
public int java.lang.String.compareTo(java.lang.String)
public int java.lang.String.compareTo(java.lang.Object)
```

Figure 2-19   First three lines of output from running the `ListStringMethods` program

In the class ListStringMethods, the main method declares an array of Method objects, ma, which is assigned the object reference obtained by calling the method **String.class.getMethods**. This one method call acquires a lot of information: Every method in the **String** class is described in an element of the returned array. The **Method** class overrides the **Object.toString** method so you can easily print out all the information about the method, including its access specifier.

Calling Methods with the Reflection API

You can do more with the Reflection API than receive a great deal of useful information about a class. Now you have two ways to execute a method or a constructor:

- Call the method by name or create an object with the **new** keyword in the usual way. This is the obvious approach to take when you know the name of the method or type of the object as you are entering source code.

- Use a **Method** object or a **Constructor** object. This approach works when you must use the Reflection API to discover which methods are available, or to determine the type of an object.

To call a method with the Reflection API, use the following instance method of the **Method** class:

```
Object invoke( Object object, Object[] args )
```

In the first argument of **invoke**, pass an object reference for the object on which the called method is to run, or specify **null** for class methods. Create an array of type **Object** for the arguments of the method and insert an object reference for the first argument of the method into the first element of the array, for the second argument into the second element, and so on. If an argument has a primitive type, wrap it with the appropriate wrapper class and insert the object reference for the wrapper instance in the array. Specify the array as the second argument of **invoke**.

If the called method returns a value, you retrieve the value through the object reference returned by **invoke**. If the return type is a primitive type, **invoke** returns an instance of the appropriate wrapper class.

If the called method does not return a value, **invoke** returns an object reference of type **Void**.

To create an instance of a class with the Reflection API, use the following instance method of the **Constructor** class:

```
Object newInstance( Object[] args )
```

The only argument of **newInstance** is an array that contains the arguments for the constructor. Build up this array in exactly the same way as you build up the array argument of **Method.invoke**. The **newInstance** method returns a reference to the newly created object, which you can cast to the appropriate class type.

The method `Constructor.newInstance` has one great advantage over the method `Class.newInstance`: You can pass arguments to the constructor.

 In the original Java platform, the only way to call a constructor explicitly was to use the method `Class.newInstance`. The Reflection API introduced the method `Constructor.newInstance` with version 1.1. The method `Class.newInstance` still works, but only if the class has a constructor with no arguments.

Figure 2-20 is an example program that creates instances of classes using `Constructor.newInstance`.

```java
package examples.rtti;
import java.lang.reflect.*;
/** A class defined to demonstrate the Reflection API
  */
class FirstType {
   private String name;
   public FirstType( String name ) {
      this.name = name;
   }
   public FirstType() {
      this.name = "DefaultFirst";
   }
   public String toString() {
      return ( "A FirstType object named " + name );
   }
}
/** A class defined to demonstrate the Reflection API
  */
class SecondType {
   // explicit constructor needed for Reflection API
   public SecondType() {
      // intentionally left empty
   }
   public String toString() {
      return ( "A SecondType object" );
   }
}
/** A class used to show how the Reflection API can
  * be used to construct objects
  */
public class Construct {
   /** Test method for the class
     * @param args the class name to be constructed
     *    followed by any constructor arguments
     */
```

Figure 2-20   Construct: an example of how to use the Reflection API to construct objects

```java
public static void main( String [] args ) {
    if ( args.length == 0 ) {
        System.out.println( " usage: Construct"
                            + " classname"
                            + " [ctor_arg]" );
        return;
    }
    // get the class object for the specified class
    Class classObj = null;
    try {
        classObj = Class.forName( args[0] );
    } catch ( ClassNotFoundException ex ) {
        System.err.println( " Unknown class "
                            + args[0] );
        return;
    }
    // get constructor for class
    Constructor ctor = null;
    Class[] ctorTypes = new Class[args.length-1];
    for ( int i = 0; i < args.length-1; i ++ ) {
        ctorTypes[i] = java.lang.String.class;
    }
    try {
        ctor = classObj.getConstructor( ctorTypes );
    } catch ( NoSuchMethodException ex ) {
        String msg = "No constructor: ";
        msg += classObj.getName() + "(";
        for ( int i = 0; i < ctorTypes.length; i++ ) {
            msg += ctorTypes[i].getName();
            if ( i < ctorTypes.length-1 ) {
                msg += ", ";
            }
        }
        msg += " )";
        System.err.println( msg );
        return;
    }
    // build up the array of arguments
    // for the constructor from the
    // command-line arguments
    String[] ctorArgs
        = new String[ctorTypes.length];
    System.arraycopy( args, 1, ctorArgs, 0,
                      ctorTypes.length );
    // call the constructor
    Object obj = null;
```

Figure 2-20   Construct: an example of how to use the Reflection API to construct objects (continued)

```
     try {
        obj = ctor.newInstance( ctorArgs );
     } catch ( Exception ex ) {
        ex.printStackTrace();
        return;
     }
     // print the object created
     System.out.println( obj );
   }
 }
```

Figure 2-20   `Construct`: an example of how to use the Reflection API to
construct objects (continued)

This program tries to create instances of either `FirstType` or `SecondType`, depending
on which class name is specified in the argument list `Construct.main`. It may be useful
to look at the code from Figure 2-20 in more detail. The following are code fragments
taken from Figure 2-20 that are followed by detailed descriptions of their content:

```
class FirstType {
   private String name;
   public FirstType( String name ) {
      this.name = name;
   }
   public FirstType() {
      this.name = "DefaultFirst";
   }
   public String toString() {
      return ( "A FirstType object named " + name );
   }
}
```

The class `FirstType` has two constructors shown in the preceding code: one with no
arguments, and one that takes a single string as an argument. This simple class does no
more than store either the string supplied to the constructor or a default string in the
private field, name, and provide a **toString** method so that the contents of the class
can be printed.

```
class SecondType {
   public SecondType() {}
   public String toString() {
      return ( "A SecondType object" );
   }
}
```

The class `SecondType` has only the no-argument constructor shown in the previous
code and a **toString** method. If a constructor is not explicitly supplied, the compiler
can supply one, and this program compiles successfully. However, the Reflection API
does not recognize the compiler-supplied constructor, and one must be supplied here.

```
        public static void main( String [] args ) {
            if ( args.length == 0 ) {
                System.out.println( " usage: Construct"
                                    + " classname"
                                    + "[ctor_arg]" );
                return;
        }
```

The work happens in the **main** method of the test class **Construct** in the preceding code. This program expects the name of a class and the arguments of a constructor for that class to be supplied as command-line arguments. For simplicity, the program assumes that the type of all arguments for the constructor is **String**. If no arguments are supplied, the program stops with a usage message that explains what is missing from the command line.

```
        Class classObj = null;
        try {
            classObj = Class.forName( args[0] );
        }
        catch ( ClassNotFoundException ex ) {
            System.err.println( " Unknown class "
                                + args[0] );
            return;
        }
```

The first step is to determine what kind of class the user wants to instantiate. The **Class.forName** method in the preceding code fragment loads the specified class into the JVM and returns the **class** object for that class. If no such class can be found, the JVM throws a **ClassNotFoundException** exception. Because **forName** expects the full class name, the exception is thrown if the user enters just **FirstType**, **SecondType**, or any other unknown class name. For the program to work with the example classes supplied in this file, the user must enter **examples.rtti.FirstType** or **examples.rtti.SecondType**.

The exception handler provided by this catch clause for the **ClassNotFoundException** exception prints an appropriate message identifying the unknown class and then terminates the program.

```
        Constructor ctor = null;
        Class[] ctorTypes = new Class[args.length-1];
        for ( int i = 0; i < args.length-1; i++ ) {
            ctorTypes[i] = java.lang.String.class;
        }
```

Having determined that the class exists, the program prepares to call a constructor to instantiate the class. It declares a **Constructor** object, ctor, in the first line of the preceding code fragment, but needs to look at the argument list before identifying a specific constructor. Therefore, the next step is to build an array of type **Class**, `ctorTypes`, in which each element encapsulates the type of one argument for the constructor. In Figure 2-20, all arguments have type **String**, and the number of arguments is determined by the command-line arguments entered by the user.

```
try {
   ctor = classObj.getConstructor( ctorTypes );
}
catch ( NoSuchMethodException ex ) {
   String msg = "No constructor: ";
   msg += classObj.getName() + "(";
   for ( int i = 0; i < ctorTypes.length; i++ ) {
      msg += ctorTypes[i].getName();
      if ( i < ctorTypes.length-1 ) {
         msg += ", ";
      }
   }
   msg += " )";
   System.err.println( msg );
   return;
}
```

The purpose of the preceding **try** block is to get a **Constructor** object for the required constructor. If such a constructor is available, the **getConstructor** method returns the **Constructor** object to ctor. Otherwise, the **getConstructor** method throws a **NoSuchMethodException** exception. The **catch** clause handles this exception by printing a message and terminating the program. In this case, the catch clause builds the message to contain the name of the constructor and the argument list. Notice that the method **getName** is used to return a printable representation of the type of each argument.

```
String[] ctorArgs = new String[ctorTypes.length];
System.arraycopy( args, 1, ctorArgs, 0,
                  ctorTypes.length );
```

Having determined that the required constructor is available, the program sets up the array of objects to pass to the constructor, `ctorArgs`, declared in the first line of the previous code fragment. For this array, every element in the array is a **String**.

```
Object obj = null;
try {
   obj = ctor.newInstance( ctorArgs );
}
catch ( Exception ex ) {
   ex.printStackTrace();
   return;
}
System.out.println( obj );
}
```

reference that will be assigned to the new object after it is created. The call of **newInstance** that creates the object is enclosed in another **try** block in case something unanticipated goes wrong while the program instantiates the object. The **catch** clause for this **try** block catches any checked exception, prints the call stack at the point where the exception occurs, and terminates the program. Ultimately, the program may create a new object. The program announces this success by printing the object.

The output for this program depends on the command-line input. Figure 2-21 lists several possible input arguments for the **Construct** program in Figure 2-20 and the resulting output. Some of the messages are split because they are too long to fit on one line in this table.

Command-Line Arguments	Output
examples.rtti.FirstType Hello	A FirstType object named Hello
examples.rtti.FirstType one two three	No constructor: examples.rtti.FirstType(java.lang.String, java.lang.String, java.lang.String)
examples.rtti.SecondType	A SecondType object
SecondType	Unknown class SecondType
java.lang.String "Hello World"	Hello World

Figure 2-21   Possible input arguments for the **Construct** program in Figure 2-20

NESTED CLASSES AND INTERFACES

You can certainly use the Java programming language without using inner classes. You do not even sacrifice program functionality by not using them. On the other hand, you can make your code more elegant and greatly improve the structure of your classes by using inner classes.

Nesting classes is an excellent way to collect a group of cooperating classes or interfaces. Up to this point, the only technique available to you for gathering related classes together has been to define a package similar to the **java.lang** or **java.io** packages that are part of the Java platform. Packages are a rather coarse-grained way to collect classes. Often you combine classes into packages when, really, the classes have no logical grouping except convenience or the fact that the files reside in the same folder. You can take advantage of inner and nested classes to indicate more clearly how classes interact with each other. The enclosing class and all that it encloses must still, however, belong to one package.

With enclosed classes, you can group classes with a finer granularity than you can with packages. In addition, the enclosed classes can share full access to private members of other enclosed classes in the same enclosing class.

The relationship between an enclosed class and enclosing class does not involve inheritance. A completely different set of rules determines the scope and accessibility of members between the enclosed and enclosing class. In fact, you can combine inner and nested classes with inheritance, by defining inner or nested classes that are subclasses and superclasses.

A class or interface may be nested inside another class or interface. The simplest way to enclose a class inside another class is to nest their definitions one inside the other. You can even nest classes within interfaces, and interfaces within classes.

To define a nested class or interface, you must qualify the enclosed class with the keyword **static**. Do not omit this qualifier because, syntactically, the keyword **static** is all that distinguishes a nested class from an inner class.

Syntax for Defining a Nested Class or Interface

```
[public] [qualifiers] class enclosing _name {
        // . . .
        [access_specifier] [qualifiers] static class enclosed _name  {
                // . . .
    }
}
```

Dissection

- The syntax of the enclosing class or interface definition is like any class or interface definition.

- You can declare nested classes to be public, protected, or private. If you omit an access specifier, the class has the default package access.

- Classes nested within interfaces are implicitly static, like fields defined in interfaces.

- The qualifiers **abstract** and **final** have their usual meaning when applied to nested classes.

Code Example for Defining a Nested Class or Interface

```
public interface outer {
//. . .
    public static class inner {
        // . . .
    }
}
```

Code Dissection

Here, the class **inner** is nested inside the interface **outer**.

The keyword **static** is appropriate for nested classes. Nested classes are not associated with instances of the enclosing class. It is the classes or interfaces, not objects, that are nested. The term *top-level class* refers to a class that is contained only in packages.

Nested classes are top-level classes just like all the classes we have seen so far in this book. They are enclosed in other classes, but are not members of the enclosing classes. Creating a nested class is a useful technique to show a close relationship between the nested enclosing class, but a relationship that does not extend to a tight coupling of the data within the two classes.

What do access specifiers mean when applied to nested classes? The rules for accessing a nested class resemble the rules for accessing members of the enclosing class. Only the enclosing class can instantiate a private nested class. All classes in the same package can access a nested class with the default package. Protected nested classes can be accessed by classes in the same package and by classes that inherit from the enclosing class. You can always access public nested classes.

A nested class has no special privileges for accessing members of the enclosing class or other enclosed classes in the same enclosed class. It has the same access privileges as any other class in the same package. Nested classes can extend other classes and can be extended by other classes.

The names of nested classes consist of package name, enclosing class names, and the simple name of the nested class, separated by dots. For example, in the program shown in Figure 2-22, the class `Node` belongs to the package examples and subpackage `inner` and is enclosed in the class `Graph1`. The name of the class is `examples.inner.Graph1.Node`.

To import all the classes nested within a class, use the asterisk, `*`, just as you do to import all the classes in a package. For example, you can import all the classes in the `Graph1` class with the following statement:

```
import examples.inner.Graph1.*;
```

Figure 2-22 is a small application in which a class called `Node` is nested inside a class called `Graph1`.

```
package examples.inner;
import java.util.Hashtable;
import java.util.Enumeration;
/** Class representing an undirected graph composed
  * of nodes.  The node class is a top-level class
  * nested within the Graph1 class.
  */
```

Figure 2-22   `Graph1:` an example of the use of nested classes

```java
public class Graph1 {
   private Hashtable nodeList = new Hashtable();
   /** Add a node to the graph
     * @param x the x coordinate of the node
     * @param y the y coordinate of the node
     */
   public void addNode( int x, int y ) {
     Node n = new Node( x, y );
     if ( ! nodeList.containsKey( n.key() ) ) {
        nodeList.put( n.key(), n );
     }
   }
   /** Get the object as a string
     * @return the object as a string
     */
   public String toString() {
     StringBuffer sb = new StringBuffer( "[ " );
     Enumeration e = nodeList.elements();
     while ( e.hasMoreElements() ) {
        sb.append( e.nextElement().toString()
                    + " " );
     }
     sb.append( "]" );
     return sb.toString();
   }
   /** Test method
     * @param args not used
     */
   public static void main( String[] args ) {
     System.out.println( "creating the graph" );
     Graph1 g = new Graph1();
     System.out.println( "adding nodes" );
     g.addNode( 4, 5 );
     g.addNode( -6, 11 );
     System.out.println( g );
   }
   /** The class representing nodes within the graph
     */
   private static class Node {
     private int x, y;
     public Node( int x, int y ) {
        this.x = x;
        this.y = y;
     }
```

Figure 2-22 Graph1: an example of the use of nested classes (continued)

```
      /** Determine the key value for a node
       * @return the key as a String
       */
      public Object key() {
         return x + "," + y;
      }
      /** Get the object as a string
       * @return the object as a string
       */
      public String toString() {
         return "(" + x + "," + y + ")";
      }
   }    // end of Node class
}    // end of Graph1 class
```

Figure 2-22 `Graph1`: an example of the use of nested classes (continued)

The output from running the program is shown in Figure 2-23.

```
creating the graph
adding nodes
[ ( 4,5 ) ( -6,11 ) ]
```

Figure 2-23 Output from running the `Graph1` program

The order in which the nodes in the graph appear in the output of Figure 2-23 may be reversed, because the hash table data structure used to hold the nodes has no specified ordering. More information about hash tables is provided in Chapter 4.

A `Graph1` object contains a collection of nodes stored in a hash table. The field `nodeList` is of type **Hashtable**. The core class **Hashtable** is defined in the package **java.util** and provides hash table objects. In the next chapter, you learn more about using **Hashtable** and the other collection classes. The first statement in the definition of the **Graph1** class declares the `nodeList` field:

```
public class Graph1 {
   private Hashtable nodeList = new Hashtable();
```

The method **addNode** in Figure 2-22 uses two methods from the **Hashtable** class:

- `containsKey` determines whether an object with a particular key is already stored in the hash.

- `put` adds a node object to the hash table.

The method **key** in the nested class **Node** in Figure 2-22 generates identifying keys for the node objects. Note that `Graph1` has exclusive use of `Node` because `Node` is private, and that `Graph1` can access the members of `Node`. The methods **addNode** and **main** of `Graph1` use `Node` exactly as they would use any class to which they have access.

INNER CLASSES

Inner classes are very different in nature from top-level classes. The term *top-level* applies to classes that are the top level of containment, excluding packages, and inner classes are always contained in other classes.

To understand why top-level classes and inner classes are so different in nature, you must consider the *state data* of objects. All instances of classes have state data. For objects of top-level classes, the state data is equivalent to the current instance of the class. The state data for an instance includes all the fields that it contains. The object reference **this** refers to the state data of one instance. The complicating factor for inner classes is that the object reference **this** relates not only to the current instance of the inner class, but also to the enclosing instances of all enclosing classes.

Compare what happens with subclasses to what happens with inner classes. An instance of a subclass has an independent copy of all the fields declared in the subclass and of all the fields inherited from its superclass. With inheritance you cannot create two objects that share the same copies of instance variables. If you instantiate a subclass and its super-class, you create two objects that can have some of the same fields, but different copies, or instances, of those fields. The superclass and subclass objects are completely separate objects.

In contrast, when you instantiate an inner class and the class that encloses it, the two objects are created with access to the same copies of the fields defined in the enclosing class. In fact, you must have an instance of the enclosing class with which to create the inner class. The inner class state data contains the inner class fields. The enclosing class state data contains the enclosing class fields. The object reference **this** for the inner class instance refers to both the inner and enclosing state data. In Figure 2-24, the gray boxes are included in the state data of both the enclosing and inner class objects.

This situation is analogous to the way in which all instances of the same class share class variables. Just as all instances of a class have access to the class variables and share a single copy of these fields, all inner class instances that share an enclosing instance have access to the fields of the enclosing instance and share a single copy of them.

Three kinds of inner classes are possible:

- *Member inner classes* are defined inside another class, at the same level as fields and methods. They are members of the enclosing class.
- *Local inner classes* are defined inside blocks of code. They are local to the enclosing method or block.
- *Anonymous inner classes* are local inner classes that have no name.

2

```
class Superclass {

    private int a;
    private int b

}

class Subclass extends Superclass {

    private int c;
    private int d:

}
Superclass S1 = new Superclass();
```

S1.a	S1.b

```
Subclass S2 = new Subclass();
```

S2.a	S2.b	S2.c	S2.d

```
class Enclosing {

    private int a;
    private int b;

    private class Inner {

        private int c;
        private int d;

    }

}
Enclosing T1 = new Enclosing();
```

T1.a	T1.b

```
Inner T2 = T1.new Inner();
```

T1.a	T1.b	T2.c	T2.d

Figure 2-24   Comparing inner classes to subclasses

Understanding the Reasons for Using Inner Classes

Programming inner classes is an advanced technique, and you may be wondering whether inner classes are worth the complications that they bring to the Java programming language. For example, you must use an expanded form of the **new** keyword to instantiate anonymous inner classes, and you must learn a new way to use the **super** method when inner classes have subclasses.

One benefit is the elegant way in which you can use them to create *adapter classes* within an existing class. Adapter classes are a programming design pattern intended to create a wrapper for the data of a class in order to present it within a different interface that the class does not implement. You can define adapter classes that are implemented as inner classes, in the places where they are used. The resulting classes also have access to the internal variables and methods of the enclosing class or block, effectively providing an entirely different type that is adapted to fit another interface. The example class `Equation1` in Figure 2-30 demonstrates using inner classes in this way.

An inner class is an elegant way to implement an interface when the interface defines only one method. Such one-method interfaces are common when you program graphical user interfaces. The Java platform provides many interfaces for classes that react to user actions, and several of these interfaces contain only one method for a single user action. You write tidier source code if you define an anonymous inner class to implement the interface than if you define and create an instance of another top-level class. Using inner classes to implement one-method interfaces is a technique that can be used to package a block of statements so that it can be passed as an argument. The method that receives the instance of the inner class can then use the instance by calling the method as defined in the interface.

The impact of inner classes on your code depends on how you use them. They are not as critical as inheritance, without which object-oriented programming is severely limited. On the other hand, some awkward techniques become elegant when implemented with inner classes. You may even be tempted to take advantage of all the nuances of inner classes. If you are, take care not to create programs that are difficult to understand and maintain. If you use inner classes in a straightforward manner and for the purposes for which they were designed, you can reap considerable benefits from minimal effort.

Defining Member Inner Classes

Inner classes are instance members of their enclosing classes. Define a member inner class like you define a nested top-level class, but do not qualify the inner class with the keyword **static**. Following is the syntax you need to know for defining such a class, as well as tips for doing this effectively.

Syntax for Defining a Member Inner Class

```
[public] [qualifiers] class enclosing_class_name {
    // . . .
    [access_specifiers] [qualifiers] class enclosed_class_name  {
      // . . .
    }
}
```

Dissection

- The syntax of the enclosing class definition is like any class definition.

- You can declare inner classes to be **public**, **protected**, or **private** because they are members of the enclosing class. If you omit an access specifier, the class has the default package access.

- The qualifiers **abstract** and **final** have their usual meaning when applied to inner classes, but you cannot use the qualifier **static**. If you declare the enclosed class to be static, it becomes a nested class, but not an inner class.

2

Code Example for Defining a Member Inner Class

```
public class Outer {
   //. . .
   private class Inner {
      // . . .
   }
}
```

Code Dissection

Here the class `Inner` is an inner class enclosed in the class `Outer`. Only `Outer` and other classes enclosed in `Outer` can access `Inner`, because `Inner` is private.

Every instance of the inner class must exist within an instance of the enclosing class. An inner class cannot be instantiated without an instance of the outer class. Therefore, you must associate the keyword **new** with an instance of the enclosing class to create an instance of an inner class.

Syntax for Instantiating a Member Inner Class

```
enclosing_instance.new inner_class( arguments )
```

Dissection

■ The enclosing class instance must be an object reference for an existing object. If you are creating the inner class object in an instance method of the enclosing class, the object reference **this** is implied.

Code Example for Instantiating a Member Inner Class

```
public static void main( String[] args ) {
   Outer O = new Outer();
   Inner I = O.new Inner();
      // . . .
}
```

The program in Figure 2-25 is a reworking of the undirected graph class `Graph1` from the example program in Figure 2-22. This new class is called `Graph2`. The class `Node` is now a member of an inner class instead of a nested class. The lines that have changed since `Graph1` appear in boldface.

```
package examples.inner;
import java.util.Hashtable;
import java.util.Enumeration;
/** Class representing an undirected graph composed
  * of nodes. The node class is a top-level class
  * nested within the Graph2 class.
  */
public class Graph2 {
    private Hashtable nodeList = new Hashtable();
    /** Add a node to the graph
      * @param x the x coordinate of the node
      * @param y the y coordinate of the node
      */
    public void addNode( int x, int y ) {
      // The use of "this." is not required here
      this.new Node( x, y );
    }
    /** Get the object as a string
      * @return the object as a string
      */
    public String toString() {
       StringBuffer sb = new StringBuffer( "[ " );
       Enumeration e = nodeList.elements();
       while ( e.hasMoreElements() ) {
          sb.append( e.nextElement().toString()
                       + " " );
       }
       sb.append( "]" );
       return sb.toString();
    }
    /** Test method
      * @param args not used
      */
    public static void main( String[] args ) {
       System.out.println( "creating the graph" );
       Graph2 g = new Graph2();
       System.out.println( "adding nodes" );
       g.addNode( 4, 5 );
       g.addNode( -6, 11 );
       System.out.println( g );
    }
```

Figure 2-25   Graph2: an example of the use of member inner classes

```
/** The class representing nodes within the graph
 */
private class Node {
   private int x, y;
   public Node( int x, int y ) {
      this.x = x;
      this.y = y;
      // The use of "Graph2.this." is not
      // required here
      if ( ! Graph2.this.nodeList
                  .containsKey( key() ) ) {
         nodeList.put( key(), this );
      }
   }
   /** Determine the key value for a node
     * @return the key as a String
     */
   public Object key() {
      return x + "," + y;
   }
   /** Get the object as a string
     * @return the object as a string
     */
   public String toString() {
      return "( " + x + "," + y + " )";
   }
}     // end of Node class
}    // end of Graph2 class
```

Figure 2-25   `Graph2`: an example of the use of member inner classes (continued)

Although the structure of the program may have changed, the overall function of this program remains the same as the `Graph1` program in Figure 2-22, and so the output from running the `Graph2` program is the same as that shown in Figure 2-23.

In this program, the single line that starts the definition of the enclosed class `Node` determines its nature. This definition omits the keyword **static**. Because `Node` does not have the **static** qualifier, it is an inner class:

```
private class Node {
```

The method `addNode` of the enclosing class `Graph2` method has changed. Whereas the same method of `Graph1` in Figure 2-22 created an object of the nested class `Node` and then conditionally called method `addNode` for the `nodeList` field, the `addNode` method of `Graph2` in Figure 2-25 has just one line:

```
this.new Node( x, y );
```

Because Node is a member of Graph2, its constructor can call addNode for the nodeList field. To create the Node object, you must specify an enclosing instance of the Graph2 class. Here, the object reference this indicates the current Graph2 object. Because addNode is an instance method, the implicit this object reference would have sufficed, but the expression this.new emphasizes the fact that an enclosing instance is being associated with the object being created. The sample program in Figure 2-26 demonstrates a situation in which you cannot omit the object reference this.

Now consider the constructor of the Node class, and consider in particular the use of the this object reference, reproduced here from Figure 2-25:

```
public Node( int x, int y ) {
    this.x = x;
    this.y = y;
    if ( ! Graph2.this.nodeList
                .containsKey( key() ) ){
        nodeList.put( key(), this );
    }
}
```

The state data of an inner class object includes current instances of the enclosing class as well as the immediate current instance of the inner class. These lines use two current instances: this and Graph2.this.

For the inner class object, this refers to the enclosed instance containing the fields defined in the inner class. Thus, this for a Node object relates to the node's x and y fields. This constructor passes the current Node object, this, to the put method of the Hashtable class because put must receive the object reference for the object to add to the hash table in its first argument.

You can always access the current instance of an enclosing class with a qualified this object reference. In this constructor, the object reference, called Graph2.this, explicitly qualifies the nodeList field. In this case, the explicit qualification is not necessary because ambiguity exists and the conditional expression could read as follows:

```
( ! nodeList.containsKey( key() ) )
```

The only time you must explicitly qualify a member name is when a name conflict exists between a member in an enclosing class and a name inherited from a superclass.

Resolving Name Conflicts in Inner Classes

The potential for name conflicts is one of the complications inner classes add to the Java programming language. When such a conflict occurs, you will be unable to compile your program successfully until the conflict is resolved. An inner class belongs to two hierarchies—its containment hierarchy and its inheritance hierarchy—and these hierarchies are defined as follows:

- The containment hierarchy for an inner class is the sequence of classes that enclose it, up to and including the top-level class at package scope.

inner class inherits, up to and including the class **Object**.

If your inner class inherits a member from a superclass with the same name as a member of an enclosing class, the unqualified name of the member is ambiguous. If a method of the inner class uses the member name without qualifying it, a compiler error results. Figure 2-26 demonstrates how name conflicts can arise.

Ideally, name conflicts between superclasses and enclosing classes are resolved by renaming one or both of the conflicting members. Realistically, the freedom to rename these members does not exist, and so the only way to resolve the conflict is by fully qualifying the names of the members so that the references are no longer ambiguous.

```
class Outer {
    int x;
    class Inner extends Super {
        void setx( int value ) {
            Outer.this.x = value;
            this.x = value;
            x = value;          ?
        }
    }
}
                              public class Super {
                                  int x;
                                  // ...
                              }
```

Figure 2-26   Name conflicts in inner classes

Enclosing Objects of Inner Classes

You have seen what happens when you create a member inner class within an instance method of an enclosing class: The enclosing object defaults to the instance of the enclosing class for which the instance method is run. What happens when you create an instance of an inner class in a class method of the enclosing class? In this case, you must qualify the **new** keyword with an object reference for the enclosing object. When you create an instance of an inner class in a class method of the enclosing class, the enclosing object can be any instance of the enclosing class.

The state data of an inner class object includes the instance of the inner class and one instance of the enclosing class for every enclosing level. The fact that inner class objects have more than one instance has the following implications:

- More than one instance of inner classes can share the same enclosing object.
- Inner class objects have access to private members of enclosing classes. The members of the enclosing objects are extensions of the states of the inner class objects.

- If an enclosing class has more than one member inner class definition, each of the inner classes has access to the private members of the others.

- Every instance of an inner class is permanently associated with its enclosing instance. You cannot move an inner class object from one enclosing instance to another. The references to enclosing objects are immutable, just as the **this** reference is immutable. For example, a statement such as the following is not allowed:

```
outer_class.this

    = new outer_class( argument );   // not valid
```

- Inner classes may not contain class methods or class variables. The Java programming language specifies that the keyword **static** can qualify only the definition of a top-level construct. Because the entire body of an inner class is within the scope of one or more enclosing instances, an inner class cannot contain a top-level construct.

Figure 2-27 is a sample program in which an inner class, `HardDrive`, is instantiated in the `main` method of a class called `Computer`. Indeed, the `Computer` object `atWork` has two instances of `HardDrive`: `IDE1` and `IDE2`. Therefore, the two instances of `HardDrive` share the same enclosing object, `atWork`. Notice that the `HardDrive` class can use the private members of `Computer`. Further notes about the code follow the example program.

```
package examples.inner;
/** Class to represent the memory and hard drive
  * information of a computer
  */
public class Computer {
   /** Maximum number of hard drives in a computer */
   public static final int MAX_DRIVES = 4;
   private int installedDrives = 0;
   private HardDrive[] drives
      = new HardDrive[MAX_DRIVES];
   private int memMegs;
   /** Test method
     * @param args not used
     * @exception
     */
   public static void main( String[] args )
                       throws Exception {
      Computer atWork = new Computer( 64 );
      System.out.println( atWork );
      // must specify the enclosing object here
      HardDrive IDE1 = atWork.new HardDrive( 1024 );
      HardDrive IDE2 = atWork.new HardDrive( 2048 );
      System.out.println( atWork );
```

Figure 2-27   Computer: an example of how inner class objects may share an enclosing object

2

```
/** Construct a Computer object
 * @param memSize the amount of memory in MB
 */
public Computer( int memSize ) {
   memMegs = memSize;
}
/** Provide a string representing the computer
 * @return string representation of the object
 */
public String toString() {
   StringBuffer sb
      = new StringBuffer( "Memory: " + memMegs
                               + "MB" );
   for ( int i=0; i<installedDrives; i++ ) {
      sb.append( ", Drive" + i + ": " );
      sb.append( drives[i].size + "MB" );
   }
   return sb.toString();
}
/** Class representing a hard drive within
 * a computer
 */
public class HardDrive {
   private int size;
   /** Construct a hard drive object and add it
    * to the list of installed drives
    * if there is room
    * @param size Size of the drive in MB
    * @exception Exception thrown
    *      if there isn't room for
    *      the hard drive being added
    */
   public HardDrive( int size ) throws Exception {
      this.size = size;
      // add this drive to the enclosing computer
      if ( installedDrives < MAX_DRIVES ) {
         drives[installedDrives++] = this;
      } else {
         throw new Exception( "Sorry, no "
                               + "more room." );
      }
   }
}
}
```

Figure 2-27   Computer: an example of how inner class objects may share an enclosing object (continued)

The output from executing the Computer program in Figure 2-27 is shown in Figure 2-28.

```
Memory: 64MB
Memory: 64MB, Drive0: 1024MB, Drive1: 2048MB
```

Figure 2-28   Output from running the `Computer` program

Because the code that creates the `HardDrive` objects is in the class method **main**, the **new** keyword that constructs `HardDrive` objects must be qualified with the enclosing object, `atWork`, as in the following lines:

```
HardDrive IDE1 = atWork.new HardDrive( 1024 );
HardDrive IDE2 = atWork.new HardDrive( 2048 );
```

Notice that the constructor of `HardDrive` adds each new `HardDrive` object to an array called **drives**, which is a private field of `Computer`. The array **drives** is an array of object references for the inner `HardDrive` objects that share the enclosing instance. The `HardDrive` constructor freely uses the private members of `Computer`, regardless of whether they are class variables, such as `MAX_DRIVES`, or instance variables, such as `installedDrives` and `drives`, as in the following lines:

```
if ( installedDrives < MAX_DRIVES ) {
    drives[installedDrives++] = this;
}
```

If you were to add another member inner class, `HardDriveController`, to the `Computer` class, objects of the `HardDrive` class would have access not only to all the members of the `Computer` class, but also to all the members of the `HardDriveController` class. Likewise, objects of the `HardDriveController` class would have access to all the members of the `Computer` and `HardDrive` classes.

Similarly, the enclosing class has access to private members of the inner class. The **toString** method, which overrides the default **toString** of the **Object** class so that you can print a report on the hard drives, can use the instance variable size.

Working with Subclasses of Member Inner Classes

You can extend a member inner class to create a new class with added fields or methods to give your new subclass additional capabilities or to override inherited methods to customize or complete their implementation. Inheritance works in the same way for inner classes as it does for top-level classes, except that some new syntax is required to deal with inner classes. Figure 2-29 is the declaration of a subclass of the `Computer.HardDrive` class, defined in Figure 2-27.

```
package chapter2.inner;
/** A class definition to show how it is possible
 * to use an inner class as a superclass
 */
public class SCSIHardDrive extends Computer.HardDrive {
  private static final int DRIVE_CAPACITY = 512;
  /** Construct a SCSI hard drive object within an
    * enclosing Computer instance
    * @param c the enclosing computer instance
    * @exception Exception is thrown if there is no
    *    room to put the hard drive into the computer
    */
  public SCSIHardDrive( Computer c ) throws Exception {
    c.super( DRIVE_CAPACITY );
  }
}
```

Figure 2-29   `SCSIHardDrive:` an example that uses an inner class as a superclass

A subclass constructor can explicitly call the constructor of the superclass. If **super** is not called explicitly, the default constructor of the superclass, for example, the superclass constructor without input parameters, is called implicitly. Inner classes add a complication: If the superclass is an inner class, an object of the superclass cannot be constructed without an enclosing object. Where should the enclosing object be specified? The most obvious place is within the call to the superclass constructor. The Java programming language puts the onus on you to call **super** explicitly when the constructor must be qualified or take arguments. The constructor of the `SCSIHardDrive` class calls the constructor of its superclass, the `Computer.HardDrive` class. You qualify the call with the `Computer` object passed as an argument to the constructor of `SCSIHardDrive`, so that the superclass object can be successfully constructed.

LOCAL INNER CLASSES

Classes declared inside methods are called *local inner classes* to distinguish them from member inner classes that were discussed earlier in this chapter and demonstrated in Figure 2-23. The only kind of class you can define inside a method is an inner class, and you define it by simply including the definition within a block of code.

Local inner classes differ from member inner classes in the following ways:

- They are private to the blocks in which they are defined and cannot be declared with the keywords **public**, **private**, or **protected**. For this reason, the names of the classes cannot be used anywhere except in the method in which they are defined.

- The methods of a local inner class have access to much more than just the fields defined within them. The state of a local inner class object includes

  - Its own fields, which cannot be qualified with **static**

  - All local variables marked **final** within any enclosing method or local block

  - All arguments of enclosing methods that are marked **final**

  - One enclosing instance of each enclosing class up to and including the top-level class at package scope

- Objects of a local inner class and all the objects within their extended states live beyond the scopes in which they are created.

The extended lifetime of local inner classes arises because of the way the Java Virtual Machine (JVM) instantiates local inner classes. The JVM builds all objects of reference types, including instances of local inner classes, not on the stack, but in a separate area of memory from which only the garbage collector can remove them. When creating objects of a local inner class, the JVM copies local variables and the method arguments into the object. If the arguments or local variables have reference types, objects of the local inner class hold object references for the arguments or variables and prevent the garbage collector from sweeping the referenced objects away. Therefore, the lifetime of method arguments and local variables continues after the method execution ends.

The compiler for the Java programming language must impose one condition so that instances of local class objects can have this extended lifetime: All arguments and local variables of the enclosing methods that are referenced by a local inner class must be qualified with **final**. The compiler rejects an inner class that breaks this rule because the inner class object has only copies of the arguments and local variables. If the inner classes could change these copies, the JVM would not properly propagate the changes to the enclosing objects.

Local inner classes can be defined within both class and instance methods. When defined in an instance method, the local class can use all members of the enclosing class. When defined in a class method, the local class can use only class variables and class methods of the enclosing class. In all other ways, it does not matter whether the enclosing method is a class method.

The sample program in Figure 2-30 demonstrates many of the characteristics of local inner classes. Each instance of the class **Equation1** has a **getResult** method to solve an equation. The actual equation solved in this example has no particular meaning and is not based on any known mathematical formula. The interesting aspect of **Equation1** is that the method that returns the solution to the equation has an inner class that implements an interface. Because it implements the interface, the inner class must implement the method defined in that interface, which in this case is the method that solves the equation. Therefore, this example shows how an inner class can be an adapter class by implementing an interface that the enclosing class does not implement.

face, `Equation1.Result`, is nested inside `Equation1`. The interface contains one method, `getAnswer`. The method `Equation1.getResult` has an inner class, `MyResult`, that implements `Equation1.Result` and therefore implements `getAnswer`. You look in more detail at some of the interesting constructs in the class immediately following Figure 2-30.

```java
package examples.inner;
/** A class definition to explore the use of local
  * inner classes
  */
public class Equation1 {
   private int equationInput;
   /** An interface defining the result from an
     * equation
     */
   public interface Result {
      public double getAnswer();
   }
   /** Constructor method
     * @param ei the equation input
     */
   public Equation1( int ei ) {
      equationInput = ei;
   }
   /** Create the result of the equation for the given
     * input values
     * @param input1 the first equation input
     * @param input2 the second equation input
     * @return the result object
     */
   public Result getResult(final int input1,
                           final int input2 ) {
      final int[] localVar={ 2,6,10,14};
      class MyResult implements Result {
         private int normalField;
         public MyResult() {
            normalField = 2;
         }
         public double getAnswer() {
           return (double) input1 / input2
                          - equationInput + localVar[2]
                          - normalField;
         }
      }
   }
}
```

Figure 2-30 `Equation1`: an example of the use of local inner classes

```
      return new MyResult();
   }
   /** The test method for the class
    * @param args not used
    */
   public static void main( String[] args ) {
      Equation1 e = new Equation1( 10 );
      Result r = e.getResult( 33, 5 );
      System.out.println( r.getAnswer() );
   }
}
```

Figure 2-30   `Equation1`: an example of the use of local inner classes (continued)

The definition of the interface `Result` is nested inside the class `Equation1`, so this example is a complete solution. If you move the definition of `Result` out of the class and provide it elsewhere in the same package, there would be no impact on the rest of the `Example1` class. The interface `Result` contains one method, `getAnswer`, and all classes that implement this interface must implement this method. `getAnswer` returns a value of type **double**.

```
public class Equation1 {
  public interface Result {
    public double getAnswer();
  }
```

The class `Equation1` has a method, `getResult`, to solve the equation. The actual calculation is performed by the method `getAnswer` of the class `MyResult`, which is a local class defined in `getResult`. Because `MyResult` implements `Result`, the class must provide an implementation of the method `getAnswer`. This particular implementation, reproduced in the following code from Figure 2-30, is interesting because it uses data stored in different places to demonstrate the different kinds of extended states that a local inner class may have:

```
public Result getResult( final int input1,
                         final int input2 ) {
   final int[] localVar= {2,6,10,14};
   class MyResult implements Result {
      private int normalField;
      public MyResult() {
         normalField = 2;
      }
      public double getAnswer() {
         return ( double ) input1/input2
                      - equationInput
                      + localVar[2]
                      - normalField;
      }
   }
}
```

2

in different ways:

- `equationInput` is a private instance variable of the enclosing class.

- `input1` and `input2` are arguments of the instance method in which the local class is defined.

- `localVar[2]` is an element of an array that is a local variable of the instance method in which the local class is defined.

- `normalField` is a private instance variable of the local inner class.

Notice that the `getResult` method returns an object that it creates. There would be nothing special about such a construct if the type of `MyResult` were defined outside the method:

```
return new MyResult();
```

You must look in the `main` method to see where the object of the class `MyResult` is actually used. The `main` method calls `getAnswer` and writes the value to the standard output stream. Thus, a `MyResult` object is actually used long after the end of the scope in which the object is created. The arguments and the local variables of the method are available even though the method has finished:

```
public static void main( String[] args ) {
    Equation1 e = new Equation1( 10 );
    Result r = e.getResult( 33, 5 );
    System.out.println( r.getAnswer() );
}
```

When you run the program `Equation1`, the output from the program is simply the number `4.6`.

ANONYMOUS LOCAL INNER CLASSES

The name given to the local inner class in the previous example of Figure 2-30 may seem somewhat pointless. The name of a local inner class cannot be used outside the block in which the local class is defined. As in the `Equation1` example, all references to the type of an object of a local class use the name of the interface that the local class implements or the class that the local class extends. If you do not need to refer to a local class by its name inside the method, you can make it an *anonymous inner class*. Anonymous inner classes are always local to a code block.

Creating Anonymous Inner Classes

Here is another example of inner classes adding complexity to the Java programming language. The **new** keyword has an enhanced form so that a class definition can follow it. Use the enhanced **new** keyword to declare anonymous inner classes. Following is the syntax you need to know for declaring such a class, as well as tips for doing this effectively.

Syntax for Declaring an Anonymous Inner Class

```
new [class_or_interface_name()] { body_of_class }
```

Dissection

- As always, the **new** keyword creates an object and returns the object reference for the new object. An anonymous inner class cannot have a constructor; if you supply arguments with the **new** keyword, they are passed to the constructor of the superclass.

- The optional *class_or_interface_name* is the name of either a class that is extended or an interface that is implemented by the anonymous class being defined. If you omit a class or interface name, the anonymous class extends the **Object** class.

- The members of the class are defined in the body of the class and enclosed in braces in the usual manner.

Code Example for Declaring an Anonymous Inner Class

```
new {
    String msg() {
        return "anonymous inner class";
    }
}
```

Code Dissection

This anonymous inner class contains one method that returns a **String**. You can call this method with the object for which the inner class is instantiated.

Using Instance Initializers

Anonymous inner classes have neither names nor constructors. To initialize an object, use an instance initializer. The syntax of instance initializers is simple and is shown following, along with tips for using them effectively.

Syntax of an Instance Initializer

```
{
    initialization_statements
}
```

Dissection

- An instance initializer is a nameless block of code surrounded by braces and placed anywhere inside the definition of a class.

- An instance initializer has the same syntax as a static initializer, but without the keyword **static**.

include an instance initializer block in any class definition, even if you also define one or more constructors. Instance initializer blocks are executed before the constructor, but after the superclass constructor. They provide a handy way to collect common initialization statements into one place when a class has more than one constructor.

The `Equation1` example program shown in Figure 2-30 has been reworked to use an anonymous inner class, and the resulting class is called `Equation2`. All the changes required to convert the local inner class from the `Equation1` example to the anonymous inner class of the `Equation2` example are confined to the `getResult` method that follows and are shown in boldface in Figure 2-31.

```
/** Create the result of the equation for the given
 * input values
 * @param input1 the first equation input
 * @param input2 the second equation input
 * @return the result object
 */
 public Result getResult( final int input1,
                          final int input2 ) {
    final int[] localVar = { 2,6,10,14 };
    return new Result() {
       private int normalField;
       public double getAnswer() {
          return ( double ) input1 / input2
                          - equationInput
                          + localVar[2]
                          - normalField;
       }
       // this is an instance initializer block
       {
          normalField = 2;
       }
    };
 }
```

Figure 2-31   Reworked `getResult` method from `Equation2` program that uses an anonymous inner class

The changes to the `getResult` method can be summarized as follows:

- The definition of the local class is moved into the **return** statement and combined with the enhanced form of the **new** keyword.
- The constructor in the local class definition is eliminated and replaced by an instance initializer for the field `normalField` in the body of the anonymous class.

CLASS FILES FOR NESTED AND INNER CLASSES

The `.class` file-naming scheme implemented by the JVM contends with inner and nested classes a bit differently than it does with classes you have used up to this point. A few extra naming rules and conventions apply:

- For the purpose of gaining access from other packages, all classes have either public or package access. If you declare a member class to be **protected**, its `.class` file defines it as a public class. If you declare a member class to be **private**, its `.class` file defines it as having package scope.

- Each nested top-level class or inner class is stored in its own `.class` file.

- The filename generated for `.class` files consists of the enclosing class name, followed by a dollar sign character (**$**), and then by the enclosed class name, for every level of nesting.

- An anonymous class is identified by a number.

For example, the Java compiler creates three `.class` files when it compiles the `Equation2.java` file:

- `Equation2.class`

  This file contains the public class `Equation2`.

- `Equation2$Result.class`

  This file contains the nested interface `Result`.

- `Equation2$1.class`

  This file is for the anonymous inner class.

CHAPTER SUMMARY

- Classes should be the implementation of a design, or object model, that reflects the types of real-world objects, relationships between objects, and scenarios that your programs are representing.

- The **new** keyword calls the constructor of the class. Automatic garbage collection is used to free memory when required.

- You can perform cleanup actions as the program terminates by using shutdown hook threads.

- Copying objects is not as simple as it sounds. For the primitive types, you can copy with the assignment operator. For the reference types, the assignment operator does not make a copy.

❑ The **Object** class defines a method that you should use to copy objects:

`Object clone()`

❑ All objects of reference type, including arrays, can use the **clone** method. By default it performs a shallow copy. In other words, it copies the values of all fields that are contained in the object being cloned, regardless of whether the fields are primitive types or object references. Usually a deep copy is preferable.

❑ A deep copy duplicates contained objects, creates new object references for the duplicates, and inserts the new object references into the copy of the containing object.

❑ If your classes contain fields that have reference types, you should override the **clone** method to perform a deep copy, with the understanding that a shallow copy is adequate for immutable, contained objects. You should start the implementation of **clone** with the statement **super.clone()** so that every class in the hierarchy can correctly copy the fields it defines.

❑ To be cloneable, an object must be an instance of a class that implements the interface **Cloneable**. This is a marker interface that indicates whether a class allows cloning. The **clone** method throws an exception when called for an instance of a class that is not cloneable.

❑ You can define classes that are cloneable or not cloneable. You can force subclasses of your classes to be cloneable, or prevent them from being cloneable. You have great flexibility because you can do the following in different combinations:

   - Override or inherit **clone**.

   - Optionally define your class to implement **Cloneable**.

   - Optionally throw the exception **CloneNotSupportedException**.

   - Optionally catch the exception **CloneNotSupportedException**.

   - List or omit the exception in the throws clause of the **clone** method.

❑ Run-time type information (RTTI) is particularly important in the Java platform. Your class may be using classes from other sources, such as networks, and you sometimes cannot know the type of objects at development time. RTTI is also useful with dynamic binding.

❑ The simplest form of RTTI involves using the **instanceof** operator:

`object_reference instanceof class_or_interface_name`

❑ The **instanceof** operator returns **true** if the first operand is an instance of the class, a subclass of the class, or a class that implements the interface specified in the second operand. It returns **false** otherwise.

❐ For every class known to the JVM, an object of type **Class** exists. Every instance of a class has a field named **class** that is an object reference to a **Class** object. The **Class** class provides several methods that are described in this chapter. You can call these methods to find out, for example, whether a class is an interface, what its name is, and what the name of its superclass is. Three ways to access the **Class** object exist:

- Use the field **class**.

- Call the following method of the **Class** class and supply the fully qualified class name as the argument:

```
Class forName( String class_name )
```

- Call the following method of the **Object** class for an object:

```
Class getClass()
```

❐ Even the primitive types have **Class** objects; you access them by using the object reference **TYPE** that is a field of each wrapper class for the primitive types.

❐ You also receive run-time type information when you are warned that you are trying to cast class types in an unsafe manner. The compiler rejects casts between classes that are not a direct or indirect superclass and subclass of each other. But some casts from superclass to subclass must be checked at runtime, especially when dynamic binding is involved. The JVM throws a **ClassCastException** exception if you try performing an unsafe cast at runtime.

❐ For more extensive run-time type information, the Java platform provides the Reflection API. This API consists of five classes in the package **java.lang. reflect** (**Field, Method, Constructor, Array**, and **Modifier**) along with some other features, such as the **Class** objects, for the primitive types.

❐ The classes **Field, Method**, and **Constructor** provide many methods that describe the building blocks of classes.

❐ To find out what methods are available for an object at runtime, call the following method of the **Class** class:

```
Method[] getMethods()
```

❐ To call a method for which you do not know the name at compile time, use the following method of the **Method** class:

```
Object invoke( Object object, Object[] args )
```

❐ You can create instances of classes three ways:

- Use the **new** operator in the usual fashion.

- If you can use the no-argument constructor, call the **newInstance** method of the **Class** class.

2

To use any constructor first get the Constructor object for the

structor by calling the `getConstructor` method of the **Class** class and then call the **newInstance** method of the **Constructor** class.

❐ A top-level class is a class that is contained only in packages and not in other classes. In the Java programming language, classes can also be contained in other classes.

❐ You can define a class inside the definition of another class. The enclosed class is a nested class. Depending on how you define it, the enclosed class falls into one of the following categories:

- Nested top-level classes

- Member inner classes

- Local inner classes

- Anonymous local inner classes

❐ Nested top-level classes are declared with the keyword **static**. Except for the fact that they are defined within another class, they have the same behavior and characteristics of top-level classes defined at package scope.

❐ Member inner classes are defined inside another class. Their definitions are syntactically identical to those of nested classes except that they are not declared **static**.

❐ Member inner classes must be instantiated as part of an instance of their enclosing class. Therefore, you can qualify the **new** keyword with an object reference to specify the enclosing object. You must qualify **new** if the object of an inner class is created in a class method.

❐ The state data of an inner class object includes the current instance of the inner class and every enclosing object, up to and including the enclosing object of the top-level class at package scope. Thus, inner class objects have an extended state compared to top-level class objects. More than one inner class object can share enclosing objects.

❐ Local inner classes are defined within a method, and their definitions are private to that method. Like member inner classes, local inner classes have state data that extends to include the enclosing object. In addition, the state data includes all method parameters and method local variables that are declared **final**.

❐ After an object of a local inner class has been created, its lifetime continues even after the scope in which the class is declared ends.

❐ Anonymous inner classes are local inner classes that do not have a name. Objects of such classes are created using an enhanced syntax for the **new** keyword:

```
new [class_or_interface_name()] { body_of_class }
```

❏ Anonymous inner classes do not have constructors, but you can initialize their fields with instance initializer blocks. You can also use instance initializer blocks within top-level classes.

REVIEW QUESTIONS

1. Examine the following code:

```
public class Quiz2_1 {
    private static int a;
    private static int b;
    public static void main( String[] args ) {
        System.out.println( a + " " + b );
    }
    static {
        a = 100;
    }
    static {
        b = 200;
    }
}
```

Which of the following statements correctly describe the behavior when this program is compiled and run? Select all that apply.

a. The compiler rejects the attempt to define a method called **static**.

b. The compiler rejects the attempt to define two static initialization blocks.

c. Compilation is successful and the output is 0 0.

d. Compilation is successful and the output is 100 200.

e. Compilation is not successful because the argument of **main** must be(String[] args).

2. Which of the following methods are defined in the **Cloneable** interface? Select all that apply.

a. toString

b. clone

c. equals

d. hashCode

e. finalize

3. Which of the following are references to objects of the class **Class**? Select all that apply.

a. Object.TYPE

b. StringBuffer.class

c. Long.TYPE

d. Class.class

e. `Class.TYPE`

4. True or False: The **instanceof** operator returns **true** when the class of an object exactly matches the class specified.

5. Examine the following code:

```
public class Quiz2_5 {
    String s = "Good morning!";
    public Object clone()
            throws CloneNotSupportedException {
        Quiz2_5 result = ( Quiz2_5 ) super.clone();
        return result;
    }
    public static void main( String[] args )
            throws CloneNotSupportedException {
        Quiz2_5 x = new Quiz2_5();
        Quiz2_5 y = ( Quiz2_5 ) x.clone();
        System.out.println( y.s );
    }
}
```

Which of the following statements are true when the code is compiled and run? Select all that apply.

a. The compiler rejects the definition of the method `Quiz2_5.clone` because it returns a reference of type **Object**, not `Quiz2_5`.

b. Compilation is successful, but a **CloneNotSupportedException** exception is thrown when `Quiz2_5.main` executes.

c. Compilation is successful and the output is `Good morning!`

d. Compilation is successful, but the `Quiz2_5.clone` method does not give a correct result because the field s is not cloned.

6. Examine the following code:

```
public class Quiz2_6 implements Cloneable {
    StringBuffer sb
        = new StringBuffer( "Good morning!" );
    public Object clone()
            throws CloneNotSupportedException {
        Quiz2_6 result = ( Quiz2_6 ) super.clone();
        result.sb = this.sb;
        return result;
    }
    public static void main( String[] args )
            throws CloneNotSupportedException {
        Quiz2_6 x = new Quiz2_6();
        Quiz2_6 y = ( Quiz2_6 ) x.clone();
        x.sb.append( " How are you today?" );
```

```
            System.out.println( y.sb );
    }
}
```

Which of the following statements are true when the code is compiled and run? Select all that apply.

a. The compiler rejects the definition of the method **Quiz2_6.clone** because it returns a reference of type **Object**, not Quiz2_6.

b. Compilation is successful, but a **CloneNotSupportedException** is thrown when Quiz2_6.main executes.

c. Compilation is successful and the output is Good morning!

d. Compilation is successful and the output is Good morning!
   How are you today?

e. The two Quiz2_6 objects share the same **StringBuffer** object.

7. Examine the following code:

```
public class Quiz2_7 {
    public static void main( String[] args ) {
      Class c = Integer.TYPE;
      System.out.println( c.getName() );
    }
}
```

Which of the following statements are true when the code is compiled and run? Select all that apply.

a. The compiler rejects **Class** as an unknown type because the following statement is missing: import java.lang.reflect.*;

b. Compilation is successful and the output is **Integer**.

c. Compilation is successful and the output is **int**.

d. The compiler rejects the expression **Integer.TYPE** because it is missing parentheses.

8. Examine the following code:

```
class A { }
class B extends A { }
public class Quiz2_8 {
    public static void main( String[] args ) {
      A a = new A();
      System.out.println( a instanceof B );
    }
}
```

Which of the following statements are true when the code is compiled and run? Select all that apply.

a. The compiler rejects the definitions of classes **A** and **B** because they are empty.

b. Compilation is successful and the output is **true**.

2

a. Compilation is successful and the output is false.

d. The compiler rejects the following expression because the result of the **instanceof** operator cannot be printed:

```
System.out.println( a instanceof B )
```

9. Whether you should implement the **clone** method for a class that implements **Cloneable** depends on the types of the fields in the class. For which of the following types of instance variables should you consider implementing **clone**? Select all that apply.

   a. Integer

   b. StringBuffer

   c. int

   d. String

   e. double[ ]

10. Examine the following code:

```
public class Quiz2_10 {
    public static void main( String[] args ) {
        Integer i = new Integer( 6 );
        Long l = new Long( 10000000067L );
        Double d = new Double( 4.567 );
        Number n;
        n = d;
        d = i;
        l = (Long) i;
        System.out.println( l );
    }
}
```

Which of the following statements are true when the code is compiled and run? Select all that apply.

   a. Compilation is successful and the output is 6.

   b. The compiler rejects the expression n = d.

   c. The compiler rejects the expression d = i.

   d. The compiler rejects the expression l = (Long) i.

   e. Compilation is successful, but a **ClassCastException** exception is thrown when the program is run.

11. Which interface is implemented by all of the classes in the **java.lang.reflect** package that represent the contents of a class definition?

12. Examine the following code:

```
public class Quiz2_12 {
    private int a = 200;
    public static void main( String[] args ) {
        Quiz2_12 x = new Quiz2_12();
        B y = new B();
    }
    public class B {
        private int b = 100;
    }
}
```

Which of the following statements are true? Select all that apply.

a. The compiler rejects the definition of the B class because it is not declared with the **static** keyword.

b. Compilation is successful.

c. Class B is a member inner class.

d. The compiler rejects the expression **new B( )** because it does not provide an enclosing instance for the object being created.

13. Examine the following code:

```
public class Quiz2_13 {
    // -X-
}
```

Which of the following class definitions are valid when placed at the line marked -X-? Select all that apply.

a. public class A { }

b. protected class B { }

c. public static class C { }

d. private static class D { }

e. static class E { }

14. Examine the following code taken from a single source file:

```
public class Quiz2_14 {
    private int x;
    static public void main( String[] args ) {
        class A { };
    }
    protected class B { }
    public int getX() {
        class C { }
        return x;
    }
    private static class D { }
```

```
    }
    class E { }
```

Which of the classes are inner classes? Select all valid answers.

a. A

b. B

c. C

d. D

e. E

15. Examine the following code taken from a single source file:

```
interface Y {
    public void f();
}
abstract class Z {
    public abstract void g();
    public void h() {
        System.out.println( "Hello!" );
    }
}
public class Quiz2_15 {
    public static void main( String[] args ) {
        // -X-
    }
}
```

Which of the statements include valid definitions of anonymous inner classes when placed at position -X-? Select all that apply.

a.
```
Object y = new Y() {
    public void f() {
        System.out.println( "Choice a)" );
    }
};
```

b.
```
Z z = new Z() {
    public void g() {
        System.out.println( "Choice b)" );
    }
};
```

c.
```
Object y = new Y, Z() {
    public void f() {
        System.out.println( "Choice c)" );
    }
    public void g() {
```

```
            System.out.println( "Choice c)" );
        }
    };
d. Z z = new Z() {
    public void h() {
        System.out.println( "Choice d)" );
    }
};
e. Object z = new Z() {
    public void g() {
        System.out.println( "Choice e)" );
    }
    public void h() {
        System.out.println( "Choice e)" );
    }
};
```

16. Examine the following code taken from a single source file:

```
public class Quiz2_16 {
    public int calculate() {
        return a + b + c + d + e;
    }
    static public void main( String[] args ) {
        class A {
            private int a;
        };
    }
    protected class B {
        private int b;
    }
    class C {
        private int c;
    }
    private static class D {
        private int d;
    }
}
class E {
    private int e;
}
```

Which of the following statements are true? Select all that apply.

a. The compiler rejects the expression a + b + c + d + e because the variable a is undefined at that place in the file.

b. The compiler rejects the expression a + b + c + d + e because the variable b is undefined at that place in the file.

able c is undefined at that place in the file.

d. The compiler rejects the expression a + b + c + d + e because the variable d is undefined at that place in the file.

e. The compiler rejects the expression a + b + c + d + e because the variable e is undefined at that place in the file.

17. Examine the following code:

```
public class Quiz2_17 {
    public class C {
    }
}
```

Which of the following statements best describes the type of the class called C? Select the best answer.

a. Local inner class

b. Member inner class

c. Member inner class at package scope

d. Static member class

e. Anonymous inner class

18. Examine the following code taken from a single source file:

```
public class Quiz2_18 {
    static public void main( String[] args ) {
        class A {
            private int a;
        };
    }
    protected class B {
        private int b;
        public int calculate() {
            return a + b + cObj.c + dObj.d + e;
        }
    }
    class C {
        private int c;
    }
    private static class D {
        private int d;
    }
    private D dObj = new D();
    private C cObj = new C();
    private int e;
}
```

Which of the following statements are true? Select all that apply.

a. The compiler rejects the expression **a + b + cObj.c + dObj.d + e** because the variable **a** is undefined at that place in the file.

b. The compiler rejects the expression **a + b + cObj.c + dObj.d + e** because the variable **b** is undefined at that place in the file.

c. The compiler rejects the expression **a + b + cObj.c + dObj.d + e** because the variable **cObj.c** is undefined at that place in the file.

d. The compiler rejects the expression **a + b + cObj.c + dObj.d + e** because the variable **dObj.d** is undefined at that place in the file.

e. The compiler rejects the expression **a + b + cObj.c + dObj.d + e** because the variable **e** is undefined at that place in the file.

19. True or False: When you are creating an instance of any inner class, specifying an enclosing instance is optional.

20. Examine the following code:

```
public class Quiz2_20 {
    public void calculate() {
        // -X-
    }
}
```

Which of the following class definitions are valid when placed at the line marked **-X-**? Select all that apply.

a. `public class A { };`

b. `protected class B { };`

c. `class C { };`

d. `private class D { };`

e. `static class E { };`

21. Examine the following code:

```
public class Quiz2_21 {
    class A {
        // -X-
    }
}
```

Which of the following definitions are valid when placed at the line marked **-X-**? Select all that apply.

a. `static int v;`

b. `private int w;`

c. `static final int x = 10;`

d. `transient int y;`

e. `final int z = 20;`

PROGRAMMING EXERCISES

Debugging

1. Correct all the errors in the following program:

```
package questions.c2;
public class Debug2_1 {
    private double x;
    public Debug2_1( double input ) {
        x = input;
    }
    public String toString() {
        return String.valueOf( x );
    }
    void finalize() throws Throwable {
        System.out.println( "Goodbye!" );
    }
    public static void main( String[] args ) {
        Debug2_1 a = new Debug2_1( -7.3 );
        System.out.println( a );
        System.gc();
        System.runFinalize();
    }
}
```

2. Correct all the errors in the following program:

```
package questions.c2;
public class Debug2_2 implements Cloneable {
    StringBuffer sb
        = new StringBuffer( "Sales Report for " );
    public Debug2_2 clone()
                throws CloneNotSupportedException {
        Debug2_2 result = super.clone();
        result.sb
            = new StringBuffer( this.sb.toString() );
        return result;
    }
    public static void main( String[] args )
                throws CloneNotSupportedException {
        Debug2_2 x = new Debug2_2();
        Debug2_2 y = x.clone();
        x.sb.append( "October" );
        System.out.println( y.sb );
    }
}
```

3. The output in the following program should be:

```
Inventory count 300
```

Correct all the errors in the program:

```
package questions.c2;
class Debug2_3_Base {
   private int x;
   int getX() {
      return x;
   }
   public void setX( int newX ) {
      x = newX;
   }
}
public class Debug2_3 extends Debug2_3_Base
         implements Cloneable {
   StringBuffer sb
      = new StringBuffer( "Inventory count" );
   public Object clone()
            throws CloneNotSupportedException {
      Debug2_3 result = new Debug2_3();
      result.sb
         = new StringBuffer( this.sb.toString() );
      return result;
   }
   public static void main( String[] args )
         throws CloneNotSupportedException {
      Debug2_3 a = new Debug2_3();
      a.setX( 300 );
      Debug2_3 b = ( Debug2_3 ) a.clone();
      System.out.println( b.sb + " " + b.getX() );
   }
}
```

4. Correct all the errors in the following program without making any changes to the main method:

```
package questions.c2;
class Debug2_4_Base {
   private StringBuffer name;
   public String getName() {
      return name.toString();
   }
   public void setName( String newName ) {
      name = new StringBuffer( newName );
   }
}
public class Debug2_4 extends Debug2_4_Base
         implements Cloneable {
   private double weight;
```

```
    double getWeight() {
        return weight;
    }
    public void setWeight( double newWeight ) {
        weight = newWeight;
    }
    public static void main( String[] args ) {
        Debug2_4 a = new Debug2_4();
        a.setWeight( 11.567 );
        a.setName( "Steel girders" );
        Debug2_4 b = ( Debug2_4 ) a.clone();
        System.out.println( b.getName() + " "
                                  + b.getWeight() );

    }
}
```

5. Correct all the errors in the following program so that it takes a string from the command line, creates an instance of the class named in the string, and then outputs the class name without directly using the input string:

```
package questions.c2;
public class Debug2_5 {
    public static void main( String[] args ) {
        if ( args.length >= 1 ) {
            Object x = Class.newInstance( args[0] );
            System.out.println( x.getName );
        }
    }
}
```

6. The output for the following program is:

```
Name: int is a primitive type.
```

Correct all the errors in the program:

```
package questions.c2;
public class Debug2_6 {
    public static void printClassInfo( Class c ) {
        System.out.print( "Name: " + c.getName() );
        if ( c.isPrimitive() ) {
            System.out.println( " is a primitive "
                                  + "type." );
        } else {
            System.out.println( " is not a primitive
                                  + "type." );
        }
    }
    public static void main( String[] args ) {
        int x = 1;
        printClassInfo( x.class );
    }
}
```

7. Correct all the errors in the following program:

```
package questions.c2;
public class Debug2_7 {
    public Debug2_7() {
        class A {
            int a = 6;
        }
        Debug2_7.A x = new Debug2_7.A();
        System.out.println( x.a );
    }
    public static void main( String[] args ) {
        new Debug2_7();
    }
}
```

8. Correct all the errors in the following program:

```
package questions.c2;
public class Debug2_8 {
    A x;
    public static void main( String[] args ) {
        Debug2_8 a = new Debug2_8();
        a.x = new A();
        System.out.println( a.x.getValue() );
    }
    class A {
        private String s = "pork chops and applesauce";
        public String getValue() {
            return s;
        }
    }
}
```

9. Correct the errors in the following program so that the output of the program is as follows:

```
Shopping List:
eggs & cheese
```

Here's the program listing:

```
package questions.c2;
interface ShoppingList {
    public void f();
    public void g();
}
public class Debug2_9 {
    public static void main( String[] args ) {
        ShoppingList y = new ShoppingList() {
            public void f() {
                System.out.println( "Shopping List:" );
```

```
        }
        y.f();
        y.g();
    }
}
```

10. Correct the errors in the following program without adding initializers to the definitions of the strings ON_MSG and OFF_MSG:

```
package questions.c2;
interface Switch {
    public void on();
    public void off();
}
public class Debug2_10 {
    public static void main( String[] args ) {
        Switch s = new Switch() {
            public Switch() {
                ON_MSG = "Switch on";
                OFF_MSG = "Switch off";
            }
            public void on() {
                System.out.println( ON_MSG );
            }
            public void off() {
                System.out.println( OFF_MSG );
            }
            final String ON_MSG;
            final String OFF_MSG;
        };
        s.on();
        s.off();
    }
}
```

11. Correct the errors in the following program so that the output, correct to two decimal places, is 148.41:

```
package questions.c2;
public class Debug2_11 {
    public static double calculate( double x,
                                     double y ) {
        class Helper {
            double doSomething() {
                return Math.sqrt( x ) + Math.sqrt( y );
            }
        }
        Helper h = new Helper();
        return Math.exp( h.doSomething() );
    }
```

```
        public static void main( String[] args ) {
           System.out.println( calculate( 4.0, 9.0 ) );
        }
  }
```

Complete the Solution

1. Extract the file `X:\Data\questions\c2\Point3D.java` from the CD-ROM, where `X:` is the drive letter of the CD-ROM. Complete the `Point3D` class definition by adding a **finalize** method that prints the final contents of the `Point3D` object to **System.out** just before the object is destroyed.

2. Extract the file `X:\Data\questions\c2\Fibonacci.java` from the CD-ROM, where `X:` is the drive letter of the CD-ROM. The `main` method of the `Fibonacci` class calculates the first 25 numbers in the `Fibonacci` sequence and provides a method to return the value of any particular value in the sequence. Complete the `Fibonacci` class definition by providing a static initialization block that calculates the first `MAXFIB` numbers in the sequence. The first two numbers in the sequence are 0 and 1. Every other number in the sequence is the sum of the two numbers that precede it in the sequence. For example, the Fibonacci sequence starts 0, 1, 1, 2, 3, 5, 8, 13...

3. Extract the file `X:\Data\questions\c2\Complete2_3.java` from the CD-ROM, where `X:` is the drive letter of the CD-ROM. Complete the definition of the class `questions.c2.Complete2_3` by adding a **clone** method.

4. Extract the file `X:\Data\questions\c2\Complete2_4.java` from the CD-ROM, where `x:` is the drive letter of the CD-ROM. Complete the definition of the class `questions.c2.Complete2_4` by adding a **clone** method.

5. Extract the file `X:\Data\questions\c2\Complete2_5.java` from the CD-ROM, where `x:` is the drive letter of the CD-ROM. Complete the definition of the class `questions.c2.Complete2_5` by adding statements to the method `f` that use the **instanceof** operator to handle two specific subclasses of **Number**. If the parameter of `f` is an **Integer**, output the integer value divided by 2. If the parameter of `f` is a **Double**, output the double value divided by 2.5. Otherwise, do nothing.

6. Extract the file `X:\Data\questions\c2\Complete2_6.java` from the CD-ROM, where `X:` is the drive letter of the CD-ROM. Complete the definition of the class `questions.c2.Complete2_6` by adding a try block and a catch clause for **ClassCastException** to method `f`. Write the exception handler to treat one specific subclass of **Number** differently from other **Number** subclasses. If the parameter of `f` is a **Long**, output the long value multiplied by 2. If the parameter of `f` is any other subclass of **Number**, output its value as a double multiplied by 3.

7. Extract the file `X:\Data\questions\c2\Complete2_7.java` from the CD-ROM, where `X:` is the drive letter of the CD-ROM. Complete the program so that it takes a **String** as a command-line argument and prints a message if the class named in the string has a constructor without parameters.

CD-ROM, where **X:** is the drive letter of the CD-ROM. Complete the **main** method of the **Complete2_8** class by adding a definition of an anonymous class that implements the **TapeRecorder** interface. Test your **TapeRecorder** object by calling all four of its methods.

9. Extract the file **X:\Data\questions\c2\Automobile.java** from the CD-ROM, where **X:** is the drive letter of the CD-ROM. Complete the **Automobile** program by creating four instances of the **Tire** class that all share the **Automobile** object **a** as their enclosing instance.

10. Extract the file **X:\Data\questions\c2\Complete2_10.java** from the CD-ROM, where **X:** is the drive letter of the CD-ROM. Complete the definition of the class **Complete2_10** by adding a top-level nested class called **StockItem**. Add a statement to the **main** method of the **Complete2_3** class to create the **StockItem** object **x**. Your **StockItem** class must implement the methods required by **main**.

11. Extract the file **X:\Data\questions\c2\Complete2_11.java** from the CD-ROM, where **X:** is the drive letter of the CD-ROM. Complete the definition of the class **Complete2_11** by defining a local class inside the **main** method. Your class definition should implement both the **Nameable** and **Identifiable** interfaces defined inside **Complete2_11**.

12. Extract the file **X:\Data\questions\c2\Complete2_12.java** from the CD-ROM, where **X:** is the drive letter of the CD-ROM. Complete the definition of the class **Complete2_12** by completing the **concatenate** method. Your method should define a class that implements the **Concatenates** interface. The method should then create a **Concatenates** object and use the object to create a string that is equivalent to the result of the expression s1 + s2.

Discovery

1. Create a class called **ObjectStack** that encapsulates an array of **Object** objects and provides methods for pushing a value onto the stack, popping a value off the stack, and peeking at the value on the top of the stack. There should also be a method, **isEmpty**, that returns a **boolean** value to indicate whether the stack is empty. Since the stack is being built around an array that will have a fixed size, you should add another method, **isFull**, to return a value indicating whether room exists for another item on the stack. Add exception classes with a common superclass called **StackException**. The subclasses should be **EmptyStackException**, which is thrown when an attempt is made to pop or peek at an empty stack, and **FullStackException**, which is thrown when an attempt is made to push an item onto a full stack. Add a **clone** method to the **ObjectStack** class that delegates the cloning of individual stack elements by calling the **clone** method of each element. Don't forget to write a **main** method that tests all of your methods.

2. Create a class called `PropertyFinder` that has a method that analyzes the method input parameter of type **Object**. Using the Reflection API, the class will look for method pairs of the form `void setX( T )` and `T getX()`, where `X` is some arbitrary string and T is a type. For every such pair that it finds, the class will write a message saying that the object has a property X of type T.

3. Expand the `Graph2` example class in this chapter to include edges as well as nodes, and call the new class `EdgeNodeGraph`. You can start with the code in the file `X:\Data\examples\inner\Graph2.java` from the CD-ROM where `X:` is the drive letter of the CD-ROM. In a graph, a start node and an end node define an edge. Create another member inner class called `Edge` that is nested in `EdgeNodeGraph` and is a peer of `Node`. You will need to expand the methods and fields of `EdgeNodeGraph` to allow the user to create edges and to query edges already in the graph. Add a **main** method to `EdgeNodeGraph` that tests the class by adding several nodes and edges.

4. Create a class called `MusicCollection`. This class must have member inner classes called `Artist` and `Recording`. The `Recording` class must have an inner class called `Track` that represents a single piece of music within a `Recording` object. A `MusicCollection` object must have an array of `Artist` objects and an array of `Recording` objects. `Recording` objects must have a single `Artist` object, for simplicity, and an array of `Track` objects. Add a **main** method to `MusicCollection` that tests the creation of all of these objects.

3

INPUT/OUTPUT AND SERIALIZATION

In this chapter you will:

- ◆ Learn how the Java platform supports I/O
- ◆ Understand file I/O basics
- ◆ Understand character streams
- ◆ Use the new I/O (NIO) programming interface
- ◆ Understand object serialization
- ◆ Write appropriate code to read, write, and update files
- ◆ Describe the permanent effects on the file system of constructing and using **FileInputStream**, **FileOutputStream**, and **RandomAccessFile** objects
- ◆ Describe the connection between object serialization and I/O streams
- ◆ Distinguish between classes that can be serialized and those that cannot
- ◆ Write code to define a class that can be serialized
- ◆ Learn about the compatibility of serialization formats

HOW THE JAVA PLATFORM SUPPORTS I/O

It is time to turn your attention to the matter of input and output, which is generally referred to as I/O. A mastery of I/O concepts is essential to creating programs that people will use, because even the most complex or sophisticated algorithm is truly useless if people are unable to supply data to or extract results from your program. In addition, the concepts in this chapter are the foundation for network programming that will be discussed in detail in Chapter 11. The first part of this chapter examines the package **java.io** and how it supports console I/O and file I/O:

- **Console I/O** is character keyboard input and output without the mouse graphics of a graphical user interface and is typically associated with command-line windows.

- **File I/O** involves reading and writing data to and from a mass storage device, typically the computer's hard drive. The data is put in named files that are organized using a structure of directories.

Both I/O categories have I/O streams in the **java.io** package that are designed for raw data bytes, and I/O streams that are designed for characters and respect the fact that a character may occupy more than one byte. The importance of supporting I/O for multibyte characters is increasing with the demand for software that is internationalized. Multibyte characters enable not only the North American and Western European character sets, but also the Middle Eastern, Asian, and other character sets.

The latter part of this chapter examines the new I/O (NIO) package **java.nio**, introduced in the 1.4 release of the Java 2 platform to supplement the original I/O package and then examines object serialization. The **java.nio** package has significant improvements over the original **java.io** package that make I/O programming easier and the resulting programs more efficient.

Not all forms of user interaction that may be considered I/O are covered in this chapter. For example, a different mechanism manages user input through graphical user interfaces (GUIs). Chapters 6 and 7 describe how to program a GUI. The **java.io** and **java.nio** packages support data transfer between the program and the console, files, or network. These packages do not provide facilities for drawing or displaying graphical components on the screen.

PROGRAMMING I/O

Most I/O in the Java platform operates through streams in which data is considered to be one contiguous group of information from beginning to end. In stream I/O, characters or bytes are read or written sequentially. For example, when a file is opened as a stream, all input or output starts at the beginning of the file and proceeds character by character or byte by byte to the end of the file. There is no inherent blocking into records or lines and no direct access to any locations in the file other than the next byte or character position. These simplifications make the stream I/O model broadly applicable, and so it is not difficult to write a program that can handle console I/O and file I/O interchangeably.

The core classes do not offer much formatting control for the output streams. However, if you are writing applets or applications for a graphical environment, you use a different output mechanism to send your output to the screen. Therefore this limitation of the stream classes affects far fewer programs than it may at first seem. Console I/O is often used only for debugging or for quick and simple utilities. Most of the tools that come with the Java 2 SDK, including the Java compiler itself, use console I/O. Console I/O on the Java platform is not flexible. You may be disappointed if you want to set the width of fields or precision of floating-point numbers when you write to the console or a formatted file.

When you program for the international market, you should format numbers, dates, times, and similar items according to the local customs of the users. The Java platform includes classes, such as **Locale**, **ResourceBundle**, **DateFormat**, and **NumberFormat**,

the classes and interfaces for handling local customs. You can use the core class **DecimalFormat** in the package **java.text** to set patterns for formatting and parsing numbers. For example, you can specify grouping by thousands with commas as separators, set the minimum or maximum number of digits on either side of the decimal point, provide a different pattern for negative numbers, and specify how to represent percentages. Even if internationalization is not your goal, you may find that the classes in **java.text** can meet your number-formatting requirements. "Internationalization" in Chapter 4 describes the programming techniques and core classes you can use to make your program international and provides examples on how to employ them.

The Java platform includes two dual hierarchies of classes that support streams: byte-oriented input and output, and character-oriented input and output. The byte-oriented streams are widely used, partly because they have been available since the original version of the Java platform and partly because they are adequate for the ASCII character set used by English-language North American personal computers. The structure of the hierarchy of character-oriented stream classes mirrors that of the byte-oriented classes.

Object streams support object serialization and are the last set of streams described in this chapter. Figure 3-14 provides a detailed example of the use of object streams for serializing objects to and from a file.

 The character-oriented streams and object serialization became available in version 1.1 of the Java platform. The original version of the Java platform lacked support for I/O to character sets other than ASCII and had no object serialization. Version 1.1 of the Java platform also introduced the package **java.text** and full support for internationalization.

Not all I/O in the Java platform is stream I/O. The package **java.io** includes the core class **RandomAccessFile**, which you can use to read and write arbitrary locations within a file without first having to read or write all the bytes or characters that precede that location. There can be significant performance advantages to using this capability of moving directly to the desired data, for example. However, most I/O, including sequential file reading and writing, operates through streams.

BYTE-ORIENTED STREAM CLASSES

The hierarchies of the byte-oriented stream classes have a superclass for output, **java.io.OutputStream**, and another superclass for input, **java.io.InputStream**. All the classes in these hierarchies extend the input and output superclass directly or indirectly and ultimately extend **Object**. Figure 3-1 shows the classes that support byte-oriented streams and how they are related. The shaded boxes represent abstract classes. The next sections of this chapter present highlights of the subclasses of **InputStream** and **OutputStream**.

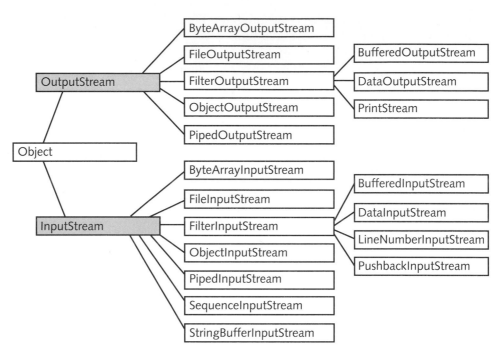

Figure 3-1   Byte-oriented stream classes in the `java.io` package

Predefined Stream Objects

All Java programs can use three stream objects that are defined in the **System** class of the **java.lang** package: **System.in**, **System.out**, and **System.err**.

Class

`java.lang.System`

Purpose

The **System** class provides the standard stream objects.

Fields

- **System.in**

  The field **System.in** is a **java.io.BufferedInputStream** object. The field is often called the standard input stream. By default, this object encapsulates keyboard input. You can wrap a character-oriented stream around **System.in** to get buffered, character-oriented input from the console. This is desirable, because it gives the user the opportunity to backspace over errors and relieves you of responsibility of processing every keystroke individually.

3

The field **System.out** is a **java.io.PrintStream** object. The field is often called the standard output stream. By default, this object encapsulates output to a command-line window and is used for most command-line mode output. When you run a program with the **java** command, you can use features of your operating system to redirect the output to a file.

■ **System.err**

The field **System.err** is a **java.io.PrintStream** object. It is often called the standard error stream. Output sent to **System.err** goes to a command line and can be mixed with output to **System.out.** The difference between **System.err** and **System.out** is that **System.err** is usually reserved for error messages, or log or trace information. Therefore, by directing **System.out** or **System.err** to a file, you can separate the desired program output from other messages.

The overloaded methods of the **PrintStream** class, **print** and **println**, are particularly useful for console output. Most of the example programs in early chapters of this book use these methods. The difference between them is that **println** appends a line separator to its argument to produce a complete line of output. The **print** method does not add the line separator, so you can build up one line of output with several calls of **print**.

For example, examine the code in Figure 3-2.

```
for ( int i = 0; i < 10; i++ ) {
    System.out.print( '*' );
}
for ( int i = 0; i < 2; i++ ) {
    System.out.println( "one line" );
}
```

Figure 3-2   Comparing the usage of the **print** and **println** methods

These lines produce the output in Figure 3-3.

```
**********one line
one line
```

Figure 3-3   Output of the **print** and **println** methods

The methods **print** and **println** are overloaded to create versions specifically for the primitive types, for **char[ ]**, and for **String**. All other reference types use the version of **print** or **println** that takes an **Object** as input. This catch-all version essentially calls the **toString** method for the object and then outputs the resulting **String** object in the normal way. As a result, you can easily print textual representations of objects of any class that implements **toString**. Usually, when you anticipate that you will need to display a class in textual format, you implement **toString**.

Input and Output Methods

You perform most byte-oriented I/O operations by calling methods that are defined in the **InputStream** and **OutputStream** classes. The subclasses of **InputStream** and **OutputStream** add value by overriding and overloading these methods for specific circumstances.

Class

```
java.io.InputStream
```

Purpose

The **InputStream** class is the superclass of all byte-oriented input streams.

Constructor

The constructor of this class, **InputStream()**, takes no arguments.

Methods

- **int available()**

  The **available** method returns the number of bytes that can be read without blocking.

- **void close()**

  The **close** method closes the input stream and frees the resources it was using.

- **void mark(int** *readlimit* **)**

  The **mark** method is used to set a bookmark in the stream. You can return to the marked spot until the number of bytes specified in the argument has been read.

- **boolean markSupported()**

  The **markSupported** method indicates whether the stream supports the setting of bookmarks.

- **int read()**

  int read(byte[] *buffer* **)**

  int read(byte[] *buffer*, **int** *offset*, **int** *length* **)**

  The **read** method reads bytes from the input stream. To read one byte, supply no arguments and receive the data in the return value. The **int** value returned can be cast to type **char** as required with no loss of information. To read bytes into an array, pass the array as a parameter. No more bytes are read than can be stored in

~~the array and the return value is the actual number of bytes read. You can also spec~~ify the first position in the array to fill as an integer argument, and the maximum number of bytes to read as a second integer argument. This third approach provides for maximum flexibility, because it does not make the assumption that the entire buffer is available for input and allows the user to identify the starting place and length of the available space in the buffer.

- **void reset()**

The **reset** method repositions the stream to the bookmark.

- **long skip(long** *bytecount* **)**

The **skip** method reads but discards up to the number of bytes specified in the argument and returns the actual number of bytes skipped.

Class

java.io.OutputStream

Purpose

The **OutputStream** class is the superclass of all byte-oriented output streams.

Constructor

The constructor of this class, **OutputStream()**, takes no arguments.

Methods

- **void close()**

The **close** method closes the stream and frees the resources it was using.

- **void flush()**

The **flush** method forces any buffered bytes to be written.

- **void write(int** *b* **)**

  void write(byte[] *bytebuffer* **)**

  void write(byte[] *bytebuffer*, **int** offset, **int** count **)**

The **write** method writes a single byte or an array of bytes. If you specify an array of bytes, you can optionally specify the first element in the array to write, and the number of bytes to write.

Filter Streams

Earlier in this chapter, you were introduced to the **print** and **println** methods of the **PrintStream** class that converted data to text to make it easier to read. This conversion of data to text is a form of filtering. **PrintStream** is one of the filtered stream classes. Refer to Figure 3-1 for all the classes that subclass either **FilterOutputStream** or **FilterInputStream**. A subclass of **FilterInputStream** contains some other input stream, which it uses as its basic source of data, transforming the data along the way or providing additional functionality. Similarly, a **FilterOutputStream** subclass stream sits on top of an already existing output stream, which it uses as its basic output target of data, transforming the data or providing additional functionality.

The class **FilterInputStream** extends **InputStream**, and the class **FilterOutputStream** extends **OutputStream**. These abstract classes are designed to act as wrappers for the **InputStream** and **OutputStream** classes. To use a filter stream, you must already have an **InputStream** or an **OutputStream** object. When you create the filter stream object, specify an **InputStream** object or an **OutputStream** object as the argument of the constructor, as shown in Figure 3-4.

BufferedInputStream and **BufferedOutputStream**	These classes provide buffering for input and output operations. Use these classes to increase efficiency. **System.in** is a **BufferedOutputStream** object.
DataInputStream and **DataOutputStream**	These classes transmit data of specific types across a stream instead of treating a stream as a sequence of independent bytes. You can also call methods of these classes to read and write the binary representations of the primitive types.
PushbackInputStream	This class maintains a one-byte push-back buffer. With a push-back buffer, you can peek at the next byte in the input stream, and then either treat it as read or push it back into the input stream to be read later.
PrintStream	**PrintStream** implements methods for displaying data types textually. Two familiar methods in this class are **print** and **println**, and two familiar objects are **System.out** and **System.err**. To convert the output into the representation of the characters native to the operating system, use the class **PrintWriter** instead of this class.

Figure 3-4   Byte-oriented filter streams

Other Byte I/O Classes

The **java.io** package defines many classes. Extensions of **InputStream** include the following classes listed for your awareness:

- The class **ByteArrayInputStream** lets you read an array of bytes as though it were an **InputStream** object. To create a **ByteArrayInputStream** object, supply a parameter of type **byte[]** to the constructor.

- The class **SequenceInputStream** provides a mechanism for concatenating the data from two or more **InputStream** objects into a single, seamless stream.

- The class **PipedInputStream** implements half of a pipe to connect the input stream of one thread or process to the output stream of another thread or process. Pipes are especially useful for communication between threads. Chapter 11 tells you how to develop multithreaded programs that use pipes.

Extensions of **OutputStream** include the following classes listed for your awareness:

- The class **ByteArrayOutputStream** sends its output into an object of type **byte[]**. You can use this class to perform your own buffering, or to build an object that another piece of code reads as a **ByteArrayInputStream**.

- The class **PipedOutputStream** is the complementary class to **PipedInputStream**. Together, these two classes comprise a pipe that you can use for communication between threads.

Exploring a Console I/O Sample Program

The program listing in Figure 3-5 does a bit of everything in terms of simple console input and output. Notice that the declaration of **main** contains a throws clause because the **java.io** package can throw exceptions for certain input and output error conditions. Because it is a public class, it is found in a file called **ConsoleTest.java**. You will find this file in the **X:\Data\examples\io** directory on the CD-ROM. (Here **X:** is the drive letter of the CD-ROM.) This program will be dissected in more detail in later sections.

```
package examples.io;
import java.io.*;
import java.util.StringTokenizer;
/** A class to demonstrate how console I/O is used
  */
public class ConsoleTest {
    /** The test method for the class
      * @param args Not used
      * @exception java.io.IOException
      *            Unspecified I/O exception
      */
    public static void main( String[] args )
          throws java.io.IOException {
      int i = 10;
      int j = 20;
      double d = 99.101;
      System.out.print( "Here are some values: " );
      System.out.println( i + " " + j + " " + d );
      System.out.println(
          "Enter an integer, a float, and a string:" );
      BufferedReader br
          = new BufferedReader(
            new InputStreamReader( System.in ) );
      String line = br.readLine();
      StringTokenizer st = new StringTokenizer( line );
      int k = Integer.parseInt( st.nextToken() );
      float f = Float.parseFloat( st.nextToken() );
      String s = st.nextToken();
      while( st.hasMoreTokens() ) {
          s += " " + st.nextToken();
      }
      System.out.println( "Here's your data: " );
      System.out.println( k );
      System.out.println( f );
      System.out.println( s );
    }
}
```

Figure 3-5 `ConsoleTest`: an example of how console I/O is used

```
Here are some values: 10 20 99.101
Enter an integer, a float, and a string:
13 34.6 Quick brown fox
Here's your data:
13
34.6
Quick brown fox
```

Figure 3-6 A possible console session resulting from running the `ConsoleTest` program

following:

```
// prints one line: hello number 2
int id = 2;
System.out.println( "hello number " + id );
```

The **PrintStream** class provides several methods, including **print** and **println**. These two methods have one argument, which can be an object of any primitive or reference type. The most common way to build up the argument to print is to give an argument of type **String** and to use the string concatenation operator, **+**, to concatenate elements in a string expression. If an item is a number, as **id** is in the preceding line of code, it is converted to a string during the evaluation of the string expression. When you are concatenating numbers, be careful that at least one operand of each **+** is a **String**. Otherwise, the **+** performs arithmetic addition, which may not be what you intended.

```
System.out.println( 1 + 2 + 3 );        // output is 6
System.out.println( "1" + 2 + 3 );      // output is 123
System.out.println( "1" + ( 2 + 3 ) );  // output is 15
```

Programming console input is more complicated than programming console output. The reason is that you usually want to read a full line at a time, so you wait for the user to press Enter and let the operating system handle the pressing of Backspace and other inline edits.

Code that reads one line from the console is usually similar to the following lines extracted from Figure 3-5:

```
BufferedReader br
   = new BufferedReader(
      new InputStreamReader( System.in ) );
String line = br.readLine();
```

To understand these lines, you must be comfortable with the concept of wrapping an object of one class around an object of another class. Many of the classes in the I/O package **java.io** are wrapper classes. A *wrapper class* is essentially a class that provides different behavior for an object than the behavior established by the class of the object. In other words, a wrapper class gives you another way of using the object it wraps. The preceding lines of code provide a good example of wrapper classes.

For console input, you start with the standard stream object **System.in**. The first layer of wrapping creates an **InputStreamReader** object for **System.in**. The core class **InputStreamReader** is in the package **java.io**. This class implements a character-input stream that reads bytes from a byte-oriented input stream and converts the bytes to characters. For **System.in**, **InputStreamReader** converts the input from the character encoding of the native operating system to Unicode. In the following expression, the **new** keyword creates an **InputStreamReader** object:

```
new InputStreamReader( System.in )
```

The next step is to instantiate a **BufferedReader** object. In other words, the second layer of wrapping creates a **BufferedReader** object for the **InputStreamReader** object.

```
BufferedReader br
  = new BufferedReader(
    new InputStreamReader( System.in ) );
```

The reason for using a **BufferedReader** object is that the **BufferedReader** class provides the **readLine** method, which is the easiest way to read a complete line into a **String** object. This **BufferedReader** object is called br, and the **readLine** method returns an object reference for a **String**, so the following line actually reads the input:

```
String line = br.readLine();
```

All this wrapping of one object inside another may seem like a lot of trouble to go through just to read in a line of text. However, the alternative of reading each character individually and having to detect the end of the input line requires more programming effort and is an approach that is more prone to errors. **InputStreamReader** and **BufferedReader** are considered filter classes, because the bytes from the input stream pass through them and are converted into the format in which the program chooses to receive them.

Parsing an Input String

Often, the next step after reading a line of input is to parse it, or break it into separate tokens. A token usually consists of a sequence of characters that does not include a space, newline, tab, or other nonprinting character. These characters are often called *whitespace*. The following lines show how to extract numbers and words from a string. For demonstration, the first token in this line is interpreted as an integer, the second as a floating-point number, and all remaining tokens as one string:

```
StringTokenizer st = new StringTokenizer( line );
int k = Integer.parseInt( st.nextToken() );
float f = Float.parseFloat( st.nextToken() );
String s = st.nextToken();
while ( st.hasMoreTokens() ) {
    s += " " + st.nextToken();
}
```

added as part of the Java 2 platform. Previously, parsing a **String** to extract a floating-point value required a temporary object of type **Float** or **Double**, as in the following line: `float f = Float.valueOf( st.nextToken() ).floatValue();`

3

To tokenize a string, you can use the **StringTokenizer** class provided by the **java.util** package. Use a **StringTokenizer** object as a wrapper for a **String** object. The first of the statements in the preceding code fragment creates a **StringTokenizer** object called **st** to manipulate an existing **String** called **line**:

```
StringTokenizer st = new StringTokenizer( line );
```

By default, a **StringTokenizer** object interprets whitespace characters as delimiters between tokens. You can call methods of **StringTokenizer** to customize this behavior. For example, you can specify that the delimiter be a comma. The following sections provide details about how to construct a **StringTokenizer** object along with useful methods of the class.

Class

java.util.StringTokenizer

Purpose

This utility class extracts tokens from a string, one by one.

Constructors

- **StringTokenizer(String** *s* **)**

  StringTokenizer(String *s*, **String** *delim* **)**

  StringTokenizer(String *s*, **String** *delim*, **Boolean** *retDelim* **)**

  The constructor builds a **StringTokenizer** object for the **String** specified in the first argument. By default, whitespace separates tokens, but you can specify one or more alternative delimiter characters in a second argument of type **String**. If you want each delimiter to be returned as a **String** of length one, set the **boolean** argument to **true**. If this argument is **false** or omitted, delimiters are skipped.

Methods

- `String nextToken()`

  This method returns the next token in the **StringTokenizer** object, or throws an exception if no more tokens are available.

- `boolean hasMoreTokens()`

  This method returns **true** if another token can be extracted from the **StringTokenizer** object, or **false** otherwise. You should call **hasMoreTokens** before **nextToken**, and call **nextToken** only if **hasMoreTokens** returns **true**.

Continuing with our dissection of the program in Figure 3-5, the next three lines perform equivalent tasks for an integer, a floating-point number, and a string. In all three cases, the code extracts the next token from `line` by applying the method **nextToken** to **st** and converts it to the required type.

The method **parseInt** of the **Integer** class returns the **int** value represented by a string. The argument is the object returned by **nextToken**.

```
int k = Integer.parseInt( st.nextToken() );
```

The method **parseFloat** of the **Float** class returns the **float** value represented by a string. The argument is the object returned by **nextToken**.

```
float f = Float.parseFloat( st.nextToken() );
```

To get the third token as a string, simply call **nextToken**. However, building up **s** to contain all the tokens that remain on the input line involves repeatedly calling **nextToken** until the method **hasMoreTokens** returns **false**.

```
String s = st.nextToken();
while( st.hasMoreTokens() ) {
    s += " " + st.nextToken();
}
```

One potential disadvantage of a **StringTokenizer** object is that it folds multiple, adjacent whitespace characters into one delimiter. You cannot use the default delimiter if you want to preserve multiple spaces between words.

FILE I/O BASICS

Programming stream I/O to and from files is much like programming stream I/O to and from the console. After a stream is established, its usage is the same regardless of whether the ultimate destination is a file or the console.

However, major differences exist between files and the standard console I/O objects **System.in**, **System.out**, and **System.err**:

- Before you can use a file, you must associate the file with a **FileInputStream** or **FileOutputStream** object.

- If you want to access the data in a file in random-access order, you must open it as a **RandomAccessFile** object, not as a **FileInputStream** object.

- In a network environment, the default security restrictions do not let applets perform any file I/O on the client workstation. Applets can perform I/O only on files that reside on the server from which the applet originated.

When you perform stream I/O on a file, you are actually manipulating a **FileInputStream** object or a **FileOutputStream** object. First you must set up the association between the object and the actual file. You can do this in one of two ways:

- You can pass the name of the file, as a **String**, to the constructor of the **FileInputStream** or **FileOutputStream** class.

- You can create a **File** object, passing the name of the file to the constructor of the **File** class. Then, create the stream object and pass the **File** object as a parameter of the constructor.

The second method has two steps, which are a little more work. Creating a **File** object has advantages:

- When you create the **File** object, you can perform checks, such as whether an input file exists and is read-only or has read-write capabilities. Use this approach if you want to check the status of the file before you open it. If you check the **File** object, as in the sample code shown in Figure 3-7, you may be able to avoid throwing **IOException** objects for reasons such as writing to a read-only file.

- The **File** class provides a level of insulation from platform-dependent conventions such as whether a separator between subfolder names is a forward slash (/) or backslash (\).

File Navigation Methods

The **File** class gives you more than a way of checking the status of a file before you perform I/O on it. This class provides several methods that you can use to navigate the file system on your workstation, or on the server of an applet or application, in a platform-independent manner. It is worth noting that the Java platform does not define a separate class for folders. The **File** class does double duty as a representative of both kinds of file system objects.

If you have had the experience of programming with the API for different operating systems to perform simple file manipulations or to move around the file system on a variety of platforms, you will appreciate the **File** class. Following are the details about how to construct a **File** object along with a listing of the most useful methods of the **File** class.

Syntax

```
java.io.File
```

Purpose

The **File** class encapsulates most of the platform-dependent complexities of files and path names in a portable manner.

Constructors

- **File(String** *filename* **)**

  File(File *folder***, String** *filename* **)**

  File(String *folder***, String** *filename* **)**

  You can create a **File** object by specifying only the filename or the filename and the folder in which it resides. You can specify the folder by path name or with an existing **File** object. Be aware, however, that creating a **File** object does not create an actual file on the computer's hard drive.

Methods

- **boolean canRead()**

  The **canRead** method returns **true** if the file is readable, and **false** otherwise.

- **boolean canWrite()**

  The **canWrite** method returns **true** if you can write to the file, and **false** otherwise.

- **File createTempFile(String** *prefix***, String** *suffix* **)**

  File createTempFile(String *prefix***, String** *suffix***, File** *folder***)**

3

The `createTempFile` method creates a temporary file with a name generated using the given prefix and suffix. The prefix must be at least three characters long. The suffix may be **null**, in which case it defaults to `.tmp`. If you specify a folder, the file is created in that folder. Otherwise it is created in the default temporary file directory.

■ **boolean delete()**

The **delete** method deletes the file. The return value indicates success or failure.

■ **void deleteOnExit()**

The **deleteOnExit** method marks a file to be deleted on normal termination of the JVM. It is particularly useful for cleaning up temporary files created by an application. The result of this method is irreversible, so you should use it with care.

■ **boolean exists()**

The **exists** method returns **true** if the file already exists on disk, and **false** otherwise.

■ **String getAbsolutePath()**

The **getAbsolutePath** method returns the platform-specific absolute path to the **File** object for which the method is called.

■ **String getName()**

The **getName** method returns the name of the file. The value returned is the portion of the path that follows the last file separator character.

■ **String getParent()**

The **getParent** method returns the name of the folder in which the file resides, or **null** if the file is in the root folder.

■ **File getParentFile()**

The **getParentFile** method is similar to **getParent**, but returns a **File** object instead of a **String**. Using **getParentFile** may be more convenient for navigating through the file system because you do not have to create a **File** object from a returned **String**.

■ **boolean isDirectory()**

The **isDirectory** method returns **true** if the file is a folder, and **false** otherwise.

■ **boolean isFile()**

The **isFile** method returns **true** if the file is an ordinary file and **false** if it is a folder.

- **long lastModified()**

  The **lastModified** method returns the system-specific time when the file was last modified.

- **String[] list()**

  String[] list(FilenameFilter *filter* **)**

  If the file is a folder, the **list** method returns an array that contains a list of the names of files that reside in the folder. You can specify an object of a class that implements the interface **java.io.FilenameFilter** to get only filenames accepted by a filter object.

- **File[] listFiles()**

  File[] listFiles(FileFilter filter)

  File[] listFiles(FilenameFilter *filter* **)**

  The **listFiles** method is similar to **list**, but returns a **File[]** object instead of a **String[]**. Using **listFiles** may be more convenient for navigating through the file system because it saves you from having to create **File** objects from a returned **String** array.

- **File[] listRoots()**

  This method returns all file-system roots. Some file systems have more than one root. For example, Windows platforms have a file root associated with each drive letter; whereas UNIX file systems have only a single file-system root called "/".

- **boolean mkdir()**

  The **mkdir** method creates a folder with the name of this file. The return value indicates success or failure.

- **boolean setReadOnly()**

  The **setReadOnly** method sets the file-system attributes of the file so that only read operations are allowed.

- **URL toURL()**

  This method returns the file path name into a **URL** object of the form **file: //***pathname*. If the path name is a folder, the **URL** ends with a slash character. The **URL** class is discussed in Chapter 11.

Figure 3-7 is a sample program that checks whether a file can be written to. This program defines the class **FileChecking**.

```
package examples.io;
import java.io.*;
/** Class used to demonstrate how to find out
  * information about a file
  */
public class FileChecking {
   /** Test method for the class
     * @param args[0] the filename to be used
     */
   public static void main( String[] args ) {
      if ( args.length < 1 ) {
         System.out.println( "Please supply a "
                                 + "filename" );
      } else {
         File f = new File( args[0] );
         if ( f.exists() ) {
            System.out.println( f.getName()
                                   + " exists:" );
            if ( f.canRead() ) {
               System.out.println( "\tand can be "
                                      + "read" );
            }
            if ( f.canWrite() ) {
               System.out.println( "\tand can be "
                                      + "written" );
            }
         } else {
            System.out.println( "Sorry, " + args[0]
                                   + " doesn't exist" );
         }
      }
   }
}
```

Figure 3-7   `FileChecking`: an example of how to find out information about a file

The two-step method does not give you the ability to reuse a **File** object for different **FileInputStream** or **FileOutputStream** objects unless it is for the same folder and filename. **File** objects are immutable and cannot be altered to reference another file.

Creating stream objects for file input does not in itself change the status of the files on the native file system. For example, creating and using a **FileInputStream** object makes no physical change to any data stored on disk. However, creating a **FileOutputStream** object or writing to a **RandomAccessFile** object does modify physical storage. You create a new file when you use an output file that did not previously exist. What you write to files is permanently stored on disk, except when your program ends prematurely. In that situation, some buffered output may be lost if it is still in a buffer when termination occurs.

Figure 3-8 is a sample program that demonstrates file I/O.

```
package examples.io;
import java.io.*;
import java.util.Random;
/** A class used to demonstrate file input and output
  */
public class CaseMixer {
    /** Method randomly sets case of characters in a
     * stream
     * @param args[0] The name of the input file
     *    ( defaults to standard in )
     * @param args[1] The name of the output file
     *    ( defaults to standard out )
     * @throws IOException
     *    if an error is detected opening or closing the
     *    files
     */
    public static void main( String[] args ) throws IOException {
        InputStream  istream;
        OutputStream ostream;
        if ( args.length >= 1 ) {
            File inputFile = new File( args[0] );
            istream = new FileInputStream( inputFile );
        } else {
            istream = System.in;
        }
        if ( args.length >= 2 ) {
            File outputFile = new File( args[1] );
            ostream = new FileOutputStream( outputFile );
        } else {
            ostream = System.out;
        }
        int c;
        Random mixer = new Random();
        try {
            while ( ( c = istream.read() ) != -1 ) {
                if ( mixer.nextFloat() < 0.5f ) {
                    c = Character.toLowerCase( (char) c );
                } else {
                    c = Character.toUpperCase( (char) c );
                }
                ostream.write( c );
            }
        }
        catch( IOException iox ) {
            System.out.println( iox );
        }
```

Figure 3-8 `CaseMixer`: an example of file input and output

```
        finally {
            istream.close();
            ostream.close();
        }
    }
}
```

Figure 3-8 `CaseMixer`: an example of file input and output (continued)

Suppose the input is as follows:

`The quick brown fox jumps over the lazy dog.`

The output may be the following:

`thE qUiCk BRown FOx JUmPs OVEr tHe lAZY DOg.`

This code reads characters from an input file, randomly forces each character into upper-case or lowercase, and prints the result to an output file. The filenames are passed as parameters to **main**. If the parameters are missing, the program substitutes **System.in** and **System.out** for files. The actual input is performed with the method **read** of the **InputStream** class, and the output is performed with the **write** method of the **OutputStream** class. Notice that **read** takes no parameters but returns an **int**, which is stored in the local variable **c**. The **write** method has one parameter, which is also of type **int**. Both **read** and **write** can throw an **IOException** exception.

Random-Access File I/O

The class **RandomAccessFile** supports byte-oriented I/O to and from random-access files. Use it to read and write data from or to any specified location within a file. **RandomAccessFile** objects are not streams. The class **RandomAccessFile** extends **Object**, not **InputStream** or **OutputStream**.

RandomAccessFile combines input and output operations in one class. It has the same **close**, **read**, and **write** methods that **InputStream** and **OutputStream** have, listed previously in this chapter in the section "Input and Output Methods." In addition, it has the same methods for reading and writing primitive types as the **DataInputStream** and **DataOutputStream** classes as described in Figure 3-4. The **seek** method distinguishes this class from the stream I/O classes. The **seek** method selects the position within the file where the next I/O operation will begin. Another important difference is that a single **RandomAccessFile** object can provide input and output to a program, unlike a stream object, which must be either input or output but not both. For an example of how to use a **RandomAccessFile** object for both input and output, refer to Figure 3-13 later in this chapter.

CHARACTER STREAMS

The **java.io** package has classes that are specifically designed to support character streams. You can use them to work with characters, character arrays, and strings. The character streams differ from the byte streams mainly in that they operate on buffered input and output and properly convert each character from the encoding scheme of the native operating system to the Unicode character set used by the Java platform. In contrast, **InputStream** and **OutputStream**, and the classes that extend them, operate on bytes and arrays of bytes. The byte-oriented streams correctly handle only seven-bit ASCII characters, which have the same value as the first 128 Unicode characters. Character streams are sensitive to different character-encoding schemes and fully support international applications.

The hierarchy of classes that support character streams mirrors the structure of the hierarchy of classes that support byte-oriented streams. The superclass of character-oriented input stream I/O is **java.io.Reader**. The corresponding output stream is **java.io. Writer**. Like **java.io.InputStream** and **java.io.OutputStream**, the **Reader** and **Writer** classes are also direct subclasses of **Object**. Most byte stream classes have a corresponding character stream class. For example, **FileReader** is the character-oriented counterpart to **FileInputStream**, and **FileWriter** is the counterpart to **FileOutputStream**. Figure 3-9 shows character stream classes and how they are related.

There are filter-stream classes for the byte streams and separate filter-stream classes for the character streams. The base classes for character filter streams are **FilterReader** and **FilterWriter**. Both are abstract classes. Only **FilterReader** has a subclass that is part of the **java.io** package. The **PushbackReader** class wraps a **Reader** object and adds the ability to push characters back into the stream. The size of the pushback buffer is an argument of the constructor parameter and has the default value of one character.

Connecting Byte and Character I/O Classes

The Java platform includes adapter classes that bridge between character I/O classes and byte I/O classes. These adapter classes are useful because programs written for old versions of the Java platform sometimes use the **InputStream** and **OutputStream** classes for stream I/O.

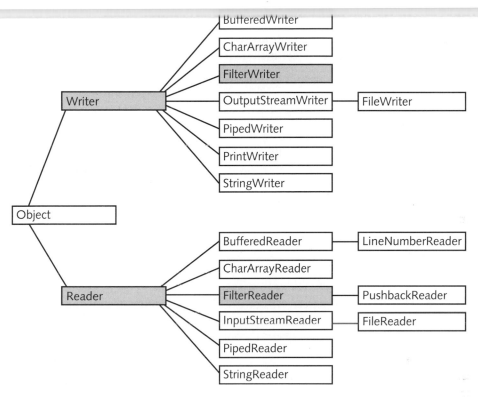

Figure 3-9 Character stream classes in the `java.io` package

The **InputStreamReader** and **OutputStreamWriter** classes perform the adaptation. For example, you can convert an existing **InputStream** object, such as **System.in**, by constructing an **InputStreamReader** object and passing the object reference for the **InputStream** object as the argument of the constructor. The resulting object can be used anywhere that a **Reader** object is required. Similarly, you can adapt the **System.err OutputStream** object for use as a **PrintWriter** object by creating an **OutputStreamWriter** object and passing a reference to the **System.err** object as an input argument. However, it is worth noting that this adaptation works in only one direction. You cannot create a stream object from a **Writer** object or a **Reader** object.

Using Other Character I/O Classes

Many other classes besides **FileReader** and **FileWriter** extend **Reader** and **Writer**. Extensions of the **Reader** object include the following:

- The class **CharArrayReader** lets you read an array of characters as though it were a **Reader** object. To create a **CharArrayReader** object, supply a parameter of type **char[ ]** to the constructor of the object.

- The class **StringReader** lets you read a **String** object as though it were a **Reader** object. To create a **StringReader** object, supply a parameter of type **String** to the constructor of the object.

- The class **PipedReader** implements half of a pipe and is especially useful for communication between threads. Chapter 11 describes developing multi-threaded programs and shows you how to create a pipe that provides input to a **Reader** object on one thread and accepts input from a **Writer** object on another thread.

Extensions of the **Writer** object include the following:

- The class **CharArrayWriter** sends its output into an object of type **char[ ]**. You can use this class to perform your own buffering, or to build an object that another piece of code reads as a **CharArrayReader** object.

- The class **StringWriter** lets you write to a **StringBuffer** object as though it were a **Writer** object. No input is necessary to create the **StringBuffer** object explicitly. Just construct the **StringWriter** object. You can accept the default initial size for the buffer, or specify an optional initial size as an argument of the **StringWriter** constructor. Use the method **getBuffer** to get the object reference for the **StringBuffer** object that contains the information that is written.

- The class **PipedWriter** is the complementary class to **PipedReader**. Together, these classes comprise a pipe that you can use for communication of character information between threads.

- The class **PrintWriter** is the character I/O equivalent of the **PrintStream** class. It has all the same methods as **PrintStream**, but has the internationalization support that **PrintStream** lacks. You can easily convert a **PrintStream** object to a **PrintWriter** object by constructing a **PrintWriter** object and passing a reference to the **PrintStream** object as the input parameter.

Reading One Token at a Time

The class **StreamTokenizer** is a utility class in **java.io** that is not related to any of the other classes by inheritance. It lets you read a file as a sequence of tokens by encapsulating a **Reader** object and grouping the stream of input bytes into tokens. This could be very useful if you wanted to read a text file as words and not as individual characters. By default, tokens are delimited by whitespace, but you can call many methods to customize a tokenizing algorithm. You can also call a method to find out on which line in the file a token appeared.

To use the **StreamTokenizer** class, first create a **Reader** object, and then pass the **Reader** object as a parameter to the constructor of the **StreamTokenizer** object.

THE NEW I/O (NIO) PROGRAMMING INTERFACE

The **java.nio** package and its subpackages were added to supplement the I/O support that has been provided in the **java.io** package since the original version of the Java platform. This supplement provides new features and improved performance. Notable among the new features is support for buffer management, a new primitive I/O abstraction called a channel, file locking at the process level, and memory mapping.

Buffers

The concept of a buffer is not new and is certainly familiar to any programmer. What is new is the explicit support for buffers in the Java platform and their close relationship with the new channel I/O abstraction. Previously, programmers had to define their own buffers and typically did so by allocating byte arrays. Now that these predefined and performance-optimized classes are available, programmers will never need to define their own buffers again. A list of all the buffer classes defined in the **java.nio** package is given in Figure 3-10.

Class Name	Description
Buffer	The abstract superclass from which all other buffer classes inherit
ByteBuffer	A byte buffer
CharBuffer	A character buffer
DoubleBuffer	A double buffer
FloatBuffer	A float buffer
IntBuffer	An integer buffer
LongBuffer	A long integer buffer
MappedByteBuffer	A subclass of **ByteBuffer**; this is directly memory mapped onto a region of a file.
ShortBuffer	A short integer buffer

Figure 3-10   Buffer classes defined in **java.nio**

All buffer classes share some common properties that you need to understand before you can use them effectively. The *capacity* of a buffer is the maximum number of data elements that the buffer can contain. This value cannot change and is never negative. The *limit* of a buffer is a reflection of the amount of data that the buffer currently contains and is defined as the index of the first element in the buffer that should not be read or written. The limit can never exceed the capacity and cannot be negative. A buffer's *position* is the *index* of the next element to be read or written and can never exceed the limit. A buffer can also have a *mark*, which is the index to which the position value will be set if the buffer is reset. With these properties in mind, the essential methods of the **Buffer** class are listed here:

Class

java.nio.Buffer

Purpose

The **Buffer** class is the superclass of all data buffer classes.

Methods

- **int capacity()**

  The **capacity** method returns the buffer's capacity.

- **Buffer clear()**

  The **clear** method makes the buffer ready for channel-read or relative write operations by setting the limit equal to the capacity and the position to zero. The updated **Buffer** object is returned.

- **Buffer flip()**

  The **flip** method makes the buffer ready for channel-write or relative read operations by setting the limit equal to the current position, then setting the position to zero. The updated **Buffer** object is returned.

■ boolean hasRemaining()

The **hasRemaining** method returns **true** if there are elements between the current position and the limit.

■ boolean isReadOnly()

The **isReadOnly** method returns **true** if the buffer is read-only.

■ int limit()
  Buffer limit(int newLimit)

The **limit** method without input parameters returns the buffer's limit. The **limit** method with one **int** as input sets the buffer's limit to the value provided, and the updated **Buffer** object is returned.

■ Buffer mark()

The **mark** method sets the buffer's mark equal to its position, and the updated **Buffer** object is returned.

■ int position()
  Buffer position(int newPosition)

The **position** method without input parameters returns the buffer's position. The **position** method with one **int** as input sets the buffer's limit to the value provided, and the updated **Buffer** object is returned.

■ int remaining()

The **remaining** method returns the number of elements between the current position and the limit.

■ Buffer reset()

The **reset** method returns the buffer's position to the previously marked position.

■ Buffer rewind()

The **rewind** method makes the buffer ready for rereading the data it already contains. It leaves the limit unchanged and sets the position to zero. The updated **Buffer** object is returned.

Channels

The **java.nio.channels** package introduces the concept of a channel to the Java plat-form. A *channel* is a flexible concept that includes any open connection to a program entity that is capable of I/O operations such as read or write. If you decide to use the NIO pro-gramming interface, you will have to learn to use channels because they are required by the NIO programming interface. Examples include a file, a network socket, or a hardware device. A list of notable channel classes defined in the **java.nio.channels** package is given in Figure 3-11.

Class Name	Description
DatagramChannel	A channel for working with network datagram sockets. The class **DatagramSocket** provides a method for returning an object of this class.
FileChannel	A channel for reading, writing, mapping, and manipulating files. The classes **FileInputStream**, **FileOutputStream**, and **RandomAccessFile** all provide methods for returning an object of this class.
Pipe.SinkChannel	A channel for use with the writable end of a pipe.
Pipe.SourceChannel	A channel for use with the readable end of a pipe.
SocketChannel	A channel for use with TCP/IP sockets. The classes **Socket** and **ServerSocket** provide methods for returning an object of this class.

Figure 3-11   Channel classes in **java.nio.channels**

To show how working with channels is different from the previous approach that uses only streams, the **CaseMixer** example class from Figure 3-8 has been reworked to make use of the new **FileChannel** class. The resulting class, **CaseMixerNIO**, is given in Figure 3-12.

```
package examples.io;
import java.io.*;
import java.nio.*;
import java.nio.channels.*;
import java.util.Random;
/** A class used to demonstrate file channel i/o
  */
public class CaseMixerNIO {
   /** Method randomly sets case of characters in a
     * file
     * @param args[0] The name of the input file
     * @param args[1] The name of the output file
```

Figure 3-12   **CaseMixerNIO**: an example of file channel I/O

3

```
 *  @throws IOException
 *    if an error is detected opening or closing the
 *    files
 */
public static void main( String[] args ) throws IOException {
    FileInputStream istream = null;
    FileOutputStream ostream = null;
    FileChannel fcin = null;
    FileChannel fcout = null;
    if ( args.length >= 2 ) try {
        File inputFile = new File( args[0] );
        istream = new FileInputStream( inputFile );
        fcin = istream.getChannel();
        File outputFile = new File( args[1] );
        ostream = new FileOutputStream( outputFile );
        fcout = ostream.getChannel();
        ByteBuffer bb = ByteBuffer.allocate( (int) fcin.size() );
        bb.clear();
        fcin.read( bb );
        char c;
        Random mixer = new Random();
        for ( int i = 0; i < bb.limit(); i++ ) {
            c = (char) bb.get( i );
            if ( mixer.nextFloat() < 0.5f ) {
                bb.put( i,
                        (byte) Character.toLowerCase( c ) );
            } else {
                bb.put( i,
                        (byte) Character.toUpperCase( c ) );
            }
        }
        bb.rewind();
        fcout.write( bb );
    }
    catch( IOException iox ) {
        System.out.println( iox );
    }
    finally {
        fcin.close();
        fcout.close();
        istream.close();
        ostream.close();
    } else {
        System.out.println( "Provide input and " +
                            "output filenames" );
    }
  }
}
```

Figure 3-12   `CaseMixerNIO`: an example of file channel I/O (continued)

Suppose the input file contains the following:

`The quick brown fox jumps over the lazy dog.`

The output file may contain the following:

`thE qUiCk BRown FOx JUmPs OVEr tHe lAZY DOg.`

As with the previous **CaseMixer** example in Figure 3-8, the **CaseMixerNIO** program reads characters from an input file, randomly forces each character into either uppercase or lowercase, and prints the result to an output file. The filenames are passed as parameters to **main**. The main difference, shown in the following code fragment, is that after constructing the **FileInputStream** and the **FileOutputStream** objects, the program takes the extra step of constructing two **FileChannel** objects, one for each stream object, and a **ByteBuffer** object that is big enough to hold the entire contents of the input file, eliminating the need to write a loop to read the contents of the file one buffer at a time.

```
File inputFile = new File( args[0] );
istream = new FileInputStream( inputFile );
fcin = istream.getChannel();
File outputFile = new File( args[1] );
ostream = new FileOutputStream( outputFile );
fcout = ostream.getChannel();
ByteBuffer bb = ByteBuffer.allocate( (int) fcin.size() );
```

The I/O operation proceeds by first clearing the buffer to prepare it for input. It then reads the entire contents into the buffer:

```
bb.clear();
fcin.read( bb );
```

A loop, reproduced in the following snippet, goes through the buffer to its limit, randomly changing the case of the characters in the buffer using individual get and put operations. At the end of the loop, the buffer is rewound to bring the position back to zero; then the buffer is written to the output **FileChannel** object:

```
for ( int i = 0; i < bb.limit(); i++ ) {
   c = (char) bb.get( i );
   if ( mixer.nextFloat() < 0.5f ) {
      bb.put( i,
              (byte) Character.toLowerCase( c ) );
      } else {
         bb.put( i,
                 (byte) Character.toUpperCase( c ) );
      }
   }
   bb.rewind();
   fcout.write( bb );
```

Mapped Buffers and File Locking

In the `CaseMixerNIO` example in Figure 3-12, the goal is to transform the contents of a file and to put the result into a different file, leaving the input file unchanged. However, if the goal is to change the input file, it is possible to map the contents of the file to a region of memory using a **MappedByteBuffer** object. This can be convenient because it allows the program to change the contents of the file directly. This technique is referred to as memory mapping. Operations that modify a file in place can be a bit risky if another process attempts to read or write the file while it is being modified. Fortunately the **java.nio** package provides a means for locking a file across processes. Figure 3-13 is an example program that demonstrates the memory mapping of a file and file locking. It is similar to the previous `CaseMixerNIO` example except that it swaps the case of the characters in the file between uppercase and lowercase (a reversible transformation).

```
package examples.io;
import java.io.*;
import java.nio.*;
import java.nio.channels.*;
/** A class used to demonstrate mapped file channel i/o
  * and file locking
  */
public class CaseReverserNIO {
    /** Method reverses the case of characters in a file
      * @param args[0] The name of the input/output file
      * @throws IOException
      *    if an error is detected opening or closing the
      *    file
      */
    public static void main( String[] args ) throws IOException {
        RandomAccessFile raf = null;
        FileChannel fc = null;
        FileLock lock = null;
        if ( args.length >= 1 ) try {
            File f = new File( args[0] );
            raf = new RandomAccessFile( f, "rw" );
            fc = raf.getChannel();
            lock = fc.lock();
            MappedByteBuffer mbb
                = fc.map( FileChannel.MapMode.READ_WRITE, 0,
                          fc.size() );
```

Figure 3-13   `CaseReverserNIO`: an example of mapped file channel I/O and file locking

```
         char c;
         for ( int i = 0; i < mbb.limit(); i++ ) {
            c = (char) mbb.get( i );
            if ( Character.isLowerCase( c ) ) {
               mbb.put( i,
                        (byte) Character.toUpperCase( c ) );
            } else if ( Character.isUpperCase( c ) ) {
               mbb.put( i,
                        (byte) Character.toLowerCase( c ) );
            }
         }
      }
      catch( IOException iox ) {
         System.out.println( iox );
      }
      finally {
         fc.close();
         raf.close();
         lock.release();
      } else {
         System.out.println( "Provide an input filename" );
      }
   }
}
```

Figure 3-13   `CaseReverserNIO`: an example of mapped file channel I/O and file locking (continued)

Suppose the input file originally contains the following:

The quick brown fox jumps over the lazy dog.

The input file will be changed to contain the following:

tHE QUICK BROWN FOX JUMPS OVER THE LAZY DOG.

Only one **File** object is used for this example. Because the file must be read and written, a **RandomAccessFile** object is used instead of **FileInputStream** or **FileOutputStream** objects. After opening the file for reading and writing, as shown in the following code fragment, a **FileChannel** object is created. Using the **FileChannel** object, the file is locked and a **MappedByteBuffer** object is obtained. This buffer is specified to be a read-write buffer that is large enough to map the entire input file and given an initial position value of 0.

3

```
File f = new File( args[0] );
raf = new RandomAccessFile( f, "rw" );
fc = raf.getChannel();
lock = fc.lock();
MappedByteBuffer mbb
    = fc.map( FileChannel.MapMode.READ_WRITE, 0,
             fc.size() );
```

With the contents of the file mapped into memory, it is a simple matter of looping through the buffer to change each character. These changes are reflected directly in the file without the need to write the buffer back into the file. After the transformation is complete, the statements contained in the **finally** block shown in the following code fragment are executed to close the file and the channel. With the channel and file safely closed by the first two statements, the lock on the file is released in the third statement so that other processes may then use the file.

```
fc.close();
raf.close();
lock.release();
```

OBJECT SERIALIZATION

Perhaps during the discussion about reading and writing numbers, strings, and the like to and from files, you have been wondering whether you could write entire objects to a file so that you can read them back later with their state intact. If so, you have anticipated the requirement to serialize objects. You may want to serialize an object to do the following:

- Transmit objects over a network.

- Save objects to files between runs of your program, or perhaps write and then read objects later in the same application.

For the primitive types, such as **int**, **double**, and **char**, the byte-oriented filter classes **DataOutputStream** and **DataInputStream** provide methods to write and read binary representations of variables of all the primitive types and **String** objects to and from a file. But what about objects of other types? The simplistic approach of saving to a file on a field-by-field basis requires discipline and constant maintenance. Every time a field is added to the class, the methods for saving and restoring the objects must be updated. What happens when a field that is an object reference field is added? Should only the reference or the whole contained object be saved and restored?

Object serialization is a general solution that lets you write objects to I/O streams and then read them, without defining any additional methods. Object serialization properly handles not only the fields defined in the class, but also inherited fields and any subfields that these fields may have.

The object serialization feature is an important component of the Java Remote Method Invocation (RMI) enterprise API. RMI is discussed in Chapter 11. For now you should know that RMI allows an object in the Java programming language on one system to invoke a method of an object in the Java programming language across a network on a different system. You need object serialization to write objects that are arguments to methods to a stream on one system and to read from the stream at the other system. Typically, the data is transferred over a TCP/IP socket.

 The Java 2 platform enhanced object serialization in a number of ways. Most of the changes affect the internal workings of serialization or are too specialized for inclusion in this description. Improvements include the addition of the `javadoc` serialization tags `@serial`, `@serialField`, and `@serialData`. The Java Object Serialization Specification hasn't changed in the 1.3 and 1.4 releases of the Java 2 platform. However, there have been numerous performance enhancements since then.

Serializing Objects

Just as not all classes of objects can be cloned, not all classes of objects support serialization. By default, classes are not serializable. To let instances of a class be serialized, define the class with **implements Serializable**. The **Serializable** interface, like the **Cloneable** interface discussed in Chapter 2, is a marker interface and contains no methods. Most of the classes in the **java.lang** package implement the **Serializable** interface. Commonly used classes in the **java.lang** package that do not implement **Serializable** are **Math**, **Process**, **Runtime**, **SecurityManager**, **System**, **Thread**, **ThreadGroup**, and **Void**. These omissions make sense for the following reasons:

- **Math** and **System** contain only class methods and variables.

- **Void** is a placeholder and is essentially empty.

- The nature of the other classes is incompatible with the rationale for object serialization. The **Process**, **Runtime**, **SecurityManager**, **Thread**, and **ThreadGroup** objects are used as a program runs.

Using Object Streams

Two stream classes support object serialization: **ObjectOutputStream** and **ObjectInputStream**. The example program in Figure 3-17 shows how to use them. **ObjectOutputStream** is a subclass of **OutputStream**. To create an

of the constructor. In the following example, the output object is an instance of
FileOutputStream that was created in the usual way, but you can use an object of any
subclass of **OutputStream**. For example, if you have established a pipe between two threads,
you can use a **PipedOutputStream** object to send an object from one thread to the other.

ObjectInputStream is a subclass of **InputStream**. To create an
ObjectInputStream object, provide an existing **InputStream** object as the argument of the constructor. In the example program in Figure 3-17, the input object has
type **FileInputStream**, but any subtype of **InputStream** is acceptable.

Suppressing Serialization of Fields

The Java programming language does not require that every field in a class be serialized.
Some fields may contain sensitive information that should not be transmitted over a network. Others may be references to objects of classes that do not implement
Serializable. Also, classes can contain fields for temporary information, such as
counters, that never need to be serialized.

You can include the qualifier **transient** when you declare fields to indicate that they
should not be serialized with instances of the class. Fields that have the **transient**
qualifier are not output when the object is serialized. When the object is deserialized
later, **transient** fields are given the default value normally used for fields of their type.

You can use the **transient** qualifier to indicate that certain fields of a class should
never be serialized, but it is not very flexible. You cannot change the declaration of a
field at runtime to include it or to exclude it from serialization.

The Java platform provides an alternative approach for run-time control: You can add a
private static final field with the name **serialPersistentFields** and type
ObjectStreamField[] to the class. Set up each **ObjectStreamField** element in the
serialPersistentFields array to represent a field to be serialized. Construct the element by specifying the name of the field as a **String**, and the **Class** object for the field.

 The qualifier **transient** has been a reserved word in the Java programming
language since the original release, but had no use until the Java platform
started to support object serialization in version 1.1.

The support for serialization that is automatically generated for a class is usually adequate. However, the designers of the Java platform know that programmers are sure to
want some ability to customize serialization for a particular class. Therefore, the designers have given you three additional methods for this purpose: **readObject**,

validateObject method, and **writeObject**. The **validateObject** method will be described in more detail later in this section. The **readObject** and **writeObject** methods have unusual characteristics:

- The **readObject** and **writeObject** methods are not part of any interface to be implemented or class to be extended. (The **validateObject** is defined as part of the **ObjectInputValidation** interface.)

- Even though the serialization support calls **readObject** and **writeObject**, they must be **private** methods.

You must define **readObject** and **writeObject** as in the following lines in Figure 3-14, which are taken from the next example program, shown in Figure 3-17. If they are defined properly, the serialization support finds them and uses them.

```
private void readObject( ObjectInputStream ois )
    throws ClassNotFoundException, IOException {
    /* whatever you want */
    ois.defaultReadObject();
    /* whatever you want */
}
private void writeObject( ObjectOutputStream oos )
    throws IOException {
    /* whatever you want */
    oos.defaultWriteObject();
    /* whatever you want */
}
```

Figure 3-14   Templates for defining the **readObject** and **writeObject** methods

Make sure you call the **defaultReadObject** and **defaultWriteObject** methods in your customized methods. The **defaultReadObject** and **defaultWriteObject** methods do the actual serialization work. If you leave them out, not much happens.

The purpose of the **validateObject** method is to provide a means for verifying that an object that has just been read is a valid object. You use this method to make sure that values of fields are within range, that any relationship between the values of fields is correct, or for any other purpose you wish. If the object is determined to be invalid, the method throws an **InvalidObjectException** exception. The use of this method can guard against data corruption, either accidental or malicious.

The use of the **validateObject** method is optional. But if you choose to use it, the class in which it is defined must implement the **ObjectInputValidation** interface. The method is defined in Figure 3-15.

```
public void validateObject()
      throws InvalidObjectException {
   /* code to verify the object is valid */
}
```

Figure 3-15   Template for defining the **validateObject** method

Providing a **validateObject** method is not sufficient for the validation to occur. An instance of the class must be registered with the associated **ObjectInputStream** object using the **registerValidation** method. A convenient place to do this is within the **readObject** method. In the following code fragment, the class that implements the **ObjectInputValidation** interface is the same class in which the **readObject** method is contained, and so it is possible to use this object reference as input to the method. The **VALIDATION_PRIORITY** parameter is an integer that allows for multiple validation methods to be sequenced with higher numbers called first, as shown in Figure 3-16.

```
private void readObject( ObjectInputStream ois )
  throws ClassNotFoundException, IOException {
  /* whatever you want */
  ois.registerValidation( this, VALIDATION_PRIORITY );
  ois.defaultReadObject();
  /* whatever you want */
}
```

Figure 3-16   Invoking the **registerValidation** method from the **readObject** method

Figure 3-17 is an example that uses object serialization. The class `ObjectToSave` is defined and implements **Serializable**.

```
package examples.io;
import java.io.*;
/** A class defined to be used in
  * serialization operations
  */
class ObjectToSave implements Serializable,
                              ObjectInputValidation {
   static final int VALIDATION_PRIORITY = 0;
   static final long serialVersionUID
     = 7482918152381158178L;
   private int i;
   private String s;
```

Figure 3-17   `ObjectSaver`: an example of serializing objects to and from a file

```
      private transient double d;
      public ObjectToSave( int i, String s, double d ) {
         this.i = i;
         this.s = s;
         this.d = d;
      }
      public String toString() {
         return "i = " + i + ", s = " + s + ", d = " + d;
      }
      public void setI( int i ) {
         this.i = i;
      }
      private void readObject( ObjectInputStream ois )
            throws ClassNotFoundException, IOException {
         ois.registerValidation( this,
                              VALIDATION_PRIORITY );
         System.out.println( "deserializing..." );
         ois.defaultReadObject();
         System.out.println( "deserialized" );
      }
      private void writeObject( ObjectOutputStream oos )
            throws IOException {
         System.out.println( "serializing..." );
         oos.defaultWriteObject();
         System.out.println( "serialized" );
      }
      public void validateObject()
            throws InvalidObjectException {
         System.out.println( "validating...");
      }
}
/** A class used to demonstrate serializing objects
  * to and from a file
  */
public class ObjectSaver {
   private static final String FILE_NAME
      = "objects.ser";
   /** Test method for the class
     * @param args not used
     */
   public static void main( String[] args ) {
      try {
         // create the object to be serialized
         ObjectToSave ots
            = new ObjectToSave( 57, "pizza", 3.14 );
         // create the target File object and erase
         // any already existing file
         File objectFile = new File( FILE_NAME );
         if ( objectFile.exists() ) {
            objectFile.delete();
         }
```

Figure 3-17   `ObjectSaver`: an example of serializing objects to and from a file (continued)

3

```
         // open the file, create the output stream,
         // and write the object
         FileOutputStream fos
            = new FileOutputStream( objectFile );
         ObjectOutputStream oos
            = new ObjectOutputStream( fos );
         oos.writeObject( ots );
         ots.setI( -4 );
         oos.writeObject( ots );
         oos.reset();
         oos.writeObject( ots );
         oos.close();
         // reopen the file and retrieve the object
         FileInputStream fis
            = new FileInputStream( objectFile );
         ObjectInputStream ois
            = new ObjectInputStream( fis );
         ObjectToSave retrieved
            = (ObjectToSave) ois.readObject();
         System.out.println( retrieved );
         retrieved
            = (ObjectToSave) ois.readObject();
         System.out.println( retrieved );
         retrieved
            = (ObjectToSave) ois.readObject();
         System.out.println( retrieved );
         ois.close();
      }
      catch ( OptionalDataException x ) {
         System.out.println( x );
         x.printStackTrace();
      }
      catch ( ClassNotFoundException x ) {
         System.out.println( x );
         x.printStackTrace();
      }
      catch ( IOException x ) {
         System.out.println( x );
         x.printStackTrace();
      }
   }
}
```

Figure 3-17 ObjectSaver: an example of serializing objects to and from a file (continued)

The output from running the `ObjectSaver` program is shown in Figure 3-18.

```
serializing...
serialized
serializing...
serialized
deserializing...
deserialized
validating...
i = 57, s = pizza, d = 0.0
i = 57, s = pizza, d = 0.0
deserializing...
deserialized
validating...
i = -4, s = pizza, d = 0.0
```

Figure 3-18   Output from the `ObjectSaver` program

This code includes its own customized serialization routines that do nothing more than print messages to the console when a serialization operation starts or finishes and when object validation occurs.

The class `ObjectSaver` does the actual work of creating `ObjectToSave` objects, opening the file, and writing the objects into the file. After closing the file, `ObjectSaver` reopens the file and retrieves the objects to verify that everything worked correctly.

Notice that when the transient field `d` is restored, it receives the default value for a **double**, which is zero.

Forcing Changed Objects to Be Serialized

In the `ObjectSaver` example in Figure 3-17, you probably noticed that, although the **writeObject** method was called three times, there are only two serialization, deserialization, and validation operations appearing in the output. This is a consequence of a potentially unexpected behavior of the `ObjectOutputStream` class in which the content of an object is copied to the output stream only the first time it is serialized. Subsequent serialization operations for the same object copy only the object reference into the stream, even if the object has changed. This explains why the output of the first two deserialized objects is the same, even though the value of the `i` field was changed between the first and second serialization operations.

Fortunately, there is a simple solution to this problem: invoke the **reset** method for the `ObjectOutputStream` object. This method causes the next serialization of an object to be treated as if it were the first. In Figure 3-17, the **reset** method is called before the third serialization operation, which causes the updated object with the new value in the `i` field to be serialized as expected.

Specifying the Version Number

In the serialization sample program (refer to Figure 3-17), did you notice the following unusual field in the `ObjectToSave` class?

```
static final long serialVersionUID
    = 7482918152381158178L;
```

Just from looking at the code, you may suspect that this field serves no purpose because it is not referenced within the program. However, this field is a unique identifier that specifies the version of the class that was serialized. The version number is saved with the serialized object. When the object is restored, this field serves as a check that the object is being restored by a class definition that matches the version that created it.

You do not arbitrarily choose a version number. The value is calculated using a formula that takes the name of the class and its interfaces, fields, and methods. You can determine the value with the `serialver` tool supplied with the SDK, by entering the following command:

```
serialver fully_qualified_class_name
```

For the class `examples.io.ObjectToSave` (note that the fully qualified class name must be used), the output is:

```
examples.io.ObjectToSave:
static final long serialVersionUID
    = 7482918152381158178L;
```

You can use copy and paste techniques to edit this number into your class definition. Alternatively, you may prefer not to define a **serialVersionUID** field and let the JVM generate one for you. The drawback when the JVM generates the number automatically is that minor changes in the class definition, such as renaming a method or adding a method that does not require any new fields, result in a new version value. Objects serialized before such a change appear to be out of date when they are not. If the needed version of the class cannot be found, the compiler throws a **ClassNotFoundException** exception.

Compatibility of Serialization Formats

The object serialization classes of the Java 2 platform write objects to object streams using a different format from earlier versions of the Java platform. As a result, objects serialized by the Java 2 API cannot be deserialized by classes compiled with versions of the Java platform before version 1.1.7. To identify the serialization stream format used, Java 2 defines two new constants, **PROTOCOL_VERSION_1** and **PROTOCOL_VERSION_2**, in the **java.io.ObjectStreamConstants** interface. Versions of the

Java platform beginning with 1.1.7 can read both serialization stream versions, but earlier Java platform versions can read only the original stream version.

For those cases where compatibility requires that objects be serialized using the original version, the method **useProtocolVersion** has been added to **ObjectOutputStream**. This method takes a protocol version constant as input and updates the **ObjectOutputStream** object to use the corresponding serialization stream version.

CHAPTER SUMMARY

- ❏ A great deal of input to and output from Java programs is stream based, regardless of whether the program is communicating with the console, disk files, or another program running on the network. The notable exception is that random-access file I/O does not use streams.

- ❏ Support for I/O is provided by the core classes in the package **java.io.**

- ❏ The Java platform supports byte-oriented streams that are usually adequate for working with the 7-bit ASCII character set used by most English-language North American PCs, and the character-oriented streams that convert characters from the native character encoding of the native operating system to Unicode.

- ❏ For byte-oriented I/O, the two classes **InputStream** and **OutputStream** are the abstract classes that are the roots of the input and output class hierarchies, respectively.

- ❏ The predefined console input stream object, **System.in**, and the console output stream objects, **System.out** and **System.err**, are **InputStream** and **OutputStream** objects. You should wrap a character-oriented stream class around **System.in** to ensure that the data is converted correctly to Unicode.

- ❏ The stream I/O model means that console I/O and file I/O are very similar. **FileInputStream** and **FileOutputStream** are the classes used for reading and writing files. Their constructors take either a string containing the filename or an object of the class **File**.

- ❏ **File** objects are constructed by providing a string containing a filename in a platform-independent manner. A **File** object offers the capability to query the physical file it represents and find out whether it exists, whether it can be read or written, and so on. You can also use a **File** object to navigate the file system on your host in a platform-independent manner.

- ❏ Filter-stream classes are designed to wrap either an **InputStream** or an **OutputStream** class. They build on the base I/O functions and add features such as buffering and data pushback.

- ❏ Several other classes extend the **InputStream** and **OutputStream** classes to provide capabilities such as reading and writing byte arrays, sequencing multiple streams as a single stream, and reading and writing pipes.

3

□ Use the class **RandomAccessFile** to read and write information at arbitrary locations within a file without first having to read or write information at the preceding locations.

□ The design of the character-stream class hierarchy is similar to that of the byte-
stream class hierarchy.

□ The **java.nio** package and its subpackages were added to supplement the I/O
support that has been provided in the **java.io** package since the original version
of the Java platform. This supplement provides new features and improved performance. Notable among the new features is support for buffer management, a new
primitive I/O abstraction called a channel, file locking at the process level, and
memory mapping.

□ To enable programmers to read and write objects as a whole, the Java programming
language provides object serialization. Objects are written to and read from
ObjectOutputStream and **ObjectInputStream** objects. Only classes that
implement the marker interface **Serializable** can be serialized. You can exclude
individual fields within a class from the serialization operation by applying the
transient qualifier.

□ Defining the methods **readObject**, **validateObject**, and **writeObject**
allows for customizing serialization operations. The **readObject** and
writeObject methods are not part of any interface to be implemented or class to
be extended and must be declared as private methods. The **validateObject**
method is defined as part of the **ObjectInputValidation** interface.

REVIEW QUESTIONS

1. Which of the following classes are subclasses of **InputStream**? Select all that apply.

   a. SequenceInputStream

   b. File

   c. ObjectInputStream

   d. StringReader

   e. RandomAccessFile

2. Which of the following classes can be passed as a parameter to the constructor of
   FilterOutputStream? Select all that apply.

   a. PipedOutputStream

   b. BufferedWriter

   c. String

   d. File

   e. ByteArrayOutputStream

3. True or False: The **RandomAccessFile** class extends neither **InputStream** nor **OutputStream**.

4. Examine the following code:

```
import java.io.*;
public class Quiz3_4 {
    public static void main( String[] args )
                            throws IOException {
        PrintWriter pr = new PrintWriter( System.out );
        pr.println( "What a lovely day." );
        pr.flush();
    }
}
```

Which of the following statements are true when the code is compiled and run? Select all that apply.

a. The compiler rejects the expression new **PrintWriter(System.out)** because it is not possible to construct a **PrintWriter** object from a **PrintStream** object.

b. The **flush** method ensures that the information in the **PrintWriter** stream is written to the console.

c. Compilation is successful and the output is What a lovely day.

d. The **throws** clause in **main** is unnecessary because none of the methods in **main** throw an **IOException**.

5. Which class is used to represent a file system folder?

6. Which of the following statements creates a physical file in the file system, assuming that the file **data1** does not already exist? Select all that apply.

a. new RandomAccessFile("data1", "rw");

b. new File("data1");

c. new FileOutputStream("data1");

d. new FileOutputStream(new File("data1"));

e. new FileWriter("data1")

7. True or False: Write operations performed on a read-write **MappedByteBuffer** object directly change the contents of the file that is mapped by the buffer.

3

buffer to zero? Select all that apply.

a. `reset()`

b. `flip()`

c. `clear()`

d. `position( 0 )`

e. `rewind()`

9. Examine the following code:

```
import java.io.*;
class SaveMe implements Serializable {
   boolean b = true;
   transient String s
      = "Something from the meat case, Linda?";
}
public class Quiz3_9 {
   private static final String FILE_NAME
      = "objects.ser";
   public static void main( String[] args ) {
      try {
         SaveMe sm = new SaveMe();
         File objectFile = new File( FILE_NAME );
         FileOutputStream fos =
         new FileOutputStream( objectFile );
         ObjectOutputStream oos =
            new ObjectOutputStream( fos );
         oos.writeObject( sm );
         oos.close();
         FileInputStream fis =
            new FileInputStream( objectFile );
         ObjectInputStream ois
            = new ObjectInputStream( fis );
         SaveMe retrieved = (SaveMe) ois.readObject();
         ois.close();
         System.out.println( retrieved.b );
         System.out.println( retrieved.s );
      }
      catch ( Exception x ) {
         System.out.println( x );
      }
   }
}
```

Which of the following statements are true when the code is compiled and run? Select all that apply.

a. The compiler rejects the method `Quiz3_9.main` because all possible exceptions have not been handled by a catch clause or been identified in a throws clause.

b. The class `SaveMe` accepts the default value of the field **serialVersionUID**.

c. Compilation is successful and the output is
```
true
null
```

d. Compilation is successful and the output is
```
true
Something from the meat case, Linda?
```

e. The compiler rejects the definition of the class `Quiz3_9` because it does not implement the **Serializable** interface.

10. Which of the following classes do not implement the **Serializable** interface? Select all that apply.

a. `Integer`

b. `Process`

c. `String`

d. `Object`

e. `Thread`

11. Which of the following methods are defined in the **Serializable** interface? Select all that apply.

a. `serialize`

b. `readObject`

c. `writeObject`

d. `getSerialVersionUID`

e. `setSerialVersionUID`

PROGRAMMING EXERCISES

Debugging

1. Correct the following program so that it uses **Reader** and **Writer** subclasses for reading and writing characters:

```
package questions.c3;
import java.io.*;
public class Debug3_1 {
    public static void main( String[] args )
            throws IOException {
        InputStream  input;
        OutputStream output;
        if ( args.length >= 2 ) {
            input = new FileInputStream( args[0] );
            output = new FileOutputStream( args[1] );
        } else {
            input = System.in;
            output = System.out;
        }
        int c;
        try {
            while ( ( c = input.read() ) != -1 ) {
                // change blanks to underscores
                if ( c == ' ' ) {
                    c = '_';
                }
                output.write( c );
            }
        }
        catch( IOException iox ) {
            System.out.println( iox );
        }
        finally {
            input.close();
            output.close();
        }
    }
}
```

2. Correct all the errors in the following program so that it outputs a message specifying the length of the line read for each line in the input file:

```
package questions.c3;
import java.io.*;
public class Debug3_2 {
    public static void main( String[] args )
            throws IOException {
```

```
                  if ( args.length >= 2 ) {
                      Reader  input;
                      Writer output;
                      String inputLine;
                      input = new FileReader( args[0] );
                      output = new FileWriter( args[1] );
                      inputLine = input.readLine();
                      try {
                         while ( inputLine != null ) {
                            output.println( "Line length = "
                                            + inputLine.length() );
                            inputLine = input.readLine();
                         }
                      }
                      catch( IOException iox ) {
                         System.out.println( iox );
                      }
                      finally {
                         input.close();
                         output.close();
                      }
                  } else {
                      System.err.println( "Usage is <input_file> "
                                          + "<output_file>" );
                  }
              }
          }
```

3. Correct all the errors in the following program so that the **StreamTokenizer** object is used to output each of the tokens in the input file:

```
package questions.c3;
import java.io.*;
public class Debug3_3 {
    public static void main( String[] args )
            throws IOException {
        if ( args.length >= 1 ) {
            Reader  input;
            StreamTokenizer st;
            input = new FileReader( args[0] );
            st = new StreamTokenizer( input );
            try {
               while ( st.moreTokens() ) {
                  System.out.println( "token = "
                                      + st.getNext() );
               }
            }
            catch( IOException iox ) {
               System.out.println( iox );
            }
```

3

```
                        finally {
                            input.close();
                        }
                    } else {
                        System.err.println( "Usage is "
                                              + "<input_file>" );
                    }
                }
            }
```

4. Correct all the errors in the following program:

```
package questions.c3;
import java.io.*;
import java.nio.*;
import java.nio.channels.*;
public class Debug3_4 {
    public static void main( String[] args )
                                throws IOException {
        FileInputStream istream = null;
        FileOutputStream ostream = null;
        FileChannel fcin = null;
        FileChannel fcout = null;
        if ( args.length >= 2 ) try {
            File inputFile = new File( args[0] );
            istream = new FileInputStream( inputFile );
            fcin = istream.getChannel();
            File outputFile = new File( args[1] );
            ostream = new FileOutputStream( outputFile );
            fcout = ostream.getChannel();
            ByteBuffer bb
                = ByteBuffer.allocate( (int) fcin.size() );
            fcin.read( bb );
            char c;
            for ( int i = 0; i < bb.limit(); i++ ) {
                c = (char) bb.get( i );
                if ( c == "/" ) {
                    bb.put( i, (byte) "\\" );
                } else {
                    bb.put( i, (byte) c );
                }
            }
            fcout.write( bb );
        }
        catch( IOException iox ) {
            System.out.println( iox );
        }
        finally {
            fcin.close();
            fcout.close();
```

```
                istream.close();
                ostream.close();
            } else {
                System.out.println( "Provide input and " +
                                          "output filenames" );
            }
        }
    }
```

5. Correct all the errors in the following program:

```
package questions.c3;
import java.io.*;
public class Debug3_5 {
    private static final String FILE_NAME
        = "debug3_5.ser";
    int count = 11;
    Thread t = new Thread();
    String title = "Placeholder";
    public static void main( String[] args ) {
        try {
            File objectFile = new File( FILE_NAME );
            Debug3_5 x = new Debug3_5();
            x.count = 57;
            x.title = "Varieties";
            FileOutputStream fos =
                new FileOutputStream( objectFile );
            ObjectOutputStream oos =
                new ObjectOutputStream( fos );
            oos.writeObject( x );
            oos.close();
            FileInputStream fis =
                new FileInputStream( objectFile );
            ObjectInputStream ois
                = new ObjectInputStream( fis );
            Debug3_5 retrieved
                = (Debug3_5) ois.readObject();
            ois.close();
            System.out.println( retrieved.count );
            System.out.println( retrieved.title );
        }
        catch ( Exception x ) {
            System.out.println( x );
        }
    }
}
```

Complete the Solution

1. Extract the file X:\Data\questions\c3\Complete3_1.java from the CD-ROM. (Here X: is the drive letter of the CD-ROM.) Complete the definition of the class questions.c3.Complete3_1 by finishing the initialize method so that it fills the character array with characters read from the specified file.

2. Extract the file X:\Data\questions\c3\Complete3_2.java from the CD-ROM. (Here X: is the drive letter of the CD-ROM.) Complete the definition of the class questions.c3.Complete3_2 by finishing the getInt method so that it reads an integer from the specified starting position in the specified file.

3. Extract the file X:\Data\questions\c3\Complete3_3.java from the CD-ROM. (Here X: is the drive letter of the CD-ROM.) Complete the definition of the class questions.c3.Complete3_3 by finishing the main method so that it uses a MappedByteBuffer object to simplify the operation of reversing the order of bytes in the file, and a FileLock object to ensure that this reversal operation isn't interrupted by another process accessing the file.

4. Extract the file X:\Data\questions\c3\Complete3_4.java from the CD-ROM. (Here X: is the drive letter of the CD-ROM.) Complete the definition of the class questions.c3.Complete3_4 by adding methods readObject, validateObject, and writeObject to have them print messages indicating status of the serialization store and retrieve operations.

5. Add to the definition of class questions.c3.Complete3_4 by calculating and defining the appropriate serialVersionUID field for the class.

Discovery

1. Using the classes from the java.io and java.nio packages, create a simple copy utility in a class called FileCopyUtility that can copy the contents of an entire folder into a different folder. For an additional challenge, add support to your utility that allows the user to specify an option that will also recursively copy any subfolders of the specified folder.

2. Create a class called HasAProfile that maintains name, address, and phone number information in serialized form on disk so that it can be retrieved whenever a new HasAProfile object is constructed. If an error occurs when retrieving the information during object construction, the object will prompt the user for name, address, and phone number information and use the information to create a new serialized profile on disk.

4

COLLECTIONS AND A WEALTH OF UTILITIES

In this chapter you will:

- ♦ Explore a wide variety of utilities provided by utility and text packages of the J2SDK
- ♦ Learn the architecture of the Java collections framework
- ♦ Select appropriate collection classes and interfaces for specific behavioral requirements
- ♦ Create, build, and traverse collections using the provided collection classes
- ♦ Define your own collections that conform to the collections framework
- ♦ Set up an event-notification mechanism using **Observer** and **Observable** objects
- ♦ Generate random numbers
- ♦ Use **Locale** objects that encapsulate cultural environments
- ♦ Format and transform numbers, currency values, dates, and times using locale-sensitive classes
- ♦ Use resource bundles and properties files to separate literal data from executable code
- ♦ Parse strings using the **StringTokenizer** class
- ♦ Use regular expressions for character and string pattern recognition

INTRODUCTION

The classes and interfaces included in the Java 2 Software Development Kit (J2SDK) are grouped into packages. Most packages contain classes that are usually used together to solve certain types of programming problems. Some packages are more specialized than others. For example, the package `java.io` contains classes and interfaces that support input and output and is described in Chapter 3 of this book. As you might expect, the J2SDK contains a number of utilities for which the only logical grouping could be considered "miscellaneous." This chapter covers the packages `java.util`, some related packages with names beginning `java.util`, and some supporting classes in the package `java.text`.

Among other things, the package `java.util` includes several classes and interfaces that make up what is commonly called the collections framework. The collections framework occupies most of the first half of this chapter. You can use this discussion as a primer on the architecture of Java collections and a guide to encapsulating the data structures that your programs require in collections. The framework supports many kinds of collections. Selecting the most appropriate and efficient implementation for data in your program can have a major impact on the performance and robustness of your programs.

The discussion of the collections framework includes a brief review of some conceptual data aggregations including sets, bags, lists, trees, hash tables, and maps. To benefit fully from this discussion, you should have prior knowledge of basic abstract data structures including queues, stacks, linked lists, and binary trees.

It would be misleading to consider `java.util` as just the collections package. It contains classes that have no relation to collections, but provide solutions to common programming problems. For example, the types **Observer** and **Observable** provide an implementation of an event-notification design pattern, and there are classes for handling time and date information.

This chapter describes how to use classes in `java.util.regex` to parse regular expressions. Other specialized utility packages are listed in Figure 4–1 but not covered in detail. In addition, this chapter shows how to adapt the representation of data to the cultural environment within which your program runs by using locales and some classes in the `java.text` package.

THE UTILITY PACKAGES

Before concentrating on the collections framework, you should be aware of the other classes in the package `java.util` and related packages. The rationale for some of the groupings of classes into packages is no doubt historical. In the first version of Java, the package `java.util` was a relatively small set of general purpose utility classes and interfaces, and included some classes that implement common data structures. When

building the collections framework to provide more flexible support for aggregations of
data, the designers of the Java 2 platform decided to add the new types to **java.util**
rather than create a new package for collections. However, over time, classes and interfaces
that support other specific tasks were added as separate packages.

The first column of Figure 4-1 lists the packages in the J2SDK that can be considered
utility packages. Note that all the package names start with **java.util**. The second
column of Figure 4-1 states the version of the SDK that first contained each package.

Package name	Since	Description
java.util	1.0	Contains the collections framework and a number of utility types not related to collections; Figure 4.2 shows noncollection types.
java.util.jar	1.2	Contains classes to read and write Java Archive (jar) files, including maintaining the manifest file for the jar.
java.util.logging	1.4	Contains types used to format and write logging messages that monitor activities of programs. You typically use logs as diagnostic aids when maintaining or servicing programs deployed to a production environment.
java.util.prefs	1.4	Contains types for storing and accessing user or system preferences in an implantation-dependent persistent storage media. For example, user preferences could include the initial location and size of the window that holds a program's graphical user interface, and a system preference could be the location of files.
java.util.regex	1.4	Contains classes for matching character sequences against patterns presented as regular expressions. Using these classes and regular expressions is discussed in the latter half of this chapter.
java.util.zip	1.1	Contains types for reading and writing files in standard zip and gzip formats, compressing and decompressing data using the algorithm used in zip and gzip files, and calculating CRC-32 and Adler-32 checksums for streams of characters.
java.text	1.1	Contains types for handling text, dates, times, and numbers including monetary values and messages. The classes are locale sensitive so you can use them to format output according to the user's cultural environment. Some examples are supplied later in this chapter.

Figure 4-1   Utility and related packages

Figure 4-2 shows the types defined in **java.util** that are not part of the collections
framework. It also shows the inheritance relationships between them. The shaded boxes
represent abstract classes, and the rounded boxes represent interfaces. Grey lines between
types indicate that these types are often used together.

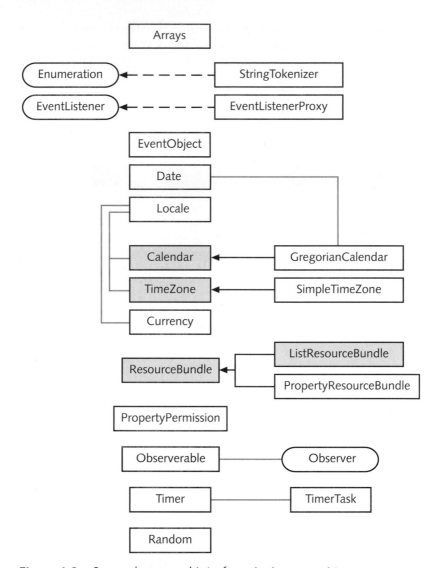

Figure 4-2 Some classes and interfaces in `java.util`

Most of the types shown in Figure 4-2 are discussed in the second half of this chapter. The following are not covered in this chapter because you do not use them directly or they are covered elsewhere in this book:

- The **EventObject** and **EventListenerProxy** classes and **EventListener** interface support user interaction with a graphical user interface.

- Class **PropertyPermission** extends **java.security.BasicPermission** and is used to grant access to properties, such as environmental variables.

■ You can use a **Timer** object to schedule activities encapsulated in instances of **TimerTask** on a system-generated thread, as described in the section "Using the JVM to Schedule Tasks" of Chapter 5.

THE COLLECTIONS FRAMEWORK

When you write a program requiring data that is more than a single element, you usually define a data structure to hold the data. In this context, a *data structure* is a programming construct that contains more than one element, and each element is a unit that can be accessed by the program. For example, you can use a data structure to represent all the students in a class, the items in a purchase order, or accounts managed by a bank. In object-oriented terms, a data structure is an *aggregation* and the elements are objects.

In Java, collections are aggregations implemented by the classes and interfaces that make up the collections framework or by types that extend the classes defined in the collections framework. The collections framework consists of

- ■ Interfaces that define the behavior of collections (for example, they define methods to add and remove elements)

- ■ Concrete classes that provide general-purpose implementations of the interfaces that you can use directly

- ■ Abstract classes that implement the interfaces of the collections framework that you can extend to create collections for specialized data structures

These types make up a large part of the **java.util** package.

 The classes and interfaces that make up the collections framework have been part of the Java platform since J2SDK 1.2. Six collection classes and one interface were included in the original Java 1 platform, and some of the original classes have been reengineered to be compatible with the collections framework in the Java 2 platform. The original classes, sometimes called the legacy collection classes, are **BitSet**, **Dictionary**, **Hashtable**, **Properties**, **Stack**, and **Vector**.

To fully understand the flexibility of the collections framework, you must be familiar with some concepts that programmers use to describe aggregations. The following list contains terms for aggregations used by Java programmers. You may already be familiar with them, because these abstract data structures can be implemented in many programming languages. They are not specific to Java or even to object-oriented programming:

- ■ A *bag* is a group of elements. No order or relationship between the elements is implied. A bag is an abstract concept, and there are no types in the collections framework that implement bags.

- A *set* is a group of unique elements. A set is a bag that does not allow two different elements to be identical, and therefore, contains no duplicates. A set is an abstraction. To implement a set, you must implement a strategy for storing and retrieving the elements.

- A *list* is a group of elements that are accessed in order. Having an order does not mean being sorted. It means that each element has a position, or index, and comes after another element (unless it is the first in the list) and before another element (unless it is the last in the list). A list has a linear structure, as shown in Figure 4-3. In a linked list, each element contains a link to the element before it, or to the element after it, or to both. Figure 4-3 shows a doubly linked list. Depending on how a list is implemented, you can access one element directly using its index, or by following the links from one end of the list until you find the element.

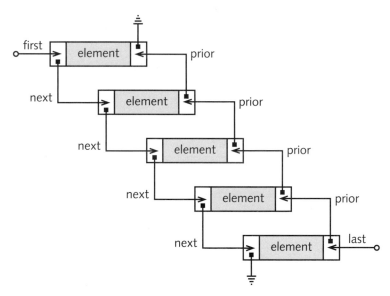

Figure 4-3   A doubly linked list

- A *tree* is a group of elements with a hierarchical structure, as shown in Figure 4-4. Elements in a tree are called *nodes*, and the first node is the *root* of the tree. The links from one node to other nodes make up *branches*, and branches end at *leaf nodes*. Figure 4-4 shows a binary tree. In a binary tree, each node can have up to two branches. Elements are accessed in order and are usually accessed by traversing the branches of the tree. Trees can be traversed in different orders, such as right branch – root – left branch, root – right branch – left branch, and left branch – root – right branch. Trees are most appropriate for storing sorted elements so that they can be located later by value. The maximum number of comparisons required to find any element by value is limited to the depth of the tree.

4

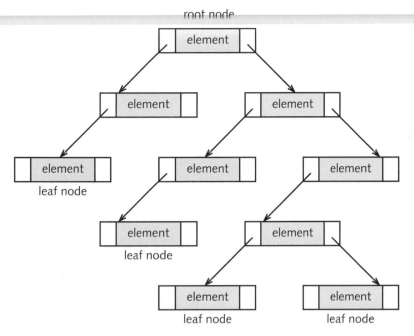

Figure 4-4 A binary tree

- A *hash*, or *hash table*, is a group of elements, each of which is stored in a known location that is selected based on the value of the element. To picture a hash table, imagine an arrangement of buckets and a mechanical arm that can reach into any bucket. Each bucket has a code that is some arbitrary value, different from the code of any other bucket. Given an element to store, the arm calculates the code for the element, called a *hash code*, based on an internal algorithm and usually the value of the element, and then puts the element in the bucket with the matching code. If necessary, the arm can create a new bucket.

  Hash tables provide fast element storage and retrieval if the algorithm to calculate the hash code is efficient. As soon as the arm knows the hash code, it can move directly to the right bucket without having to compare element values or traverse from bucket to bucket. Therefore, hash tables are an efficient way of storing many items when no ordering is required. However, they provide no features for navigation from one element or bucket to another.

A Note on Hash Tables and Hash Codes:

Hash tables are particularly interesting because the Java platform maintains a number of hash tables internally. You do not need to worry about these tables, and you cannot access them directly. Because hash tables are efficient in many situations, they are used pervasively by the JVM, operating systems, and what is generally called system software.

You may be familiar with the concept of hash codes and know that whenever you create a class and override the default **equals** method you should also override **hashCode**. Default **equals** and **hashCode** methods defined in the **Object** class often are not adequate for your classes. The default **equals** method returns **true** when two object references have the same value, in other words when they refer to the same object. The default **equals** method returns **false** when two object references refer to different objects—regardless of whether those objects have identical contents. Usually you override **equals** to return **true** when the fields in two instances of the same type have identical values. The **equals** method is related to the **hashCode** method, because the Java platform states that the following criteria must be met to ensure that all hash tables perform as expected:

- When the **equals** method considers two objects to be equal, they must have the same hash code.
- The hash code for an object must not change unless the state of the object—meaning the set of values stored in its fields—also changes.

A common way to override **hashCode** is to calculate and return a value such as the concatenation of the values of key fields in the object. This approach is optimized for simplicity rather than efficiency, but is adequate for many Java programs. Devising efficient hash code algorithms is an interesting problem that is beyond the scope of this book.

You may be wondering why collections are necessary because arrays are aggregations that are easy to use. Like many programming languages, Java supports arrays and includes the index operator, [ ], to access individual elements. For example, the following code snippet declares an array that can contain 10 integers and then assigns the values 0 through 9 to the elements in the array:

```
int [ ] value = new int[10];
for ( int i=0; i < value.length; i++; ) {
    value[i] = i;
}
```

In Java, elements in arrays can be primitive types or objects. The elements in collections must have reference types. However, an easy workaround to this limitation is to use the wrapper classes for the primitive types, such as **Integer** and **Double**. In practice, Java

ing limitations:

- All elements of an array must have the same type. For example, you cannot create an array in which one element is a **String** and another is a **Date**. You can define an array to have type **Object[ ]**, but then you must use the wrapper classes for primitives just as you do for collections. Elements in any collection can have unrelated object types, such as **String**, **Date**, Car, **Policy**, and **Account**.

- The capacity of an array is fixed when the array is defined. You must request enough storage to accommodate the maximum number of elements ever required, and the array has exclusive use of that storage for the duration of its lifetime. Therefore, arrays can force you to use memory inefficiently.

- Programs that use arrays are error-prone because the only way to access an element is through its index. Therefore, you should take care to ensure that every index is in the range defined for the array or wrap all operations on the array in try blocks and with catch blocks that handle **ArrayIndexOutOfBounds** exceptions.

- Arrays provide convenient access to individual elements, but you must do a lot of work to represent structures such as linked lists or trees.

The goals of the collections framework are to

- Reduce the programming effort of developers by providing the most common data structures.

- Provide a set of types that are easy to use, extend, and understand.

- Increase flexibility by defining a standard set of interfaces for collections to implement. As a result, you can easily convert from one kind of data structure to another or change the implementation of a collection without changing how it is used by other classes.

- Improve program quality through the reuse of tested software components.

In addition to the collection classes and interfaces, the **java.util** package includes support classes and methods that enhance the collections framework and make it more powerful. The API that provides commonly required algorithms for sorting and searching is described in the section "Algorithms for Collections." Classes described in the section "Wrapper Implementations for Collections" provide methods for creating wrapper objects that make a collection read-only or synchronized for use in multithreaded applications.

Three Key Interfaces in the Collections Framework

The fundamental design principle behind the collections framework is that Java interfaces define the standard behavior of collections. When you use a collection, you call methods defined in these interfaces to perform operations such as adding an element to a collection or removing an element from a collection. This section introduces three basic interfaces. Following sections introduce classes that implement these interfaces and then move on to more specialized collection types.

Different classes can become collections by implementing the standard interfaces. These classes provide implementations that model data structures, such as linked lists and trees. Thus, using collections effectively has two aspects:

- Selecting the most appropriate implementing class. For this, you consider which abstract data structure performs best for the way you use the collection.

- Manipulating the collection using the methods defined in the interface. After you have selected the implementing class, using the collection is straightforward.

Another design principle is that the collection interfaces do not contain the methods that traverse the collection. Instead they include a method that returns an **Iterator** object. An iterator is a *cursor*, a helper object that clients of the collections use to access elements one at a time. Different abstract data structures use different cursors to navigate from element to element. For example, a tree cursor navigates the branches of the tree and a linked list cursor follows the links between elements.

The Collection Interface

The root interface of the framework is **Collection**. **Collection**, and **Map** interfaces define the behavior common to all classes in the framework. The elements in maps are more specialized than those in general collections and are discussed in the section "Maps." The methods of the **Collection** interface add and remove elements and operate on elements of type **Object**. Because all classes directly or indirectly extend the class **Object**, a **Collection** can hold any type of object. The **Collection** interface is defined to be general enough to be implemented by any class that defines a collection of individual objects. No assumption is made about whether the collection is a set or bag, and whether the elements are sorted or ordered.

Some of the methods defined in the **Collection** interface are optional. Optional methods modify a collection object. Of course, any class that implements an interface must implement all its methods. But an immutable class that implements the interface can provide implementations of the optional methods that throw an **UnsupportedOperationException** exception when the method is called.

The collections framework does not include a class that directly implements the **Collection** interface. Such a class would implement a bag. The creators of the framework decided that programmer requirements for bags are not strong enough to merit providing a standard bag class.

~~Here is a detailed description of the API defined by the Collection interface.~~

Interface

`java.util.Collection`

Purpose

Instances of classes that implement **Collection** are objects that contain an aggregation of other objects.

4

Methods

- **boolean add(Object** *element* **)**

  The **add** method ensures that this collection contains the specified element. This is an optional operation.

- **boolean addAll(Collection** *c* **)**

  Call **addAll** to add all the elements in the specified collection to this collection. This is an optional operation.

- **void clear()**

  The **clear** method removes all the elements from the collection. This is an optional operation.

- **boolean contains(Object** *element* **)**

  This method returns **true** if the collection contains the specified element.

- **boolean containsAll(Collection** *c* **)**

  The **containsAll** method returns **true** if the collection contains all the elements in the specified collection.

- **boolean equals(Object** *o* **)**

  This method is patterned after the **equals** method of the **Object** class. It compares the specified object with this collection for equality.

- **int hashCode()**

  This method is patterned after the **hashCode** method of the **Object** class. Here, it returns the hash code value for the collection.

- **boolean isEmpty()**

  The **isEmpty** method returns **true** if this collection contains no elements.

- **Iterator iterator()**

  Use the **iterator** method to obtain an iterator for traversing the elements in the collection.

- **boolean remove(Object** *element* **)**

  The **remove** method removes a single instance of the specified element from this collection, if it is present. This is an optional operation.

- **boolean removeAll(Collection** *c* **)**

  The **removeAll** method removes all of this collection's elements that are also contained in the specified collection. This is an optional operation.

- **boolean retainAll(Collection** *c* **)**

  Use the **retainAll** method to retain only the elements in the collection that are contained in the specified collection. This is an optional operation.

- **int size()**

  The number of elements in the collection is returned by the **size** method.

- **Object[] toArray()**

  Object[] toArray(Object[] *a* **)**

  Use the **toArray** method to create an array containing all the elements in the collection. The resultant array has type **Object[]** if no input array is specified. If an input array is specified, the returned array has the same type as the argument. The size of the input array does not matter and may be zero.

The Set Interface

The **Set** interface extends the **Collection** interface to define the standard behavior for a collection that does not allow duplicate elements. The **Set** interface does not introduce any additional methods beyond those defined in the **Collection** interface. The interface does, however, add restrictions to prevent duplicate elements.

The following description of the **Set** interface lists only methods that differ from methods in **Collection** to ensure that every element in a **Set** is unique:

Interface

java.util.Set

Purpose

Instances of classes that implement **Set** are objects that contain a collection of unique objects.

Methods

- **boolean add(Object** *element* **)**

  The **add** method ensures that this collection contains the specified element. If the element is already part of the set, **false** is returned. This is an optional operation.

Call **addAll** to add all the elements in the specified collection to this collection. If all the elements in the specified collection are already part of the set, **false** is returned. This is an optional operation.

The List Interface

The **List** interface extends the **Collection** interface to define the standard behavior for ordered collections, often referred to as *sequences*. Typically, a **List** implementation allows duplicate elements. Elements in collections that implement this interface have a position within the collection that is specified by an integer index value. As with arrays, these index values begin at zero and have a maximum value equal to the size of the list minus one.

The following description of the **List** interface lists only methods added or changed from the **Collection** interface to support ordered collections:

Interface

java.util.List

Purpose

Instances of classes that implement **List** are objects that contain an ordered collection of other objects.

Methods

■ **boolean add(Object** *element* **)**

void add(int index, Object *element* **)**

The **add** method ensures that this collection contains the specified element. If you supply an index, this method inserts the element at the specified position. Otherwise, this method appends the element to the end of the list. Existing elements are not overwritten by this method. The single-argument method returns **false** when the collection is not changed by the call (the collection does not accept duplicates and already contains an object equal to the argument) and **true** otherwise. This is an optional operation.

■ **boolean addAll(Collection** *c* **)**

boolean addAll(int *index***, Collection** *c* **)**

Call **addAll** to insert all the elements in the specified collection into this collection. If you supply an index, this method inserts the contents of the collection at the specified position. Otherwise, the elements are appended to the end of the list. Existing elements are not overwritten. The method returns **true** when the collection is changed by the call. This is an optional operation.

- `Object get( int `*`index`*` )`

  This method returns the element of the list at the specified index.

- `int indexOf( Object `*`element`*` )`

  Use this method to find the position of the first occurrence of the specified element in the list. If the element is not found, this method returns the value -1.

- `int lastIndexOf( Object `*`element`*` )`

  Use this method to find the position of the last occurrence of the specified element in the list. If the element is not found, the value -1 is returned.

- `ListIterator listIterator()`

  `ListIterator listIterator( int `*`index`*` )`

  Use the **`listIterator`** method to obtain an iterator for traversing the elements in the collection in proper sequence. If an index is supplied, the traversal begins at the specified position in the list.

- `boolean remove( Object `*`element`*` )`

  `Object remove( int `*`index`*` )`

  The **remove** method removes an element from the collection. If you specify an object, this method locates and then removes the first occurrence of that object. If you specify an index, this method removes the element at that position and returns the removed element. The **boolean** return value indicates whether an element was removed. This is an optional operation.

- `Object set( int `*`index`*`, Object `*`element`*` )`

  The **set** method puts the specified object into the collection at the specified position, overwriting the existing element at that position. The method returns the element that is overwritten. This is an optional operation.

- `List subList( int `*`beginIndex`*`, int `*`endIndex`*` )`

  The **subList** method returns a view of the portion of the list between the specified *beginIndex*, inclusive, and *endIndex*, exclusive.

Note that the **List** interface enforces the behavior that all implementing classes can get the element located at a specified index, set the element located at a specified index, and insert an element at a specified index. In addition, a list can return the index of the first and last occurrences of an element. You may have used lists that did not operate on indexes in other languages or other contexts. The **List** interface sets the behavior of lists built upon the Java collections framework and does not attempt to define the abstract concept of a list.

Traversing Collections with Iterators

Clients of a collection use a separate cursor object to traverse the collection and, in ordered collections, to access individual elements in the proper order. The key design issues are that the cursor is not built into the class that implements the collection and no collection is limited to one cursor. There may be several cursors, including at least one for every client object that uses one collection. This is a common situation in multithreaded programs.

Even one client can request and use more than one cursor. For example, the client may open a cursor to access all patients in a collection of patients. The client can add patient ages and release the cursor when it has the total. From the total age and number of patients, the client can calculate the average patient age. Then the client can open another cursor and access all patients again, this time performing some analysis on only patients over the average age.

For all but the legacy collection types, the cursor implements the **Iterator** interface. You do not directly create the iterators for collections. Instead, you call the **iterator** method of the collection to obtain one.

All cursors provide methods that indicate whether there are more elements in the collection and to return the next element. Some **Iterator** objects provide a **remove** method for removing elements from a collection as the collection is being traversed. When the client uses an iterator that supports the **remove** method, the client can visit an element, operate on it, and then remove it from the collection, all using the cursor. The advantage is that the client does not have to perform a separate operation on the collection to locate and then remove the element, because the client already has a reference to the element returned by the cursor.

Here is a description of the **Iterator** interface:

Interface

java.util.Iterator

Purpose

You can use instances of classes that implement **Iterator** to traverse a collection and to remove elements from the collection during traversal.

Methods

- **boolean hasNext()**

  This method returns **true** if there are more elements in the traversal.

- **Object next()**

  This method returns the next element in the traversal.

- **void remove( )**

  This method removes the most recently returned element from the collection associated with the iterator. This is an optional operation.

Because all legacy collection classes have a method that returns an iterator, you can navigate all collections of all nonlegacy types with code similar to the following snippet. Here, assume objects of a defined type **ActivityRecord** have been added to the collection object called **activityLog**:

```
Iterator it = activityLog.iterator();
   while ( it.hasNext() ) {
         ActivityRecord activity = (ActivityRecord) it.next( );
         // process the activity record
   }
```

Do not be fooled into assuming that the declaration of **it** instantiates **Iterator**. Instead, it declares an object reference for an object of unknown type that implements the **Iterator** interface. The method **List.iterator** for the collection creates the cursor. The actual type of the cursor is unimportant. All that matters is that it implements the **Iterator** interface.

Collections that implement the **List** interface also support **Iterator** objects that implement the **ListIterator** interface. The **ListIterator** interface extends **Iterator**, allowing forward and backward traversal through a list and to provide additional methods for modifying a list while it is being traversed. Only the additional methods are included in this description of the **ListIterator** interface.

Interface

java.util.ListIterator

Purpose

You can use instances of classes that implement **ListIterator** to traverse a list forward and backward and to insert, replace, and remove elements from the list during traversal.

Methods

- **void add(Object** *element* **)**

  This method inserts the specified element into the list. This is an optional operation.

- **boolean hasPrevious( )**

  This method returns **true** if there are more elements for backward traversing.

■ int nextIndex()

This method returns the index of the element that would be returned by the subsequent call of the **next** method.

■ **Object previous()**

This method returns the next element in backward traversing.

4

■ **int previousIndex()**

This method returns the index of the element that would be returned by a subsequent call of the **previous** method.

■ **void set(Object** *element* **)**

This method replaces the element returned by the most recent call to **next** or **previous** with the specified element. This is an optional operation.

One of the differences between the behavior of cursors defined in the collections framework and cursors used by the legacy collection classes relates to how the classes and cursors control concurrent access to collections in multithreaded programs. Multithreading is covered in Chapter 5. For an example of the complications that multithreading adds, consider what should happen when code executing on one thread inserts an element into a collection that another thread is navigating at the same time. This issue is discussed in the section "Comparing Legacy and Collections Framework Cursors" later in this chapter.

General Purpose Implementations

Before you can actually use a collection, you need a concrete class that implements one of the collection interfaces. Figure 4-5 shows the general purpose implementations included in the collections framework with the interfaces and abstract classes they implement.

The seven concrete classes—**HashSet**, **LinkedHashSet**, **TreeSet**, **ArrayList**, **LinkedList**, **Vector**, and **Stack**—are suitable for most programming requirements.

- **HashSet** is described in the section "General Purpose Sets."

- **TreeSet** is described in the section "Sorted Collections."

- **LinkedList**, **LinkedHashSet**, and **ArrayList** are described in the section "General Purpose Lists."

- **Vector** and **Stack** are described in the section "Legacy Collection Classes."

A number of hash table implementations of **Set** and **Map** interfaces are also provided and discussed in the section "Maps."

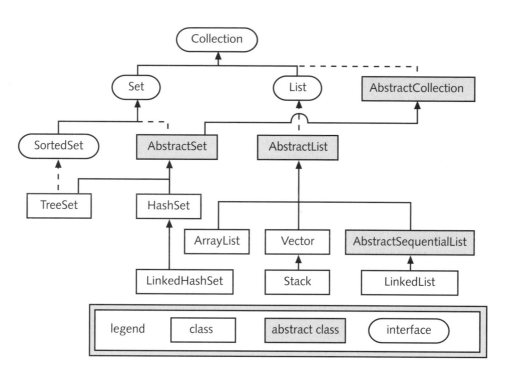

Figure 4-5   General purpose types in the collections framework

For special cases, you may have to define new implementation classes. How to do that is discussed in the section "Extending the Collections Framework."

The collections framework is designed to let programmers exploit the polymorphic, or dynamic binding, feature of Java. When you write methods that use collections, manipulate them using references of the interface types, not of the implementation types. For example, if you pass a **LinkedList** object to a method, refer to the argument as a **List** in the method. If the method knows only that the argument is a **List**, it can work with all classes that implement **List**. This technique hides the implementation class and forces you to code the program to the higher level of abstraction.

The polymorphic nature of collections built on the collections framework gives your programs two main advantages:

- You gain the ability to change the implementation at any time without affecting the code that uses the collection.

- You can use methods of a utility class supplied with the collections framework and described in the section "Algorithms for Collections" to perform operations such as sorting, searching, and reversing the order of elements in a collection.

All the general-purpose implementation classes in the framework implement the interfaces **Cloneable** and **Serializable**. **Cloneable** is described in Chapter 2, and

lection interfaces do not extend **Cloneable** or **Serializable**. This is by design and means that programmers who create their own classes that implement the standard interfaces for collections are not forced to implement **Cloneable** and **Serializable**. If you create a class that implements one of the collection interfaces, you must explicitly implement **Cloneable** and **Serializable** to let users of your collection clone or serialize instances of your collection class.

General Purpose Sets

Three framework classes implement the **Set** interface: **HashSet**, **TreeSet**, and **LinkedHashSet**. **TreeSet** also implements the **SortedSet** interface and is a sorted collection. **HashSet** is the most general implementation class in the collections framework. Nothing is revealed about the underlying organization of the elements and there is no ordering. A hash is never sorted. No guarantee is made as to the ordering of the elements in **HashSet**, and the ordering may even change as elements are added and removed. This implementation allows the **null** element.

Here is a description of the **HashSet** class:

Class

java.util.HashSet

Purpose

Instances of the **HashSet** class implement the **Set** interface. Objects of this class should be manipulated using methods from the **Set** interface. **HashSet** collections allow elements with value **null**.

Constructors

- **HashSet( )**

  The no-argument constructor creates an empty set with a default size of 16 and load factor of 0.75.

- **HashSet(Collection** *c* **)**

  The set is constructed and initialized with the elements from the specified collection in the order returned by the collection's iterator. Any duplicate elements in the specified collection are ignored.

- **HashSet(int** *initialCapacity* **)**

  This constructor creates an empty set with the specified initial capacity. Setting a large initial capacity improves performance when you know that the set will grow to be very large.

- **HashSet(int** *initialCapacity,* **float** *loadFactor***)**

  This constructor creates an empty set with the specified initial capacity and load factor. Setting a large initial capacity improves performance for cases in which you know that the set will become very large. The load factor is a number between 0.0 and 1.0 and a measure of how full the set can become. A larger load factor uses memory more efficiently but can increase the time required to find elements.

The `HashSetExample` class in Figure 4-6 demonstrates how to create and initialize a `Set`, add elements, and retrieve elements.

```
package examples.collections;
import java.util.*;
/** A class to demonstrate the use of the Set
  * interface in the java.util package
  */
public class HashSetExample {
    /** Test method for the class
      * @param args not used
      */
    public static void main( String[] args ) {
        // create a set and initialize it
        Set s1 = new HashSet();
        s1.add( new Integer( 6 ) );
        s1.add(  "Hello" );
        s1.add( new Double( -3.423 ) );
        s1.add( new java.util.Date( ) );
        // iterate to display the set values
        Iterator i1 = s1.iterator();
        while ( i1.hasNext() ) {
            System.out.print( i1.next() + " " );
        }
    }
}
```

Figure 4-6   Sample class using a **HashSet** collection

Here is breakdown of key lines in this `HashSetExample` class:

```
Set s1 = new HashSet();
```

This line creates an empty collection of type **HashSet**. All you need to do is call a default constructor. The class knows internally how to manage elements that you give it. You do not need to allocate storage because the collection grows as required.

```
s1.add( new Integer( 6 ) );
s1.add( "Hello" );
s1.add( new Double( -3.423 ) );
s1.add( new java.util.Date( ) );
```

Four lines add four elements to the collection. To simplify this program, only objects of types defined in the J2SDK are used, but any types visible to a program can be added to a collection. Note that the two numbers, 6 and −3.423, must be wrapped in wrapper classes and be added as objects to the collection.

```
Iterator i1 = s1.iterator();
```

Acquiring a cursor to access the elements involves calling the **iterator** method on the collection object. You never know the actual type of the iterator, but need only be assured that it is an instance of a class that implements the **Iterator** interface.

```
while ( i1.hasNext() ) {
```

The most common way to traverse a collection is to code a loop that repeats as long as the **hasNext** method returns **true** to indicate there is another element stored in the collection. How the collection navigates to the next element depends upon the type of the collection. In **HashSet**, you cannot predict which element will be returned next, only that a different element is returned on every call until the **hasNext** method returns **false**.

```
    System.out.print( i1.next() + " " );
}
```

The last step is to access the element by calling **next**. The type returned from **next** is always **Object**, so you must cast if you are going to assign the object to an object reference with any type other than **Object**. This means that you should know what is in the collection or use the reflection to ask the object to tell you its type. This program avoids the issue by simply printing the value on the console using **System.out.print**. As a result, the **toString** methods are called on each **Object**, and dynamic binding ensures that the value is converted for output by the right **toString** method.

The output is similar to

```
6 -3.423 Hello Sat Mar 01 17:52:51 EST 2004
```

If you run this program, you may see the values appear in a different order and the date and time should reflect your current date and time.

The **LinkedHashSet** class is a subclass of **HashSet** that maintains a doubly linked list of its entries. Note that **LinkedHashSet** does not implement **List** and therefore is not used like a **List**: You cannot access individual elements by an index. Nor does **LinkedHashSet** implement **SortedSet**. A **LinkedHashSet** object has a fixed order but is not sorted. Unlike the **Iterator** for a **HashSet** object, the **Iterator** for a **LinkedHashSet** object accesses entries in a predictable order. The result is an ordered set that incurs less overhead than a **TreeSet** object and more overhead than **HashSet**.

To modify this program to use a collection of type **LinkedHashSet** instead of **HashSet**, you need only change one line:

```
Set s1 = new LinkedHashSet();
```

The output of the modified program is

```
6 Hello -3.423 Sat Mar 01 18:11:30 EST 2004
```

The order of elements in the output cannot vary. If you run this program, the only difference you should see from this output is your current date and time.

Use the **LinkedHashSet** class exactly as you would the **HashSet** class. Both classes have the same constructors and set of inherited methods. The only difference is that iterators for **LinkedHashSet** objects access elements in a consistent order. Even if you create a copy by instantiating a **LinkedHashSet** object with a statement such as the following, the second **LinkedHashSet** accesses elements in the same order as the original:

```
Set duplicateLinkedHashSet = new LinkedHashSet( existingHashSet );
```

Note that the previous statement creates two collections with identical contents. They are independent objects, and changes made to one after the preceding statement has been executed are not reflected in the other.

 IdentityHashSet is new with version 1.4 of the J2SDK.

General Purpose Lists

Four concrete classes in the framework are implementations of the **List** interface: **ArrayList**, **LinkedList**, **Vector**, and **Stack**. **Vector** and **Stack** are discussed in the section "Legacy Collection Classes."

The **ArrayList** class implements **List** using arrays. The great advantage of using **ArrayList** instead of an ordinary array is that you have an array with expandable capacity, that you access through a standard collection interface, and that you can easily convert to other collection types. However, you lose the handy array syntax based on the index operator, [ ]. The **LinkedList** class implements a doubly linked list using elements that contain object references to the next and prior element, as shown in Figure 4-3.

Which **List** implementation should you use? That depends on the performance impact of the operations you perform most often on the collection.

- When you access an individual element, usually by calling the **get** method passing the index of the element as argument, the **ArrayList** class is efficient. The implementation of the **get** method can use the argument as the array index and go directly to the element. In contrast, the **LinkedList.get** method must navigate the chain of pointers until it reaches the element at the specified index.

4

- **ArrayList** collections are much less efficient than **LinkedList** collections
on insert and delete. The reason is that the physical location of each element
in an array is tied to the index of the element. When you insert an element
into an **ArrayList** object, the collection class may have to create a new
array with more capacity than the current array and then copy all the elements. Even if there is room for the new element, every element after the
insertion point must be copied into a new position. Similarly, if you delete an
element, all the following elements must be moved forward one position.

In contrast, inserting into a linked list involves creating the new element,
navigating to the insertion point, and then modifying two pointers. The
next-element reference of the element before the insertion point must refer
to the new element. The prior-element reference in the element after the
insertion point must also refer to the new element. Similarly, to delete from a
linked list, alter the next-element reference in the element before the deletion
point to refer to the element after the deletion, and alter the prior-element
reference in the element after the deletion point to refer to the element
before the deletion. Figure 4-7 may help you visualize how an insert or
delete works.

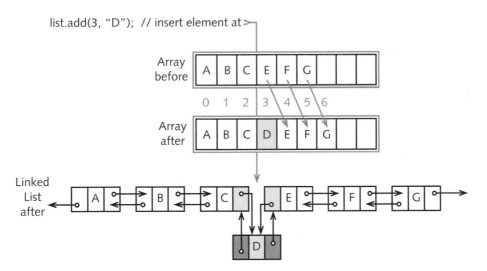

Figure 4-7   Comparing insert on an **ArrayList** and a **List**

Always consider using an **ArrayList** or **LinkedList** collection instead of declaring
an array.

Veteran Java programmers often choose **Vector** in preference to
ArrayList or **LinkedList**. Often the reason is familiarity or habit,
because **Vector** is one of the legacy collection classes. The **Vector** class has
implemented **List** since J2SDK version 1.2.

Use **ArrayList** when you add and remove elements relatively rarely but access elements by index frequently. Following is a description of the **ArrayList** class:

Class

java.util.ArrayList

Purpose

Instances of the **ArrayList** class implement the **List** interface using arrays.

Constructors

- **ArrayList( )**

  The no-argument constructor creates an empty list.

- **ArrayList(Collection** *c* **)**

  The list is constructed and initialized with the elements from the specified collection in the order returned by the collection's iterator.

- **ArrayList(int** *initialCapacity* **)**

  An empty list is created with the specified initial capacity. Setting a large initial capacity improves performance when you know that the list will grow very large.

Use **LinkedList** to reduce the impact of many insert and delete operations on the performance of your program when the set of elements contained in the collection changes frequently. Following is a description of the **LinkedList** class:

Class

java.util.LinkedList

Purpose

Instances of the **LinkedList** class implement the **List** interface using a linked list data structure.

Constructors

- **LinkedList( )**

  The no-argument constructor creates an empty list.

- **LinkedList(Collection** *c* **)**

  The list is constructed and initialized with the elements from the specified collection in the order returned by the collection's iterator.

Recall from the section "Traversing Collections with Iterators" that the `List` interface has two methods to return a cursor: **iterator** and **listIterator**. If you need only the methods **hasNext**, **next**, and **remove**, you can use the generic **iterator**. But when you want to navigate the list both forwards and backwards, and add as well as delete elements, use the **ListIterator** cursor.

The following program, shown in Figure 4-8, demonstrates the use of the **ArrayList** class and the **ListIterator** interface. The class **Line** manipulates an **ArrayList** collection of `java.awt.Point` objects. The class **Point** stores the x and y coordinates of a two-dimensional point and implements the **toString** method to return a textual representation of a point. As with most general-purpose collection classes, this program uses a constructor to get the collection and then operates on the collection using methods of the underlying interface.

```java
package examples.collections;

import java.util.List;
import java.util.ArrayList;
import java.util.ListIterator;
import java.io.PrintStream;
import java.awt.Point;

/** A class to demonstrate the use of the ArrayList
  * and ListIterator types in the java.util package
  */
public class Line {

    private List points = new ArrayList();

    /** Set the starting point for a line
      * @param p the starting point
      */
    public void setStart( Point p ) {
        points.clear();
        points.add( p );
    }

    /** Set the next point in a line
      * @param p the next point
      */
    public void addPoint( Point p ) {
        points.add( p );
    }

    /** Print all the points in a line
      * @param ps the stream where the points
      *                will be printed
      */
```

Figure 4-8   Sample class demonstrating `java.util.ArrayList`

```
public void listPoints( PrintStream ps ) {
   ListIterator li = points.listIterator();
   while ( li.hasNext() ) {
      ps.println( li.next() );
   }
}

/** Test method for the class
 * @param args not used
 */
public static void main( String[] args ) {
   Line x = new Line();
   x.setStart( new Point( 4, 11 ) );
   x.addPoint( new Point( -6, 1 ) );
   x.addPoint( new Point( 2, 3 ) );
   x.listPoints( System.out );
}
}
```

Figure 4-8   Sample class demonstrating `java.util.ArrayList` (continued)

The output is

```
java.awt.Point[x=4,y=11]
java.awt.Point[x=-6,y=1]
java.awt.Point[x=2,y=3]
```

The **main** method of the **Line** class creates the **ArrayList** instance. Notice that the type of the object reference is **List**, not **ArrayList**. Using the **List** interface gives you the option of substituting a different **List** implementation without requiring any change to the rest of the program. The class provides these methods:

- **setStart** starts a new line with one point.

- **addPoint** adds a point to the line.

- **listPoints** outputs a textual representation of the points in the line.

The last of these methods uses a **PrintStream** object, ps, to output each point and a **ListIterator** object, li, to visit each point in turn.

Arrays as Collections

In recognition of the fact that arrays are also aggregations, the collections framework provides the method **toArray** in the **Collection** interface for converting a **Collection** object into an array. Because the reverse conversion is also commonly required the class **Arrays** defines the static method **asList** that converts an array of **Object** instances into a **List** object. Here is a description of the **Arrays** class:

Class

java.util.Arrays

Purpose

This class provides a number of static methods that operate on array objects.

Methods

- **List asList(Object[]** *a* **)**

   This method returns a fixed-size list backed by the supplied array. The returned **List** object does not support operations that increase its size.

You may find the **Arrays** class useful when integrating your programs with APIs that require that arguments of methods be arrays or that return arrays.

Sorted Collections

Whether a collection is sorted is a different matter than whether it is ordered. For example, a collection of dates may be stored in no consistent order, as in a **HashSet** object or in the order in which they were added to the collection, as in as **LinkedHashSet** object. You can also order a **LinkedHashSet** object to visit most-recently used first. In contrast to ordering, sorting imposes some order based on the values contained in the elements in the collection. For example, when a collection of dates is sorted, the order is usually chronological. **String** and **Character** objects sort into lexicographic order, and numbers sort into numerical order.

Lexicographic order is more precise and comprehensive than alphabetic order because case (as in A and a) and accents (as in é, å, and ç) affect the ordering. Also, non-alphabetic characters (digits, punctuation, and control characters) are included in the sort order. In Java, **String** sort order is based on the Unicode value of each character in the string. In Unicode, all uppercase letters come before all lowercase letters, and accented letters come after unaccented letters. See Appendix A for more information on Unicode.

Chronological, lexicographic, and numeric sort orders are the *natural ordering* of dates, character data, and numbers, respectively. You can set up collections to sort on natural order, ascending or descending. You can also create collections that sort in a custom order. For example, a listing of colors custom sorted to the order they appear in a rainbow is red, orange, yellow, green, blue, violet.

Interfaces for Sorted Collections in the Collections Framework

The **SortedSet** interface extends the **Set** interface to define the standard behavior for **Set** objects with iterators that always traverse the elements in sort order. The traversal follows either the ordering defined when the **SortedSet** instance is created or the natural order of the elements. Following is a description of the **SortedSet** interface:

Interface

```
java.util.SortedSet
```

Purpose

Instances of classes that implement **SortedSet** contain a collection of objects and keep the elements in sort order. Duplicate elements are prohibited. All the methods of the **Set** interface operate in the same fashion on instances of **Set** and **SortedSet**, with two exceptions:

- The **Iterator** object returned by the **iterator** method traverses the set in sort order.

- The elements in the array returned by the **toArray** method are stored in sort order.

SortedSet provides the methods listed here in addition to the methods defined by the **Set** interface:

Methods

- **Comparator comparator()**

  Use the **comparator** method to obtain a reference to the **Comparator** object currently in use by the set. If the set uses natural ordering, the value **null** is returned.

- **Object first()**

  The **first** method returns the first element in the set.

- **SortedSet headSet(Object *element*)**

  Use the **headSet** method to obtain a **SortedSet** collection containing all the elements of the set that come before the specified element.

- **Object last()**

  The **last** method returns the last element in the set.

- **SortedSet subSet(int *beginElement,* int *endElement*)**

  The **subSet** method returns a view of the portion of the set between the specified values *beginElement*, inclusive, and *endElement*, exclusive.

- SortedSet tailSet(Object element)

Use the **tailSet** method to obtain a **SortedSet** collection containing all the elements that come after or are equal to the specified element.

Classes of elements that have a natural ordering implement the **java.lang.Comparable** interface. This interface has a single method, **compareTo**, that compares the current object with another object of the same type. Following is a description of the **Comparable** interface:

Interface

java.lang.Comparable

Purpose

The **Comparable** interface defines methods that determine the sort order of elements in a collection where the sort rule defines a natural order that applies to all elements in the collection.

Method

- **int compareTo(Object o)**

This method compares the current object with the specified object and returns a negative integer, a zero, or a positive integer to indicate whether the current object is less than, equal to, or greater than the specified object, respectively.

Figure 4 –9 is an excerpt from a class for which each instance contains a **String** object. The natural order is based on the length of the contained **String**. Objects with shorter strings come before objects with longer strings. If the contained strings have equal length, the objects are considered identical.

```
public class ComparableString implements Comparable {
   String contents;
   ComparableString( String s) {
      contents = s;
   }
   public int compareTo( Object o ) {
      return contents.length() -
         ( (ComparableString) o ).getContents().
         length();
   }
   // rest of class definition
}
```

Figure 4-9   Implementing the **Comparable** interface

In a set of `ComparableString` objects, each element contains a **String** object that is longer than the **String** object in the previous element, and no two elements contain **String** objects with the same length.

If a class does not have a natural ordering, you can use a **Comparator** object to define the ordering. You can also define a **Comparator** class for a collection that has a natural ordering to add a custom order. In other words, a class that defines elements in a collection that implements **SortedSet** can implement either **Comparable**, or **Comparator**, or both interfaces. Implementing **Comparator** is appropriate when the rule for which of two elements comes first varies for every pair of elements. For example, it is hard to express the order red, orange, yellow, green, blue, violet as a parameterized rule. In contrast, the rule in the `ComparableString` class is based on the lengths of the **String** field and can be coded in a common way for all pairs of `ComparableString` objects in the **compareTo** method.

The **Comparator** interface defines two methods. Here is a description of the **Comparator** interface:

Interface

`java.util.Comparator`

Purpose

The **Comparator** interface defines methods that determine the relative ordering of elements in a collection where the sort rule must be stated specifically for each pair of elements.

Classes that implement **Comparable** use classes that implement **Comparator** to compare pairs of objects and to determine their relative ordering.

Methods

- `int compare( Object first, Object second )`

  This method takes two objects as input and returns a negative integer, a zero, or a positive integer to indicate whether the first **Object** argument is less than, equal to, or greater than the second **Object** argument, respectively.

- `boolean equals( Object o )`

  This method is patterned after the **equals** method of the **Object** class. It compares the specified object with this collection for equality.

The next section, "Sorted Set Implementations," contains an example of a collection in which the elements implement **Comparator**.

Sorted Set Implementations

The **TreeSet** class is an implementation of **Set** that uses a binary tree structure internally. By default, the elements are sorted based on a natural ordering, and **TreeSet** guarantees that the elements are kept in ascending order.

Decide which implementation of **Set** to use based on the requirement for data to be stored or visited in order. The **HashSet** and **LinkedHashSet** implementations are not sorted, but **LinkedHashSet** preserves the original insertion order. If this is adequate, use **LinkedHashSet** to avoid the overhead that **TreeSet** consumes in sorting. To keep the elements sorted even when not inserted in the desired order, use **TreeSet**. Here is a description of the **TreeSet** class:

Class

`java.util.TreeSet`

Purpose

Instances of the **TreeSet** class implement both the **Set** and **SortedSet** interfaces and maintain a sorted set. Objects of this class should be manipulated using methods from either the **Set** or **SortedSet** interfaces.

Constructors

- `TreeSet()`

   The no-argument constructor creates an empty set.

- `TreeSet( Collection c )`

   The set is constructed and initialized with the elements from the specified collection according to the natural order of the elements as defined by an implementation of the **Comparable** interface. Duplicate elements in the collection are ignored.

- `TreeSet( Comparator c )`

   This constructor creates an empty set that keeps its elements sorted according to the ordering defined by the supplied **Comparator** object.

- `TreeSet( SortedSet s )`

   This constructor constructs and initializes the set with the elements from the specified collection according to the same order as the specified sorted set. Duplicate elements in the collection are ignored.

Figure 4-10 is a listing of a sample program demonstrating two collections, one that uses a natural order and one that uses a custom order, for a collection of objects of type `ComparativeString`. A `ComparativeString` object contains a field of type **String** with values limited to word representations of the decimal digits, case-insensitive.

Therefore, a `ComparativeString` collection can hold zero, One, Two, ...NINE. The natural order sorts on the length of the contained **String** field, so one comes before zero and zero comes before three. A custom order sorts on the numeric value of the digit represented.

In this listing, the implementation of the methods in the **Comparator** interface is shown in bold.

```
package examples.collections;
import java.util.*;
/** A class to demonstrate the use of Comparable
 * and Comparator interfaces with a TreeSet
 */
public class ComparativeString implements
       Comparable, Comparator {
  String contents = null;
  final String[] digits =
      { "zero", "one", "two", "three", "four",
        "five", "six", "seven", "eight", "nine" };
/** Default constructor needed to use as Comparator
 */
  ComparativeString() {
  };
/** Constructor that builds an instance that has
 * contents used with comparator. Allows only
 * words that represent digits: "zero", "ONE",...
 * @param the string reprentation of a digit
 * @throws java.lang.Exception if String not
 * recognized
 */
  ComparativeString(String s) throws Exception {
     for (int i = 0; i < digits.length; i++) {
         if (digits[i].equals(s.toLowerCase())) {
             contents = s;
             break;
         }
     }
     if (contents == null) {
        throw new Exception(s +
           " is not allowed in collection");
     }
  }
/**
 * CompareTo implements method defined in Camparable
 * @param The object to compare with the current
 * @return <0 if this is shorter, 0 if both strings
 * have the same length and > 0 if this is longer
 */
```

Figure 4-10   A program that uses **Comparable**, **Comparator**, and **TreeSet**

```
    public int compareTo( Object o ) {
        return contents.length() -
            ( (ComparativeString) o ).getContents().
                length();
    }
/**    Compare implements method defined in Comparator
 * @param Two objects to compare
 * @return <0, 0, or >0 based value of digits
 * represented by contained strings
 */
    public int compare(Object o1, Object o2) {
        int i1 = -1, i2 = -1;
        String c1 = ((ComparativeString) o1).
          getContents().toLowerCase();
        String c2 = ((ComparativeString) o2).
          getContents().toLowerCase();
        for (int i = 0; i < digits.length; i++) {
            if (i1 < 0 && c1.equals(digits[i])) {
                i1 = i;
                if (i2 >= 0)
                    break;
            }
            if (i2 < 0 && c2.equals(digits[i])) {
                i2 = i;
                if (i1 >= 0)
                    break;
            }
        }
        return i1 - i2;
    }
/**    Equals implements method defined in Comparator
 * @param object to test against current
 * @return true if contained Strings are equal
 * represented by contained strings
 */
    public boolean equals(Object o) {
        String c = ((ComparativeString) o).
            getContents().toLowerCase();
        return contents.toLowerCase().equals(c);
    }
/**    Test method for Compative strings
 * @param arguments not used
 */
    public static void main(String[] args) {
        TreeSet mySet = new TreeSet(
            new ComparativeString() );
        try {
            mySet.add(new ComparativeString("FiVe"));
            mySet.add(new ComparativeString("Zero"));
            mySet.add(new ComparativeString("Six" ));
            mySet.add(new ComparativeString( "oNe" ));
```

Figure 4-10   A program that uses Comparable, Comparator, and TreeSet
            (continued)

```
                  mySet.add(new ComparativeString("five"));
                  mySet.add(new ComparativeString("two"));
                  mySet.add(new ComparativeString("EiGhT"));
                  mySet.add(new ComparativeString("three"));
                  mySet.add(new ComparativeString("NINE"));
                  mySet.add(new ComparativeString("fOUr"));
                  mySet.add(new ComparativeString("ten"));
                  mySet.add(new ComparativeString("SEVEN"));
               } catch (Exception e) {
                  System.err.println(e.getMessage());
               }
               Iterator i1 = mySet.iterator();
               while (i1.hasNext()) {
                  String s = ((ComparativeString) i1.next()).
                     getContents();
                  System.out.println(s);
               }
               TreeSet yourSet = new TreeSet( );
               try {
                  yourSet.add(new ComparativeString("FiVe"));
                  yourSet.add(new ComparativeString("Zero"));
                  yourSet.add(new ComparativeString("Six"));
                  yourSet.add(new ComparativeString("oNe"));
                  yourSet.add(new ComparativeString("five"));
                  yourSet.add(new ComparativeString("two"));
                  yourSet.add(new ComparativeString("EiGhT"));
                  yourSet.add(new ComparativeString("three"));
                  yourSet.add(new ComparativeString("NINE"));
                  yourSet.add(new ComparativeString("fOUr"));
                  yourSet.add(new ComparativeString("ten"));
                  yourSet.add(new ComparativeString("SEVEN"));
               } catch (Exception e) {
                  System.err.println(e.getMessage());
               }

               Iterator i2 = yourSet.iterator();
               while (i2.hasNext()) {
                  String s = ((ComparativeString) i2.next()).
                     getContents();
                  System.out.println(s);
               }
            }
            /**
             * Returns the contents.
             * @return String
             */
            public String getContents() {
               return contents;
            }
```

Figure 4-10   A program that uses `Comparable`, `Comparator`, and `TreeSet`
(continued)

```
/**
 * Sets the contents.
 * @param contents The String contents to set
 */
public void setContents(String contents) {
    this.contents = contents;
}
}
```

4

Figure 4-10   A program that uses `Comparable`, `Comparator`, and `TreeSet` (continued)

The first part of the **main** method creates a **TreeSet** instance using the custom order defined by the method `ComparativeString.compare`, adds `ComparativeString` elements, and then displays the contents of **TreeSet**. The output of this first part is

```
ten is not allowed in collection
Zero
oNe
two
three
fOUr
FiVe
Six
EiGhT
NINE
```

The test **main** method next creates a **TreeSet** collection using the natural order of `ComparativeString` (defined by the method `ComparativeString.compareTo`), adds elements, and then displays the contents of the **TreeSet** object. The output of this second part is:

```
ten is not allowed in collection
Six
FiVe
EiGhT
```

Note that when the natural order is used, elements that contain **String** objects with the same length are considered identical. Therefore, the collection stores only Six, the first three-character string; FiVe, the first four-character string; and EiGhT, the first five-character string.

For another example of a class that implements **Comparator**, see Figure 14-14. There, the **Comparator** is declared as an anonymous inner class of the **TreeMapExample** class.

Maps

A map is an abstraction for an aggregation of key-value, or name-value, pairs. Each entry is an object that has two parts and is therefore sometimes called a pair. One part is called the key or name, and the other part is called the value. The key part has a value that identifies an entry in the map and sometimes determines where the entry is stored. The value part is the information stored in the element. For example, if a university course catalog is viewed as a map, each course has a key, such as "CSC101," and a value that could include the course description, scheduling information, instructor's name, and lecture location.

Typically, the key is a single value that is sufficient to identify one element. For example, in a registry of vehicles, the key could be the license number and the value could be other information about the vehicle. Usually, keys must be unique but duplication of values is allowed.

Maps are extremely useful for managing large numbers of objects that lend themselves to being identified by a key. For example, if map entries represent records stored in databases, the key part of an entry can represent the primary key of a row in a table while the value part of the entry represents the remaining fields in the row. The collections framework includes a set of types that encapsulate maps and entries in maps. Figure 4-11 shows these types, how they are related to each other, and some of the collection types.

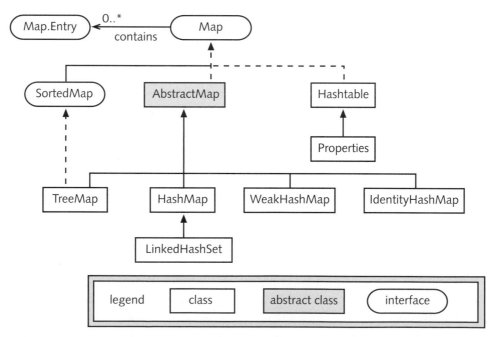

Figure 4-11   The types in the collections framework for maps

~~LinkedHashMap~~ and ~~IdentityHashMap~~ are new with version 1.4 of the J2SDK. **Hashtable** and **Properties** have been available since the original version of Java, but were retrofitted to implement **Map** in the Java 2 platform. All other types were introduced in version 1.2 of the J2SDK. **WeakHashMap** was added at the same time as weak references in version 1.2.

Interfaces for Maps

Two interfaces in the collections framework define the behavior of maps: **Map** and **SortedMap**. A third interface, **Map.Entry**, defines the behavior of elements extracted from **Map**. The fundamental behavior of a **Map** collection is that entries are stored according to their keys, and the most efficient way to access an element is by its key.

The **Map** interface does not extend the **Collection** interface. Instead, it is the fundamental interface for aggregations that contains key-value pairs and in which keys must have unique values. Both the keys and the values are object references, because the **Map** interface defines methods that work on instances of **Object**.

- The method **keySet** returns all the keys in the **Map** as a **Set** object.

- The method **values** returns a **Collection** containing all the values in the **Map**.

- The method **entrySet** returns the entire contents of the **Map** as a **Set** of **Map.Entry** objects.

The **Map.Entry** interface is described after the **Map** interface.

Interface

java.util.Map

Purpose

Instances of classes that implement **Map** are objects that contain key-value pairs with unique keys.

Methods

- **void clear()**

  The **clear** method removes all the key-value pairs from the map. This is an optional operation.

- **boolean containsKey(Object** *key* **)**

  This method returns **true** if the map contains the specified key.

- **boolean containsValue(Object** *value* **)**

  This method returns **true** if the map contains the specified value.

- **Set entrySet( )**

  To obtain a view of the key-value pairs as a set of **Map.Entry** objects, use this method. The object returned is an instance of **Set** because keys guarantee unique **Map.Entry** objects. The **Set** object returned does not support the **add** or **addAll** methods.

- **boolean equals(Object o)**

  This method is patterned after the **equals** method of the **Object** class. For this interface, it compares the specified object with the current instance of **Map** for equality.

- **Object get(Object key)**

  Use this method to obtain the value that is stored with the specified key.

- **int hashCode( )**

  This method is patterned after the **hashCode** method of the **Object** class. Here, it returns the hash code value for this map.

- **boolean isEmpty( )**

  The **isEmpty** method returns **true** if this map contains no key-value pairs.

- **Set keySet( )**

  To obtain a view of the keys contained in this map, use this method. The object returned is an instance of **Set** because keys in **Map** must be unique. The **Set** object returned does not support the **add** or **addAll** methods.

- **Object put(Object key, Object value)**

  The **put** method adds a key-value pair to this map and returns the previous value associated with the given key. It returns **null** if the key did not previously exist in the map. This is an optional operation.

- **void putAll(Map map)**

  Use the **putAll** method to add all the key-value pairs from the specified map. This is an optional operation.

- **Object remove(Object key)**

  The **remove** method removes the key-value pair associated with the given key and returns the value associated with the key. If the key does not exist in this map, **null** is returned. This is an optional operation.

- **int size( )**

  The number of key-value pairs in this map is returned by the **size** method.

- Collection values()

  Use the **values** method to obtain a copy of the values in this map as a
  Collection object. Because values are not guaranteed to be unique, the type of
  the returned object is **Collection** and not **Set**. The object returned does not
  support the **add** or **addAll** methods.

The definition of the **Map.Entry** interface is nested within the definition of the **Map**
interface. See Chapter 2 for an explanation of nested type definitions.

Interface

java.util.Map.Entry

Purpose

Instances of classes that implement **Map.Entry** represent key-value pairs when a **Map**
object is viewed as a **Set**.

Methods

- **boolean equals(Object** *o* **)**

  This method is patterned after the **equals** method of the **Object** class. For this
  interface, **equals** compares the specified object with this map entry for equality.

- **Object getKey()**

  Use this method to obtain the key for the map entry.

- **Object getValue()**

  Use this method to obtain the value for the map entry.

- **int hashCode()**

  This method is patterned after the **hashCode** method of the **Object** class. Here, it
  returns the hash code value for the map entry.

- **Object setValue(Object** *value* **)**

  The **setValue** method changes the value for the key-value pair and returns the
  previous value. This is an optional operation.

The **SortedMap** interface extends the **Map** interface to define the standard behavior for
a map in which the key-value pairs are always sorted. The sort order is the natural ordering of the keys or some other ordering defined when **SortedMap** is created. Classes of
keys that have a natural ordering implement the **java.lang.Comparable** interface.
Create a **Comparator** object to define a custom ordering.

Interface

`java.util.SortedMap`

Purpose

Instances of classes that implement **SortedMap** are objects that contain key-value pairs that are maintained in sorted order by key. All the methods of the **Map** interface operate in the same fashion for objects of classes that implement **SortedMap**. The methods that the **SortedMap** interface defines and the methods that the **Map** interface defines are listed here:

Methods

- **Comparator comparator( )**

  Use the **comparator** method to obtain a reference to the **Comparator** object currently in use by this map for ordering its keys. If this map uses the natural ordering of its keys, the value **null** is returned.

- **Object firstKey( )**

  The **firstKey** method returns the key of the first key-value pair for this map.

- **SortedMap headMap(Object *key*)**

  Use the **headMap** method to obtain a **SortedMap** collection containing all the key-value pairs of this map for which the key is less than the specified key.

- **Object lastKey( )**

  The **lastKey** method returns the key of the last key-value pair in this map.

- **SortedMap subMap(int *beginKey*, int *endKey*)**

  The **subMap** method returns a view of the portion of this map with key-value pairs having a key value between the specified *beginKey*, inclusive, and *endKey*, exclusive.

- **SortedMap tailMap(Object *key*)**

  Use the **tailMap** method to obtain a **SortedMap** collection containing all the key-value pairs of this map with a key value that is greater than or equal to the specified key.

Unsorted Map Implementations

Seven concrete framework classes implement the **Map** interface: **HashMap**, **IdentityHashMap**, **LinkedHashMap**, **TreeMap**, **WeakHashMap**, **Hashtable**, and **Properties**. The **TreeMap** class also implements the **SortedMap** interface and is

discussed in the section "Sorted Map Implementations." The Hashtable and
Properties legacy classes are discussed in the section "Legacy Collection Classes."

The **HashMap** class uses a hash table as its underlying data structure for organizing the key-value pairs. No guarantee is made as to the ordering of the keys in a **HashMap** collection, and the ordering may change as key-value pairs are added and removed. This implementation allows both **null** values and the **null** key.

4

Class

```
java.util.HashMap
```

Purpose

Instances of the **HashMap** class implement the **Map** interface using a hash table data structure. Objects of this class should be manipulated using methods from the **Map** interface.

Constructors

- **HashMap( )**

  The no-argument constructor creates an empty map.

- **HashMap(Map *m*)**

  This constructor creates and initializes the map with the elements from the specified map in the order returned by the map's iterator.

- **HashMap(int *initialCapacity*)**

  This constructor creates an empty map with the specified initial capacity. Setting a large initial capacity improves performance when you know that the map will become very large.

- **HashMap(int *initialCapacity*, float *loadFactor*)**

  This constructor creates an empty map with the specified initial capacity and load factor. Setting a large initial capacity improves performance when you know that the map will become very large. The load factor is a number between 0.0 and 1.0 and a measure of how full the map is allowed to become. A larger load factor uses memory more efficiently, but can increase the time required to find keys.

The sample program in Figure 4-12 is the **HashMap** example class. The **main** method creates a **HashMap** collection and populates it with data. It then demonstrates several of the **Map** methods by retrieving and printing information about **Map**, including **Set** of keys and **Collection** of values.

```
package examples.collections;
import java.util.*;
/** A class to demonstrate the use of the HashMap
  */
public class HashMapExample {
   /** Test method for the class
     * @param args not used
     */
   public static void main(String[] args) {
      // create a map and intialize it
      Map m1 = new HashMap();
      m1.put("height", new Integer(72));
      m1.put("weight", new Integer(180));
      m1.put("age", new Integer(21));
      m1.put("shoe", new Integer(11));
      m1.put("sleeve", new Integer(35));
      // print information about the HashMap
      System.out.println("The HashMap holds " +
         m1.size() + " elements");
      System.out.println("The keys are: ");
      Set keySet = m1.keySet();
      Iterator ikey = keySet.iterator();
      while (ikey.hasNext()) {
         System.out.println("\t" + ikey.next());
      }
      System.out.println("The values are: ");
      Collection valueCol = m1.values();
      Iterator ival = valueCol.iterator();
      while (ival.hasNext()) {
         System.out.println("\t" + ival.next());
      }
      System.out.print(
         "The value for key \"age\" is ");
      System.out.println(
         ( (Integer) m1.get("age") ).toString() );
      System.out.print(
         "The value for key \"hat\" is ");
      System.out.println( (
         (Integer) m1.get("hat") ).toString() );
   }
}
```

Figure 4-12   Using a `HashMap`

The output of the program listed in Figure 4–12 is

```
The HashMap holds 5 elements
The keys are:
   age
   shoe
```

```
        height
        sleeve
        weight
    The values are:
        21
        11
        72
        35
        180
    The value for key "age" is 21
    The value for key "hat" is      java.lang.NullPointerException
        at examples.collections.HashMapExample.main
            (HashMapExample.java:38)
    Exception in thread "main"
```

Note that the map does not contain an entry with the key "hat" so the attempt to get that entry causes an exception of type **NullPointerException**.

The **LinkedHashMap** class extends class **HashMap** and not only adds the behavior of maintaining a doubly linked list running through its elements, but also lets you select whether the element order is based on insertion sequence or last retrieval time. The **Iterator** object for a **LinkedHashMap** collection follows the linked list to access elements in a predictable order.

Class

java.util.LinkedHashMap

Purpose

The **LinkedHashMap** class extends class **HashMap** with an implementation that provides a predictable order of element access by the **Iterator** object.

Constructors

- **LinkedHashMap()**

  The no–argument constructor creates an empty **LinkedHashMap** instance with a default size of 16 and load factor of 0.75.

- **LinkedHashMap(Map *m*)**

  This constructor builds a **LinkedHashMap** object that holds the same elements as the supplied **Map**. If the supplied **Map** is also a **LinkedHashMap** object, the order of the original map carries over into the new map.

- **LinkedHashMap(int *initialCapacity*)**

  This constructor creates an empty **LinkedHashMap** instance with the specified initial capacity. Setting a large initial capacity improves performance when you know that the map will become very large.

- **LinkedHashMap(int** *initialCapacity,* **float** *loadFactor* **)**

   This constructor creates an empty **LinkedHashMap** instance with the specified initial capacity and load factor. Setting a large initial capacity improves performance when you know that the map will become very large. The load factor is a number between 0.0 and 1.0 and is a measure of how full the map is allowed to become. A larger load factor uses memory more efficiently, but can increase the time required to find keys.

- **LinkedHashMap(int** *initialCapacity,* **float** *loadFactor,* **boolean** *accessOrder* **)**

   In addition to building an empty map with the specified initial capacity and load factor, this constructor gives you some control over the order in which elements are accessed. When the third argument is **false**, the default cursor lists elements in the order in which they were originally inserted into the map. When the third argument is **true**, the cursor lists most recently accessed first.

Methods

- **void clear( )**

   The **clear** method removes all elements from this map.

- **boolean containsValue(Object** *value* **)**

   The **containsValue** method returns **true** if the map contains one or more keys mapped to the specified value.

- **Object get(Object** *key* **)**

   The **get** method returns the value for the specified key.

- **boolean removeEldestEntry(Map.Entry** *eldest* **)**

   This protected method is called by methods **put** and **putAll** after they insert a new entry into the map. When you subclass the **LinkedHashMap** class, you can implement this method to create a map that can grow until a criteria is reached, and then stay the same size by deleting the oldest entry when a new entry is added.

Figure 4-13 shows how you can create a subclass of the **LinkedHashMap** class that not only returns elements in order, but has a size limit and retains only the most recent elements when the size limit is reached. The method that enforces the size limit is shown in bold.

```
                                        4
         extends LinkedHashMap {
   private static final int MAX_ENTRIES = 5;
   protected boolean removeEldestEntry(
      Map.Entry eldest) {
      return size( ) > MAX_ENTRIES;
   }
/** Test method for the class
 * @param args not used
 */
   public static void main(String[] args) {
      // create a set and initialize it
      Map lhmap5 = new LinkedHashMapFive();
      for (int i = 0; i < 10; i++) {
         lhmap5.put(new Integer(i), "*" );
         Set contents= lhmap5.entrySet();
          String output = "LinkedHashMap5 contents:";
          Iterator cursor = contents.iterator();
         while (cursor.hasNext()) {
            Map.Entry  me = (Map.Entry)
               cursor.next();
            output += " " + me.getKey() +
                      ":" + me.getValue();
         }
         System.out.println( output );
      }
   }
}
```

Figure 4-13   A subclass of `LinkedHashMap` that retains a fixed number of most recent elements

The output from the `LinkedHashMapFive` class is

```
LinkedHashMap5 contents: 0:*
LinkedHashMap5 contents: 0:* 1:*
LinkedHashMap5 contents: 0:* 1:* 2:*
LinkedHashMap5 contents: 0:* 1:* 2:* 3:*
LinkedHashMap5 contents: 0:* 1:* 2:* 3:* 4:*
LinkedHashMap5 contents: 1:* 2:* 3:* 4:* 5:*
LinkedHashMap5 contents: 2:* 3:* 4:* 5:* 6:*
LinkedHashMap5 contents: 3:* 4:* 5:* 6:* 7:*
LinkedHashMap5 contents: 4:* 5:* 6:* 7:* 8:*
LinkedHashMap5 contents: 5:* 6:* 7:* 8:* 9:*
```

Sorted Map Implementations

The collections framework contains one general-purpose class that implements a sorted map: **TreeMap**. The **TreeMap** class sorts elements based on key values and guarantees they will be kept in order. If the natural ordering of elements is used, a **TreeMap** object guarantees that the elements are kept in ascending order.

Class

java.util.TreeMap

Purpose

Instances of the **TreeMap** class maintain a sorted map. Objects of this class should be manipulated using methods from the **Map** or **SortedMap** interfaces.

Constructors

- **TreeMap( )**

  The no-argument constructor creates an empty map.

- **TreeMap(Map *m*)**

  This constructor creates and initializes a new instance of **TreeMap** with the elements from the specified map according to the elements' natural order.

- **TreeMap(Comparator *c*)**

  This constructor creates an empty map that will keep its keys sorted according to the ordering defined by the supplied **Comparator** object.

- **TreeMap(SortedMap *s*)**

  This constructor creates and initializes the map with the elements from the specified map maintaining the same order as the specified sorted map.

The criteria for choosing one of the **Map** implementations should be based first on whether the order of element access matters. If order is not important, use **HashMap** because it is the fastest of the three. Then consider whether the options provided by **LinkedHashMap** are adequate. **LinkedHashMap** does not have the sorting overhead of **TreeMap**. But if you want the map sorted by key value, use **TreeMap**.

The sample program in Figure 4-14 builds a **TreeMap** collection from a **HashMap object**. The comparator for the new subclasss of **TreeMap** is an anonymous inner class declared in the bold lines in Figure 4-14. See Chapter 2 for a description of inner classes. This comparator has the effect of reversing the natural order of the elements in the **Map**. The keys are **String** objects, so the natural order is lexicographic. In the output from this class, you can see that the **Map.Entry** elements are retrieved in reverse lexicographic order.

```
package examples.collections;
import java.util.*;
/** A class to demonstrate the use of the Map
  * and SortedMap interfaces in the java.util package
  */
public class TreeMapExample {
    /** Test method for the class
      * @param args not used
      */
    public static void main(String[] args) {
        // create a map and intialize it
        Map m1 = new HashMap();
        m1.put("height", new Integer(72));
        m1.put("weight", new Integer(180));
        m1.put("age", new Integer(21));
        m1.put("Shoe", new Integer(11));
        m1.put("sleeve", new Integer(35));
        // use an anonymous inner class to define the
        // Comparator for the SortedMap
        SortedMap m2 = new TreeMap(new Comparator() {
            public int compare(Object o1, Object o2) {
                // reverse the natural ordering
                Comparable c1 = (Comparable) o1;
                Comparable c2 = (Comparable) o2;
                return - (c1.compareTo(c2));
            }
        });
        m2.putAll(m1);
        // get a view of the map as a set
        Set s2 = m2.entrySet();
        // iterate to display the set values
        Iterator i2 = s2.iterator();
        while (i2.hasNext()) {
            Map.Entry me = (Map.Entry) i2.next();
            System.out.print(me.getKey() + ":" +
                me.getValue() + " ");
        }
        System.out.println();
    }
}
```

Figure 4-14   Using a `TreeMap`

The output of the `TreeMapExample` program is:

```
weight:180 sleeve:35 height:72 age:21 Shoe:11
```

Two subclasses of **HashMap** are designed for use in specialized purposes: **IdentityHashMap** and **WeakHashMap**.

- In an **IdentityHashMap** collection, two keys are considered equal when comparing them with the equality operator returns **true**, regardless of what the **equals** method returns. In other words, **key1** is equal to **key2** only if the expression **key1==key2** is **true**. This behavior does not conform to the contract of the **Map** interface because the **equals** operator should be used to compare key objects in implementations of **Map**. However, the deviation is intentional to allow for scenarios where reference-equality is required.

Possible uses for an **IdentityHashMap** collection involve serialization or deep copying. For an explanation of deep copying, see the section "Cloning Objects" in Chapter 2. Another possibility is maintaining proxy objects. *Proxies* are objects that stand in for other objects in your application.

■   The **WeakHashMap** implementation of **Map** takes advantage of the support for weak references. See the Section "Reference Objects and the Garbage Collector" in Chapter 2 for an introduction to weak references. In a **WeakHashMap** collection, the references to the keys are weak references. If the only reference to a key is in the collection, the weak reference does not prevent the garbage collector from deleting the key. When the key has been removed by the garbage collector, the entry is effectively deleted from the map.

One possible use of a **WeakHashMap** is to provide a cache of objects that represents data extracted from a database.

The behavior of **WeakHashMap** is such that entries can disappear when there is nothing in the code to explain the change. For example, two calls of the **size** method may return different values for no apparent reason. Typically, this behavior is desirable when the collection is used as an object cache. For example, the map may be loaded with data extracted from a database. As long as some other class in the application is holding a reference to the key and potentially working with the entry, the key has a strong reference and is not a candidate for garbage collection. When all references outside the map are gone, only the weak reference remains, and the garbage collector may call the **finalizer** method on the key object.

WeakHashMap collections are useful because they save you the work of explicitly removing obsolete entries. Before you use a collection of this type, consider carefully the implications of weak references, as explained in Chapter 2. To avoid unexpected behavior, use key classes that are compared for equality using the == operator. You cannot re-create a key when all strong references to it are gone. Instead, for a database cache, you may have to implement an algorithm that returns to the database to retrieve data and reload the cache when necessary.

WeakHashMap is the only the general-purpose implementation class in the framework that does not implement the interfaces **Cloneable** and **Serializable**.

Legacy Collection Classes

Before the collections framework was added to Java in the Java 2 platform, there were six collection classes in the **java.util** package: **BitSet**, **Stack**, **Vector**, **Dictionary**, **Hashtable**, and **Properties**; and one cursor interface: **Enumeration**. Figure 4-15 shows how these types relate to the types introduced in version 1.2 of the J2SDK.

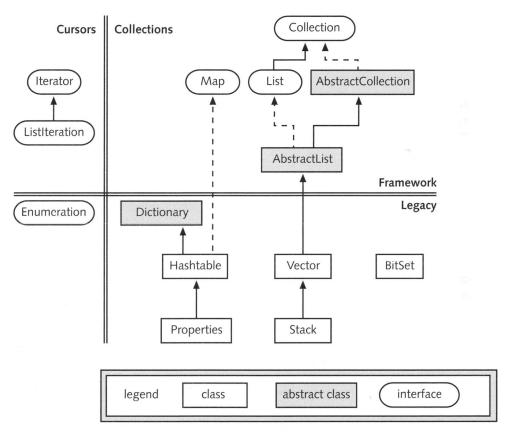

Figure 4-15   Relationships among legacy and newer collection classes

These classes were, and still are, useful, but they do not have common interfaces. Therefore, they lack the flexibility of the classes introduced with the collections framework. Most of the legacy collection types have been retrofitted into the framework by modifying them to implement one of the interfaces in the framework. In Figure 4-15, you can see that **Vector** and **Stack** now implement **List**; **Hashtable** and **Properties** now implement **Map**.

The legacy classes are not deprecated; you can continue to use them. The exception is that the abstract **Dictionary** class is obsolete and has been replaced by the **Map** interface. The other five classes provide aggregations that are not duplicated in the collections framework, and some are required by other core APIs. Figure 4-16 summarizes the purpose of the six legacy classes.

Legacy Class	Purpose
BitSet	Use **BitSet** collections to contain sets of bits or true-false flags. The collection is dynamically sized, so you can add elements without worrying about exceeding limits. Simply setting or clearing a value at an index value that is beyond the current size extends the set. When you extend a **BitSet** object, all the added elements are given the default value of **false**. A **BitSet** collection never shrinks.
Dictionary	This abstract class defines methods for storing elements of type **Object**, according to key values that are also of type **Object**. **Dictionary** is the superclass of the **Hashtable** class, but is otherwise not available for use. For new collections, implement **Map** and do not extend **Dictionary**.
Hashtable	Instances of the **Hashtable** class are hash tables.
Properties	The **Properties** class extends **Hashtable** to a collection of key-value pairs, where each key and each value is a **String** object. The key for each item in the **Properties** table is the name of a property.
Stack	The **Stack** class has methods for adding and removing objects according to the last-in first-out rule. The **Stack** class extends **Vector** and adds methods for pushing, popping, and peeking into the stack.
Vector	An instance of **Vector** is an indexed list of objects, much like an array. Use a **Vector** when you need greater flexibility than arrays provide. The main advantage is that a **Vector** collection can grow and shrink in size as required, but an array has a fixed size. The **Vector** class also has several methods that are not available for arrays. Because **Vector** objects are ordered, they are more efficient than **Hashtable** objects for enumeration purposes.

Figure 4-16   Legacy collection classes

Do the new collection classes replace the legacy classes? The **BitSet**, **Properties**, and **Stack** legacy classes have no close equivalent. However, an **ArrayList** is usually appropriate in the same situations as **Vector**, and **HashSet** can be used rather than **Hashtable**. There are some subtle differences between **ArrayList** and **Vector** and between **HashSet** and **Hashtable**, especially with regard to using their cursors in multithreaded programs. See the section "Comparing Legacy and Collections Framework Cursors" for more details.

Comparing Legacy and Collections Framework Cursors

Before the collections framework was introduced, using the **Enumeration** interface was the standard way to traverse collections. All the legacy collection classes except **BitSet** implement or inherit the method **elements**. Call **elements** to obtain an **Enumeration** object for the current collection and then use the returned **Enumeration** object as your cursor.

Interface

```
java.util.Enumeration
```

Purpose

This interface defines the methods you can use to traverse the objects in a collection of type **Vector**, **Stack**, **Hashtable**, or **Properties**.

Methods

- **boolean hasMoreElements()**

  Call **hasMoreElements** to determine whether you can extract an object from the collection. The method returns **true** if an object is available and **false** if the collection is empty or has been completely traversed.

- **Object nextElement()**

  Call **nextElement** to obtain the next object in a collection. If no object is available, the method throws the exception **NoSuchElementException**. You can prevent the exception by calling **hasMoreElements** first and then calling this method only if **hasMoreElements** returns **true**.

As with **Iterator** objects, you cannot create **Enumeration** cursors for collections directly. Instead, call the **elements** method on a legacy collection, much like you call **iterator** or **listIterator** on one of the classes introduced with the framework. Do not write any new collections to use **Enumeration** objects for iterators. Using **Iterator** objects instead is strongly recommended.

Using an **Enumeration** is similar to using an **Iterator**. Here is a snippet of code that navigates **Vector** object v:

```
Enumeration e = v.elements( );
While ( e.hasMoreElements( ) ) {
   Element element = (Element) e.nextElement( );
   // work with element
}
```

There are some issues related to using collections in multithreaded programs. Chapter 5 describes multithreaded programs in detail. For this discussion, accept that more than one client class can run your program simultaneously. When that happens, each client has what is called a *thread*. All threads share one copy of the code and access the same instance and class variables, including data in collections. In other words, they concurrently access collections. If one thread changes an element in a collection, deletes it, or moves it by inserting another element while another thread is working with the same collection, the net effect can be unpredictable. Certainly the data becomes suspect. What should happen if two threads make different changes to the same element at the same time?

This is a particular concern for collections, because they are often used to store data for relatively long periods during execution time. If the contents of the collections are written to a database, it is very important that the integrity of the data not be corrupted. Otherwise the ramifications could extend far beyond the correct operation of one program.

The methods of the legacy collection classes are *synchronized*. That means that only one thread can call the method at a time. Concurrent execution of individual methods is prohibited. This helps to make the collections thread-safe. The classes in the collections framework do not have synchronization built in, for performance reasons, so you should consider using the wrapper classes described in the section "Wrapper Implementations for Collections."

Synchronization does not eliminate another thread-related problem. What if one thread deletes or inserts an element when another thread is using a cursor to navigate the collection? If the cursor is an **Enumeration** object, its position may be invalidated. In contrast, the **Iterator** objects returned by implementations in the collections framework are fail-fast cursors. A *fail-fast cursor* does not allow processing to continue if the collection it is traversing changes in ways that are out of the cursor's control.

The methods of **Iterator** objects throw a **ConcurrentModificationException** exception if the collection is modified structurally using methods other than those of the **Iterator** interface after the **Iterator** object is created. The rationale for throwing the exception is that it is better to trap the potential source of a problem than to suffer the undefined behavior to which such a modification could lead. Unfortunately there are situations where the exception mechanism cannot guarantee integrity of the cursor. You should consider building in additional checks if your application allows no tolerance for any lost or corrupted operations on the collection.

Note that **Vector** and **Stack** implement **List**. Therefore, you can use an object of type **Iterator**, **ListIterator**, or **Enumeration** as the cursor.

Legacy Collection Implementations

This section introduces the five legacy collection classes that you can use, in alphabetic order.

Typical use of a **Bitset** collection is to model a mask that is a collection of 1/0 or yes/no or on/off flags. Use a **Bitset** object in preference to an array of **boolean** values, or instead of performing bit manipulations on an integer in which you treat every bit as a separate item of data.

Class

```
java.util.BitSet
```

Purpose

A **BitSet** object contains a number of bits, each of which represents a **true** or **false** value.

4

Constructors

- **BitSet( )**

  BitSet(int *size* **)**

  The constructor creates an empty set. You can optionally specify an initial size.

Methods

- **void and(BitSet** *b* **)**

  The **and** method performs a logical AND operation on the bits in the current object and specified **BitSet** object.

- **void andNot(BitSet** *b* **)**

  The **andNot** method clears all of the bits in the current **BitSet** object whose corresponding bit is set in the specified **BitSet** object.

- **void clear(int** *position* **)**

  The **clear** method clears the bit in the specified position so that its value, when returned by **get**, is **false**.

- **boolean get(int** *position* **)**

  The **get** method returns **true** if the bit in the specified position is set and **false** otherwise.

- **int length( )**

  The **length** method returns the index of the highest bit set in the **BitSet** object plus one.

- **void or(BitSet** *b* **)**

  The **or** method performs a logical OR operation on the bits in the current object and specified **BitSet** object.

- **void set(int** *position* **)**

  The **set** method sets the bit in the specified position so that its value, when returned by **get**, is **true**.

- **int size( )**

  The **size** method returns the number of positions of space actually in use by the **BitSet** object.

- **void xor(BitSet** *b* **)**

  The **xor** method performs a logical EXCLUSIVE OR operation on the bits in the current object and the specified **BitSet** object.

A **Hashtable** is similar in purpose to a **HashSet** except that it is the superclass to the **Properties** collection and can be traversed using an **Enumeration**.

Class

```
java.util.Hashtable
```

Purpose

The **Hashtable** class extends **Dictionary** and implements **Map**. You can use a **Hashtable** collection for key-value pairs when the keys are instances of classes that implement the **hashCode** and **equals** methods.

Constructors

- **Hashtable( )**

  Hashtable(int *capacity* **)**

  Hashtable(int *capacity***, float** *load* **)**

  When you create an empty **Hashtable**, you can optionally specify a capacity and load factor. The load factor must be a number between 0.0 and 1.0 and is a measure of how full the **Hashtable** is allowed to become. A larger load factor uses memory more efficiently, but can increase the time required to look up keys. The default initial capacity is 11 and load factor is 0.75.

Method

- **Enumeration elements( )**

  The **elements** method returns an **Enumeration** cursor for **Hashtable**.

Use the methods of the **Map** interface to operate on a hash table.

Collections of type **Properties** contain key-value pairs where both the key and value are **String** objects. Key-value pairs of this form are used in diverse situations, so **Properties** is a useful class. For example, you can use a **Properties** collection to record initialization parameters for a program. Then, store the parameters to a file by calling the **save** method on the **Properties** object. On a subsequent run, call the **load** method to reinstate the **Properties** object. For example, if your program has a graphical user interface (GUI), you can store the size and position of the window for the GUI just before the program ends. On the next run, get the window information from the restored **Properties** object and draw the GUI so that it looks the same as when the user last left it.

Class

```
java.util.Properties
```

4

Purpose

The **Properties** class extends **Hashtable**. The key and value are **String** objects, suitable for writing to or reading from I/O streams. A **Properties** object can contain another **Properties** object that gives default values.

Constructors

- **Properties()**

  Properties(Properties *default*)

  When you create a **Properties** object, you can optionally supply another **Properties** object to serve as a table of default values.

Methods

The **Properties** class indirectly implements the **Map** interface. Some useful methods that are not part of the interface have been added to the **Properties** class.

- **String getProperty(String *key*)**

  String getProperty(String *key*, String *default*)

  The **getProperty** method first searches the property table, and then the default table, for an occurrence of the specified key. If it finds the key, it returns the associated value. Otherwise, it returns **null** or the default **String** specified in the optional second argument.

- **void load(InputStream *in*)**

  The **load** method reads a property list from an input stream.

- **Enumeration propertyNames( )**

  The **propertyNames** method returns an **Enumeration** object you can use to iterate through the keys in the **Properties** object.

- **void list(PrintStream *out*)**

  void list(PrintWriter *out*)

  The **list** method prints the property list on the specified output stream.

- **void save(OutputStream *out*, String *header*)**

  The **save** method outputs first the header **String** and then the contents of the **Properties** table to the specified output stream.

The JVM maintains a **Properties** collection that contains system information such as the version of the Java platform installed, the installation directory, the folder separator on the host operating system ("\" on Windows and "/" on Unix), and much more.

Figure 4-17 is a listing of a program that prints the system properties table. When the user supplies the names of specific system properties as command-line arguments to the **SystemProperties** program, the class prints just the named properties and associated values in the system properties table. When the user supplies no arguments, the program prints the entire system properties table.

```
 package examples.collections;
import java.util.*;
/** A class to help demonstrate how to work with
  * system properties
  */
public class SystemProperties {
   /** Display the system properties specified as
    * input parameters or, if no input is given,
    * all the system properties
    * @param args the list of system properties
    *              to be displayed
    */
   public static void main( String[] args ) {
      if ( args.length > 0 ) {
         // dump selected system properties
         for ( int i=0; i<args.length; i++ ) {
            System.out.println( args[i] + ": " +
               System.getProperty( args[i],
                  "not found" ) );
         }
      } else {
         // dump all system properties
         Properties sysProps = System.getProperties();
         Enumeration e = sysProps.propertyNames();
         while ( e.hasMoreElements() ) {
            String propName = (String)e.nextElement();
            System.out.println( propName + ": " +
               sysProps.getProperty( propName ) );
         }
      }
   }
}
```

Figure 4-17   Using a **Properties** collection

If you run the program, you should see output similar to the following lines, except that several lines have been deleted from this listing and your results will reflect your installation of the Java platform:

```
java.runtime.name: Java(TM) 2 Runtime Environment, Standard Edition
sun.boot.library.path: C:\j2sdk1.4.1_01\jre\bin
java.vm.version: 1.4.1_01-b01
java.vm.vendor: Sun Microsystems Inc.
java.vendor.url: http://java.sun.com/
```

```
java.vm.name: Java HotSpot(TM) Client VM
file.encoding.pkg: sun.io
user.country: US
...
sun.cpu.endian: little
sun.io.unicode.encoding: UnicodeLittle
sun.cpu.isalist: pentium i486 i386
```

4

You can specify specific properties as command-line arguments. For example, to determine what the classpath is when your program runs, enter the following on one command line:

```
java examples.collections.SystemProperties java.class.path
```

If you set your classpath to run the samples that come with this book from the CD-ROM, as explained in Chapter 1, and your CD-ROM is drive X:, the output may be

```
java.class.path: X:\Data
```

If you enter a program argument that is not a known system property name, say "whatever," you receive output similar to

```
whatever: not found
```

The **Vector** class is the favorite collection of many Java programmers who have been writing Java since before the Java 2 platform became available. Often **Vector** is the first collection class new programmers see, because it is a flexible alternative to one-dimensional arrays and easy to use.

Class

java.util.Vector

Purpose

The **Vector** class supports a dynamically resizable list of object references. The **Vector** class implements the **List** interface.

Constructors

- **Vector()**

  Vector(int *capacity* **)**

  Vector(int *capacity*, **int** *increment* **)**

  When you create a **Vector** collection, you can optionally specify an initial capacity, or the number of elements for which to reserve space, and by how much the capacity should be incremented every time **Vector** must grow. The size of a **Vector** collection is the number of elements actually contained in **Vector**. The capacity is always equal to or greater than the size.

Methods

Because the **Vector** class implements the **List** interface, **Vector** collections should be manipulated using the methods of **List**. Many legacy methods of the **Vector** class are not part of the **List** interface:

- **addElement(Object** *o* **)**

- **capacity( )**

- **copyInto(Object [ ]** *array* **)**

- **elementAt(int** *index* **)**

- **firstElement( )**

- **insertElementAt(Object** *o,* **int** *index* **)**

- **lastElement( )**

- **removeAllElements( )**

- **removeElement(Object** *o* **)**

- **removeElementsAt(int** *index* **)**

- **setElementAt(Object** *o,* **int** *index* **)**

You may see Java programs that use these methods. Avoid using any of these methods in new programs because they eliminate the possibility of interchanging a **Vector** implementation with any other implementation that uses the **List** interface.

If you know in advance approximately how many elements will be stored in the **Vector** object, pass that number as the capacity argument of the constructor. This improves efficiency, especially if the **Vector** object grows gradually to a large size. Every time a **Vector** object grows, the object references it contains are copied into a new instance of **Vector** and the old **Vector** object is available for garbage collection.

The program **LegacyLine**, in Figure 4-18, is a reworked version of the **ArrayList** Line program in Figure 4-8. This version demonstrates the **Vector** class using the **List** interface. The class **LegacyLine** manipulates a **Vector** of **java.awt.Point** objects. The class **Point** stores the x and y coordinates of a two-dimensional point and implements the **toString** method to return a textual representation of a point.

4

```
package examples.collections;
import java.util.*;
import java.io.PrintStream;
import java.awt.Point;
/** A class to demonstrate the use of the Vector and
  * Enumeration classes in the java.util package
  */
public class LegacyLine {
   private Vector points = new Vector();
   /** Set the starting point for a line
     * @param p the starting point
     */
   public void setStart( Point p ) {
      points.removeAllElements();
      points.add( p );
   }
   /** Set the next point in a line
     * @param p the next point
     */
   public void addPoint( Point p ) {
      points.add( p );
   }
   /** Print all the points in a line
     * @param ps the stream where the points
     *            will be printed
     */
   public void listPoints( PrintStream ps ) {
      ListIterator i = points.listIterator();
      while ( i.hasNext() ) {
         ps.println( i.next() );
      }
   }
   /** Test method for the class
     * @param args not used
     */
   public static void main( String[] args ) {
      LegacyLine x = new LegacyLine();
      x.setStart( new Point( 4, 11 ) );
      x.addPoint( new Point( -6, 1 ) );
      x.addPoint( new Point( 2, 3 ) );
      x.listPoints( System.out );
   }
}
```

Figure 4-18   Manipulating **Vector** with the **List** interface

The output of the LegacyLine program is

```
java.awt.Point[x=4,y=11]
java.awt.Point[x=-6,y=1]
java.awt.Point[x=2,y=3]
```

The **Stack** class extends **Vector** and adds methods for last-in first-out behavior. The **Stack** class indirectly implements the **List** interface through its superclass, **Vector**. For a **Stack** object to be useful, it needs to be manipulated with its legacy methods such as **push**, **pop**, and **peek**, which are defined outside of the **List** interface.

Class

`java.util.Stack`

Purpose

The **Stack** class provides a collection with first-in last-out or last-in first-out behavior.

Constructor

■ `Stack()`

The **Stack** class has only the no-argument constructor.

Methods

■ `boolean empty()`

The **empty** method returns **true** if **Stack** is empty and **false** if at least one element is in the instance of **Stack**.

■ `Object peek()`

The **peek** method returns an object reference last added to, but not removed from, the **Stack** object. Unlike **pop**, this method does not remove the element from the collection. If the collection is empty, **peek** throws the exception **EmptyStackException**.

■ `Object pop()`

The **pop** method returns the object reference last added to, but not removed from, the instance of **Stack**. It also removes the element from the collection. If the collection is empty, **pop** throws the an exception of type **EmptyStackException**.

■ `Object push( Object object )`

The **push** method adds an element to the instance of **Stack** and returns the object reference that is passed as an argument.

The **search** method returns the position of the specified object reference in the instance of **Stack**, or minus one (-1) if the object reference is not stored on the **Stack** object.

Extending the Collections Framework

If none of the implementation classes provided by the collections framework meets your requirements, you can define your own collection class. To simplify the process, the framework includes a number of abstract classes that have already done much of the work for you. These are the same abstract classes on which the framework's implementation classes were built. The classes are **AbstractCollection**, **AbstractList**, **AbstractSet**, **AbstractSequentialList**, and **AbstractMap**. Refer to Figure 4-5 and Figure 4-11 to see how these classes relate to the interfaces and implementation classes defined in the framework. The API documentation for the Java 2 platform describes in detail how to create an implementation class that extends each of the abstract classes.

Algorithms for Collections

Algorithms for sorting, searching, and reversing are commonly applied to collections. Because of the consistent design of the collections framework, the framework can include many polymorphic algorithms that you can apply to collections that implement the framework's interfaces.

The algorithms are not defined in an interface because all implementations would then have to provide them. Instead, the algorithms are collected into a single class, **Collections**, as class methods (declared with **static**). Most of the algorithms take a **List** object as input because they require the indexed methods defined in the **List** interface, but some operate on **Collection** objects.

Class

java.util.Collections

Purpose

This class provides methods that implement polymorphic algorithms on **List** and **Collection** objects.

Methods

- **int binarySearch(List** *list,* **Object** *target* **)**

  int binarySearch(List *list,* **Object** *target,* **Comparator** *c* **)**

  Before using the **binarySearch** method, the list must be sorted in ascending order using the elements' natural ordering or the **Comparator** object specified.

Assuming the list is sorted, the method finds the target within the specified list and returns its index if the target is found. If the target cannot be found, the value returned is (-(*insertion_point*)-1), where *insertion_point* is defined as the place at which the target would be inserted into the list. (See Figure 4-19 for an example.)

■ void copy(List *target*, List *source*)

This method copies all the elements of the source list into the target list.

■ void fill(List *target*, Object *fill*)

This method replaces all elements of the list with the specified fill object.

■ Object max(Collection *coll*)

Object max(Collection *coll*, Comparator *comp*)

This method returns the maximum object as defined by the elements' natural ordering or the **Comparator** object, if one is supplied.

■ Object min(Collection *coll*)

Object min(Collection *coll*, Comparator *comp*)

This method returns the minimum object as defined by the elements' natural ordering or the **Comparator** object, if one is supplied.

■ void reverse(List *list*)

This method reverses the order of the elements of the supplied list.

■ void shuffle(List *list*)

void shuffle(List *list*, Random *r*)

This method shuffles the order of the elements of the supplied list to create a random ordering. If **random** object is supplied, it is used by the shuffling algorithm.

■ void sort(List *list*)

void sort(List *list*, Comparator *c*)

The **sort** method sorts the specified list in ascending order using the elements' natural ordering or the **Comparator** object specified. The sort algorithm used is a modified merge-sort algorithm.

The **ArraySortExample** class in Figure 4-19 demonstrates how to create a **List** object from an array. The resulting **List** object can be sorted and traversed just like any other kind of **List**.

```
package examples.collections;
import java.util.*;
/** A class to demonstrate the use of the sort and
 * search algorithms in the java.util package
 */
public class ArraySortExample {
   /** Test method for the class
    * @param args not used
    */
   public static void main( String[] args ) {
       // create a list and intialize it
       Object[] data = {  new Double( 3.45 ),
                          new Double( -0.2 ),
                          new Double( 100.3 ),
                          new Double( 89.67 ),
                          new Double( 11.0 ),
                          new Double( 23.132 )
                       };
       List list = Arrays.asList( data );
       // iterate to display the set values
       Iterator i1 = list.iterator();
       while ( i1.hasNext() ) {
          System.out.print( i1.next() + " " );
       }
       System.out.println();
       Collections.sort( list );
       Iterator i2 = list.iterator();
       while ( i2.hasNext() ) {
          System.out.print( i2.next() + " " );
       }
       System.out.println();
       for( int j=0; j<data.length; j++ ) {
          System.out.print( data[j] + " " );
       }
       System.out.println();
   }
}
```

Figure 4-19   Sample class that uses the `Collections` class

The output looks like:

```
3.45 -0.2 100.3 89.67 11.0 23.132
-0.2 3.45 11.0 23.132 89.67 100.3
-0.2 3.45 11.0 23.132 89.67 100.3
```

Notice that the second and third lines of output match, because the sort operation on the list also sorts its backing array object.

Wrapper Implementations for Collections

Except for the legacy implementation classes **Vector**, **Stack**, **Hashtable**, and **Properties** none of the implementation classes supplied in the collections framework have built-in synchronization to prevent concurrent execution in a multithreaded program. Therefore, these collections are not considered thread-safe. The problems and solutions related to multithreaded programs are discussed in detail in Chapter 5. For now, just note that you can easily create a thread-safe wrapper for a **Collection** object by using a method in the class **Collections**.

The **Collections** class has a set of static methods, one for each of the six interfaces. These methods take a **Collection** object as input and return a thread-safe collection that is backed by the original collection passed as input to the method. The definitions of the methods all follow the same pattern. The name of the method is the name of the interface prefixed with **synchronized**. The input and output of the method is a single collection of the interface type. For example, the method to create a synchronized wrapper for a **SortedSet** object is **synchronizedSortedSet**; it takes **SortedSet** as input and returns **SortedSet** as output.

Another kind of collection wrapper that can be generated by methods of the **Collections** class is a read-only wrapper class. These methods take a collection as input and return a collection that will throw an **UnsupportedOperationException** exception if any method that modifies the collection is called. The definition of these methods also follows a pattern. Each method name is the name of the collection prefixed by the string **unmodifiable**. So the method to create a read-only wrapper for a **TreeMap** object is **unmodifiableTreeMap**. The method takes a **TreeMap** object as input and returns a read-only **TreeMap** object as output.

The **ReadOnlyExample** class in Figure 4-20 demonstrates how to create a read-only **TreeMap** object from an existing **TreeMap** object. The line that creates the wrapper class is bold. The result of the attempt to add a mapping to the read-only sorted map by the second bold line in this listing is an **UnsupportedOperationException** exception.

```
public class ReadOnlyExample {
   /** Test method for the class
    * @param args not used
    */
   public static void main( String[] args ) {
      // create a map and intialize it
      SortedMap m1 = new TreeMap();
      m1.put( "beans", new Float( 2.99 ) );
      m1.put( "carrots", new Float( 1.69 ) );
      m1.put( "peas", new Float( 2.19 ) );
      m1.put( "cabbage", new Float( 3.29 ) );
      m1.put( "squash", new Float( 1.89 ) );
```

Figure 4-20   Sample class creating a collection wrapper class

```
    // create a read-only collection, then try to
    // change it
    m1 = Collections.unmodifiableSortedMap( m1 );
    try {
       m1.put( "parsnips", new Float( 1.59 ) );
     } catch ( UnsupportedOperationException x ) {
        System.out.println( x + " caught!" );
    }
  }
}
```

4

Figure 4-20   Sample class creating a collection wrapper class (continued)

The output looks like:

```
    java.lang.UnsupportedOperationException caught!
```

IMPLEMENTING AN OBSERVER-OBSERVABLE DESIGN PATTERN

In many situations, you want to create a class that is responsive to asynchronous events. An *asynchronous event* is anything that happens outside the context of a piece of code that may affect the code. The word asynchronous refers to the fact the event is not expected, specifically that the code in question is not waiting for it or regularly check-ing whether it has occured. For example, a resource may become available or unexpected input may arrive. When the event is of no interest, the running program can ignore it. However, sometimes classes must react to asynchronous events by performing some appropriate action.

For example, consider an application that lets many users run the program at the same time and communicate with each other. The user interface for each user shows a list of all users who are active, and that list is updated every time a user arrives or departs. If users may arrive or depart at any time, and the program has no control over when, then an arrival or a departure is an asynchronous event. It is possible for the program to loop, repeatedly checking the status of all possible user connections, but constantly executing a loop in which nothing happens most of the time is inefficient use of processing power and can reduce the capacity of the computer to do meaningful work. Therefore, you do not want the program component that maintains the user list to poll the set of users proactively. A much better approach is to let the component be passive, but somehow notified and activated when a user arrival or departure event occurs.

Sometimes a fast response is important. The Java platform provides a mechanism that you can use in situations where an asynchronous event changes the state of an object. Such an event occurs when a field changes value.

How can you create objects that respond to changes in instances of other classes? The Java platform provides the **Observable** class and **Observer** interface to set up an event-notification mechanism. These types provide an implementation of a design pattern based on the principle that if the state of certain objects changes, those objects are responsible for notifying other objects that have registered an interest. Each class in which such a change of state occurs must also maintain the list of interested objects. Two other event notification mechanisms are implemented in the J2SDK:

- If you have written programs with a Java GUI, you have used a different and more comprehensive event-handling mechanism. Asynchronous events occur when users interact with GUIs, for example by clicking buttons or resizing windows. Asynchronous events also occur when the data displayed in Swing lists, tables, and trees changes. Chapters 6 and 7 cover Java GUIs and show how to create programs driven by user-initiated events. The classes that represent user-interface events extend **java.util.EventObject**. Objects that handle the user-interface events are instances of classes that implement listener interfaces that extend **java.util.EventListener**.

- Yet another notification mechanism is used in multithreaded programs. Chapter 5 shows how to create and launch threads, and how to program inter-thread communication.

The **Observable** class and **Observer** interface provide a simple event-notification mechanism. Events are changes in the state of **Observable** objects, and instances of classes that implement the **Observer** interface can react to these events.

The **Observable** class drives the event-notification mechanism. If you define a class upon which other classes depend, you can define the class to extend **Observable**. The **Observable** class defines the method **addObserver** that other objects call to register as observers, and the method **notifyObservers** to alert the observers of possible state changes. If the **Observable** object has changed, the JVM notifies the observers. The observing objects must implement **Observer** and therefore have **update** methods. The JVM notifies observers by calling their **update** methods.

Most professional programmers follow a design pattern known as the model-view separation. Programs that contain a layer of classes for the user interface or presentation of data, and a separate layer for the business logic or core activities, are generally easier to maintain and extend than those with a non-layered architecture. One way to implement model-view separation is to make the objects that contain the data in the model **Observable**. A refinement of model-view separation is the Model View Controller (MVC) design pattern. The controller is a set of classes that connect the view to the model. **Observer** objects in the controller layer can update the view so that the state displayed for the user is consistent with the state of the model.

Class

java.util.Observable

Purpose

Instances of classes that extend **Observable** are observable objects.

Constructor

- `Observable()`

  The no-argument constructor is the only constructor available for this class.

Methods

- `void addObserver( Observer object )`

  Call **addObserver** to register an object as an observer for this object.

- `void deleteObserver( Observer object )`

  Call **deleteObserver** to remove the object from the list of observers.

- `void notifyObservers()`

  `void notifyObservers( Object object )`

  Calling **notifyObservers** calls the **hasChanged** method. If **hasChanged** returns **true**, **notifyObservers** calls the **update** method of every registered **Observer** object and then calls **clearChanged**. You can optionally supply an object to be passed to the **update** methods. If you use the no-argument version, object reference **null** is passed.

- `void setChanged()`

  Call **setChanged** to set the changed condition for the current object.

- `boolean hasChanged()`

  The **hasChanged** method returns **true** if **setChanged** has been called since the last call of **clearChanged**, and **false** otherwise.

- `void clearChanged()`

  Call **clearChanged** to clear the changed condition for the current object.

To create an observer, define a class that implements the interface **Observer**. To register the observer, call **addObserver** for the **Observable** object and pass the **Observer** object as the argument of the method. Because **Observer** is an interface rather than a class, you can easily adapt existing classes to be **Observers**. The **Observer** interface contains one method, **update**, which the JVM calls automatically whenever the **Observable** object for the **Observer** calls **notifyObservers**.

Interface

`java.util.Observer`

Purpose

Instances of classes that implement **Observer** can be notified of changes in **Observable** objects.

Methods

- **void update(Observable** *object*, **Object** *argument* **)**

   This method is called when the state of the **Observable** object has changed. If not **null**, the second argument is an object passed to the **notifyObservers** method of the **Observable** object.

In the sample program in Figure 4-21, the class **Pump** encapsulates an application in which **Valve** is an **Observable** object and **Buzzer** is an **Observer** object.

```
package examples.utilities;
import java.util.Observable;
import java.util.Observer;
/** Class to demonstrate the use of the Observer
  * interface and the Observable class
  */
public class Pump {
   /** Method for creating a Pump, a Valve and
     * a Buzzer object and connecting the Valve
     * and Buzzer objects together
     * @param args not used
     */
   public static void main( String[] args ) {
      Pump p = new Pump();
      Valve v = p.new Valve();
      Buzzer b = p.new Buzzer();
      v.addObserver( b );
      v.setPressure( 150 );
      v.setPressure( 200 );
      v.setPressure( 75 );
   }
   /** A class representing a valve in a pump
     * that can be observed by other objects
     */
   private class Valve extends Observable {
      private int pressure;
      /** Method used to set the pressure at
        * the valve. It notifies its
        * observers of the change
        * @param p Updated pressure value
        */
```

Figure 4-21   A sample class demonstrating **Observer** and **Observables** objects

```
       public void setPressure( int p ) {
          pressure = p;
          setChanged();
          notifyObservers();
       }
       public int getPressure() {
          return pressure;
       }
   }
   /** Class representing the warning buzzer on a
    * pump. The buzzer sounds when the pressure
    * of the valve it is observing exceeds the
    * threshold and goes silent when the pressure
    * drops back below the threshold
    */
   private class Buzzer implements Observer {
      private int threshold = 100;
      private boolean buzzerOn;
      /** This method is called whenever the valve
       * being observed changes
       * @param o the object under observation
       * @param arg optional argument, not used
       */
      public void update( Observable o, Object arg ) {
         Valve v = (Valve) o;
         if ( v.getPressure() > threshold
             && buzzerOn == false ) {
           buzzerOn = true;
           System.out.println( "Buzzer on" );
         } else if ( v.getPressure() < threshold
                    && buzzerOn == true ) {
           buzzerOn = false;
           System.out.println( "Buzzer off" );
         }
      }
   }
}
```

Figure 4-21   A sample class demonstrating `Observer` and `Observables` objects (continued)

The **main** method of the `Pump` class creates a `Pump` object. It also creates the `Buzzer` and `Valve` objects that are contained in the `Pump` object. Next, the **main** method registers the `Buzzer` object as an observer for the `Valve` object. During execution, the **main** method sets the valve pressure to three different levels.

The **setPressure** method of the `Valve` class sets the pressure and then calls two methods that class `Valve` inherits from **Observable** first **setChanged** and then **notifyObservers**.The `Buzzer` class implements the **update** method of the **Observer** interface to print the message "Buzzer on" or "Buzzer off," depending on the pressure in the `Valve` object and whether the buzzer is currently on or off.

Notice that the first argument of the **update** method has type **Observable** and must be cast to the type of the **Observable** object. The value of the second argument is **null** because the **setPressure** method does not pass an explicit object in the call of **notifyObservers**.

GENERATING RANDOM NUMBERS

In many situations you need some numbers to work with, but do not have any real data. For example, you may be testing an application and want some sample data to exercise your code. If you are writing a simulation, you usually want data that is not only realistic but also variable so that different runs can simulate different sequences of events. A common solution for the problem of how to get artificial but realistic data is to generate values as you need them. A *pseudo-random number generator* is a program component that produces a sequence of values, one at a time, so that resulting data can pass statistical tests of randomness. The key requirements of pseudo-random numbers are

- Each value generated seems to be independent of all other numbers generated. In other words, you cannot look at one value or the sequence produced so far and predict what the next value will be.

- The distribution of values is consistent with a known probability distribution. One common probability distribution is uniform. In the uniform distribution, numbers fall within a range, but the probability of any particular value occurring is equal for all values in the range. This is what most people think of as " random." Another common distribution is the Normal or Gaussian distribution, commonly known as "the Bell curve." In the Gaussian distribution values nearer the desired mean (a measurement of average) occur more frequently than numbers farther away from the mean, and a parameter called the standard deviation determines how tightly the clustering is to the mean. A small standard deviation produces a tall, thin bell. A large standard deviation gives a broad, shallow bell.

Pseudo-random number generators require a *seed*, or original value. Each time the generator is called, it manipulates the current value, or the seed on the first call, to produce the next number in the sequence. Therefore, you can get a repeatable sequence by supplying the same seed more than once. Most pseudo-random number generators produce realistic uniformly distributed values and then perform transformations as required to produce numbers for Gaussian and other distributions. The values produced are not truly random numbers because they are computer generated and, therefore, are called "pseudo-random numbers." However, such numbers can satisfy requirements of many situations.

A pseudo-random number generator is the sort of handy class you can expect to find in the utility package, and class **java.util.Random** is that class. You may be familiar with the random method in the **java.lang.Math** class, which generates uniformly distributed pseudo-random double values in the range 0.0 to 1.0. The method **Math.random** is a convenience method; it calls method **java.util.Random.nextDouble**. The **Random** class provides more flexibility than the **Math.random** method, but is also just a handy class for generating pseudo-random numbers.

Class

java.util.Random

Purpose

The **Random** class generates pseudo-random numbers or data of a variety of types.

Constructors

- **Random( )**

  Random(long *seed* **)**

  Use the no-argument constructor to generate a sequence based on a seed supplied by the **Random** class. To increase the probability that every **Random** object generates unique sequences of numbers, the default constructor uses a seed based on the current time. If two random objects are created within a millisecond of each other, they may have the same seed and therefore produce the same numbers. If you want the same sequence of numbers from different **Random** objects or different runs of your program, you can supply an initial seed.

Methods

- **void setSeed(long** *seed* **)**

  Use the **setSeed** method to change the seed for a **Random** object after instantiating it.

- **Boolean nextBoolean( )**

  double nextDouble( )

  float nextFloat( )

  int nextInt( )

  long nextLong( )

  These methods return the next uniformly distributed pseudo-random number converted desired type and range of return values. Method **nextBoolean** returns value **true** or **false**. Methods **nextDouble** and **nextFloat** return a real numbers in the range 0.0 to 1.0. Methods **nextInt** and **nextLong** return integers.

- void nextBytes(byte [ ] *byte*)

  The **nextBytes** method fills the supplied byte array with pseudo-random bytes.

- int nextInt(int *n*)

  The **nextInt** method with integer argument returns an integer in the range 0 to the value of the argument.

- double nextGaussian( )

  The **nextGaussian** method returns a pseudo-random number drawn from the Gaussian distribution with mean value of 0.0 and standard deviation 1.0. To convert to a different range of values than Normal (0.0, 1.0), multiply by the desired standard deviation and add the desired mean.

The algorithm used by the **Random** class uses a well-established linear congruence formula. Figure 4-22 is a slightly more interesting version of the **Pump** example program. Only the **main** method is listed because only it has been changed. The example now changes the pressure in the value to randomly generated values based on the Normal distribution with mean 90 and standard deviation 10.

```
public class PumpRandom {

   public static void main( String[] args ) {
      PumpRandom p = new PumpRandom();
      Valve v = p.new Valve();
      Buzzer b = p.new Buzzer();
      v.addObserver( b );
      Random rng = new Random();
      for ( int i =0; i < 12; i++) {
       // generate random pressures based on N( 90, 10 )
         int pressure = (int) (rng.nextGaussian()
         * 10 + 90);
         System.out.println("Setting pressure to: "
         + pressure);
         v.setPressure( pressure );
      }
   }
}
```

Figure 4-22   Sample class using pseudo-random numbers

On one run, the output is

```
Setting pressure to: 77
Setting pressure to: 86
Setting pressure to: 83
Setting pressure to: 101
Buzzer on
```

```
Setting pressure to: 79
Buzzer off
Setting pressure to: 102
Buzzer on
Setting pressure to: 93
Buzzer off
Setting pressure to: 83
Setting pressure to: 106
Buzzer on
Setting pressure to: 94
Buzzer off
Setting pressure to: 97
Setting pressure to: 78
```

FORMATTING OUTPUT AND USING LOCALES

With considerable foresight, the developers of Java designed the output formatting capabilities and other capabilities with internationalization in mind. Many features of the Java platform for presenting information make no assumptions about the cultural environment within which the program is used. Instead, the Java platform implements the concept of locales. As explained more fully in the next section, a *locale* stores settings about a language or country—including what alphabet is used, how dates and numbers are written, and other culture-specific aspects of information processing. A number of classes are locale-sensitive. The beauty of this solution is that dates, numbers, monetary values, and the like are formatted by default according to the default locale for the implementation of Java that you are using. In other words, the output is usually as you expect, unless for some reason you are working with a Java implementation from a different cultural environment.

Introducing Locales

There are many good reasons for learning about locales and the locale-sensitive classes. One is that you may use some of these classes to format output even if you are not preparing your code for use in other countries. An even more compelling reason may be the importance of creating program components that work around the world—in other locales—especially if you are building reusable components or applications to deploy on the World Wide Web. What sort of program elements are locale-sensitive? Here are a few examples:

- Language and translation is the most obvious problem. With some care, you can separate all textual elements that appear in your user interface and other output from Java code. The section "Using Resources and Properties Files" in this chapter describes how to put all literal strings and values that may be sensitive to cultural environment in text files outside your code.

- The interpretation of dates varies from country to country. For example, the unforgettable date 09/11/01 to the British represents the less memorable date November 9, 2001. Other countries use a wholly different calendar.

- The number 1,000 means one thousand in the United States, and means 1 accurate to 3 decimal places in French-speaking cultures.

- Different countries use different symbols for currency.

- Different languages have different alphabets. For this reason, Java uses Unicode, in which each character is a 16-bit representation. Unicode can accommodate many alphabets, and is described in more detail in Appendix A of this book. The ASCII 128-character set is a subset of the Latin 1 (ISO 8859-1) 256-character set that is adequate for many western European languages. Latin 1 is a subset of Unicode.

- The way strings are sorted into alphabetic or alphanumeric order is determined by a collating sequence, which must also account for punctuation, accented letters, and the other characters used in the cultural environment.

This chapter deals only with the locale-sensitive classes that you might use to format output within your native cultural environment.

In Java, locales are objects that encapsulate the facets that make up a cultural environment. Locales are a mature concept originally introduced in C in the 1980s and expanded in C++ before the Java platform adopted them. The previous list mentions just a few of the facets that make up a locale.

In Java, locales are represented by instances of the class **Locale**. Conceptually, a **Locale** object is a data structure in which each facet is described by the values of a number of fields. For example, one facet relates to how numbers are represented. One field in that facet is the character separator between thousands, and another is the character that separates the whole number part from the fractional part of real numbers. Therefore, this facet determines whether 1,234 is the integral value one thousand two-hundred and thirty-four or a specific real value between one and two.

Class

java.util.Locale

Purpose

Locale objects encapsulate a cultural environment. A number of locales are predefined as static members of the class. To set the locale for a locale-sensitive operation, you need a **Locale** object.

Constructors

Locale(String *language* **)**

~~Locale(String language, String country)~~

Locale(String *language*, **String** *country*, **String** *variant* **)**

To create a **Locale** object, specify a two-letter language code, optional two-letter country code, and optional two-letter variant. Use codes defined by ISO standards ISO-639 for language codes and ISO-166 for country codes. The predefined default **Locale** object, U.S. English, is specified by (**"en"**, **"US"**).

4

Methods

- **Locale getDefault()**

  This method is a class (static) method. It returns an object encapsulating the current default locale.

- **void setDefault (Locale** *newLocale* **)**

  This method is a class (static) method. It changes the default locale to the locale encapsulated in the specified **Locale** object.

When you create a **Locale** object, no exception is thrown if you request a combination of language, country, and variant that is not recognized. Any combination is accepted. The actual **Locale** instance used may not be the one you intended because of the way locales are organized into a hierarchy. The predefined **Locale** object that best matches the arguments of the constructor defines the chosen locale. The first in the following set of criteria to be satisfied determines which locale is used:

1. The language, country, and variant match exactly.

2. The language and country match.

3. The language matches.

4. Nothing matches. In this case, the default locale is used.

For example, if you ask for a locale supporting French as spoken in the Canadian province of New Brunswick, you may have to settle for the locale that supports French as spoken in Canada. If that is not available, the next best match is the default French locale. Failing even that, the default locale is used.

At times, a particular instance of **Locale** is needed only briefly and changing the default locale is inappropriate. For such situations, many methods take a **Locale** object as input to override the default locale with the specified locale only for the duration of the method.

Figure 4-23 lists several locale-sensitive classes. They are split between two packages: **java.util** and **java.text**.

Class name	Description
`java.util.Date`	A `Date` object represents a moment in time to the nearest millisecond. This class is an anomaly because it is not locale-sensitive. The `Date` class was included in the original Java version 1.0 platform, and locales were introduced in version 1.1. As a result, it contains a number of deprecated methods and should be used only to hold and compare dates and times.
`java.util.Calendar`	This abstract class is the base for converting `Date` objects into objects for which you can manipulate fields such as `DAY`, `MONTH`, `DAY_OF_MONTH`, `YEAR`, `DAY_OF_YEAR`, `HOUR`, `MINUTE`, `SECOND`, `AM_PM`, and many more. Use a class (static) method `Calendar.getCalendar` to get a `Calendar` object for an instance of `Locale` or `TimeZone`.
`java.util.GregorianCalendar`	This concrete subclass of `Calendar` supports the calendar used in North America and Western Europe, and recognized in most of the world.
`java.util.TimeZone`	This abstract class is the basis for obtaining time zone information such as the name and ID for a time zone and difference from GMT. The class handles daylight savings time. Use static methods `getTimeZone` or `getDefault` to get a `TimeZone` object.
`java.util.SimpleTimeZone`	This concrete subclass of `TimeZone` supports time zones for use with the Gregorian calendar.
`java.util.Currency`	Instances of this concrete class represent a currency, and provide information such as its symbol and ISO code. Call a class (static) `getInstance` method to obtain a `Currency` object for a locale or ISO currency code.
`java.util.ResourceBundle`	You can use a `ResourceBundle` object to work with literal data stored in locale-specific properties files. This class is described in detail in the section "Using Resources and Property Files."
`java.text.Collator`	This abstract class supports locale-sensitive comparison of strings. Call class (static) `getInstance` methods to obtain a `Collator` object for a locale.
`java.text.RuleBasedCollator`	Use this concrete subclass of `Collator` to build a table-based custom `Collator` object.

Figure 4-23   Some of the locale-sensitive classes

4

Class name	Description
java.text.CollationKey	Instances of **CollationKey** represent specific strings according to the rules of a **Collator** object. When **String** objects are compared, many times you can improve performance by creating **CollationKey** objects and then calling method **CollationKey.compareTo** instead of calling the method **Collator.compare**.
java.text.Format	This abstract class is the base for locale-sensitive formatters.
java.text.DateFormat	This abstract subclass of **Format** parses and formats date and time data, and is described in this chapter. Call static methods **getDateInstance** or **getDateTimeInstance** to obtain a **DateFormat** object.
java.text.SimpleDataFormat	This concrete subclass of **DateFormat** lets you apply patterns to the parsing and formatting of date and time information.
java.text.NumberFormat	This abstract subclass for **Format** parses and formats numerical data including percentages and monetary values, and is described in this chapter.
java.text.DecimalNumberFormat	This concrete subclass of **NumberFormat** applies patterns to parsing and formatting numbers.
java.text.ChoiceFormat	Use this concrete subclass of **NumberFormat** to apply formatting rules to a range of numbers. Typically a **ChoiceFormat** is used in a **MessageFormat** object to determine whether to use singular or plural form, as in "1 item" or "2 items."
java.text.MessageFormat	Use this concrete subclass of **Format** to construct messages by concatenating formatted elements. Obtain a **MessageFormat** object by using a constructor and passing a pattern that controls how the message is built. This class provides more options than can be discussed in a book such as this.

Figure 4-23   Some of the locale-sensitive classes (continued)

Formatting Dates and Times

Formatting dates and times manually requires a lot of string manipulation. The Java platform provides utilities to format this data in a number of different ways. For example, for the first day of 2004 you may want to display "01/01/04" or "January 1, 2004." Moreover, conventions for representing dates and times vary around the world. Use two abstract classes in the **java.util** package to work with dates and times: **Calendar** and **TimeZone**. These two classes and their corresponding concrete subclasses, **GregorianCalendar** and **SimpleTimeZone**, provide formatting options for the different locales.

The **Date** class contains a number of methods that have been deprecated and moved to the **Calendar** class since the original release of the Java platform. When looking for methods and constants for processing date and time information, look first to the **Calendar** class.

Class

```
java.util.Calendar
```

Purpose

The **Calendar** class is an abstract class that you can use to convert a **Date** object into locale-sensitive representations for the year, month, day, and the like.

Constructor

- **Calendar( )**

To get a **Calendar** object, call the class (static) method **getInstance**.

Methods

- **Calendar getInstance( )**

Calendar getInstance(TimeZone *zone* **)**

Calendar getInstance(Locale *locale* **)**

Calendar getInstance(TimeZone *zone*, **Locale** *locale* **)**

These are class (static) methods. Each returns a reference to an instance of a subclass of **Calendar**. If you do not specify a **Locale** object, you get a **Calendar** instance for the default locale. Supply a **TimeZone** object if your application uses the time offset from Greenwich Mean Time (GMT).

Use the **DateFormat** class to format date and time data in a locale-sensitive manner.

Class

```
java.text.DateFormat
```

Purpose

The **DateFormat** class is an abstract class that provides methods you can use to parse and format date and time information according to a locale.

Fields

- **DEFAULT**

  DateFormat.DEFAULT is a constant you can use to specify that date and time be formatted with the default style. For an example of this style, see the output of the sample program in Figure 4-24.

DateFormat.FULL is a constant you can use to specify the full style pattern for formatting date and time data. For an example of this style, see the output of the sample program in Figure 4-24.

- **LONG**

  DateFormat.LONG is a constant you can use to specify a long style pattern for formatting date and time data. For an example of this style, see the output of the sample program in Figure 4-24.

- **MEDIUM**

  DateFormat.MEDIUM is a constant you can use to specify a medium-length style pattern for formatting date and time data. For an example of this style, see the output of the sample program in Figure 4-24.

- **SHORT**

  DateFormat.SHORT is a constant you can use to specify a short style pattern for formatting date and time data. For an example of this style, see the output of the sample program in Figure 4-24.

Constructor

- **DateFormat()**

  To get a **DateFormat** object, call a method that returns an instance of **DateFormat** for the format of information you require.

Methods

- **DateFormat getDateInstance()**

  DateFormat getDateInstance(int *style*)

  DateFormat getDateInstance(int *style*, Locale *locale*)

  These are class (static) methods. Each returns a reference to a **DateFormat** object. You can optionally specify the style pattern to control the formatting by supplying a constant that is defined in this class. You can also specify a **Locale** object or accept the current default locale.

- **DateFormat getDateTimeInstance()**

  DateFormat getDateTimeInstance(int *datestyle*, int *timestyle*)

  DateFormat getDateInstance(int *datestyle*, int *timestyle*, Locale *locale*)

These are class (static) methods. Each returns a reference to a **DateFormat** object. You can optionally specify the style patterns to control the formatting of the date and time values independently, by supplying constants that are defined in this class. You can also specify a **Locale** object or accept the current default locale.

- **DateFormat getTimeInstance()**

  DateFormat getTimeInstance(int *style*)

  DateFormat getTimeInstance(int *style*, Locale *locale*)

These are class (static) methods. Each returns a reference to a **TimeFormat** object. You can optionally specify the style pattern to control the formatting, by supplying a constant that is defined in this class. You can also specify a **Locale** object or accept the current default locale.

The example program in Figure 4-24 demonstrates how you can use the **Calendar** and **DateFormat** classes with different locales and formats. In this case, the program prints the current date for the default and Italian locales in all the supported styles.

```
package examples.utilities;
import java.text.DateFormat;
import java.util.Calendar;
import java.util.Date;
import java.util.Locale;
/** Class to demonstrate the use of the Calendar
  * class and date formatting
  */
public class DateFormatter {
    /** main entrypoint - starts the application
      * @param args not used
      */
    public static void main( String[ ] args) {
        Calendar calDefault = Calendar.getInstance();
        Date today = calDefault.getTime();
        test( "DEFAULT style",
              DateFormat.DEFAULT, today );
        test( "FULL style", DateFormat.FULL, today );
        test( "LONG style", DateFormat.LONG, today );
        test( "MEDIUM style", DateFormat.MEDIUM, today );
            test( "SHORT style", DateFormat.SHORT, today );
    // print the current time
    System.out.println( "\nCurrent Time: "
              + DateFormat.getTimeInstance().format(today)
              + " " + DateFormat.getTimeInstance().
                getTimeZone().getDisplayName());
    }
```

Figure 4-24   Sample class showing locale-date sensitive formatting

```
/** Common test routine
 * @param label the label for the test
 * @param style the DateFormat style to be used
 * @param date the date to be formatted
 */
static void test( String label, int style, Date date ) {
   System.out.println( label );
   DateFormat df
      = DateFormat.getDateInstance( style );
   System.out.print( "\tDefault locale:    " );
   System.out.println( df.format( date ) );
   df = DateFormat.getDateInstance( style,
                             Locale.ITALY );
   System.out.print( "\tLocale for Italy: " );
   System.out.println( df.format( date ) );
   }
}
```

Figure 4-24   Sample class showing locale-date sensitive formatting (continued)

When run during the morning of the 26th day of October in 2004, the program prints the following:

```
DEFAULT style
    Default locale:   Oct 26, 2004
    Locale for Italy: 26-ott-2004
FULL style
    Default locale:   Tuesday, October 26, 2004
    Locale for Italy: martedì 26 ottobre 2004
LONG style
    Default locale:   October 26, 2004
    Locale for Italy: 26 ottobre 2004
MEDIUM style
    Default locale:   Oct 26, 2004
    Locale for Italy: 26-ott-2004
SHORT style
    Default locale:   10/26/04
    Locale for Italy: 26/10/04
Current Time: 11:47:01 AM Eastern Standard Time
```

Formatting Percentages, Monetary Values, and Numbers

The **java.text** package provides utilities for formatting numerical values in the abstract class **NumberFormat** and its concrete subclass **DecimalFormat**. Like **Calendar** and **TimeZone**, these classes are locale sensitive, and use the default locale unless you specify otherwise.

Class

java.text.NumberFormat

Purpose

`NumberFormat` is an abstract class for formatting and parsing currency values, percentages, and numbers according to a locale.

Constructor

- `NumberFormat( )`

To get an object of a concrete subclass of `NumberFormat` object, call a class (static) method of `NumberFormat`.

Methods

- `NumberFormat getNumberInstance()`

  `NumberFormat getNumberInstance( Locale locale )`

  These are class (static) methods. Each returns a `NumberFormat` object for general purpose numbers. If you do not specify a `Locale` object, the method uses the current default locale.

- `NumberFormat getCurrencyInstance()`

  `NumberFormat getCurrencyInstance( Locale locale )`

  These are class (static) methods. Each returns a `NumberFormat` object for monetary value numbers. If you do not specify a `Locale` object, the method uses the current default locale.

- `NumberFormat getPercentInstance()`

  `NumberFormat getPercentInstance( Locale locale )`

  These are class (static) methods. Each returns a `NumberFormat` object for percentage values. If you do not specify a `Locale` object, the method uses the current default locale.

- `NumberFormat getInstance()`

  `NumberFormat getInstance( Locale locale )`

  These are class (static) methods. Each returns a `NumberFormat` object to format numeric values in the default manner of the locale. If you do not specify a `Locale` object, the method uses the current default locale.

The sample program in Figure 4-25 applies the three kinds of number formatting for two locales, the default locale of U.S. English and the locale of Germany, to the same value. Note that currency formatting does not apply exchange rates to convert between monetary values. The formatter merely controls the presentation of the supplied number.

4

```java
package examples.utilities;
import java.text.NumberFormat;
import java.util.Locale;
/** Class to demonstrate the use of the NumberFormat
  * class for currency and other numbers
  */
public class NumberFormatter {
   /** Test program for the class
     * @param args not used
     */
   public static void main( String[] args ) {
      double x = 102030405.0607;
      NumberFormat nfDefault
         = NumberFormat.getInstance();
      NumberFormat nfGermany
         = NumberFormat.getInstance( Locale.GERMANY );
      test( "Default number format",
            nfDefault, nfGermany, x );
      nfDefault.setMaximumFractionDigits( 6 );
      nfGermany.setMaximumFractionDigits( 6 );
      test( "Default number format, more precision",
            nfDefault, nfGermany, x );
      double y = 0.12345;
      NumberFormat nfDefaultPc
         = NumberFormat.getPercentInstance();
      NumberFormat nfGermanyPc
         = NumberFormat.getPercentInstance(
            Locale.GERMANY );
      test( "Percent format",
            nfDefaultPc, nfGermanyPc, y );
      double z = 12345.6789;
      NumberFormat nfDefaultCr
         = NumberFormat.getCurrencyInstance();
      NumberFormat nfGermanyCr
         = NumberFormat.getCurrencyInstance(
            Locale.GERMANY );
      test( "Currency format",
            nfDefaultCr, nfGermanyCr, z );
   }

      /** Test method
     * @param label the name of the test
     * @param defNf the NumberFormat object for the
     *     default locale
     * @param gerNf the NumberFormat object for the
     *     GERMANY locale
     * @param value the value to be formatted.
     */
```

Figure 4-25   Sample class showing locale-sensitive number formatting

```
    public static void test( String label,
                             NumberFormat defNf,
                             NumberFormat gerNf,
                             double value ) {
    System.out.println( label );
    System.out.println( "\tdefault locale: "
                        + defNf.format( value ) );
    System.out.println( "\tGerman locale:  "
                        + gerNf.format( value ) );
    }
}
```

Figure 4-25   Sample class showing locale-sensitive number formatting (continued)

The program produces the following output:

```
Default number format
    default locale: 102,030,405.061
    German locale:  102.030.405,061
Default number format, more precision
    default locale: 102,030,405.0607
    German locale:  102.030.405,0607
Percent format
    default locale: 12%
    German locale:  12%
Currency format
    default locale: $12,345.68
    German locale:  12.345,68 €
```

The final line of your output may end with a different character than €. Germany uses the common European monetary unit, the euro, and the euro symbol, €, may not be supported by your operating system.

To get a currency symbol as it would be represented in your default locale, you can use the **Currency** class. For example, the following expression has the value "EUR" in the U.S. English locale:

```
Currency.getInstance(Locale.GERMANY).getSymbol()
```

In the German locale, the U.S. dollar is represented by USD instead of $.

This is not the whole story for formatting numbers and values of other types. The **NumberFormat** class lets you build patterns to represent numbers in flexible ways. For example, you can use scientific notation or put parentheses around negatives values, or insert spaces in arbitrary places. Look at the J2SDK `javadoc` for the **NumberFormat** class for details.

If you may be building messages at runtime, you should look at the **ChoiceFormat** and **MessageFormat** classes. Use a **MessageFormat** object to build a message out of parts where each part may be formatted by a **NumberFormat**, **DateFormat**, or **ChoiceFormat** object, or a pattern of your own. These classes provide far too many options to describe in this book.

USING RESOURCES AND PROPERTIES FILES

This book concentrates on the capabilities of the Java language rather than good programming practices, but it does mention recommended practices when features of the language are designed to support them. Using model-view separation is an example of generally accepted best practice. Another recommended practice is removing literal text strings and any literal values from your classes. Rather than hard coding them in Java, consider literal values to be resources and store them in properties files.

Storing literal values outside your code is particularly beneficial in programs written for the international market. To make translation for users who work in another language as painless as possible, do not embed these literal strings in your code.

Similarly, configuration data or catalogs of messages that may change should not be embedded in your code. For example, if your program uses a database, configuration data, such as the location of the database and user ID and password with which to access the database, must be stored somewhere. Should any of these values change, it is much easier to change values in external files than modify and recompile your code.

Maintaining programs is cheaper and less error-prone if you minimize the potential need to change Java code. Treating literal textual elements and other literal values that may change in different production environments as external resources is strongly recommended.

In this context, a resource is a single entity, such as a text message, that your program can access and use. The important characteristic of resources is that they are external objects that your program can manipulate. Use the **ResourceBundle** class to collect resources into one manageable object. The resources can reside in a separate file called a *properties file* or in a class definition created for the purpose of holding resources.

Creating versions of your program for users who work in another language or for an environment that requires different configuration data essentially involves three steps:

- Create a properties file that stores the literal values as strings, or define a class that extends **ListResourceBundle** to contain the values. You can include other resources such as images and audio clips.

- Modify or translate the strings in the properties file or the **ListResourceBundle** object as required. The result will be a set of files, one for each language or run-time environment. These files can have a common root name and a suffix that specifies the variant to use.

- Modify or write your program to use the **ResourceBundle** class or its subclasses to load resources by calling the **getBundle** method.

Using Resource Bundles

This section describes how to use existing resources in a properties file or a class that extends **ListResourceBundle**. The next section describes properties files and how to create them. The section "Retrieving and Formatting Messages" shows how to use properties files not only for fixed text, but also to build messages dynamically at runtime.

To access resources in a Java class, you need a **ResourceBundle** object. Individual resources are stored as key-value pairs.

Class

java.util.ResourceBundle

Purpose

This abstract class encapsulates resources that are loaded from a property file or a class that extends **ListResourceBundle**.

Constructor

- **ResourceBundle( )**

  To acquire an instance of this class, call the method **getBundle**.

Methods

- **ResourceBundle getBundle(String** *basename* **)**

  ResourceBundle getBundle(String *basename,* **Locale** *locale* **)**

  These are final class (static) methods. Each returns an instance of **ResourceBundle**. Use the returned object to load resources into a program. You must specify a base filename and can optionally specify a **Locale** object. The locale-specific variants are distinguished by suffixes that identify the associated locale.

- **Enumeration getKeys( )**

  The abstract method **getKeys( )** returns an **Enumeration** object that you can use to access keys in a **ResourceBundle** object.

- **Object getObject(String** *key* **)**

  The final method **getObject** returns the object that is the value of the resource specified by the key argument.

- **String getString(String** *key* **)**

  The final method **getString** returns a **String** object that is the value of a resource that is specified by the key argument. Use this convenience method to avoid casting when the object with the given key is known to be a string.

4

■ String[ ] getStringArray(String key)

The final method **getStringArray** returns an array of **String** objects that are the value of a resource that is specified by the key argument. Use this convenience method to avoid casting when the object with the given key is known to be a **String** array.

The next two sample programs (Figures 4-26 and 4-27) demonstrate how to use a **ResourceBundle** object. The **getBundle** method locates a **.class** file or a **.properties** file, parses the file, and then creates a **ResourceBundle** object containing the resource information. You can then call methods of the **ResourceBundle** class, such as **getString**, to get the value's individual resources as needed by your program.

ResourceBundle has two subclasses, **ListResourceBundle** and **PropertyResourceBundle**, that provide implementations for abstract methods of the **ResourceBundle** class. The class **ListResourceBundle** is an abstract class with an abstract method of its own, **getContents**, which returns resources to your program as a two-dimensional **Object** array. For resources that have types other than **String**, you should extend the class **ListResourceBundle** and include an implementation of **getContents**. When all your resources are strings, creating a properties file is a convenient way to work with resources.

Class

java.util.ListResourceBundle

Purpose

The abstract class **ListResourceBundle** is commonly extended to create a class definition used to hold program resources.

To specify the language associated with a **ListResourceBundle**, append an underscore to the class name followed by the standard abbreviation for the language. To specify a country in addition to language, append another underscore and append the standard abbreviation for the country. For example, **MyListResourceBundle_fr_CA** should define resources in French as spoken in Canada. Specifying a language and country is optional, but you must specify a language to specify a country.

Constructor

■ **ListResourceBundle()**

You must define a concrete subclass of the **ListResourceBundle** class to use.

Method

- **Object [ ] [ ] getContents()**

  When you extend **ListResourceBundle**, you must implement **getContents**. The method returns an array of pairs of objects in which each resource is a key-value pair. The key must have type **String**, but the value can have any type, including **java.awt.Image** or **java.applet.AudioClip**.

The class **PropertyResourceBundle** is a concrete class. To use it, you need one or more external properties files in which the resources are stored.

Class

java.util.PropertyResourceBundle

Purpose

You can use this subclass of **ResourceBundle** as an interface to properties files.

Constructor

- **PropertyResourceBundle(InputStream *is*)**

  When you create an instance of **PropertyResourceBundle**, specify an input stream on which to read the properties file.

Methods

- **Object handleGetObject(String *key*)**

  The method **handleGetObject** implements the abstract method of the **ResourceBundle** class to return the value of a resource. The argument identifies the required resource. To get the keys, call the **getKeys** method.

- **Enumeration getKeys( )**

  Method **getKeys** implements the abstract method of the **ResourceBundle** class to return an **Enumeration** object you can use to access the keys in a **ResourceBundle**.

Figure 4-26 demonstrates the use of the **ListResourceBundle** class. This example consists of two public classes: WebResourceBundle and TestWebResourceBundle. The resources are set up in the body of the method **getContents** in the public class WebResourceBundle.

```
package examples.utilities;
import java.util.ListResourceBundle;
/** A class to demonstrate how to extend the
  * ListResourceBundle class
  */
public class WebResourceBundle
   extends ListResourceBundle {
   /** This method must be overridden by this class
     * @return Object[][] containing the key and
     * resource pairs
     */
   protected Object[][] getContents() {
      Object[][] myContents = {
                       { "protocol", "http" },
                       { "URL", "localhost" },
                       { "port", new Integer(8080) },
                       { "context root", "myTestWeb" }
      };
      return myContents;
   }
}
```

Figure 4-26   Sample class extending `ListResourceBundle`

The class `TestWebResourceBundle` uses the method **getBundle**, providing the name of the `WebResourceBundle` class and using the default locale. The test class prints the resources defined in the bundle, as shown in Figure 4-27.

```
package examples.utilities;
import java.util.ResourceBundle;
import java.util.Enumeration;
import java.util.Locale;
public class TestWebResourceBundle {
   /** Test method for the class
     * @param args not used
     */
   public static void main( String[] args ) {
      ResourceBundle rb;
      String bundleName =
         "examples.utilities.WebResourceBundle";
      rb = ResourceBundle.getBundle( bundleName );
      print( rb );
   }
   /** Print the contents of a resource file
     * @param label the label given to the output
     * @param rb the ResourceBundle object to print
     */
```

Figure 4-27   Sample class extracting resources from `ResourceBundle`

```
public static void print( ResourceBundle rb ) {
   System.out.println(
      "Extracted from " +
      rb.getClass().getName() );
   Enumeration e = rb.getKeys();
   String key;
   while( e.hasMoreElements() ) {
      key = (String) e.nextElement();
      System.out.println( "\t" + key + " = "
         + rb.getObject( key ) );
   }
}

}
```

Figure 4-27   Sample class extracting resources from `ResourceBundle` (continued)

The output contains the following lines; however, the lines may appear in a different order, because the collection of keys extracted from the resource bundle is neither sorted nor ordered:

```
Extracted from examples.utilities.WebResourceBundle
   context root = myTestWeb
   protocol = http
   port = 8080
   URL = localhost
```

Creating Properties Files

The attraction of using properties files instead of classes that extend **ListResourceBundle** is that you can use simple text-editing tools to create and maintain properties files. Knowledge of the Java programming language is not required, so translators and nonprogrammers can maintain these files. Translation involves making a copy of the file and then using a text editor to translate all the strings.

A properties file is a line-oriented text file. You should create it with an editor that inserts no formatting codes into the text. It can have any base filename allowed on your operating system. The file extension is **.properties**. Often, it is convenient to give the file the same base name as the class that uses it. To specify the language used in a properties file, append an underscore to the base filename followed by the standard abbreviation for the language. To specify a country, append another underscore after the language and append the standard abbreviation for the country.

A properties file can contain the following kinds of lines:

Syntax

```
# comment
key = value
```

Dissection

- You can insert comments. Comments can occupy a full line or follow resource information on the same line. Either way, start a comment with the octothorpe character (#). Comments end at the end of the line.

- Specify one resource on each line. Each resource is a key-value pair. The key is the name used by a program to identify and extract the resource. The value is the definition of the resource and is the information returned to the program. The value can have embedded spaces and is not enclosed in quotation marks or other delimiting characters.

- Single quotation marks are treated as special characters within the file. If you want to put a single quote in a text value, use two consecutive single quotes.

- To indicate that a resource definition continues onto the next line, end the line with a backslash character (\ ).

- Placeholders for substitution strings provided by the program are represented by {n}. The value of n is zero for the first substitution in the line, one for the second, and so on. Substitution strings are described in the section "Retrieving and Formatting Messages."

Figure 4-28 is a sample properties file. It is used in the sample program in Figure 4-29. It could be called `RegistrationForm_en.properties`. However, because English is the default language, this file is simply named `RegistrationForm.properties`.

```
# RegistrationForm.properties
# This file contains the strings used in the
# Registration Example when run for default
# English US locales.
instructions=please complete the following form
contact.name=Name
address.street=Street
address.city=City
address.region=State
address.code=Zip Code
contact.phone=telephone
# thank-you=Thank-you
messages.missing_resource=Could not find resource "{0}".
```

Figure 4-28   A sample properties file

You can also create a properties file for a language as spoken in a particular country. For example, Canada has provinces rather than states and post codes rather than Zip codes. To create a Canadian version of the registration form, use

RegistrationForm_en_CA.properties. As with locale names, you must append the language suffix named before the country suffix:

```
# RegistrationForm_en_CA.properties
# This file contains the strings used in the Registration Example
# when run for English Canadian locales.
address.region=Province
address.code=post code
```

This file does not repeat every message in the default properties file: it includes only the differences. When the JVM looks for resources in the resource bundles, the search always begins with the bundle for the specific country and language. If the JVM fails to find the resource there, the search looks in the bundle for the language. If that search also fails, the JVM uses the default bundle. For example, if you request the locale for French as spoken in Canada, the file search order is as follows:

- RegistrationForm_fr_CA.properties

- RegistrationForm_fr.properties

- RegistrationForm.properties

If the JVM does not find the key-value pair for the resource in any resource bundle, the program throws the exception **MissingResourceException**. Note that the thank-you message is commented out in the default **RegistrationForm.properties** file to demonstrate this exception.

Using Properties Files

Figure 4-29 is a simple application from which all text has been stripped and placed in a properties file. For simplicity, it is a command-line program that prints prompts to the command line and reads responses entered by the user. In a similar manner, you can extract all the labels and text that appear in a Java GUI. Of course you can also move to properties files text that never appears in the user interface but is sensitive to the run-time environment. Following the code is a breakdown of key lines.

```
package examples.utilities;
import java.io.*;
import java.text.MessageFormat;
import java.util.Locale;
import java.util.MissingResourceException;
import java.util.ResourceBundle;
/** An example class used to demonstrate the basics
  * of separating all text from code by placing
  * strings in a properties file accessed through
  * a Resource Bundle object.
  */
```

Figure 4-29   Sample class using properties files

```
public class Registration {
  /** The test method for the class
    * @param args optional language and country
    */
  public static void main(String[] args)
        throws IOException {
    String language, country;
    language =
      args.length < 1 ? "default" : args[0];
    country =
      args.length < 2 ? "default" : args[1];
    Locale.setDefault(
      new Locale(language, country ) );
    ResourceBundle rb =
      ResourceBundle.getBundle(
        "examples\\utilities\\RegistrationForm" );
    completeForm(rb);
  }
  /** The method that prints form and accepts input
    * @param rb is the ResourceBundle
    */
  static void completeForm(ResourceBundle rb) {
    try {
      BufferedReader br =
        new BufferedReader(
        new InputStreamReader( System.in ) );
      System.out.println(
        rb.getString( "instructions" ) );
      System.out.print(
        rb.getString( "contact.name" )
        + ":\t" );
      String name = br.readLine();
      System.out.print(
        rb.getString( "address.street" )
        + ":\t" );
      String street = br.readLine();
      System.out.print(
        rb.getString( "address.city" ) + ":\t" );
      String city = br.readLine();
      System.out.print(
        rb.getString("address.region" ) + ":\t");
      String region = br.readLine();
      System.out.print(
        rb.getString("address.code" ) + ":\t");
      String code = br.readLine();
      System.out.print(
        rb.getString("contact.phone" ) + ":\t");
      String phone = br.readLine();
```

Figure 4-29 Sample class using properties files (continued)

```
      System.out.print(
         rb.getString( "thank-you" ) );
   } catch (MissingResourceException mrx) {
      String message;
      try {
         message = rb.getString(
            "messages.missing_resource" );
      } catch (MissingResourceException mrx2) {
         message =
            "Missing resource(s) in properties file";
      }
      MessageFormat mf =
         new MessageFormat(message);
      Object[] messageArgs = { mrx.getKey()};
      System.out.println(mf.format(messageArgs));
   } catch (IOException ioe) {
      ioe.printStackTrace();
   }
  }
 }
}
```

Figure 4-29   Sample class using properties files (continued)

In the following lines, the **main** method accepts two optional parameters, `language` and `country`, that identify a **Locale** object. If less than two command-line arguments are provided, the program substitutes default values that are ignored. The program then retrieves a **ResourceBundle** for the **Locale** based on the base filename of `RegistrationForm`. The properties file should reside in the same folder as the file `Registration.class`. The **main** method then calls `completeForm` to display the form and accept user input, passing the **ResourceBundle** object as an argument.

```
public static void main(String[] args)
      throws IOException {
   String language, country;
   language =
      args.length < 1 ? "default" : args[0];
   country =
      args.length < 2 ? "default" : args[1];
   Locale.setDefault(
      new Locale(language, country));
   ResourceBundle rb =
      ResourceBundle.getBundle(
         "examples\\utilities\\RegistrationForm");
   completeForm(rb);
}
```

In the following lines, the method `completeForm` uses a **BufferedReader** to accept user input. For all informational output and prompts, it extracts the string from the

exceptions of type **IOException** or **MissingResourceException** may occur.

```
static void completeForm(ResourceBundle rb) {
    try {
        BufferedReader br =
            new BufferedReader(
            new InputStreamReader( System.in));
        System.out.println(
            rb.getString( "instructions"));
        System.out.print(
            rb.getString( "contact.name")
            + ":\t" );
        String name = br.readLine();
```

If the program uses a key that is not found in the **ResourceBundle** object, the code enters the catch block for the instance of exception class **MissingResourceException**. The handler simply prints a message saying the resource cannot be found. To make the exception message available for translation, the handler tries to retrieve the message from the **ResourceBundle** and must do so in an inner try block. The inner catch block stores the message in a **String** literal as a last resort. It is better to present a message in the wrong language than no message at all. The following lines show the exception handlers:

```
} catch (MissingResourceException mrx) {
        String message;
        try {
            message = rb.getString("messages.
            missing_resource");
        } catch (MissingResourceException mrx2) {
            message = "Missing resource(s) in
            properties file";
        }
```

The last lines of the outer catch clause are a sneak preview of the next section that describes message retrieval and formatting.

```
        MessageFormat mf = new MessageFormat
        (message);
        Object[] messageArgs = { mrx.getKey()};
        System.out.println(mf.format(messageArgs));
    }
```

The program requires properties files to run. Folder **examples\utilities** contains three properties files:

- **RegistrationForm.properties** is the default properties file, and is set up for the U.S. English locale.

- **RegistrationForm_en_CA.properties** is the properties file for English as spoken in Canada.

- `RegistrationForm_fr_CA.properties` is the properties file for French as spoken in Canada, and is listed here. The hexadecimal character `code` `\u00E9` represents the é character. The last line is split to fit this page, but is not split in the actual properties file.

```
# RegistrationForm_fr_CA.properties
# This file contains the string used in the Registration
Examples
# when run for French Canadian locales.
instructions=Veuiller remplier le formularie d'inscription ici-dessus
contact.name=Nom
address.street=Rue
address.city=Ville
address.region=Province
address.code=code postal
contact.phone=t\u00E9l\u00E9phone
thank-you=merci
messages.missing_resource=La ressource "{0}"
         n''est pas trouv\u00E9e.
```

Run this program from the **Data** folder as described in Chapter 1. Try running in different locales, by entering the following commands:

- `java examples\utilities\Registration`

- `java examples\utilities\Registration en CA`

- `java examples\utilities\Registration fr CA`

In French, the result may look like

```
Veuiller remplier le formularie d'inscription ici-dessus
Nom:        Jeanne Trudeau
Rue:        83422 Rue Inconnue
Ville:      Montréal
Province:   Québec
code postal:    H3R 1Y3
téléphone: 514-332-9932
merci
```

Note, the é character may not appear correctly in your output if your Java installation or OS does not support this Unicode value.

Retrieving and Formatting Messages

The final step in separating textual information into properties files is to manipulate the messages stored in the properties files. If the entire message is a literal string, you can treat it like any other resource. Sometimes, however, you cannot know the parts of a message when you create the properties file. In that circumstance, you can insert substitute text when it uses the following line from the `RegistrationForm.properties` file:

```
messages.missing_resource=Could not find resource "{0}".
```

In this case, the {0} is a placeholder for the name of the missing resource. To handle the substitution, wrap an instance of **MessageFormat** around the message retrieved from the resource bundle. Then, declare an array of type **Object[ ]** to hold the substitution arguments for the message. This example uses only the key from the **MissingResourceException** object, so the array has only one element. The array is passed to the **format** method of the **MessageFormat** object, and the result is the final message as in the following code:

```
MessageFormat mf = new MessageFormat( message );
Object[] messageArgs = { mrx.getKey() };
System.out.println( mf.format( messageArgs ) );
```

When more than one element must be substituted, the program gives the elements sequential values: {0}, {1}, {2}, and so on. The symbols are matched to the contents of the **Object[ ]** array in order. However, these symbols can appear within the message in another order. For example, the following line defines a legitimate message in a properties file:

```
messages.example=Error {2}:Item {0} in container {1}
```

The flexibility of positioning substitution symbols in messages allows for the different grammatical structures of different languages.

You can include additional information within the substitution symbol to specify how it should be formatted. For example, if the substitution value 0 should be formatted as a time value using the long style, specify the substitution symbol as { 0, time, long }. Other format types that can be specified are date, number, and choice. Each of these can also have a format style specified to control the output format more precisely. For more details, look in the documentation supplied with the Java 2 platform and in the help or documentation provided with your choice of application development software.

PARSING STRINGS WITH `StringTokenizer`

The **java.util** package provides one helpful class for a common string manipulation task: Use the **StringTokenizer** class to parse a string to break it into separate tokens. Often you want to do this after reading a line of input.

A *token* usually consists of a sequence of characters that does not include a space, newline, tab, or other nonprinting characters. These characters are often called whitespace. By default, a **StringTokenizer** object interprets whitespace characters as delimiters between tokens. You can call methods of **StringTokenizer** to customize this behavior. For example, you can specify that the delimiter be a comma.

Class

`java.util.StringTokenizer`

Purpose

This utility class extracts tokens from a **String** object, one by one.

Constructors

- **StringTokenizer(String** *s* **)**

  StringTokenizer(String *s* **, String** *delimiter* **)**

  StringTokenizer(String *s* **, String** *delimiter* **,**

                      boolean *returnDelimiters* **)**

  The constructor builds a **StringTokenizer** for the **String** object specified in the first argument. By default, whitespace separates tokens, but you can specify one or more alternative delimiter characters in a second argument of type **String**. If you want each delimiter to be extracted as a token, set the **boolean** argument to **true**. Then each delimiter is returned as a **String** object of length one. If this argument is **false** or omitted, delimiters are skipped.

Methods

- **String nextToken()**

  This method returns the next token in the **StringTokenizer** object, or throws an exception if no more tokens are available.

- **boolean hasMoreTokens()**

  This method returns **true** if another token can be extracted from the **StringTokenizer** object, or **false** otherwise. You should call **hasMoreTokens** before **nextToken**, and call **nextToken** only if **hasMoreTokens** returns **true**.

Figure 4-30 shows how to extract numbers and words from a line of input entered by the user. For demonstration purposes, the first token in the input line is interpreted as an integer, the second as a floating-point number, and all remaining tokens as one **String** object.

```
package examples.utilities;
import java.io.*;
import java.util.StringTokenizer;
/**
 * A class to demonstrate the StringTokenizer
 */
public class InputParser {
   public static void main(String[] args) {
      try {
        BufferedReader br =
           new BufferedReader(
           new InputStreamReader( System.in ) );
```

Figure 4-30   Sample class using **StringTokenizer**

4

```
        System.out.println(
            "Enter an integer, real number, " +
            "and string on one line");
        String line = br.readLine();
        StringTokenizer st =
            new StringTokenizer( line );
        int k = Integer.parseInt( st.nextToken() );
        System.out.println( "integer:\t" + k );
        float f =
            Float.parseFloat( st.nextToken() );
        System.out.println( "float:\t" + f);
        String s = st.nextToken();
        while ( st.hasMoreTokens() ) {
            s += " " + st.nextToken();
        }
        System.out.println( "String:\t" + s );
    } catch (NumberFormatException nfe ) {
        System.out.println(
            "Incorrect number format" );
    } catch( IOException ioe ) {
        System.out.println( ioe.getMessage() );
    }
  }
}
```

Figure 4-30 Sample class using **StringTokenizer** (continued)

One potential disadvantage of **StringTokenizer** is that it folds multiple, adjacent whitespace characters into one delimiter. You cannot use the default delimiter if you want to preserve multiple spaces between words. Consider, for example, this output from the program in Figure 4-30:

```
Enter an integer, real number, and string on one line
1234 -342.3245 this is  a   string
integer:   1234
float:     -342.3245
String:    this is a string
```

Note that the input included two spaces between "is" and "a" and three spaces between "a" and "string," but the output includes only one space between each token in the string.

PATTERN RECOGNITION WITH REGULAR EXPRESSIONS

Many sorts of problems require pattern recognition in sequences of characters. Text search-and-replace or data validation can involve determining whether a string contains either a specific sequence of characters or a pattern of characters. For example, you may want to locate all words that start with a prefix "contra" in a document, or check whether a proposed identifier conforms to some application-specific pattern such as starting with two letters followed by ten digits with optional spaces between groups of four characters. For tasks such as these, you can use regular expressions.

A *regular expression* is a string of characters that describe a sequence of characters as a pattern. The pattern can be a mixture of literals and special or meta-characters. For example, all three-letter words starting with "m" and ending with 't' could be represented by a pattern "m.t". The dot is a special character that acts as a wildcard for almost any character, so "m<t", "m5t", and "m t" also match the pattern "m.t". A pattern that limits the matches to words mat, met, mit, mot, and mut is "m[aeiou]t". The next section, "Syntax of Regular Expressions," introduces the most frequently used regular expression constructs.

The classes that provide regular expressions in Java compose the **java.util.regex** package. This package contains only two classes, **Pattern** and **Matcher**, plus one exception class, **PatternSyntaxException**. A common set of programming steps for using regular expressions is to

1. Create a **Pattern** object that encapsulates a regular expression. You pass the regular expression as a **String** object to the class (static) method **Pattern.compile**. This factory method returns an instance of **Pattern**.

2. Acquire a **CharSequence** object that encapsulates the sequence of characters you want to test. Classes **java.lang.String**, **java.lang.StringBuffer**, and **java.nio.CharBuffer** implement the **CharSequence** interface.

3. Get a **Matcher** object by calling the **matcher** method on the **Pattern** object, passing as argument the **CharSequence** of interest.

4. Call a method on the **Matcher** object. For example, call **find** to see if the **CharSequence** contains a sequence of characters that conform to the pattern, or call **matches** to determine whether the whole **CharSequence** object conforms to the pattern.

Regular expressions have been used in many contexts for many years. Several scripting languages, such as Perl, operating systems, including UNIX, high-feature editors, and other text manipulation tools support regular expressions. However, they are new to the Java platform. Version 1.4 of the J2SDK added package **java.util.regex** to support regular expressions. In earlier versions, you used the **String**, **StringBuffer**, and **StringTokenizer** classes for character operations or imported non-standard packages to handle regular expressions. The **CharSequence** interface is also new with version 1.4.

Syntax of Regular Expressions

Before looking in detail at the **Pattern** and **Matcher** classes, you should learn how to build and read regular expressions. The Java implementation is close to Perl 5 regular expressions. See the J2SDK **javadoc** for a full description of the Java implementation and comparison of the differences between Java and Perl regular expression syntax.

Figure 4-31 introduces some of the characters used in regular expressions and gives descriptions and examples of their usage.

Pattern	Description	Example
x	Any nonspecial character is taken literally	d in "dog", a in "cat"
xyz	Sequence of literals to match exactly	dog in "dog" or cat in "scatter"
.	Wildcard character	h... is any four-character sequence starting with "h"
[ ]	Delimit a character class	[abc] matches "a" or "b" or "c"
-	Inside a class indicates a range	[0-9] matches any decimal digit [a-zA-Z] matches any non-accented letter
|	Performs explicit OR	e|ea|ee|ei matches one of "e", "ea", "ee", "ei" 1[2|44|888]1 matches "121" or "1441" or "18881"
^	Inside a class negates the match criteria Outside a class indicates start of line	[^@] matches any character except "@" [^0-9] matches any character except a digit ^// matches a line that starts with two slashes
&&	Inside a class defines union	[a-z&&[^y]] matches any lowercase letter except y
\	Arming character	\\ matches "\"; \. matches "." ; \$ matches "$"
^	Outside a class indicates start of line	^//.* matches a line starting with "//"
$	End of the line	/index.html$ matches lines ending "/index.html"
( )	Grouping	([a-zA-z])([0-9]) delimits one letter followed by one digit as a group

Figure 4-31   Characters in regular expressions

Note that when you code regular expressions in **String** literals, you must use a Java escape sequence for each backslash. For example, to code the regular expression to match a dollar sign, use \\$ as in:

```
\\ the pattern for price less than 10 dollars
Pattern.compile( "\\$[0-9].[0-9][0-9]" );
```

Use the special characters shown in Figure 4-32 to indicate multiplicity, or the number of occurances, of an element or character, class, or group at the current position in a pattern.

Qualifier	Description	Example
None	Exactly one occurrence	f in "gif", cat in "catalog"
?	Zero or one occurrences	\-? indicates an optional hyphen
*	Zero, one, or more occurrences	&* matches "" or "&" or "&&" or "&&&" ...
+	One or more occurrences	[0-9]+ matches a sequence of all digits
{n}	Exactly n times	[aeiou]{2} matches any two-vowel sequence
{n,m}	Between n and m times, inclusive	[*]{3,5} matches "***" or "****" or "*****"

Figure 4-32   Multiplicity in regular expressions

For convenience, a number of short forms for sets of characters are defined. Figure 4-33 lists just a few of them. Note that some standard Java escape characters are included.

Character	Represents	Character	Represents
\t	Tab	\d	Digit, equivalent to [0-9]
\r	Carriage return	\D	Nondigit [^0-9]
\n	Newline	\w	Word character [a-zA-Z0-9]
\f	From feed	\W	Nonword character [^\w]
\cx	Control character corresponding to x	\s	Whitespace [\t\n\f\r]
\uhhhh	Unicode character in hexadecimal digits	\S	Non whitespace

Figure 4-33   Escape characters in regular expressions

If your implementation of Java uses U.S. ASCII, you have also the convenient representations shown in Figure 4-34. Several standard POSIX (an IEEE standard based on UNIX) character classes are included.

Class	Value	Class	Value
\p{Lower}	Lowercase [a-z]	\p{Punch}	Punctuation including symbols
\p{Upper}	Uppercase [A-Z]	\p{Space}	Whitespace character
\p{Alpha}	[\p{Lower}\p{Upper}]	\p{Blank}	Space or tab
\p{Digit}	Digit [0-9]	\p{Cntrl}	Control character
\p{Alnum}	[\p{Alpha}\p{Digit}]	\p{Graph}	Visible character
\p{ASCII}	Hex values 00 to FF	\p{Print}	Printable character

Figure 4-34   POSIX character classes in regular expressions

Groups

Patterns within a regular expression can be grouped using parentheses. Groups can be captured or stored by the **Matcher** object. Use this feature if you want to recall a subsequence of a character sequence that conforms to a regular expression. Groups are identified by number from left to right. The entire expression is always group 0. For example, you can parse a 12-digit bank account number in which the first two digits indicate the banking institution, the next four digits indicate a branch, and the last six digits are the account number, with this expression:

```
([0-9]{2})-?([0-9]{4})-?([0-9]{6})
```

This pattern allows for optional hyphens between the parts of the account number. After matching the character sequence, you can work with the groups. Group 0 is the entire input string.

In the sequence 04-1823-312430

- Group 1 identifies the banking institution as 04.
- Group 2 indicates bank branch 1823.
- Group 3 holds the bank account number 312430.

Processing Regular Expressions

Use the pattern class to store a regular expression for processing.

Class

java.util.regex.Pattern

Purpose

A **Pattern** object holds a compiled representation of a regular expression.

Constructor

Use the class (static) method **compile** to build a **Pattern** object.

Methods

- **Pattern compile(String** *regex* **)**

  Pattern compile(String *regex***, int** *flags* **)**

  The **compile** method compiles the supplied regular expression into a pattern. You can optionally specify flags defined as fields of this class. To use the ^ and $ characters for start and end of a line, compile with the flag **MULTILINE**. In multiline mode, set flag **DOTALL** if you want the . wildcard character to match the line terminator as well as other characters.

- `Matcher matcher( CharSequence `*`input`*` )`

  The **matcher** method creates a matcher that you can use to apply the pattern to the specified input.

- `boolean matches( String `*`regex`*`, CharSequence `*`input`*` )`

  The class (static) method **matches** provides a convenient way to see whether a character sequence matches the regular expression. Calling this method is equivalent to

  ```
  Pattern p = Pattern.compile( regularExpressionString );
  Matcher m = p.matcher( inputCharSequence );
  m.matches();
  ```

- `String [ ] split(Charsequence `*`input`*` )`

  `String [ ] split(Charsequence `*`input,`*` int `*`limit`*` )`

  The **split** method breaks the input sequence into an array of strings around occurrences of the pattern in the input. The regular expression acts as a delimiter and is not included in the returned strings. You can optionally specify how many times to apply the pattern up to the size of the return array.

The **Pattern** class collaborates closely with the **Matcher** class. As well as checking for pattern matches, **Matcher** can modify the input character sequence. A typical operation is to replace all occurrences of the sequence that conform to the regular expression with alternative characters. **Matcher** can also return information about instances of regular expression groups.

Class

`java.util.regex.Matcher`

Purpose

Matcher performs the analysis of a **CharSequence** according to a regular expression.

Constructor

Obtain **Matcher** by calling the **matcher** method on the associated **Pattern** object.

Methods

- `Matcher appendReplacement( StringBuffer `*`sb,`*`
                            String `*`replacement`*`)`

  `Matcher appendTail( StringBuffer `*`sb`*` )`

  Use the **appendReplacement** and **appendTail** methods together to perform text substitution on a character sequence. The **appendReplacement** method

the next subsequence that conforms to the pattern. Then it appends the contents of the supplied replacement **String** object to the **StringBuffer** instead of the matching subsequence. Typically you use this method in a loop to replace subsequences one at a time. When there are no more matching subsequences, call **appendTail** to append characters that follow the last match to the **StringBuffer**, as in

```
boolean found = m.find( );
StringBuffer sb = new StringBuffer( );
  while ( found) {
    m.appendReplacement(  sb, "newChars" ) )
    found = m.find( );
 }
 m.appendTail( sb );
```

■ **boolean find( )**

boolean find (int *start* **)**

The **find** method looks for a sequence of characters in the input sequence that matches the pattern. By default, the search starts at the first character in the input sequence on the first call or immediately after the last match on subsequent calls. You can optionally specify a start index.

■ **int groupCount( )**

The **groupCount** method returns the number of capturing groups found in the last find or match operation.

■ **String group( )**

String group(int *i* **)**

The **group** method returns the capturing group identified by the supplied number in the last match or find operation. If no group number is supplied, the entire input sequence for this **Matcher** is returned.

■ **boolean lookingAt( )**

The **lookingAt** method tests whether the input sequence starts with a sequence of characters that conform to the pattern.

■ **boolean matches( )**

The **matches** method tests whether the entire input sequence conforms to the pattern.

■ **String replaceAll(String** *replacement* **)**

The **replaceAll** method replaces every occurrence of a sequence that conforms to the pattern in the input sequence with the supplied replacement **String** object, and returns the resulting string.

- **String replaceFirst(String** *replacement* **)**

  The **replaceFirst** method replaces the first occurrence of a sequence that conforms to the pattern in the input sequence with the supplied replacement **String** object, and returns the resulting string.

- **Matcher reset( )**

  Matcher reset(CharSequence *replacement* **)**

  The **reset** method clears all state information about this **Matcher** and sets the append position to 0. When a **CharSequence** is supplied, it replaces the current input sequence.

A common use of regular expressions is to test whether string data conforms to format rules. The first step in validating user input often involves checking the pattern of the input. For example, did the user supply a feasible Zip or post code? If yes, the program may go on to a second stage of validation and check that the code is consistent with the city supplied. You can perform the first stage with regular expressions.

A variation on the **Registration** program from the discussion of properties files earlier in this chapter reads the user input and checks the format of user-supplied Zip or post codes. The entire program is provided in the class **examples.utilities.RegistrationVerification**, but only the new method **verifyPostCode** uses regular expressions. The argument of this method is the user input. The output is **true** if the input conforms to the required pattern and **false** otherwise. Figure 4-35 shows the **verifyPostCode** method.

```
protected static boolean VerifyPostCode(
      String code) {
   Locale locale = Locale.getDefault();
   Pattern p;
// determine the country from the current Locale
   if (locale.getCountry().equals( "CA" ) ) {
      // Canadian postcodes look like a1a1a1
      p = Pattern.compile( "([a-zA-Z][0-9]){3}" );
   } else {
      // US Zip codes look like  ddddd
      // or ddddd dddd or ddddd-dddd
      p = Pattern.compile(
         "\\d{5}([ \\-]\\d{4})?" );
   }
   Matcher m = p.matcher( code );
   return m.matches();
}
```

Figure 4-35 Sample method using regular expressions

Two things to note:

1. All backslashes must be represented in Java code as the escapes sequence \\. Here, the \d notation represents a digit and appears in Java as \\d.

2. The pattern for a Zip code contains a group. In this case, the use of parentheses is to group the optional hyphen with the four-digit part of the Zip code so that the hyphen can appear only when Zip codes take the nine-digit form. The ability to recall the value of the final four digits is not used in this program.

Another common use of regular expressions is to find and replace text in files. Figure 4-36 is a sample program that locates instances of the tab character and replaces them with a number of spaces. The program takes three command-line arguments: an input filename, an output filename, and an optional number of spaces to substitute for each tab character. The default is three spaces.

```java
package examples.utilities;
import java.io.*;
import java.util.regex.Matcher;
import java.util.regex.Pattern;
/** An example class  to demonstrate using regular
  * expressions to perform text replacement
  */
public class Tab2SpaceConverter {
   /** The test method for the class
     * @param args inputfile, outputfile, optional
     * number of spaces that replace one tab.
     * The default is 3.
     */
   public static void main(String[] args) {
      if ( args.length < 2 ) {
         System.out.println( "usage: "
            + "inputFileName outputFileName"
            + "[numSpaces]" );
         System.exit( 0 );
      }
      // prepare the input and output files
      try {
         File fin = new File( args[0] );
         FileInputStream fis =
            new FileInputStream( args[0] );
         BufferedReader bri = new BufferedReader(
            new InputStreamReader(fis) );
         File fout = new File( args[1] );
         FileOutputStream fos = new FileOutputStream(
            args[1] );
         BufferedWriter bro = new BufferedWriter(
            new OutputStreamWriter( fos ) );
         // set up the replacement string
         int nspace = 3;
```

Figure 4-36   Sample class using regular expressions for text replacement

```
         try {
            nspace = Math.max(
                Integer.parseInt( args[2] ), 0 );
         } catch( Exception e ) {
            nspace = 3;
         }
         String spaces = "";
         while ( spaces.length() < nspace ) {
            spaces += " ";
         }
         // match and replace all tab characters
         Pattern p = Pattern.compile( "\\t" );
         Matcher m = p.matcher( "" );
         String line = null;
         String oline = null;
         while ( ( line = bri.readLine() )
                 != null ) {
            m.reset(line);
            bro.write( m.replaceAll( spaces) );
            bro.newLine();
         }
         // end of file
         System.out.println ( "File " + args[1] +
            " created." );
         bri.close();
         bro.close();
      } catch( IOException ioe ) {
         System.out.println( ioe.getMessage() );
      }
   }
}
```

Figure 4-36 Sample class using regular expressions for text replacement (continued)

Here is a sample input file called `days.in`:

```
My list of days
   Week
                Monday        1
                Tuesday       2
                Wednesday     3
                Thursday      4
                Friday        5
      Weekend
                Saturday      6
                Sunday        7
```

If you have set your classpath to run samples directly from the CD-ROM as described in Chapter 1, you can run the class by typing all of the following on one line:

```
java examples.utilities.Tab2SpaceConverter
     X:\data\examples\utilities\days.in
```

                          2

Note that the output must be sent to a drive to which you can write.

Here is the `days.out` file produced by running the program:

```
My list of days
   Week
      Monday     1
      Tuesday     2
      Wednesday  3
      Thursday   4
      Friday     5
   Weekend
      Saturday   6
      Sunday     7
```

The Java API for regular expressions is contained in two classes and a small number of methods. However, the grammar of regular expressions is worthy of study in its own right. You may find it far easier to code the programs that use regular expressions than to formulate regular expressions that match all the strings you want to match and no others. Regular expressions can be terse and cryptic, but they do provide a powerful and flexible tool for processing character sequences.

CHAPTER SUMMARY

- The Java platform provides classes that support a variety of data structures and other useful features in the packages **java.util**, **java.util.jar**, **java.util.logging**, **java.util.prefs**, **java.util.regex**, and **java.util.zip** and character formatting in **java.text**.

- The collections framework defines interfaces that define the behavior of a variety of data structures. Interfaces **List**, **Set**, and **SortedSet** extend **Collection**. The interface **SortedMap** extends **Map**.

- Each collection class has an **iterator** method that provides an **Iterator** object you use to traverse the collection one element at a time.

- The following ready-to-use implementations are provided by classes:

```
LinkedList      ArrayList       Vector       Stack
HashSet         LinkedHashSet   TreeSet
HashMap         LinkedHashMap   TreeMap
IdentityHashMap WeakHashMap     Hashtable
```

- To increase the usefulness of the collections framework, commonly used algorithms, such as search, sort, and reverse, are implemented in polymorphic methods that are gathered into the classes **Collections** and **Arrays**.

- The **Collections** class also provides methods for creating wrapper collections to add synchronization and read-only characteristics to existing collection objects.

- ❑ Legacy collection classes **Bitset**, **Hashtable**, **Properties**, **Vector**, and **Stack** have been available since the Java 1 platform.

- ❑ All legacy collection classes except **Bitset** have been retrofitted into the collections framework so that instances of **Vector** and **Stack** are **List** objects and instances of **Hashtable** are **Map** objects. However, they retain old methods and cursor objects of type **Enumeration**.

- ❑ Some classes in the utility package and related packages are not associated with collections but perform miscellaneous useful tasks.

- ❑ Use **Observer** and **Observable** to set up an automatic event-notification mechanism. Classes that implement the interface **Observer** are notified when an object of a class that extends the **Observable** class changes.

- ❑ The **Random** class generates pseudo-random numbers.

- ❑ Locales are data structures that encapsulate cultural environments. The **Locale** class provides many predefined **Locale** objects for different spoken languages and countries.

- ❑ Use locale-sensitive classes **Calendar**, **Timezone**, **NumberFormat**, **DecimalFormat**, and **DateFormat** to manipulate and format date, time, monetary value, percentage, and number data.

- ❑ A best programming practice is to separate literal strings and other fixed values from your code by storing the values as resources in properties files. Use **ResourceBundles** to access these resources. Using resources is also helpful when preparing programs for translation or storing configuration data.

- ❑ The **StringTokenizer** class gives you limited ability to parse strings.

- ❑ The classes **Pattern** and **Matcher** in **java.util.regex** provide flexible pattern recognition in character sequences using regular expressions.

REVIEW QUESTIONS

1. Which of the following collection classes store elements as key-value pairs? Select all that apply.
   a. **HashMap**
   b. **TreeMap**
   c. **BitSet**
   d. **Properties**
   e. **LinkedList**

2. Which of the following collection classes allow duplicate data values? Select all that apply.
   a. **ArrayList**
   b. **HashMap**

d. **LinkedList**

e. **Vector**

3. Which of the following interfaces do you implement for an unordered collection that allows duplicate elements?

a. **Collection**

b. **Set**

c. **List**

d. **Bag**

e. **Map**

4. Which of the following methods does a **SortedSet** use to determine the order of elements that have no natural ordering?

a. **java.lang.Comparable.compareTo**

b. the inherited or overridden method **Object.equals**

c. **java.lang.Comparator.compare**

d. **java.util.Comparator.equals**

e. **java.util.Comparable.compareTo**

5. Examine the following code:

```
import java.util.List;
import java.util.ArrayList;
public class Quiz4_5 {
    public static void main( String[] args ) {
        List list = new ArrayList( 100 );
        double x = -34.678;
        list.add( x );
        System.out.println( list.get( 0 ) );
    }
}
```

Which of the following statements are true when the code is compiled and run? Select all that apply.

a. The compiler rejects the expression new **ArrayList(100)** because no constructor parameters are allowed when creating an **ArrayList** object.

b. Compilation is successful, and the output is -34.678.

c. Compilation is successful, and the output is 100.

d. The compiler rejects the expression list.add(x) because x cannot be converted to the type **Object**.

e. The compiler rejects the expression list.add(x) because **List** objects can contain only integer values, not floating-point values.

6. Which of the following methods are defined in the **Observer** interface? Select all that apply.

   a. `observe`

   b. `update`

   c. `toString`

   d. `hashCode`

   e. `equals`

7. Which of the following should you not extend to create your own collection class?

   a. `AbstractCollection`

   b. `AbstractMap`

   c. `AbstractSet`

   d. `AbstractList`

   e. `Dictionary`

8. You can find out what keys are available from **ResourceBundle** in which of the following ways?

   a. Call `getKeys` to get `Iterator`. Use `Iterator` to traverse the keys.

   b. Call `getKeys` to get `Enumeration`. Use `Enumeration` to traverse the keys.

   c. Call `getKeys` to return an object of type `ArrayList`.

   d. Call `getResources` to get the keys and values in an array of type `String[ ] [ ]`.

   e. Call `nextKey` to get the next key pair. The `ResourceBundle` supplies them one at a time.

9. Which of the following regular expressions match the word "911" ? Select all that apply.

   a. `\d\d\d`

   b. `91*`

   c. `9.1`

   d. `[911]`

   e. `91{2}`

10. Most of the western world uses the Gregorian calendar. Which of the following snippets of Java code are correct ways to get an appropriate object to manipulate dates and times? Select all that apply.

    a. `Calendar  c  =  Locale.getDefault().getCalendar();`

    b. `Calendar  c  =  new GregorianCalendar();`

    c. `Calendar  c  =  GregorianCalendar.getInstance();`

    d. `Calendar  c  =  Calendar.getInstance();`

    e. `Calendar  c  =  Calendar. getCalendar( Locale.getDefault() );`

11. Examine the following code:

```
import java.util.StringTokenizer;
public class Quiz4_11 {
   private static final String text
      = "The quick, brown fox";
   public static void main( String[] args ) {
      StringTokenizer st
         = new StringTokenizer( text, "," );
      while( st.hasMoreTokens() ) {
         System.out.println( st.nextToken( " " ) );
      }
   }
}
```

Which of the following statements are true when the code is compiled and run? Select all that apply.

a. Compilation is successful, and the output is

```
The
quick,
brown
fox
```

b. Compilation is successful, and the output is

```
The quick,
brown
fox
```

c. Compilation is successful, and the output is

```
The quick,
brown fox
```

d. The compiler rejects the expression new `StringTokenizer( text, "," )` because only `String` objects can be passed as parameters to `StringTokenizer` constructors.

e. The compiler rejects the use of the methods `hasMoreTokens` and `nextToken` because they are not defined in the `Enumeration` interface.

12. You can use methods defined in the `java.text.NumberFormat` class to control the format of which of the following types of numerical values? Select all that apply.

a. monetary values including the currency symbol

b. floating-point numbers accurate to a specific number of decimal points

c. time in hours, minutes, and seconds

d. percentages

e. numbers in scientific notation

PROGRAMMING EXERCISES

To get the files required for the Debugging and Complete the Solution exercises, copy the folder \Data\questions\c4 from the CD that accompanies this book to the folder Data\questions\c4 on your hard drive. Work in the folder that contains questions. Make sure questions contains the folder c4 and c4 contains the original Java source files.

Debugging

1. Correct all the errors in the following program:

```java
package questions.c4;
import java.util.*;
public class Debug4_1 {
    private static final int SIZE = 100;
    public static void main( String[] args ) {
        List list = new ArrayList( SIZE );
        for ( int i=0; i<=SIZE; i++ ) {
            list.add( new Integer( i*i ) );
        }
        Integer x = list.getLast();
        System.out.println( x.intValue() );
    }
}
```

2. Correct all the errors in the following program so that both output statements print true:

```java
package questions.c4;
public class Debug4_2 {
    private String name = "";
    public String getName() {
        return name;
    }
    public void setName( String newName ) {
        name = newName;
    }
    public boolean equals( Object other ) {
        return name.equals( ( (Debug4_2) other).name );
    }
    public static void main( String[] args ) {
        Debug4_2 x = new Debug4_2();
        Debug4_2 y = new Debug4_2();
        x.setName( "Bono" );
        y.setName( "Bono" );
        System.out.println( x.equals( y ) );
        System.out.println(
                x.hashCode() == y.hashCode() );
    }
}
```

3. Correct all the errors in the following program

```
package questions.c4;
import java.text.Collator;
class Debug_3 {
   public static void main( String[] args ) {
      String s1 = "Smith, John";
      String s2 = "Smith, Joan";
      Collator c = new Collator();
      int result = c.compare( s1, s2 );
      switch( result ) {
         case -1:
             System.out.println( s1 + " < " + s2 );
            break;
         case 0:
             System.out.println( s1 + " == " + s2 );
            break;
         case 1:
             System.out.println( s1 + " > " + s2 );
            break;
      }
   }
}
```


4. Correct all the errors in the following program so that the **ResourceBundle** subclass is correctly defined and its data is displayed:

```
package questions.c4;
import java.util.ResourceBundle;
import java.util.ListResourceBundle;
public class Debug4_4 {
   protected Object[] getContents() {
      Object[] myContents = {
         { "price", new Double( 3.79 ) },
         { "name", "Shimmer floor wax" }
      };
      return myContents;
   }   public static void main( String[] args ) {
      ResourceBundle rb = new Debug4_4();
      String key = "price";
      System.out.println( key + " = "
                                 + rb.getObject( key ) );
      key = "name";
      System.out.println( key + " = "
                                 + rb.getObject( key ) );
   }
}
```

5. Correct all the errors in the following program:

```java
package questions.c4;
import java.util.Observable;
import java.util.Observer;
public class Debug4_5 {
    public static void main( String[] args ) {
        FireStation fs = new FireStation();
        FireAlarm fa = new FireAlarm();
        fa.addObserver( fs );
        fa.soundAlarm();
        fa.clearAlarm();
    }
    static private class FireAlarm {
        private boolean alarmOn;
        public boolean isAlarmOn() {
            return alarmOn;
        }
        public void soundAlarm() {
            alarmOn = true;
            setChanged();
            notifyObservers();
        }
        public void clearAlarm() {
            alarmOn = false;
            setChanged();
            notifyObservers();
        }
    }
    static private class FireStation
                        implements Observer {
        public void update( FireAlarm fa, Object arg ) {
            if ( fa.isAlarmOn() ) {
                System.out.println( "Go to fire!" );
            } else {
                System.out.println( "Go back to"
                                    + " station." );
            }
        }
    }
}
```

6. Correct all the errors in the following class definition so that the program displays today's date correctly for France in its long format:

```java
package questions.c4;
import java.text.DateFormat;
import java.util.Calendar;
import java.util.Date;
import java.util.Locale;
```

```
        public static void main( String[] args) {
            Calendar cal = Calendar.getInstance();
            Date today
                = cal.getTime( LONG, Locale.FRANCE );
            System.out.println(  today  );
        }
    }
```

4

Complete the Solution

1. Modify the source for class `questions.c4.Complete4_1` in the file `questions\c1\ Complete4_1.java`. This program calculates a percentage and prints the resulting double value. Modify the program to format the output using the `NumberFormat` class to display the percentage accurate to two decimal digits as written in Italy.

2. Modify the source for class `questions.c4.Complete4_2` in the file `questions\c1\ Complete4_2.java`. This program does some whimsical manipulation on dates using `GregorianCalendar`, `Calendar`, and `LinkedList` classes. Insert code as directed by comments to get an appropriate `Calendar` object and extract from it `Date` objects to insert into `LinkedList`. Then implement the method that uses `ListIterator` to access and print the items in the list.

3. Start with the sample program `RegistrationVerifcation` listed in Figures 4-29 and 4-35. Add methods that use regular expressions to verify the name, city, region, and telephone number input by the user. Ensure the input conforms to the following rules:

    a. Names contain one or more words separated by a space and each word must start with a capital letter.

    b. City names must follow the same rules as person names.

    c. The region must be a recognized two-character abbreviation for a state or province. For example, Canadian provinces can be AB, BC, MB, NB, NF, NS, ON, PE, PQ, or SK.

    d. Telephone numbers must be 10 digits, optionally split into groups of three, and four digits by spaces, dashes, or periods. For an optional challenge, also let the first three digits be enclosed in parentheses, as in (123)456-7890.

4. Modify the source for class `questions.c4.Complete4_4` in the file `questions\c4\Complete4_4.java`. This class uses a `Properties` collection. It writes properties to a file and then retrieves them. Complete the definition of class `Complete4_4` by implementing the methods for setting and getting the address and phone number fields. Also implement methods that store the properties in a file and load them from a file.

5. Modify the source for class `questions.c4.Complete4_5` in the file `questions\c4\Complete4_5.java`. Complete the program `Complete4_5` by providing the missing class `Motorist`. This class should be defined as an `Observer` of the `Observable` class `StopLight`. A motorist should respond when a `StopLight` object changes color.

Discovery

1. Write a program that simulates a telephone that records missed incoming calls. A missed call is any incoming call that the user did not answer in person. For each missed call, store the time of call, telephone number of origin, and name of caller if the name is available. For unlisted numbers, set the name to "private caller". Choose or extend the most appropriate collection class and provide the following features:

   a. Numbers are recalled in the order they arrive.

   b. Up to 10 numbers are recorded. When the eleventh call comes in, it is stored and the oldest call is deleted so that no more than 10 numbers are ever recorded.

   c. When the user presses the missed-calls button, the telephone displays the number of calls bumped (stored but then deleted because there were more than 10 missed calls). Next, the telephone displays the number of origin of each missed call that is still stored, one at a time.

   d. After each number display, the user can select (1) to delete the call, (2) to go on to the next missed call, or (3) to display the call details (number, caller name, and time).

   e. After each number-detail display, the user can select (1) to delete the call or (2) to go on to the next call.

   f. If there are no missed calls, at the end of the display of missed calls, the telephone prints "End of Missed Calls".

   Write a helper class to represent an incoming call with fields to hold the number, name of caller, and time of call. Write a tester class that stores several numbers, simulates the user pressing the missed-calls button, and finally prints the entire collection of stored calls. Make sure that if more than one call comes from the same person or number of origin, all calls are recorded.

2. Create a collection class called `IntegerSet` that imposes the restriction that all elements in the collection must be integer values and that no duplicate values are allowed. The `IntegerSet` class should have methods for adding and removing values, checking to see if a value is already in the set, and removing all values. The class should also have a method that returns an `Iterator` object that will iterate through the set.

3. The trickiest part of working with regular expressions
expression that matches all strings that you want to match, and no others. Write a program to test regular expressions. Use the program to test the syntax of a regular expression, and then to make sure it accepts and rejects the correct candidate strings. The solution can be a command-line program that prompts the user to enter a regular expression. After compiling the expression, the program can repeatedly invite the user to enter strings. It should test whether each string conforms to the regular expression or contains subsequences that conform.

For an additional challenge, if at least one subsequence is a match, replace all occurrences of the regular expression with "***" and print the resulting string. Print all the capturing groups found in the string.

4. The package **java.util.zip** contains a class **ZipFile**. Use this class to write your own unzip utility. Call methods of **ZipFile** to obtain an array of **ZipEntry** objects and represent the contents of the file and the **InputStream** objects that correspond to each **ZipEntry**. For simplicity, unzip the entire file into the current directory.

4

CHAPTER

5

MULTITHREADING

In this chapter you will:

- ♦ Explore the concepts of threads and multithreading
- ♦ Understand the lifecycle of a thread
- ♦ Create, start, and stop threads using `java.lang.Thread` and `java.lang.Runnable`
- ♦ Create daemon threads
- ♦ Use the JVM and `java.util.Timer` objects to schedule execution of `java.util.TimerTask` objects
- ♦ Make your multithreaded programs robust
- ♦ Make class variables thread-safe using the `ThreadLocal` class
- ♦ Synchronize threads using the keyword `synchronized`
- ♦ Set up interthread communication using the methods `Object.wait`, `Object.notify`, and `Object.notifyAll`
- ♦ Create and use `ThreadGroup` objects that contain sets of threads

THREADS AND MULTITHREADING

If you draw a line through your code to trace how control moves from statement to statement as your program runs, you are tracing a thread of execution. All programs have at least one thread. A multithreaded program allows more than one thread to run through the code at a time. In other words, in some programs, rather than sticking to the single sequential order, the flow of control splits and executes your program as though it were two or more separate processes. Here are some situations in which multiple threads are commonly used:

- Execution of a single-threaded program must wait after prompting the user for input until the user submits the input. If your program has two threads—one for user I/O and another for processor-heavy tasks—the number-crunching thread can continue while the I/O thread waits for user input.

- Any program that is used simultaneously by more than one user probably performs processing for each user concurrently. A common technique is to start a thread for each user. Applications with a client-server architecture often have a main or daemon thread that listens for client requests and creates a new thread to process each client request as it arrives.

- Programs that model multiple objects that perform activities concurrently lend themselves to multithreading. You can create a thread for each object and use interthread communication to model interactions between the objects. For example, imagine sets of moving objects such as flowing traffic, or separate but related processes such as ordering stock, adding items to stock, selling items from stock, and delivering purchased items in a store and warehouse.

All the programs you have seen so far in this book are single threaded. This chapter describes the features that the Java platform provides for creating multithreaded programs. Java is unlike many programming languages in that the Java platform includes an API for creating, running, and managing threads in a wholly portable way. Even multithreaded Java programs are portable: They can be compiled from source code or run from bytecode on any standard implementation of the Java platform. Understanding the material in this chapter is essential for writing multithreaded programs.

When you launch a new path through your code, you start a thread. Typically, you use more than one thread to improve the performance or responsiveness of your application. For example, you can run the graphical user interface (GUI) for your application in one thread and separate processor-heavy or file manipulation tasks in other threads. You may want a separate thread for animation.

If you have created multithreaded programs in other environments, you may be familiar with the complications that multithreading introduces to your code. Threads can interfere with each other, especially when two or more threads that can run concurrently operate on the same variables or objects. At times, you must synchronize your threads so that they do not write to the same storage or contend for the same resources. You also want to eliminate the potential for threads to corrupt the values of objects used by other threads, or to go into deadlock when they all wait on the same condition or on each other. In short, you need a way for your threads to communicate with each other.

Java includes the following features for multithreading:

- The class **java.lang.Thread** provides methods your program can use to create and control threads, described in the section "Creating and Running Threads."

- The interface **java.lang.Runnable** is implemented by a class that runs on a thread, described in the section "Creating and Running Threads."

- The classes **java.util.TimerTask** and **java.util.Timer** provide methods for requesting that the JVM generate threads to run scheduled tasks, described in the section "Using the JVM to Schedule Tasks."

- The class **java.lang.ThreadLocal** provides methods for making class
  (static) variables local to a thread, described in the section "Making Variable
  Values Thread-Safe."

- The keyword **synchronized** makes the JVM's internal mechanism for
  thread synchronization accessible to programmers, described in the section
  "Synchronizing Threads."

- All objects can use the methods **wait**, **notify**, and **notifyAll** inherited
  from **java.lang.Object** to participate in interthread communication,
  described in the section "Communicating Between Threads."

- Instances of the class **java.lang.ThreadGroup** contain sets of threads
  with common characteristics, described in the section "Grouping Threads."

Therefore, you do not have to call any operating system API to manage threads or to use
platform-dependent features for interthread communication. The close connection between
the Java virtual machine (JVM) and the Java programming language breaks down traditional
borders between the programming language, supporting libraries, and system APIs.

Even if you are familiar with the concepts of multithreading and have created multithreaded programs in other environments, you should read this chapter carefully. The
Java platform provides a comprehensive set of services for managing threads that may be
unlike operating system APIs or class libraries you have used in the past.

THE LIFECYCLE OF A THREAD

Threads can come into being, start running, pause, resume, and finally stop dynamically
during program execution. One thread, the main thread, is launched by the JVM when
you run an application or by a Web browser when it starts an applet. But how do other
threads that you define in your Java source code come into being, start running, share the
processor, and finally stop? The bulk of this chapter discusses the constructs in the Java
programming language and the core classes that you use to manage threads. Before looking into the details, you may find it helpful to see an overview of the lifecycle of threads.

After a single-threaded program starts, it has sole control of the process in which it runs
until it ends. It may wait from time to time for user input or for some I/O operation to
complete, but no other activities occur in the JVM except internal operations such as
garbage collection that run on other threads behind the scenes. The left side of Figure 5-1
represents this situation. Your program can explicitly create one or more objects that can
run as separate threads. After an object capable of running as a thread is created, your
program can call a method to begin running the thread. Your threads can also launch
other threads. Your program can consist of several threads, all sharing the JVM.

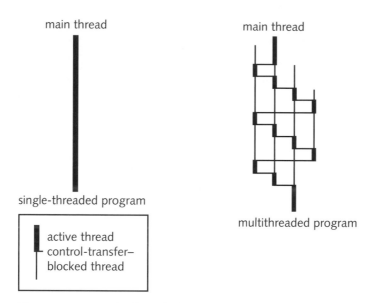

Figure 5-1   Single-threaded and multithreaded programs

How do threads share processing time? The simple story is that they each get a turn at running, and the JVM is in charge of scheduling processor time according to the priorities assigned to the threads. A more complete story depends on whether the native operating system uses preemptive or cooperative multitasking and whether you are running on a single-processor or a multiprocessor machine. Do not assume that threads are dispatched in the same way on all platforms and that they are given the same length of time every time they have an opportunity to run. For example, on a multiprocessor system, the JVM may be able to run more than one thread at the same time on different processors.

When a thread does not have control, it pauses like a movie when the projection freezes on a single frame and the JVM executes or tries to execute methods in another thread. The states of all threads except the thread that the JVM is currently executing cannot change, with the important exception that objects shared among threads may be modified by the executing thread or may be affected by external factors; for example, the state of I/O buffers can change. To the user, it may appear that all threads are running simultaneously, but the reality is more like that depicted on the right side of Figure 5-1.

By default, the JVM tries to distribute control equally to all threads. If you have some threads that require more immediate attention than others, such as threads that encapsulate the user interface and in which response time is very important, you can assign priority values to your threads. Threads with high priority values tend to preempt lower priority threads. In Java, you cannot have complete control over thread scheduling; use the Java API to state your intentions and let the JVM do the best it can with the multithreading features of the native operating system.

CREATING AND RUNNING THREADS

The two fundamental types that Java programs use for multithreading are the **Thread** class and **Runnable** interface. Both are included in the **java.lang** package. The **Thread** class is introduced first in this chapter because it gives the most straightforward way of creating and controlling threads. All programs that explicitly use multithreading create **Thread** objects. However, when designing a class that runs on a thread, you have a choice of extending **Thread** or implementing **Runnable**. Implementing **Runnable** is the more flexible and therefore usually preferred approach. The **Runnable** interface and how to use **Runnable** objects together with **Thread** objects is explained in the section "Using the **Runnable** Interface."

5

Using the Thread Class

A Java program creates a thread by instantiating a **Thread** object and manipulates the thread by calling methods of the **Thread** class. Creating and launching a thread is sometimes called *spawning* a thread. In most programming environments, you must use a low-level operating system API to spawn a thread. Unlike most high-level languages, which give programmers no access to threads. The Java platform lets programmers control threads by calling methods of the **Thread** class. All the methods listed in the following overview of the **Thread** class are explained in this chapter.

Class

java.lang.Thread

Purpose

The **Thread** class provides the infrastructure for multithreaded programs in the Java platform. It implements the interface **java.lang.Runnable**, which is introduced after the first sample multithreaded program.

Constructors

- **Thread()**

  Thread(Runnable *object* **)**

  Thread(String *name* **)**

  Thread(Runnable *object***, String** *name* **)**

  Thread(ThreadGroup *group***, Runnable** *object* **)**

  Thread(ThreadGroup *group***, String** *name* **)**

  Thread(ThreadGroup *group***, Runnable** *object***, String** *name* **)**

  When you construct a **Thread** object, you can optionally specify a name for the thread in the argument of type **String**.

When you create a thread by instantiating a class that is defined to implement **Runnable**, you must provide the **Runnable** object as an argument of the constructor. Thread groups are discussed in the section "Grouping Threads."

Methods

- **Thread currentThread()**

  The class (static) method **currentThread** returns a reference to the currently executing thread.

- **int getPriority()**

  The **getPriority** method returns the priority of the thread.

- **void interrupt()**

  The **interrupt** method interrupts the current thread.

- **boolean isDaemon()**

  The **isDaemon** method returns **true** if the **Thread** object is a daemon thread, and **false** otherwise. Daemon threads are discussed in the section "Creating Service Threads."

- **boolean isAlive()**

  The **isAlive** method returns **true** if the thread has been started and has not yet died, and **false** otherwise.

- **void join()**

  void join(long *milliseconds*)

  The **join** method waits for the thread object to terminate. You can optionally specify a maximum number of milliseconds to wait for the lifetime of the thread to end.

- **void run()**

  A subclass of **Thread** must provide an implementation of **run** because it implements the **Runnable** interface. If the **Thread** object is created with a **Runnable** object, that object's **run** method is called. Otherwise this method does nothing and returns.

- **void setDaemon(boolean *on*)**

  The **setDaemon** method determines whether the thread is a daemon thread. When the **boolean** argument has the value **true**, the **Thread** object becomes a daemon. If the argument is **false**, the thread runs as a regular thread.

- **void setPriority(int *priority*)**

  The **setPriority** method sets the priority of a thread to the specified value, or the maximum allowed for the group to which the thread belongs if that maximum is less than the specified value.

■ void sleep(long milliseconds)

The **sleep** method makes the thread pause for the specified number of milliseconds.

■ **void start()**

The **start** method causes the thread to begin execution.

■ **void yield()**

The **yield** method makes the thread pause so another thread can execute.

5

When a class extends **Thread**, it inherits all the methods and fields required to be manipulated as a separate thread, with one important exception: the **Thread** class does have a **run** method, but it is empty. You must override the inherited **run** method with one from your class if your thread is to accomplish anything.

You do not call the **run** method to start a thread. After you have created the thread, make it active by calling the **start** method. The JVM then passes control to the appropriate **run** method. After a thread starts, it can be in a runnable or blocked state. While it is *runnable*, the thread is either executing or ready to execute as soon as the JVM gives it control. The thread can be *blocked* as the result of a call to **sleep** or **Object.wait**, or because it is waiting for an I/O operation. Figure 5-2 shows how a thread can change states during its lifecycle.

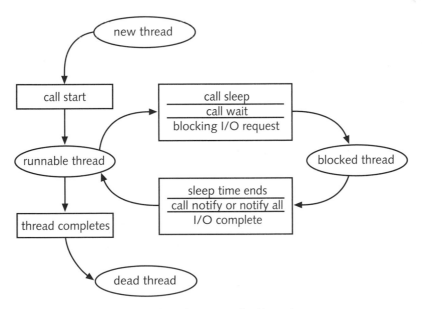

Figure 5-2   State Transition diagram of a thread

Figure 5-3 is a listing of a multithreaded program that contains three classes, each of which runs on a different thread. The main class, **SpawnTwoThreads**, runs on the main thread. It starts a thread `HelloName` to do some simple I/O and then starts the thread `NumberCrunch` to perform some processor-intensive activity while the `HelloName` thread is waiting for user input. The code contains some elements that are explained later in this chapter, but you should be able to see how the two **Thread** objects are created and then started by the **SpawnTwoThreads** class. A detailed breakdown follows the listing. All three classes reside in one source file.

```
package examples.threads;
import java.io.*;
/**
 * Class to demonstrate spawning threads
 * that are subclasses of the Thread class
 */
public class SpawnTwoThreads {
    public static void main(String[] args)
        throws InterruptedException {
            Thread one = new HelloName();
            one.start();
            Thread two = new NumberCrunch();
            two.start();
            one.join();
            ( (NumberCrunch) two ).end();
    }
}
/**
 * Class that performs I/O and runs on a thread
 */
class HelloName extends Thread {
    public void run() {
        try {
            System.out.print( "What is your name? " );
            BufferedReader br =
                new BufferedReader(
                new InputStreamReader( System.in ) );
            String name = br.readLine();
            System.out.println( "Hello " + name );
        } catch ( IOException ioe ) {
            System.out.println( ioe.getMessage() );
        }
    }
}
/**
 * Class that performs processor-heavy calculations
 * and runs on a thread
 */
class NumberCrunch extends Thread {
    private static boolean stopflag = false;
```

Figure 5-3   Running classes that extend **Thread** in multithreaded programs

```
public void run() {
    try {
        int i = 1;
        double d = 0;
        while ( !stopflag ) {
            d = Math.log( i++ );
            sleep( 1 );
        }
        System.out.println(
            "The log of " + i + " is " + d );
    } catch ( InterruptedException ie ) {
        System.out.println( ie.getMessage() );
    }
}
public void end() {
    stopflag = true;
}
}
```

5

Figure 5-3   Running classes that extend **Thread** in multithreaded programs (continued)

Here is a breakdown of the SpawnTwoThreads program.

```
public class SpawnTwoThreads {
    public static void main(String[] args)
        throws InterruptedException {
```

The main class, SpawnTwoThreads, runs on the main thread. It has only a **main** method. All threads in a multithreaded program can be interrupted, so the **main** method must either catch the **java.lang.InterruptedException** exception or list it in its throws clause. The **InterruptedException** exception is explained in the section "Stopping a Thread."

```
Thread one = new HelloName();
one.start();
```

These two lines create a second thread and start it. This call of **start** starts the **run** method in the **HelloName** object. At this point, the main thread and the **HelloName** thread are active.

```
Thread two = new NumberCrunch();
two.start();
```

These two lines create a third thread and start it. This call of **start** starts the **run** method in the **NumberCrunch** object. At this point, all three threads are active, unless the **HelloName** thread is already blocked awaiting user input.

```
one.join();
( (NumberCrunch) two ).end();
```

The first of these two lines calls **join** on the **HelloName** thread to wait for it to end. Then the main thread tells the **NumberCrunch** thread to end by calling its **end** method.

This is necessary because the `NumberCrunch` thread loops until a stop flag is set. Note that the object reference `two` must be cast because there is no `end` method in the `Thread` class.

The `run` method in the `HelloName` class is straightforward. As well as a `run` method, the `NumberCrunch` class contains an instance variable called `stopflag` and a method `end` to set `stopflag`. The section "Stopping a Thread" explains how this variable and method are used to stop the thread. For now, just look at the `run` method of the `NumberCrunch` class.

```
public void run() {
    try {
      int i = 1;
      double d = 0;
```

The `run` method in the `NumberCrunch` class contains a loop that is enclosed in a try block because an exception could occur during the loop. Code in the loop performs calculations on variables `i` and `d`.

```
while ( !stopflag ) {
    d = Math.log( i++ );
    sleep( 1 );
}
```

The loop repeats until `stopflag` has the value `true`. On each pass, the code in the loop performs the processor-heavy operation of calculating the natural logarithm of a number and then increments the number. Without the call of `sleep`, this loop could hog the processor because there is nothing in it to block execution. Therefore, it calls `sleep` to force the thread to release control for one millisecond and let the other active threads take a turn.

```
System.out.println(
    "The log of " + i + " is " + d );
```

When the loop ends, the `NumberCrunch` thread prints the number of passes through the loop and the natural logarithm of the number that serves as loop counter.

```
} catch ( InterruptedException ie ) {
   System.out.println(ie.getMessage());
}
```

The `NumberCrunch` thread could be interrupted during one of the sleep periods. Therefore, the `run` method must handle **InterruptedException**.

The output of this class varies each time you run it, because it depends upon the time taken to supply input to the `HelloName` thread. Following is sample output.

```
What is your name? student
Hello student
The log of 5704 is 8.648747631156539
```

The first two lines of output come from the `HelloName` thread. The last line is from the `NumberCrunch` thread and shows that 5704 passes through the while loop were completed while the other threads were blocked.

Three methods of the **Thread** class are deprecated in the Java 2 platform.
Previous versions of the Java platform made the method **stop** available to terminate execution of a thread, **suspend** to suspend execution of a thread, and **resume** to restore a suspended thread to a runnable state. These methods are still available, but they are considered unsafe and you should not use them. If you call them or compile an existing class that calls them, the compiler produces a deprecation warning and you should rewrite the offending code to avoid calling **stop**, **suspend**, or **restore**. See the section "Stopping a Thread" for further explanation and a safe way to halt execution of a thread.

Using the Runnable Interface

The problem with extending **Thread** to define a class that can run on a thread is that the class cannot be a subclass of some other type. For example, if you design **Car** objects, **Bus** objects, and **Truck** objects to run on separate threads by extending **Thread**, classes **Car**, **Bus**, and **Truck** cannot also extend **Vehicle**. Therefore, the Java platform provides the interface **java.lang.Runnable** that defines the **run** method and is designed to be used with a separate **Thread** object. An object can be run as a thread if it is a **Runnable** object. In other words, any object that instantiates a class that implements the interface **Runnable** can be launched as a new thread by the main thread or by any other active thread.

Interface

java.lang.Runnable

Purpose

The **Runnable** interface defines the protocol that must be followed by all threads.

Method

- **void run()** is the only method in the **Runnable** interface.

  You must provide an implementation of the **run** method in every class that can be run as a spawned thread. This method is the entry point for the thread, and is analogous to **main** in a class you start with the **java** command.

Generally, implementing **Runnable** is considered a better technique than extending **Thread**, for the following reasons:

- If your class already has a superclass other than **Object**, extending **Thread** is not an option.

- A class that implements **Runnable** inherits less overhead than one that extends **Thread**. This does not affect the efficiency of the code because you must always have a **Thread** object for each thread, but does reduce the number of inherited members.

You can always implement **Runnable**. The only catch is that you must wrap the **Runnable** object in a **Thread** object to use it as a thread. Do this by creating a **Thread** object and passing your **Runnable** object as an argument of the **Thread** constructor. When a **Thread** object is constructed with a **Runnable** object as input, the **Thread** object uses the **run** method of the **Runnable** object in place of its own **run** method.

The program listed in Figure 5-4 is a variation on the SpawnTwoThreads class. Minimal changes have been made to allow for the following difference:

- The main class is renamed RunTwoThreads.

- The class HelloName is renamed HelloOne and implements **Runnable** instead of extending **Thread**.

- The class NumberCrunch is renamed NumberCruncher and implements **Runnable** instead of extending **Thread**.

All lines changed since the program listed in Figure 5-3 are highlighted in bold.

```
package examples.threads;
import java.io.*;
/**
 * Class to demonstrate spawning threads
 * that are implement Runnable
 */
public class RunTwoThreads {
   public static void main(String[] args)
      throws InterruptedException {
         Thread one = new Thread( new HelloOne() );
         one.start();
         NumberCruncher nc = new NumberCruncher();
         Thread two = new Thread( nc );
         two.start();
         one.join();
         nc.end();
   }
}
/**
 * Class that performs I/O and runs on a thread
 */
class HelloOne implements Runnable {
   public void run() {
      try {
         System.out.print( "What is your name? " );
         BufferedReader br =
            new BufferedReader(
            new InputStreamReader(System.in) );
         String name = br.readLine();
         System.out.println( "Hello " + name );
```

Figure 5-4   Running classes that implement **Runnable** in multithreaded programs

```
            } catch (IOException ioe) {
                System.out.println( ioe.getMessage() );
            }
        }
    }
}
/**
 * Class that performs processor-heavy calculations
 * and runs on a thread
 */
class NumberCruncher implements Runnable {
    private static boolean stopflag = false;
    public void run() {
        try {
            int i = 1;
            double d = 0;
            while (!stopflag) {
                d = Math.log(i++);
                Thread.currentThread().sleep(1);
            }
            System.out.println(
                "The log of " + i + " is " + d);
        } catch (InterruptedException ie) {
            System.out.println(ie.getMessage());
        }
    }
    public void end() {
        stopflag = true;
    }
}
```

Figure 5-4 Running classes that implement **Runnable** in multithreaded programs
(continued)

Stopping a Thread

The **Thread** class provides the **start** method to begin the execution of a thread, but no methods to stop or suspend the execution. In the original version of the Java platform, the **Thread** class provided methods **stop**, **suspend**, and **resume**. However, these methods have been deprecated since version 1.2 of the Java platform. This section explains why the methods were deprecated and how you should stop a thread.

Why Were stop, suspend, and resume Deprecated?

The designers of the Java platform found the methods **stop** and **suspend** to be inherently unsafe because they may make the stopped thread leave data in an inconsistent state if that data is accessed concurrently by more than one thread. The **resume** method is deprecated because, without **suspend**, you never need to call it.

In the section "Writing Robust Multithreaded Programs," you learn how to prevent threads from interfering with each other, or corrupting data that different threads share, by applying locks to a class or an object. You learn how to set up locks so that only one thread at a time can alter the value of critical variables. Stopping an active thread asynchronously from the outside, by calling **stop** or **suspend**, releases all locks without giving the thread an opportunity to complete potentially critical operations. Because other threads may then pick up corrupt information, the integrity of all threads that share variables with a stopped or suspended thread is compromised.

How to Stop a Thread

A thread should run to its natural termination. In other words, you should let a thread return under its own control; you should never terminate it from the outside. What about threads that loop continuously? Without some signal to stop, some threads would run forever. Here is the recommended way to make all threads stop gracefully:

- Define an instance variable in the thread's class that acts as a flag indicating whether it is time to stop.

- Make sure that the variable itself is not affected by concurrent access from other threads. As explained in the section "Synchronizing Threads," you can do this by declaring the variable with the keyword **volatile**, or by declaring all code that accesses it to be **synchronized**.

- In the thread, check the value of the variable frequently. Typically, you test the value in the condition controlling a loop. If the thread waits for long periods, you can call the **interrupt** method to interrupt the wait.

- Return from the **run** method as soon as possible when the flag indicates that the thread should stop.

The sample programs in this chapter use this approach. The lines in Figure 5-5 are taken from the program in Figure 5-6, the `RepeatedMessage` class.

```
// declaration of a class that runs as a thread
// other field declarations omitted
   private volatile boolean stopFlag;
// other methods omitted
   public void run() {
      stopFlag = false;
      try {
         while ( ! stopFlag ) {
         // body of main processing loop
         }
      } catch( InterruptedException ie ) {
         return;
      }
   }
   public void finish() {
      stopFlag = true;
      return;
   }
```

Figure 5-5 A coding technique for stopping a thread

Unfortunately you cannot name the method that sets the flag **stop** for compatibility with existing code that called the deprecated **Thread.stop** method, because **Thread.stop** is a **final** method. If you try to override **Thread.stop**, you receive an error and a warning that you are overriding a deprecated method.

The **RepeatedMessage** program in Figure 5-6 has three threads: a main thread and two threads launched by the main thread. This program demonstrates one kind of problem that can occur when you do not synchronize your threads.

```
package examples.threads;
/** A class to demonstrate why synchronized methods
  * are needed by showing what can happen when they
  * are not synchronized.
  */
public class RepeatedMessage implements Runnable {
   private String message;
   private int pauseTime;
   /**  field stopFlag tells thread when to stop
     * declared volatile to ensure every thread sees
     * change immediately
     */
   private volatile boolean stopFlag;
   /** Construct a repeating message
     * @param inputMessage the message to be
     *     repeated
     * @param inputPauseTime the time, in ms,
     *     paused between each letter of the
     *     message
     */
   public RepeatedMessage( String inputMessage,
                           int inputPauseTime ) {
     message = inputMessage;
     pauseTime = inputPauseTime;
   }
   /** Display a repeating message
     * @param rm the message to be repeated
     * @exception InterruptedException if the thread
     *    does not sleep for the full time specified
     */
   public static void
       displayMessage( RepeatedMessage rm )
       throws InterruptedException {
     for( int i=0; i < rm.message.length(); i++ ) {
        System.out.print( rm.message.charAt( i ) );
        Thread.currentThread().sleep( 50 );
     }
     System.out.println();
   }
   /** The workings of the thread
     */
```

Figure 5-6   A class that shows why thread synchronization is needed

```
    public void run() {
        stopFlag = false;
        try {
            while ( ! stopFlag ) {
                displayMessage( this );
                Thread.currentThread().sleep( pauseTime );
            }
        } catch( InterruptedException ie ) {
            return;
        }
    }
    /** A method to set a flag to stop the thread
      */
    public void finish() {
        stopFlag = true;
        return;
    }
    /** The test method for the class
     * @param args not used
     */
    public static void main( String[] args ) {
        try {
            RepeatedMessage m1
                = new RepeatedMessage( "bonjour!", 500 );
            Thread m1t = new Thread( m1 );
            m1t.start();
            RepeatedMessage m2
                = new RepeatedMessage( "HELLO!", 111 );
            Thread m2t = new Thread( m2 );
            m2t.start();
            // pause to let the threads run,
            // then stop them
            Thread.currentThread().sleep( 5000 );
            m1.finish();
            m2.finish();
        } catch( InterruptedException ie ) {
            ie.printStackTrace();
        }
        finally {
            // flush the output buffer
            System.out.println();
        }
    }
}
```

Figure 5-6   A class that shows why thread synchronization is needed (continued)

This program allows the output to be scrambled by printing messages one character at a time from different threads, and by pausing between characters. The output may look different on different installations of the Java platform, and may vary from run to run. Figure 5-7 shows one possible output.

```
bHoEnLjLoOu!r
!
HELLO!
HEbLoLnOj!o
urH!E
LLO!
HELLbOo!n
jouHrE!L
LO!
HELLOb!o
njHoEuLrL!O
!
HELLO!
bonHjEoLuLrO!!

HELLO!
bHoEnLjLoOu!r
!
H
ELLO!
```

Figure 5-7   Possible output from the `RepeatedMessage` class

In this program, `m1` and `m2` are **Runnable** objects and instances of the class `RepeatedMessage`. The **main** method of the class `RepeatedMessage` runs on the main thread. In the `m1` and `m2` threads, the **run** method repeatedly calls `displayMessage` to output a message and sleeps briefly after each call. The **sleep** method suspends execution for the specified number of milliseconds. Meanwhile, the main thread sleeps. Note the use of the static method **Thread.currentThread** to access the thread on which a **Runnable** object is running.

Notice that the **run** method is coded as an unending while loop. This looks like terrible programming style, but it is acceptable here because **main** stops the threads after five seconds, by calling **finish**. In fact, many event-driven applications rely on similar logic. Threads often loop continuously, monitoring their input buffers or waiting to be notified of an event.

Any thread that is executing can call **interrupt** on another thread. When a thread is interrupted, it becomes active and an **InterruptedException** exception occurs on the interrupted thread. This exception can occur when **sleep** is running in `m1` and `m2`, so the **run** method of these two threads must catch and handle **InterruptedException**. The **run** method does not have the option of listing the exceptions in a throws clause, because **run** is defined in **Runnable** to throw no exceptions. Therefore, the call of **sleep** must be enclosed in a try block with a catch clause that handles **InterruptedException**.

CREATING SERVICE THREADS

Service threads typically contain a never-ending loop for the sole purpose of receiving and handling requests. You can convert such threads into daemon threads. A *daemon* thread runs continuously in the background. You can call the **setDaemon** method for a thread to specify that it is a daemon thread and call the **isDaemon** method to determine whether a thread is a daemon thread.

The JVM does not expect daemon threads, unlike regular user threads, to finish. However, a Java application is assumed to be complete when all its threads have terminated. How can a program that starts daemon threads ever end? The JVM can detect when your program reaches a point where only daemon threads are running. The JVM then assumes your application is finished and terminates the daemon threads.

In client-server configurations, one or several client processes make requests on a server process. Each server is usually a separate program from the clients and may reside on a different processor. A common technique for programming servers that communicate over TCP/IP connections is to create a daemon thread to monitor each TCP/IP port for incoming client requests. When it receives a request, the server typically launches another thread to process the request and return a response to the client. The threads dedicated to individual requests terminate when their response has been sent, but the monitoring thread is kept alive as long as the server is required.

Just as the Java platform provides an API to simplify the task of creating multithreaded programs, it provides core classes in the package **java.net** to support networking. In Chapter 11, you see how client and server programs can communicate over TCP/IP sockets. A sample server program is supplied and, like many servers, it is a multithreaded program.

USING THE JVM TO SCHEDULE TASKS

Sometimes you want to schedule tasks to be completed later during execution of your program. For example, you can check the value of a variable that many threads are updating after 10 seconds or you can check the value regularly at one-second intervals. You can do so by launching a thread, programming it to sleep for the desired interval and then perform the required task. Alternatively, you can use two handy classes provided by the **java.util** package to ask the JVM to provide the thread for you.

Class **java.util.TimerTask** implements **Runnable**, and class **java.util.Timer** provides the facility to run a **TimerTask** object on a background thread generated by the JVM. A **Timer** object can run a task once or repeatedly at regular intervals. Use these classes only for short-lived tasks, because long-running tasks can interfere with the scheduling of subsequent tasks.

Class

`java.util.TimerTask`

Purpose

The **`TimerTask`** class encapsulates a task that can be scheduled by a **`Timer`** object.

Constructor

- **`TimerTask()`**

  Define a subclass of **`TimerTask`** to perform the required activity.

Methods

- **`void cancel()`**

  The **`cancel`** method cancels the task.

- **`void run()`**

  The implementation of the **`run`** method defines the task to perform.

- **`long scheduledExecutionTime()`**

  The method **`scheduledExecutionTime`** returns the scheduled time of the most recent actual execution of the task.

Several threads can share a **`Timer`** object; it is thread–safe. A **`Timer`** object maintains a queue of tasks and can handle a very large number of tasks efficiently. The **`Timer`** object is available for garbage collection when there are no more references to it and all scheduled tasks are completed.

Class

`java.util.Timer`

Purpose

The **`Timer`** class is a facility for scheduling tasks. An instance of **`Timer`** runs on a background thread supplied by the JVM.

Constructors

- **`Timer()`**

  `Timer( boolean isDaemon )`

  By default, the thread on which a **`Timer`** object runs is not a daemon thread. Ensure that this thread does not prevent your program from terminating. To run the **`Timer`** on a daemon thread, call the constructor with one **`boolean`** argument and set the value to **`true`**.

Methods

- `void cancel()`

  The **cancel** method cancels the timer and discards scheduled tasks.

- `void schedule( TimerTask` *task*`, Date` *time* `)`

  `void schedule( TimerTask` *task*`, Date` *time*`, long` *period* `)`

  `void schedule( TimerTask` *task*`, long` *delay* `)`

  `void schedule( TimerTask` *task*`, long` *delay* `, long` *period* `)`

  The **schedule** method schedules the specified task at a specific time or after a specified delay. To execute the task repeatedly, specify the period in milliseconds between successive executions.

- `void scheduleAtFixedRate(TimerTask` *task*`, Date` *time*`, long` *period* `)`

  `void scheduleAtFixedRate(TimerTask` *task*`, long` *delay* `, long` *period* `)`

  The method **scheduleAtFixedRate** schedules tasks to be executed at a fixed time or after the specified delay, and to repeat at regular intervals separated by the specified period in milliseconds.

The program composed of the `ScheduledTask` class listed in Figure 5-8 and the `ScheduleTasks` class listed in Figure 5-9 is a bit of whimsy: It schedules tasks to print statements that give the impression of a conversation. The task is simply to print a message to the console.

```
package examples.threads;
/** A class to demonstrate using the Timer utility to schedule
  * tasks on a background thread.
  */
public class ScheduledTask extends java.util.TimerTask {
   String message;
/** construct a task
  * @param message is a String to be displayed by the task
  */
   ScheduledTask(String message) {
      this.message = message;
   }
/** The task is simply to print the message to the console
  */
   public void run() {
      System.out.println(message);
   }
}
```

Figure 5-8 A class that extends `java.util.TimerTask`

The main class creates the `Timer` and `TimerTask` objects and leaves the rest to the JVM, as shown in Figure 5-9.

```java
package examples.threads;
/**A lass to demonstrate using the Timer utility to schedule
 * tasks on a background thread.
 */
public class ScheduleTasks {
    public static void main(String[] args) {
        ScheduledTask hello1 = new ScheduledTask("Hello Joe");
        ScheduledTask hello2 = new ScheduledTask("Hello Paula");
        ScheduledTask howareyou = new ScheduledTask("How are you?");
        ScheduledTask fine = new ScheduledTask("I'm fine thank-you, and you?");
        ScheduledTask fine2 = new ScheduledTask("I'm fine too");
        ScheduledTask goodbye1 = new ScheduledTask("Goodbye Joe");
        ScheduledTask goodbye2 = new ScheduledTask("Goodbye Paula");
        // run the timer thread as a daemon
        java.util.Timer timer = new java.util.Timer(true);
        timer.schedule(hello1, 1000);
        timer.schedule(goodbye2, 6000);
        System.out.println("Two old friends meet.");
        timer.schedule(howareyou, 3000);
        timer.schedule(fine2, 4500);
        System.out.println("They haven't seen each other in years.");
        timer.schedule(fine, 4000);
        System.out.println("They have gone their separate ways.");
        timer.schedule(goodbye1, 5500);
        timer.schedule(hello2, 1000);
        try {
            Thread.currentThread().sleep(7000);
        } catch (InterruptedException e) {};
    }
}
```

Figure 5-9   A class that creates a `java.util.Timer` object and schedules tasks

The times in the **main** method of the `ScheduleTasks` class are rigged to produce the following output, one line at a time:

```
Two old friends meet.
They haven't seen each other in years.
They have gone their separate ways.
Hello Joe
Hello Paula
How are you?
I'm fine thank-you, and you?
I'm fine too
Goodbye Joe
Goodbye Paula
```

WRITING ROBUST MULTITHREADED PROGRAMS

Creating and running threads is straightforward. Making sure the threads work well together is a far more difficult task. The program in Figure 5-6 demonstrates one way in which things can go wrong in multithreaded programs. The Java programming language has two keywords for the specific purpose of eliminating concurrent access problems:

- You can qualify variables with the keyword **volatile** to suppress compiler optimizations that have the potential to lose or ignore changes made by different threads to the values of the variables. Changes made to a variable by another thread are called *asynchronous* changes, because the flow of control through the current thread does not determine when the changes occur. Asynchronous changes are invisible to the compiler.

  In reality, you rarely need to declare variables to be **volatile**, because the JVM updates memory frequently. However, you should use **volatile** for shared variables for which you adopt none of the synchronization techniques described in this chapter.

- If you qualify the declaration of a method with **synchronized**, the method can be run for a particular object or class by only one thread at a time. You can synchronize threads to avoid race situations: You cannot know which thread will execute code that accesses a shared variable first, and the order in which threads read or set shared values can affect the results.

Deadlock can occur when all threads are in a blocked state, rather like a gridlock in road traffic. Java provides no automatic way of detecting and resolving deadlock. To avoid deadlock, carefully analyze the interactions between your threads. Unfortunately, a good debugger is sometimes your best tool for detecting deadlock.

You are responsible for ensuring that your threads do not interfere with each other and that at least one thread is active until your program is meant to terminate.

MAKING VARIABLE VALUES THREAD-SAFE

Making variables thread-safe removes the danger of their values being changed asynchronously by threads other than the current one. *Thread-safe* variables belong to one thread alone; different threads have separate copies.

So far you have seen variables with the following scopes:

- *Local variables* are variables declared within method bodies. Local variables are inherently thread-safe because each thread has a separate storage area for local variables.

- *Instance variables* are fields that are specific to each instance of the class, but shared by all threads that access an instance. Therefore, whether instance variables are thread-safe depends on how your program is structured. An instance variable of an object declared as a local variable is thread-safe. But the fields of a class whose

the safety you need for instance variables; the concern relates to conflicts due to concurrent access of fields of a single object. One object can contain only one copy of each field, not separate copies of certain fields on different threads.

■ *Class variables* are fields declared with the qualifier **static** and are shared by all instances of the class on all threads. Class variables are stored only once and are therefore not thread-safe.

The J2SDK does provide a way to make fields declared as **static** common to instances of the class on a single thread, but different for instances on separate threads. Classes **ThreadLocal** and **InheritableThreadLocal** provide variables that are local to each thread and therefore thread-safe.

Typically you declare a field to be **private static ThreadLocal** when it holds data that is associated with the state of a thread. For an example from an online banking application, say you spawn a thread for each user and that each user may run several banking transactions. You may want all instances of class **BankingTransaction** on a thread to have the same value in the field **userID**. But you want all instances on a different thread to have another value in the field **userID**. You can do that by declaring the field **userID** to have type **ThreadLocal**. Typically, a **ThreadLocal** field has these characteristics:

■ It is declared to be **private** and **static**.

■ It holds a value that is identified with the thread.

■ Its value does not change during the execution of the thread.

If the thread has child threads, you can use **InheritableThreadLocal** so that values from the parent thread are inherited by the child thread.

When a thread ends, its **ThreadLocal** objects become available for garbage collection.

Class

java.lang.ThreadLocal

Purpose

The **ThreadLocal** class provides a thread-safe static field of a class. It can hold an object of any reference type.

Constructor

■ **ThreadLocal()**

Methods

■ **Object get()**

The **get** method returns the value of the **ThreadLocal** variable on the current thread.

- **Object initialValue()**

  The **initialValue** method returns the initial value of the **ThreadLocal** variable on the current thread.

- **void set(Object** *value* **)**

  The **set** method changes the value of the **ThreadLocal** variable on the current thread to the specified value.

The design problems solved by **ThreadLocal** fields are quite specialized. The sample scenario consists of three classes listed in Figure 5-10, Figure 5-11, and Figure 5-12 and is based on a business transaction that can run simultaneously for multiple clients on multiple threads. In this case, a number that is incremented every time a new thread starts identifies the transaction. In this program, class **Transaction** records transaction state information, **TransactionThread** does the work for one transaction, and **TestTransactionThreads** is the main class that launches three transactions on three threads. Figure 5-10 shows the **Transaction** class. The bolded lines show the declaration and initialization of the **ThreadLocal** variable **threadTranId**. The initializer is an anonymous inner class that overrides the **ThreadLocal.initialValue** method. This is a common technique for initializing **ThreadLocal** objects. The instance variable **tranId** is set in the constructor to a value equal to the number of **Transaction** objects created.

```
package examples.threads;
/**
 * Class Transaction demonstrates ThreadLocal
 * static variables. It contains an instance
 * Variable for comparison purposes.
 */
public class Transaction {
    // use counter to issue sequential transaction numbers
    private static int tranCount = 0;
    // tranId and threadTranId demonstrate the impact of ThreadLocal
    private int tranId = 0;
    private static ThreadLocal threadTranId = new ThreadLocal() {
            protected synchronized Object initialValue() {
             return new Integer(tranCount);
             }
        };
    public Transaction() {
       tranId=(++tranCount);
    }
    public static int getThreadTranId() {
       return ((Integer) (threadTranId.get())).intValue();
    }
    public void setThreadTranId( int id) {
       threadTranId.set(new Integer(id));
    }
```

Figure 5-10   A class that declares a **ThreadLocal** class variable

```
   public int getTranId() {
      return tranId;
   }
   public void setTranId( int id) {
      tranId = id;
   }
}
```

Figure 5-10   A class that declares a **ThreadLocal** class variable (continued)

The `TransactionThread` class runs on a thread. It creates a `Transaction` object and calls `actionA`, `actionB`, and `actionC` methods to perform tasks within the context of a transaction. After `actionB`, a new instance of `Transaction` is created for `actionC` to use in a task such as recovery from an error condition or logging transaction state. For demonstration purposes, all action methods simply print the transaction identification information. The lines in bold in Figure 5-11 show how this class accesses the **ThreadLocal** variable of the `Transaction` object `tran`.

```
package examples.threads;
/**
 * Class TransactionThreads creates objects that
 * contain ThreadLocal variables and illustrates
 * how these variables work
 */
public class TransactionThread extends Thread {
   private Transaction tran;
   TransactionThread() {
      tran = new Transaction();
   }
   public void run() {
      try {
         doActionA();
         sleep(50);
         doActionB();
         sleep(50);
         // restart transaction due to rollback or error
         tran = new Transaction();
         doActionC();
         sleep(50);
      } catch (InterruptedException e) {
         System.out.println("Thread Interrupted");
      }
   }
   public void doActionA() {
      System.out.println(
```

Figure 5-11   A class that uses a **ThreadLocal** variable

```
                "Action A for thread-safe id = "
                + tran.getThreadTranId()
                + ". Transaction instance = "
                + tran.getTranId()
                + ".");
      }
      public void doActionB() {
         System.out.println(
                "Action B for thread-safe id = "
                + tran.getThreadTranId()
                + ". Transaction instance = "
                + tran.getTranId()
                + ".");
      }
      public void doActionC() {
         System.out.println(
                "Action C for thread-safe id = "
                + tran.getThreadTranId()
                + ". Transaction instance = "
                + tran.getTranId()
                + ".");
      }
}
```

Figure 5-11   A class that uses a **ThreadLocal** variable (continued)

The **TestTransactionThreads** class simply launches three threads, simulating three clients accessing the same transaction, and is listed in Figure 5-12.

```
package examples.threads;
/**
 * Class TestTransactionThreads demonstrates
 * ThreadLocal variables
 * in the threads that it creates
 */
public class TestTransactionThreads {
   public static void main(String[ ] args) {
      for (int i=1; i < 4; i++) {
            TransactionThread tThread = new TransactionThread();
            tThread.start();
            try {
               Thread.currentThread().sleep(50);
            } catch (InterruptedException e) {}
      }
   }
}
```

Figure 5-12   The main class for the **ThreadLocal** sample program

Here is the output from the TestTransactionThreads program:

```
Action A for thread-safe id = 1. Transaction instance = 1.
Action B for thread-safe id = 1. Transaction instance = 1.
Action A for thread-safe id = 2. Transaction instance = 2.
Action C for thread-safe id = 1. Transaction instance = 3.
Action B for thread-safe id = 2. Transaction instance = 2.
Action A for thread-safe id = 4. Transaction instance = 4.
Action C for thread-safe id = 2. Transaction instance = 5.
Action B for thread-safe id = 4. Transaction instance = 4.
Action C for thread-safe id = 4. Transaction instance = 6.
```

As in all these multithreaded programs, you may receive different output because the threads are scheduled differently by the native operating system. In this output, the three threads correspond to threadTranId values 1, 2, and 4. This thread-safe transaction ID is shared for both transactions on each thread. In contrast, the instance variable tranId has values 1 and 3 for the two transactions with threadTranId of 1; 2 and 5 for the two transactions with threadTranId of 2; and 4 and 6 for the two transactions with threadTranId of 4. The thread-safe transaction ID is unique for each thread, unlike an ordinary class variable.

SYNCHRONIZING THREADS

Recall the RepeatedMessage class listed in Figure 5-6 and its output listed in Figure 5-7. The output from two threads is intermixed because control switched between the two threads at times that appear random from the point of view of the program code. The RepeatedMessage class is rather contrived but demonstrates the point that, after an activity starts on a thread, correct operation of your program may depend on exclusive use of some code to keep objects being manipulated in a consistent state. The output of the RepeatedMessage class is scrambled because its displayMessage method is not synchronized.

For a more serious example, consider online stock trading. Suppose a client issues a sell command followed by a buy command to purchase a different stock with the proceeds from the first stock sale. If the two commands are issued in rapid succession but completing the operations takes some time, two threads, one trying to sell and another trying to buy, may be concurrently accessing the client's portfolio. If the buy operation reads the cash balance before the sell updates the balance, the buy may fail thinking that the client does not have enough funds. The solution is to ensure that only one transaction for each client portfolio runs at a time. In other words, the method that performs a buy or sell transaction must be synchronized across different threads.

Synchronizing threads has the effect of serializing access to blocks of code running on the thread. Serializing in this context means giving one thread at a time the right to execute specific blocks of code. For an analogy, picture a group discussion where there is only one microphone. To speak, a speaker must gain control of the microphone. When each speaker ends, the microphone is passed to another speaker. The result is an orderly meeting in which the business of the day can be accomplished much more efficiently than if everyone spoke at once.

Serialization does not control the order in which threads gain control, but it ensures that only one thread executes the synchronized code at a time. The order is controlled by the native operating system and the JVM, and is beyond the control of your program.

Synchronizing threads involves setting *locks*. You can conceive of locks as objects that indicate whether objects or classes are available for threads to use or are already in use. In the meeting analogy, the microphone is the lock on the right to speak. Locks are the Java concept for flags maintained by the operating system. Sometimes the term *monitor* is used to describe a lock. You can apply locks to methods or blocks of code to prevent them from running simultaneously on more than one thread. You do not have to apply locks to all methods in a class. Use locks only for code that requires exclusive access to an object or class while the code is running. Also, you can use locks for code that cannot tolerate changes to fields while it executes. Java supports two kinds of locks:

- *Object locks* apply to instance methods. The lock controls whether a method can be run when it is called for a particular object. For example, a lock in the stock trading application may apply to each client portfolio. Before the method can run, it must acquire the lock on the object and may have to wait for the lock to become free. The method releases the lock automatically when it ends. Only one thread can have the lock at a time. Therefore, synchronized methods cannot operate on the same object in more than one thread at a time. Other objects of the same class and instance methods that do not require a lock are not affected. All class methods are also unaffected.

- *Class locks* apply to all the class (static) methods. When a thread has the lock for a class, it is the only thread that can execute any of the class methods that require a lock. Class methods that do not require a lock are unaffected. All instance methods are also unaffected.

Apply the keyword **synchronized** to a method as follows:

Syntax

```
[access_specifier] synchronized [other_qualifiers]
  return_type method_name ( argument_list )
  [throws exception_list]
  block
```

Dissection

- If the method is not declared with the qualifier **static**, the qualifier **synchronized** applies an object lock to the object for which the instance method is called.

- If the method is declared **static**, the qualifier **synchronized** applies a class lock to class methods.

language—just qualify the declaration of methods with the keyword **synchronized**. You lock classes and objects independently by synchronizing class and instance methods separately.

You do not operate on the locks explicitly. The **synchronized** keyword tells the JVM that the method requires a lock to run. The JVM together with the native operating system create the lock and manage the allocation of the lock to threads during execution, as follows:

- The request for a lock is automatic and is always satisfied if the lock is available.
- A lock is always available unless a thread has requested and been granted the lock.
- When a synchronized method ends, it releases the lock. If another thread with a synchronized method is waiting for that lock, that thread acquires the lock and can proceed.

Synchronized methods are mutually exclusive in the sense that they can be run by only one thread at a time for the locked object. As a simple solution to the synchronization problem in the `RepeatedMessage` program, you can declare the `displayMessage` method to be synchronized so that the code is as shown in Figure 5-13.

```
public static synchronized
    void displayMessage ( RepeatedMessage rm )
        throws InterruptedException {
        for( int i=0; i < rm.message.length(); i++ ) {
            System.out.print( rm.message.charAt( i ) );
            sleep( 50 );
        }
        System.out.println();
    }
```

Figure 5-13   A synchronized method

The `displayMessage` method is a class method in this example. As a result, the lock applies to the class `RepeatedMessage`.

You can also indicate that an object lock is required for a single statement or block of code by using the **synchronized** statement.

Syntax

synchronized (*object_to_be_locked*)
        statement_or_block

Dissection

- When preceding a block of code, the **synchronized** keyword synchronizes the code for the specified object. You can name any object, and a common technique is to declare a field specifically to act as a lockable object.

Code Example

```
// object used by all instances for its lock
private static Object sharedLock = new Object();
public static
      void displayMessage( RepeatedMessage rm )
throws InterruptedException {
   synchronized ( sharedLock ) {
      for( int i=0; i<rm.message.length(); i++ ) {
         System.out.print( rm.message.charAt( i ) );
         sleep( 50 );
      }
      System.out.println ();
   }
}
```

Code Dissection

In this code, the `displayMessage` method acquires the lock just for the duration of the for statement that prints the messages one character at a time. The only reason for creating the object `sharedLock` is to apply its lock to this block of code.

This section presents two approaches to locking code: qualifying a method with the keyword **synchronized** and synchronizing a block of code using a specific object to represent the lock. Which approach is better? Synchronizing a method is often preferred because it is simple to do and clear to understand. However, you should consider the performance implications of serialized access. A lock is a potential bottleneck. The longer the synchronized code takes to run and the more threads that may request the lock, the larger the potential bottleneck may grow. In general you should try to synchronize the smallest block of code that adequately protects objects from concurrent access. As a rule of thumb, if the method is long or likely to run on many threads, look for opportunities to synchronize specific statements using a lockable object. When the performance degradation is not a concern or the method contains little code outside the lines that require serialized access, synchronizing the method is usually adequate.

When to Synchronize Code

The most difficult aspect of the **synchronized** keyword is deciding when to use it. You pay a performance penalty for using synchronized methods. However, internal algorithms introduced to the JVM since the original version of Java have greatly improved the performance of multithreaded programs. The result is that synchronized methods now run much closer to the speed of methods that have no locking considerations. Regardless of the size of the overhead for synchronization, it is a reasonable price to pay to ensure correctness of your program. In general, consider synchronizing whenever the value of class or instance variables may change or methods may produce output to the same destination in code that can run on more than one thread.

To determine the level of synchronization that your application requires, consider how the threads within it share classes and objects. You can use one of the following approaches:

- The first and simplest level of synchronization is no synchronization at all. This is acceptable only for single-threaded programs and for multithreaded programs that use all classes containing only class methods in a single thread. You need synchronization when different threads share objects. If none of the class methods modifies any objects, maintaining object integrity does not require synchronization.

- In the second level of synchronization, you synchronize all class methods to safeguard the integrity of class variables that the methods use. If you adopt this approach, you can access class variables only by calling synchronized class methods, even from within methods of the same class. In this model, different threads can freely share class variables because they are protected from simultaneous access and modification. This level of synchronization is not adequate when instances of the class may be used by more than one thread.

- In the third level of synchronization, all class methods and instance methods are synchronized to protect the integrity of all fields. This allows different threads to share objects and classes because the fields have been protected from simultaneous access and modification.

Never synchronize a constructor. The JVM runs constructors only to create objects, and you cannot use the **new** keyword to tell the JVM to create the same object on two different threads. Therefore, the compiler rejects a constructor qualified with the keyword **synchronized** as an error.

When you override a synchronized method, you do not have to synchronize the method in the subclass. The superclass method remains synchronized, even if the subclass method is not synchronized. The Java programming language has no rules about overriding synchronized methods beyond the usual rules about overriding methods.

Synchronizing Methods of Inner Classes

Inner classes can complicate the synchronization of methods. In Chapter 2, you learned that an inner class has access to the fields of the enclosing instances and that several inner class objects can share the same enclosing instance. Therefore, you should design inner class objects in such a way that they do not undermine the synchronization of the methods of the enclosing instances.

No special relationship exists between the synchronized methods of an inner class and its enclosing class. As a result, simply qualifying the methods of the inner and enclosing classes with the **synchronized** keyword does not provide proper synchronization between them. Using such an approach allows one thread to call a method of the enclosing class while another thread calls a method of the inner class. If these methods may access and modify the same fields, further synchronization is probably required.

Synchronizing access to fields of enclosing classes by inner classes is straightforward, if not automatic. The methods of the inner class that access the fields of the enclosing class can use a synchronized statement to obtain a lock on the enclosing instance before accessing or modifying the fields of the enclosing instance.

In Figure 5-14, the inner and enclosing classes have methods for accessing the name field.

```
package examples.threads; /**
  * Enclosing and inner classes to demonstrate how
  * to synchronize methods between them.
  */
public class Enclosing {
   private String name = "";
   /** get the name value
    * @return the name
    */
   public synchronized String getName() {
     return name;
   }
   /** set the name value
    * @param s the input name value
    */
   public synchronized void setName( String s ) {
     name = s;
   }
   /** Example inner class
    */
   public class Insider {
     /** convert the name to all upper case
      */
     public void upperCaseName() {
       synchronized( Enclosing.this ) {
          name = name.toUpperCase();
       }
     }
   }
   /** Test method for the class
    * @param args not used
    */
   public static void main( String[] args ) {
     Enclosing enc = new Enclosing();
     enc.setName( "Maria" );
     Insider ins = enc.new Insider();
     ins.upperCaseName();
     System.out.println( enc.getName() );
   }
}
```

Figure 5-14   Synchronization in inner and enclosing classes

The output is

```
MARIA
```

In this example, the methods of the inner class use a synchronized statement to obtain a lock on the enclosing instance, **Enclosing.this**, before accessing the **name** field and changing it.

Do the methods of the inner class need the **synchronized** qualifier in addition to the **synchronized** statement? In this simple case, the answer is no. Because the inner class does not define any fields of its own, you need to provide synchronization only for the enclosing class. In general, use the synchronization qualifier for methods of inner classes only when code running in more than one thread may use fields of the inner classes.

When you synchronize methods of inner and outer classes and then run the classes in a multithreaded program, the principle of hierarchical locking specifies that the inner class acquires the lock first.

COMMUNICATING BETWEEN THREADS

In multithreaded programs, you need some form of interthread communication so that threads can notify each other when conditions change. You often want threads to tell each other to wait or to stop waiting when a condition has been satisfied. The following description of the **Object** class describes three methods for interthread communication—**wait**, **notify**, and **notifyAll**—that are inherited by all objects:

Class

java.lang.Object

Purpose

The common ancestor class **Object** defines the common behavior of all classes.

Methods

- **void wait()**

  void wait(long *timeout* **)**

  void wait(long *timeout***, int** *nanoseconds* **)**

  The **wait** methods put the current thread object into a blocked state so that the thread cannot continue to execute code. You can call **wait** only from a method that owns a lock. Calling **wait** releases the lock. If you do not specify a time period, the thread waits until notified by another thread. You can specify a timeout period, in milliseconds, after which the thread stops waiting, regardless of whether it has been notified. You can also specify a number of nanoseconds to add to the wait period.

- **void notify()**

  The **notify** method wakes up a single thread that is blocked because it is in a wait state. The thread is put into a ready-to-run state, but does not automatically start running. A synchronized method must still wait for the lock on the class or object.

- **void notifyAll()**

  The **notifyAll** method sends wake-up messages to all threads waiting for the lock. All the threads go into a runnable state, but only one can actually acquire the lock and start running. So which thread actually gets control? The JVM selects the thread to run. It may be the one that has been waiting longest, but there is no guarantee and you should not base the logic of your application on any assumptions about the order in which the JVM gives locks to threads. The other threads that have been awakened from their **wait** calls will continue as soon as they can reacquire the lock. In other words, you do not need to notify them again unless they call **wait** again.

You can use these methods for objects within single-threaded applications. However, no gain exists unless you are designing a class for use in either single-threaded or multi-threaded programs.

The **wait**, **notify**, and **notifyAll** methods are final methods of the **Object** class. You cannot override them and can rest assured that no other class has overridden them. You can call these methods for a particular object only when the current thread has a lock on the object. Otherwise, the JVM throws an exception of type **IllegalMonitorStateException**. In this context, the term *monitor* refers to the locking mechanism.

The program in Figure 5-15 demonstrates correct and incorrect uses of the **notifyAll** method. An explanation of the exception thrown follows the program and output listings.

```
package examples.threads;
  /**
   * A class to demonstrate the run-time error that
   * occurs if wait, notify, or notifyAll are used
   * when no lock has been obtained.
   */
public class ShowThreadError {
    private int value;
}
    /** Set the value of an object
      * This method is synchronized
      * @param v the object's new value
      */
    public synchronized void setValue( int v ) {
      value = v;
      doTheNotificationThing();   // okay here
    }
```

Figure 5-15   A class demonstrating the **notifyAll** method

```
    /** Get the value of the object
     * This method is synchronized
     * @return the object's value
     */
    public synchronized int getValue() {
       return value;
    }
    /** Notify waiting objects of a change
     * This method is not synchronized
     */
    public void doTheNotificationThing() {
       notifyAll();
    }
    /** Test method for the class
     * @param args not used
     */
     public static void main( String[] args ) {
     ShowThreadError t = new ShowThreadError();
     t.setValue( 10 );
     System.out.println( "value has been set to "
                          + t.getValue() );
     // the next statement causes a run-time error
     t.doTheNotificationThing();
    }
 }
```

Figure 5-15   A class demonstrating the `notifyAll` method (continued)

In the output shown here, some lines have been split and the indenting has been modified to fit on the printed page. Because the program listing has also been reformatted to fit the printed page, the line numbers given in the stack trace may not match the line numbers in Figure 5-15.

```
    value has been set to 10
    Exception in thread "main"
       java.lang.IllegalMonitorStateException:
       current thread not owner
       at
       java.lang.object.notifyAll(Native Method)
       at
       examples.threads.ShowThreadError.
          doTheNotificationThing(ShowThreadError.java:32)
       at
         examples.threads.ShowThreadError.
           main(ShowThreadError.java:39)
    Exception in thread "main")
```

This program has only one thread, but can still use the locking mechanism for the `ShowThreadError` object that it creates in the **main** method. If this class is used in a multithreaded application, the synchronized methods `getValue` and `setValue` cannot run at the same time on more than one thread. When `setValue` calls doTheNotificationThing, the lock obtained by the setValue method is released by the call of **notifyAll** in doTheNotificationThing. Because the doTheNotificationThing method is not synchronized but calls **notifyAll**, an **IllegalMonitorStateException** exception always occurs when doTheNotificationThing is called by a method that is not synchronized, including the **main** method.

Making Threads Wait

The **wait** method suspends execution of the thread and releases the lock that the thread holds on the object for which **wait** is called. Call this method when your code must wait for a condition to be satisfied before it can continue. For example, your method may be waiting for input that is not yet available or for a numeric value to reach a certain threshold. For efficiency and to help avoid deadlock, you should call **wait** to suspend the thread, release the lock that it has on the object, and let other threads run during what otherwise may be wasted processor cycles.

Usually, the thread remains suspended until you call the **notify** or **notifyAll** method for the object from another thread. You can call **wait** with a time-out as an alternative to calling **sleep**, or use the time-out as a fail-safe measure in case the JVM does not always notify the thread as you intended.

Typically you put a call to **wait** in a loop, in the following form:

```
while ( condition ) {
    wait();
}
```

Using a loop is the safest approach. The thread may be awakened for many different reasons, and you should not assume that the value of the condition has changed. Every time you regain control, the while loop gives you an opportunity to check the reason you were waiting and wait again if the condition is still true.

Threads release locks when they call **wait**. Take care not to create opportunities for deadlock when you call **wait**. Consider what can happen when you program a design that allows access to one class, called B, from only synchronized methods of another class, called A. Suppose a synchronized method of A calls a synchronized method of B. All is well until the thread in which the method of B runs calls **wait**. The call of **wait** releases the lock on the instance of B, but the lock on the instance of A remains. Deadlock can result, because the synchronized methods of A are locked out and no other methods can access B to wake up the blocked thread.

Waking a Single Thread

You can call **notify** to wake up a thread. You cannot specify which thread should be given control. The JVM decides which thread to notify. This method is most useful when all threads are waiting on the same condition.

Calling **notify** is more efficient than calling **notifyAll**. However, the result of **notify** can be that the JVM wakes up a thread that should not be given control of the object at that moment and leaves the thread that should have awakened waiting. When you use **notify**, be careful that deadlock is not a possible outcome.

Waking All Threads

The **notifyAll** method wakes up all waiting threads for the object. If different threads are waiting on different conditions, you should call this method rather than **notify**. The threads should each check their conditions. At least one thread should be able to continue, and threads whose conditions are not yet satisfied should use the **wait** method to return to the blocked state.

It is important to note that even though more than one thread may be awakened by the **notifyAll** method, only one can obtain the lock for the object and be allowed to execute.

An Example of Communicating Between Threads

The next example is a relatively long program. Setting up a multithreaded program often involves several classes. The sample program is a simple banking application composed of four classes, **BankAccount** listed in Figure 5-16, **Saver** listed in Figure 5-17, **Spender** listed in Figure 5-18, and **Banking** listed in Figure 5-19. Sample output is listed in Figure 5-20. For demonstration purposes, it maintains a bank account and performs deposits and withdrawals against the same bank account on separate threads. The **BankAccount.withdraw** method may call the **wait** method to force a withdrawal to wait until an account has enough money to maintain a positive bank balance. The **BankAccount.deposit** method calls **notifyAll** whenever the bank balance changes so that all threads waiting on that bank account object receive notice of the change and can evaluate the situation to determine whether they can proceed.

The first of the four classes encapsulates a bank account.

```
package examples.threads.bank;
/** A class to demonstrate wait and notify methods
  */
```

Figure 5-16   The BankAccount class in the banking sample of interthread
                    communication

```
public class BankAccount {
   private int balance = 0;
   private boolean isOpen = true;
   /** The method withdraws an amount from the
     * account. If funds are insufficient, it will
     * wait until the funds are available or the
     * account is closed.
     * @param amount The amount to be withdrawn from
     *     the account
     * @return true if the withdrawal is successful,
     *     false otherwise
     * @exception InterruptedException If another
     *     thread calls the <b>interrupt</b> method
     */
   public synchronized boolean withdraw( int amount )
              throws InterruptedException {
      while ( amount > balance && isOpen() ) {
         System.out.println( "Waiting for "
                           + "some money ..." );
            wait();
      }
      boolean result = false;
      if ( isOpen() ) {
         balance -= amount;
         result = true;
      }
      return result;
   }
   /** The method to deposit an amount into the
     * account provided that the account is open.
     * When the deposit is  successful, it will notify
     * all waiting operations that there is now more
     * money in the account
     * @param amount The amount to be deposited into
     *     the account
     * @return true if the deposit is successful,
     *     false otherwise
     */
   public synchronized boolean deposit( int amount ) {
      if ( isOpen() ) {
         balance += amount;
         notifyAll();
         return true;
      } else {
         return false;
      }
   }
```

Figure 5-16   The BankAccount class in the banking sample of interthread communication (continued)

```
    /** Check to see if the account is open
     * @return true if it is open, otherwise false
     */
  public synchronized boolean isOpen() {
      return isOpen;
  }
  /** Close the bank account */
  public synchronized void close() {
      isOpen = false;
      notifyAll();
  }
}
```

Figure 5-16   The BankAccount class in the banking sample of interthread communication (continued)

The BankAccount class has the following characteristics:

- The methods deposit and withdraw are synchronized instance methods. Therefore, the JVM applies a lock to the BankAccount object for which they are called.

- If the account has insufficient funds, the method withdraw calls wait and prints a message. Because withdraw calls wait, an InterruptedException exception can occur and must be listed in the throws clause.

- The deposit method calls notifyAll to alert all threads whenever the balance in the account changes.

- The methods isOpen and close are also synchronized.

- The BankAccount class provides the isOpen method to determine whether transactions are allowed on the BankAccount object. The isOpen method returns true until the method close is called to close an account.

- The close method is synchronized so that it can call notifyAll to stop any transactions that are in progress when the account is closed and to prevent the account from being closed in the middle of a transaction or while another thread is checking to see if the bank account is open.

The listing in Figure 5-17 is the thread that makes deposits. It contains a class called Saver that implements Runnable. The Saver object operates on a BankAccount object that the class Banking passes to the Saver constructor. The Banking class is the test program for the banking application and is listed in Figure 5-19.

```
package examples.threads.bank;
/**
  * A class to demonstrate wait and notify methods
  */
public class Saver implements Runnable {
   private BankAccount account;
      /** Class constructor method
        * @param ba The bank account where this saver
        *    puts the money
        */
      public Saver( BankAccount ba ) {
         account = ba;
      }
/** The method the saver uses to put away money */
public void run() {
   while( account.isOpen() ) {
      try {
         if ( account.deposit( 100 ) ) {
            System.out.println(
            "$100 successfully deposited." );
         }
         Thread.currentThread().sleep( 1000 );
      } catch ( InterruptedException iex ) {
         // display the exception, but continue
         System.err.println( iex );
      }
   }
}
}
```

Figure 5-17   The Saver class that makes deposits in the banking sample

These classes demonstrate how the threads interact, rather than how a banking application should be designed. The **run** method of the Saver class tries repeatedly to deposit $100, as long as the account is open. After making a deposit, **run** sleeps for a second. The threads sleep to stagger deposit and withdrawal transactions for demonstration purposes. If an **InterruptedException** exception is thrown while the thread sleeps, and that exception awakens the thread, the catch block catches but ignores the exception.

The listing in Figure 5-18 shows the thread that makes withdrawals. It contains a class called Spender that extends **Thread**. It also could have implemented **Runnable** in the same manner that the Saver thread implements **Runnable**, but Spender extends **Thread** to demonstrate both techniques. Like the Saver class, Spender operates on a BankAccount object that the Banking class passes as an argument to the constructor.

```
package examples.threads.bank;
/**
  * A class to demonstrate wait and notify methods
  */
public class Spender extends Thread {
   private BankAccount account;
   /** Class constructor method
     * @param ba The bank account from which
     *     this spender takes the money
     */
   public Spender( BankAccount ba ) {
      account = ba;
   }
   /** The method the spender uses
     * to take out money
     */
   public void run() {
      while( account.isOpen() ) {
         try {
            if ( account.withdraw( 500 ) ) {
               System.out.println(
               "$500 successfully withdrawn." );
            }
            sleep( 1000 );
         } catch ( InterruptedException iex ) {
            // display any interruptions but continue
            System.err.println( iex );
         }
      }
   }
}
```

Figure 5-18   The Spender class that makes withdrawals in the banking application

Like the Saver class, the Spender class is not designed to model realistic banking activity. The **run** method of the Spender class tries repeatedly to withdraw $500 as long as the account is open. Like a Saver object, a Spender object sleeps for a second after each withdrawal, and catches, but ignores, exceptions thrown during the sleep period.

The listing in Figure 5-19 is the test class for the banking application. The **main** method creates a BankAccount object ba. Then it creates a Spender thread named spenderThread and a Saver object named aSaver for the account ba. The Spender class extends **Thread**, but the Saver class implements **Runnable**. Therefore, the main method must create a separate **Thread** object, saverThread, for aSaver. Finally, the **main** method starts the Spender and Saver threads.

```
package examples.threads.bank;
/**
  * A class to demonstrate wait and notify methods
  */
public class Banking {

   /** The test method for the class
     * @param args[0] Time in seconds for which
     *     this banking process should run
     */
   public static void main( String[] args ) {
      BankAccount ba = new BankAccount();
      // create the spender thread
      Spender spenderThread = new Spender( ba );
      // create the saver thread, which is a two-step
      // process because Saver implements Runnable
      Saver aSaver = new Saver( ba );
      Thread saverThread = new Thread( aSaver );
      spenderThread.start();
      saverThread.start();
      int time;
      if ( args.length == 0 ) {
         time = 10000;
      } else {
         time = Integer.parseInt( args[0] ) * 1000;
      }
      try {
         Thread.currentThread().sleep( time );
      } catch ( InterruptedException iex ) {
         /* ignore it */
      }
      // close the bank account
      ba.close();
   }
}
```

Figure 5-19   The main class, `Banking`, for the interthread-communication sample program

The code that runs on the spawned threads deposits and withdraws money regularly, so the main thread can go to sleep. Like the **Saver** and **Spender** classes, **Banking** catches and ignores any exceptions that wake it up during a sleep period. When its sleep period ends, **main** wakes up and closes the bank account. This, in turn, causes the other threads to end.

By default, the **main** method sleeps for 10 seconds, but you can specify a different time interval in a command-line argument. For example, you can run the program for 12 seconds by issuing the following command:

```
java examples.threads.bank.Banking 12
```

Then, the output may be as shown in Figure 5-20.

```
Waiting for some money ...
Waiting for some money ...
$100 successfully deposited.
$100 successfully deposited.
Waiting for some money ...
Waiting for some money ...
$100 successfully deposited.
Waiting for some money ...
$100 successfully deposited.
$500 successfully withdrawn.
$100 successfully deposited.
Waiting for some money ...
Waiting for some money ...
$100 successfully deposited.
Waiting for some money ...
$100 successfully deposited.
Waiting for some money ...
$100 successfully deposited.
Waiting for some money ...
$100 successfully deposited.
$500 successfully withdrawn.
$100 successfully deposited.
Waiting for some money ...
$100 successfully deposited.
Waiting for some money ...
Waiting for some money ...
$100 successfully deposited.
```

Figure 5-20   Sample output of the banking interthread-communication example

GROUPING THREADS

The Java platform lets you separate or gather (depending on your point of view) your threads into groups. Creating thread groups has the following advantages:

- **Thread** objects in separate groups can be protected from each other.
- Some **Thread** operations are simplified if you perform them on an entire group at once. You can do this rather than iterate through a list of threads and perform the same operation on each of them.

For example, you can group sets of threads that load images from files or perform network operations. Then you can assign the same priority to the entire group of threads with one method call, or interrupt all threads involved in an operation when the user clicks a Stop button you include in your GUI.

Use the **ThreadGroup** class to create and manipulate groups of threads.

Class

java.lang.ThreadGroup

Purpose

A **ThreadGroup** object represents a set of threads. It can include other groups, and you can build a hierarchical structure of thread groups. Each **Thread** object can access information about its own group or its subgroups, but not about the parent groups, if any exist, or any other groups.

Constructors

- **ThreadGroup(String** *name* **)**

  ThreadGroup(ThreadGroup *parent*, **String** *name* **)**

  When you create a thread group, you must specify the name of the group as a **String** object. You cannot change the name after creating the group. If the new group is to be a subgroup of an existing group, supply the object reference for the parent group as the first argument of the constructor.

Methods

- **int activeCount()**

  The **activeCount** method returns an estimate of the number of active threads in the group.

- **int activeGroupCount()**

  The **activeGroupCount** method returns an estimate of the number of groups in the current group.

- **void checkAccess()**

  The **checkAccess** method is a security manager and is called by several other methods in the **ThreadGroup** class. If the thread does not have permission to modify the group, this method throws the exception **SecurityException**.

- **int enumerate(Thread[]** *list* **)**

  int enumerate(Thread[] *list*, **boolean** *recurse* **)**

  int enumerate(ThreadGroup[] *list* **)**

  int enumerate(ThreadGroup[] *list*, **boolean** *recurse* **)**

  The **enumerate** method copies object references for every active thread or thread group into the specified array. You should call **activeCount** or **activeGroupCount** before calling **enumerate**, and pass an array that has enough entries. If you supply a **boolean** argument with the value **true**, all threads or groups in subgroups of the current group are included, recursively. Due to the dynamic nature of threads, it

5

is possible for the number of threads and groups to change between the calling of **activeCount** or **activeGroupCount** and **enumerate**. It is wise to allocate an array larger than required, because the list of threads will be truncated without any error indication if the array is too small.

- **int getMaxPriority()**

The **getMaxPriority** method returns the highest priority value allowed for the threads in the group.

- **String getName()**

The **getName** method returns the name of the group.

- **ThreadGroup getParent()**

The **getParent** method returns an object reference to the group that is the parent of the current group, or **null** if there is no parent group.

- **boolean isDaemon()**

The **isDaemon** method returns **true** if the group is a daemon thread group, or **false** otherwise.

- **interrupt()**

This method calls **interrupt** on all threads in this group.

- **void list()**

Call the **list** method to output information that is useful for debugging to the stream **System.out**.

- **void setDaemon(boolean *daemon*)**

Call the **setDaemon** method with a **boolean** value that establishes whether the group is a daemon group.

- **void setMaxPriority(int *priority*)**

Call **setMaxPriority** to set the highest priority value allowed for the threads in the group.

Since version 1.2 of the J2SDK, the methods **stop**, **suspend**, **resume**, and **allowThreadSuspension** of the **ThreadGroup** class are deprecated for the same reasons that **stop**, **suspend**, and **resume** are deprecated in the **Thread** class.

ThreadGroup objects provide security because a thread is allowed to modify another thread only if both threads reside in the same group, or if the modified thread resides in a group that is nested within the group of the modifying thread. For example, if a thread calls the **setPriority** method to lower the priority of a **Thread** object in another group that is not a subgroup, the JVM throws an exception.

Every thread belongs to a group. By default, a new thread is placed in the same group as the thread that created it. When you create a thread, you can assign it to a different group by supplying a **ThreadGroup** reference to the group as an argument to the constructor for the **Thread** object. After you create a thread, you cannot change its group.

The sample program in Figure 5-21 creates two **ThreadGroup** objects and creates one thread in each group. This program also demonstrates using piped input and output streams in multithreaded programs. Chapter 3 introduces piped input and output streams but does not include a multithreaded program to show their use.

```
package examples.threads;
import java.io.*;
/**
  * A class to demonstrate threads and piped streams
  */
public class PlumbingThreads implements Runnable {
    private PipedInputStream pipeIn;
    private PipedOutputStream pipeOut;
    /** Create a PlumbingThreads object to connect with
      * an existing PipedOutputStream
      */
    public PlumbingThreads( PipedOutputStream p ) {
        pipeOut = p;
    }
    /** Create a PlumbingThreads object to connect with
      * an existing PipedInputStream
      */
    public PlumbingThreads( PipedInputStream p ) {
        pipeIn = p;
    }
    /** Read from standard input and echo
      * the characters to the output pipe
      * @exception IOException general I/O error
      */
    public void sendKeystrokes() throws IOException {
        int c;
        while ( ( c = System.in.read() ) != -1 ) {
            pipeOut.write( c );
        }
        pipeOut.close();
    }
    /** Read characters from the input pipe
      * and echo them to standard out
      * @exception IOException general I/O error
      */
    public void receiveKeystrokes() throws IOException {
        int c;
        while ( ( c = pipeIn.read() ) != -1 ) {
            System.out.write( c );
        }
```

Figure 5-21   A class that demonstrates **ThreadGroup** objects

```
        pipeIn.close();
    }
    /** The workings of the threads
     */
    public void run() {
        try {
            // determine if this is an input or
            // output thread and go to work
            if ( pipeIn != null ) {
                receiveKeystrokes();
            } else if ( pipeOut != null ) {
                sendKeystrokes();
            }
        } catch ( IOException ioe ) {
            System.err.println( ioe );
        }
    }
    /** The test method for the class
     * @param args not used
     */
    public static void main( String[] args ) {
        try {
            // create the input and output pipes
            PipedInputStream istream
                = new PipedInputStream();
            PipedOutputStream ostream
                = new PipedOutputStream( istream );
            // construct the plumbing threads,
            // specifying the newly created pipes
            PlumbingThreads in
                = new PlumbingThreads( istream );
            PlumbingThreads out
                = new PlumbingThreads( ostream );
            // put the threads into separate groups
            ThreadGroup inputGroup
                = new ThreadGroup( "input thread group" );
            ThreadGroup outputGroup
                = new ThreadGroup( "output thread group" );
            // construct threads with existing
            // plumbing threads
            Thread inputThread
                = new Thread( inputGroup, in,
                              "input pipe" );
            Thread outputThread
                = new Thread( outputGroup, out,
                              "output pipe" );
            // start the threads and let them go!
            inputThread.start();
            outputThread.start();
```

Figure 5-21   A class that demonstrates **ThreadGroup** objects (continued)

```
        } catch ( IOException ioe ) {
            System.err.println( ioe );
        }
    }
}
```

Figure 5-21   A class that demonstrates `ThreadGroup` objects (continued)

`PlumbingThread` objects communicate through a pipe. If the argument of the constructor is a `PipedInputStream` object, the thread reads from the pipe. If the argument of the constructor is a `PipedOutputStream` object, the thread writes to the pipe. Notice how the **run** method determines which end of the pipe is attached to the `PlumbingThread` object.

The **main** method creates two `PlumbingThread` objects, in and out. Then, **main** creates two **ThreadGroup** objects, inputGroup and outputGroup, and the **Thread** objects inputThread and outputThread. The constructor of **Thread** is called with three arguments:

- The **ThreadGroup** to which the JVM is to add the newly created thread
- The **Runnable** object
- A **String** that becomes the name of the thread

Finally, **main** starts the two threads. What they actually do is trivial. The input thread reads characters from **System.in** and puts them into the pipe. The output thread reads characters from the pipe and writes them to **System.out**.

The only complication that can occur is an **IOException** exception, which can be thrown during a read or write operation. The **run** method of `PlumbingThread` can catch the exception and print a message.

CHAPTER SUMMARY

- This chapter shows how to create threads and gives some techniques for synchronizing threads and performing interthread communication.
- A class can run as a separate thread if it extends the **Thread** class or implements the **Runnable** interface. The **Thread** class provides the full infrastructure for multithreading, and implements **Runnable**.
- All classes that implement **Runnable** must implement the method **run**. This method is the entry point for the thread. Your multithreaded program must call **Thread.start** to launch all but the main thread.
- The **Thread** class provides many methods that you can call to control your threads, including **yield**, **sleep**, and **setPriority**.

❑ Daemon threads are threads that run in the background and typically have no associated user interface.

❑ The JVM creates background threads for you if you use the **Timer** and **TimerTask** classes from the **java.util** package to schedule tasks for future execution.

❑ Programming for multithreading ensures that your threads do not interfere with each other or go into deadlock by entering a wait state. This chapter describes features you can use to help, but you are responsible for ensuring that your threads do not corrupt each other or create a deadlock.

❑ You can declare variables to be **volatile** if other threads may change them. Do this if optimization may generate code that could lose or ignore the changes made to the variables on other threads.

❑ You can associate variables with the thread instance by giving them type **ThreadLocal**. **ThreadLocal** static variables are shared by all instances on a thread but not by instances of the same class on other threads.

❑ Declare instance methods of a class with the keyword **synchronized** if only one thread at a time should be able to execute the method on the instance. While a synchronized method is active, no other synchronized methods defined for the same object can run.

❑ Declare a class method with **synchronized** if only one thread at a time should be able to execute the method. In addition, no other synchronized class methods defined for the same class can run while the method is active.

❑ The mechanism of thread synchronization places locks on objects. Object and class locks are independent.

❑ No special relationship exists between the synchronized methods of an inner class and its enclosing class. If a method of an inner class needs to participate in the synchronization of fields in the enclosing class, it should use a **synchronized** statement to obtain a lock for the enclosing class instance.

❑ You can program one form of interthread communication by calling the methods **wait**, **notify**, and **notifyAll**. All classes inherit these final methods from the **Object** class.

❑ Call the **wait** method if a thread reaches an inactive state while waiting for input. This method suspends the thread and gives other threads a chance to run. The best way to call **wait** is in a loop with the following form:

```
while ( condition ) { wait() }
```

❑ When two or more threads are synchronized on the same lock, the active thread can wake up other threads by calling **notify** or **notifyAll**. The **notifyAll** method is safer, but less efficient, because it wakes up all threads that are waiting on the lock. Each thread can call **wait** again or continue processing. Use **notifyAll** to reduce the risk of deadlock.

❑ For greater security and convenience, you can collect **Thread** objects into **ThreadGroup** objects.

Review Questions

1. Which of the following qualifiers is applied to a method to indicate that it requires serialized access to an object or class? Select the best answer.

   a. `volatile`

   b. `transient`

   c. `locked`

   d. `synchronized`

   e. `serialized`

2. When you create a **TimerTask** object to perform a scheduled activity, which type of object do you use to schedule the activity?

   a. `Thread`

   b. `ThreadLocal`

   c. `ThreadGroup`

   d. `Timer`

   e. `Runnable`

3. Examine the following code:

   ```
   public class Quiz5_3 {
       // —X—
   }
   ```

   Which of the following definitions are valid when placed at the line marked —X—? Select all that apply.

   a. `public synchronized Quiz5_3() {}`

   b. `private synchronized void b() {}`

   c. `public volatile void c() {}`

   d. `public static synchronized void d() {}`

   e. `public static volatile void d() {}`

4. In which of the following classes are the methods **wait**, **notify**, and **notifyAll** defined? Select all that apply.

   a. `Thread`

   b. `ThreadLocal`

   c. `ThreadGroup`

   d. `Timer`

   e. `Object`

5. Examine the following code:

```
public class Quiz5_5 extends Thread {
    private int limit;
    public Quiz5_5( int l ) {
        limit = l;
    }
    public void run() {
        int i;
        for( i = 0; i <= limit - 1; i++ ) {
            System.out.print( i + ", " );
        }
        System.out.println( i );
    }
    public static void main( String[] args ) {
        Quiz5_5 x = new Quiz5_5( 5 );
        x.run();
    }
}
```

Which of the following statements are true when the code is compiled and run? Select all that apply.

a. The compiler rejects the definition of the **run** method because it does not have the **synchronized** keyword.

b. Compilation is successful and the output is

0, 1, 2, 3, 4, 5

c. The output of the program is written using a different thread than the thread executing the **main** method.

d. The compiler rejects the class definition because **Quiz5_5** does not implement the **Runnable** interface.

e. The output of the program is written using the same thread as that which executes the **main** method.

6. Which of the following methods are defined in the **Runnable** interface? Select all that apply.

a. **start**

b. **run**

c. **setPriority**

d. **interrupt**

e. **isDaemon**

7. Examine the following code:

```
public class Quiz5_7 implements Runnable {
    private int limit;
    public Quiz5_7( int l ) {
        limit = l;
```

```
            }
            public void run() {
                int i;
                for( i=0; i <= limit - 1; i++ ) {
                    System.out.print( i + ", " );
                }
                System.out.println( i );
            }
            public static void main( String[] args ) {
                Quiz5_7 x = new Quiz5_7( 5 );
                Thread t = new Thread( x );
                t.start();
            }
        }
```

Which of the following statements are true when the code is compiled and run? Select all that apply.

a. The compiler rejects the definition of the **run** method because it does not have the **synchronized** keyword.

b. Compilation is successful and the output is

```
0, 1, 2, 3, 4, 5
```

c. The output of the program is written using a different thread than the one executing the **main** method.

d. The output of the program is written using the same thread as the one executing the **main** method.

e. The compiler rejects the expression new **Thread(x)** because the **Thread** class does not have any constructor that takes a **Quiz5_7** object as a parameter.

8. Which of the following statements are true of daemon threads? Select all that apply.

a. You can create groups of daemon threads by calling **ThreadGroup.setDaemon**.

b. You can keep a program alive by creating a daemon thread that continues to execute after all other threads terminate.

c. To define a class that runs on a dacmon thread, you can either extend **Thread** or implement **Runnable**.

d. You can supply the JVM a daemon thread on which to schedule a **TimerTask** object.

e. All variables on daemon threads are inherently thread–safe.

9. Examine the following code:

```
public class Quiz5_9 {
    private String name;
    private int count;
```

```
public quiz_5( String n, int c ) {
        name = n;
        count = c;
    }
    public static void main( String[] args ) {
        // —X—
    }
}
```

Which of the following statements are valid synchronized blocks if placed at the line marked —X—? Select all that apply.

a. `synchronized {}`

b. `synchronized ( String ) {}`

c. `synchronized ( a ) {}`

d. `synchronized ( a.name ) {}`

e. `synchronized ( a.count ) {}`

10. Examine the following code:

```
public class Quiz5_10 {
    public Quiz5_10() throws InterruptedException {
        // A
    }
    public void f1() throws InterruptedException {
        // B
    }
    public static void f2()
                        throws InterruptedException {
        // C
    }
    private void f3() throws InterruptedException {
        // D
    }
    public synchronized void f4()
                        throws InterruptedException {
        // E
        f3();
    }
}
```

Which of the locations marked within the class definition are valid locations from which the **wait** method can be called?

a. A

b. B

c. C

d. D

e. E

PROGRAMMING EXERCISES

To get the files required for the Debugging and Complete the Solution exercises, copy the folder \Data\questions\c5 from the CD that accompanies this book to folder Data\questions\c5 on your hard drive. Work in the folder that contains questions. Make sure questions contains folder c5 and c5 contains the original Java source files.

Debugging

1. Correct all the errors in the following program:

```
package questions.c5;
public class Debug5_1 {
   private int count;
   public Debug5_1( int c ) {
      count = c;
   }
   public void run() {
      int powerOf2 = 1;
      for( int i=1; i < count; i++ ) {
         powerOf2 = 2*powerOf2;
         System.out.println( powerOf2 );
      }
   }
   public static void main( String[] args ) {
      Debug5_1 x = new Debug5_1( 10 );
      x.start();
   }
}
```

2. Correct all the errors in the following program, but do not change the fact that the class implements the **Runnable** interface:

```
package questions.c5;
public class Debug5_2 implements Runnable {
   private int count;
   public Debug5_2( int c ) {
      count = c;
   }
   public void run() {
      int powerOf2 = 1;
      for( int i=1; i < count; i++ ) {
         powerOf2 = 2*powerOf2;
         System.out.println( powerOf2 );
      }
   }
   public static void main( String[] args ) {
      Debug5_2 x = new Debug5_2( 12 );
      x.start();
   }
}
```

3. Correct all the errors in the following program without removing the synchronized blocks:

```
package questions.c5;
public class Debug5_3 {
    private double balance = 0.0;
    public void increaseBalance( double increase ) {
        synchronized( balance ) {
            balance += increase;
        }
    }
    public void decreaseBalance( double decrease ) {
        synchronized( balance ) {
            balance -= decrease;
        }
    }
    public static void main( String[] args ) {
        Debug5_3 x = new Debug5_3();
        x.increaseBalance( 100.75 );
        x.decreaseBalance( 50.50 );
    }
}
```

4. Correct the following program so that all methods of the enclosing class and the inner class are synchronized:

```
package questions.c5;
public class Debug5_4 {
    private String name;
    class HomeAddress {
        private String street;
        private String city;
        public String getStreet() {
            return street;
        }
        public String getCity() {
            return city;
        }
        public void setStreet( String s ) {
            street = s;
        }
        public void setCity( String s ) {
            city = s;
        }
    }
    public synchronized String getName() {
        return name;
    }
    public synchronized void setName( String s ) {
        name = s;
    }
```

```
        public static void main( String[] args ) {
            Debug5_4 person = new Debug5_4();
            HomeAddress address = person.new HomeAddress();
            person.setName( "Mike Edotsuc" );
            address.setStreet( "23 Elm Street" );
            address.setCity( "Toronto" );
            System.out.println( person.getName() );
            System.out.println( address.getStreet() );
            System.out.println( address.getCity() );
        }
    }
```

5. Correct all the errors in the following program:

```
    package questions.c5;
    public class Debug5_5 extends Thread {
        private int samples;
        private double average;
        public Debug5_5( int s ) {
            samples = s;
        }
        public synchronized void run() {
            java.util.Random r = new java.util.Random();
            double sum = 0.0;
            for( int i=0; i < samples; i++ ) {
                sum += r.nextDouble();
            }
            average = sum / samples;
        }
        public double getAverage() {
            while ( average == 0.0 ) try {
                wait();
            } catch ( InterruptedException ix ) {
                System.out.println( ix );
            }
            return average;
        }
        public static void main( String[] args ) {
            Debug5_5 x = new Debug5_5( 500000 );
            x.start();
            System.out.println( "Average = "
                                + x.getAverage() );
        }
    }
```

Complete the Solution

1. Modify the source for class questions.c5.Complete5_1 in the file
   questions\c5\ Complete5_1.java. Define the **main** method of the
   Complete5_1 class to create and start a thread that executes the **run** method of

~~the Completed_1 class. The master method should let the thread run long~~
enough to print its message approximately 10 times. The **main** method should
then request that the thread stop.

2. Modify the source for class **questions.c5.Complete5_2** in the file
questions\c5\ Complete5_2.java. Complete the definition of class
Complete5_2 by having the class extend **Thread** and by adding a **run** method.
The **run** method should count characters and output the result to the console in
a fashion similar to what the **main** method of the **Complete5_2** class does.

3. Start with the version of class **Complete5_2** that is the answer to the previous
exercise, and complete the solution by having the character counting operation
take place on a different thread. But instead of having the top-level class extend
Thread, add a method called **backgroundCount** that creates an anonymous
inner class that extends **Thread**. The **run** method of the anonymous inner class
should do the same thing as the method in the previous exercise.

4. Modify the source for class **questions.c5.Complete5_5** in the file
questions\c5\ Complete5_5.java. Complete the definition of the class
Complete5_5 by providing a definition for the missing inner class
MessageReader and by completing the method **addMessage**.

5. Modify the source for class **questions.c5.Complete5_2** in the file
questions\c5\ Complete5_2.java. Complete the definition of class
Complete5_2 by adding lines to use the **Timer** and **Tick** objects to print a
countdown from 10 to 1 on the console, followed by "blastoff." Make sure the
program terminates properly.

Discovery

1. Create a class called **FileWatcher** that can be given several filenames that may
or may not exist. The class should start a thread for each filename. Each thread
will periodically check for the existence of its file. If the file appears, the thread
will write a message to the console and then end. Put all the threads within a
new **ThreadGroup** object created by the **FileWatcher** class.

2. Review the pump, valve, and buzzer example that demonstrates the **Observer**
interface and **Observable** class in Chapter 4. Rewrite the example using threads,
and use interthread communication. In addition to inner classes **Valve** and **Buzzer**,
add an inner class **ValveSetter** that extends **TimerTask** to the **Pump** class. In
the **main** method of **Pump**, use a **Timer** object to schedule pressure changes to
150 after 200 milliseconds, 200 after 400 milliseconds, and 75 after 600 milliseconds.
The inner class **Valve** records the pressure, and its **setPressure** method calls
notifyAll whenever the pressure changes. This version of **Valve** does not
extend **Observable** and does not need to implement **Runnable** because its
setPressure method is called by an instance of **ValveSetter**. The inner class
Buzzer does not implement **Observer** but instead extends **Thread** or implements
Runnable. In this version of the pump program, the buzzer is a thread that

sleeps most of the time but wakes up at regular intervals, say every 90 milliseconds, to check pressure of the valve. Let the pump program run for 1000 milliseconds and make sure that the buzzer goes on when the pressure rises above 100 and goes off when the pressure falls below 100.

3. Write a program that finds all the prime numbers from 1 to 100. A positive integer is prime if the only positive integers that divide evenly into it are 1 and the number itself. To exercise multithreading, follow the algorithm presented here in pseudo code:

   ❑ Set up an array of 100 **boolean** elements and initialize every element to **true**. Each element is a flag, and **true** indicates a potential prime number. Set an element to **false** when its index is proven not to be prime.

   ❑ Loop through the array. If the element is **true**, meaning the number is a potential prime, launch a thread for the index of the element and in that thread, set elements to **false** for all multiples of the number. For example, the first thread you launch this way eliminates multiples of 2 (4, 8, 16 ...) from the set of potential primes. The next thread eliminates multiples of 3, and so on.

   ❑ When all the threads except the main thread have ended, print the numbers for which the corresponding element is still **true**. The output should show 26 prime numbers starting with 1, 2, 3, 5, 7, 11....

6

COMMON ELEMENTS OF GRAPHICAL USER INTERFACES

In this chapter you will:

♦ Learn the characteristics of a graphical user interface

♦ Explore the contents of the Java Foundation Classes

♦ Discover how the JFC supports creating GUIs for the Java platform

♦ Design GUIs with layouts that dynamically adjust to screen resolution and window size

♦ Include predefined components such as text fields, buttons, and multimedia elements in your GUI

♦ See how the JFC provides a framework for interacting with the user in event-driven programs

♦ Write code using component, container, and layout manager classes of the AWT and Swing

♦ State the name of the event class for any specified listener interface in the `java.awt.event` package

♦ Write code to implement the `paintComponent` method of a `javax.swing.Jcomponent` component

INTRODUCTION

This chapter explains the main elements of a graphical user interface (GUI), gives an overview of the Java Foundation Classes (JFC), and shows by example how to program a GUI using the Abstract Windowing Toolkit (AWT) and the Swing APIs of the JFC. You can effectively use it in conjunction with Chapter 7, which presents the detailed descriptions for the classes and interfaces that constitute the APIs.

Modern computer operating systems include presentation services that provide the user with a graphical user interface (GUI). As a result, computer users now demand application programs that also provide GUIs. Fortunately, the Java platform provides extensive support for building them, and programmers have made the most of this support. For instance, in your studies of existing programs, have you ever downloaded source files for Java applets or applications that run in a windowing environment? You may be surprised by how much of that code is concerned with the user interface to the applet or application. When a program has a GUI, a large portion of the code services the GUI.

GUIs display in graphical form on the screen. So far, you have used sample programs with console input and output. In other words, they were command-line programs with the look and feel of operating systems like DOS. The reason for this is simplicity; many aspects of the Java programming language and the packages in the Java platform are better explained without the distracting complexities of programming for a GUI. Programmers can use the forms of I/O described in Chapter 3 even when they are programming a GUI. For example, the program may open a file and write information into the file to be used to trace the flow of the program and as an aid for debugging errors.

To program a GUI, you must master event-driven programming because GUI-oriented programs are event driven. The user initiates most events by moving and clicking the mouse or by pressing keys on the keyboard. Unlike command-line programs that operate in a batch-processing mode or perhaps pause occasionally to solicit user input, GUI-based programs must always be responsive to and take directions from the user.

Java Foundation Classes provides a flexible and extensive set of GUI-building objects that are easy to use. For example, many features, such as support for toolbars, borders, tables, trees, and pluggable look and feel, have been added since the original version of the Java platform in which support for GUI development was limited. Although some APIs of the JFC, most notably Swing, were first available as add-ons to version 1.1 of the Java platform, the JFC did not exist as a complete set until the release of the Java 2 platform. The size of the JFC may be overwhelming at first, but these classes provide programmers with the objects necessary for creating the powerful and polished GUIs that users demand.

Main Features and Terminology of a GUI

All interactive output and input should pass through your program's GUI. Therefore, the GUI consists of what the user sees on the screen and code to process user actions such as clicking the mouse or typing on the keyboard. Your program must properly relate those actions to the elements displayed in the GUI and perform the appropriate activities in response.

To be consistent with object-oriented design, you should separate a program's GUI from a program's processing, just as you distinguish between the interface to a class and the implementation of the class. This design pattern, known as Model View Controller (MVC), structures your application effectively because all logic for an application is separated from visible elements and the controller controls all interactions between them.

Model-view separation is the technique for separating a program's GUI from its data processing. It occurs when you run the GUI in one thread to give the user a quick response, or at least to acknowledge a user action, and then perform more time-consuming tasks, such as file I/O or number crunching, in

other threads. The proportion of the program that is part of the GUI depends
on the program's nature and purpose. For applets, which tend to be short and
highly interactive, the GUI often makes up most of the code. For an application, the GUI could be a simple interface to a complex program.

Components comprise a major part of a GUI. In the Java platform, components are predefined standard elements, such as buttons, text fields, frame windows, and dialog boxes.
The Swing and AWT APIs provide a large repertoire of components. This chapter mentions a few of the most commonly used components. Discussions of additional components will come in the following chapters.

The display space on the screen is also a component. Like all GUI-based applications, a
Java application window is a frame window. Frame windows have a title and a border; buttons for closing, minimizing, and maximizing the window; and can contain a menu bar.
The browser or applet viewer that is used in a Java application controls the display space
for an applet. Thus, applets run in a simpler and displayable component called a panel.

Controls, such as check boxes, labels, scrollbars, text areas, dialog boxes, and list boxes, are
also components. Some components, such as buttons, are used individually. Others, aptly
called containers, are components that house other components. Frame windows, panels,
and dialog boxes are all containers.

Consider the dialog box, which is a window that opens to present information to or
receive information from the user. A dialog box is a container, because it can have buttons, text fields, and other components within it. A file dialog box is also a container. It
lets you select or enter a filename in a window. The Java platform has a class for file dialog boxes.

You can use one of the core classes—the layout managers—to control the way components are arranged within a container. For each container, you select the layout manager
that controls the size and position of components within the container. This separation
of container classes from layout manager classes gives you the freedom to select the container you want, and then select a layout manager you want. Containers have no built-in
limitations on how you can position components within them.

Components that comprise the Swing and AWT APIs take responsibility for how they
are drawn as part of a GUI. However, your GUI is not limited to the available components. You can custom draw your own components directly onto the graphics context
of a window or panel. The term *graphics* refers to drawing in the graphics context for a
component. A *graphics context* is the area on the display screen where a component is
positioned. You can obtain the graphics context from a window or panel and then call
methods to draw entities, such as lines, text, and images. To Java, images are graphical
objects, such as pictures or icons, stored in a format supported by your implementation
of the Java platform.

Painting is the process of displaying components or refreshing the display of components
on the screen. Painting can occur when the GUI for an application or an applet starts;

when you call methods to redraw the GUI; or when the application or applet window is resized, moved, or exposed on the screen after being covered. Objects of the component classes handle the painting of themselves. When you perform custom drawing directly to a graphics context, your code must also handle the painting. To ensure that a program does not have to wait for every paint operation to complete, GUIs use a separate thread called the event dispatch thread for drawing and forwarding all paint requests to that thread.

Handling events is an important part of GUI programming. Events can be triggered by the operating system or by user actions, such as clicking or moving the mouse or pressing keys on the keyboard, and action events occur when the user acts on components. For example, the user may click a check box, select an item from a list, or type characters into a text field. Components encapsulate not only the look of visual elements of the GUI, but also the set of events that the components generate.

You should structure your user interface so that it is directed by events. To do this, you provide handlers that react to events that can occur while your program runs. When you first learned how the Java platform implemented exception handling, you were introduced to the concept of handlers in the discussion of catch clauses for exceptions. However, the JFC supports a much broader use of handlers than is used for exceptions. Exception handlers interrupt the usual flow of control to deal with an error or unexpected situation. In a GUI, event handlers let you pass control of the program to the user so that your program proceeds by responding to user activities.

The mechanism for event handlers is different from that of exception handlers. The GUI event-handling mechanism has been revised since the original version of the Java platform, and it now uses a set of interfaces called listeners, which are similar to the `java.util.Observer` interface explained in Chapter 4. Each listener interface is targeted for a specific type of GUI event, such as a mouse click. You create handlers for user-initiated events by defining classes that implement the listener interfaces. The appropriate listener interface method is called automatically whenever the component generates an event. You establish the relationship between each handler and an event by registering the listener with the component for which the event is generated.

Each listener interface that has more than one method also has a corresponding adapter class. The adapter is a class that implements all the methods of the interface in a trivial way by providing empty methods for all of them. Thus, you can choose between implementing a listener and extending an adapter. The advantage of extending an adapter class is that you can provide implementations for only the events that are of interest and inherit the trivial handlers for the other events from the adapter class.

 Programmers use the term 1.0.2 event model to describe GUI event handling in the original version of the Java platform that was based on the inheritance relationships of AWT API classes. The much-improved delegation event model described in this chapter was introduced in version 1.1 of the Java platform.

handler implements an interface with a name that ends with `listener` or extends a class with a name that ends with `adapter`, the programmer coded it using the delegation event model for version 1.1 or later of the Java platform. The use of the method `handleEvent` indicates that the program uses the original inheritance-based event model.

INTRODUCING THE JAVA FOUNDATION CLASSES

The developers of the Java platform responded to popular demand and invested considerable effort into providing powerful and flexible support for creating GUIs for applications in the JFC. The goal of the JFC is to simplify the development of 100% Pure Java programs for network or standalone environments. The classes let you design GUIs that reflect the operating system that is host to the JVM, to create your own platform–independent interface, or to use a look and feel that is defined for the Java platform and common across all implementations of the JVM.

Figure 6-1 lists the five APIs that make up the JFC. This chapter and Chapter 7 focus on the Abstract Windowing Toolkit (AWT) API and the Swing API, because they are fundamental for the creation of GUIs. The Java2D API builds on the basic drawing support provided in the AWT to provide support for advanced graphics and imaging. The Accessibility API provides the programming interface necessary for assistive technologies, such as Braille screen readers and speech-recognition software, to interact with GUIs built with the JFC. This support is provided in the form of interfaces, GUI components that report their current state, and utilities that allow assistive technologies to plug easily into system services such as the user interface event queue. The Drag and Drop API provides support for transferring data within a Java application, between two Java applications, and between a Java application and a native application. A user performs a drag-and-drop operation by picking up an icon in one window, dragging it to another window, and dropping it. The Accessibility API and the Drag and Drop API are specialized topics that are beyond the scope of this text.

API	Description
Abstract Windowing Toolkit	The original toolkit for developing GUIs for the Java platform. It provides the foundation for the JFC with its support for colors, fonts, graphics, images, events, listeners, layout managers, and so forth.
Swing	An extensive set of mostly lightweight components built on top of the AWT component classes that feature a pluggable look and feel. Lightweight components do not have a window of their own but are drawn directly on their container's window.
Java2D	Provides a variety of painting styles and features for defining complex shapes and controlling the rendering process. It provides enhanced font and drawing capabilities that build on those in the AWT.

Figure 6-1   The JFC APIs

API	Description
Accessibility	Provides an interface that allows assistive technologies, such as screen readers, screen magnifiers, and speech-recognition software, to be easily integrated into applications.
Drag and Drop	Provides the ability to move data between programs created with the Java programming language. With applications developed in other languages, it provides for interoperability between applications.

Figure 6-1   The JFC APIs (continued)

Abstract Windowing Toolkit API

To program a GUI-oriented application or an applet, you need extensive support from your application development software. The Java platform provides a relatively simple set of GUI-building classes in the package **java.awt** and its subpackages.

This book cannot cover all the options of the AWT, and you could spend many weeks focusing on the AWT and Swing classes. The goal of this chapter and Chapter 7 is to show you the most commonly used features of the AWT and Swing classes. If you ultimately plan to write code based on the AWT or the Swing classes that are introduced in the next section of this chapter, you should become familiar with the JFC API documentation. Alternatively, you can assemble GUI programs by combining JavaBeans using RAD tools that will generate the code for you. Chapter 8 explains what JavaBeans are and how you can reuse them as building blocks for new programs.

This book discusses the most commonly used AWT classes so that you can confidently explore the rest of the package independently. This section and the next section of this chapter provide an overview of the classes and architecture of the AWT and Swing APIs. The rest of this chapter and Chapter 7 describe in detail how to use some of these classes and give simple examples.

The discussion begins with the classes in the **java.awt** package and its subpackages. The classes fall into six major categories, as shown in Figure 6-2.

Category	Description
Graphics	This set of classes in **java.awt** encapsulates fonts, colors, images, polygons, and so forth.
Components and containers	This set of classes extends **Component** to provide objects such as buttons, check boxes, labels, scrollbars, and text components. The class **Container** extends **Component** for components that can contain other components, such as windows, panels, and dialog boxes. The AWT components make up a basic set of GUI building blocks. The Swing API provides a more extensive and flexible set of components. Although the Swing components are ultimately based on the AWT components, you should not mix Swing and AWT. Generally, the Swing set of components is replacing the AWT as the most popular GUI-building API.

Figure 6-2   Categories of classes in the AWT

Category	Description
Layout managers	To select a predefined strategy for positioning components in a container, set up an association between a class that extends **LayoutManager** or **LayoutManager2** and a container. You can set a wide range of format controls and let the layout manager dynamically determine where to put the components. With layout managers, you do not specify coordinate positions for components. To specify actual screen coordinates would make your program inflexible, probably build in dependence on a platform and screen resolution, and perhaps constrain your ability to translate labels into other languages. You can use the AWT layout managers for AWT and Swing containers. The Swing API adds some new layout managers for Swing containers only.
Events	This set of classes in the package **java.awt.event** extends **AWTEvent** to encapsulate the information about a user interaction with the application. For example, some classes are **MouseEvent**, **TextEvent**, and **FocusEvent**. Each kind of event has an associated listener interface. The Swing components use the AWT event model, although some of the Swing components add new types of events.
Listeners and adapters	Listeners and adapters handle events. To create a listener, implement one or more of the listener interfaces in the **java.awt.event** package. If you register an instance of a listener with one or more components, one of the listener methods is called whenever an event is generated by a component with which the event is registered. You can extend an adapter class rather than implement a listener. Extending an adapter can be more efficient, because you need to override only the methods that are of interest and do not have to provide your own empty methods for the events to be ignored. As with events, listeners and adapters work in the same way for Swing and AWT components.
Peers	Peers are classes that implement the elements of a GUI built from AWT components on the platform that is host to your Java platform. You do not use these classes directly. Instead, you use the corresponding subclasses of **Component** classes. For example, a button peer on Mac OS uses a Mac OS button and on Solaris uses a Motif button. You can create a **Button** object and not worry about the peer class behind the scenes. When your code runs on a different platform from the development platform, the look of AWT components adjusts automatically.

Figure 6-2   Categories of classes in the AWT (continued)

Inside the package **java.awt,** the AWT encapsulates the platform specifics for the implementation of the AWT in the class **Toolkit.** This class is the bridge between the platform–dependent AWT classes and their corresponding peers. The class does have some useful methods that provide information on the screen size, screen resolution, available fonts, and so forth.

EVENT MODEL

The AWT event model takes advantage of a hierarchy of event classes and associated listener interfaces. You can define any class to be an event handler, regardless of its superclass, by implementing a listener interface. Call a method of a component class to register the listener with the component. Chapter 7 describes how to do so and how to write the handler. When an event that relates to the component occurs, only the registered listeners are notified and passed a copy of the event. If no listeners are registered, the event is not delivered.

The event model is consistent with the JavaBeans interface. Although they are certainly not limited to GUI applications, JavaBeans do facilitate encapsulating GUI components in such a way that developers can easily build GUI-based programs, complete with event handling, by loading JavaBeans into tools and connecting them together.

Swing API

The AWT API described in this chapter and Chapter 7 provides a user interface framework with which you can continue to develop GUIs. When the Java platform was introduced in 1995, the AWT was the only API for creating GUIs. The set of components provided by the AWT is adequate for simple tasks, but it has some significant limitations. For example, creating a new type of component by directly subclassing **Component** is difficult because you must also create a peer object. For components that are built on windows, the result is that each new component has its own opaque native window. This one-to-one mapping between components and native windows has disadvantages:

- Native windows can consume a lot of system resources. Therefore, you should create a minimum number of custom components.

- Native windows are handled differently across platforms. Therefore, maintaining a consistent view across varied platforms is difficult and error-prone.

In version 1.1 of the Java platform, the AWT introduced a framework for creating lightweight GUI components. The lightweight GUI framework lets you extend the **java.awt.Component** and **java.awt.Container** classes directly, without creating native peer objects. The Swing API builds upon this lightweight GUI framework to create a set of GUI components that are independent of the native windowing system. Because the components do not need native support, you don't have to supply any native code to process them. Therefore, handling lightweight components is 100% Pure Java. The result is common code and consistency across platforms.

Not every Swing component is a lightweight component. For a Java application to have a GUI that appears on the user's desktop, at least the top-level window on which the lightweight components are drawn must be a heavyweight component with a native peer. There are only a few heavyweight Swing components: **JApplet**, **JDialog**, **JFrame**, and **JWindow**. (Refer to Figure 6-3 for brief descriptions of these components.) They are based on `java.applet.Applet` and the AWT components `Dialog`, `Frame`, and `Window`, respectively.

The Swing API contains 100% Pure Java versions of the AWT components, plus many additional components that are also 100% Pure Java. Because Swing does not contain or depend on native code, none of the Swing components are constrained to conform to a single style. Instead, Swing components have a pluggable look and feel. They are adaptable to different operating system platforms or to a custom look and feel. The Swing API consists of more than 250 classes and 75 interfaces grouped into the following categories:

- A component named **JComponent** that extends the AWT class **Container** and a set of components that are subclasses of **JComponent**. All these components have names beginning with the letter J. Examples of these classes are **JButton**, **JLabel**, and **JOptionPane**.

- Nonvisible support classes that provide important services, such as event classes, and that implement the model, or logic, portion of the Swing design model. These classes do not begin with the letter J. Examples of these classes are **EmptyBorder**, **TreeSelectionEvent**, and **SwingUtilities**.

- A set of related interfaces that are implemented by Swing component and support classes. Examples of these interfaces are **Icon**, **ListSelectionModel**, and **Document**.

Figure 6-3 lists the most frequently used components of the Swing API and states which Swing components have a corresponding AWT component.

Frequently Used Components	Corresponding AWT Component
`JApplet`	The superclass of all Swing applets. It is a heavyweight component that implements the `RootPaneContainer` interface. It is an extension of the original applet superclass, `java.applet.Applet`.
`JButton`	A button that contains text and graphics. The corresponding AWT component is `Button`.
`JCheckBox`	A check box that can contain text and graphics. The corresponding AWT component is `Checkbox`.
`JCheckBoxMenuItem`	A check box menu item. The corresponding AWT component is `CheckBoxMenuItem`.
`JColorChooser`	A component that provides the interface to allow a user to select a color with visual feedback of the color selected.
`JComboBox`	Combines a text field and drop-down list that lets the user type a value or select it from a list that appears in response to a user request. `JComboBox` provides a superset of the functions provided by the AWT component `Choice`.

Figure 6-3   Swing components

Frequently Used Components	Corresponding AWT Component
JDesktopPane	A container intended to hold internal frame windows.
JDialog	The superclass of all Swing dialog boxes. JDialog is a heavyweight component that implements the RootPaneContainer interface. The corresponding AWT component is Dialog.
JEditorPane	Provides a text pane that lets the user edit content of various kinds.
JFileChooser	A component that provides the interface to allow a user to select a file. The corresponding AWT component is FileDialog.
JFormattedTextField	A text field for which there are defined rules for the legal set of characters that may be entered in the field.
JFrame	An external frame that encloses Java application GUIs. It is a heavyweight component that implements the RootPaneContainer interface. The corresponding AWT component is Frame.
JInternalFrame	Similar in function to a frame window but can be placed inside the top-level frame application. An internal frame is confined to the visible area of the container that holds it. It implements the RootPaneContainer interface.
JLabel	A label that can contain text and graphics. The corresponding AWT component is Label.
JList	A component that presents a list of items for single or multiple selection. The corresponding AWT component is List. Unlike its AWT counterpart, a **JList** component does not have scrollbars and should be placed in a **JScrollPane** component if scrollbars are required.
JMenu	A menu that can be attached to a menu bar or placed in another menu to create a cascading menu. The corresponding AWT component is Menu.
JMenuBar	A set of menus usually positioned beneath a frame window's title bar. The corresponding AWT component is MenuBar.
JMenuItem	An item in a menu. The corresponding AWT component is MenuItem.
JOptionPane	Provides a straightforward mechanism for creating commonly required dialog boxes. For example, use **JOptionPane** to display a message, ask a yes-no question, or prompt for a single input.
JPanel	A basic container. The corresponding AWT component is Panel.

Figure 6-3   Swing components (continued)

Frequently Used Components	Corresponding AWT Component
JPasswordField	A component that lets the user edit a single line of text. Feedback shows that characters are entered but does not display the input characters.
JPopupMenu	A pop-up menu component. The corresponding AWT component is PopupMenu.
JProgressBar	Can be used to indicate the progress of an activity by displaying its percentage of completion.
JRadioButton	Provides a round button with two possible states: selected or deselected.
JRadioButtonMenuItem	Provides a radio button item within a menu.
JScrollBar	A scrollbar component. The corresponding AWT component is Scrollbar.
JScrollPane	A container with available vertical and horizontal scrollbars. The corresponding AWT component is ScrollPane.
JSeparator	A horizontal or vertical separator.
JSlider	Lets the user graphically select a value by moving an indicator along a bounded range.
JSpinner	A single line input field that lets the user select a number or an object value from an ordered set. This is similar to JComboBox, but without the drop-down list.
JSplitPane	A component intended to contain two components and divided horizontally or vertically. The user can interactively resize the split between the two components.
JTabbedPane	A component that lets the user switch from one group of components to another by clicking a tab with a given title or icon.
JTable	A component to present data in a two-dimensional table format.
JTableHeader	A heading for a table.
JTextArea	A component for entering and displaying multiple lines of text. The corresponding AWT component is TextArea. Unlike its AWT counterpart, a **JTextArea** component does not have scrollbars and should be placed in a **JScrollPane** component if scrollbars are required.
JTextField	A component for entering a single line of text. The corresponding AWT component is TextField.
JTextPane	A simple text-editor component.
JToggleButton	Implements a two-state button that alternates between pressed and released. **JToggleButton** is the superclass of both **JRadioButton** and **JCheckBox**.

Figure 6-3   Swing components (continued)

6

Frequently Used Components	Corresponding AWT Component
`JToolBar`	Displays commonly used actions or controls as a horizontal row or vertical column of buttons.
`JToolTip`	Creates a pop-up text window that can display a brief textual description of a component when the mouse pointer lingers over the component.
`JTree`	A component to display a set of hierarchical data as an outline. The display has branches that the user can expand and collapse.
`JViewport`	A viewport for displaying scrollable components.
`JWindow`	A heavyweight component that implements the `RootPaneContainer` interface. The corresponding AWT component is `Window`.

Figure 6-3   Swing components (continued)

Figure 6–3 does not list all the Swing components, but it includes the most notable. All the listed Swing components are in the package **javax.swing**. All AWT components are in the package **java.awt**.

The Swing components **JSpinner** and **JFormattedTextField** were introduced in version 1.4 of the Java 2 platform.

GUI applications use Swing components and AWT components in much the same way. Swing components use the same layout managers, event objects, and listener interfaces as the AWT components. However, there are some notable differences. For example, it is not possible to add components directly to a container that implements the **RootPaneContainer** interface. Such containers have a content–pane container where all components are to be placed. The **RootPaneContainer** interface defines the method **getContentPane** for accessing this container. The **JFrame**, **JApplet**, **JDialog**, **JWindow**, and **JInternalFrame** classes all fall into this category. Another key difference is in the use of scrollbars. The AWT components **TextArea** and **List** both have available scrollbars, but the corresponding Swing components **JTextArea** and **JList** do not have scrollbars. If scrollbars are required, **JTextArea** and **JList** components can be placed in a **JScrollPane** container.

Separable Model Architecture

A fundamental difference between the Swing architecture and AWT architecture is that Swing components separate the manipulation of data associated with a component from the rendering or graphical-representation component and its contents. The benefits are greatest for the more complicated containers, such as **JTree**, **JList**, and **JTable**, that

contain structured data. However, the separation is implemented for all Swing components. One of the limiting factors of AWT-based GUIs is the absence of model and view
separation, with the result that the appearance of AWT GUI components cannot be
altered without impacting their implementation and that there is exactly one implementation of a component.

The designers of the Swing API implemented prototypes that conformed fully to the
MVC design pattern. Each component had a model object as well as view and controller
objects that defined the component's look and feel. Experimentation with this separation led to the realization that a component's view and controller objects are tightly coupled and that it made sense to collapse these two objects into a single object. In the
Swing API, this combined view-controller object is referred to as the component's UI
delegate. Because Swing has these UI delegate objects in place of view and controller
objects, it cannot be said to implement the true MVC separation. Instead, Swing is said
to use a *separable model architecture*.

The separation of the model from its UI delegate gives programmers a great advantage
over the AWT: Programmers can design their applications around operations on data
rather than around operations that display data. A simple example of this is how the
JToggleButton.ToggleButtonModel class provides a model for user interface
options that can be turned on and off. Both the **JRadioButton** and **JCheckBox** components use this model, so it is easy to switch between these two GUI components without requiring any change to the program's data model. The Swing API defines a set of
model interfaces that are implemented by various components. Figure 6-4 lists the various model interfaces and the components that use them.

Model Interfaces	Components
ButtonModel	JButton JToggleButton JCheckBox JRadioButton JMenu JMenuItem JCheckBoxMenuItem JRadioButtonMenuItem
ComboBoxModel	JComboBox
BoundedRangeModel	JProgressBar JScrollBar JSlider
SingleSelectionModel	JTabbedPane
SpinnerModel	JSpinner
ListModel	JList

Figure 6-4   Swing model interfaces

6

Model Interfaces	Components
ListSelectionModel	`JList`
TableModel	`JTable`
TableColumnModel	`JTable`
TreeModel	`JTree`
TreeSelectionModel	`JTree`

Document	`JEditorPane`
	`JFormattedTextField`
	`JTextPane`
	`JTextArea`
	`JTextField`
	`JPasswordField`

Figure 6-4   Swing model interfaces (continued)

Because the models are separate from the components, several components can share the same model. For example, you can create a split-window view, similar to that used in many word processors, by placing two **JTextPane** objects sharing the same model document into a **JSplitPane** object. Any changes made in one half of the split pane would be immediately reflected in the other half of the split pane because both are based on the same model.

Model objects must be able to notify their UI delegates whenever their data values change, so that the UI delegates always present current information. To do this, all Swing models use the JavaBeans event model. This event model is discussed in Chapter 8, when JavaBeans are presented in detail. For now, consider this event model as similar in concept to the **Observer/Observable** model presented in Chapter 4.

Swing models use two different styles of notification: lightweight and stateful. *Lightweight notification* does nothing more than indicate that something in the model has changed and provides no details. This means event objects used for lightweight notification can be reused, saving the cost of creating a new event object every time. *Stateful notification* provides the details of the change, saving the cost of calling the methods of the model to determine what changed. Event objects used for stateful notification are not reused.

The choice of notification style depends on the frequency of the events. For models, such as **BoundedRangeModel** used by sliders and scrollbars that can generate frequent events, a lightweight notification style is used to avoid the cost of creating many event objects. For most other models, **DocumentModel** for example, stateful notification is used to provide as much information as possible in the event object and to avoid the need to call additional methods.

JFC SAMPLE PROGRAMS

You get a feel for what the JFC can do by looking at the small sample programs in this section. They introduce some of the most commonly used classes in the JFC. You can start to experiment by writing short programs that are similar to these samples and then expand your knowledge by trying to program variations that use different classes and methods.

The sample programs are applications, not applets. The main difference is that Swing-based applets extend the **javax.swing.JApplet** class, and Swing-based applications extend the **javax.swing.JFrame** class. Both **JApplet** and **JFrame** are indirect sub-classes of **Container**. Similarly, an AWT-based applet extends **java.applet.Applet** and an AWT-based application extends **java.awt.Frame**.

As a further distinction between the two, you should know that a Web browser displays an applet as a panel within the browser window, so that the applet does not have a title bar or minimize, maximize, or close buttons. Also, applets do not have a **main** method, but are instead controlled by the browser using an event-driven mechanism. Apart from these differences, you can use the Swing or AWT classes in an applet just as you can in an application.

A Java Hello World! Program

The first sample JFC program (see Figure 6-5) is a version of the classic starter program that most programmers write when they first work with a new language or programming environment. This program defines the class **HelloWorld**. Because **HelloWorld** is a public class, it is located in a file called **HelloWorld.java**. The structure of packages mirrors the file system, so you will find this source code in the **X:\Data\examples\windows** directory on the CD-ROM. (Here **X:** is the drive letter of the CD-ROM.) This program displays the string **"Hello World!"** centered in a window on the screen (see Figure 6-6). As with most applications, the GUI for this program is contained in a frame window, which is an independent window with its own frame, title, and control boxes.

Although this is a simple program, the code is longer than a command-line version because it contains a minimal GUI.

```
package examples.windows;
import javax.swing.JFrame;
import javax.swing.JLabel;
import java.awt.BorderLayout;
/** An example of a very simple windowed program
  */
```

Figure 6-5   HelloWorld: an example of a very simple windowed program

```
public class HelloWorld extends JFrame {
   /** Class constructor
    * @param titleText window's title bar text
    */
   public HelloWorld( String titleText ) {
      super( titleText );
      setDefaultCloseOperation( JFrame.EXIT_ON_CLOSE );
      JLabel greeting = new JLabel( "Hello World!",
                                    JLabel.CENTER );
      getContentPane().add( greeting,
                            BorderLayout.CENTER );
      setSize( 300, 100 );
      setVisible( true );
   }
   /** The test method for the class
    * @param args not used
    */
   public static void main( String[] args ) {
      new HelloWorld( "Hello World! Sample" );
   }
}
```

Figure 6-5 `HelloWorld`: an example of a very simple windowed program (continued)

The output is similar on all platforms, but it does vary in small ways because the frame takes on the appearance and behavior of the application windows of the native operating system. Therefore, your output may look different from the output shown in Figure 6-6, particularly in the buttons that are specific to the operating system and the borders of the frame.

Figure 6-6 Output from the `HelloWorld` program

The `HelloWorld` program is contained in one class, `HelloWorld`. The `HelloWorld` class extends **JFrame**. The **JFrame** class is a component class for frame windows, which are the usual top-level windows in which applications run. Because it extends **JFrame**, `HelloWorld` inherits functioning minimize, maximize, and close buttons, and a title bar. The first line of the class definition that establishes the inheritance relationship is as follows:

```
public class HelloWorld extends JFrame {
```

The following lines from Figure 6-5 are the first lines of the constructor for HelloWorld. The constructor has one argument, which is the string to be used in the title bar. It passes the string to the constructor of the superclass **JFrame** so that the string becomes the text in the title bar of the frame window.

```
public HelloWorld( String titleText ) {
    super( titleText );
```

You do not have to write the code for the event loop that controls a GUI program. The JFC APIs handle that. All you must do is plug in handlers for various events. The next statement provides direction on what should happen to the Java application when the user closes the window. The method **setDefaultCloseOperation** is a member of the **JFrame** class, and when the constant **EXIT_ON_CLOSE** is provided as input, the Java application exits when the window is closed. This is not the default, and so it is important to include this statement. You will see it appear over and over again in examples throughout this text that have a GUI.

```
setDefaultCloseOperation( JFrame.EXIT_ON_CLOSE );
```

Caution

The method **setDefaultCloseOperation** was introduced in version 1.3 of the Java platform. Before it was available, programmers had to go to much more trouble to achieve the same effect. A **WINDOW_CLOSING** event occurs when the user closes the application window. This event does not automatically terminate execution, but it is reported to the **JFrame** object so that the program has an opportunity to close. A call of **addWindowListener** registers an object to listen to window events for the current component. The argument becomes the registered handler for window events. In this call, the handler is an instance of the **WindowAdapter** class. See the following code:

```
addWindowListener( new WindowAdapter() {
        /** End the program when the user
          * closes the window
          */
        public void
        windowClosing( WindowEvent e ) {
          HelloWorld.this.dispose();
          System.exit( 0 );
        }
    }
);
```

An adapter class is appropriate because this program needs to handle only one of the events for which the **WindowListener** interface defines handlers. The method **windowClosing** overrides the default method of the **WindowAdapter** class to handle the **WINDOW_CLOSING** event. The method disposes of the current **JFrame** object and then calls **System.exit** to terminate the application.

6

The constructor of the `HelloWorld` class also sets the size of its window in pixels, by calling **setSize**. The width is 300 pixels, and the height is 100. The window appears at the upper-left corner of the screen because this constructor does not call **setLocation** to override the default location of the frame window. The constructor must call **setVisible** and pass the value **true** to make the window visible to the user and bring the window to the front of other windows.

```
setSize( 300, 100 );
setVisible( true );
```

The text message to be displayed is put into the **JLabel** object greeting, and the justification of the text is set so that it is centered within the label. The label must be added to the **JFrame** object in order for it to appear within the frame window, but it cannot be added directly. Objects of the **JFrame** class have a **JRootPane** object to which they delegate control of the components they contain via the **JRootContainer** interface. You can access the container that holds the components by calling the **getContentPane** method defined in the **JRootContainer** interface. The method then adds the label to the content-pane container.

```
JLabel greeting = new JLabel( "Hello World!",
                          JLabel.CENTER );
getContentPane().add( greeting,
                    BorderLayout.CENTER );
```

By default, the content-pane container of a **JFrame** object uses a **BorderLayout** object to arrange its components. A border layout can contain up to five components, arranged as shown on the left in Figure 6-7. This program uses only the center section. Therefore, the north, south, west, and east drop out, the center component expands, and the arrangement is as shown on the right of Figure 6-7.

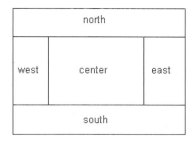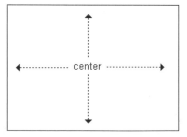

Figure 6-7   Border layouts

Because the `HelloWorld` class is an application, it must have a **main** method. For this application, **main** creates a `HelloWorld` object and passes the title of the frame window as an argument of the constructor:

```
public static void main( String[] args ) {
    new HelloWorld( "Hello World! Sample" );
}
```

After the **JFrame** object has been created, the application runs until the user closes the window. The reason that the program does not end after calling the **HelloWorld** constructor is that the JFC APIs create an event dispatch thread when the **JFrame** class is instantiated. An application remains active as long as a nondaemon thread is running and the event dispatch thread is not a daemon thread. Refer to Chapter 5, "Multithreading," for more details regarding the difference between daemon and nondaemon threads.

Three Panels Example

The **HelloWorld** example is about as simple as a GUI program can be. The next program is a bit more complex. It makes greater use of layout managers; includes buttons with icons, a text field, and a check box; and has labeled borders.

The program in Figure 6-8 uses **JPanel** objects nested in the **JFrame** object's content-pane container to provide a more flexible approach to positioning components. The **JPanel** class, like **JFrame**, is a subclass of **java.awt.Container**, and instances of **JPanel** are the simplest objects that can hold other components. Panels are widely used to group objects. You can arrange one or more panels within a window by using a layout manager.

The program in Figure 6-8 is called the **ThreePanels** program because it has three **JPanel** objects. The panels are arranged vertically to occupy the top, middle, or bottom slices of a window. Often, event handling deals with user actions, such as clicking a button. The **ThreePanels** program demonstrates three buttons and one check box.

ThreePanels is a simple application that displays the string **Change the color of this text** across the top panel of the frame window. The middle panel has three buttons labeled Black, Red, and Green. When the user clicks a button, the sentence above the buttons changes color accordingly. The bottom panel has a check box labeled **Disable changes**. The user clicks the check box to disable or enable the buttons.

```
package examples.windows;
import javax.swing.*;
import java.awt.*;
import java.awt.event.*;
/** An example class used to demonstrate the basics of
 * creating components such as panels, arranging
 * components using layout objects, and nesting
 * components inside each other
 */
public class ThreePanels extends JFrame {
    private JPanel upper, middle, lower;
    private JTextField text;
    private JButton black, red, green;
    private JCheckBox disable;
```

Figure 6-8 **ThreePanels:** an example of the basics of GUI programming

```
/** Class constructor method
  * @param titleText Window's title bar text
  */
public ThreePanels( String titleText ) {
   super( titleText );
   setDefaultCloseOperation( JFrame.EXIT_ON_CLOSE );
   upper = new JPanel();
   upper.setBorder(
      BorderFactory.createTitledBorder(
      "Sample text" ) );
   upper.setLayout( new BorderLayout() );
   text = new JTextField(
      "Change the color of this text" );
   upper.add( text, BorderLayout.CENTER );
   middle = new JPanel();
   middle.setBorder(
      BorderFactory.createTitledBorder(
      "Text color control" ) );
   middle.setLayout( new FlowLayout(
      FlowLayout.CENTER ) );
   black = new JButton( "Black",
               new ColorIcon( Color.black ) );
   black.addActionListener(
      new ButtonListener( Color.black ) );
   middle.add( black );
   red = new JButton( "Red",
               new ColorIcon( Color.red ) );
   red.addActionListener(
      new ButtonListener( Color.red ) );
   middle.add( red );
   green = new JButton( "Green",
               new ColorIcon( Color.green ) );
   green.addActionListener(
      new ButtonListener( Color.green ) );
   middle.add( green );
   lower = new JPanel();
   lower.setLayout( new FlowLayout(
      FlowLayout.RIGHT ) );
   disable = new JCheckBox( "Disable changes" );
   disable.addItemListener( new ItemListener() {
         /** Disable and enable the buttons
           */
         public void
         itemStateChanged( ItemEvent e ) {
            boolean enabled
               = ( e.getStateChange()
                     == ItemEvent.DESELECTED );
```

Figure 6-8   ThreePanels: an example of the basics of GUI programming (continued)

```
                    black.setEnabled( enabled );
                    red.setEnabled( enabled );
                    green.setEnabled( enabled );
                }
            }
        );
        lower.add( disable );
        Container cp = getContentPane();
        cp.add( upper, BorderLayout.NORTH );
        cp.add( middle, BorderLayout.CENTER );
        cp.add( lower, BorderLayout.SOUTH );
        pack();
        setVisible( true );
    }
    /** The class representing the button event
      * listeners
      */
    class ButtonListener implements ActionListener {
        private Color c;
        /** Class constructor
          * @param c the color for this button
          */
        public ButtonListener( Color c ) {
            this.c = c;
        }
        /** Respond to the action events
          * @param e The click event
          */
        public void actionPerformed( ActionEvent e ) {
            text.setForeground( c );
        }
    }
    /** The class representing the colored icons on
      * the buttons
      */
    class ColorIcon implements Icon {
        private Color c;
        private static final int DIAMETER = 10;
        /** Class constructor
          * @param c the color for this button
          */
        public ColorIcon( Color c ) {
            this.c = c;
        }
        /** Paint the color icon with a black border
          * @param cp the component holding the icon
          * @param g the graphics context for the icon
```

Figure 6-8   `ThreePanels`: an example of the basics of GUI programming (continued)

6

```
    * @param x the x draw start position
    * @param y the y draw start position
    */
   public void paintIcon( Component cp, Graphics g,
                          int x, int y ) {
      g.setColor( c );
      g.fillOval( x, y, DIAMETER, DIAMETER );
      g.setColor( Color.black );
      g.drawOval( x, y, DIAMETER, DIAMETER );
   }
   /** Get the icon's height
     * @return the height of the icon
     */
   public int getIconHeight() {
      return DIAMETER;
   }
   /** Get the icon's width
     * @return the width of the icon
     */
   public int getIconWidth() {
      return DIAMETER;
   }
}
/** The test method for the class
  * @param args not used
  */
public static void main( String[] args ) {
   new ThreePanels( "Three Panels Sample" );
}
}
```

Figure 6-8   `ThreePanels`: an example of the basics of GUI programming (continued)

The output looks similar to Figure 6-9.

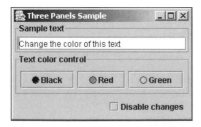

Figure 6-9   Output of the `ThreePanels` program

The class of this program is called `ThreePanels`. Like the `HelloWorld` example in Figure 6-5, it extends **JFrame**. The components used in this application are private fields of the `ThreePanels` class, as follows:

```
public class ThreePanels extends JFrame {
   private JPanel upper, middle, lower;
```

```
private JTextField text;
private JButton black, red, green;
private JCheckBox disable;
```

Also like the **HelloWorld** class, the constructor of **ThreePanels** passes the string that becomes the title of the frame window to the constructor of its superclass, **JFrame**:

```
public ThreePanels( String titleText ) {
    super( titleText );
```

The following statement uses the same technique as the **Hello World** program to make sure the program ends when the user closes the window :

```
setDefaultCloseOperation( JFrame.EXIT_ON_CLOSE );
```

The rest of the constructor creates the components, sets their attributes, and adds the components to the **JPanel** objects and the panels to the frame. The constructor assigns one **JPanel** field, **upper**, to a new **JPanel** object, sets its border to be a labeled border with the text **Sample text**, and then gives the panel a border layout.

```
upper = new JPanel();

upper.setBorder(
    BorderFactory.createTitledBorder(
    "Sample text" ) );
upper.setLayout( new BorderLayout() );
```

The next object created is a **JTextField** object. The private field **text** is assigned the object reference to **JTextField**. The **JTextField** class extends the **JTextComponent** class to define objects that hold a single line of text, and the method passes the text as a string to the constructor. The method **add** in these lines adds the text component to the upper container. Here, the argument **BorderLayout.CENTER** positions the component in the central area of the upper panel. Because only the center portion of the border layout for the upper panel has contents, the center portion expands to fill the entire upper panel.

```
text = new JTextField(
    "Change the color of this text" );
upper.add( text, BorderLayout.CENTER );
```

The second of the three panels is assigned to the private field **middle**. Like the upper panel, the middle panel has its border set to be a labeled border with the text **Text color control**. Unlike the upper panel, the middle panel has a flow layout. A flow layout places components side by side, from left to right, in the order they are added to the container and wraps to the next row as required. The argument of the constructor of a **FlowLayout** object is a constant provided by the **FlowLayout** class. Here, **FlowLayout.CENTER** specifies that the rows of components in the middle panel be centered within the panel. By default, **JPanel** objects have a centered flow layout, so this statement was added for clarity.

```
middle = new JPanel();
middle.setBorder(
    BorderFactory.createTitledBorder(
    "Text color control" ) );
middle.setLayout( new FlowLayout(
    FlowLayout.CENTER ) );
```

You specify the label that appears on a **JButton** object as the argument of the constructor for the **JButton** object. The second constructor parameter specified for each of the buttons is a **ColorIcon** object. **ColorIcon** is an inner class that implements the **javax.swing.Icon** interface. It is described in detail later in this section. The class **java.awt.Color** provides public-class variables for many colors, including **Color.red**, **Color.green**, and **Color.black**. Instead of using **Color** constants, you can construct a **Color** object from eight-bit values for red, green, and blue.

To handle button-click events, you must register an **ActionListener** object with each **JButton** object, by calling the method **JButton.addActionListener**. Here, instances of the inner class **ButtonListener** are constructed to specify the color associated with the button and are registered to handle the action events for the buttons.

```
black = new JButton( "Black",
            new ColorIcon( Color.black ) );
black.addActionListener(
    new ButtonListener( Color.black ) );
middle.add( black );
red = new JButton( "Red",
            new ColorIcon( Color.red ) );
red.addActionListener(
    new ButtonListener( Color.red ) );
middle.add( red );
green = new JButton( "Green",
            new ColorIcon( Color.green ) );
green.addActionListener(
    new ButtonListener( Color.green ) );
middle.add( green );
```

The last of the three panels is assigned to the object reference **lower**. This panel also has a flow layout, but this flow layout is right-justified. As a result, the **JCheckBox** component labeled **Disable changes** that is placed in the panel appears on the lower right of the application frame window.

```
lower = new JPanel();
    lower.setLayout( new FlowLayout(
        FlowLayout.RIGHT ) );
```

The **JCheckBox** object **disable** requires an **ItemListener** object so that it can enable or disable the buttons when the user checks or unchecks the box.

```
disable = new JCheckBox( "Disable changes" );
disable.addItemListener( new ItemListener() {
    public void
    itemStateChanged( ItemEvent e ) {
        boolean enabled
            = ( e.getStateChange()
                == ItemEvent.DESELECTED );
        black.setEnabled( enabled );
        red.setEnabled( enabled );
        green.setEnabled( enabled );
    }
  }
);
lower.add( disable );
```

Now that the three panels are complete, the next four statements can add them to the content-pane container of the frame window:

```
Container cp = getContentPane();
cp.add( upper, BorderLayout.NORTH );
cp.add( middle, BorderLayout.CENTER );
cp.add( lower, BorderLayout.SOUTH );
```

The final statements in this rather long constructor are calls to **pack** and **setVisible**. Call **pack** to give the layout managers a chance to arrange all components for optimal size. When you call **pack**, the layout managers determine how much space each of the components needs and dynamically adjusts the component positions. Call **setVisible** to make the **ThreePanels** object and all the contained panels and components visible and available for display.

```
pack();
setVisible( true );
```

The **ButtonListener** class implements the **ActionListener** interface. It also implements the **actionPerformed** method to handle the **ActionEvent** objects for button clicks. When an instance of the **ButtonListener** class is created, the color of its button is specified. Because each **ButtonListener** object is associated with only one button, when its **actionPerformed** method is called, the appropriate action is to set the foreground color for the **JTextField** text by calling the method **JComponent.setForeground**. The **JTextField** class inherits this method from the **JComponent** class.

```
class ButtonListener implements ActionListener {
    private Color c;
```

```
        public ButtonListener( Color c ) {
           this.c = c;
        }
        public void actionPerformed( ActionEvent e ) {
           text.setForeground( c );
        }
     }
```

The `ColorIcon` class implements the **Icon** interface and its three methods: **paintIcon**, **getHeight**, and **getWidth**. The purpose of the `ColorIcon` class is to draw a very simple color icon that consists of a solid circle of a specified color with a black border. The size of the circle is fixed by the class constant `DIAMETER`, and the color of the circle is set by the constructor parameter.

```
     class ColorIcon implements Icon {
        private Color c;
        private static final int DIAMETER = 10;
        public ColorIcon( Color c ) {
           this.c = c;
        }
```

Both **getHeight** and **getWidth** are simple methods that return the circle's diameter. The **paintIcon** method is more involved. It must draw the circle and its border using the provided graphics context at the specified x and y coordinates. An object of the class **java.awt.Graphics** represents the graphics context. This class provides many methods for performing basic drawing operations. In this case, the two methods used are **fillOval** and **drawOval**. They draw a solid circle and an outline of a circle, respectively.

```
     public void paintIcon( Component cp, Graphics g,
                            int x, int y ) {
        g.setColor( c );
        g.fillOval( x, y, DIAMETER, DIAMETER );
        g.setColor( Color.black );
        g.drawOval( x, y, DIAMETER, DIAMETER );
     }
     public int getIconHeight() {
        return DIAMETER;
     }
     public int getIconWidth() {
        return DIAMETER;
     }
```

The **main** method of the `ThreePanels` class, which follows, does very little. It simply creates a `ThreePanels` object. This instance of **JFrame** contains all the panels set up in the constructor. The driving force behind the application is the user who triggers events by clicking one of the three color buttons or the check box.

```
public static void main( String[] args ) {
    new ThreePanels( "Three Panels Sample" );
}
```

All the coding and GUI design for the **ThreePanels** class was done by entering Java source statements into a text file using an editor. Using this approach, it can be difficult to visualize how the resulting GUI will look when the program executes, which means getting the right look for the GUI can become a trial-and-error process. The next section discusses how a GUI can be designed visually to get the right look—the first time—for the GUI.

LAYOUT MANAGERS

6

Layout managers automate the positioning of components within containers. They free you from the tricky task of figuring out how much space each component requires and at what pixel coordinates to position it. Usually, the exact position of components isn't important, but they should be arranged neatly. For example, you probably want components, such as buttons and labels, to be aligned and not to overlap or crowd into one area of the screen.

Layout managers make optimal use of space and automatically align buttons and similar components. Moreover, they adjust for factors such as different screen resolutions, platform-to-platform variations in the appearance of components, and font sizes. It would be very difficult to program a GUI if you could not depend on layout managers to figure out the best layout on the target platform at runtime.

In the Java platform, two interfaces—**java.awt.LayoutManager** and **java.awt.LayoutManager2**—provide the base for all layout manager classes. As its name implies, the **LayoutManager2** interface is an extension of **LayoutManager**. It has additional layout management methods to support layout constraints that are typically used in the more complicated layout managers.

These interfaces define the methods necessary for arranging **JComponent** objects inside containers. The relationship between the layout manager interfaces and classes that implement them is shown in Figure 6-10. Note that ovals represent interfaces.

Each layout manager supports a different strategy for arranging components within a container component. Of course, the individual components can, in turn, be containers, which gives you the option of nesting layout managers within layout managers. You can nest a layout of one kind within a layout of a different kind, which means you can create an amazing variety of effects by manipulating just a few layout manager classes.

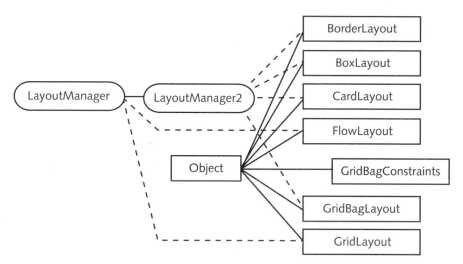

Figure 6-10   Layout managers and related interfaces

When you create a new container component, you should call the method **setLayout** for it by specifying an object of one of the classes that implement **LayoutManager**. Each container class has a default layout manager, but the defaults are not the same for all types of containers. Therefore, it is best to set the layout manager for a container explicitly.

Although the AWT API provides five layout manager classes to give you five different layout strategies, the Swing API adds one more: **BoxLayout**. In addition, two containers in the Swing API—**javax.swing.JTabbedPane** and **javax.swing.JSplitPane**—have built-in layout characteristics that make it easy to create effects not possible with the AWT alone. You can also create your own layout manager class by defining a class that implements the **LayoutManager** interface, but the many layout manager classes that already exist mean it's unlikely you'll ever have to resort to that.

Figure 6-11 contains the code for the **ExampleLayouts** program that exercises several of the available layout managers by positioning **JButton** objects. A **JTabbedPane** object is used to organize the different layouts. After presenting the code for the program in its entirety, the code fragment related to each of the various layout managers will be examined individually in the sections that follow.

```
package examples.windows;
import javax.swing.*;
import java.awt.*;
import java.awt.event.*;
/** An example class used to demonstrate the basics of
  * using many of the available layout managers by
```

Figure 6-11   **ExampleLayouts:** example usage of many available layout managers

```
   * positioning JButton objects
   */
public class ExampleLayouts extends JFrame {
   private JPanel flow
      = new JPanel( new FlowLayout( FlowLayout.CENTER ) );
   private Box box = new Box( BoxLayout.Y_AXIS );
   private JPanel boxPanel = new JPanel();
   private JPanel grid
      = new JPanel( new GridLayout( 3, 2 ) );
   private JPanel gridBag
      = new JPanel( new GridBagLayout() );
   private JPanel border
      = new JPanel( new BorderLayout() );
   /** Class constructor method
     * @param titleText Window's title bar text
     */
   public ExampleLayouts( String titleText ) {
      super( titleText );
      setDefaultCloseOperation( JFrame.EXIT_ON_CLOSE );
      // Add the buttons to the flow layout
      flow.add( new JButton( "One" ) );
      flow.add( new JButton( "Two" ) );
      flow.add( new JButton( "Three" ) );
      flow.add( new JButton( "Four" ) );
      // Add the buttons to the box
      box.add( new JButton( "One" ) );
      box.add( new JButton( "Two" ) );
      box.add( new JButton( "Three" ) );
      box.add( new JButton( "Four" ) );
      // Add the buttons to the grid layout
      grid.add( new JButton( "One" ) );
      grid.add( new JButton( "Two" ) );
      grid.add( new JButton( "Three" ) );
      grid.add( new JButton( "Four" ) );
      grid.add( new JButton( "Five" ) );
      grid.add( new JButton( "Six" ) );
      // Add the buttons to the grid-bag layout
      GridBagConstraints c = new GridBagConstraints();
      c.fill = GridBagConstraints.BOTH;
      c.weightx = 1.0;
      c.weighty = 1.0;
      c.gridwidth = GridBagConstraints.REMAINDER;
      gridBag.add( new JButton( "One" ), c );
      c.gridy = 1;
      c.gridx = 1;
      gridBag.add( new JButton( "Two" ), c );
      c.gridy = 2;
      gridBag.add( new JButton( "Three" ), c );
      c.gridy = 1;
```

Figure 6-11   `ExampleLayouts`: example usage of many available layout managers (continued)

```
            c.gridx = 0;
            c.gridheight = 2;
            c.gridwidth = 1;
            gridBag.add( new JButton( "Four" ), c );
            // Add the buttons to the border layout
            border.add( new JButton( "One" ),
                        BorderLayout.NORTH );
            border.add( new JButton( "Two" ),
                        BorderLayout.WEST );
            border.add( new JButton( "Three" ),
                        BorderLayout.CENTER );
            border.add( new JButton( "Four" ),
                        BorderLayout.EAST );
            border.add( new JButton( "Five" ),
                        BorderLayout.SOUTH );
            // create a tabbed pane and put the panels into it
            JTabbedPane tp = new JTabbedPane();
            tp.addTab( "Flow", flow );
            boxPanel.add( box );
            tp.addTab( "Box", boxPanel );
            tp.addTab( "Grid", grid );
            tp.addTab( "GridBag", gridBag );
            tp.addTab( "Border", border );
            setContentPane( tp );
            setSize( 300, 175 );
            setVisible( true );
        }
        /** The test method for the class
         * @param args not used
         */
        public static void main( String[] args ) {
            new ExampleLayouts( "Example Layouts" );
        }
    }
```

Figure 6-11   `ExampleLayouts`: example usage of many available layout managers (continued)

Border Layouts

The **BorderLayout** class implements the **LayoutManager2** interface to support a container that holds up to five components. The components are sized to fill all the space in the container and arranged as shown in Figure 6-12. The relative sizes of the areas are determined at runtime from the contents of each area. If you do not fill all areas, the empty ones collapse so that they take up no space, and the other areas expand to fill the container.

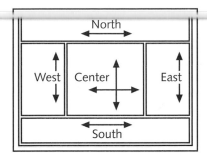

Figure 6-12   The **BorderLayout** strategy

When a container with a **BorderLayout** object is resized to be wider or narrower, the north and south regions change in width, but the sizes of the west and east regions do not change. When the window is stretched vertically, the west and east regions get taller or shorter, but the north and south regions do not change. The central region can expand and contract in both directions.

When you add a component to a container using a **BorderLayout** object, you specify in which area of the layout to place the component by using one of the constants (**NORTH**, **SOUTH**, **EAST**, **WEST**, and **CENTER**) that are defined in the **BorderLayout** class. For example, the following lines of code give a container a border layout and add a component called newPanel to the center of the layout:

```
setLayout( new BorderLayout() );
add( newPanel, BorderLayout.CENTER );
```

You can put only one component into each area, and the size of the component adjusts to fill the area. This is not as restrictive as it might seem, because each component can also be a container. That container can have its own layout manager and can hold any number of components. When the window is displayed, the border layout manager investigates the component in each area to see how much space it needs. If the component is a container, the sizing algorithm recursively determines how much space the components within the container need. As a result, border layouts give you great flexibility to group components and create a wide variety of arrangements.

By default, the **JWindow**, **JFrame**, and **JDialog** containers have border layouts.

The following lines, reproduced here from the **ExampleLayouts** program in Figure 6-11, were used to implement the border layout strategy shown in Figure 6-12 and to produce the output that appears in Figure 6-13:

```
private JPanel border
   = new JPanel( new BorderLayout() );
// Add the buttons to the border layout
border.add( new JButton( "One" ),
          BorderLayout.NORTH );
```

```
border.add( new JButton( "Two" ),
            BorderLayout.WEST );
border.add( new JButton( "Three" ),
            BorderLayout.CENTER );
border.add( new JButton( "Four" ),
            BorderLayout.EAST );
border.add( new JButton( "Five" ),
            BorderLayout.SOUTH );
```

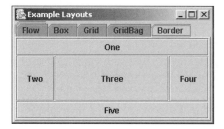

Figure 6-13   A **BorderLayout** example produced by the **ExampleLayouts** program

Flow Layouts

The class **FlowLayout** implements the **LayoutManager** interface to support flow layouts. If the container uses a flow layout, components are arranged in a row across the area of the container. When you add a component, it is added to become the rightmost component in the row. If there is not enough room, the row wraps so that the new component starts a new row. Figure 6-14 shows one possible effect of positioning four buttons in a container with a flow layout, with alignment set to **FlowLayout.CENTER**.

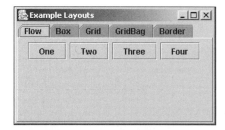

Figure 6-14   The **FlowLayout** example produced by the **ExampleLayouts** program

When you create a **FlowLayout** object, you can specify, with an argument to the constructor, whether components are centered, right-justified, or left-justified. By default, the components are centered. The following line of code gives a container a centered flow layout and adds a button labeled **Cancel** to the container:

```
setLayout( new FlowLayout( FlowLayout.CENTER ) );
add( new Button( "Cancel" ) );
```

Unlike a component in a border layout that expands to fill the area in which it is placed, components in a flow layout retain their preferred size. Resizing the window does not change the size of the components in a flow layout but may adjust their positions.

By default, **JPanel** objects have flow layouts.

The following lines, reproduced from the **ExampleLayouts** program in Figure 6-11, were used to implement the **FlowLayout** strategy shown in Figure 6-14:

```
private JPanel flow
   = new JPanel( new FlowLayout( FlowLayout.CENTER ) );
// Add the buttons to the flow layout
flow.add( new JButton( "One" ) );
flow.add( new JButton( "Two" ) );
flow.add( new JButton( "Three" ) );
flow.add( new JButton( "Four" ) );
```


Grid Layouts

The class **GridLayout** implements the **LayoutManager2** interface to support grid layouts. This layout manager divides the area of the container into a grid of equally sized rows and columns. When you add a component to the container, it automatically goes into the next cell in the grid. Components are put into cells in row order, as shown in Figure 6-15.

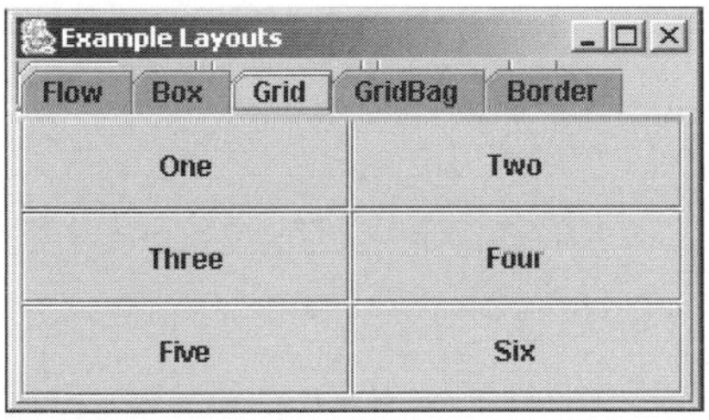

Figure 6-15 A **GridLayout** example produced by the **ExampleLayouts** program

When you set up a grid layout, you specify the number of rows and columns as arguments to the constructor. You can specify zero to mean an unlimited number. However, you cannot specify a row or column position when you add a component to the container. Components are automatically put into the next cell, in a left to right order, filling rows from top to bottom. You cannot skip cells or insert a component into an arbitrarily selected cell. When the user resizes a window that has a grid layout, the cells in the grid change size uniformly, and the appearance of components in those cells adjusts accordingly.

The following lines, reproduced from the `ExampleLayouts` program in Figure 6-11, were used to implement the `GridLayout` strategy shown in Figure 6-15:

```
private JPanel grid
   = new JPanel( new GridLayout( 3, 2 ) );
// Add the buttons to the grid layout
grid.add( new JButton( "One" ) );
grid.add( new JButton( "Two" ) );
grid.add( new JButton( "Three" ) );
grid.add( new JButton( "Four" ) );
grid.add( new JButton( "Five" ) );
grid.add( new JButton( "Six" ) );
```

Grid-Bag Layouts

The class **GridBagLayout** implements the **LayoutManager2** interface to support grid-bag layouts. This layout manager is more flexible than a grid layout, because components can be put in any cell and can span more than one row or column. A grid-bag layout is based on a rectangular grid, just like a grid layout, but it uses a helper class, **GridBagConstraints**, to specify how each component should be located within the grid. With the grid-bag layout, you can create effects such as the arrangement shown in Figure 6-16.

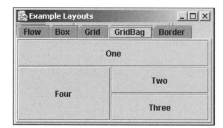

Figure 6-16   A `GridBagLayout` example produced by the `ExampleLayouts` program

Using a grid-bag layout is not as simple as using a grid, border, or flow layout. You should create a **GridBagConstraints** object for each component that you put in the container. In the **GridBagConstraints** object, you set fields to indicate factors such as the following:

- The number of vertical or horizontal cells to span

- The position of the component in the container, and whether that position should be relative to that of the previous component

- The orientation of the component if it does not fill its cell

- How to display a component that is too big for its cell

The Java platform documentation describes the full set of methods for the **GridBagLayout** class and fields in the **GridBagConstraints** class.

You must do some extra work to take advantage of the power of a grid-bag layout. For instance, the lines from the **ExampleLayouts** program in Figure 6-11, reproduced here for convenience, implemented the **GridBagLayout** strategy to generate the output shown in Figure 6-16. Note that the constraints apply to the next cell put into the container. For example, the button labeled **One** goes into the default cell (0, 0) and fills the row because its width is set to the remainder of the row. Then, the button labeled **Two** goes into cell (1, 1) and button **Three** goes into cell (2, 1). Finally, the button labeled **Four** goes into cell (0, 1) but is two rows high. You can vary the **weightx** constraint from row to row and **weighty** constraint from column to column. The **weightx** field controls the relative height of rows, and **weighty** controls the relative width of columns. Setting both to 1.0 makes all rows and columns expand uniformly to fill the container.

```
private JPanel gridBag
   = new JPanel( new GridBagLayout() );
// Add the buttons to the grid-bag layout
GridBagConstraints c = new GridBagConstraints();
c.fill = GridBagConstraints.BOTH;
c.weightx = 1.0;
c.weighty = 1.0;
c.gridwidth = GridBagConstraints.REMAINDER;
gridBag.add( new JButton( "One" ), c );
c.gridy = 1;
c.gridx = 1;
gridBag.add( new JButton( "Two" ), c );
c.gridy = 2;
gridBag.add( new JButton( "Three" ), c );
c.gridy = 1;
c.gridx = 0;
c.gridheight = 2;
c.gridwidth = 1;
gridBag.add( new JButton( "Four" ), c );
```

Card Layouts

The class **CardLayout** implements the **LayoutManager2** interface to support card layouts. If a container has a card layout, the components are stacked on top of each other, like a deck of cards, so that only one component is visible at a time. This layout is not used frequently, but it may work when you want users to be able to view the components in a container one component at a time, and in order. The **CardLayout** class provides the methods **first**, **last**, and **next** that you can call to make a component visible.

Box Layouts

The class **Box** is a Swing container that uses the **BoxLayout** strategy. **BoxLayout** implements the **LayoutManager2** interface to define a layout strategy that is similar to the **FlowLayout** strategy. However, unlike the flow layout, the box layout does not wrap to create additional lines when the components on a line do not fit in the given space. All components are placed in a single line, which may be arranged horizontally or vertically. Figure 6-17 shows a box layout with the components stacked vertically.

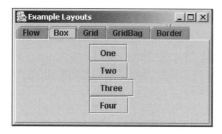

Figure 6-17   A **BoxLayout** example produced by the **ExampleLayouts** program

The following lines, reproduced from the **ExampleLayouts** program in Figure 6-11, implement the **BoxLayout** strategy to generate the output shown in Figure 6-17:

```
private Box box = new Box( BoxLayout.Y_AXIS );
private JPanel boxPanel = new JPanel();
// Add the buttons to the box
box.add( new JButton( "One" ) );
box.add( new JButton( "Two" ) );
box.add( new JButton( "Three" ) );
box.add( new JButton( "Four" ) );
```

Tabbed Panes

The class **JTabbedPane** isn't a true layout manager in the sense that it does not implement the **LayoutManager** interface. However, from the point of view that a tabbed pane does control the positioning and presentation of components, it can be considered a type of layout manager.

In the **ExampleLayouts** program in Figure 6-11, the following lines positioned the panels containing the button layouts shown in Figures 6-13 through 6-17:

```
// create a tabbed pane and put the panels into it
JTabbedPane tp = new JTabbedPane();
tp.addTab( "Flow", flow );
boxPanel.add( box );
tp.addTab( "Box", boxPanel );
tp.addTab( "Grid", grid );
```

```
tp.addiab(  GiiuBay , giiuBay );
tp.addTab( "Border", border );
setContentPane( tp );
```

Split Panes

Similar to the class **JTabbedPane**, the class **JSplitPane** is not a true layout manager because it does not implement the **LayoutManager** interface. However, from the point of view that a split pane does control the positioning and presentation of components, it can be considered a type of layout manager.

For an example program that includes a split pane, refer to the **TextExamples** program and its output in the section "Text-Entry Components" in Chapter 7.

Positioning Components Manually

If you want to position components manually, you can suppress the layout manager with the following method call:

```
setLayout( null );
```

You may want to undertake the considerable effort of arranging components for the following reasons:

- To gain more precise control than an available layout manager provides
- As part of creating a layout manager of your own

  If you turn off the layout manager by specifying a null layout manager, you must position and shape all the components in the container. The **Component** class provides methods for doing this. In particular, you can call **setBounds** to specify the height, width, and upper-left corner of a component. You can use the **setLocation** method to reposition a component relative to the upper left of its container, and **setSize** to resize a component. All of these methods operate on pixel addresses.

EVENTS

A user interface usually displays components and graphics, but it is not just output. It must interact with user input as well.

In a GUI for a Java application, *events* are objects that encapsulate changes in state that are initiated by the user or the operating system. Generally, the user triggers events by pressing and releasing keys on the keyboard or by moving and clicking the mouse. Some events, such as button clicks or text entry, have meaning for only specific components in your GUI. Others, such as resizing a window or moving focus from window to window, are also recognized by the native operating system.

The AWT API includes the package **java.awt.event**, in which you will find the classes from this API that encapsulate the events that relate to the GUI components in your application or applet. All classes in this package that define events are subclasses of the class **java.awt.event.AWTEvent**, which is a subclass of **java.util.EventObject**. **EventObject** is the superclass of all Java platform classes that define events, whether they are GUI events or not.

The Swing API separates its event-related classes into a package called **javax.swing.event**. It is worth noting that most Swing event classes are direct subclasses of **EventObject**, not **AWTEvent**.

A large part of programming a GUI involves providing handlers for events. In the Java programming language, this task is straightforward because you create event handlers by implementing predefined listener interfaces or extending predefined adapter classes. Listeners and adapters are described later in this chapter.

To catch and handle events, you adopt the "Hollywood model" of programming: "Don't call us, we'll call you." In other words, you do not poll the environment looking for events. When an event occurs, the event dispatch thread calls you. In parts of your code not directly related to events, you can ignore events. Like different threads in a multi-threaded application, these parts of your code carry on with their usual business. When events occur, the JVM or your Web browser receives messages from the operating system. The classes in the **java.awt.event** package determine the nature of the event and identify the appropriate component. The JVM calls the object that implements the listener interface registered for the event. Through listeners, events call you.

Figure 6-18 lists the types of common AWT events. Figure 6-19 lists common Swing events.

Event class	Description
AdjustmentEvent	Indicates a change to an object of a class that implements the Adjustable interface. The **JScrollBar** class is an example of an Adjustable class of objects.
ComponentEvent	Occurs when a component has been moved, resized, shown, or hidden. The event dispatch thread typically handles such events.
ContainerEvent	Occurs when the contents of a container have changed or when a component has been added or removed. Use this event as notification only, because the event dispatch thread handles these events.
FocusEvent	Lets a user open more than one window simultaneously, but only one window at a time can be highlighted and brought to the foreground. The foreground window is said to have focus, and the user usually brings a window into focus by clicking the mouse over it. A focus event occurs when a component gets or loses focus.
InputEvent	The superclass for both keyboard and mouse events. It has no corresponding listener interface.

Figure 6-18 Description of common AWT event classes

Event class	Description
ItemEvent	Occurs when the state of an item within a component that implements the ItemSelectable interface has changed. **JCheckBox**, **JComboBox**, and **JList** are examples of selectable components. The **JComboBox** and **JList** classes are discussed later in this chapter.
KeyEvent	Occurs when the user releases a key on the keyboard.
MouseEvent	The events encapsulated by this class are clicking the mouse button, releasing the button, dragging the mouse, and moving the mouse.
PaintEvent	Indicates that a component should have its update method invoked. The event dispatch thread handles these events automatically.
TextEvent	Occurs when the user edits the text value in components such as **JTextField** or **JTextArea**. The classes that provide text components are discussed later in this chapter.
WindowEvent	User actions relating to windows generate instances of this event class.

Figure 6-18   Description of common AWT event classes (continued)

Event class	Description
ChangeEvent	Used to notify interested parties that the state has changed in the event source. It carries no details about the change that has happened.
InternalFrameEvent	Inherits from AWTEvent and adds support for **JInternalFrame** objects as the event source.
ListSelectionEvent	Used to indicate a change in the current list selection.
MenuEvent	Used to notify interested parties that the menu that is the event source has been posted, selected, or canceled. It carries no details about the change that has happened. Menus are described later in this chapter.
TableModelEvent	Used to notify listeners that a date in a table model has changed. Like all Swing components, there is a separate model class to hold the data displayed in the component. For tables, lists, and trees, the ability to deal with the model separately from the component adds great power to the Swing classes. The **JTable** class and its model are explained later in this chapter.
TreeSelectionEvent	Indicates a change in the current tree selection.

Figure 6-19   Description of common Swing event classes

Each event object contains the appropriate data for the event. You can call methods of the event classes to access this information. Figure 6-20 shows some methods you can call to get information about an event in an event handler.

6

Class	Method	Description
AWTEvent	int getID()	Returns the type of the current event.
ComponentEvent	Component getComponent()	Returns the component involved in the event.
ItemEvent	Object getItem()	Returns the object that was either selected or deselected.
ItemEvent	int getStateChange()	The return value is ItemEvent.SELECTED or ItemEvent.DESELECTED. A method to indicate the change of state is required because the only handler in the ItemListener interface, itemStateChanged, does not make this distinction.
KeyEvent	int getKeyChar()	Returns the Unicode character that was typed.
MouseEvent	int getClickCount()	Distinguishes between single and double mouse clicks.
InputEvent	int getModifiers()	The return value indicates which mouse button is involved. Different operating systems support one, two, or three mouse buttons.
MouseEvent	Point getPoint()	Returns the location for the mouse event.
PaintEvent	Rectangle getUpdatedRect()	Returns the rectangle representing the area to be painted.
WindowEvent	Window getWindow()	Returns the window that is the source of the event.

Figure 6-20   Select methods of the event classes

To make the method **AWTEvent.getID** easier to use, each event that subclasses it defines integer constants for events associated with the class. For example, the **FocusEvent** class defines the two constants **FOCUS_GAINED** and **FOCUS_LOST**. Very often, the context of each event handler gives you the same information as the **getID** method, so you do not have to call this method. For example, there are two handlers for **FocusEvent** objects in the **FocusListener** interface: **focusGained** and **focusLost**.

Listener Interfaces and Their Adapter Classes

The AWT and Swing APIs define a set of interfaces called *listeners*. Each kind of event has a listener interface, and each listener has methods for every event that can occur in its event class. For example, the **TextListener** interface corresponds to the **TextEvent**

contents of the text component. Thus, the only method in the **TextListener** interface is **textValueChanged**. The **TextListener** interface has only one method, so it does not have an adapter class. The **MouseListener** class, however, has five methods—**mouseClicked**, **mouseEntered**, **mouseExited**, **mousePressed**, and **mouseReleased**—and so it does have an associated adapter class called **MouseAdapter**.

Use listener interfaces to create handlers for events. You must complete two steps to create a handler for an event:

1. Define a class that implements the appropriate listener interface. Your class provides the handler by implementing the methods that are declared in the interface.

2. Register an instance of the class with the component affected by the event.

The following syntax boxes give details on the methods used to register listener objects with a component and also on the listener interfaces. They are presented using generic names because all of these methods and interfaces follow the same naming pattern.

6

Class

Any component class

Methods

- **void add*xxx*Listener (*xxx*Listener *object*)**

  The **add*xxx*Listener** methods register a listener with a component; they all return **void**. The ***xxx*** is the type of the listener. All components have the methods **addComponentListener**, **addFocusListener**, **addMouseListener**, and **addMouseMotionListener**.

Code Example

```
class myHandler implements TextListener {
   public void textValueChanged( TextEvent e ) {
      // implementation of textValueChanged omitted
   }
}
TextListener tl = new myHandler();
JTextArea t = new JTextArea();
t.addTextListener( tl );
```

Code Dissection

These lines of code are excerpts from a program that handles text events.

The structure of the listener interfaces is regular and predictable. All the methods of all the interfaces follow the same form.

Interface

xxxListener

Dissection

Each event class has an associated listener interface. The **xxx** represents the name of an event class.

Methods

- **void xxxEvent (xxxEvent E)**

- All listener methods have return type **void**.

- All listener methods take one argument: an object of an event class.

- All listener methods begin with the same word as the listener.

- For example, all the methods in the **ComponentListener** interface begin with **Component**, have an argument of type **ComponentEvent**, and return **void**. The methods in a **ComponentListener** object are **componentMoved**, **componentShown**, and **componentHidden**.

- Mouse events are the one exception to this pattern. Mouse event handlers are split over two interfaces: **MouseListener** and **MouseMotionListener**. The methods in these two interfaces all begin with **mouse**, and all take a single **MouseEvent** object as a parameter. The **MouseListener** methods are **mouseClicked**, **mousePressed**, **mouseReleased**, **mouseEntered**, and **mouseExited**. The **MouseMotionListener** methods are **mouseDragged** and **mouseMoved**.

You can implement a listener interface directly. For listener interfaces with more than one method, you can alternatively implement the listener indirectly by extending its adapter class. It makes no sense to have an adapter class for an interface with only one method, because the reason to extend an adapter class is to provide fewer method implementations than the interface defines and accept the trivial (in other words, empty) implementations for the other methods. Of course, you can't implement less than one method in a class!

The AWT and Swing APIs provide several adapter classes that implement listener interfaces for you. The adapters provide empty implementations of all the methods in the interface. The advantage of the adapter classes is that classes that extend them can implement only the handlers of interest and inherit the empty implementations of all other methods.

The adapter classes follow a naming pattern similar to that of the listener interfaces, except that the names are *xxx*Adapter rather than *xxx*Listener, where *xxx* is the type of event for which the interface is listening.

Generally, extending adapter classes is preferable when a minority of the methods in the interface are of interest. Using an adapter simplifies the coding but does not change the mechanism.

The listener interfaces in **java.awt.event** all extend the interface **EventListener** from the package **java.util**, just as the adapter classes extend **Object** from **java.lang**. The predefined adapter classes for listeners are all abstract classes.

Any class can handle events, not just GUI components; a class needs only to implement the appropriate interface and register itself with the object that generates the events.

Events that Start Long Operations

At times, a user action will begin a long operation. For the purpose of this discussion, a long operation is one that is unlikely to complete within the normal user interface response time of a second or two. For example, clicking a menu item that causes the contents of a file to be retrieved from another computer somewhere on the Internet starts an operation that could take a minute or longer. In such cases, it is important that the long operation be executed on a separate thread and not on the event dispatch thread. Failing to do so causes the user interface to become unresponsive, because no other events can be handled until the long operation completes and frees the event dispatch thread.

However, using separate threads to handle long operations can cause problems because Swing components are not thread-safe. If more than one thread attempts to access a Swing component at the same time, errors will result, because, for the sake of speed, the methods of Swing components are not synchronized. So, if the thread that retrieves the contents of a file from the Internet attempts to write those contents into a text area in the user interface, it may conflict with the event dispatch thread as it updates the same text area.

The solution is to make sure that the event dispatch thread makes all updates to the user interface. Obviously, if only one thread updates the user interface, no conflicts will occur. In the **javax.swing.SwingUtilities** class, the **invokeLater** and **invokeAndWait** methods allow other threads to define updates to Swing components for the event dispatch thread to execute. The only difference between these two methods is that **invokeAndWait** blocks the thread that calls it until the event dispatch thread completes the updates. The **invokeLater** method does not block. Both **invokeLater** and **invokeAndWait** take a single **Runnable** object as input.

Figure 6-21 is the outline of a class that would execute on a thread separate from the event dispatch thread. In its **run** method, it uses the **invokeLater** method to update a text field to indicate when the operation begins and when it ends. Anonymous inner classes are used to create the **Runnable** objects that are passed as input to the **invokeLater** method.

```
package examples.windows;
import javax.swing.*;
public class ReadFromInternet extends Thread {
   private JTextField status;
   public ReadFromInternet( JTextField tf ) {
      status = tf;
   }
   public void run() {
      SwingUtilities.invokeLater( new Runnable() {
            public void run() {
               status.setText(
                  "Beginning the operation" );
            }
         }
      );

      // read the file from the Internet

      SwingUtilities.invokeLater( new Runnable() {
            public void run() {
               status.setText( "Operation complete" );
            }
         }
      );
   }
}
```

Figure 6-21   `ReadFromInternet`: an example showing how to handle events that start long operations

PAINTING

Painting is the act of producing the graphics image of windows and everything that they contain on the screen. This is a different task from making a window visible by calling the **setVisible** method. A window can be fully rendered, or painted, and, at the same time, not visible because it is minimized or hidden behind another window. Painting occurs when it is necessary to refresh what the user can see. For example, when the window is resized or covered by another window and then uncovered, it must be repainted.

All paint operations are performed by a central thread: the event dispatch thread. When your code requests that a component be painted or repainted, the JVM passes the request to the event dispatch thread. Your code then continues to execute in its own thread while the event dispatch thread does the actual painting.

All objects that are instances of subclasses of **java.awt.Component** handle their own painting. Unless your application has special requirements for graphics, such as drawing directly on the graphics context or performing animation, you do not have to implement the **paint** method. Generally, it is better to let the Java platform use its own methods for the painting of components.

Four key methods are involved in painting components:

■ A Swing component should override the

```
void paintComponent ( Graphics context )
```

method to control how it is displayed:

The **paintComponent** method provides control over the way the component itself is displayed but maintains the default behavior for displaying the component's border and child components. It draws the entire component automatically when the component is first displayed, exposed after being covered, resized, or scrolled into view. Unless the component is intended to be transparent, the first statement in a component's **paintComponent** method should be a call to **super.paintComponent**.

Do not call **paintComponent** directly. Only the event dispatch thread schedules the painting of objects. It does this to make sure that painting operations always complete and do not have unpredictable results, such as leaving half of a window on the screen while the application does something else.

■ The method of the component class that renders components for display is

```
void paint ( Graphics context )
```

The **paint** method draws the entire component automatically when the component is first displayed, exposed after being covered, resized, or scrolled into view. Do not call **paint** directly. Only the event dispatch thread schedules the painting of objects. It does this to make sure that painting operations always complete and do not have unpredictable results, such as leaving half of a window on the screen while the application does something else.

■ To make sure a component is painted, you can call the following method:

```
void repaint ( long time )
```

When you call **repaint**, the JVM calls **update** and then **paint** for the current component. Unlike **paint**, **repaint** can be called directly. You can call the overloaded version of the **repaint** method with no arguments to request that **repaint** begin immediately. Because painting occurs on a separate event dispatch thread, specifying a time interval in milliseconds before the next **paint** is to begin can give better performance than tying up the processor by repainting frequently in a tight loop.

- The fourth essential painting method is

void update (Graphics *context* **)**

Unlike **paint**, which must be able to render the entire component, **update** can be used to update selective areas. One reason to override **update** is to create smooth animations. The default implementation can produce a flickering image because it floods the entire area of the component with the background color before calling **paint**.

The **JComponent** class overrides the **update** method to call **paint** directly to reduce flicker when drawing.

When you override the **paint**, **paintComponent**, or **update** methods, make sure that your code can execute very quickly. Include all the statements you need for painting, but no more. For example, try to remove all calculations and retain only the drawing statements. You do not want to slow down the event dispatch thread by making it perform any operations that you can perform elsewhere. If the **paint** or **paintComponent** methods for one component hog time, they can prevent other components from being painted in a timely fashion and potentially cause a situation in which the display for a program does not match its internal state.

Basic Support for Graphics

Many programs produce graphical output. Lines, characters, and any shapes drawn directly onto a component's display area make up graphical output. Graphical output can be part of your GUI. The AWT API provides basic graphics support through the class **Graphics**, which includes many methods you can use for drawing. This class is one of many utility classes that reside in the package **java.awt**.

The drawing methods are instance methods of the **Graphics** class, and each instance of **Graphics** is the graphics context for a component. The **paint** and **update** methods provide a **Graphics** object as an argument of the method for you to use when you override the method.

The sample program in Figure 6-22 defines the **Drawings** class and provides a demonstration of using the methods of the **Graphics** class.

Drawing in the graphics context of a component is a very different process than adding a component to a container. The main differences are the following:

- No core Java platform layout manager class can work with graphics, and you must specify coordinates.

■ ~~Components automatically redraw themselves when the window in which~~
they appear is displayed, resized, or uncovered on the screen. You must
redraw graphical output as required. Usually, you effect redraw operations
by including in the **paint** method calls to the methods that your application uses for drawing.

■ If your program uses only components and never draws to the graphics context, there is no need to implement **paint**.

Details about the **Graphics** class are provided next, along with a list of commonly used
methods defined in this class.

Class

```
java.awt.Graphics
```

Purpose

The **Graphics** class provides a number of methods for drawing onto a component.

Methods

■ **void drawString (String** *str***, int** *x***, int** *y* **)**

The **drawString** method draws the string provided by the first argument so that
the lower-left corner of the first character is at pixel coordinate (*x, y*). The
characters appear in the current font and color, which you can set with other
methods of the **Graphics** class.

■ **void drawLine(int** *x1***, int** *y1***, int** *x2***, int** *y2* **)**

The **drawLine** method draws a line from (*x1, y1*) to (*x2, y2*), in the
coordinates of the graphics context.

■ **void drawRect(int** *x***, int** *y***, int** *width***, int** *height* **)**

The **drawRect** method draws the outline of a rectangle from (*x, y*) to
(*x+width, y+height*).

■ **void drawPolygon(int[]** *xPoints***, int[]** *yPoints***, int** *nPoints* **)**

The **drawPolygon** method draws the closed polygon defined by the arrays of *x*
and *y* coordinates. It is also possible to create an instance of the **Polygon** class and
use the version of **drawPolygon** with a single **Polygon** parameter.

■ **void drawArc(int** *x***, int** *y***, int** *width***, int** *height***,**
int *startAngle***, int** *arcAngle* **)**

The **drawArc** method draws an arc of an ellipse or circle bounded by the coordinates
x and *y* and the specified *width* and *height* arguments. The arc rotates counter-
clockwise from *startAngle* degrees to *startAngle* + *arcAngle* degrees.

- **boolean drawImage(Image** *img*, **int** *x*, **int** *y*,
                      ImageObserver *observer* **)**

The **drawImage** method draws an image at the coordinates specified. The **Image** class is defined in **java.awt** for GIF files, JPEG files, and URLs. Loading an image can take some time. Therefore, the method returns without waiting, and a return value of **false** indicates the image is not completely loaded. The **ImageObserver** object is notified when the operation is complete. Chapter 14 describes how to display **Image** objects.

- **void fillRect(int** *x*, **int** *y*, **int** *width*, **int** *height* **)**

  void fillPolygon(int *xPoints*[], **int** *yPoints*[], **int** *nPoints* **)**

  void fillArc(int *x*, **int** *y*, **int** *width*, **int** *height*,
                int *startAngle*, **int** *arcAngle* **)**

These methods of the **Graphics** class fill areas of the screen with color rather than draw outlines. The result of a draw or fill operation depends on various settings that you can specify by calling the following methods of the **Graphics** class:

- **void setColor(Color** *c* **)**

The **setColor** method sets the color used for subsequent drawing and fill coloring.

- **void setFont(Font** *f* **)**

This method sets the font for subsequent text operations.

- **void setPaintMode()**

  void setXORMode(Color *c* **)**

The **setPaintMode** and **setXORMode** methods set alternative paint modes. Call **setPaintMode** to overwrite whatever is already drawn on the screen. Call **setXORMode** to display pixels in the color that results from an exclusive OR (XOR) operation between the current color and the color specified in the argument. Predicting the resulting colors from XOR mode is difficult, and this mode can create bizarre effects. However, the colors are reversible, and you can restore pixels to the original color by redrawing the same area.

It is important to note that the values set for a particular **Graphics** object used in a **paint** method are lost at the end of the **paint** method, because each **paint** method gets a fresh **Graphics** object with which to work. To make such changes last, you should make them to the component object.

Although the **Graphics** class is useful, it does have limitations. For example, you cannot specify the width of a line or use a fill pattern. The Java 2D API introduces a new

~~class called GraphicsDB that extends the original Graphics class and addresses the~~
shortcomings of the basic 2D graphics support in the AWT API.

Figure 6-22 is a program that exercises several methods of the **Graphics** class. It also demonstrates using the **java.awt.Font** class to set the size of characters to draw and working with the **java.awt.Color** class. The program does not have much substance, pretense to art, or even amusing output, but it provides a representative sample of the methods in the **Graphics** class. As with the other sample programs, a breakdown of this code follows the output.

6

```
package examples.windows;
import java.awt.*;
import javax.swing.*;
/** An example class used to demonstrate various
  * drawing techniques including text, lines,
  * shapes, and filled shapes
  */
public class Drawings extends JFrame {
   /** Class constructor method
     * @param titleText name to be put in the
     *     window's title bar
     */
   public Drawings( String titleText ) {
      super( titleText );
      setDefaultCloseOperation( JFrame.EXIT_ON_CLOSE );
      DrawingPanel dp = new DrawingPanel();
      getContentPane().add( dp, BorderLayout.CENTER );
      setSize( 500, 500 );
      setVisible( true );
   }
   public class DrawingPanel extends JPanel {
      /** Class constructor
        */
      public DrawingPanel() {
         setBackground( Color.white );
         setBorder( BorderFactory.createTitledBorder(
            "Sample output from drawing methods:" ) );
      }
      /** Draws the text, lines, and shapes in the
        * specified graphics context
        * @param g the component's graphics context
        */
      public void paintComponent( Graphics g ) {
         super.paintComponent(g);
         g.drawString( "Hello World!", 100, 60 );
```

Figure 6-22   `Drawings`: example usage of basic drawing techniques

```
        Font cFont = g.getFont();
        Font newFont = new Font( cFont.getName(),
                                 cFont.getStyle(),
                                 cFont.getSize() + 20 );
        g.setFont( newFont );
        g.drawString( "Here I am!", 200, 80 );
        g.drawLine( 50, 50, 100, 200 );
        g.setColor( Color.blue );
        g.drawRoundRect( 150, 300, 100, 125, 15, 15 );
        g.setColor( Color.red );
        g.fillOval( 400, 200, 50, 180 );
    }
}
/** The test method for the class
  * @param args not used
  */
public static void main( String[] args ) {
  new Drawings( "Drawings Sample" );
}
}
```

Figure 6-22 `Drawings`: example usage of basic drawing techniques (continued)

Allowing for differences in operating systems, the output should be similar to Figure 6-23.

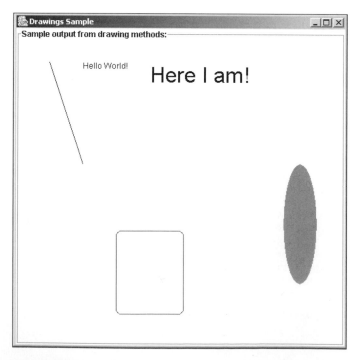

Figure 6-23 Output of the `Drawings` program

usual, begins by passing the title for the **JFrame** object to the constructor of the **JFrame** superclass.

```
public Drawings( String titleText ) {
    super( titleText );
```

As with the other sample programs in this chapter, you must call the method **setDefaultCloseOperation** and specify that the application should exit when the user closes the window, as shown next:

```
setDefaultCloseOperation( JFrame.EXIT_ON_CLOSE );
```

Then, an instance of the **DrawingPanel** class is constructed. This object is positioned in the center section of the border layout of the frame window.

```
DrawingPanel dp = new DrawingPanel();
getContentPane().add( dp, BorderLayout.CENTER );
```

The second to last statement of the constructor calls the method **setSize** that is inherited from the **Component** class. The call to **setSize** sets the size of **JFrame**, in pixels. Finally, **JFrame** is displayed by a call to **setVisible**. The **setVisible** method is implemented in the **JComponent** class to make the component visible.

```
setSize( 500, 500 );
setVisible( true );
```

A nested class defines the component where the actual drawing will take place. This class extends the **JPanel** class. The constructor sets the background color for the panel and adds a titled border to it.

```
public class DrawingPanel extends JPanel {
    public DrawingPanel() {
        setBackground( Color.white );
        setBorder( BorderFactory.createTitledBorder(
            "Sample output from drawing methods:" ) );
    }
```

This application only draws some shapes, so most of the action occurs in the **paintComponent** method. The first statement calls **paintComponent** of the superclass:

```
public void paintComponent( Graphics g ) {
    super.paintComponent(g);
```

The **paintComponent** method draws two strings—Hello World! and Here I am!—in different sizes. The Hello World! string is drawn in the default font. To be bigger than Hello World!, Here I am! must be drawn with a different font. The **Font** class is a utility class in **java.awt** that encapsulates fonts, and the **Font** constructor has arguments for the name, style, and size of the required font. Here, the new font is a variation on the default font because only the size changes, so the **paint** method creates a **Font** object and specifies it as the font for the graphics context. The **paint** method executes the following steps in the order presented:

1. Obtains an object reference for the current font of the graphics context, by calling **Graphics.getFont**.

2. Retrieves the current **Font** object to determine its name, style, and size by calling **getName**, **getStyle**, and **getSize**. The name of a font is specified in a **String** object. You can call the method **getAvailableFontFamilyNames** using an instance of the class **GraphicsEnvironment** to get the names of the fonts available on your installation of the Java platform. The possible styles are **Font.PLAIN**, **Font.BOLD**, and **Font.ITALIC**. The size is expressed in points.

3. Uses the **new** keyword to create a new **Font** object with the same characteristics as the current font, except that the size is increased by 20 points.

4. Calls **Graphics.setFont** to set the new font as the current font for the current graphics context.

The following lines of the **paint** method draw the two strings using the process described previously:

```
g.drawString( "Hello World!", 100, 60 );
Font cFont = g.getFont();
Font newFont = new Font( cFont.getName(),
                         cFont.getStyle(),
                         cFont.getSize() + 20 );
g.setFont( newFont );
g.drawString( "Here I am!", 200, 80 );
```

The remaining lines of the **paint** method draw a line in the default foreground color, a rounded rectangle in blue, and a solid oval shape in red.

```
g.drawLine( 50, 50, 100, 200 );
g.setColor( Color.blue );
g.drawRoundRect( 150, 300, 100, 125, 15, 15 );
g.setColor( Color.red );
g.fillOval( 400, 200, 50, 180 );
```

The **main** method for the **Drawings** class simply creates a **Drawings** object and passes the title bar text as the parameter for the constructor.

```
public static void main( String[] args ) {
    new Drawings( "Drawings Sample" );
}
```

Java 2D API

The basic support for drawing that had been available since the first version of the Java platform was generally considered to be lacking when high-quality graphics were needed. In response, the Java 2D API was created and included as part of the JFC. This new API enhanced the existing **java.awt** and **java.awt.image** packages and added half a dozen new packages. Figure 6-24 lists notable features that the Java 2D API provides.

Java 2D API Feature	Use
Antialiasing	The use of curves in shapes and fonts can lead to jagged edges in drawing, but the antialiasing support that is built into the Java 2D API takes care of this.
Filling	Shapes can be filled not only with a solid color, but also with a pattern, a color gradient, or anything else that can be imagined.
Fonts	The Java 2D API can make use of any TrueType or Type 1 font that is available on the system and isn't limited to those known by the Toolkit class. Refer to the **java.awt.font** package.
Printing	The Java 2D API was the first package to make printing within a Java application bearable. Since that time, more printing enhancements have come along that make printing easier for the programmer, especially multipage documents. Printing will be discussed in depth in Chapter 7.
Shapes	Along with the expected standard shapes, it is possible to create arbitrary shapes by combining lines and curves using the contents of the **java.awt.geom** package.
Strokes	The use of the new **Stroke** class makes it possible to create lines with any width, and these lines can also be solid, dotted, or patterns of dashes. The **Stroke** class can be found in the **java.awt.geom** package.
Transformations	A comprehensive library of transformations makes it possible to rotate, translate, stretch, or squish everything you can draw. Details can be found in the **java.awt.geom** package.

Figure 6-24   Notable Java 2D features

Because the goal was to create an API that addressed the needs of graphics professionals, the complexity of many of the features including compositing, rendering, and transformations means that a detailed discussion of the API is beyond the scope of this text. However, much of the API is simple to use; to show this, the **Drawings** example has been reworked to use the 2D API, and the resulting **Drawings2D** class is provided in Figure 6-25. The differences between the two programs in Figures 6-22 and 6-25 are highlighted in bold in Figure 6-25.

```
package examples.windows;
import java.awt.*;
import java.awt.geom.*;
import javax.swing.*;
/** An example class used to demonstrate various
  * drawing techniques including text, lines,
  * shapes, and filled shapes for the 2D Graphics
  * library
  */
public class Drawings2D extends JFrame {
    /** Class constructor method
      * @param titleText name to be put in the
      *     window's title bar
      */
    public Drawings2D( String titleText ) {
        super( titleText );
        setDefaultCloseOperation( JFrame.EXIT_ON_CLOSE );
        DrawingPanel dp = new DrawingPanel();
        getContentPane().add( dp, BorderLayout.CENTER );
        setSize( 500, 500 );
        setVisible( true );
    }
    public class DrawingPanel extends JPanel {
        /** Class constructor
          */
        public DrawingPanel() {
            setBackground( Color.white );
            setBorder( BorderFactory.createTitledBorder(
                "Sample output from 2D Graphics" +
                " drawing methods:" ) );
        }
        /** Draws the text, lines, and shapes in the
          * specified graphics context
          * @param g the component's graphics context
          */
        public void paintComponent( Graphics g ) {
            super.paintComponent(g);
            Graphics2D g2 = (Graphics2D) g;
            g2.setRenderingHint(
                RenderingHints.KEY_ANTIALIASING,
                RenderingHints.VALUE_ANTIALIAS_ON);
            g2.setStroke( new BasicStroke( 4.0f ) );
            g2.drawString( "Hello World!", 100, 60 );
            Font cFont = g2.getFont();
            Font newFont = new Font( cFont.getName(),
                                     cFont.getStyle(),
                                     cFont.getSize() + 20 );
            g2.setFont( newFont );
            g2.drawString( "Here I am!", 200, 80 );
            Line2D line
                = new Line2D.Double( 50.0, 50.0,
                                     100.0, 200.0 );
```

Figure 6-25   Drawings2D: example usage of drawing techniques for the Java 2D API

```
            g2.draw( line );
            g2.setPaint( Color.blue );
            RoundRectangle2D rndrect
               = new RoundRectangle2D.Double( 150.0, 300.0,
                                              100.0, 125.0,
                                              15.0, 15.0 );
            g2.draw( rndrect );
            g2.setPaint( Color.red );
            Ellipse2D oval
               = new Ellipse2D.Double( 400.0, 200.0,
                                       50.0, 180.0 );
            g2.fill( oval );
      }
   }
   /** The test method for the class
     * @param args not used
     */
   public static void main( String[] args ) {
      new Drawings2D( "Drawings2D Sample" );
   }
}
```

Figure 6-25   `Drawings2D`: example usage of drawing techniques for the Java 2D API
(continued)

Allowing for differences in operating systems, the output should be similar to Figure 6–26.

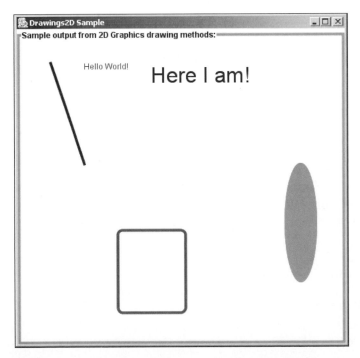

Figure 6-26   Output of the `Drawings2D` program

All the essential differences between the `Drawings` and the `Drawings2D` classes are found in the **paintComponent** method. The method begins with the same call to the superclass' **paintComponent** method, but then casts the received `Graphics` object to be a `Graphics2D` object. This cast operation to reveal the "hidden" `Graphics2D` object is necessary to be able to use the new methods of the `Graphics2D` class later in the method.

```
super.paintComponent(g);
Graphics2D g2 = (Graphics2D) g;
```

The powerful antialiasing support is easily enabled by a single method call to the following **setRenderingHint** method, in order to set the value of the antialiasing key to be turned on. This produces a noticeable improvement in the smoothing of curves as compared to the `Drawings` example. If this difference isn't evident from the figures in this text, run both examples side by side to see the difference.

```
g2.setRenderingHint(
    RenderingHints.KEY_ANTIALIASING,
    RenderingHints.VALUE_ANTIALIAS_ON);
```

To control the width of the line used for drawing, a **BasicStroke** object is constructed using the following statement with an input value to the constructor, `4.0f`, that makes the line four units wide. By passing this object as input to the **setStroke** call, all lines and shapes are drawn with this stroke until you specify another stroke.

```
g2.setStroke( new BasicStroke( 4.0f ) );
```

The sequence of method calls to draw text strings is exactly the same without any need for changes.

```
g2.drawString( "Hello World!", 100, 60 );
Font cFont = g2.getFont();
Font newFont = new Font( cFont.getName(),
                         cFont.getStyle(),
                         cFont.getSize() + 20 );
g2.setFont( newFont );
g2.drawString( "Here I am!", 200, 80 );
```

The drawing of the line is accomplished by first creating an object representing the line to be drawn, then by calling the general purpose **draw** method to draw the line. This contrasts with the use of the special-purpose method, **drawLine**, used in the previous example. Note that the line that is drawn is thicker in this example because of the stroke specified.

```
Line2D line
   = new Line2D.Double( 50.0, 50.0,
                        100.0, 200.0 );
g2.draw( line );
```

The drawing of the rounded rectangle is also accomplished in two steps by first creating the shape to be drawn, then by calling the general purpose **draw** method to draw the shape. Note that the line used for this shape is blue because of the **setPaint** call and thick because the stroke has not changed.

```
g2.setPaint( Color.blue );
RoundRectangle2D rndrect
    = new RoundRectangle2D.Double( 150.0, 300.0,
                                   100.0, 125.0,
                                    15.0, 15.0 );
g2.draw( rndrect );
```

The drawing of the filled ellipse is accomplished by first creating the shape to be drawn, then by calling the general purpose **fill** method to draw the filled shape. Note that the fill used for this shape is red because of the **setPaint** call.

```
g2.setPaint( Color.red );
Ellipse2D oval
    = new Ellipse2D.Double( 400.0, 200.0,
                             50.0, 180.0 );
g2.fill( oval );
```

6

CHAPTER SUMMARY

This chapter and the next are complementary. Chapter 7 builds on the understanding that you gain in this chapter to provide more comprehensive coverage of the JFC. This chapter explained that the JFC is part of the Java platform.

❑ The JFC consists of five major APIs, including the classes and interfaces in the AWT and Swing APIs that you use to program a GUI for an application or applet.

❑ The Swing API includes classes for the standard elements of GUIs, many of which are components. For example, **JButton**, **JCheckBox**, and **JTextField** are Swing component classes. You build the GUI for your program with components.

❑ To make a class into an application that runs in a top-level window, define your class to extend the class **javax.swing.JFrame** or **java.awt.Frame**. Coding the GUI for an applet is similar to coding a GUI-based application, except that the applet class must extend the class **javax.swing.JApplet** or **java.applet.Applet** and does not need a **main** method.

❑ You can add components to containers by creating objects of the component class and calling the **add** method of the container, passing the component as an argument.

❑ Use layout managers to arrange the components in a way that adjusts for screen resolutions and window resizings. Specify a layout manager by calling the **setLayout** method for the container.

❏ An equally important aspect of programming GUIs consists of responding when the user moves the mouse, clicks the mouse, or types on the keyboard. These kinds of user input are events. Each component class supports a number of events that are appropriate to its type of component.

❏ To handle an event, define a class to implement the appropriate listener interface. Call a method for the component to register the listener with the component. The methods in the listener interface are automatically called when events occur and receive an event object as an argument. Therefore, the listener can interrogate and handle the event.

❏ You can use adapter classes that implement the interfaces to reduce the number of methods that you must implement to only those events that are of interest.

❏ Each container has a layout manager that arranges components dynamically. Standard layout managers include **BorderLayout**, **FlowLayout**, **GridLayout**, **GridBagLayout**, **Box**, and **CardLayout**. You can nest components and layout managers for flexible arrangements. **JPanel** objects are useful containers for this purpose.

❏ The AWT contains a hierarchy of event classes for different kinds of user-initiated events, such as **ComponentEvent**, **MouseEvent**, **KeyEvent**, **ItemEvent**, **TextEvent**, and **ActionEvent**.

❏ Create handlers for the various kinds of events by instantiating classes that implement listener interfaces. The listener interfaces are named ***xxxListener***, where ***xxx*** is the kind of event. Register a listener with a component by calling the component method **add*xxx*Listener**, where ***xxx*** is the kind of event.

❏ For most listeners, there is an associated adapter class. Often, it is more convenient to extend the adapter class than to implement the interface.

❏ Painting is the act of drawing onto the graphics context of a component. Usually, you call drawing methods of the **Graphics** class in overloaded **paintComponent**, **paint**, and **update** methods of a component. The graphics context is a **Graphics** object passed as an argument to these methods. Do not call **paint**, **paintComponent**, or **update** directly.

❏ The basic support for drawing that had been available since the first version of the Java platform was generally considered to be lacking when high-quality graphics were needed. In response, the Java 2D API was created and included as part of the JFC.

REVIEW QUESTIONS

1. Which of the following major groups of the AWT API is/are responsible for the strategy of placing GUI elements within an interface? Select the best answer.

   a. graphics

   b. components

c. layout managers

d. events

e. listeners and adapters

2. Name the class in the AWT API that is the superclass of events generated by all classes that extend `java.awt.Component`.

3. Which of the following are subpackages of the **java.awt** package? Select all that apply.

   a. **java.awt.components**

   b. **java.awt.event**

   c. **java.awt.image**

   d. **java.awt.graphics**

   e. **java.awt.peer**

4. Which of the following classes are superclasses of Swing applets? Select all that apply.

   a. **java.lang.Object**

   b. **javax.swing.JFrame**

   c. **java.awt.Panel**

   d. **javax.swing.JApplet**

   e. **java.awt.Window**

5. How many components can be added to a container using a **BorderLayout** layout manager?

6. Which of the following are heavyweight Swing components? Select all that apply.

   a. **JApplet**

   b. **JPanel**

   c. **JInternalFrame**

   d. **JDialog**

   e. **JFrame**

7. Which of the following Swing components implement the **RootPaneContainer** interface? Select all that apply.

   a. **JFrame**

   b. **JOptionPane**

   c. **JApplet**

   d. **JPanel**

   e. **JDesktopPane**

8. What interface must a class implement if it needs to handle the event that occurs when a user clicks a button?

9. What class in the **java.awt.event** package implements all of the methods defined in the **WindowListener** interface?

10. Which method is used to obtain a reference to the content-pane container of a frame window?

11. Which of the following method definitions can be used to override the **paintComponent** method of the **JComponent** class? Select all that apply.

    a. `protected void paintComponent( ) { }`

    b. `protected boolean paintComponent( ) { return false; }`

    c. `public boolean paintComponent( ) { return false; }`

    d. `public void paintComponent( ) { }`

    e. `protected void paintComponent( ) throws Throwable { }`

12. Assuming that g is a **Graphics** object, what does the following statement do when executed? Select the best answer.

    `g.drawString( "Hello!", 100, 60 );`

    a. It writes the string "Hello!" into g in an area 100 pixels wide by 60 pixels high.

    b. It writes the string "Hello!" into g in an area 60 pixels wide by 100 pixels high.

    c. It writes the string "Hello!" into g in an area 60 pixels from the top edge of the area and 100 pixels from the left edge of the area.

    d. It writes the string "Hello!" into g in an area 100 pixels from the top edge of the area and 60 pixels from the left edge of the area.

    e. It writes the string "Hello!" into g in an area 100 pixels from the top edge of the area and 60 pixels from the right edge of the area.

13. Which of the following statements draws a horizontal line 100 pixels long into a **Graphics** object g? Select all that apply.

    a. `g.drawLine( 50, 50, 150, 50 );`

    b. `g.drawLine( 50, 50, 100 );`

    c. `g.drawLine( 100 );`

    d. `g.drawLine( 50, 50, 50, 150 );`

    e. `g.drawLine( 100, 50, 50 );`

PROGRAMMING EXERCISES

Debugging

1. Correct all the errors in the following program:

```
package questions.c6;
import javax.swing.*;
import java.awt.*;
import java.awt.event.*;
```

```
public class Debug6_1 {
    public Debug6_1( String titleText ) {
        setDefaultCloseOperation( JFrame.EXIT_ON_CLOSE );
        JLabel greeting = new JLabel( "Debug Question",
                                      JLabel.CENTER );
        getContentPane().add( greeting,
                              BorderLayout.CENTER );
        setSize( 300, 100 );
        setVisible( true );
    }
    public static void main( String[] args ) {
        new Debug6_1( "Debug Question" );
    }
}
```

2. Correct all the errors in the following program:

```
package questions.c6;
import javax.swing.*;
import java.awt.*;
import java.awt.event.*;

public class Debug6_2 extends JFrame {
    public Debug6_2( String titleText ) {
        super( titleText );
        setDefaultCloseOperation( JFrame.EXIT_ON_CLOSE );
        JLabel greeting = new JLabel( "Debug Question",
                                      JLabel.CENTER );
        getContentPane().add( greeting,
                              BorderLayout.CENTER );
    }
    public static void main( String[] args ) {
        new Debug6_2( "Debug Question" );
    }
}
```

3. Correct all the errors in the following program:

```
package questions.c6;
import javax.swing.*;
import java.awt.*;
import java.awt.event.*;

public class Debug6_3 extends JFrame {
    public Debug6_3( String titleText ) {
        super( titleText );
        setDefaultCloseOperation( JFrame.EXIT_ON_CLOSE );
        JLabel greeting = new JLabel( "Debug Question",
                                                 JLabel.CENTER );
        setSize( 300, 100 );
        setVisible( true );
    }
```

```
        public static void main( String[] args ) {
            new Debug6_3( "Debug Question" );
        }
    }
```

4. Correct all the errors in the following program so that a single button with the label Debug appears in the middle of the frame window:

```
package questions.c6;
    import javax.swing.*;
    import java.awt.*;
    import java.awt.event.*;

    public class Debug6_4 extends JFrame {
        private JButton debugButton;
        public Debug6_4( String titleText ) {
        super( titleText );
        setDefaultCloseOperation( JFrame.EXIT_ON_CLOSE );
        Container cp = getContentPane();
        cp.setLayout( new BorderLayout() );
        cp.add( debugButton, BorderLayout.CENTER );
        pack();
        setVisible( true );
    }
    public static void main( String[] args ) {
        new Debug6_4( "Debug Question" );
    }
}
```

5. Correct all the errors in the following program so that the three buttons appear within the frame in a single row:

```
package questions.c6;
import javax.swing.*;
import java.awt.*;
import java.awt.event.*;

public class Debug6_5 extends JFrame {
    private JButton black, red, green;
    public Debug6_5( String titleText ) {
        super( titleText );
        setDefaultCloseOperation( JFrame.EXIT_ON_CLOSE );
        black = new JButton( "Black" );
        red = new JButton( "Red" );
        green = new JButton( "Green" );
        Container cp = getContentPane();
        cp.add( black );
        cp.add( red );
        cp.add( green );
        pack();
        setVisible( true );
    }
```

```
public static void main( String[] args ) {
        new Debug6_5( "Debug Question" );
    }
}
```

6. Correct all the errors in the following program so that a pattern of alternating black and white squares begins with a black square in the upper-left corner of the window:

```
package questions.c13;
import javax.swing.*;
import java.awt.*;
import java.awt.event.*;
// extend the Frame class
public class Debug6_5 extends JFrame {
    public Debug6_5( String titleText ) {
        super( titleText );
        setDefaultCloseOperation( JFrame.EXIT_ON_CLOSE );
        setSize( 500, 300 );
        setVisible( true );
    }
    public void paintComponent( Graphics g ) {
        int squareSize = 30;
        Dimension d = getSize();
        g.setColor( Color.white );
        g.fillRect( 0, 0, d.width, d.height );
        g.setColor( Color.black );
        for( int y=0; y<d.height; y+=squareSize*2 ) {
            for( int x=0; x<d.width; x+=squareSize*2 ) {
                g.fillRect( x, y,
                            squareSize, squareSize );
            }
        }
    }
    public static void main( String[] args ) {
        new Debug6_5( "Debug Question" );
    }
}
```

Complete the Solution

1. Extract the file X:\Data\questions\c6\Complete6_1.java from the CD-ROM. (Here X: is the drive letter of the CD-ROM.) Complete the Complete6_1 class definition by adding a **JLabel** object with the string, "I completed the solution!"

2. Extract the file X:\Data\questions\c6\Complete6_2.java from the CD-ROM. (Here X: is the drive letter of the CD-ROM.) Complete the Complete6_2 class definition by adding a **JTextField** that can hold 40 characters in the center of the frame window.

3. Extract the file `X:\Data\questions\c6\Complete6_3.java` from the CD-ROM. (Here `X:` is the drive letter of the CD-ROM.) Complete the `Complete6_3` class definition by creating a **JPanel** object and a **JCheckBox** object. Put the check box into the center of the panel and put the panel into the North section of the frame window.

4. Extract the file `X:\Data\questions\c6\Complete6_4.java` from the CD-ROM. (Here `X:` is the drive letter of the CD-ROM.) Complete the `Complete6_4` class definition by adding code to the **actionPerformed** method that will change the label of the button to "Thanks!" when the user clicks it.

5. Extract the file `X:\Data\questions\c6\Complete6_5.java` from the CD-ROM. (Here `X:` is the drive letter of the CD-ROM.) Complete the `Complete6_5` class definition by putting a check box in the middle of the window. When the check box is selected, the text should be green; when the check box is not selected, the text should be red.

6. Extract the file `X:\Data\questions\c6\Complete6_6.java` from the CD-ROM. (Here `X:` is the drive letter of the CD-ROM.) Complete the `Complete6_6` class definition by writing a **paint** method that draws a chessboard pattern of eight rows and eight columns of black and white squares with a black outline around the entire board.

7. Extract the file `X:\Data\questions\c6\Complete6_7.java` from the CD-ROM. (Here `X:` is the drive letter of the CD-ROM.) Complete the `Complete6_7` class definition by adding a **MouseEvent** handler that responds to mouse clicks and puts their locations into either the **singleClicks** or the **doubleClicks Vector** object, depending upon whether or not they are single or double clicks. The definition provides a **paint** method that draws blue dots (for single clicks) and green dots (for double clicks) at the click location.

Discovery

1. Create a class called **SquareRoots** that implements a special purpose calculator that finds only square roots. The user interface for this calculator should have an entry field where the user enters the input number for the calculation, and a second entry field that displays the answer. Put two buttons in the window: one called Calculate that causes the square root to be calculated and displayed, and another called Cancel that ends the program.

2. Add a user interface to the **JUnzip** class described in the Discovery questions in Chapter 4. Call the new class **JUnzip2**. The user interface should display the files contained in a zip file and provide two buttons: one to unzip the file and the other to end the program. The name of the zip file is passed as a command-line argument.

COMPONENTS AND FACILITIES FOR RICH GRAPHICAL USER INTERFACES

In this chapter you will:

♦ Become familiar with the extensive library of GUI components offered by the Swing API

♦ Write code that uses the methods of the **javax.swing. JComponent** class

♦ Learn to add windows, dialog boxes, and panels to a GUI application

♦ Learn to add labels, buttons, and check boxes to a GUI application

♦ Learn to add menus, toolbars, and actions to a GUI application

♦ Learn to add sliders, spinners, progress bars, and scrollbars to a GUI application

♦ Learn to add lists and combo boxes to a GUI application

♦ Learn to add text-entry components to a GUI application

♦ Learn to add file and color choosers to a GUI application

♦ Learn to add tables and trees to a GUI application

♦ Add printing support to a GUI application using the 2D API

♦ Learn how to discover what print facilities are available to an application using the Java Print Service API

PROGRAMMING WITH THE JFC

If you are planning to write applets or applications that have graphical user interfaces (GUIs), you will be using the Java Foundation Classes (JFC) of the Java platform. The JFC consists of a set of classes that supports the programming of a GUI. This chapter builds upon the common elements for writing a GUI that were discussed in Chapter 6, such as event handling and layout management. It describes the classes that implement the concepts introduced in that chapter and demonstrates how to use them in succinct sample programs.

You do not have to use the JFC if you are programming only for console I/O, but users of applications usually demand GUI operation, and the nature of applets mandates that you program for a windowing environment. Therefore, many, if not all, of your programs that directly interact with users are likely to use the JFC.

Java 2 gives you a choice between using the AWT or Swing component classes to build your GUI, whereas prior to version 1.2 of the Java platform, the AWT was the only option. The AWT has been available since the original Java platform, although the event-handling model was radically redesigned for version 1.1 of the Java platform.

One of the advantages of the Java platform is that core classes and interfaces provide support for creating a GUI. The Abstract Windowing Toolkit (AWT), Drag and Drop, and Java 2D APIs are contained in the core package **java.awt** and related packages, as shown in Figure 7-1.

Package Name	Description
`java.awt.color`	A part of the Java 2D API that provides classes for color spaces.
`java.awt.datatransfer`	Provides classes that support data transfer between applications. For example, you can give users access to the operating system clipboard and let them perform cut-and-paste operations to and from the Clipboard.
`java.awt.dnd`	Provides interfaces and classes for supporting drag-and-drop operations for the Drag and Drop API.
`java.awt.event`	Provides classes that encapsulate the various kinds of user activities. Other classes and interfaces provide the framework within which you create customized handlers for the events.
`java.awt.font`	A part of the Java 2D API that provides enhanced support for fonts.
`java.awt.geom`	A part of the Java 2D API that provides classes for defining and performing operations on objects related to two-dimensional geometry.
`java.awt.im`	Provides classes and an interface for the input method framework used for entering characters for languages such as Japanese.
`java.awt.im.spi`	Provides interfaces that enable the development of input methods that can be used with any Java run-time environment.

Figure 7-1   Packages of the AWT

Package Name	Description
`java.awt.image`	Contains classes that support different color models and image filters for image processing. However, the **Image** class itself is in the `java.awt` package.
`java.awt.image.renderable`	A part of the Java 2D API that provides classes and interfaces for producing images that are described and have operations applied to them independent of any specific rendering of the image.
`java.awt.peer`	The classes that bridge between the AWT classes and their implementations that depend on the native operating system. Usually, you do not use the classes in this package directly. The component classes in the Swing API do not use peers and have no native code. AWT components always adopt the look and feel of the native operating system. An advantage of Swing is greater flexibility in designing the look and feel of a GUI than is possible with the AWT.
`java.awt.print`	A part of the Java 2D API that provides classes and interfaces for general printing.

Figure 7-1   Packages of the AWT (continued)

The Swing and Accessibility APIs are contained in the core package `javax.swing` and its related packages, as shown in Figure 7-2.

Package Name	Description
`javax.swing`	The base Swing package, and provider of all the Swing components.
`javax.swing.border`	Provides classes and an interface for drawing specialized borders around Swing components.
`javax.swing.colorchooser`	Contains classes and interfaces used by **JColorChooser** objects. However, the **JColorChooser** class is in the `javax.swing` package.
`javax.swing.event`	Provides for events used by Swing components.
`javax.swing.filechooser`	Contains classes and interfaces used by **JFileChooser** objects. However, the **JFileChooser** class is in the `javax.swing` package.
`javax.swing.plaf`	Provides one interface and many abstract classes that Swing uses to provide its pluggable look-and-feel capabilities.

Figure 7-2   The Swing packages

Package Name	Description
javax.swing.plaf.basic	Provides user interface objects built according to the Basic look and feel.
javax.swing.plaf.metal	Provides user interface objects built according to the cross-platform look and feel called metal.
javax.swing.plaf.multi	Provides the multiplexing look and feel used by the Accessibility API to combine auxiliary looks and feels (for example, audio, large type, and so on) with the default look and feel.
javax.swing.table	Provides classes and interfaces for dealing with the JTable component. However, the **JTable** class is in the **javax.swing** package.
javax.swing.text	Provides classes and interfaces that deal with editable and noneditable text components.
javax.swing.text.html	Provides the classes for creating HTML text editors.
javax.swing.text.html.parser	Provides the default HTML parser, along with support classes.
javax.swing.text.rtf	Provides a class for creating Rich Text Format (RTF) text editors.
javax.swing.tree	Provides classes and interfaces for dealing with the JTree component. However, the **JTree** class is in the **javax.swing** package.
javax.swing.undo	Provides support for undo/redo capabilities in an application such as a text editor.

Figure 7-2   The Swing packages (continued)

SWING API COMPONENTS

The Java platform provides two sets of classes that implement the Swing and AWT visual components. These visual components, common in GUIs, include buttons, check boxes, text areas, and windows. By using them you avoid the need to design your own classes for standard elements.

When using visual components, this chapter focuses on the components in the Swing API because their design is improved over the original AWT API visual components; the functionality of Swing visual components is more extensive; and the Swing visual components are easier to implement. And, although it may be tempting if you are doing maintenance work on older Java GUI applications, don't mix Swing and AWT visual components in the same program. AWT components will be given focus first and will obscure Swing components from view.

~~Each component includes the support required to draw itself. For example, if you cre-~~ ate an instance of the **JButton** class and add it to a container, the button appears fully rendered on the screen when the object is displayed. Components also support the framework for GUI interaction that is appropriate for the component. For example, the **JButton** class can generate events when the user clicks a **JButton** object. That is why most GUI applications and applets make heavy use of the component classes provided by the Java platform and rarely create their own custom visual components. The following sections discuss commonly used Swing component classes, beginning with the **JComponent** class.

JComponent CLASS

The **JComponent** class is the superclass of all Swing components. The **JButton** objects, **JCheckBox**, and **JTextField** that you saw in the **ThreePanels** program in Chapter 6 are all examples of **JComponent** subclasses.

The **JComponent** class is a direct subclass of the **java.awt.Container** class that, in turn, is a direct subclass of **java.awt.Component**. This inheritance hierarchy establishes two important facts for all Swing components: they are all containers, and they are all connected to the original AWT component hierarchy.

In addition to their overloaded constructors, the various subclasses of the **JComponent** class inherit several methods that establish the common behavior of all components. The following description of the **JComponent** class lists some of the most frequently used methods. In addition, for each method listed for the **JComponent** class that sets the value of a property, there is a method to retrieve the value of the property. For example, you can call **setSize** and pass a **Dimension** object to specify the exact size of a component in pixels. To find out the size of a component, call **getSize**, which returns a **Dimension** object.

Class

javax.swing.JComponent

Purpose

The **JComponent** class is the abstract superclass for all Swing components.

Methods

- **void addxxxListener(xxxListener object)**

  All components have a set of methods in which the name of each method begins with the word **add** and ends with **Listener.** Each **addxxxListener** method registers a listener for a specific type of event with the component. Use listeners to handle user-initiated events that relate to the component. Different listeners handle different

7

types of events. The *xxx* in the method name varies, depending on the type of the listener. Events and listeners were discussed in detail in Chapter 6.

■ void repaint()

void repaint(long *msec*)

void repaint(int *x*, int *y*, int *height*, int *width*)

void repaint(long *msec*, int *x*, int *y*, int *height*, int *width*)

You can call the **repaint** method to have the current component repainted. If you do not supply a parameter, the **repaint** request is sent immediately to the AWT thread. You can schedule the repainting operation by specifying that the repaint operation begin in *msec* (milliseconds). If it is not necessary to repaint the entire component, you can specify the area to be repainted.

■ void setBackground(Color *c*)

Call **setBackground** to set the background color. For the argument, you can use one of the constants defined in the class **java.awt.Color**. Several color constants are available, including **red**, **green**, **blue**, **yellow**, **black**, and **white**. Also, you can specify colors as 24-bit values in which the first eight bits are the intensity of red, the middle eight bits are the intensity of green, and the last eight bits are the intensity of blue. To do that, use **Color** objects created by passing integer values in the range zero to 255 for the red, green, and blue integer arguments to the **Color** constructor.

■ void setBorder(Border *b*)

Call **setBorder** to add a border to the component. Use a border to outline a component, add a title to a component, or create space around a component. By default, components have no borders. The simplest way to create a border is to use one of the many static methods defined in the **javax.swing.BorderFactory** class. The **BorderFactory** class defines static methods to create all the styles of borders that Swing supports.

■ void setDoubleBuffered(boolean *b*)

Call **setDoubleBuffered(true)** to let a component prepare component updates in an off-screen buffer before they are copied to the screen. Double buffering helps eliminate screen flicker. Components are enabled for double buffering by default. Specify the argument **false** to turn off double buffering.

■ void setEnabled(boolean *b*)

Call **setEnabled(true)** to enable the component to respond to user input and to generate events. Components are enabled by default. When the argument is **false**, the component does not respond to events.

■ void setFont(Font *f*)

Call **setFont** to specify the font for all textual data in the component. The argument should be an instance of the class **java.awt.Font**. When you create a **Font** object, you specify the name of the font, the style, and the point size in arguments of the constructor. The `FontSliderSpinner` program, shown in Figure 7-11 later in this chapter, demonstrates creating and modifying **Font** objects.

- **void setForeground(Color *c*)**

  Call **setForeground** to set the foreground color. Specify the argument exactly as you would specify the argument to the method **setBackground**.

- **void setPreferredSize(Dimension *d*)**

  Call **setPreferredSize** to specify the ideal size for the component. For example, the preferred size of a button is the size large enough to hold the button's label with a visually attractive border around it. A smaller size may truncate the label, and a larger size puts the label in the middle of wasted, unused space.

  The argument should be an instance of the class **java.awt.Dimension**. You can create a **Dimension** object with an **int** argument for width, followed by an **int** argument for height, or just one argument for a square shape. Layout managers use the preferred size when positioning and shaping components whenever possible.

- **void setSize(Dimension *d*)**

  Call **setSize** to set the size of a component in pixels.

- **void setToolTipText(String *s*)**

  Call **setToolTipText** to associate a string with a component. This string is displayed in a pop-up window near the component when the user's mouse pauses over the component.

- **void setVisible(boolean *b*)**

  Call **setVisible** and pass the value **true** to show the component. Pass **false** to hide it.

- **void update(Graphics *context*)**

  The **update** method calls **paint** to repaint the component. The Drawings and Drawings2D example programs in Chapter 6 demonstrate the use of this method in detail.

WINDOWS, DIALOG BOXES, AND PANELS

Generally, graphical designers do not place windows, dialog boxes, and panels in user interfaces. However, these containers are key for programmers because containers organize and, with the help of layout managers, establish the visual design of a GUI by providing the surfaces on which other components are placed.

Although all Swing components inherit from the **java.awt.Container** class, only the components **JDesktopPane**, **JInternalFrame**, **JOptionPane**, **JPanel**,

`JApplet`, `JDialog`, `JFrame`, and `JWindow` can hold other Swing components. Other Swing components are restricted to containing things such as icons and text. For example, Figure 7-6, later in the chapter, demonstrates how the `JToggleButton` class can be a container for an `ImageIcon` object.

A container can also hold other containers, because every container is a component. The ability to nest components within containers, and containers within containers, gives you the flexibility to create an enormous variety of designs for your user interface. Adding a component to a container involves calling the method **add** for the container object and passing the `JComponent` object as the argument of **add**.

Class

`java.awt.Container`

Purpose

The `Container` class provides several methods for adding and removing components or working with layouts.

Methods

- **`void add( Component `*`comp`*` )`**

- **`void add( Component `*`comp`*`, Object `*`constraint`*` )`**

  The **add** method adds the specified component to the container using default placement rules. For some layout managers, you should specify an object that constrains where the layout manager places the component. For example, if your container has a border layout, specify the area in which to put the component as a string in the second argument of the **add** method. Border layouts and other layout managers are described later in this chapter. Some overloaded **add** methods return the object reference passed as an argument to the method.

- **`Component[ ] getComponents()`**

  The **getComponents** method returns an array containing all the components within the container.

- **`LayoutManager getLayout()`**

  The **getLayout** method returns the layout manager for the container.

- **`void remove( Component `*`comp`*` )`**

  The **remove** method removes the component from the container.

- **`void setLayout( LayoutManager `*`mgr`*` )`**

  The **setLayout** method determines which layout manager controls the arrangement of components as they are added to the container.

Swing has several top-level container components that you will use as the basis for your GUI programs: **JApplet**, **JDialog**, **JFrame**, and **JWindow**. These heavyweight components extend components in the AWT API. As mentioned in Chapter 6, a heavyweight component is one that has a peer component in the underlying native windowing support of the operating system.

Unlike their AWT counterparts, top-level Swing containers have a separate container called the content pane to which you add all components. To add a component to a **JApplet**, **JDialog**, **JFrame**, or **JWindow** object, you must first call the method **getContentPane** and add the component to the returned object, as shown in the examples in this section. At first, this content pane may seem an unnecessary complication, but Swing containers use it to provide flexibility in positioning other components in layers and in controlling mouse events. All the containers need this capability, so it makes good sense to separate this capability into its own class that is distinct from the containers but available to them all.

Descriptions of the **JDialog**, **JFrame**, and **JWindow** classes as well as the details of the constructors that are available for creating objects of these classes follow.

Class

javax.swing.JDialog

Purpose

The **JDialog** class extends **java.awt.Dialog**. Typically, you use a dialog box to solicit input from the user. You can display labels and other information, provide components in which users enter data or select items from a list, and add buttons that users can click to submit or cancel their input.

By default, the layout manager for a **JDialog** object is a **BorderLayout** object.

Constructors

- **JDialog(Frame** *parent***)**

  JDialog(Frame *parent***, boolean** *modal* **)**

  JDialog(Frame *parent***, String** *title* **)**

  JDialog(Frame *parent***, String** *title***, boolean** *modal* **)**

  A **JDialog** object must have a parent window, which usually is the **JFrame** object for an application. By default, **JDialog** windows are not modal. A *modal dialog box* is one that captures and holds the focus of the application and prevents the user from doing anything else with the application until the dialog box has been dismissed. If you want to prevent the user from interacting with other windows while **JDialog** is visible, include the **boolean** argument with the value **true**. To give the **JDialog** window a title, specify it with the **String** argument.

Class

`javax.swing.JFrame`

Purpose

The **JFrame** class extends **java.awt.Frame**. A **JFrame** object is a window with borders and a title bar. It can have a menu bar also. All the sample programs in this and the previous chapter are created and displayed as **JFrame** objects. A GUI-driven application usually has at least one frame window, and the main class of the application often extends **JFrame**. Applets and applications can open additional frame windows.

By default, the layout manager for a **Frame** object is a **BorderLayout** object.

Constructors

- `JFrame()`

  `JFrame( String title )`

  If you pass a **String** object to the constructor, the content of the string appears in the title bar of the frame window.

Class

`javax.swing.JWindow`

Purpose

JWindow objects are empty windows that have no title or menu bar. Typically, Swing programmers use them as the basis for creating custom components.

By default, the layout manager for a **JWindow** object is a **BorderLayout** object.

Constructors

- `JWindow( Frame parent )`

  You usually specify the **JFrame** object for your application as the parent of a **JWindow** object. In this context, the parent is the owner of the window. When a parent window is closed, its child windows are also closed automatically. The parent-child relationship does not place any constraints on the positioning of child windows, as is the case in some windowing systems that require the placement of child windows on top of parent windows.

There are other container components that Swing programs use within the top-level containers just described. **JDesktopPane**, **JInternalFrame**, **JOptionPane**, and **JPanel** are lightweight components that extend **JComponent**.

Class

javax.swing.JDesktopPane

Purpose

The **JDesktopPane** class is a container for **JInternalFrame** objects. You can use this class to give your GUI a work area that resembles the desktop provided by a native GUI-oriented operating system.

Constructor

- **JDesktopPane( )**

  No parameters are allowed when constructing a **JDesktopPane** object. By default, a **JDesktopPane** object uses a null layout manager that requires the user to control absolute positioning.

Class

javax.swing.JInternalFrame

Purpose

The **JInternalFrame** class extends **JComponent**, but not any heavyweight AWT components. A **JInternalFrame** object does not have its own window and is almost always contained in a window within **JDesktopPane**. You can add several panels to the internal frame's window to divide the area of the window into regions, as you did in the **ThreePanels** program in Chapter 6. You can use layout managers and nested panels to create almost any arrangement of components on the screen.

Constructors

- **JInternalFrame( )**

  JInternalFrame(String *title* **)**

  JInternalFrame(String *title***, boolean** *resizable* **)**

  JInternalFrame(String *title***, boolean** *resizable***, boolean** *closable* **)**

  JInternalFrame(String *title***, boolean** *resizable***, boolean** *closable***,**
  boolean *maximizable* **)**

  JInternalFrame(String *title***, boolean** *resizable***, boolean** *closable***,**
  boolean *maximizable***, boolean** *iconifiable* **)**

  If you pass a **String** object to the constructor, the content of the string appears in the title bar of the internal frame window. The **boolean** constructor parameters set the allowable actions for the window. The default is **false** in all cases. When a frame or internal frame has its iconifiable property set to be **true** in the constructor or by using the **setIconifiable** method, the user can minimize it so that an icon, but not the whole object, is displayed on the desktop or desktop pane.

Class

javax.swing.JOptionPane

Purpose

The **JOptionPane** class provides an easy way to create and display the most common kinds of dialog boxes. It supports message, confirmation, and input dialog boxes, and combinations of dialog box types.

Constructors

- **JOptionPane( )**

  JOptionPane(Object *message* **)**

  JOptionPane(Object *message*, **int** *messageType* **)**

  JOptionPane(Object *message*, **int** *messageType*, **int** *optionType* **)**

  JOptionPane(Object *message*, **int** *messageType*, **int** *optionType*, **Icon** *icon* **)**

  JOptionPane(Object *message*, **int** *messageType*, **int** *optionType*, **Icon** *icon*, **Object[]** *options* **)**

  JOptionPane(Object *message*, **int** *messageType*, **int** *optionType*, **Icon** *icon*, **Object[]** *options*, **Object** *initialValue* **)**

  JOptionPane objects are highly configurable. The constructor builds a dialog box based on the specified message, type, options, icon, and an initially selected option.

Class

javax.swing.JPanel

Purpose

The **JPanel** class extends **JComponent** but is not a heavyweight component. A **JPanel** object does not have its own window and is almost always contained in a window. You can add several panels to a panel's window to divide the area of the window into regions, as you did in the **ThreePanels** program in Chapter 6. You can use layout managers and nested panels to create almost any arrangement of components on the screen.

Constructors

- `JPanel()`

  `JPanel( boolean isDoubleBuffered )`

  `JPanel( LayoutManager layout )`

  `JPanel( LayoutManager layout, boolean isDoubleBuffered )`

  If you do not want the default arrangement of components on a panel, specify one of the **LayoutManager** classes demonstrated in Chapter 6. It is also possible to specify whether double buffering is turned on or off. By default, a **JPanel** object uses a **FlowLayout** layout manager.

Figure 7-3 is a program that exercises the **JDesktopPane, JInternalFrame**, and **JOptionPane** classes described in the preceding discussion. A breakdown of this code follows the output. This program defines the class **DesktopAndDialog**. Because **DesktopAndDialog** is a public class, it is located in a file called **DesktopAndDialog.java**. The structure of packages mirrors the file system, so you will find this source code in the **X:\Data\examples\windows** directory on the CD-ROM. (Here **X:** is the drive letter of the CD-ROM.)

```
package examples.windows;
import javax.swing.*;
import java.awt.*;
/** An example class used to demonstrate the use of
  * the JDesktopPane, JInternalFrame, and JOptionPane
  * components
  */
public class DesktopAndDialog extends JFrame {
   private static final boolean RESIZABLE = true;
   private static final boolean CLOSABLE = true;
   private static final boolean MAXIMIZABLE = true;
   private static final boolean ICONIFIABLE = true;
   private static final boolean MODAL = false;
   /** Class constructor method
     * @param titleText Window's title bar text
     */
   public DesktopAndDialog( String titleText ) {
      super( titleText );
      setDefaultCloseOperation( JFrame.EXIT_ON_CLOSE );
      JInternalFrame ifrm = new JInternalFrame(
         "Internal Frame",
         RESIZABLE, CLOSABLE, MAXIMIZABLE, ICONIFIABLE );
```

Figure 7-3   `DesktopAndDialog`: an example using the **JDesktopPane**, **JInternalFrame**, and **JOptionPane** components

```
        ifrm.setPreferredSize( new Dimension( 375, 300 ) );
        ifrm.setVisible( true );
        JDesktopPane dt = new JDesktopPane();
        dt.setLayout( new FlowLayout() );
        dt.add( ifrm );
        getContentPane().add( dt, BorderLayout.CENTER );
        setSize( 500, 400 );
        setVisible( true );
        JOptionPane.showMessageDialog(
            ifrm, "This is a JOptionPane" );
    }
    /** The test method for the class
     * @param args not used
     */
    public static void main( String[] args ) {
        new DesktopAndDialog(
            "Example Desktop with Dialog" );
    }
}
```

Figure 7-3   `DesktopAndDialog`: an example using the **`JDesktopPane`**,
    `JInternalFrame`, and **`JOptionPane`** components (continued)

Allowing for differences in operating systems, the output should be similar to Figure 7-4. You may notice that the internal frame does not look like a native frame on your platform. That is because, by default, Swing uses a cross-platform look and feel known as the Metal look and feel for its components. The Metal look and feel was designed to be distinctive from existing looks and feels provided by Windows, MacOS, and Motif. Its name comes from the fact that it is reminiscent of embossing on sheets of metal.

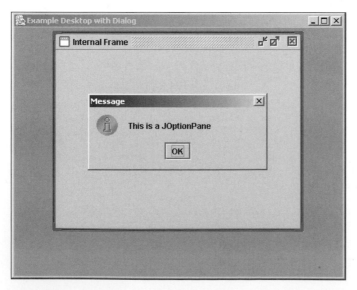

Figure 7-4   Output of the `DesktopAndDialog` class

The class encapsulating the drawing program is called DesktopAndDialog. The constructor, as usual, begins by passing the title for the **JFrame** object to the constructor of the **JFrame** superclass.

```
public DesktopAndDialog( String titleText ) {
    super( titleText );
```

The close operation is set so that users exit the program when they close the window.

```
setDefaultCloseOperation( JFrame.EXIT_ON_CLOSE );
```

The next two statements create a **JInternalFrame** object that can be resized, closed, maximized, and iconified. They also set the preferred size of the object and specify that it should be made visible.

```
JInternalFrame ifrm = new JInternalFrame(
    "Internal Frame",
    RESIZABLE, CLOSABLE, MAXIMIZABLE, ICONIFIABLE );
ifrm.setPreferredSize( new Dimension( 375, 300 ) );
ifrm.setVisible( true );
```

A **JDesktopPane** object is needed to contain the internal frame, and the following lines create the pane and give it a flow layout manager before adding the internal frame to the pane:

```
JDesktopPane dt = new JDesktopPane();
dt.setLayout( new FlowLayout() );
dt.add( ifrm );
```

The desktop pane is then added to the center of the **JFrame** object's content pane that is retrieved using the method **getContentPane**.

```
getContentPane().add( dt, BorderLayout.CENTER );
```

The next step is to set the size of the **JFrame** and make it visible.

```
setSize( 500, 400 );
setVisible( true );
```

The last statement of the constructor uses a static method of the **JOptionPane** class to display a message dialog box. This dialog box is created using the internal frame object as its parent. The text of the message is also provided. You can use this static method to create a **JOptionPane** object that contains a **JDialog** object and display it with one method call.

```
JOptionPane.showMessageDialog(
    ifrm, "This is a JOptionPane" );
```

The **main** method simply creates a `DesktopAndDialog` object and provides it with the text for the **JFrame** object's title bar.

```
public static void main( String[] args ) {
    new DesktopAndDialog(
        "Example Desktop with Dialog" );
}
```

LABELS, BUTTONS, AND CHECK BOXES

Labels, buttons, and check boxes are fundamental parts of a GUI. Labels add text that typically explains the purpose of the other elements of a user interface. They can also display a message, such as a status line, to the user. Buttons and check boxes provide the opportunity to make selections and trigger actions.

The **JLabel** class inherits directly from **JComponent**, but all the button classes extend the class **AbstractButton**. The **AbstractButton** class extends **JComponent** and provides the implementation of behavior that is common to all button classes. Figure 7-5 shows **AbstractButton** and its button subclasses.

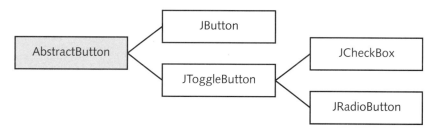

Figure 7-5 **AbstractButton** and its subclasses

Details about each of the Swing label, button, and check box classes are provided next. Lists of all the constructors that are available for creating objects of these classes are provided also.

Class

`javax.swing.JLabel`

Purpose

A **JLabel** object is a single line of read-only text. A common use of **JLabel** objects is to position descriptive text above or beside other components.

Constructors

■ `JLabel()`

 `JLabel( Icon icon )`

```
JLabel( String text )

JLabel( String text, int horizontalAlignment )

JLabel( String text, Icon icon, int horizontalAlignment )
```

The constructor without any arguments creates a horizontally left–justified, empty **JLabel** object. Use the **String** argument to specify the contents of the **JLabel** object and the **Icon** argument to add a graphic picture. The alignment is an integer, and you can specify any one of the following fields: **JLabel.LEFT**, **JLabel.CENTER**, **JLabel.RIGHT**, **JLabel.LEADING**, or **JLabel.TRAILING**. Use the methods **setHorizontalTextPosition** and **setVerticalTextPosition** to specify the position of the text relative to the graphic.

Class

javax.swing.JButton

Purpose

A **JButton** object is a push button with a text label.

Constructors

- **JButton()**

  ```
  JButton( Icon icon )

  JButton( String label )

  JButton( String label, Icon icon )
  ```

  When you create a button, you can specify the text that appears on the button as a **String** argument of the constructor. It is also possible to add a graphic to the button by specifying an **Icon** object. Use the methods **setHorizontalTextPosition** and **setVerticalTextPosition** to specify the position of the button label relative to the graphic.

Class

javax.swing.JToggleButton

Purpose

A **JToggleButton** object is a push button with a text label. Clicking the button causes the button to alternate between the pressed and released states.

Constructors

- **JToggleButton()**

  ```
  JToggleButton( Icon icon )
  ```

```
JToggleButton( String label )

JToggleButton( String label, Icon icon )

JToggleButton( Icon icon, boolean pressed )

JToggleButton( String label, boolean pressed )

JToggleButton( String label, Icon icon, boolean pressed )
```

When you create a button, you can specify the text that appears on the button as a **String** argument of the constructor. Use the **boolean** parameter to specify whether the button is initially pressed or released. Also, you can add a graphic to the button by specifying an **Icon** object. Use the methods **setHorizontalTextPosition** and **setVerticalTextPosition** to specify the position of the button label relative to the graphic. You also can create groups of toggle buttons. A **ButtonGroup** object may contain a set of **JToggleButton** objects and permit the user to select only one button in the group at a time. To combine a **JToggleButton** object with others in a group, construct a **ButtonGroup** object and add the toggle button to the group. Toggle buttons in a **ButtonGroup** object are mutually exclusive, which means that when the user selects one, all others in the same group are deselected automatically.

Class

javax.swing.JCheckBox

Purpose

A **JCheckBox** object is a check box with a text label.

Constructors

- **JCheckBox()**

  ```
  JCheckBox( Icon icon )

  JCheckBox( String label )

  JCheckBox( String label, Icon icon )

  JCheckBox( Icon icon, boolean selected )

  JCheckBox( String label, boolean selected )

  JCheckBox( String label, Icon icon, boolean selected )
  ```

  The **String** argument contains the text that labels the check box. The **boolean** parameter indicates whether the check box is on or off; it is set to off, or **false**, by default. You can also add a graphic to the check box by specifying an **Icon** object, or you can create groups of check boxes. A **ButtonGroup** object may contain a set of **JCheckBox** objects from which the user can check only one box in the group at a time. To combine **JCheckBox** with others in a group, construct a

ButtonGroup object are mutually exclusive, which means that when the user selects one, all others in the same group are deselected automatically.

Class

`javax.swing.JRadioButton`

Purpose

A **JRadioButton** object is a radio button with a text label.

Constructors

- `JRadioButton()`

  `JRadioButton( Icon icon )`

  `JRadioButton( String label )`

  `JRadioButton( String label, Icon icon )`

  `JRadioButton( Icon icon, boolean selected )`

  `JRadioButton( String label, boolean selected )`

  `JRadioButton( String label, Icon icon, boolean selected )`

  The **String** argument contains the text that labels the radio button. The **boolean** parameter indicates whether the radio button is on or off; it is set to off, or **false**, by default. It is also possible to add a graphic to the button by specifying an **Icon** object. You can create groups of radio buttons. A **ButtonGroup** object may contain a set of **JRadioButton** objects from which the user can select only one button in the group at a time. To combine a **JRadioButton** object with others in a group, construct a **ButtonGroup** object and add the button to the group. Radio buttons in a **ButtonGroup** object are mutually exclusive, which means that when the user selects one, all others in the same group are deselected automatically.

Class

`javax.swing.ButtonGroup`

Purpose

A **ButtonGroup** object is a group of mutually exclusive buttons. A **ButtonGroup** object may contain a set of button objects from which the user can check only one box in the group at a time. You can mix **JToggleButton**, **JRadioButton**, and **JCheckBox** objects in one group, but groups usually contain sets of radio buttons. Buttons in a **ButtonGroup** are mutually exclusive, which means that when the user selects one, all others in the same group are deselected automatically.

Constructor

■ **ButtonGroup( )**

Only the default constructor is available. Use the **add** method to add a button to the group.

Class

javax.swing.ImageIcon

Purpose

The **ImageIcon** class defines objects representing small fixed-size pictures that are typically used to decorate components. This class implements the **Icon** interface.

Constructors

■ **ImageIcon( )**

ImageIcon(byte[] *imageData* **)**

ImageIcon(byte[] *imageData***, String** *description* **)**

ImageIcon(Image *image* **)**

ImageIcon(Image *image***, String** *description* **)**

ImageIcon(String *filename* **)**

ImageIcon(String *filename***, String** *description* **)**

ImageIcon(URL *location* **)**

ImageIcon(URL *location***, String** *description* **)**

You can build **ImageIcon** objects from binary data by supplying an array of bytes from an existing **Image** object, from an image stored in a file (typically, in **.gif** format), or from a URL. Also, you can supply a **String** object that contains a description of the image to the constructor.

Figure 7-6 is a program that exercises many of the classes described previously. A breakdown of this code follows the output. This program defines the class **ButtonsAndBoxes** to demonstrate the use of radio buttons, check boxes, and toggle buttons. Each type of button has its own panel, and the panels have titled borders to indicate the type of button. The program uses colorful icons to show the flexibility of these classes and to make the GUI more appealing. Before you run this program, copy all the **.gif** files from the **X:\Data\examples\windows** directory into the current directory. Alternatively, you could run the program with **X:\Data\examples\windows** as the current directory. (Here **X:** is the drive letter of the CD-ROM.) If the JVM cannot find the **.gif** files, the program runs, but the icons do not display.

```
package examples.windows;
import javax.swing.*;
import java.awt.*;
import java.util.Enumeration;
/** An example class used to demonstrate the use of
  * the JToggleButton, JCheckBox, and JRadioButton
  * components
  */
public class ButtonsAndBoxes extends JFrame {
    /** Class constructor method
      * @param titleText Window's title bar text
      */
    public ButtonsAndBoxes( String titleText ) {
        super( titleText );
        setDefaultCloseOperation( JFrame.EXIT_ON_CLOSE );
        JPanel left = new JPanel( new GridLayout( 0, 1 ) );
        left.setBorder(
            BorderFactory.createTitledBorder(
                "Button group" ) );
        ButtonGroup bg = new ButtonGroup();
        bg.add( new JRadioButton( "ribeye" ) );
        bg.add( new JRadioButton( "filet mignon" ) );
        bg.add( new JRadioButton( "T-bone" ) );
        Enumeration e = bg.getElements();
        while( e.hasMoreElements() ) {
            JRadioButton rb = (JRadioButton) e.nextElement();
            rb.setIcon( new ImageIcon( "bulb1.gif" ) );
            rb.setSelectedIcon(
                new ImageIcon( "bulb2.gif" ) );
            left.add( rb );
        }
        JPanel right = new JPanel( new GridLayout( 0, 1 ) );
        right.setBorder(
            BorderFactory.createTitledBorder(
                "Independent check boxes" ) );
        right.add( new JCheckBox( "cake" ) );
        right.add( new JCheckBox( "pie" ) );
        right.add( new JCheckBox( "soft drink" ) );
        right.add( new JCheckBox( "fries" ) );
        JPanel bottom = new JPanel();
        bottom.setBorder(
            BorderFactory.createTitledBorder(
                "Toggle buttons" ) );
        bottom.add( new JToggleButton(
            "burger", new ImageIcon( "burger.gif" ) ) );
        bottom.add( new JToggleButton(
            "hot dog", new ImageIcon( "hotdog.gif" ) ) );
        bottom.add( new JToggleButton(
            "pizza", new ImageIcon( "pizza.gif" ) ) );
```

Figure 7-6   ButtonsAndBoxes: an example using the **JToggleButton**, **JCheckBox**, and **JRadioButton** components

```
            Container cp = getContentPane();
            cp.setLayout( new GridBagLayout() );
            GridBagConstraints c = new GridBagConstraints();
            c.fill = GridBagConstraints.BOTH;
            c.weightx = 1.0;
            c.weighty = 1.0;
            cp.add( left, c );
            c.gridwidth = GridBagConstraints.REMAINDER;
            cp.add( right, c );
            cp.add( bottom, c );
            pack();
            setVisible( true );
        }
        /** The test method for the class
         * @param args not used
         */
        public static void main( String[] args ) {
            new ButtonsAndBoxes(
                "Example Buttons and Check Boxes" );
        }
    }
```

Figure 7-6   `ButtonsAndBoxes`: an example using the **`JToggleButton`**,
`JCheckBox`, and `JRadioButton` components (continued)

When you run this program, you will see that the `ButtonsAndBoxes` GUI could be the menu of a fast-food outlet. The radio buttons display as labeled images instead of the default labeled circle, and the buttons have icons showing pictures of menu items. Allowing for differences in operating systems, the output should be similar to Figure 7-7.

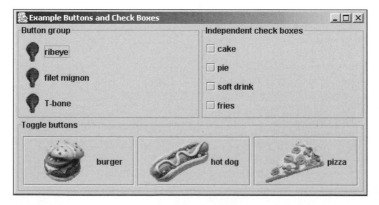

Figure 7-7   Output of the `ButtonsAndBoxes` class

The class encapsulating the menu-drawing program is called `ButtonsAndBoxes`. The structure of this example is similar to the preceding examples in this chapter; so only those program statements that pertain to the classes presented in this section are discussed in the code breakdown.

First, a panel is created with a one-column grid layout and a border titled Button group. This panel will be put in the upper-left part of the frame window.

```
JPanel left = new JPanel( new GridLayout( 0, 1 ) );
left.setBorder(
   BorderFactory.createTitledBorder(
      "Button group" ) );
```

A button group is created to hold a mutually exclusive set of buttons. In this case, three radio buttons are created and added to the group. These buttons are initially created with only a text label.

```
ButtonGroup bg = new ButtonGroup();
bg.add( new JRadioButton( "ribeye" ) );
bg.add( new JRadioButton( "filet mignon" ) );
bg.add( new JRadioButton( "T-bone" ) );
```

The radio buttons must then be added to the panel. A **while** loop uses a **java.util.Enumeration** object to iterate through the list of radio buttons in the group and place each one into the panel. At the same time, each of the radio buttons is assigned two images: one to be used when the button is selected and the other when the button is not selected. The images are pictures of lightbulbs. A lighted bulb indicates the selected button.

```
Enumeration e = bg.getElements();
while( e.hasMoreElements() ) {
   JRadioButton rb = (JRadioButton) e.nextElement();
   rb.setIcon( new ImageIcon( "bulb1.gif" ) );
   rb.setSelectedIcon(
      new ImageIcon( "bulb2.gif" ) );
   left.add( rb );
}
```

Another panel with a single-column grid layout is created to hold the list of check boxes that appear in the upper-right part of the frame window. This panel is also given a border titled Independent check boxes because these boxes are not in a group.

```
JPanel right = new JPanel( new GridLayout( 0, 1 ) );
right.setBorder(
   BorderFactory.createTitledBorder(
      "Independent check boxes" ) );
```

Four check boxes are created and added to the panel. Because they are not part of a button group, any number of the check boxes may be selected at the same time. These check boxes do not have associated images.

```
right.add( new JCheckBox( "cake" ) );
right.add( new JCheckBox( "pie" ) );
right.add( new JCheckBox( "soft drink" ) );
right.add( new JCheckBox( "fries" ) );
```

7

The panel to be used at the bottom of the window is created with the panel's default flow layout and is given a border titled `Toggle buttons`. Three toggle buttons are added to the panel, each with a text description and a graphic image.

```
JPanel bottom = new JPanel();
bottom.setBorder(
   BorderFactory.createTitledBorder(
      "Toggle buttons" ) );
bottom.add( new JToggleButton(
   "burger", new ImageIcon( "burger.gif" ) ) );
bottom.add( new JToggleButton(
   "hot dog", new ImageIcon( "hotdog.gif" ) ) );
bottom.add( new JToggleButton(
   "pizza", new ImageIcon( "pizza.gif" ) ) );
```

After the panels are created and filled, they must be added to the frame window's content pane. A grid-bag layout is used for the frame window and a constraints object is created to hold positioning information.

```
Container cp = getContentPane();
cp.setLayout( new GridBagLayout() );
GridBagConstraints c = new GridBagConstraints();
```

The default constraints are accepted for use by the method with a few exceptions. First, the fill attribute is set so that the components will stretch to fill the frame in both directions. The weighting of 1.0 for both the x and y directions that is used by all components causes all components to share equally when the frame is stretched or shrunk, because the extra horizontal space is distributed to each column in proportion to its weight and extra vertical space is distributed to each row in proportion to its weight.

```
c.fill = GridBagConstraints.BOTH;
c.weightx = 1.0;
c.weighty = 1.0;
```

The upper-left panel is added first. Then, the grid width constraint is set so that the next two components added stretch to fill the two rows of the layout.

```
cp.add( left, c );
c.gridwidth = GridBagConstraints.REMAINDER;
cp.add( right, c );
cp.add( bottom, c );
```

MENUS, TOOLBARS, AND ACTIONS

Even before GUIs became commonplace in application software, applications had menu bars and menu items for organizing the functions available within the application. As GUIs proliferated and became more sophisticated, another element for organizing functions, the toolbar, also became common. So it should come as no surprise that the Swing API would have components for implementing menu systems and toolbars.

tem, Swing provides a mechanism, the **Action** interface, for defining objects that can be put into toolbars and menus. These action objects provide a single point of control and avoid duplication.

Within the Swing component hierarchy, menus and menu items are subclasses of the **AbstractButton** class. Figure 7-8 shows how the menu classes fit within this hierarchy.

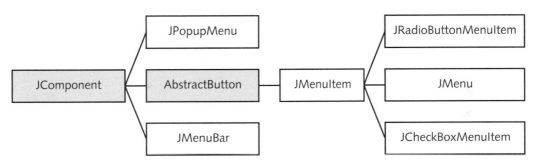

Figure 7-8   Menu classes in `javax.swing`

You can create instances of all the classes in the following syntax discussions and combine them into menus by using these guidelines:

- To create a main menu for an application, use a **JMenuBar** object. Use the **add** method to add menus to the menu bar and the **setJMenuBar** method to add the menu bar to its window.

- For a menu that is associated with a component and pops up when the user clicks a component, create a **JPopupMenu** object.

- For every item in a menu, use an instance of **JMenuItem** or a subclass of **JMenuItem**.

- To nest menus, use **JMenu** objects. A **JMenu** object is a **JMenuItem** object that is itself a menu.

- For a menu item that is also a check box, use a **JCheckBoxMenuItem** object.

- For a menu item that is also a radio button, use a **JRadioButtonMenuItem** object.

Class

`javax.swing.JMenuBar`

Purpose

JMenuBar objects encapsulate the sort of menu bars you often see directly under the title of the frame window for an application. Items in the menu are arranged side by side starting on the left. Often each item is itself a pull-down menu.

Constructor

- **JMenuBar( )**

  A **JMenuBar** object can be set for the top-level containers **JApplet**, **JDialog**, **JFrame**, or **JInternalFrame**. Use the method **setJMenuBar** to associate a **JMenuBar** object with one of these top-level containers.

Class

javax.swing.JMenuItem

Purpose

JMenuItem objects encapsulate standard menu items that do not take the form of a check box or a radio button.

Constructors

- **JMenuItem( )**

  JMenuItem(Icon *icon* **)**

  JMenuItem(String *label* **)**

  JMenuItem(String *label***, Icon** *icon* **)**

  JMenuItem(String *label***, int** *mnemonic* **)**

  Usually, you give every item a label, an icon, or both so users can identify the menu item. You pass the label to the constructor as a string and the icon as an **Icon** object. A mnemonic character can be specified also. Use the method **setMnemonic** to add or change the mnemonic character after constructing the object. The mnemonic character is underlined when the menu item is displayed, and then the user can type that key as an alternative to clicking the item. If you want to set up an accelerator key (such as Ctrl+S for save) that is available regardless of whether the menu item is visible, use the method **setAccelerator** and specify a **java.awt.Keystroke** object as input.

Class

javax.swing.JMenu

Purpose

A **JMenu** object is a **JMenuItem** object that is itself a pull-down menu from a **JMenuBar** object.

Constructors

- **JMenu( )**

  JMenu(String *label* **)**

```
JMenu( String label, boolean tearoff )
```

The **String** argument is the label of the **JMenu** object in the **JMenuBar** object or other **JMenu** object of which this object is a submenu. By default, **JMenu** objects disappear when the user releases the mouse button. If your native operating system supports tear-off menus—pull-down menus that can be detached from the menu bar and dragged to another position for convenient access—you can create a tear-off menu by setting the **boolean** argument to **true**.

Class

javax.swing.JPopupMenu

Purpose

A **JPopupMenu** object is a menu that is not tied to the menu bar and can appear at a dynamically determined position within a component.

Constructors

- **JPopupMenu()**

  JPopupMenu(String name)

  When you create a **JPopupMenu** object, you can give it a specific name to be used as a title by supplying a **String** argument to the constructor. Associate a popup menu with a component by calling the following method:

  Component.add(JPopupMenu popup)

  The **add** method of the **Component** class adds the specified **JPopupMenu** object to the component.

Class

javax.swing.JCheckBoxMenuItem

Purpose

A **JCheckBoxMenuItem** object is a **JMenuItem** object that includes a check box.

Constructors

- **JCheckBoxMenuItem()**

  JCheckBoxMenuItem(Icon icon)

  JCheckBoxMenuItem(String label)

  JCheckBoxMenuItem(String label, Icon icon)

  JCheckBoxMenuItem(String label, boolean selected)

  JCheckBoxMenuItem(String label, Icon icon, boolean selected)

When you create a **JCheckBoxMenuItem** object, you can optionally specify a label, a graphic, or both to appear beside the check box. The **boolean** argument indicates whether the check box is checked initially. Include this argument with the value **true** to override the default state, in which the check box is not checked.

Class

`javax.swing.JRadioButtonMenuItem`

Purpose

A **JRadioButtonMenuItem** object is a **JMenuItem** object that includes a radio button.

Constructors

- JRadioButtonMenuItem( )

  JRadioButtonMenuItem(Icon *icon*)

  JRadioButtonMenuItem(Icon *icon*, boolean *selected*)

  JRadioButtonMenuItem(String *label*)

  JRadioButtonMenuItem(String *label*, Icon *icon*)

  JRadioButtonMenuItem(String *label*, boolean *selected*)

  JRadioButtonMenuItem(String *label*, Icon *icon*, boolean *selected*)

  When you create a **JRadioButtonMenuItem** object, you can optionally specify a label, a graphic, or both to appear beside the check box. The **boolean** argument indicates whether the check box is initially checked. Include this argument with the value **true** to override the default state, in which the check box is not checked.

Class

`javax.swing.JToolBar`

Purpose

JToolBar objects encapsulate the list of buttons you often see directly under the title or the menu bar for an application. By default, items in the toolbar are arranged side by side starting on the left.

Constructors

- JToolBar( )

- JToolBar(int *orientation*)

  When a **JToolBar** object is created, specifying its orientation is optional. The two possible values are **JToolBar.HORIZONTAL** and **JToolBar.VERTICAL**. The default orientation is horizontal.

Class

javax.swing.AbstractAction

Purpose

The **AbstractAction** class implements the **Action** interface and provides default implementations of all methods except the **actionPerformed** method. Subclassing **AbstractAction** greatly simplifies the job of defining classes that implement the **Action** interface.

Constructors

- **AbstractAction( )**

  AbstractAction(String *name* **)**

  AbstractAction(String *name*, **Icon** *icon* **)**

  AbstractAction is an abstract class so it is not possible to construct instances of this class. Instead, you are expected to create subclasses of this class. When you construct a subclass of **AbstractAction**, you can call the superclass constructor and optionally specify the name of the action, an icon for the action, or both.

Figure 7-9 is a program that exercises many of the classes described previously. A breakdown of this code follows the output. This program defines the class **MenusToolbar** and five inner classes that extend **AbstractAction** to represent actions for creating and saving files, as well as the clipboard operations of cut, copy, and paste. The constructor creates instances of each of these **AbstractAction** subclasses and puts each object into a toolbar and a menu. Before you run this program, copy all the **.gif** files from the **X:\Data\examples\windows** directory into the current directory. Alternatively, you could run the program with **X:\Data\examples\windows** as the current directory. (Here **X:** is the drive letter of the CD-ROM.) If the JVM cannot find the **.gif** files, the program runs, but the icons do not display.

```
package examples.windows;
import javax.swing.*;
import java.awt.*;
import java.awt.event.*;
/** An example class used to demonstrate the use of
  * menus and toolbars
  */
public class MenusToolbar extends JFrame {
    private JLabel actionInfo
        = new JLabel( "Action information", JLabel.CENTER );
```

Figure 7-9   **MenusToolbar:** an example using menus and toolbars

```
    /** Class constructor method
     * @param titleText Window's title bar text
     */
    public MenusToolbar( String titleText ) {
        super( titleText );
        setDefaultCloseOperation( JFrame.EXIT_ON_CLOSE );
        JToolBar tb = new JToolBar();
        JMenu file = new JMenu( "File" );
        JMenu edit = new JMenu( "Edit" );
        JMenuBar mb = new JMenuBar();
        mb.add( file );
        mb.add( edit );
        NewAction na = new NewAction();
        file.add( na ).setMnemonic( 'N' );
        tb.add( na );
        SaveAction sa = new SaveAction();
        KeyStroke ks
            = KeyStroke.getKeyStroke( KeyEvent.VK_S,
                                      Event.CTRL_MASK );
        file.add( sa ).setAccelerator( ks );
        tb.add( sa );
        tb.addSeparator();
        CutAction cta = new CutAction();
        edit.add( cta );
        tb.add( cta );
        CopyAction cpa = new CopyAction();
        edit.add( cpa );
        tb.add( cpa );
        PasteAction pa = new PasteAction();
        edit.add( pa );
        tb.add( pa );
        setJMenuBar( mb );
        Container cp = getContentPane();
        cp.add( tb, BorderLayout.NORTH );
        cp.add( actionInfo, BorderLayout.CENTER );
        setSize( 350, 200 );
        setVisible( true );
    }
    class NewAction extends AbstractAction {
        public NewAction() {
            super( "new", new ImageIcon( "new.gif" ) );
        }
        public void actionPerformed( ActionEvent e ) {
            actionInfo.setText( "new selected" );
        }
    }
    class SaveAction extends AbstractAction {
        public SaveAction() {
            super( "save", new ImageIcon( "save.gif" ) );
        }
```

Figure 7-9   MenusToolbar: an example using menus and toolbars (continued)

```
         public void actionPerformed( ActionEvent e ) {
            actionInfo.setText( "save selected" );
         }
      }
      class CutAction extends AbstractAction {
         public CutAction() {
            super( "cut", new ImageIcon( "cut.gif" ) );
         }
         public void actionPerformed( ActionEvent e ) {
            actionInfo.setText( "cut selected" );
         }
      }
      class CopyAction extends AbstractAction {
         public CopyAction() {
            super( "copy", new ImageIcon( "copy.gif" ) );
         }
         public void actionPerformed( ActionEvent e ) {
            actionInfo.setText( "copy selected" );
         }
      }
      class PasteAction extends AbstractAction {
         public PasteAction() {
            super( "paste", new ImageIcon( "paste.gif" ) );
         }
         public void actionPerformed( ActionEvent e ) {
            actionInfo.setText( "paste selected" );
         }
      }
      /** The test method for the class
        * @param args not used
        */
      public static void main( String[] args ) {
         new MenusToolbar( "Example Menus and Toolbar" );
      }
   }
```

Figure 7-9   `MenusToolbar:` an example using menus and toolbars (continued)

Allowing for differences in operating systems, the output should be similar to Figure 7–10.

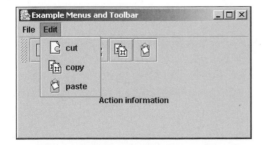

Figure 7-10   Output of the `MenusToolbar` class

The class encapsulating the drawing program is called `MenusToolbar`. The structure of this example is similar to that in the preceding examples, so only those program statements that pertain to the classes presented in this section are discussed in the code breakdown.

Consider the following code. To demonstrate that an action has been invoked without going to all the trouble of actually implementing the action, a label object called `actionInfo` is created. It appears in the center of the frame window and reports which menu item or toolbar button was last selected. This is done to keep the example simple and focused on the implementations of the menus and toolbars without cluttering it up with a lot of additional code.

```
private JLabel actionInfo
    = new JLabel( "Action information", JLabel.CENTER );
```

This example uses a toolbar, so, with the following code, a toolbar object is created with the default horizontal orientation:

```
JToolBar tb = new JToolBar();
```

Two menus for file-related and edit-related actions are created. Then a menu bar object is created, and the menus are added to the menu bar.

```
JMenu file = new JMenu( "File" );
JMenu edit = new JMenu( "Edit" );
JMenuBar mb = new JMenuBar();
mb.add( file );
mb.add( edit );
```

Then, an instance of the `NewAction` class is created and added to the File menu and the toolbar. This is possible because the `NewAction` class extends **AbstractAction**. The **add** method for the menu returns a **JMenuItem** object that is used to set the mnemonic character for the menu item. Similarly, the toolbar's **add** method returns a **JButton** object, but it is not used.

```
NewAction na = new NewAction();
file.add( na ).setMnemonic( 'N' );
tb.add( na );
```

Consider the following code. The `SaveAction` class also extends **AbstractAction**, so the `SaveAction` object also can be added to both the menu bar and the toolbar. For the save action, an accelerator key is set to be Ctrl+S. The difference between an accelerator key and a mnemonic is that an accelerator key is always active, even if the menu is not visible. Mnemonic keys are active only when the menu is displayed. The **getKeyStroke** method is a static method of the **KeyStroke** class that returns a **KeyStroke** object given a base key and any modifying keys with which it must be

argument is a key modifier specifying that the control key must be pressed also.

```
SaveAction sa = new SaveAction();
KeyStroke ks
   = KeyStroke.getKeyStroke( KeyEvent.VK_S,
                                Event.CTRL_MASK );
file.add( sa ).setAccelerator( ks );
tb.add( sa );
```

To separate the file-related actions from the edit-related actions on the toolbar, a separator is added to the toolbar between the Save and Cut buttons.

```
tb.addSeparator();
```

Then, an instance of the `CutAction` class is created and added to the Edit menu and the toolbar. Similarly, instances of `CopyAction` and `PasteAction` also are added in both places.

```
CutAction cta = new CutAction();
edit.add( cta );
tb.add( cta );
```

When the menu bar is complete, it is added to the frame window.

```
setJMenuBar( mb );
```

Toolbars have no special method for adding them to a container. Typically, you add them to the **NORTH** section of the container's border layout, as the following code shows:

```
Container cp = getContentPane();
cp.add( tb, BorderLayout.NORTH );
```

All the classes that extend **AbstractAction** take the same form. Each defines a default constructor that passes its text and icon to its superclass. Also, each must define the **actionPerformed** method that will be invoked when the toolbar button is clicked or the menu item is selected. Only the `NewAction` class is shown here. The `SaveAction`, `CutAction`, `CopyAction`, and `PasteAction` classes are similar to `NewAction`.

```
class NewAction extends AbstractAction {
   public NewAction() {
      super( "new", new ImageIcon( "new.gif" ) );
   }
   public void actionPerformed( ActionEvent e ) {
      actionInfo.setText( "new selected" );
   }
}
```

Sliders, Spinners, Progress Bars, and Scrollbars

Most of the GUI components discussed in the preceding sections, such as buttons and menu items, are useful for selecting among a fixed set of choices that are few in number. Usually, a different approach is more appropriate for selecting or displaying a value within a range of values, especially if the number of selections between the minimum and maximum values is very large. Swing provides four controls—**JProgressBar**, **JScrollBar**, **JSlider**, and **JSpinner**—that allow users to select or display a value within a bounded range. Figure 7-12 shows a **JSlider** control and a **JSpinner** control being used to adjust the font size of a label. The **JScrollPane** control uses **JScrollBar** controls to specify the visible portion of a viewport. Figure 7-14 shows a **JScrollPane** control.

Details about each of these classes are provided next. Lists of all the constructors that are available for creating objects of these classes are provided also.

The **JSpinner** control was added in version 1.4 of the Java platform. Before it was available, programmers would use either a **JComboBox** control (for list selection) or a **JSlider** control (for numeric selection), but neither of these alternatives is as compact as **JSpinner**.

Class

javax.swing.JProgressBar

Purpose

Use a **JProgressBar** object to display a value within a bounded range. Most commonly, programs use **JProgressBar** objects to indicate the progress (for example, percent completed) of a long-running operation. For situations in which the amount of work cannot be determined, **JProgressBar** can be put into indeterminate mode using the method **setIndeterminate**. In this mode, the control uses an animation to indicate that work is being done without being specific about how much work remains to be done. If, at some point, the amount of work remaining can be determined, the control can then switch back to determinate mode.

The ability to switch **JProgressBar** into and out of indeterminate mode was added in version 1.4 of the Java platform.

Constructors

- **JProgressBar()**

  JProgressBar(BoundedRangeModel *brm* **)**

~~JProgressBar(int orientation)~~

```
JProgressBar( int min, int max )

JProgressBar( int min, int max, int value )

JProgressBar( int orientation, int min, int max, int value )
```

By default, a slider is created with a vertical orientation, a minimum value of zero, a maximum value of 100, and an initial value in the middle of the range at 50. If you choose to specify the orientation, supply either **JProgressBar.HORIZONTAL** or **JProgressBar.VERTICAL**.

Class

javax.swing.JScrollBar

Purpose

Use a **JScrollBar** object to control the visible contents of a component. This component is not usually used on its own, but is used indirectly as part of a **JScrollPane** component.

Constructors

- **JScrollBar()**

```
JScrollBar( int orientation )

JScrollBar( int orientation, int value, int extent,
            int min, int max )
```

By default, a scrollbar is created with a vertical orientation, an initial value of zero, an extent of 10, a minimum value of zero, and a maximum value of 100. If you choose to specify the orientation, its value should be **JScrollBar.HORIZONTAL** or **JScrollBar.VERTICAL**. The initial position of the sliding knob is on the top or left. The extent is a measure of how much of the component is visible when the knob is in any particular position.

Class

javax.swing.JScrollPane

Purpose

Use a **JScrollPane** object to display a component with contents that are likely to exceed the available visible area. The **JScrollPane** class adds scrollbars automatically to control scrolling operations. A common use of this component is to contain **JTextArea** objects and **JList** objects, because these classes do not provide scrollbars.

Constructors

- JScrollPane()

  JScrollPane(Component *view*)

  JScrollPane(int *vsbPolicy*, int *hsbPolicy*)

  JScrollPane(Component *view*, int *vsbPolicy*, int *hsbPolicy*)

  By default, scrollbars are included as needed so the user can view the entire component by scrolling. You also can specify an integer representing the horizontal and vertical scrollbar display policies. The *hsbPolicy* value should be one of the following:

  ```
  JScrollPane.HORIZONTAL_SCROLLBAR_ALWAYS
  JScrollPane.HORIZONTAL_SCROLLBAR_AS_NEEDED
  JScrollPane.HORIZONTAL_SCROLLBAR_NEVER
  ```

  The vsbPolicy value should be one of the following:

  ```
  JScrollPane.VERTICAL_SCROLLBAR_ALWAYS
  JScrollPane.VERTICAL_SCROLLBAR_AS_NEEDED
  JScrollPane.VERTICAL_SCROLLBAR_NEVER
  ```

Class

```
javax.swing.JSlider
```

Purpose

Use a **JSlider** object to allow selection of a value within a bounded range. **JSlider** objects support labels for their minimum and maximum values as well as major and minor ticks along their range.

Constructors

- JSlider()

  JSlider(BoundedRangeModel *brm*)

  JSlider(int *orientation*)

  JSlider(int *min*, int *max*)

  JSlider(int *min*, int *max*, int *value*)

  JSlider(int *orientation*, int *min*, int *max*, int *value*)

  By default, a slider is created with a vertical orientation, a minimum value of zero, a maximum value of 100, and an initial value in the middle of the range at 50. If you choose to specify the orientation, its value should be **JSlider.HORIZONTAL** or **JSlider.VERTICAL**.

Class

javax.swing.JSpinner

Purpose

Use a **JSpinner** object to allow selection of a value within a bounded range from a predetermined list of legal values. How the **JSpinner** object will function depends upon which subclass of the abstract **SpinnerModel** class is used for the control. **SpinnerNumberModel** is designed for sequences of numbers; **SpinnerListModel** is designed for values that are provided in the form of an array or **List** object. If a sequence of dates is required, the best choice for a model class is **SpinnerDateModel**.

Constructors

■ JSpinner( )

  JSpinner(SpinnerModel *sm*)

  By default, a spinner is created with an **Integer SpinnerNumberModel** class, with initial value of zero and no minimum or maximum limits.

7

Figure 7-11 is a program that uses the **JSlider** and **JSpinner** classes to change the size of the text in a **JLabel** object that is centered in a frame window. For an example that uses **JScrollPane**, refer to the "Text-Entry Components" section later in this chapter. A breakdown of this code follows the output. This program defines the class **FontSliderSpinner**.

```
package examples.windows;
import javax.swing.*;
import javax.swing.event.*;
import java.awt.*;
import java.awt.event.*;
/** An example class used to demonstrate the use of
  * the JSlider and JSpinner components
  */
public class FontSliderSpinner extends JFrame {
   private JLabel text = new JLabel( "Sample Text",
                              JLabel.CENTER );
   private static final int MIN_POINTS = 8;
   private static final int MAX_POINTS = 36;
   private JSlider slideSizer = new JSlider();
   private JSpinner spinSizer = null;
   private SpinnerNumberModel snm = null;
```

Figure 7-11   FontSliderSpinner: an example using the **JSlider** and **JSpinner** components

```
/** Class constructor method
  * @param titleText Window's title bar text
  */
public FontSliderSpinner( String titleText ) {
   super( titleText );
   setDefaultCloseOperation( JFrame.EXIT_ON_CLOSE );
   getContentPane().add( text, BorderLayout.CENTER );
   int initValue = text.getFont().getSize();
   slideSizer.setMinimum( MIN_POINTS );
   slideSizer.setMaximum( MAX_POINTS );
   slideSizer.setValue( initValue );
   slideSizer.setMajorTickSpacing( 4 );
   slideSizer.setMinorTickSpacing( 1 );
   slideSizer.setPaintLabels( true );
   slideSizer.setPaintTicks( true );
   slideSizer.addChangeListener( new ChangeListener() {
         public void stateChanged( ChangeEvent e ) {
            int newSize = slideSizer.getValue();
            Font of = text.getFont();
            Font nf = new Font( of.getName(),
                                of.getStyle(),
                                newSize );
            text.setFont( nf );
            snm.setValue( new Integer( newSize ) );
            text.repaint();
         }
      }
   );
   int step = 1;
   snm = new SpinnerNumberModel( initValue, MIN_POINTS,
                                 MAX_POINTS, step );
   spinSizer = new JSpinner( snm );
   spinSizer.addChangeListener( new ChangeListener() {
         public void stateChanged( ChangeEvent e ) {
            int newSize = snm.getNumber().intValue();
            Font of = text.getFont();
            Font nf = new Font( of.getName(),
                                of.getStyle(),
                                newSize );
            text.setFont( nf );
            slideSizer.setValue( newSize );
            text.repaint();
         }
      }
   );
   JPanel sizerPanel
      = new JPanel( new BorderLayout() );
   sizerPanel.setBorder(
      BorderFactory.createTitledBorder( "Font size" ));
```

Figure 7-11 FontSliderSpinner: an example using the JSlider and JSpinner components (continued)

```
        sizerPanel.add( spinSizer, BorderLayout.WEST );
        sizerPanel.add( slideSizer, BorderLayout.EAST );
        getContentPane().add( sizerPanel,
                            BorderLayout.SOUTH );
        setSize( 275, 175 );
        setVisible( true );
    }
    /** The test method for the class
      * @param args not used
      */
    public static void main( String[] args ) {
        new FontSliderSpinner( "Example Slider Usage" );
    }
```

Figure 7-11   `FontSliderSpinner:` an example using the `JSlider` and `JSpinner` components (continued)

Allowing for differences in operating systems, the output should be similar to Figure 7–12.

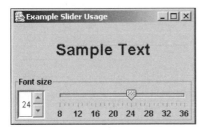

Figure 7-12   Output of the `FontSliderSpinner` class

The class encapsulating the example program is called `FontSliderSpinner`. The structure of this example is similar to the preceding examples, so only those program statements that pertain to the classes presented in this section will be discussed in the following code breakdown.

This program uses a slider and a spinner to control the font size of a `JLabel` object, `text`, which is centered in the window above the slider. With the following code, this label object is created with default horizontal centering and with vertical centering explicitly specified as the second constructor parameter:

```
    private JLabel text = new JLabel( "Sample Text",
                                JLabel.CENTER );
```

Consider the following code. The minimum and maximum value for this font size slider are defined as class constants, and the `JSlider` object is created. No constructor parameters are specified because the initial value has not yet been calculated and the default initial value, 50, is not within the valid range. Using an initial value that is outside of the valid range would cause an exception when the program runs.

```
private static final int MIN_POINTS = 8;
private static final int MAX_POINTS = 36;
private JSlider slideSizer = new JSlider();
```

The class fields for the **JSpinner** object and its model are declared but no object is constructed. These objects will be constructed later when all the information needed for the model is known.

```
private JSpinner spinSizer = null;
private SpinnerNumberModel snm = null;
```

Within the constructor, the minimum, maximum, and initial values of the slider control can be set. The initial value is the current font size of the label object.

```
int initValue = text.getFont().getSize();
slideSizer.setMinimum( MIN_POINTS );
slideSizer.setMaximum( MAX_POINTS );
slideSizer.setValue( initValue );
```

The difference between the minimum and maximum values is 24, so setting the slider's major ticks to be four units apart yields a reasonable number of major ticks, as the following code shows. Minor ticks don't have labels and can be closer together, so the minor tick spacing is set at one. These tick marks are not painted by default, so the **setPaintTicks** method is used to enable painting.

```
slideSizer.setMajorTickSpacing( 4 );
slideSizer.setMinorTickSpacing( 1 );
slideSizer.setPaintLabels( true );
slideSizer.setPaintTicks( true );
```

As the knob of the slider is moved, the slider fires **ChangeEvent** objects. The following statements define an anonymous inner class that implements the **ChangeListener** interface and register it to handle the events. The interface has only one method, **stateChanged**, and this method is implemented to get the current font of the label. Then, the method creates a new font with the same font name and style, but with a font size that is taken from the current value of the slider. **Font** objects are immutable, so you cannot simply change the size of the current font. The new **Font** object is set for the label, and the label is repainted after updating the current value in the spinner's model so that the two controls remain synchronized.

```
slideSizer.addChangeListener( new ChangeListener() {
    public void stateChanged( ChangeEvent e ) {
        int newSize = slideSizer.getValue();
        Font of = text.getFont();
```

```
           of.getStyle(),
           newSize );
      text.setFont( nf );
      snm.setValue( new Integer( newSize ) );
      text.repaint();
    }
  }
);
```

The model for the spinner control uses the same maximum, minimum, and initial values as the slider. The spinner doesn't have tick marks, but the step amount to be used when the user increments or decrements the spinner must be specified. After the model is constructed, the spinner control is constructed to use this model.

7

```
int step = 1;
snm = new SpinnerNumberModel( initValue, MIN_POINTS,
                              MAX_POINTS, step );
spinSizer = new JSpinner( snm );
```

Just as for the slider control, **ChangeEvent** objects are fired by the spinner as its value is altered and so a similar handler is defined to handle these events and update the font size of the label. The value of the slider control is also updated so that the two controls remain synchronized.

```
spinSizer.addChangeListener( new ChangeListener() {
    public void stateChanged( ChangeEvent e ) {
        int newSize = snm.getNumber().intValue();
        Font of = text.getFont();
        Font nf = new Font( of.getName(),
                            of.getStyle(),
                            newSize );
        text.setFont( nf );
        slideSizer.setValue( newSize );
        text.repaint();
    }
  }
);
```

The following statements give the user an explanation of the slider and spinner controls by placing the two controls in a panel with a titled border. They give the panel a border layout and add the spinner to the **WEST** area and the slider to the **SOUTH** area so that the controls sit next to each other and stretch horizontally, but not vertically, as the window resizes.

```
JPanel sizerPanel
    = new JPanel( new BorderLayout() );
sizerPanel.setBorder(
    BorderFactory.createTitledBorder( "Font size" ));
sizerPanel.add( spinSizer, BorderLayout.WEST );
sizerPanel.add( slideSizer, BorderLayout.EAST );
```

Finally, the panel containing the slider is added to the **SOUTH** section of the frame window so that it is positioned beneath the text that is being controlled.

```
getContentPane().add( sizerPanel,
                        BorderLayout.SOUTH );
```

LISTS AND COMBO BOXES

Swing provides two components for presenting lists from which the user can select single or multiple items. The **JComboBox** component is a drop-down list that is useful for lists with a small number of items, because it does not have scrolling capability. **JComboBox** can provide an entry field where users enter values not present in the list. For long lists of items, you should use the **JList** class because **JList** objects can be contained within **JScrollPane** and scrolled to view the entire list. Users cannot directly enter new values into a **JList** object.

Details about the list and combo box classes are provided next. Lists of all the constructors that are available for creating objects of these classes are provided also.

Class

javax.swing.JComboBox

Purpose

A **JComboBox** object displays a drop-down list of choices from which the user can select one or more items. A combo box can provide an entry field into which the user can enter a value instead of selecting from the presented list.

Constructors

- JComboBox()

  JComboBox(ComboBoxModel *model*)

  JComboBox(Object[] *items*)

  JComboBox(Vector *items*)

  You can specify that the list be built from an existing model, or the list of items can be specified and a new model will be created to contain them. If no parameter is specified, an empty default model is created.

Class

javax.swing.JList

Purpose

A **JList** object displays a list of choices from which it is possible to select one or multiple items. List contents cannot be edited by the user. Because lists can be long, they are typically contained within **JScrollPane** objects so scrollbars are available for controlling the visible portion of the list.

Constructors

- **JList()**

  JList(ListModel *model* **)**

  JList(Object[] *items* **)**

  JList(Vector *items* **)**

  The model for a list is a separate object that contains the data displayed in the list. You can specify that the list be built from an existing model or provide data from which a new model will be created. If no parameter is specified, an empty default model is created.

Figure 7-13 is a program that exercises both **JComboBox** and **JList** classes. A breakdown of this code follows the output. This program defines the class **ListsAndComboBoxes** to create a GUI for ordering a pizza. A list is used to present the available toppings, because the number of choices is large and selecting more than one topping is possible. A combo box is used to present the pizza crust choices. A combo box is appropriate because the number of choices is small, and only one of the choices can be selected. The button used to place the order includes a colorful icon to make the GUI more appealing. When the order button is clicked, a confirmation dialog box is presented so that the customer has one last chance to verify that the order is correct.

Before you run the program shown in Figure 7-13, copy the **pizza.gif** file from the **X:\Data\examples\windows** directory on the CD-ROM into the current directory. Alternatively, you could run the program with **X:\Data\examples\windows** as the current directory. (Here **X:** is the drive letter of the CD-ROM.) If the JVM cannot find the **.gif** file, the program runs, but the icon on the button does not display.

```
package examples.windows;
import javax.swing.*;
import java.awt.*;
import java.awt.event.*;
/** An example class used to demonstrate the use of
  * the JList and JComboBox components
  */
```

Figure 7-13   ListsAndComboBoxes: an example using the **JList** and **JComboBox** components

```
public class ListsAndComboBoxes extends JFrame {
   private JComboBox crustBox;
   private JList toppingList;
   /** Class constructor method
     * @param titleText Window's title bar text
     */
   public ListsAndComboBoxes( String titleText ) {
      super( titleText );
      setDefaultCloseOperation( JFrame.EXIT_ON_CLOSE );
      crustBox = new JComboBox( new Object[] {
            "thick and chewy",
            "thin and crispy",
            "Chicago deep dish"
         }
      );
      toppingList = new JList( new Object[] {
            "pepperoni",
            "sausage",
            "ham",
            "grilled chicken",
            "mushrooms",
            "green peppers",
            "hot peppers",
            "black olives",
            "tomato slices",
            "sun-dried tomatoes",
            "extra cheese",
            "pineapple",
            "anchovies"
         }
      );
      toppingList.setSelectionMode(
         ListSelectionModel.MULTIPLE_INTERVAL_SELECTION);
      JScrollPane scrollToppingList
         = new JScrollPane( toppingList );
      JPanel lists = new JPanel( new GridBagLayout() );
      GridBagConstraints c = new GridBagConstraints();
      c.fill = GridBagConstraints.HORIZONTAL;
      c.anchor = GridBagConstraints.NORTHWEST;
      c.insets = new Insets( 10, 10, 10, 10 );
      c.weightx = 0.0;
      c.weighty = 0.0;
      lists.add( new JLabel( "Toppings:" ), c );
      c.gridwidth = GridBagConstraints.REMAINDER;
      c.weightx = 1.0;
      c.weighty = 1.0;
      lists.add( scrollToppingList, c );
      c.gridwidth = 1;
      c.weightx = 0.0;
      c.weighty = 0.0;
```

Figure 7-13   ListsAndComboBoxes: an example using the JList and JComboBox
              components (continued)

```
        lists.add( new JLabel( "Crust type:" ), c );
        c.gridwidth = GridBagConstraints.REMAINDER;
        c.weightx = 1.0;
        c.weighty = 1.0;
        lists.add( crustBox, c );
        JPanel buttons = new JPanel();
        JButton order = new JButton( "Place order",
           new ImageIcon( "pizza.gif" ) );
        order.addActionListener( new ActionListener() {
             public void actionPerformed( ActionEvent e ) {
                confirmOrder();
             }
          }
        );
        buttons.add( order );
        Container cp = getContentPane();
        cp.add( lists, BorderLayout.CENTER );
        cp.add( buttons, BorderLayout.SOUTH );
        setSize( 400, 350 );
        setVisible( true );
     }
     /** Confirm a customer's order
       */
     public void confirmOrder() {
        StringBuffer question = new StringBuffer();
        question.append( "Order a " +
           crustBox.getSelectedItem() +
           " crust pizza topped with" );
        Object[] toppings = toppingList.getSelectedValues();
        for ( int i=0; i < toppings.length; i++ ) {
           question.append( " " + toppings[i] );
           question.append ( ( i + 1 < toppings.length)
              ? " and" : "?" );
        }
        JOptionPane.showConfirmDialog( this,
                                       question );
     }
     /** The test method for the class
       * @param args not used
       */
     public static void main( String[] args ) {
        new ListsAndComboBoxes(
           "Example Lists and Combo Boxes" );
     }
}
```

Figure 7-13   ListsAndComboBoxes: an example using the **JList** and **JComboBox** components (continued)

Allowing for differences in operating systems, the output should be similar to Figure 7-14.

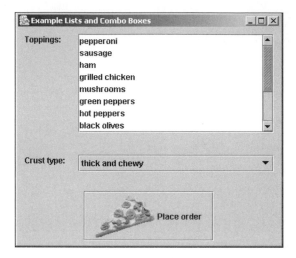

Figure 7-14   Output of the `ListsAndComboBoxes` class

The class encapsulating the drawing program is called `ListsAndComboBoxes`. The structure of this example is similar to the preceding examples, so only those program statements that pertain to the classes presented in this section are discussed in the following code breakdown.

The program defines a combo box called `crustBox` for presenting a list of possible pizza crust types and a list called `toppingList` that will contain a list of all the available pizza toppings. These are fields of the class so that they are accessible to both the constructor and the `confirmOrder` method defined next.

```
private JComboBox crustBox;
private JList toppingList;
```

When the combo box is constructed, it is initialized with an anonymous array of three **String** objects:

```
crustBox = new JComboBox( new Object[] {
     "thick and chewy",
     "thin and crispy",
     "Chicago deep dish"
   }
);
```

Another anonymous array initializes the contents of the list with all the possible pizza toppings:

```
toppingList = new JList( new Object[] {
     "pepperoni",
     "sausage",
     "ham",
```

```
            "mushrooms",
            "green peppers",
            "hot peppers",
            "black olives",
            "tomato slices",
            "sun-dried tomatoes",
            "extra cheese",
            "pineapple",
            "anchovies"
        }
    );
```

Because we want to let users select as many pizza toppings as they want, the multiple-selection mode is set for the list:

```
toppingList.setSelectionMode(
    ListSelectionModel.MULTIPLE_INTERVAL_SELECTION );
```

JList objects do not have any scrollbars of their own, so the topping list is wrapped in a **JScrollPane** object that will provide the scrollbars and handle the scrolling operations:

```
JScrollPane scrollToppingList
    = new JScrollPane( toppingList );
```

A grid-bag layout is used to position the combo box and the list along with their labels. All four objects are put into a single panel called **lists**. Within the grid bag, all four objects are set to stretch horizontally and anchored in the northwest corner of their cells. They also have a 10-pixel border around them, as the following code shows:

```
JPanel lists = new JPanel( new GridBagLayout() );
GridBagConstraints c = new GridBagConstraints();
c.fill = GridBagConstraints.HORIZONTAL;
c.anchor = GridBagConstraints.NORTHWEST;
c.insets = new Insets( 10, 10, 10, 10 );
```

The x and y weights for the label are set to zero so that it will not stretch with the window. This will allow the combo box to do the stretching, as the following code shows:

```
c.weightx = 0.0;
c.weighty = 0.0;
lists.add( new JLabel( "Toppings:" ), c );
```

The combo box takes the remainder of the first row and is given x and y weightings so that it will stretch.

```
c.gridwidth = GridBagConstraints.REMAINDER;
c.weightx = 1.0;
c.weighty = 1.0;
lists.add( scrollToppingList, c );
```

The **gridwidth**value is reset to its default value of 1 and, again, the weightings are set so that the label won't stretch:

```
c.gridwidth = 1;
c.weightx = 0.0;
c.weighty = 0.0;
lists.add( new JLabel( "Crust type:" ), c );
```

The last component that the method puts into the layout is the list, which is set to take the remainder of the second row:

```
c.gridwidth = GridBagConstraints.REMAINDER;
c.weightx = 1.0;
c.weighty = 1.0;
lists.add( crustBox, c );
```

Then, a panel is created for the Place order button and the button is created with both text and a graphic of a piece of pizza:

```
JPanel buttons = new JPanel();
JButton order = new JButton( "Place order",
    new ImageIcon( "pizza.gif" ) );
```

The next statement defines an action listener as an anonymous inner class and adds it to the button, so that the `confirmOrder` method is invoked when the user clicks the button:

```
order.addActionListener( new ActionListener() {
        public void actionPerformed( ActionEvent e ) {
            confirmOrder();
        }
    }
);
```

The button is added to the panel, and then both of the panels are added to the frame window's content pane. The lists are set in the center of the window and the button at the bottom, as the following code shows:

```
buttons.add( order );
Container cp = getContentPane();
cp.add( lists, BorderLayout.CENTER );
cp.add( buttons, BorderLayout.SOUTH );
```

The `confirmOrder` method begins by creating a string with the type of crust the user selected:

```
public void confirmOrder() {
    StringBuffer question = new StringBuffer();
    question.append( "Order a " +
        crustBox.getSelectedItem() +
        " crust pizza topped with" );
```

~~Thus, the list of toppings that were selected is added to the string so that all the details~~
of the order are now in the string:

```
Object[] toppings = toppingList.getSelectedValues();
for ( int i=0; i < toppings.length; i++ ) {
   question.append( " " + toppings[i] );
   question.append ( ( i + 1 < toppings.length)
      ? " and" : "?" );
}
```

Presenting a dialog box to the user so that the order can be confirmed is a simple matter of calling the static **showConfirmDialog** method of the **JOptionPane** class. The two parameters are the parent window for the dialog box and the question to be displayed. Although it is not shown in this example, this method returns an integer with one of the following values that indicates the user's action: **YES_OPTION**, **NO_OPTION**, **CANCEL_OPTION**, **CLOSED_OPTION**.

```
JOptionPane.showConfirmDialog( this,
                               question );
```

TEXT-ENTRY COMPONENTS

No set of GUI components would be complete without components that allow the user to enter text. Swing provides several such components from the most basic single-line text field to the sophisticated multiline components that understand and support HTML and RTF. Swing also provides a convenience class of entry fields specifically suited for entering passwords.

Figure 7-15 shows **JTextComponent** and its subclasses. Following the figure, the syntax discussion gives details about each of the text components. Lists of all the constructors that are available for creating objects of these classes are also provided.

The class **JFormattedTextField** was introduced in version 1.4 of the Java platform. Before it was available, programmers had to use **JTextField** controls and control the formatting of the entry field contents manually.

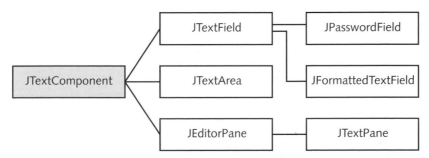

Figure 7-15 TextComponent and its subclasses

Class

`javax.swing.JEditorPane`

Purpose

A **JEditorPane** object is a region that is designed to parse and edit specific types of structured text content. If a scrollable region is required, this component should be placed inside a **JScrollPane** object.

Constructors

- **JEditorPane( )**

  JEditorPane(String *url* **)**

  JEditorPane(String *mimeType*, **String** *text* **)**

  JEditorPane(URL *url* **)**

  The text pane requires that a MIME type be specified for its content. If a URL is given as input to the constructor, the URL will determine the MIME type. However, it is possible to construct a **JEditorPane** object specifying both the MIME type and the actual text to be displayed. By default, three MIME types of content are known:

  text/plain: Plain text, which is the default if the type given isn't recognized. This produces a wrapped plain text view.

  text/html: HTML text, as defined by HTML version 3.2.

  text/rtf: Rich Text Format (RTF), for which limited support is provided.

Class

`javax.swing.JFormattedTextField`

Purpose

A **JFormattedTextField** object is an entry field in which the data that the user enters must meet the specified formatting rules.

Constructors

- **JFormattedTextField()**

  JFormattedTextField (Format *format* **)**

  JFormattedTextField (FormattedTextField.AbstractFormatter *formatter* **)**

  JFormattedTextField (FormattedTextField.AbstractFormatterFactory *factory* **)**

factory, Object *initialValue*)

JFormattedTextField (Object *initialValue*)

The simplest way to use a **JFormattedTextField** object is by constructing it and providing an initial value. The control then uses the type of that object, for example **Date**, to determine the format to be applied to the control. Other constructors allow the programmer to take more control over the formatting to be used.

Class

`javax.swing.JPasswordField`

Purpose

JPasswordField can display a single line of text and lets the user enter or edit the text. The field provides feedback as characters are entered, but the actual characters typed are not displayed.

Constructors

- JPasswordField()

  JPasswordField(String *text*)

  JPasswordField(int *columns*)

  JPasswordField(String *text*, int *columns*)

  JPasswordField(Document *docModel*, String *text*, int *columns*)

  If you supply an initial text string, it is displayed in **JPasswordField**; otherwise, the **JPasswordField** object is initially empty. The text field uses a model object that implements the **javax.swing.text.Document** interface if one is specified; otherwise, a new model is constructed. The **int** argument is the width of the **JPasswordField** object expressed as the number of feedback characters that can be displayed. For a fixed-pitch or monospace font, the width is equivalent to the number of columns of characters that fit on the line. For a variable-pitch or proportional font, the width is an approximation based on medium-size letters. You may see more characters if the feedback string contains several occurrences of narrow letters, such as *l* or *i,* and fewer characters if the string contains several occurrences of wide letters, such as *m* or *w.* If you do not specify a width, the **JPasswordField** object is wide enough to display either the specified **String** object or a minimum of one character.

  Unlike the other text components, you should not use the **getText** method to retrieve the value of the entered password. The **getText** method has been deprecated for this class and has been replaced by the method **getPassword**, which returns a **char[]** array that contains the text in the component. After retrieving and processing the password, the characters in the array should be set to zero as a security precaution to prevent inadvertently disclosing the password.

Class

`javax.swing.JTextArea`

Purpose

JTextArea is a region that can contain several lines of text. If a scrollable region is required, this component should be placed inside a **JScrollPane** object.

Constructors

- `JTextArea()`

  `JTextArea( String text )`

  `JTextArea( Document docModel )`

  `JTextArea( int rows, int columns )`

  `JTextArea( String text, int rows, int columns )`

  `JTextArea( Document docModel, String text, int rows, int columns )`

  You can specify the size of the **JTextArea** object in terms of the number of rows and the number of characters or columns that are displayable at one time. The text area will use a **Document** model object if one is specified; otherwise, a new model is constructed. As with a **JTextField** object, the number of columns is exact for a fixed-pitch font and approximate for a variable-pitch font. If you specify a string to the constructor, the content of the string is displayed when the **JTextArea** object is displayed.

Class

`javax.swing.JTextField`

Purpose

JTextField can display a single line of text and lets the user enter or edit the text.

Constructors

- `JTextField()`

  `JTextField( String text )`

  `JTextField( int columns )`

  `JTextField( String text, int columns )`

  `JTextField( Document docModel, String text, int columns )`

wise, the **JTextField** object is initially empty. The text field will use a **Document** model object if one is specified; otherwise, a new model is constructed. The **int** argument is the width of **JTextField** expressed as the number of characters that can be displayed. If you do not specify a width, the **JTextField** object is wide enough to display either the specified **String** object or a minimum of one character.

Class

javax.swing.JTextPane

Purpose

A **JTextPane** object is a region that can contain several lines of text. This text can be given styles that can be represented graphically. If a scrollable region is required, this component should be placed inside a **JScrollPane** object.

Constructors

- **JTextPane()**

  JTextPane(StyledDocument *docModel*)

  The text pane will use a **StyledDocument** model object if one is specified; otherwise, a new model is constructed.

Figure 7-16 is a program that exercises the **JTextField** and **JTextArea** classes described previously. A breakdown of this code follows the output. This program defines the class **TextExamples** to create a GUI in which the user enters a filename in the text field at the top of the frame window and the contents of the file are displayed in two text areas. The text areas are put into a **JSplitPane** object that is split horizontally. The two text areas share the same underlying document model, so any change that is made in one text area will be immediately reflected in the other text area. Before you run this program, copy the file **TextExamples.java** from the **X:\Data\examples\ windows** directory into the current directory. Alternatively, you could run the program with **X:\Data\examples\windows** as the current directory. (Here **X:** is the drive letter of the CD-ROM.)

```
package examples.windows;
import javax.swing.*;
import java.awt.*;
import java.awt.event.*;
import java.io.*;
import java.nio.*;
import java.nio.channels.*;
```

Figure 7-16   TextExamples: an example using the **JTextField** and **JTextArea** components

```java
/** An example class used to demonstrate the use of
  * the JTextField and JTextArea components
  */
public class TextExamples extends JFrame {
   /** Class constructor method
     * @param titleText Window's title bar text
     */
   public TextExamples( String titleText ) {
      super( titleText );
      setDefaultCloseOperation( JFrame.EXIT_ON_CLOSE );
      final JTextArea upper = new JTextArea();
      final JTextArea lower
         = new JTextArea( upper.getDocument() );
      JScrollPane upperScroll = new JScrollPane( upper );
      JScrollPane lowerScroll = new JScrollPane( lower );
      JSplitPane sp
         = new JSplitPane( JSplitPane.VERTICAL_SPLIT,
                           upperScroll,
                           lowerScroll );
      sp.setOneTouchExpandable( true );
      sp.setDividerLocation( 0.5 );
      final JTextField fName = new JTextField();
      fName.setToolTipText( "Enter a file name" );
      fName.addActionListener( new ActionListener() {
            public void actionPerformed( ActionEvent e ) {
               if ( fName.getText() != null ) try {
                  FileInputStream fis
                     = new FileInputStream( fName.getText() );
                  FileChannel fc = fis.getChannel();
                  ByteBuffer bb
                     = ByteBuffer.allocate( (int) fc.size() );
                  fc.read( bb );
                  upper.setText( new String( bb.array() ) );
                  fc.close();
                  fis.close();
               } catch( IOException ioe ) {
                  System.out.println( ioe );
               }
            }
         }
      );
      JPanel entry = new JPanel( new BorderLayout() );
      entry.add( new JLabel( "File: " ),
                 BorderLayout.WEST );
      entry.add( fName, BorderLayout.CENTER );
      getContentPane().add( entry, BorderLayout.NORTH );
      getContentPane().add( sp, BorderLayout.CENTER );
      setSize( 500, 400 );
      fName.requestFocus();
      setVisible( true );
   }
```

Figure 7-16 `TextExamples`: an example using the **JTextField** and **JTextArea** components (continued)

```
   /** The test method for the class
    * @param args not used
    */
   public static void main( String[] args ) {
      new TextExamples( "Example Text Components" );
   }
}
```

Figure 7-16   `TextExamples`: an example using the `JTextField` and `JTextArea` components (continued)

Allowing for differences in operating systems, the output should be similar to Figure 7-17.

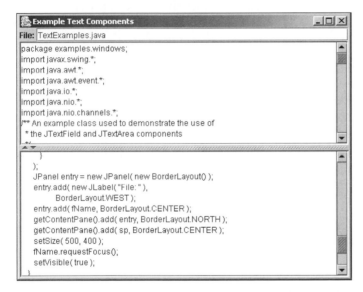

Figure 7-17   Output of the `TextExamples` class

The class encapsulating the drawing program is called **TextExamples**. The structure of this example is similar to the preceding examples, so only those program statements that pertain to the classes presented in this section are discussed in the following code breakdown.

Consider the following code, which uses two **JTextArea** objects that share a single document model. The first **JTextArea** object is constructed using all the defaults, and then the second **JTextArea** object is constructed specifying the document model of the first **JTextArea** object as input. The result is two text areas that are two different views of the same document model.

```
final JTextArea upper = new JTextArea();
final JTextArea lower
   = new JTextArea( upper.getDocument() );
```

The two text–area components are put into **JScrollPane** objects so that they will have scrollbars if they are needed:

```
JScrollPane upperScroll = new JScrollPane( upper );
JScrollPane lowerScroll = new JScrollPane( lower );
```

Then, the two scroll panes are put into a split pane, one on top of the other:

```
JSplitPane sp
   = new JSplitPane( JSplitPane.VERTICAL_SPLIT,
                     upperScroll,
                     lowerScroll );
```

Examine the following code. By setting the **oneTouchExpandable** property of the split pane to **true**, a control is added to the bar that divides the split pane. This makes it easy to expand the split pane to show one component or the other. The **dividerLocation** property is set so that it is initially in the middle of the pane:

```
sp.setOneTouchExpandable( true );
sp.setDividerLocation( 0.5 );
```

A text field is created for inputting the name of the file to be displayed in the two text-area components. A ToolTip is associated with the entry field to help the user to know its use:

```
final JTextField fName = new JTextField();
fName.setToolTipText( "Enter a file name" );
```

Then, an **ActionListener** listener object is needed for the text area to listen for **ActionEvent** objects so that when the user presses Enter, the value in the text field can be used as a filename for loading the text areas.

```
fName.addActionListener( new ActionListener() {
      public void actionPerformed( ActionEvent e ) {
```

As long as the specified string isn't **null**, the string will be used to create a file input stream and the file will be read into the text area:

```
FileInputStream fis
   = new FileInputStream( fName.getText() );
FileChannel fc = fis.getChannel();
ByteBuffer bb
   = ByteBuffer.allocate( (int) fc.size() );
fc.read( bb );
upper.setText( new String( bb.array() ) );
fc.close();
fis.close();
```

If an I/O exception occurs, the contents of the I/O exception object will be written to the standard output stream:

```
} catch( IOException ioe ) {
   System.out.println( ioe );
}
```

A panel is created for combining the entry field along with its label. This panel is added to the **NORTH** section of the frame window, and the split pane with the two text-area objects is put into the center of the frame window, as shown next:

```
JPanel entry = new JPanel( new BorderLayout() );
entry.add( new JLabel( "File: " ),
        BorderLayout.WEST );
entry.add( fName, BorderLayout.CENTER );
getContentPane().add( entry, BorderLayout.NORTH );
getContentPane().add( sp, BorderLayout.CENTER );
```

Finally, just before the window is made visible, a request is made to have the focus put on the entry field so that if the user begins typing, the input text will go into the entry field:

```
fName.requestFocus();
```

7

COLOR AND FILE CHOOSERS

Some panels are used so commonly for user input that they have been added to Swing as standard components. This is just as well, because both the **JColorChooser** and **JFileChooser** standard components are complex panels that would be difficult for most programmers to create on their own. Like the panels of the **JOptionPane** class, the **JColorChooser** and **JFileChooser** components typically are embedded with **JDialog** components. (Another possibility is to embed them in an internal frame.) Both classes provide convenient static methods that do the work of creating the panel, creating the dialog box, and putting the panel into the dialog box and making it visible.

Details about these chooser classes are provided next. Lists of all the constructors that are available for creating objects of these classes are provided also.

Class

javax.swing.JColorChooser

Purpose

JColorChooser is a panel that allows users to browse a palette of available colors and select one.

Constructors

- **JColorChooser()**

  JColorChooser(Color *initialSelection* **)**

  JColorChooser(ColorSelectionModel *model* **)**

  If the default constructor is used, a dialog box is displayed with white as the initial selection. If a color is specified, it will be indicated to be the initial selection. By default, a new selection model is created for the chooser, but it is possible to specify that the chooser use an existing selection model at construction time.

Class

---

javax.swing.JFileChooser

Purpose

JFileChooser is a panel that allows users to browse the contents of the file system and select a file to open or a file to save.

Constructors

- **JFileChooser()**

  JFileChooser(File *currentDirectory* **)**

  JFileChooser(FileSystemView *fsView* **)**

  JFileChooser(String *currentDirectoryPath* **)**

  JFileChooser(File *currentDirectory*, **FileSystemView** *fsView* **)**

  JFileChooser(String *currentDirectoryPath*, **FileSystemView** *fsView* **)**

  The file selection begins in the user's home directory if no current directory is specified as either a **File** object or a string. The **FileSystemView** object is an object that encapsulates the details of the host system's file system. To display the chooser, typically you use either the method **showOpenDialog** or the method **showSaveDialog**.

Figure 7-18 is a program that exercises both of the chooser classes described previously. A breakdown of this code follows the output. The program defines the class **Choosers** to implement a simple file browser program. The file to be displayed is selected using a **JFileChooser** object that is invoked from the item File open on the File menu. The browser allows the text color to be changed using a **JColorChooser** object that is placed within a **JDialog** object. The menu item used to change the text color is found on the Edit menu.

```
package examples.windows;
import javax.swing.*;
import java.awt.*;
import java.awt.event.*;
import java.io.*;
import java.nio.*;
import java.nio.channels.*;
```

Figure 7-18   **Choosers:** an example using the color and file choosers

```
/** An example class used to demonstrate the use of the
  * color and file choosers
  */
public class Choosers extends JFrame {
   private JTextArea text = new JTextArea();
   private JFileChooser fileChoose
      = new JFileChooser();
   private JDialog colorDlg;
   private JColorChooser colorChoose
      = new JColorChooser();
   /** Class constructor
     * @param titleText Title bar text
     */
   public Choosers( String titleText ) {
      super( titleText );
      setDefaultCloseOperation( JFrame.EXIT_ON_CLOSE );
      setJMenuBar( buildMenuBar() );
      text.setEditable( false );
      Container cp = getContentPane();
      cp.add( new JScrollPane( text ),
            BorderLayout.CENTER );
      setSize( 500, 400 );
      setVisible( true );
   }
   /** Present a dialog box to have the user select
     * the file for browsing */
   public void loadFile() {
      int result = fileChoose.showOpenDialog(
         Choosers.this );
      File file = fileChoose.getSelectedFile();
      if ( file != null
           && result == JFileChooser.APPROVE_OPTION )
      try {
            FileInputStream fis
               = new FileInputStream( file );
         FileChannel fc = fis.getChannel();
         ByteBuffer bb
            = ByteBuffer.allocate( (int) fc.size() );
         fc.read( bb );
         text.setText( new String( bb.array() ) );
         fc.close();
         fis.close();
      } catch( IOException ioe ) {
         ioe.printStackTrace();
      }
   }
   /** Build the menu bar, menus, and menu items for
     * the file browser */
   public JMenuBar buildMenuBar() {
      JMenuBar menuBar = new JMenuBar();
```

Figure 7-18   Choosers: an example using the color and file choosers (continued)

```
      JMenu fileMenu = new JMenu( "File" );
      JMenu editMenu = new JMenu( "Edit" );
      JMenuItem exitItem = new JMenuItem( "Exit" );
      JMenuItem fileOpenItem
         = new JMenuItem( "File open..." );
      JMenuItem colorsItem
         = new JMenuItem( "Change Color..." );
      fileMenu.setMnemonic( KeyEvent.VK_F );
      editMenu.setMnemonic( KeyEvent.VK_E );
      fileOpenItem.setMnemonic( KeyEvent.VK_O );
      exitItem.setMnemonic( KeyEvent.VK_X );
      colorsItem.setMnemonic( KeyEvent.VK_C );
      fileOpenItem.addActionListener(
         new ActionListener() {
            public void actionPerformed( ActionEvent e ) {
               loadFile();
            }
         }
      );
      exitItem.addActionListener(
         new ActionListener() {
            public void actionPerformed( ActionEvent e ) {
               dispose();
               System.exit( 0 );
            }
         }
      );
      colorsItem.addActionListener(
         new ActionListener() {
            public void actionPerformed( ActionEvent e ) {
               if ( colorDlg == null ) {
                  colorDlg = JColorChooser.createDialog(
                     Choosers.this,
                     "Select Text Color",
                     true,
                     colorChoose,
                     new ColorOKListener(),
                     null
                  );
               }
               colorChoose.setColor(
                  text.getForeground() );
               colorDlg.setVisible( true );
            }
         }
      );
      menuBar.add( fileMenu );
      menuBar.add( editMenu );
      fileMenu.add( fileOpenItem );
      fileMenu.add( exitItem );
      editMenu.add( colorsItem );
```

Figure 7-18   Choosers: an example using the color and file choosers (continued)

```
      return menuBar;
   }
   class ColorOKListener implements ActionListener {
      public void actionPerformed( ActionEvent e ) {
         Color c = colorChoose.getColor();
         text.setForeground( c );
         text.repaint();
      }
   }
   /** The test method for the class
     * @param args not used
     */
   public static void main( String[] args ) {
      new Choosers( "File and Color Choosers" );
   }
}
```

Figure 7-18   `Choosers:` an example using the color and file choosers (continued)

Allowing for differences in operating systems, Figure 7-19 represents what you will see if you choose the **Change Color** item from the Edit menu.

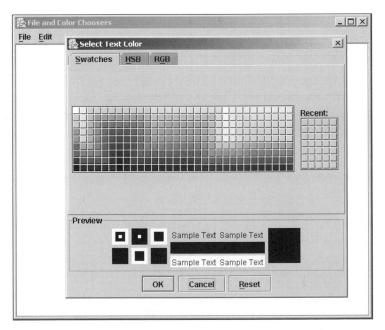

Figure 7-19   Output of the `Choosers` class

The class encapsulating the drawing program is called **Choosers**. The structure of this example is similar to the preceding examples, so only those program statements that pertain to the classes presented in this section are discussed in the following code breakdown.

Consider the following code that defines the fields for the **Choosers** class that will be used throughout the program. The fields are the text-area component where the file contents will be shown, the file-chooser panel, and a color-chooser panel and the dialog box in which it will be displayed:

```
private JTextArea text = new JTextArea();
private JFileChooser fileChoose
    = new JFileChooser();
private JDialog colorDlg;
private JColorChooser colorChoose
    = new JColorChooser();
```

The menu bar for this class is built and returned by the **buildMenuBar** method, and then it is set for the frame window:

```
setJMenuBar( buildMenuBar() );
```

Examine the following code. You are working with a file-browser program, so editing is disabled for the text area. Text areas do not have scrollbars, so the text-area object is placed in a scroll pane (that comes with its own horizontal and vertical scrollbars) and then the scroll pane is positioned in the center of the frame window's content pane:

```
text.setEditable( false );
Container cp = getContentPane();
cp.add( new JScrollPane( text ),
        BorderLayout.CENTER );
```

The **loadFile** method is invoked when the File open menu item is selected. It begins by using the file chooser's **showOpenDialog** method to allow the user to select a file. This is a modal dialog box, so when the method completes, the user has either selected a file or quit from the dialog box.

```
public void loadFile() {
    int result = fileChoose.showOpenDialog(
        Choosers.this );
    File file = fileChoose.getSelectedFile();
```

Consider the following code. If the user does not select a file, the file string is **null**. The **int** value returned from the **showOpenDialog** method call can be used to determine which action the user took to close the dialog box. If the Open button was clicked, the result equals **JFileChooser.APPROVE_OPTION**.

```
if ( file != null
    && result == JFileChooser.APPROVE_OPTION )
try {
```

Assuming that a file was selected successfully, a **FileInputStream** object is constructed to read the file and the text area is cleared. A buffer for reading the entire

`JTextArea` component.

```
FileInputStream fis
    = new FileInputStream( file );
FileChannel fc = fis.getChannel();
ByteBuffer bb
    = ByteBuffer.allocate( (int) fc.size() );
fc.read( bb );
text.setText( new String( bb.array() ) );
fc.close();
fis.close();
```

The menu bar for the program consists of one **JMenuBar** object, two **JMenu** objects for File and Edit, and three **JMenuItem** objects for the actions.

```
public JMenuBar buildMenuBar() {
    JMenuBar menuBar = new JMenuBar();
    JMenu fileMenu = new JMenu( "File" );
    JMenu editMenu = new JMenu( "Edit" );
    JMenuItem exitItem = new JMenuItem( "Exit" );
    JMenuItem fileOpenItem
        = new JMenuItem( "File open..." );
    JMenuItem colorsItem
        = new JMenuItem( "Change Color..." );
```

Mnemonic characters are set for both menus and all the menu item objects.

```
fileMenu.setMnemonic( KeyEvent.VK_F );
editMenu.setMnemonic( KeyEvent.VK_E );
fileOpenItem.setMnemonic( KeyEvent.VK_O );
exitItem.setMnemonic( KeyEvent.VK_X );
colorsItem.setMnemonic( KeyEvent.VK_C );
```

Action listeners must be created and added for each of the three menu items. Anonymous inner classes are used in all cases. The action listener for the Open file menu item calls the `loadFile` method, as shown in the following code:

```
fileOpenItem.addActionListener(
    new ActionListener() {
        public void actionPerformed( ActionEvent e ) {
            loadFile();
        }
    }
);
```

The action listener for the Exit item disposes the frame window and exits the JVM:

```
exitItem.addActionListener(
    new ActionListener() {
        public void actionPerformed( ActionEvent e ) {
            dispose();
```

```
                    System.exit( 0 );
              }
         }
    );
```

Then, as shown in the following code, the action listener for the Change Color item creates a dialog box to hold the color chooser panel, if one does not already exist. Using this approach, you avoid creating a new dialog box every time, which would be resource intensive. The last two parameters of the `createDialog` method are the listeners for the dialog box's OK and Cancel buttons. Because this program will take no action if Cancel is selected, that handler is set to null:

```
colorsItem.addActionListener(
    new ActionListener() {
        public void actionPerformed( ActionEvent e ) {
            if ( colorDlg == null ) {
                colorDlg = JColorChooser.createDialog(
                    Choosers.this,
                    "Select Text Color",
                    true,
                    colorChoose,
                    new ColorOKListener(),
                    null
                );
            }
```

The current color of the text is set as the initial color for the color chooser, and then the dialog box is made visible:

```
            colorChoose.setColor(
                text.getForeground() );
            colorDlg.setVisible( true );
        }
    }
);
```

The last group of statements in the `buildMenuBar` method adds the menu items to the menus and then the menus to the menu bar. The finished product is returned:

```
    menuBar.add( fileMenu );
    menuBar.add( editMenu );
    fileMenu.add( fileOpenItem );
    fileMenu.add( exitItem );
    editMenu.add( colorsItem );
    return menuBar;
}
```

The `color chooser` is a graphical foreground. The action listener for the OK button for the color chooser dialog box. The selected color is determined and used as the foreground color of the text area. A call to **repaint** causes the change to take effect:

```
class ColorOKListener implements ActionListener {
    public void actionPerformed( ActionEvent e ) {
        Color c = colorChoose.getColor();
        text.setForeground( c );
        text.repaint();
    }
}
```

TABLES AND TREES

7

The two most ambitious components in Swing are **JTable** (Figure 7-21) and **JTree** (Figure 7-23). Each of these components is complex. In fact, both classes have an entire package of their own support classes. This section outlines what is possible with these components. Specifically, you will learn how to use these controls to present information.

The **JTable** component is useful for presenting information of a tabular nature. This section presents the **JTable** syntax and a sample program first. Then, the section presents the syntax and sample program for the **JTree** component.

Class

javax.swing.JTable

Purpose

JTable is a component that displays information in tabular format.

Constructors

- JTable( )

  JTable(int *rows*, int *columns*)

  JTable(Object[][] *rowData*, Object[] *columnNames*)

  JTable(Vector *rowData*, Vector *columnNames*)

  JTable(TableModel *model*)

  JTable(TableModel *model*, TableColumnModel *tcModel*)

  JTable(TableModel *model*, TableColumnModel *tcModel*,
          ListSelectionModel *lsModel*)

By default, models are created for the table, but it is possible to specify that the chooser should use existing model objects.

Figure 7-20 is a program that uses the **JTable** class just described. A breakdown of this code follows the output. This program defines the class `TableExample` to create a GUI that displays a table of statistics for five baseball players.

```java
package examples.windows;
import javax.swing.*;
import javax.swing.event.*;
import java.awt.*;
/** An example class used to demonstrate the use of
 * the JTable component
 */
public class TableExample extends JFrame {
   /** Class constructor method
     * @param titleText Window's title bar text
     */
   public TableExample( String titleText ) {
      super( titleText );
      setDefaultCloseOperation( JFrame.EXIT_ON_CLOSE );
      JTable stats = new JTable( new Object[][] {
            { "Gonzalez",  ".295", "34", "12", "6", "10" },
            { "Carter",    ".302", "27", "12", "2", "15" },
            { "Fernandez", ".285", "30", "12", "11", "1" },
            { "Greene",    ".321", "41", "12", "0", "10" },
            { "Delgado",   ".298", "34", "12", "1", "20" },
          } ,
          new Object[] {
             "Player", "avg", "1B", "2B", "3B", "HR"
          }
      );
      JScrollPane scrollStats = new JScrollPane( stats );
      getContentPane().add( scrollStats,
                            BorderLayout.CENTER );
      setSize( 500, 200 );
      setVisible( true );
   }
   /** The test method for the class
     * @param args not used
     */
   public static void main( String[] args ) {
      new TableExample( "Table Example" );
   }
}
```

Figure 7-20   `TableExample`: an example using the **JTable** component

Allowing for differences in operating systems, the output should be similar to Figure 7-21.

Player	avg	1B	2B	3B	HR
Gonzalez	.295	34	12	6	10
Carter	.302	27	12	2	15
Fernandez	.285	30	12	11	1
Greene	.321	41	12	0	10
Delgado	.298	34	12	1	20

Figure 7-21   Output of the `TableExample` class

The class encapsulating the drawing program is called `TableExample`. The structure of this example is similar to the preceding examples, so only those program statements that pertain to the classes presented in this section are discussed in the following code breakdown.

Consider the following code. The table is constructed by providing two array objects as input. The first is an anonymous two-dimensional array of **String** objects containing the table data. The second array contains the column titles defined as an anonymous array of **String** objects:

```
JTable stats = new JTable( new Object[][] {
        { "Gonzalez",  ".295", "34", "12", "6",  "10" },
        { "Carter",    ".302", "27", "12", "2",  "15" },
        { "Fernandez", ".285", "30", "12", "11", "1"  },
        { "Greene",    ".321", "41", "12", "0",  "10" },
        { "Delgado",   ".298", "34", "12", "1",  "20" },
    } ,
    new Object[] {
        "Player", "avg", "1B", "2B", "3B", "HR"
    }
);
```

Then, the table object is put into a scroll pane. This serves two purposes: It provides the table with scrollbars, and it gives the table column headers a place to reside. The scroll pane is then set in the center of the frame window's content pane:

```
JScrollPane scrollStats = new JScrollPane( stats );
getContentPane().add( scrollStats,
                      BorderLayout.CENTER );
```

Class

javax.swing.JTree

Purpose

JTree is a component that displays information in a hierarchical format.

Constructors

- `JTree()`

  `JTree( Hashtable` *hashtable* `)`

  `JTree( Object[]` *value* `)`

  `JTree( TreeModel` *model* `)`

  `JTree( TreeNode` *root* `)`

  `JTree( TreeNode` *root,* `boolean` *asksAllowsChildren* `)`

  `JTree( Vector` *value* `)`

  By default, default models are created for the tree, but it is possible to specify that the tree should use existing model objects.

The program in Figure 7-22 exercises many of the classes described previously. A breakdown of this code follows the output. This program defines the class `TreeExample` that creates a simple tree-structured GUI with three branches under the root node and a few leaf nodes under each of these three branches.

```
package examples.windows;
import javax.swing.*;
import javax.swing.event.*;
import javax.swing.tree.*;
import java.awt.*;
/** An example class used to demonstrate the use of
  * the JTree component
  */
public class TreeExample extends JFrame {
   /** Class constructor method
     * @param titleText Window's title bar text
     */
   public TreeExample( String titleText ) {
      super( titleText );
      setDefaultCloseOperation( JFrame.EXIT_ON_CLOSE );
      DefaultMutableTreeNode everything
         = new DefaultMutableTreeNode( "everything" );
      JTree avm = new JTree( everything );
      DefaultMutableTreeNode animal
         = new DefaultMutableTreeNode( "animal" );
      everything.add( animal );
      animal.add( new DefaultMutableTreeNode( "cat" ) );
      animal.add( new DefaultMutableTreeNode( "dog" ) );
      animal.add( new DefaultMutableTreeNode( "fish" ) );
      DefaultMutableTreeNode vegetable
         = new DefaultMutableTreeNode( "vegetable" );
```

Figure 7-22   `TreeExample:` an example using the **JTree** component

```
         everything.add( vegetable );
         vegetable.add(
            new DefaultMutableTreeNode( "onion" ) );
         vegetable.add(
            new DefaultMutableTreeNode( "lettuce" ) );
         vegetable.add(
            new DefaultMutableTreeNode( "carrot" ) );
         DefaultMutableTreeNode mineral
            = new DefaultMutableTreeNode( "mineral" );
         everything.add( mineral );
         mineral.add(
            new DefaultMutableTreeNode( "quartz" ) );
         mineral.add(
            new DefaultMutableTreeNode( "feldspar" ) );
         avm.addTreeSelectionListener(
            new TreeSelectionListener() {
               public void
               valueChanged( TreeSelectionEvent e ) {
                  JOptionPane.showMessageDialog(
                     TreeExample.this,
                     "You selected " + e.getPath() );
               }
            }
         );
         getContentPane().add( avm, BorderLayout.CENTER );
         setSize( 200, 300 );
         setVisible( true );
      }
      /** The test method for the class
       * @param args not used
       */
      public static void main( String[] args ) {
         new TreeExample( "Tree Example" );
      }
   }
}
```

Figure 7-22   `TreeExample:` an example using the **JTree** component (continued)

Allowing for differences in operating systems, after expanding the tree, the output should be similar to Figure 7-23.

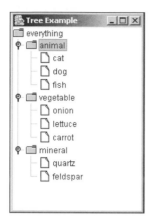

Figure 7-23   Output of the `TreeExample` class

The class encapsulating the drawing program is called **TreeExample**. The structure of this example is similar to the preceding examples, so only those program statements that pertain to the classes presented in this section are discussed in the following code breakdown.

The tree containing the information to be displayed is built one node at a time, beginning with the root node **everything**. This root node object is passed as the tree's constructor input:

```
DefaultMutableTreeNode everything
   = new DefaultMutableTreeNode( "everything" );
JTree avm = new JTree( everything );
```

Next, the node for animals is created and it is added as a child node of the root node. In turn, three animal nodes are added to the **animal** node:

```
DefaultMutableTreeNode animal
   = new DefaultMutableTreeNode( "animal" );
everything.add( animal );
animal.add( new DefaultMutableTreeNode( "cat" ) );
animal.add( new DefaultMutableTreeNode( "dog" ) );
animal.add( new DefaultMutableTreeNode( "fish" ) );
```

Next, a node for vegetables is created and added as a child node of the root node. Then, three nodes are added as children of the **vegetable** node:

```
DefaultMutableTreeNode vegetable
   = new DefaultMutableTreeNode( "vegetable" );
everything.add( vegetable );
vegetable.add(
   new DefaultMutableTreeNode( "onion" ) );
vegetable.add(
   new DefaultMutableTreeNode( "lettuce" ) );
vegetable.add(
   new DefaultMutableTreeNode( "carrot" ) );
```

then two nodes are added as children of the `mineral` node:

```
DefaultMutableTreeNode mineral
   = new DefaultMutableTreeNode( "mineral" );
everything.add( mineral );
mineral.add(
   new DefaultMutableTreeNode( "quartz" ) );
mineral.add(
   new DefaultMutableTreeNode( "feldspar" ) );
```

It is possible to detect when the user makes a selection in the tree. To do this, a tree selection listener object is added to the tree, as shown in the following code. The `valueChanged` method for this anonymous inner class displays an informational message dialog box with the path of the **TreeSelectionEvent** object, for instructional purposes:

```
avm.addTreeSelectionListener(
   new TreeSelectionListener() {
      public void
      valueChanged( TreeSelectionEvent e ) {
         JOptionPane.showMessageDialog(
            TreeExample.this,
            "You selected " + e.getPath() );
      }
   }
);
```

Finally, the **JTree** object is added to the center of the frame window's content pane:

```
getContentPane().add( avm, BorderLayout.CENTER );
```

PRINTING WITH THE 2D API

The very first version of the Java platform did not have support for printing, but ever since programmers discovered that the Java programming language was good for much more than applets, there has been a call for sophisticated and powerful printing support. The 1.1 version of the Java platform offered the **java.awt.PrintJob** class that provided rudimentary printing support. This class still exists and has not been deprecated, so you may come across it if you do maintenance work on older Java applications.

It was when the Java 2D API came along and introduced the **java.awt.print** package that printing support on the Java platform really matured. The class **java.awt.print.PrinterJob** is the central class in this package, providing the control point for displaying print-related dialog boxes, indicating what will print, and actually starting the print job.

Class

```
java.awt.print.PrinterJob
```

Purpose

The **PrinterJob** class provides the control point for displaying print-related dialog boxes, indicating what will print, and actually starting the print job.

Constructor

■ **PrinterJob getPrinterJob()**

There is no public constructor for this class. All **PrinterJob** objects are obtained by calling the static method **getPrinterJob**.

Methods

■ **PageFormat defaultPage( )**

This method creates a new **PageFormat** object with the default margins and print orientation.

■ **PrintService getPrintService()**

This method returns the printer service associated with this printer job.

■ **PageFormat pageDialog(PageFormat** *format* **)**

PageFormat pageDialog(PrintRequestAttributeSet *attrs* **)**

This method displays the platform-specific page setup dialog box with initial values provided by either the input **PageFormat** or **PrintRequestAttributeSet** object.

■ **void print()**

void print(PrintRequestAttributeSet *attrs* **)**

This method prints a set of pages using the attributes specified in the **PrintRequestAttributeSet** object, if provided.

■ **boolean printDialog()**

boolean printDialog(PrintRequestAttributeSet *attrs* **)**

This method displays the platform-specific print dialog box with initial values specified by the input **PrintRequestAttributeSet** object, if provided. The method returns **true** if the user input indicated that the print job should proceed, **false** otherwise.

■ **void setPrintable(Printable** *painter* **)**

void setPrintable(Printable *painter***, PageFormat** *format* **)**

render the pages to be printed. If a **PageFormat** object is specified, it will be passed along to the **Printable** object.

■ **void setPrintService(PrintService** *service* **)**

This method associates the **PrinterJob** object with a new **PrintService** interface. The **PrintService** interface is discussed in the **ViewPrintGIF** example in Figure 7-27.

Class

java.awt.print.PageFormat

Purpose

PageFormat provides information about the size, orientation, and area available for printing for a page of printed output.

7

Constructor

■ **PageFormat()**

The only class constructor returns a default object with portrait page orientation.

Methods

■ **double getHeight()**

This method returns the height of the page in points. One point is equivalent to 1/72 of an inch.

■ **double getImageableHeight()**

This method returns the height of the printable area of the page in points. One point is equivalent to 1/72 of an inch.

■ **double getImageableWidth()**

This method returns the width of the printable area of the page in points. One point is equivalent to 1/72 of an inch.

■ **double getImageableX()**

This method returns the **x** coordinate of the upper-left point of the printable area of the page in points. One point is equivalent to 1/72 of an inch.

■ **double getImageableY()**

This method returns the **y** coordinate of the upper-left point of the printable area of the page in points. One point is equivalent to 1/72 of an inch.

■ **int getOrientation()**

This method returns the orientation of this page. Allowable values are **LANDSCAPE**, **PORTRAIT**, and **REVERSE_LANDSCAPE**. (Reverse landscape orientation has the origin at the top right of the paper with **x** running top to bottom and **y** running right to left.)

■ **double getWidth()**

This method returns the width of the page in points. One point is equivalent to 1/72 of an inch.

Interface

java.awt.print.Printable

Purpose

Any class that is intended to be printed using a **java.awt.print.PrinterJob** object must implement the **Printable** interface.

Method

■ **int print(Graphics *g*, PageFormat *format*, int *pageIndex*)**

When the Printing API calls this method, the data to be printed will be rendered into the provided **Graphics** object using formatting information the **PageFormat** object supplies. The page to be rendered is indicated by the **pageIndex** value, beginning with zero for the first page. Requests for the same **pageIndex** value may be repeated, but the index will not decrease. This method returns **PAGE_EXISTS** if the page is rendered, or **NO_SUCH_PAGE** if the page cannot be rendered.

The program in Figure 7-24 uses the **PrinterJob** and **PageFormat** classes and **Printable** interface. A breakdown of this code follows the output. This program defines the class **FilePrinter** to create a GUI that displays the contents of a file and allows for printing the file.

```
package examples.windows;
import java.awt.*;
import javax.swing.*;
import java.awt.event.*;
import java.awt.print.*;
import java.io.*;
import java.nio.*;
import java.nio.channels.*;
/** An example class used to demonstrate the use of
  * the PrinterJob and PageFormat classes and the
  * Printable interface
  */
```

Figure 7-24   **FilePrinter**: an example using the **PrinterJob** and **PageFormat** classes and **Printable** interface

```
public class FilePrinter extends JFrame
                         implements Printable {
   private JTextField statusLine;
   private JTextArea  text;
   private File file = null;
   private PrinterJob pj = null;
   private PageFormat upf = null;
   /** Class constructor
     * @param titleText Title bar text
     */
   public FilePrinter( String titleText ) {
      super( titleText );
      setDefaultCloseOperation( JFrame.EXIT_ON_CLOSE );
      setJMenuBar( buildMenuBar() );
      Container cp = getContentPane();
      cp.setLayout( new BorderLayout() );
      text = new JTextArea();
      text.setEditable( false );
      text.setBackground( Color.white );
      JScrollPane sp = new JScrollPane( text );
      cp.add( sp, BorderLayout.CENTER );
      statusLine = new JTextField();
      cp.add( statusLine, BorderLayout.SOUTH );
      setSize( 500, 400 );
      setVisible( true );
   }
   /** Present a dialog box to have the user select
     * the file for browsing */
   public void loadFile() {
      JFileChooser fileDialog = new JFileChooser();
      int result
         = fileDialog.showOpenDialog(
                                FilePrinter.this );
      file = fileDialog.getSelectedFile();
      if ( file != null
           && result == JFileChooser.APPROVE_OPTION )
      try {
          FileInputStream fis
             = new FileInputStream( file );
         FileChannel fc = fis.getChannel();
         ByteBuffer bb
            = ByteBuffer.allocate( (int) fc.size() );
         fc.read( bb );
         text.setText( new String( bb.array() ) );
         fc.close();
         fis.close();
      } catch( IOException ioe ) {
         statusLine.setText( ioe.toString() );
      }
   }
```

Figure 7-24   FilePrinter: an example using the PrinterJob and PageFormat
classes and Printable interface (continued)

```java
/** Present a dialog box to allow the user to set up
  * the page geometry for printing */
public void setupPage() {
   if ( pj == null ) {
     pj = PrinterJob.getPrinterJob();
     }
     if ( upf == null ) {
        upf = pj.defaultPage();
     }
   upf = pj.pageDialog( upf );
}
/** Present a dialog box to allow the user to print
  * the file open for browsing */
public void printFile() {
    try {
        if ( pj == null ) {
         pj = PrinterJob.getPrinterJob();
          }
      if ( pj.printDialog() ) {
        if ( upf == null ) {
           pj.setPrintable( this );
         } else {
            pj.setPrintable( this, upf );
      }
      pj.print();
      String prtName
          = pj.getPrintService().getName();
      statusLine.setText( "Printing to "
                                  + prtName );
      }
    } catch( PrinterException pe ) {
       statusLine.setText( pe.toString() );
    }
}
/** Build the menu bar, menus, and menu items for
  * the file browser */
public JMenuBar buildMenuBar() {
   JMenuBar menuBar = new JMenuBar();
   JMenu fileMenu = new JMenu( "File" );
   JMenuItem exitItem = new JMenuItem( "Exit" );
   JMenuItem fileOpenItem
      = new JMenuItem( "File Open..." );
   JMenuItem filePrintItem
      = new JMenuItem( "Print..." );
   JMenuItem filePageSetupItem
      = new JMenuItem( "Page Setup..." );
   fileOpenItem.addActionListener(
      new ActionListener() {
         public void
```

Figure 7-24 FilePrinter: an example using the **PrinterJob** and **PageFormat** classes and **Printable** interface (continued)

```
               actionPerformed( ActionEvent event ) {
                  loadFile();
               }
            }
         );
         filePrintItem.addActionListener(
            new ActionListener() {
               public void
               actionPerformed( ActionEvent event ) {
                  printFile();
               }
            }
         );
         filePageSetupItem.addActionListener(
            new ActionListener() {
               public void
               actionPerformed( ActionEvent event ) {
                  setupPage();
               }
            }
         );
         exitItem.addActionListener(
            new ActionListener() {
               public void
               actionPerformed( ActionEvent event ) {
                  dispose();
                  System.exit( 0 );
               }
            }
         );
         menuBar.add( fileMenu );
         fileMenu.add( fileOpenItem );
         fileMenu.add( filePageSetupItem );
         fileMenu.add( filePrintItem );
         fileMenu.add( exitItem );
         return menuBar;
      }
      /** Required by the Printable interface, this method
        * defines what is printed and how that's done
        */
      public int print(Graphics g, PageFormat ppf,
                         int pageIndex) {
         int pageLen = (int) ppf.getImageableHeight();
         if ( pageIndex * pageLen > text.getHeight() ) {
            return NO_SUCH_PAGE;
         }
         Graphics2D g2 = (Graphics2D) g;
         int pageShift = pageIndex * pageLen;
         g2.translate( ppf.getImageableX(),
                      ppf.getImageableY() - pageShift );
```

Figure 7-24   `FilePrinter`: an example using the `PrinterJob` and `PageFormat` classes and `Printable` interface (continued)

```
        boolean dblbuff = text.isDoubleBuffered();
        if ( dblbuff ) {
            text.setDoubleBuffered( false );
        }
        text.paint( g2 );
        text.setDoubleBuffered( dblbuff );
        return PAGE_EXISTS;
    }
    /** The test method for the class
      * @param args not used
      */
    public static void main( String[] args ) {
        new FilePrinter( "File Printer Sample" );
    }
}
```

Figure 7-24   FilePrinter: an example using the PrinterJob and PageFormat classes and Printable interface (continued)

Allowing for differences in operating systems and available printers, the output should be similar to Figure 7-25 when the Page Setup dialog box is displayed and similar to Figure 7-26 when the Print dialog box is displayed.

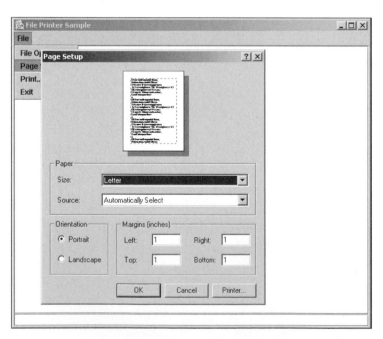

Figure 7-25   Output of the FilePrinter class with the Page Setup dialog box displayed

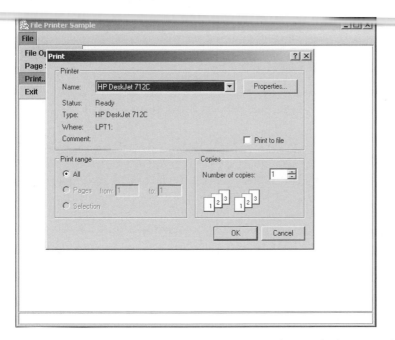

Figure 7-26   Output of the `FilePrinter` class with the Print dialog box displayed

The class encapsulating the program is called `FilePrinter`. The structure of this example is similar to the preceding examples, so only those program statements that pertain to the classes presented in this section are discussed in the following code breakdown.

The **setupPage** method is called when the user selects Page Setup from the File menu. If no **PrinterJob** object has been created, then one is created. Likewise, if no **PageFormat** object has been created, one is created with the default settings. The **pageDialog** method is called to display the dialog box, and the **PageFormat** object is the input parameter. In order to remember the user's input, the **PageFormat** object that was passed as input is replaced by the **PageFormat** object returned by the method. This object will be used later when the printer operation is initiated.

```
public void setupPage() {
    if ( pj == null ) {
        pj = PrinterJob.getPrinterJob();
    }
    if ( upf == null ) {
        upf = pj.defaultPage();
    }
    upf = pj.pageDialog( upf );
}
```

The **printFile** method is the heart of the print operation. It begins by creating a **PrinterJob** object if one has not yet been created, then calls the **printDialog** method to display the Print dialog box. Unless the user cancels the print operation, the **printDialog** method will return **true**.

```
public void printFile() {
    try {
        if ( pj == null ) {
            pj = PrinterJob.getPrinterJob();
        }
        if ( pj.printDialog() ) {
```

The next step is to set what exactly is to be printed by using the **setPrintable** method. The **FilePrinter** class implements the **Printable** interface, so **this** is used to indicate that the current object is to be printed. If the user had previously used the Page Setup dialog box to indicate page format preferences, these preferences will also be passed on the **setPrintable** method call:

```
if ( upf == null ) {
    pj.setPrintable( this );
} else {
    pj.setPrintable( this, upf );
}
```

Finally, it is the invocation of the **print** method that actually causes the job to be sent to the printer. So that the user knows that the job has been sent, the name of the printer is obtained from the print service used for the job and put into the status line:

```
pj.print();
String prtName
    = pj.getPrintService().getName();
statusLine.setText( "Printing to "
                            + prtName );
```

The discussion so far provides a high-level description of the process for creating and submitting a print job. But the details are in the **print** method that actually renders the pages of the file for printing. The **print** method begins by determining whether the requested page exists. To do that, the **pageIndex** value is multiplied by the printable height of the page and the product is compared against the height of the text area being printed. If the product of the **pageIndex** value and the printable height exceeds the height of the text area, then the page doesn't exist and **NO_SUCH_PAGE** is returned.

```
public int print(Graphics g, PageFormat ppf,
                        int pageIndex) {
    int pageLen = (int) ppf.getImageableHeight();
    if ( pageIndex * pageLen > text.getHeight() ) {
        return NO_SUCH_PAGE;
    }
```

If the input **pageIndex** value is within the range of the number of pages to be printed, the **Graphics2D** object is obtained, and the shift required to be applied to the contents of the text area so that the requested page would be rendered beginning at the upper

assumed that the lengths of the lines will not exceed the width of the printable area and so no additional translation is required in the **x** direction. If this cannot be safely assumed, then additional logic must be added to the program to divide long lines across several pages:

```
Graphics2D g2 = (Graphics2D) g;
int pageShift = pageIndex * pageLen;
g2.translate( ppf.getImageableX(),
              ppf.getImageableY() - pageShift );
```

Swing components, such as the **JTextArea** object to be rendered in this example, are by default double buffered. This means that they are first rendered in an off-screen buffer, then rendered onto the display. The result is a display image with noticeably less flicker. However, this step of rendering in an off-screen buffer is not required for printing, and actually does harm because it means that the rendering is done for the resolution of a display. Any additional resolution supported by the printer is ignored. The workaround for this is to turn off double buffering before the rendering operation, then turn it back on again afterwards. Just in case double buffering was turned off for some other reason, a test is first done to determine if it is on or off:

```
boolean dblbuff = text.isDoubleBuffered();
if ( dblbuff ) {
    text.setDoubleBuffered( false );
}
```

With all the setup compete, the text is rendered to the **Graphics2D** object. Double buffering is turned back on (assuming it was on to begin with) and then the method returns **PAGE_EXISTS** to let the Printing API know that there is a page available for printing.

```
text.paint( g2 );
text.setDoubleBuffered( dblbuff );
return PAGE_EXISTS;
}
```

Java Print Service API

A recent development in the support of printing on the Java platform is the release of the Java Print Service API. This new API is an enhancement to the Printing API described in the preceding section, but is intended to serve as a unifying Java Print API for all Java platforms including those with very small memory footprints, such as PDAs and mobile telephones. One of its most important contributions is the ability to define a list of required print job attributes, and then discover all the printers that can support these attributes and select the most appropriate one for the task at hand. Classes in the package **javax.print** and its subpackages provide all of this support.

Interface

`javax.print.Doc`

Purpose

The **Doc** interface encapsulates the interface for an object that supplies a piece of print data for a print job. You pass the print job to an object that implements this interface, and the print job calls methods on that object to obtain the print data. The class **javax.print.SimpleDoc** is an implementation of this interface that can be used in common printing requests because of its ability to handle the document types defined as static variables in the **DocFlavor** class.

Class

`javax.print.DocFlavor`

Purpose

The **DocFlavor** class encapsulates the format in which data will be supplied to a **DocPrintJob** object and has two components: the MIME type and the fully qualified name of the class of the object from which the actual print data comes.

Constructor

- **DocFlavor (String *mimeType*, String *className*)**

  Typically, there is no need to use this constructor because static objects of the class have already been created in anticipation of the most common pairs of MIME type and class name.

Interface

`javax.print.DocPrintJob`

Purpose

This interface represents a print job that can print a specified document with a set of job attributes. An object implementing this interface is obtained from a **PrintService** object.

Class

`javax.print.attribute.HashPrintRequestAttributeSet`

Purpose

The class **HashPrintRequestAttributeSet** is an implementation of the **PrintRequestAttributeSet** interface that can be used for collecting attributes for the print request.

Constructors

- **HashPrintRequestAttributeSet ()**
  HashPrintRequestAttributeSet (PrintRequestAttribute *attr* **)**
  HashPrintRequestAttributeSet (PrintRequestAttribute[ ] *attrs* **)**
  HashPrintRequestAttributeSet (PrintRequestAttributeSet *attrs* **)**

  These constructors create a set for storing attributes for a print request. The set can be constructed as an empty set or as a set with one or more attributes.

Interface

javax.print.attribute.PrintRequestAttributeSet

Purpose

The **PrintRequestAttributeSet** interface specifies the interface for a set of print request attributes. It is used to specify the settings to be applied to a whole print job and to all the documents in the print job. The class **javax.print.attribute. HashPrintRequestAttributeSet** is an implementation of this interface that can be used for collecting attributes for the print request.

Interface

javax.print.PrintService

Purpose

The **PrintService** interface is the factory for **DocPrintJob** objects. An object that implements the **PrintService** interface describes the capabilities of a printer and can be queried regarding a printer's supported attributes.

Class

javax.print.SimpleDoc

Purpose

The **SimpleDoc** class is an implementation of the **Doc** interface that can be used in common printing requests because of its ability to handle the doc flavors defined as static variables in the **DocFlavor** class.

Constructor

- **SimpleDoc (Object** *printData***, DocFlavor** *flavor***,**
          DocAttributeSet *attrs* **)**

  This constructor creates a simple document with the given print data, document flavor, and document attribute set. The attribute set can be **null**.

Figure 7-27 is a program that uses the **DocFlavor**, **HashPrintRequestAttributeSet**, **PrintRequestAttributeSet**, and **SimpleDoc** classes and the **DocPrintJob**, **Doc**, and **PrintService** interfaces. A breakdown of this code follows the output. This program defines the class **ViewPrintGIF** to create a GUI that displays the contents of a GIF (Graphics Interchange Format) file and allows for printing the file to a printer that has been found to support printing this file format.

```
package examples.windows;
import java.awt.*;
import javax.swing.*;
import javax.swing.filechooser.FileFilter;
import java.awt.event.*;
import java.io.*;
import javax.print.*;
import javax.print.attribute.*;
import javax.print.attribute.standard.*;
/** An example class used to demonstrate the
  * use of the Java Print Service
  */
public class ViewPrintGIF extends JFrame {
   private JTextField statusLine;
   private ImagePanel imgPanel;
   private File file = null;
   /** Class constructor
     * @param titleText Title bar text
     */
   public ViewPrintGIF( String titleText ) {
      super( titleText );
      setDefaultCloseOperation( JFrame.EXIT_ON_CLOSE );
      setJMenuBar( buildMenuBar() );
      Container cp = getContentPane();
      cp.setLayout( new BorderLayout() );
      imgPanel = new ImagePanel();
      cp.add( imgPanel, BorderLayout.CENTER );
      statusLine = new JTextField();
      cp.add( statusLine, BorderLayout.SOUTH );
      setSize( 500, 400 );
      setVisible( true );
   }
   /** Present a dialog box to have the user select
     * the file for browsing */
   public void loadFile() {
      JFileChooser fileDialog = new JFileChooser();
      fileDialog.setFileFilter( new GIFFilter () );
      int result
         = fileDialog.showOpenDialog( ViewPrintGIF.this );
      file = fileDialog.getSelectedFile();
      if ( file != null
           && result == JFileChooser.APPROVE_OPTION )
```

Figure 7-27   `ViewPrintGIF`: an example of the Java Print Service

```
         try {
            imgPanel.setImage( file );
         } catch( Exception e ) {
            statusLine.setText( e.toString() );
         }
      }
   /** Find a printer suitable for GIF files and print
     * the selected GIF file
     */
   public void printFile() {
      DocFlavor flavor = DocFlavor.INPUT_STREAM.GIF;
      PrintRequestAttributeSet aset
         = new HashPrintRequestAttributeSet();
      aset.add( MediaSizeName.NA_LETTER );
      aset.add( new Copies( 1 ) );
      PrintService[] pservices
         = PrintServiceLookup.lookupPrintServices( flavor,
                                                   aset );
      if (pservices.length > 0) {
         statusLine.setText( "Printing to " +
                             pservices[0].getName());
         DocPrintJob dpj = pservices[0].createPrintJob();
         try {
            FileInputStream fis
               = new FileInputStream( file );
            Doc doc = new SimpleDoc( (InputStream) fis,
                                     flavor, null );
            dpj.print( doc, aset );
         } catch( IOException ioe ) {
            statusLine.setText( ioe.toString() );
         } catch( PrintException pe ) {
            statusLine.setText( pe.toString() );
         }
      } else {
         statusLine.setText( "No printer detected" );
      }
   }
   /** Build the menu bar, menus, and menu items
     */
   public JMenuBar buildMenuBar() {
      JMenuBar menuBar = new JMenuBar();
      JMenu fileMenu = new JMenu( "File" );
      JMenuItem exitItem = new JMenuItem( "Exit" );
      JMenuItem fileOpenItem
         = new JMenuItem( "File Open..." );
      JMenuItem filePrintItem
         = new JMenuItem( "Print" );
      fileOpenItem.addActionListener(
         new ActionListener() {
            public void
```

Figure 7-27   `ViewPrintGIF`: an example of the Java Print Service (continued)

```
                        actionPerformed( ActionEvent event ) {
                            loadFile();
                        }
                }
            );
            filePrintItem.addActionListener(
                new ActionListener() {
                    public void
                    actionPerformed( ActionEvent event ) {
                        printFile();
                    }
                }
            );
            exitItem.addActionListener(
                new ActionListener() {
                    public void
                    actionPerformed( ActionEvent event ) {
                        dispose();
                        System.exit( 0 );
                    }
                }
            );
            menuBar.add( fileMenu );
            fileMenu.add( fileOpenItem );
            fileMenu.add( filePrintItem );
            fileMenu.add( exitItem );
            return menuBar;
        }
        /** GUI component class used to display an
          * image within a panel
          */
        public class ImagePanel extends JPanel {
            Toolkit tk;
            Image i = null;
            /** Class constructor
              */
            public ImagePanel() {
                setBackground( Color.white );
                tk = Toolkit.getDefaultToolkit();
            }
            /** Draws the text, lines, and shapes in the
              * specified graphics context
              * @param g the component's graphics context
              */
            public void paintComponent( Graphics g ) {
                super.paintComponent(g);
                if ( i != null ) {
                    g.drawImage( i, 0, 0, this );
                }
            }
```

Figure 7-27   `ViewPrintGIF`: an example of the Java Print Service (continued)

```
        /** Specify the image to be displayed by
         * providing the name of the file containing
         * the image
         * @param f file containing the image
         */
        public void setImage( File f ) {
           i = tk.createImage( f.getPath() );
        }
    }
    /** Class for filtering GIF files and the directories
     * that contain them
     */
    public class GIFFilter extends FileFilter {
        /** Determine whether a file is accepted
         * by the filter
         * @param f the file to be tested
         */
        public boolean accept( File f ) {
           if ( f.getName().endsWith( ".gif" ) ) {
              return true;
           } else if ( f.isDirectory() ) {
              return true;
           } else {
              return false;
           }
        }
        /** Return the name of the file filter
         */
        public String getDescription() {
           return "GIF image files (*.gif)";
        }
    }
    /** The test method for the class
     * @param args not used
     */
    public static void main( String[] args ) {
        new ViewPrintGIF( "GIF File Viewer/Printer Sample" );
    }
}
```

Figure 7-27   `ViewPrintGIF:` an example of the Java Print Service (continued)

Allowing for differences in operating systems, the output should be similar to Figure 7-28 after successfully printing the contents of a GIF file.

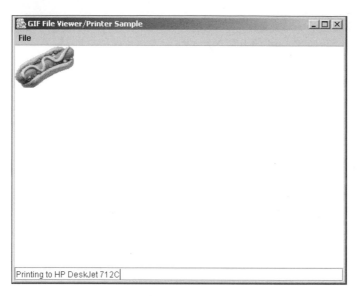

Figure 7-28   Output of the `ViewPrintGIF` class after printing an image

The class encapsulating the program is called `ViewPrintGIF`. The structure of this example is similar to the preceding examples, so only those program statements that pertain to the classes presented in this section are discussed in the following code breakdown.

The `printFile` method is called when the user selects Print from the File menu. The method begins by specifying that the doc flavor will be a GIF from an input stream and then creates a set for holding the attributes of the print job. Attributes are added to indicate that the paper size required is North American letter size, and that a single copy is required.

```
public void printFile() {
   DocFlavor flavor = DocFlavor.INPUT_STREAM.GIF;
   PrintRequestAttributeSet aset
      = new HashPrintRequestAttributeSet();
   aset.add( MediaSizeName.NA_LETTER );
   aset.add( new Copies( 1 ) );
```

The next statement is where the real power of this API comes through. With one line of code the program is able to retrieve a complete list of all the available print services that will handle the doc flavor and attributes specified.

```
PrintService[] pservices
   = PrintServiceLookup.lookupPrintServices( flavor,
                                             aset );
```

The length of the array will indicate how many matching print services were found. If at least one is found, the program will just naively take the first one to create the necessary

the user will know where to go to get the printer output:

```
if (pservices.length > 0) {
    statusLine.setText( "Printing to " +
                        pservices[0].getName());
    DocPrintJob dpj = pservices[0].createPrintJob();
```

The document to be printed must still be specified. Creating an instance of the **SimpleDoc** class does this. The constructor parameters are a file input stream to be the print data, and the same doc flavor that was used to find the print service. No document attributes are provided, and so the third constructor parameter is **null**:

```
try {
    FileInputStream fis
        = new FileInputStream( file );
    Doc doc = new SimpleDoc( (InputStream) fis,
                             flavor, null );
```

After successfully creating the doc to be printed, the printer job's **print** method is called and the doc and the printer job attribute set are passed as input parameters:

```
dpj.print( doc, aset );
```

If any errors occur, the contents of the exception are written into the status line. Likewise, if no printer service matched the printer job attributes, a message is written into the status line to inform the user of this problem:

```
    } catch( IOException ioe ) {
        statusLine.setText( ioe.toString() );
    } catch( PrintException pe ) {
        statusLine.setText( pe.toString() );
    }
} else {
    statusLine.setText( "No printer detected" );
}
}
```

CHAPTER SUMMARY

- ❏ Support for the development of GUIs for the Java platform is provided by a combination of the AWT and Swing APIs.

- ❏ The AWT API provides the infrastructure for layout managers, events, event listeners, and basic 2D graphics support. The Swing API provides a comprehensive set of GUI components that can be assembled to produce professional applications.

- ❏ The most basic Swing class is **JComponent**, which is the superclass of all Swing components and provides the basic function common to all the Swing components.

❑ Components that are containers hold other components. Swing provides many container components. Especially useful are the top-level containers **JApplet**, **JDialog**, **JFrame**, and **JWindow**.

❑ An application runs in a **JFrame** object. An applet runs in a **JApplet** object. You build a GUI adding containers and components to the **JFrame** object of an application or the panel of an applet.

❑ Swing provides several classes of buttons and check boxes that can be used to provide selection lists and triggers for events.

❑ Use the classes **JMenuBar**, **JMenuItem**, **JMenu**, **JPopupMenu**, **JRadioButtonMenuItem**, and **JCheckBoxMenuItem** to add menus to your GUI. Swing also provides support for toolbars through the **JToolBar** class. Actions that are common to both menus and toolbars can be created as subclasses of **AbstractAction** to provide a single point of control.

❑ The classes **JSlider**, **JProgressBar**, and **JScrollBar** provide adjustable components to be added to GUIs. The classes **JList** and **JComboBox** provide selection lists to be added to GUIs. In addition, Swing provides several text entry classes with a wide variety of complexity: **JTextField**, **JTextArea**, **JPasswordField**, **JEditorPane**, and **JTextPane**.

❑ Because selecting files and colors are such common operations, Swing includes the standard classes **JFileChooser** and **JColorChooser** that implement panels and that can be embedded in dialogs or internal frames.

❑ Swing provides two sophisticated controls for structured information: **JTable** and **JTree**. The **JTable** class is best suited for tabular information, and **JTree** is ideal for hierarchical information.

❑ Print capability can be added to an application by using either the Printing API from the 2D API or by using the Java Print Service API. The print capability provided by the 2D API is well suited for printing text and graphics that are displayed within an application. The Java Print Service API can be used for that same purpose, but its strength lies in its capability to handle many flavors of documents and to search and discover print services for handling these many document flavors.

REVIEW QUESTIONS

1. Which of the following classes are subclasses of **javax.swing. AbstractButton**? Select all that apply.

a. **JButton**

b. **JComboBox**

d. JMenu

e. JMenuItem

2. Which method of the **JComponent** class allows a component to respond to user input and generate events? Select the best answer.

a. setVisible

b. setEnabled

c. setReady

d. addListener

e. setActive

3. Which of the following classes are subclasses of **javax.swing.text. JTextComponent**? Select all that apply.

a. JList

b. JTextField

c. JFileChooser

d. JEditorPane

e. JScrollPane

4. Which of the following statements construct a **JTextArea** object that can display 20 lines of text of approximately 60 characters each? Select all that apply.

a. JTextArea t = new JTextArea(60, 20);

b. JTextArea t = new JTextArea(20, 60);

c. JTextArea t = new JTextArea("Sales Projections:",
                 60, 20);

d. JTextArea t = new JTextArea("Sales Projections:",
                 20, 60);

e. JTextArea t = new JTextArea(60, 20,
                 "Sales Projections:");

5. Which of the following classes implement the **LayoutManager** interface? Select all that apply.

a. Container

b. Canvas

c. FlowLayout

d. BoxLayout

e. GridLayout

7

6. Which of the following classes is the default **LayoutManager** class for the **JPanel** class? Select the best answer.

   a. BorderLayout

   b. CardLayout

   c. FlowLayout

   d. GridBagLayout

   e. There is no default.

7. What is the return type of all methods defined in the **TreeSelectionListener** interface? Select the best answer.

   a. void

   b. boolean

   c. TreeSelectionEvent

   d. TreeSelectionListener

   e. TreeSelection

8. What model class that extends the **AbstractSpinnerModel** class should be used for a **JSpinner** component that allows the user to select a value from a predefined list?

9. True or False: The same **JFileChooser** object can be used to open files and to save files.

10. True or False: If the method **PrintServiceLookup.lookupPrintServices** is unable to find a print service that matches the specified attributes, a **PrintException** exception is thrown.

11. What methods of the **PageFormat** class are used to determine the size of the printable area for a specific printer job?

12. How does a program indicate to the 2D API that there are no more pages left to print for the current printer job?

PROGRAMMING EXERCISES

Debugging

1. Correct all the errors in the following program so that the text in the label is green when the window appears:

```
package questions.c7;
import javax.swing.*;
import java.awt.*;
import java.awt.event.*;
```

```
public class Debug7_1 extends JFrame {
    public Debug7_1( String titleText ) {
        super( titleText );
        setDefaultCloseOperation( JFrame.EXIT_ON_CLOSE );
        JLabel l = new JLabel( "Debug question" );
        l.setColor( green );
        getContentPane().add( l, BorderLayout.CENTER );
        setSize( 300, 100 );
        setVisible( true );
    }
    public static void main( String[] args ) {
        new Debug7_1( "Debug Question" );
    }
}
```

2. Correct all the errors in the following program so that when the frame window appears it contains a text area with 80 columns and 25 rows:

```
package questions.c7;
import javax.swing.*;
import java.awt.*;
import java.awt.event.*;
public class Debug7_2 extends JFrame {
    public Debug7_2( String titleText ) {
        super( titleText );
        setDefaultCloseOperation( JFrame.EXIT_ON_CLOSE );
        JTextArea ta
            = new JTextArea( 80, 25, "Sample Text" );
        getContentPane().add( ta, BorderLayout.CENTER );
        pack();
        setVisible( true );
    }
    public static void main( String[] args ) {
        new Debug7_2( "Debug Question" );
    }
}
```

3. Correct all the errors in the following program so that the nine buttons are displayed in a three-by-three grid no matter how the frame window is resized:

```
package questions.c7;
import javax.swing.*;
import java.awt.*;
import java.awt.event.*;
public class Debug7_3 extends JFrame {
    public Debug7_3( String titleText ) {
        super( titleText );
        setDefaultCloseOperation( JFrame.EXIT_ON_CLOSE );
        JButton[] buttons = new JButton[9];
```

7

```
        for( int i=0; i<buttons.length; i++ ) {
            buttons[i]
                = new JButton( String.valueOf( i+1 ) );
            add( buttons[i] );
        }
        pack();
        setVisible( true );
    }
    public static void main( String[] args ) {
        new Debug7_3( "Debug Question" );
    }
}
```

4. Correct all the errors in the following program so that the handler defined for the **JTextField** object converts any lowercase character entered to uppercase when the Enter key is pressed:

```
package questions.c7;
import javax.swing.*;
import java.awt.*;
import java.awt.event.*;
public class Debug7_4 extends JFrame {
    public Debug7_4( String titleText ) {
        super( titleText );
        setDefaultCloseOperation( JFrame.EXIT_ON_CLOSE );
        final JTextField tf = new JTextField( 40 );
        tf.addListener( new Listener() {
                public void eventHappened( Event e ) {
                    tf.setText(
                        tf.getText().toUpperCase() );
                }
            }
        );
        getContentPane().add( tf, BorderLayout.NORTH );
        pack();
        setVisible( true );
    }
    public static void main( String[] args ) {
        new Debug7_4( "Debug Question" );
    }
}
```

5. Correct all the errors in the following program so that the program will print the message "Print this!" when the Print menu item is selected:

```
package questions.c7;
import java.awt.*;
import javax.swing.*;
import java.awt.event.*;
import java.awt.print.*;
```

```
                                      implements Printable {
   private JTextField statusLine;
   private JLabel greeting
      = new JLabel( "Print this!", JLabel.CENTER );
   public Debug7_5( String titleText ) {
      super( titleText );
      setDefaultCloseOperation( JFrame.EXIT_ON_CLOSE );
      setJMenuBar( buildMenuBar() );
      Container cp = getContentPane();
      cp.setLayout( new BorderLayout() );
      cp.add( greeting, BorderLayout.CENTER );
      statusLine = new JTextField();
      cp.add( statusLine, BorderLayout.SOUTH );
      setSize( 500, 400 );
      setVisible( true );
   }
   public void printFile() {
       try {
         PrinterJob pj = PrinterJob.getPrinterJob();
         if ( pj.printDialog() ) {
             pj.setPrintable( this );
             pj.print();
             String prtName
                 = pj.getPrintService().getName();
             statusLine.setText( "Printing to "
                                             + prtName );
         }
         } catch( PrinterException pe ) {
            statusLine.setText( pe.toString() );
      }
   }
   public JMenuBar buildMenuBar() {
      JMenuBar menuBar = new JMenuBar();
      JMenu fileMenu = new JMenu( "File" );
      JMenuItem exitItem = new JMenuItem( "Exit" );
      JMenuItem filePrintItem
         = new JMenuItem( "Print..." );
      filePrintItem.addActionListener(
         new ActionListener() {
            public void
            actionPerformed( ActionEvent event ) {
               printFile();
            }
         }
      );
```

7

```
        exitItem.addActionListener(
            new ActionListener() {
                public void
                actionPerformed( ActionEvent event ) {
                    dispose();
                    System.exit( 0 );
                }
            }
        );
        menuBar.add( fileMenu );
        fileMenu.add( filePrintItem );
        fileMenu.add( exitItem );
        return menuBar;
    }
    public int print(Graphics g, PageFormat ppf,
                        int pageIndex) {
        Graphics2D g2 = (Graphics2D) g;
        g2.print( greeting );
        return PAGE_EXISTS;
    }
    public static void main( String[] args ) {
        new Debug7_5( "Greeting Printer" );
    }
}
```

Complete the Solution

1. Extract the file X:\Data\questions\c7\Complete7_1.java from the CD-ROM. (Here X: is the drive letter of the CD-ROM.) Complete the Complete7_1 class definition by defining an inner class called CheckboxHandler. Objects of this class will handle events generated by the disableCheck object. When disableCheck is selected, all the JButton objects should be disabled.

2. Extract the file X:\Data\questions\c7\Complete7_2.java from the CD-ROM. (Here X: is the drive letter of the CD-ROM.) Complete the Complete7_2 class definition by adding statements that create a label, a list, and a panel with two buttons. Put the label in the North position of the frame, the list in the Center position, and the button panel in the South position. It isn't necessary to add event handlers for these components.

3. Extract the file X:\Data\questions\c7\Complete7_3.java from the CD-ROM. (Here X: is the drive letter of the CD-ROM.) Complete the Complete7_3 class definition by adding statements to the empty centerOnDesktop method so that the method centers the window on the user's desktop. Look to the Toolkit class for methods that provide information about the desktop.

4. Begin with the sample program ~~PrintInvoice~~ presented in this chapter, and use **JOptionPane** components to improve the usability of the printing interface. When no printer services are found that match, display an informational message. When only one printer is found, display a confirmation message before using the printer. And when multiple matches are found, display the list of print services and have the user choose which to use.

5. Extract the file **X:\Data\questions\c7\Complete7_5.java** from the CD-ROM. (Here **X:** is the drive letter of the CD-ROM.) Complete the **Complete7_5** class definition by adding statements to the empty **findPrintServices** method so that the method takes the doc flavor and attributes specified in the user interface, then finds and displays all the print service matches.

Discovery

1. Create an application called **ColoredScribble** that lets the user click, drag, and release with the mouse to draw lines in a window. Include menu items that let the user select the color of the line to be drawn, print the drawing, save the drawing to a file, and retrieve the drawing from a file. (*Hint*: Use object serialization for saving and retrieving the drawing.)

2. Continue the enhancement of your **JUnzip** class from the previous chapter's Discovery questions to allow the user either to extract all files or to extract files selectively from the zip archive.

3. Enhance the **Choosers** sample program to provide the ability to change the font used to display the file contents. Swing currently has no font chooser class, so create your own using a **JOptionPane** object to display a list of fonts from which the user can select. (*Hint*: Investigate the **GraphicsEnvironment** class to find a method that will return a list of all the available fonts.)

7

JavaBeans

INTRODUCTION

With an understanding of JavaBeans, you can create better software because you are encouraged to think and design in a modular fashion. Two groups of Java programmers need to understand the JavaBeans architecture:

- Programmers who create beanboxes, which are the tools that consume JavaBeans and allow them to be connected

- Developers who create the actual JavaBeans

This chapter focuses on the latter, and larger, group. Much of the discussion centers on using the Java programming language and the core classes and interfaces in the package **java.beans** to create beans. Because understanding how beans are used to create applications is essential for designers of beans, this chapter includes an introduction to the Beans Development Kit (BDK) from Sun. The BDK is a software package intended to encourage and support the development of JavaBeans components. It contains a tutorial, example source code, and the demonstration beanbox known as the BeanBox.

The Enterprise JavaBeans (EJB) specification describes a model for Java components that are designed to be installed on and made available from servers. The connection between EJB components and JavaBeans is that both are component models for the Java programming language. Except for the similarity in the names—JavaBeans and Enterprise JavaBeans—there are few similarities between the actual components. JavaBeans are primarily designed for use in the visual composition of programs that are constructed from reusable components. Enterprise JavaBeans extend the JavaBeans model to meet the needs of business applications used in industries such as banking, electronic commerce, and insurance. To do this, they add support for transactions, state management, and application deployment attributes. Enterprise JavaBeans are discussed in depth in Chapter 14.

JavaBeans Component Model

For many years, software developers strived to achieve modularity and reusability of software components by developing models to describe these components and the way the components should be constructed, in order to allow them to connect to each other in a straightforward fashion. The goal of software developers is to make the integration of software components a reality, so that they can build applications from existing components, or entire programs. The goal of creating reusable and interchangeable software components is emerging through the development of software component models. The Java platform's designers took a bold step by proposing the platform's own component model—JavaBeans. The JavaBeans component model provides a framework for creating reusable, connectable software components.

Increasingly, Integrated Development Environments (IDEs) for the Java platform, such as IBM's WebSphere Studio Application Developer, are being designed to accept JavaBean components. These applications provide environments in which the programmer can easily assemble JavaBean components to build complex software applications out of standard parts.

When you use a visual development environment, the distinguishing feature of components, such as JavaBeans, becomes clear: You manipulate the components at design time as binary executables. You are not modifying source statements or working with the Java platform APIs.

By no means is JavaBeans the first component model ever devised, but it is the first component model for the Java platform. Recognizing that other component models are in use, the creators of the JavaBeans component model designed the model for interoperability with other component frameworks. For example, the ActiveX bridge, which is available on 32-bit Windows platforms, can turn a bean into an ActiveX control for embedding in ActiveX-aware software.

It is possible to define classes that conform to the specification of the JavaBeans component model and are also compatible with other Java programming models. For example, you can create a class that can function as an applet and as a JavaBean. A loan interest calculator would be an example of a class that would be useful as both an applet embedded in a Web page and as a JavaBean that could be connected with other components to construct a personal finance application. Indeed, you may already be more familiar with the JavaBeans specification than you realize. All the Swing and AWT components described in Chapters 6 and 7 are JavaBeans.

JavaBeans are packaged in Java archive (.jar) files that include a manifest file. You create and manipulate these .jar files using the jar utility provided in the SDK. A .jar file

file indicates which of these `.class` files correspond to a JavaBean. A single `.jar` file can have more than one JavaBean class.

WHAT MAKES A CLASS A BEAN

The core classes and interfaces in the packages `java.beans` and `java.beans.beancontext` provide the support for creating JavaBeans. However, there is no JavaBean superclass that all JavaBeans extend and no interface that all JavaBeans implement. Creating a class that is also a JavaBean largely involves adhering to the standards of the JavaBeans component model.

> Support for the JavaBeans component model was added to the Java platform with version 1.1. Many method names in the AWT API were changed between versions 1.0 and 1.1 to follow the JavaBeans convention. The original GUI event model was deprecated, and the current model was introduced to make JavaBeans possible.

Creating a reusable, embeddable piece of software, such as a JavaBean, requires some planning. Enough of the workings of the JavaBean must be exposed to make it useful, but not so much that the user becomes overwhelmed with its complexity or hopelessly dependent on the details of the JavaBean's inner workings. Where to draw this line is something that is learned mostly by experience and by carefully considering the needs of the users of the JavaBean. Each item of a JavaBean interface falls into one of the three categories listed in Figure 8-1.

A full description of the JavaBeans specification is beyond the scope of this book. The programming conventions are summarized in Figure 8-2, and the full specifications are available from the Sun Web site at the following URL: `http://java.sun.com/beans/docs/spec.html`.

The latest news about JavaBeans and many related documents are available from the JavaBeans home page on the Sun Web site at the following URL: `http://java.sun.com/products/javabeans/`.

Some of the main characteristics of JavaBeans follow:

- If a bean has a property named `X`, it can have public methods named `setX` or `getX`, to assign and return the value of the property `X`. A variation on this convention is allowed for properties of type `boolean`, for which the methods are named `setX` and `isX`. A read-only or write-only property has only one method of the pair. A read-only property is not necessarily constant; a change to another property might change a read-only property indirectly.

- If a bean can generate events of the class `YEvent`, it should have public methods of the following forms:

```
void addYListener( YEvent )
void removeYListener( YEvent )
```

Element	Description
Methods	A method represents some action that can be executed against the JavaBean. For example, a JavaBean that displays an animation may have methods to start and stop the animation.
Properties	A property represents an attribute of the JavaBean, such as its color or font. The property does not have to be a visible attribute. For example, a property can be an abstract quality, such as a `boolean` flag that indicates whether a component is enabled for input. Properties can be single entities or indexed elements of a set. They can be passive or bound. A passive property cannot initiate any activity. A bound property can notify other beans when it changes. If a property is constrained, other beans can prevent it from changing value.
Events	JavaBean objects use events to notify other JavaBean objects that some event has occurred. These objects use the same event-handling mechanism as Swing and AWT components. JavaBeans that must be aware of a certain event register as a listener with the JavaBean that generates the event. Listener JavaBeans must implement the interface that corresponds to the event class of interest. Source JavaBeans provide registration methods for the event. When the event occurs, the source JavaBean sends a copy of the event to each registered listener. Many of the events generated by beans are `PropertyChangeEvent` objects, but you can define custom events.

Figure 8-1   Elements of a JavaBean interface

Other public methods of the class are actions that the JavaBean can execute.

- All beans should have a constructor that takes no arguments because the Sun BeanBox (and most other beanboxes) call this constructor. When the superclass constructor has required arguments, the bean constructor must call the superclass constructor and pass literal constants as arguments.

- A JavaBean class must implement the marker interface **Serializable**, because beanboxes use serialization to save the state of beans. (Chapter 3 describes object serialization.) As a result, fields that are instances of classes that do not support serialization must be qualified with the keyword **transient**. In general, attributes that depend on system-specific features, such as font sizes, should also be qualified with **transient** so that they can be recalculated when the bean is deserialized. Figure 8-2 gives a more complete list of the programming conventions for declarations in a bean.

Element of the Bean	Form of Declaration
Property X of type C	
Accessor	`public C getX()`
Mutator	`public void setX( C value )`
Boolean property X	
Accessor	`public boolean getX()` or `public boolean isX()`
Mutator	`public void setX( boolean value )`
Indexed property X of type C[ ]	
Group accessor	`public C[] getX()`
Group mutator	`public void setX( C[] value )`
Element accessor	`public C getX( int index )`
Element mutator	`public void setX( int index, C value )`
Bound property X of type C	
Accessor	`public C getX()`
Mutator	`public void setX( C value )`
Listener registration	`public void addPropertyChangeListener` `( PropertyChangeListener listener )`
Listener removal	`public void removePropertyChangeListener` `( PropertyChangeListener listener )`
Constrained property X of type C	
Accessor	`public C getX()`
Mutator	`public void setX( C value )  throws` `PropertyVetoException`
Listener registration	`public void addVetoableChangeListener` `( VetoableChangeListener listener )`
Listener removal	`public void RemoveVetotableChangeListener` `( VetoableChangeListener listener )`
Event Y	
Class name	`YEvent`
Listener interface name	`YListener`
Listener registration	`public void addYListener( YListener listener )`
Listener removal	`public void removeYListener( YListener listener )`
BeanInfo class for class JB	
Class name	`JBBeanInfo`
Property editor for type C	
Class name	`CEditor`
Constructor	Must have a no-argument constructor.
Customizer for class JB	
Class name	Any, but `JBCustomizer` is common.
Superclass	Must be `java.awt.Component` or a subclass, usually `Panel` or `JPanel`.
Constructor	One constructor must have no arguments.

Figure 8-2   Programming conventions for JavaBeans

8

BEAN DEVELOPMENT ENVIRONMENTS

When you are creating JavaBeans, it is helpful to understand how development environments operate on JavaBeans. To that end, Sun created a demonstration development environment called the BeanBox. This book uses this capitalized term when referring to this specific environment to distinguish it from a general reference to a beanbox environment coming from another source.

You can download the most recent version from the Sun Web site by following the instructions in the ReadMe file on the CD-ROM that accompanies this book. Because the BDK is freely available, it is used as the reference point for the JavaBean examples in this chapter. When using the BeanBox, keep in mind that it was developed for demonstration purposes and is not a production IDE intended to create JavaBean applications. The BDK software is no longer being enhanced and is provided by Sun for educational and demonstration purposes only. Sun's successor to the BeanBox is the Bean Builder, which was available only as a beta release at the time this text was developed. Similar to the BeanBox, the Bean Builder is a program that demonstrates new and emerging technologies within the Java platform that allow the construction of applications using component assembly mechanisms. The Bean Builder extends the capabilities of the original BeanBox by demonstrating new techniques for persistence, layout editing, and dynamic event adapter generation. Examples in this chapter use the original BeanBox because it is a proven tool and because its simplicity allows us to focus on the JavaBeans and not on the features and functions of a tool.

You can load beans into the Sun BeanBox directly from a Java archive (`.jar`) file. You create and manipulate these files using the `jar` utility.

Syntax

`jar options [manifest] destination file_list`

Dissection

Control the activities of the `jar` utility with options. The fields you include in a `jar` command depend on the actions to be performed.

- When you specify more than one option, concatenate them into one token.

- The optional manifest file holds information about the `.jar` file. A default manifest is included in the `.jar` file if you do not specify one of your own. Usually the default manifest is adequate, but not for cases where JavaBeans are included.

- You can use the wildcard characters `*` and `?` when listing files. You can also specify folder names.

- The `jar` command recursively processes subfolders when the input file is a folder.

Options of the jar command are the following:

- The option **c** creates a new or empty .jar file.

- Include the option **f** to indicate that the .jar file to create is named on the command line. Without this option, the command sends the output to standard output. When combined with the **x** or **t** options, option **f** indicates that the second field on the command line is the name of an existing .jar file to process.

- To include information from an existing manifest, include the **m** option and list the manifest file on the command line.

- If you do not want a manifest file, include the option **m** to suppress creation of a manifest.

- The option **t** lists the table of contents for the archive.

- The option **v** generates additional output, such as the size of files and when they were created.

- The option **x** extracts the files named on the command line, or all files if no specific files are listed.

- The **0** (digit zero) option tells the jar utility to store the files only when creating a .jar file and not to apply any compression.

Examples

```
jar cf mystuff.jar *.class *.au *.gif *.jpg
jar cmf mymanifest.txt mystuff.jar *.class
jar tf newjar.jar
jar xf X.class existingjar.jar
```

Example Contents of a Manifest File for a Java Archive (.jar) File

```
Name: examples/beans/ImageBean1.class
Java-Bean: True

Name: examples/beans/ImageBean2.class
Java-Bean: True

Name: examples/beans/MagentaButton.class
Java-Bean: True
```

Tool Usage Dissection

The first command in the preceding examples creates a .jar file called **mystuff.jar** and adds to the .jar file all files in the current folder with the extension .class, .au, .gif, or .jpg.

The second command creates a .jar file called **mystuff.jar**, using an existing manifest **mymanifest.txt**, and adds all .class files in the current folder to the .jar file. Each manifest entry must have a Name property that identifies where the JavaBean

.class file can be found within the .jar file, and a Java-Bean attribute that must be set to True. The BeanBox requires a blank line between the manifest file entries for each JavaBean and a blank line after the last entry.

The third command lists all the files in the .jar file newjar.jar.

The fourth command will extract the file X.class from the .jar file existingjar.jar. If only a .jar file name is specified, all files are extracted.

In general, a beanbox uses the classes of the **java.lang.reflect** package to analyze the classes contained within the .jar file. This package supports run-time type information, as described in Chapter 2. If the beanbox finds public methods of the form setX, getX, or isX, it assumes that X is a property of the JavaBean. If the beanbox finds public methods of the form addYListener and removeYListener, both of which return void and take a single argument of type YEvent, it assumes that the JavaBean fires events of the class YEvent. Some beanboxes, including the Sun BeanBox described in this chapter, have a limitation that prevents them from handling other methods, unless the methods take no arguments and return **void**. This restriction is not part of the JavaBeans specification.

USING THE SUN BEANBOX

To follow the examples in this chapter, install the Sun BeanBox as part of the BDK by following the instructions in the ReadMe file on the CD-ROM.

To start the BeanBox:

1. Open a command-line window and go to the folder in which you installed the BDK. For example, if you installed the BDK in its default location, use the command **cd C:\BDK1.1**.

2. Make the subfolder **beanbox** the current folder using the command **cd beans\beanbox**.

3. Enter **run**.

The run command executes a batch file that sets up the environment for the BDK, loads the JVM, and loads the BeanBox Java application. When the BeanBox starts, you see four windows similar to those shown in Figures 8-3, 8-4, 8-5, and 8-6.

The ToolBox window serves as a palette of the available beans. Beans are loaded when the BeanBox automatically opens and processes all .jar files that reside in the reserved subfolder called jars. If you start with only the files supplied with the BDK, the ToolBox window lists the demonstration beans included with the BDK, as shown in Figure 8-3.

Figure 8-3   The BDK BeanBox ToolBox window

The window labeled BeanBox is the composition window in which you can arrange and connect the beans. You can load a `.jar` file into the ToolBox window after the BeanBox has started by choosing LoadJar from the File menu of the window in Figure 8-4.

Figure 8-4   The BDK BeanBox composition window

8

The Properties window, shown in Figure 8-5, lists the properties of a selected bean and lets you edit those properties.

Figure 8-5   The BDK BeanBox Properties window

The Method Tracer window, shown in Figure 8-6, displays the output from the method tracing service provided by the BeanBox. This service is useful for understanding the flow of an application. JavaBeans use the BeanContext API to locate and use the method tracing service.

Figure 8-6   The BDK BeanBox Method Tracer window

Before developing this chapter's example bean, try positioning a demonstration bean in the composition window and then removing the bean.

To position a demonstration bean in the composition window:

1. Select the JellyBean bean from the ToolBox window by clicking the word **JellyBean** with the mouse. The cross-hair cursor appears.

2. Position the cross-hair cursor on the BeanBox window. Click the **BeanBox** window, and the JellyBean bean drops into place.

   The bean is surrounded by a hatched black and gray border, which indicates that the bean is selected. When a bean is selected, its properties are displayed and editable in the Properties window.

8. Try changing some properties. Click the **color** box in the Properties window. The window called sun.beans.editors.ColorEditor opens. Figure 8-7 shows the ColorEditor window.

Figure 8-7   The BeanBox property editor window

4. Change the color of the bean by selecting a color from the drop-down list on the right of the window or by changing the red, green, or blue intensity values in the middle of the window. The color on the left of the ColorEditor window and the color of the bean in the BeanBox window change immediately. Click the **Done** button when finished.

To remove the bean from the BeanBox window:

1. With the bean selected, click **Edit** from the BeanBox menu bar, and then click **Cut**.

2. Click **File** from the BeanBox menu bar, and then click **Exit** to close the BeanBox window.

   The BeanBox comes with its own documentation in HTML format, including more complete instructions for using the BeanBox than this chapter can include. You can experiment with the BeanBox until you have a feel for how it works.

When a bean is instantiated in a beanbox, the bean's methods are called in the following order:

- The constructor with no arguments is called to set up the bean.

- The **preferredSize** method returns the display dimensions of the bean.

- The **paint** method draws the bean on the BeanBox window. Recall that for Swing components, the **paint** method calls the **paintComponent** method.

CREATING A JAVABEAN CLASS

As a programmer, you may be expected to build beans that other developers load into a beanbox and use to build an application. Thus, in this section, you learn how to create a JavaBean, package it into a `.jar` file, and then load it into the BeanBox so that it can be connected with other JavaBean components.

An example JavaBean is developed throughout this chapter. The bean displays an image on a panel. The first version is a class called **ImageBean1**. It extends the class **Panel** and manipulates an object of type **Image**. The default image is a GIF file that is provided by the Sun BeanBox and that contains the familiar image of Duke the Java platform mascot as a juggler. Figure 8-10 shows what this bean looks like when it is used within the BeanBox.

The ImageBean1 bean has three properties:

- The properties **fileName** and **fillColor** have mutator methods **setFileName** and **setFillColor**, and accessor methods **getFileName** and **getFillColor**. They are read-write properties, so each property requires both a **set** and a **get** method.

- ImageBean1 has a **getPreferredSize** method but no **setPreferredSize** method. The property **preferredSize** is a read-only property of the bean.

If the image chosen is smaller than the panel, the empty space is painted using a specified fill color.

Figure 8-8 is the complete source code for the ImageBean1 JavaBean. Because **ImageBean1** is a public class, it is found in a file called **ImageBean1.java**. The structure of packages mirrors the file system, so you will find this source code in the **X:\Data\examples\beans** directory on the CD-ROM. (Here **X:** is the drive letter of the CD-ROM.)

```
package examples.beans;
import javax.swing.JPanel;
import java.awt.*;
import java.io.*;
import java.awt.image.ImageObserver;
/** A very simple JavaBean class that displays an image
  * and allows the user to specify the file containing
  * the image and the fill color to be used if the
  * image is smaller than the panel
  */
public class ImageBean1 extends JPanel {
    private String fileName = "";
    private transient Image image;
    private int width = 200;
    private int height = 150;
    private Color fill = Color.lightGray;
    /** No-argument constructor; sets the filename to a
      * default value
      */
    public ImageBean1() {
        setFileName( "..\\demo\\sunw\\demo\\juggler\\"
                    + "Juggler0.gif" );
    }
```

Figure 8-8   **ImageBean1:** A very simple JavaBean class that displays an image

```
/** Accessor for the filename property
  * @return The current image's filename
  */
public String getFileName() {
   return fileName;
}
/** The preferred size of the panel
  * @return The size of the current image
  */
public Dimension getPreferredSize() {
   return new Dimension( width, height );
}
/** Accessor for the fillColor property
  * @return The current fill color
  */
public Color getFillColor() {
   return fill;
}
/** Method for monitoring the progress of the
  * loading of the current image
  */
public boolean imageUpdate( Image img,
                            int infoflags,
                            int x, int y,
                            int w, int h ) {
   if ( (infoflags & ImageObserver.ALLBITS) != 0 ) {
      width = img.getWidth( null );
      height = img.getHeight( null );
      repaint();
      return false;
   } else {
      return true;
   }
}
/** Paint the fill color if the panel is bigger than
  * the image and then draw the image
  * @param g the panel's graphics context
  */
public void paintComponent( Graphics g ) {
   super.paintComponent( g );
   Dimension panelSize = getSize();
   Insets ins = getInsets();
   int actWidth = panelSize.width - ins.right
                     - ins.left - 1;
   int actHeight = panelSize.height - ins.top
                     - ins.bottom - 1;
   if ( panelSize.width > width ||
        panelSize.height > height ) {
      g.setColor( fill );
```

Figure 8-8   `ImageBean1`: A very simple JavaBean class that displays an
image (continued)

8

```
                g.fillRect( ins.left, ins.top,
                            actWidth, actHeight );
            }
            if ( image != null ) {
                g.drawImage( image, ins.left, ins.top, this );
            }
        }
        /** Deserialization method called for the JavaBean;
          * this is necessary because Image objects can be
          * serialized and must be regenerated manually
          * @exception IOException if an error occurs
          *             reading the serialized JavaBean
          * @exception ClassNotFoundException if the
          *             serialized JavaBean can't be found
          */
        private void readObject( ObjectInputStream ois )
                throws IOException, ClassNotFoundException {
            ois.defaultReadObject();
            image = getToolkit().getImage( fileName );
            repaint();
        }
        /** Mutator method for the fillColor property
          * @param c the new fill color value
          */
        public void setFillColor( Color c ) {
            fill = c;
            repaint();
        }
        /** Mutator method for the fileName property
          * @param fn the new image filename
          */
        public void setFileName( String fn ) {
            fileName = fn;
            image = getToolkit().getImage( fileName );
            repaint ();
        }
    }
```

Figure 8-8   `ImageBean1`: A very simple JavaBean class that displays an
             image (continued)

Breakdown of the `ImageBean1` Class

The `ImageBean1` class is in the package **examples.beans**. The `ImageBean1` class
displays an image using the **JPanel** class in the package **javax.swing**, several classes
in the packages **java.awt** and **java.io**, as well as the **ImageObserver** class in the
package **java.awt.image**.

```
package examples.beans;
import javax.swing.JPanel;
import java.awt.*;
```

```
import java.awt.image.ImageObserver;
```

The class **ImageBean1** inherits its serialization behavior from its superclass, **JPanel**. Therefore, **ImageBean1** does not have to declare explicitly that it implements the interface **Serializable**.

```
public class ImageBean1 extends JPanel {
```

The fields of the **ImageBean1** class record the state of the JavaBean. They are all given default values except for the **Image** instance. Notice that the **Image** instance variable is qualified as **transient** and so will not be serialized. The reason for this is because the **Image** class does not implement the interface **Serializable**. Therefore, the image field cannot be serialized with the other fields in an **ImageBean1** object. Because the **Image** class is not serializable, any attempt to serialize an **Image** object results in an exception.

```
private String fileName = "";
private transient Image image;
private int width = 200;
private int height = 150;
private Color fill = Color.lightGray;
```

The **ImageBean1** class has a constructor with no arguments. The beanbox calls this constructor when an object of this class is dropped onto the composition window. This constructor initializes the **fileName** property of the JavaBean. The default filename has a relative path, `..\demo\sunw\demo\juggler\juggler0.gif`, and is set on the assumption that a `.jar` file containing the **ImageBean1** class is in the jars subfolder of the folder in which the BDK is installed. You can edit the **fileName** property to point to any other valid file containing an image.

```
public ImageBean1() {
   setFileName( "..\\demo\\sunw\\demo\\juggler\\"
               + "Juggler0.gif" );
}
```

The next three methods are accessor methods that return the current values of the three properties of the JavaBean: **fileName**, **preferredSize**, and **fillColor**.

```
public String getFileName() {
   return fileName;
}
public Dimension getPreferredSize() {
   return new Dimension( width, height );
}
public Color getFillColor() {
   return fill;
}
```

The **imageUpdate** method is part of the **ImageObserver** interface that all AWT components implement. When a method is called to draw an image, the method may return before the image is fully available. For this reason, the methods to draw images take a reference to an **ImageObserver** object. Periodically, the bean's **imageUpdate** method is called to update the status of the image. As long as **imageUpdate** returns **true**, the updates continue.

As shown in the following snippet, this implementation of **imageUpdate** waits until the information flags have the ALLBITS flag set on. When that condition indicates that the entire image is drawn, the actual width and height of the image are requested and the image is repainted. The method returns **false** to indicate that no further updates are required.

```
public boolean imageUpdate( Image img,
                            int infoflags,
                            int x, int y,
                            int w, int h ) {
    if ( (infoflags & ImageObserver.ALLBITS) != 0 ) {
        width = img.getWidth( null );
        height = img.getHeight( null );
        repaint();
        return false;
    } else {
        return true;
    }
}
```

The code that follows this paragraph shows that the **paintComponent** method for this JavaBean compares the size of the panel to the size of the image. If the panel is bigger, the **paintComponent** operation begins by filling the panel with the specified fill color. Then, if the image is not **null**, it is drawn starting in the upper-left corner of the panel. By retrieving and using the inset values of the panel, care is taken not to draw the image over any border that the panel may have.

```
public void paintComponent( Graphics g ) {
    super.paintComponent( g );
    Dimension panelSize = getSize();
    Insets ins = getInsets();
    int actWidth = panelSize.width - ins.right
                        - ins.left - 1;
    int actHeight = panelSize.height - ins.top
                        - ins.bottom - 1;
    if ( panelSize.width > width ||
         panelSize.height > height ) {
        g.setColor( fill );
        g.fillRect( ins.left, ins.top,
                    actWidth, actHeight );
    }
    if ( image != null ) {
        g.drawImage( image, ins.left, ins.top, this );
    }
}
```

~~The instance variable image must be qualified with the transient keyword so that~~ the image is not saved when the bean is serialized and not restored when the bean is deserialized. As a result, the image must be reloaded from the GIF file when this bean is deserialized. Deserializing the bean is accomplished using the **readObject** method, as shown here:

```
private void readObject( ObjectInputStream ois )
        throws IOException, ClassNotFoundException {
    ois.defaultReadObject();
    image = getToolkit().getImage( fileName );
    repaint();
}
```

The last two methods of the JavaBean class are the mutator methods that allow the read-write properties **fileName** and **fillColor** to be changed. Both of these methods trigger a **repaint** operation. A change of the filename also causes a new image to be loaded, which may cause the **preferredSize** property to change.

```
public void setFillColor( Color c ) {
    fill = c;
    repaint();
}
public void setFileName( String fn ) {
    fileName = fn;
    image = getToolkit().getImage( fileName );
    repaint();
}
```

ImageBean1 Class Used in a BeanBox

Before you can access a JavaBean in a beanbox, you must put it in a `.jar` file. There is an additional requirement: the .jar file must include a manifest that specifies which `.class` files in the `.jar` file are JavaBeans. To do this, you simply set the JavaBean property in the manifest to be true for the JavaBean class.

To load this example bean into the BeanBox window of the BDK:

1. Create a manifest file for the bean **ImageBean1**. In a text editor, create a flat text file that contains the following two lines, followed by a blank line. Spaces are significant, so make sure both lines start in the first character position of each line.

```
Name: examples/beans/ImageBean1.class
Java-Bean: True
```

8

2. Save the file with filename **ImageBeans.manifest** in the folder that is the parent of the folder that contains the package examples.

3. Make sure the current folder is the one that contains the file `ImageBeans.manifest` and the examples folder. Type the following command on one line to create a `.jar` file named `ImageBeans.jar`:

```
jar cfm ImageBeans.jar ImageBeans.manifest
                       examples\beans\*.class
```

4. Copy the file `ImageBeans.jar` into the **jars** subfolder of the folder in which you installed the BDK.

5. To start the BeanBox, make the subfolder **beanbox** the current folder, and enter the command **run**.

When the four windows appear, you should see `ImageBean1` listed in the ToolBox window, as shown in Figure 8-9.

6. Select the ImageBean1 bean from the ToolBox window by clicking the word **ImageBean1** with the mouse. The cross-hair cursor appears. (Notice that the position of ImageBean1 in the list may not be exactly as shown in Figure 8-9.)

Figure 8-9　The `ImageBean1` in the ToolBox window

7. Position the mouse icon over the BeanBox window. Click the Bean Box window, and the ImageBean1 bean drops into place so that it looks like Figure 8-10.

Figure 8-10   The `ImageBean1` in the BeanBox window

The Properties window for the ImageBean1 bean looks like Figure 8-11 and shows many fields, although the `ImageBean1` class defines only two read-write properties. All the other fields are inherited from the superclass, **JPanel**. In the Properties window, you can enter different values for the `fillColor` and the `fileName` properties of the JavaBean. If you try this, you will see the changes immediately reflected in the BeanBox window.

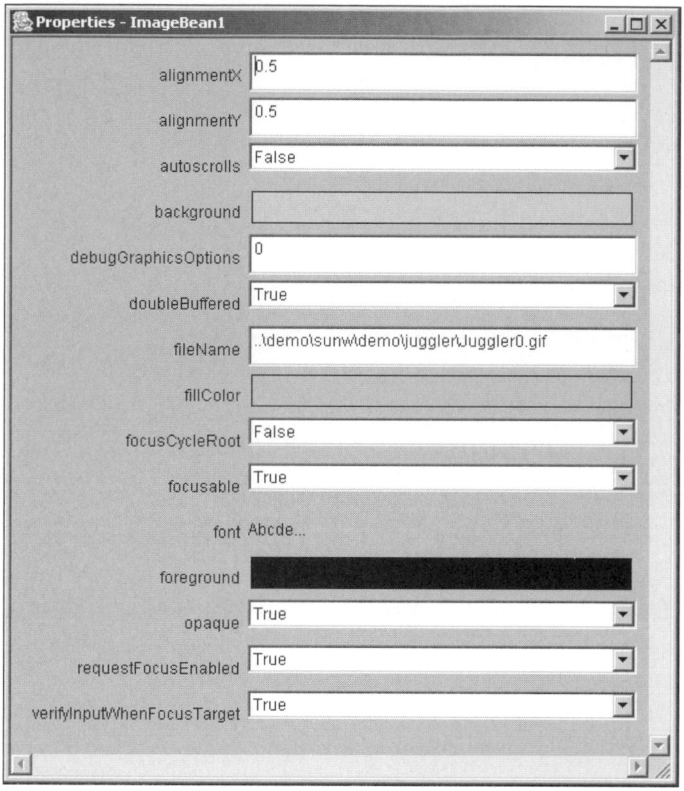

Figure 8-11 The Properties window for the `ImageBean1` bean

You can bind a property of the ImageBean1 bean to a property of another bean, if the properties have the same type. By doing this, the property of the `ImageBean1` bean will be updated automatically whenever the property it is bound to changes, guaranteeing that the values are synchronized. In the following example, the other bean used will be an instance of the JellyBean JavaBean that comes with the Sun BeanBox. The JellyBean JavaBean has a color property that will be tied in with the ImageBean1 bean.

To tie a property from the JellyBean JavaBean to the ImageBean1 JavaBean:

1. Select the **JellyBean** bean from the ToolBox window, and then drop the bean on the BeanBox composition window.

2. To indicate that it is selected, the JellyBean will have a hatched black and gray border. If it does not, click the **JellyBean** to select it.

3. Click **Edit** on the menu bar of the BeanBox window, and then click **Bind property**.

4. The PropertyNameDialog box appears, as shown in Figure 8-12. It lists properties of the JellyBean. Select **color**, and click **OK** to close the dialog box.

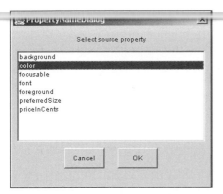

Figure 8-12   The PropertyNameDialog box

5. A red line appears. One end of the line is attached to the JellyBean, and the other end follows the mouse. Drag the moving end of the line over the ImageBean1 bean, and click.

6. The PropertyNameDialog box appears again, now showing the properties of the ImageBean1 bean. Select **fillColor**, and click **OK**.

7. The ImageBean1 bean is selected, and its fill color is the same as the color of the JellyBean.

If you select the JellyBean and change its color using the Properties window, the fill color of ImageBean1 changes to match, because the `fillColor` property of the ImageBean1 bean is now bound to the color property of the JellyBean.

You cannot do much more with the ImageBean1 bean. It is limited to being a passive participant in a beanbox. Enabling this bean to connect actively with other components involves adding events and more methods. The following section discusses JavaBean property types beyond the basic property type used in the `ImageBean1` class. The class `ImageBean2` uses one of these more advanced property types and can be a more active participant in an application or applet.

EXPLORING JAVABEAN PROPERTY TYPES

The bean ImageBean1 has a simple property type. For more flexibility, you can move beyond simple properties to use properties that are indexed, bound, or constrained.

Indexed Properties

Properties are not limited to individual values. They can be indexed under a single name with an integer index value. For example, to alter the ImageBean1 bean to display an animated sequence, you might supply several filenames for the sequence of images. In that case, `fileName` would naturally become an indexed property. In addition to providing the methods for reading and writing the entire indexed property, you can provide methods for reading and writing individual elements of the property.

Syntax

```
property_type getproperty_name( int index )
void setproperty_name( property_type x, int index )
```

Dissection

The mutator and accessor methods for an indexed property must have the arguments, names, and return types shown in the preceding syntax box. Beanboxes also recognize method signatures with these patterns and add them to the list of properties for the JavaBean. To be usable, the methods must be public.

Code Example

```
myBean.setFileName( "Juggler0.gif", 0 );
String fn = myBean.getFilename( 0 );
```

Code Dissection

The example shows the accessor and mutator methods for an indexed property called `fileName` of type **String**.

Bound Properties

Bound properties provide notification when they change so that other JavaBeans can listen for these changes and act accordingly. For example, the properties of the `ImageBean1` class are passive but are tied to the bound properties of a demonstration JavaBean of the `JellyBean` class. The `fillColor` property of the `ImageBean1` class is not bound. However, the color property of the `JellyBean` class is bound.

The package **java.beans** includes a class for use with bound properties, **PropertyChangeSupport**, that is detailed next.

Class

java.beans.PropertyChangeSupport

Purpose

You can create an instance of this class for a JavaBean object and delegate to it the tasks of maintaining a list of interested listeners and sending **java.beans.PropertyChangeEvent** objects. Using this class relieves the programmer from having to maintain a list of objects that need to be informed when the value of a property changes and also from sending out the notifications.

Constructor

- **PropertyChangeSupport(Object** *sourceBean* **)**

You can create a **PropertyChangeSupport** object for a JavaBean.

Methods

- **void addPropertyChangeListener(PropertyChangeListener** *listener* **)**

  The **addPropertyChangeListener** method adds the specified object to the list of listeners for the bean.

- **void firePropertyChange(String** *propertyName,*

                            Object *oldValue,*

                            Object *newValue* **)**

  The **firePropertyChange** method informs all listeners of a change to a bound property. The method generates no event if the new value equals the old value.

- **void removePropertyChangeListener (PropertyChangeListener**
                                            *listener***)**

  The **removePropertyChangeListener** method removes the specified object from the list of listeners for the bean.

The **ImageBean2** example program in Figure 8-15 shows how these methods are used typically:

- A class defines its own **addPropertyChangeListener** and **removePropertyChangeListener** methods, which do little more than pass the **PropertyChangeListener** parameter they receive along to the **PropertyChangeSupport** instance.

- The **set** methods for the properties are modified to call the **firePropertyChange** method to indicate that the value has changed.

Constrained Properties

The JavaBeans component model allows for the possibility that one or more of the listening objects might not allow certain changes to the value of a property. For example, a banking application may not allow a withdrawal operation that causes an account balance to go below zero. This variation is known as a *constrained property*. In this case, each listener can veto a change and stop it from happening.

The difference between implementing support for a constrained property and a bound property is mostly in the support class that is chosen. To implement a constrained property, a JavaBean class should use an object of the **VetoableChangeSupport** class. The details of this class are given next.

Class

java.beans.VetoableChangeSupport

Purpose

Use a **VetoableChangeSupport** object for constrained properties much like you use a **PropertyChangeSupport** object for bound properties.

Constructor

- **VetoableChangeSupport(Object** *sourceBean* **)**

  You can create a **VetoableChangeSupport** object for a JavaBean.

Methods

- **void addVetoableChangeListener(PropertyChangeListener** *listener* **)**

  The **addVetoableChangeListener** method adds the specified object to the list of listeners for the bean.

- **void firePropertyChange(String** *propertyName***,**

  Object *oldValue***,**

  Object *newValue* **)**

  The **firePropertyChange** method informs all listeners of a change to a bound property. The method generates no event if the new value equals the old value. Listeners can veto the change by throwing a **java.beans.PropertyVetoException** object. When this happens, the **VetoableChangeSupport** object catches this exception, notifies the other listeners that the property is reverting to its original value, and then rethrows the exception.

- **void removeVetoableChangeListener(PropertyChangeListener** *listener* **)**

  The **removeVetoableChangeListener** method removes the specified object from the list of listeners for the bean.

The event object type is **PropertyChangeEvent** for both constrained and bound properties, because the information contained in the event object is the same. Only the mechanism for delivering the event differs: Write the **set** method for a constrained property to catch the **PropertyVetoException** object and undo the change.

ADDING CUSTOM EVENT TYPES

JavaBeans are not limited to the **PropertyChangeEvent** event type. They can use any event type, even custom event types. For example, if you want to define an event that triggers only when a data structure is full, that would be a custom event. Unfortunately, implementing custom event types requires more work because there is no core class analogous to **PropertyChangeSupport** to support such events.

To create and use a custom event

1. Define the event class that extends **java.util.EventObject** or one of its subclasses. The rest of this discussion refers to this class as class **X**.

2. Define the interface, **XListener**, that the event listeners must implement. This interface should extend the marker interface **java.util.EventListener**. The methods of this interface are the event handlers. They should return **void** and take one parameter of type **X**. They have the following form:

   ```
   void handleX( X event )
   ```

3. Define the methods **addXListener** and **removeXListener**, both of which take a single parameter of type **XListener**, for the JavaBean class that can fire the event. An instance of the **Vector** class can be used to hold the list of registered listeners updated by these two methods.

4. The JavaBean class should define a method, **fireX**, that goes through the list of registered listeners and calls the **handleX** method, passing an X object for each of them.

   Follow these conventions so that a beanbox can detect the presence of the custom event type and allow it to be connected to other JavaBeans. The **ImageBean2** class in Figure 8-15 contains an example of a custom event type called **FillColorEvent**.

CREATING A JAVABEAN CLASS WITH EVENTS

The second JavaBean class, **ImageBean2**, is an enhancement of the **ImageBean1** class. This class converts all the properties into bound properties and adds a custom event type, **FillColorEvent**, that triggers when the color that fills in the background for the image changes. The code for the **FillColorEvent** event follows the discussion of the **ImageBean2** class.

The class adds two methods, **makeFillGreen** and **makeFillRed**, as conveniences to the users of the JavaBean. In a beanbox, it is easy to add a button JavaBean and then connect the button's click action to one of these methods. Creating a customized button JavaBean that extends the **javax.swing.JButton** class is simple. Figure 8-13 is the code to create the **MagentaButton** class, an extension of **JButton** with a customized background color and button text.

8

```
package examples.beans;
/**
 * A customized JavaBean push button
 */
public class MagentaButton extends javax.swing.JButton {
   public MagentaButton() {
      setBackground( java.awt.Color.magenta );
      setText( "Press" );
   }
}
```

Figure 8-13   `MagentaButton`: a customized JavaBean push button

Figure 8-14 shows how the `MagentaButton` bean appears when placed in the BeanBox window.

Figure 8-14   The `MagentaButton` in the BeanBox window

Much of the code for the `ImageBean2` class, shown in Figure 8-15, is identical to the Java source for `ImageBean1`. For convenience, the changes are highlighted in boldface. The details of the changes made from `ImageBean1` to `ImageBean2` are described in the breakdown after the complete source code.

```
package examples.beans;
import javax.swing.JPanel;
import java.awt.*;
import java.io.*;
import java.util.*;
import java.awt.image.ImageObserver;
import java.beans.*;
/** A very simple JavaBean class that displays an image
  * and allows the user to specify the file containing
  * the image and the fill color to be used if the
  * image is smaller than the panel
  */
public class ImageBean2 extends JPanel {
   private String fileName;
```

Figure 8-15   `ImageBean2`: A very simple JavaBean class that displays an image

```java
private transient Image image;
private int width = 200;
private int height = 150;
private Color fill = Color.lightGray;
private PropertyChangeSupport
   myListeners = new PropertyChangeSupport( this );
private Vector fillColorListeners = new Vector();
/** No-argument constructor; sets the filename to a
 * default value
 */
public ImageBean2() {
   setFileName( "..\\demo\\sunw\\demo\\juggler\\"
                +"Juggler0.gif" );
}
/** Send an event to all registered listeners */
public void fireFillColorEvent( FillColorEvent e ) {
   Vector snapshot
      = (Vector) fillColorListeners.clone();
   Enumeration cursor = snapshot.elements();
   while( cursor.hasMoreElements() ) {
      FillColorListener fcl
         = (FillColorListener) cursor.nextElement();
      if ( e.getID()
                  == FillColorEvent.COLOR_CHANGE ) {
         fcl.fillColorChange( e );
      }
   }
}
/** Accessor for the filename property
 * @return The current image's filename
 */
public String getFileName() {
   return fileName;
}
/** The preferred size of the panel
 * @return The size of the current image
 */
public Dimension getPreferredSize() {
   return new Dimension( width, height );
}
/** Accessor for the fillColor property
 * @return The current fill color
 */
public Color getFillColor() {
   return fill;
}
/** Method for monitoring the progress of the
 * loading of the current image
 */
```

Figure 8-15   `ImageBean2`: A very simple JavaBean class that displays an image (continued)

```
    public boolean imageUpdate( Image img,
                                int infoflags,
                                int x, int y,
                                int w, int h ) {
  if ( (infoflags & ImageObserver.ALLBITS) != 0 ) {
     int oldWidth = width;
     int oldHeight = height;
     width = img.getWidth( null );
     height = img.getHeight( null );
     if ( oldWidth != width
           || oldHeight != height ) {
        myListeners.firePropertyChange(
           "preferredSize",
           new Dimension( oldWidth, oldHeight ),
           new Dimension( width, height ) );
     }
     repaint();
     return false;
  } else {
     return true;
  }
}
/** Set the image fill color to green; the Sun
  * BeanBox recognizes only methods without
  * parameters that return void
  */
public void makeFillGreen() {
   setFillColor( Color.green );
}
/** Set the image fill color to red; the Sun
  * BeanBox recognizes only methods without
  * parameters that return void
  */
public void makeFillRed() {
   setFillColor( Color.red );
}
/** Paint the fill color if the panel is bigger than
  * the image and then draw the image
  * @param g the panel's graphics context
  */
public void paintComponent( Graphics g ) {
   super.paintComponent( g );
   Dimension panelSize = getSize();
   Insets ins = getInsets();
   int actWidth = panelSize.width - ins.right
                     - ins.left - 1;
   int actHeight = panelSize.height - ins.top
                     - ins.bottom - 1;
```

Figure 8-15   `ImageBean2`: A very simple JavaBean class that displays an image (continued)

```
            if ( panelSize.width > width ||
                panelSize.height > height ) {
              g.setColor( fill );
              g.fillRect( ins.left, ins.top,
                         actWidth, actHeight );
            }
            if ( image != null ) {
              g.drawImage( image, ins.left, ins.top, this );
            }
          }
          /** Deserialization method called for the JavaBean;
           * this is necessary because Image objects can be
           * serialized and must be regenerated manually
           * @exception IOException if an error occurs
           *            reading the serialized JavaBean
           * @exception ClassNotFoundException if the
           *            serialized JavaBean can't be found
           */
          private void readObject( ObjectInputStream ois )
                  throws IOException, ClassNotFoundException {
            ois.defaultReadObject();
            image = getToolkit().getImage( fileName );
            repaint();
          }
          /** Mutator method for the fillColor property
           * @param c the new fill color value
           */
          public void setFillColor( Color c ) {
            Color oldFill = fill;
            fill = c;
            myListeners.firePropertyChange( "fillColor",
                                            oldFill,
                                            fill );
            fireFillColorEvent( new FillColorEvent( this,
                              FillColorEvent.COLOR_CHANGE,
                              c ) );
            repaint();
          }
          /** Mutator method for the fileName property
           * @param fn the new image filename
           */
          public void setFileName( String fn ) {
            String oldFileName = fileName;
            fileName = fn;
            image = getToolkit().getImage( fileName );
            myListeners.firePropertyChange( "fileName",
                                            oldFileName,
                                            fileName );
            repaint();
          }
```

Figure 8-15   `ImageBean2`: A very simple JavaBean class that displays an image (continued)

```
        /** Add a listener interested in FillColorEvent
         * objects
         */
        public void
        addFillColorListener( FillColorListener l ) {
           fillColorListeners.addElement( l );
        }
        /** Add a listener interested in property change
         * events
         */
        public void addPropertyChangeListener(
           PropertyChangeListener l ) {
           myListeners.addPropertyChangeListener( l );
        }
        /** Remove a listener no longer interested in
         * FillColorEvent objects
         */
        public void removeFillColorListener(
           FillColorListener l ) {
           fillColorListeners.removeElement( l );
        }
        /** Remove a listener no longer interested in
         * property change events
         */
        public void
        removePropertyChangeListener(
           PropertyChangeListener l ) {
           myListeners.removePropertyChangeListener( l );
        }
    }
```

Figure 8-15   `ImageBean2`: A very simple JavaBean class that displays an
image (continued)

Breakdown of the `ImageBean2` Class

The two new fields, `myListeners` and `fillColorListeners`, support the handling
of events. The field `myListeners` provides the support for creating bound properties.
The field `fillColorListeners` is the list of listeners registered to receive
`FillColorEvent` objects.

```
public class ImageBean2 extends JPanel {
    private String fileName;
    private transient Image image;
    private int width = 200;
    private int height = 150;
    private Color fill = Color.lightGray;
    private PropertyChangeSupport
        myListeners = new PropertyChangeSupport( this );
    private Vector fillColorListeners = new Vector();
```

The method fireFillColorEvent sends a FillColorEvent object to all registered listeners. It begins by cloning the list of registered listeners to avoid any problems that could arise if the list changes while the events are being delivered. Using an **Enumeration** object, the program visits all items in the list and calls the handler method fillColorChange for each one:

```
public void fireFillColorEvent( FillColorEvent e ) {
   Vector snapshot
      = (Vector) fillColorListeners.clone();
   Enumeration cursor = snapshot.elements();
   while( cursor.hasMoreElements() ) {
      FillColorListener fcl
            = (FillColorListener) cursor.nextElement();
      if ( e.getID()
         == FillColorEvent.COLOR_CHANGE ) {
         fcl.fillColorChange( e );
      }
   }
}
```

The methods for accessing the properties have not changed, but the imageUpdate method has changed to fire a **PropertyChangeEvent** if the image loaded has a size different from the previous image. The method also saves the old width and height at the beginning of the method so that the old and new values can be put into the event object. Because the **preferredSize** property is returned as a **Dimension** object, two **Dimension** objects are created to hold the old and new values, as shown next:

```
public boolean imageUpdate( Image img,
                        int infoflags,
                        int x, int y,
                        int w, int h ) {
   if ( (infoflags & ImageObserver.ALLBITS) != 0 ) {
      int oldWidth = width;
      int oldHeight = height;
      width = img.getWidth( null );
      height = img.getHeight( null );
      if ( oldWidth != width
            || oldHeight != height ) {
         myListeners.firePropertyChange(
            "preferredSize",
            new Dimension( oldWidth, oldHeight ),
            new Dimension( width, height ) );
      }
      repaint();
      return false;
   } else {
      return true;
   }
}
```

The convenience methods `makeFillGreen` and `makeFillRed` simply call the `setFillColor` method and pass the appropriate constant value. These do not set the field `fillColor` directly, because that would bypass the property-change reporting that has been added to this class.

```
public void makeFillGreen() {
   setFillColor( Color.green );
}
public void makeFillRed() {
   setFillColor( Color.red );
}
```

The painting and deserialization methods do not change, but the mutator methods are altered to add change reporting. Both methods now begin by saving the old value of the property before changing it to the new value. After the change is made, the `firePropertyChange` method is used to fire `PropertyChangeEvent`. The `setFillColor` method not only reports a property-change event, it also fires `FillColorEvent` with an ID value of COLOR_CHANGE, as shown next:

```
public void setFillColor( Color c ) {
   Color oldFill = fill;
   fill = c;
   myListeners.firePropertyChange( "fillColor",
                                    oldFill,
                                    fill );
   fireFillColorEvent( new FillColorEvent( this,
                       FillColorEvent.COLOR_CHANGE,
                       c ) );
   repaint();
}
public void setFileName( String fn ) {
   String oldFileName = fileName;
   fileName = fn;
   image = getToolkit().getImage( fileName );
   myListeners.firePropertyChange( "fileName",
                                    oldFileName,
                                    fileName );
   repaint();
}
```

The last four methods of the class are for adding and removing event listeners. The method `addFillColorListener` puts the given listener object into the **Vector** of listeners.

```
public void
addFillColorListener( FillColorListener l ) {
   fillColorListeners.addElement( l );
}
```

The addPropertyChangeListener method delegates to the PropertyChangeSupport object, myListeners, the handling of the bound property listeners.

```
public void addPropertyChangeListener(
   PropertyChangeListener l ) {
   myListeners.addPropertyChangeListener( l );
}
```

To remove themselves from the list, listeners no longer interested in FillColorEvent objects use the method removeFillColorListener. This method then removes the element from the **java.util.Vector** object holding the list.

```
public void removeFillColorListener(
   FillColorListener l ) {
   fillColorListeners.removeElement( l );
}
```

The method removePropertyChangeListener delegates to the **PropertyChangeSupport** object the removal of the specified **PropertyChangeListener** object from the list.

```
public void
removePropertyChangeListener(
   PropertyChangeListener l ) {
   myListeners.removePropertyChangeListener( l );
}
}
```

Custom Event Class for the ImageBean2 Bean

A separate class defines the custom event used in the ImageBean2 class. The constructor takes three inputs: a reference to the object that is the source of the event, an integer constant that is the event identifier, and the color associated with the event. The source reference is passed along to the superclass constructor, **EventObject**. The other methods of the class are defined so that the receiving objects can extract information from the event, as shown in Figure 8-16.

```
package examples.beans;
import java.awt.Color;
import java.util.EventObject;
/** A user-defined event class
  */
public class FillColorEvent extends EventObject {
   /** event type identifier */
   public static final int COLOR_CHANGE = 0;
```

Figure 8-16   FillColorEvent: the custom event used in the ImageBean2 class

```
   private int id;
   private Color color;
   /** Construct an event object
     * @param source the object initiating the event
     * @param id the event identifier
     * @param c the color for the event
     */
   public FillColorEvent( Object source, int id,
                              Color c ) {
      super( source );
      id = id;
      color = c;
   }
   /** Return the color associated with the event
     * @return The color
     */
   public Color getColor() {
      return color;
   }
   /** Return the event identifier
     * @return The event identifier
     */
   public int getID() {
      return id;
   }
}
```

Figure 8-16   `FillColorEvent`: the custom event used in the `ImageBean2` class
(continued)

Listener Interface for the Custom Event Class

The last piece of code needed for this example is the definition of the
`FillColorListener` interface, as shown in Figure 8-17. It adds just one empty
method to the **EventListener** interface. This is the method that will be called when
a `FillColor` change occurs.

```
package examples.beans;
import java.util.EventListener;
public interface FillColorListener extends EventListener {
   /** The method called when a FillColor change occurs
     */
   public void fillColorChange( FillColorEvent e );
}
```

Figure 8-17   `FillColorListener`: the custom interface for FillColorEvent events

ImageBean2 Used in a BeanBox

You can test the ImageBean2 bean by loading the bean into a beanbox.

To load ImageBean2 into the BDK BeanBox:

1. Add lines to the `ImageBeans.manifest` file in the folder into which you unpacked the `examples.jar` file, so that the file lists `ImageBean1`, `ImageBean2`, and `MagentaButton`. One `.jar` file can list any number of beans. The BDK BeanBox requires a blank line between the entries for each bean and a blank line after the last entry. The manifest file should now look like the following:

```
Name: examples/beans/ImageBean1.class
Java-Bean: True

Name: examples/beans/ImageBean2.class
Java-Bean: True

Name: examples/beans/MagentaButton.class
Java-Bean: True
```

2. Type the following command, on one line, from the parent folder of the examples folder to create a `.jar` file named `ImageBeans.jar`:

```
jar cfm ImageBeans.jar ImageBeans.manifest
                       examples\beans\*.class
```

3. Copy the file `ImageBeans.jar` into the **jars** subfolder of the folder in which you installed the BDK.

4. Start the BeanBox as described earlier in this chapter in the section "Using the Sun BeanBox." See that `ImageBean2` is now listed in the ToolBox window.

5. You can have a little fun with this bean. Drop an **ImageBean2** bean onto the BeanBox window.

6. Drop two **MagentaButton** beans on to the BeanBox window and position them near, but not on top of, the `ImageBean2`. These beans look like buttons labeled `Press`.

7. Change the background property of one `MagentaButton` to red and the other `MagentaButton` to green using the BeanBox property editor window described in the section "Using the Sun BeanBox." Use the Properties window and ColorEditor the same way as when you changed the color of a JellyBean object earlier in this chapter.

8. Click the **red** button. While it is selected, click **Edit** on the menu bar, and then select **Events**. From the cascading menus, select **action**, and then click **actionPerformed**.

   A red line appears from the bean to the current mouse position.

8

9. Move over the area of the ImageBean2 bean, and click.

10. The EventTargetDialog dialog box opens, inviting you to select a target method. Click **makeFillRed**, and then click **OK**. Briefly, a message box appears saying that an adaptor class is being generated and compiled.

11. Now, try clicking the **red** button. The fill color of the ImageBean2 bean should turn red.

12. In a similar fashion, make the green button change the fill color of the ImageBean2 to green. Depending on how you arrange the beans, your BeanBox window may look similar to Figure 8-18.

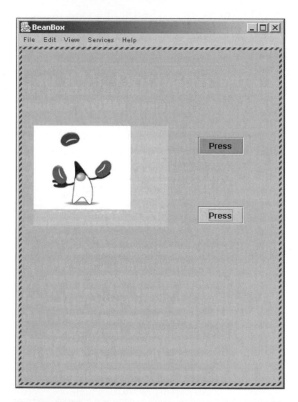

Figure 8-18   The ImageBean2 in the BDK BeanBox

13. Now, you can use the fillColor bound property of the ImageBean2. Drop a **JellyBean** onto the BeanBox window.

11. S̶e̶l̶e̶c̶t̶ ̶I̶m̶a̶g̶e̶B̶e̶a̶n̶2̶.̶ ̶C̶l̶i̶c̶k̶ ̶E̶d̶i̶t̶ ̶f̶r̶o̶m̶ ̶t̶h̶e̶ ̶m̶e̶n̶u̶ ̶b̶a̶r̶ ̶a̶n̶d̶ ̶t̶h̶e̶n̶ ̶c̶l̶i̶c̶k̶ ̶B̶i̶n̶d̶ **property**. When the PropertyNameDialog dialog box pops up, select **fillColor** and then click **OK**.

15. Use your mouse to position the end of the red line coming out from the ImageBean2 object over the JellyBean and click. When the PropertyNameDialog dialog box pops up, select **color** and then click **OK**.

Now, click the **red** and **green** buttons and see what happens. Feel free to experiment.

USING THE BEANINFO CLASSES

Beanboxes generally use the Reflection API to determine what they need to know about a JavaBean. But you cannot deduce some pieces of information from a JavaBean definition, and in some cases you may not be able to follow the programming conventions, such as method naming, that beanboxes expect. For these reasons, the JavaBeans specification allows for the definition of additional information classes to accompany a JavaBean class: BeanInfo classes.

BeanInfo classes are used only when beans are being connected in a beanbox. They have no role when the bean is executing, so you do not have to include them in the `.jar` file when you package JavaBeans into an application. The BeanInfo classes implement the **java.beans.BeanInfo** interface.

A beanbox finds the information classes as follows:

- For each JavaBean class, the beanbox looks for a class with a name formed by appending the suffix **BeanInfo** onto the name of the JavaBean class. For example, if the JavaBean class is named **JB**, the beanbox looks for class **JBBeanInfo**.

- If a class satisfies the naming convention, the beanbox checks whether the class implements the **BeanInfo** interface. For example, the beanbox accepts the following class:

```
class JBBeanInfo implements java.beans.BeanInfo
```

- If a class satisfies these requirements, the beanbox can call its methods to collect detailed information about the JavaBean. Some of the information is encapsulated in instances of other classes in the **java.beans** package that are listed in Figure 8-19.

8

Class	Description
FeatureDescriptor	FeatureDescriptor is the superclass for all the other descriptor classes. It contains methods for reading and writing information that is common to all features of a JavaBean, such as name, shortDescription, and value.
BeanDescriptor	The BeanDescriptor class contains high-level information for the entire JavaBean class.
EventSetDescriptor	The EventSetDescriptor class provides details about the set of events that are gathered under a single listener interface. Each listener interface supported by the JavaBean can have its own EventSetDescriptor object.
MethodDescriptor	The MethodDescriptor class describes one of the methods supported by a JavaBean.
ParameterDescriptor	ParameterDescriptor objects are associated with MethodDescriptor objects. Each ParameterDescriptor object describes one argument of a method.
PropertyDescriptor	A PropertyDescriptor object describes a single property of a JavaBean. If your bean has a property for which the read and write methods do not follow the JavaBeans naming convention, use the PropertyDescriptor object to identify the read and write methods.
IndexedPropertyDescriptor	The IndexedPropertyDescriptor class extends PropertyDescriptor and adds methods for the indexed read and write methods.

Figure 8-19   JavaBean information classes

Class

java.beans.BeanInfo

Purpose

You can optionally define a class that implements this interface to provide information about the methods, events, properties, and other characteristics of your JavaBean class. Development tools that consume JavaBean classes may use the classes that implement this interface. Programs that use the JavaBean class do not use BeanInfo classes.

Methods

- **BeanInfo[] getAdditionalBeanInfo()**

  Implement the **getAdditionalBeanInfo** method to specify an array of additional **BeanInfo** objects that provide information about the JavaBean.

8

BeanDescriptor getBeanDescriptor()

Implement **getBeanDescriptor** to return general information in a **BeanDescriptor** object.

- **int getDefaultEventIndex()**

  Implement **getDefaultEventIndex** to tell the beanbox which element in the **EventSetDescriptor** array to treat as the default event when a user interacts with the JavaBean.

- **int getDefaultPropertyIndex()**

  Implement the **getDefaultPropertyIndex** method to tell the beanbox which element in the **PropertyDescriptor** array to treat as the default when a user interacts with the JavaBean.

- **EventSetDescriptor[] getEventSetDescriptors()**

  Implement **getEventSetDescriptors** to return an array of **EventSetDescriptor** objects that describe the events generated by this bean.

- **Image getIcon(int *iconKind*)**

  Implement the **getIcon** method to return an icon that can be used to represent the JavaBean in toolbars and the like. The argument specifies the kind of icon required.

- **MethodDescriptor[] getMethodDescriptors()**

  Implement the **getMethodDescriptors** method to return an array of **MethodDescriptor** objects that describe the externally visible methods of the JavaBean.

- **PropertyDescriptor[] getPropertyDescriptors()**

  Implement the **getPropertyDescriptors** method to return an array of **PropertyDescriptor** objects that describe the properties of the JavaBean.

You can define a class that implements the **BeanInfo** interface and supply implementations of all the **BeanInfo** methods. A simpler approach is to define a class that extends the class **java.beans.SimpleBeanInfo**. This class implements the **BeanInfo** interface and provides methods in which the return values indicate that no information is available.

You can extend the **SimpleBeanInfo** class and override selected methods. For example, if an icon can represent your JavaBean class, you can implement the **BeanInfo.getIcon** method to return the icon. Some of the classes in the **java.beans** package that provide information about JavaBean classes are listed in Figure 8-19.

Providing a Custom Property Editor

Beanboxes can reasonably be expected to provide property editors for commonly used property types including **String**, **Font**, and **Color**. However, a programmer who creates JavaBeans may be required to provide a property editor for other kinds of properties, especially custom types that have a specific set of allowable values. For example, if you had a property that identified the temperature scale, you would need a customer editor that allowed the user to choose one of Fahrenheit, Celsius, and Kelvin. All property editors must implement the interface **java.beans.PropertyEditor**. Property editors must keep track of all objects that are interested in the property and notify all these objects when a property changes.

The class **java.beans.PropertyEditorSupport** provides a trivial property editor. For many cases, all you must do to create a custom property editor is extend this class and override a few of its methods. For example, if the editor needs only to present a list of valid choices for the property value, the support **PropertyEditorSupport** provides is sufficient. The next example program demonstrates a customized editor class that takes this approach (Figure 8-20).

For cases requiring something more complex than presenting a list of valid choices, a class that directly implements the **PropertyEditor** interface and provides implementation of all its methods may be more appropriate.

Beanboxes usually provide a dialog box containing a list of all JavaBean properties and a field for editing each one. Often, this dialog box is sufficient. Nevertheless, a complex JavaBean may require that you efficiently customize a specialized user interface. A special purpose customizer can treat the JavaBean as a whole, because it can understand the dependencies between fields and makes sure that they are respected.

A customizer class must meet the following criteria:

- The class must implement the **java.beans.Customizer** interface.
- An instance of the class must be a component that can be embedded in a dialog box. Typically, you define a customizer class to extend the **Panel** or **JPanel** classes.
- The class must have a constructor that has no arguments.

When you create a customizer class, you must also provide the method **getBeanDescriptor** in the BeanInfo class associated with the JavaBean. The **BeanDescriptor** object associates the customizer class with a particular JavaBean. To instantiate the **BeanDescriptor** class, use the form of the constructor that has two arguments so that you can specify both the JavaBean object and the **customizer** object.

Syntax

```
BeanDescriptor myBeanDescriptor
   = new BeanDescriptor( beanClass, customizerClass );
```

Dissection

The first argument of the constructor is the **Class** object for the JavaBean class.

The second argument of the constructor is the **Class** object for the customizer class.

Creating a JavaBean Class with a BeanInfo Class

The third version of the example JavaBean, the **ImageBean3** class, is expanded further by the addition of another property called scaling. It allows the image to appear at its original size or scaled to fit the panel that contains it. This property has only two allowable values, the constants **ORIGINAL_SIZE** and **SCALED_TO_FIT**, both of which are defined in the class. A custom property editor is created for this property that lets the user choose between these two values without having to know the integer values used within the class.

ImageBean3 also has an accompanying BeanInfo class. Following the prescribed naming convention, this class is called **ImageBean3BeanInfo**. The source for the scaling property editor class and the **ImageBean3BeanInfo** class follows the breakdown of the **ImageBean3** class.

Figure 8-20 is the complete source code for this third version of the ImageBean example. The differences between this version and the previous version are highlighted in boldface and described in detail after the source code. There are no differences in appearance between the two versions when they are put into the BeanBox window.

```
package examples.beans;
import javax.swing.JPanel;
import java.awt.*;
import java.io.*;
import java.util.*;
import java.awt.image.ImageObserver;
import java.beans.*;
/** A JavaBean class that displays an image and
  * allows the user to specify the file containing
  * the image and the fill color to be used if the
  * image is smaller than the panel; there is also a
  * scaling property that allows the image to be shown
  * in its original size or scaled to fit in the panel
  */
public class ImageBean3 extends JPanel {
    private String fileName;
    private transient Image image;
    private int width = 200;
    private int height=150;
    private Color fill = Color.lightGray;
```

Figure 8-20   ImageBean3: implements a scaling property to control the image display

```
private PropertyChangeSupport
   myListeners = new PropertyChangeSupport( this );
private Vector fillColorListeners = new Vector();
/** Specify how the image is drawn, must be one of
  * the constants defined below */
private int scaling;
/** Draw the image in its original size */
public static final int ORIGINAL_SIZE = 0;
/** Scale the image to fit in the panel */
public static final int SCALED_TO_FIT = 1;
/** No-argument constructor; sets the file name to a
  * default value
  */
public ImageBean3() {
   setFileName( "..\\demo\\sunw\\demo\\juggler\\"
                  + "Juggler0.gif" );
}
/** Send an event to all registered listeners */
public void fireFillColorEvent( FillColorEvent e ) {
   Vector snapshot
      = (Vector) fillColorListeners.clone();
   Enumeration cursor = snapshot.elements();
   while( cursor.hasMoreElements() ) {
      FillColorListener fcl
         = (FillColorListener) cursor.nextElement();
      if ( e.getID()
         == FillColorEvent.COLOR_CHANGE ) {
         fcl.fillColorChange( e );
      }
   }
}
/** Display the image at its original size; the Sun
  * BeanBox recognizes only methods without
  * parameters that return void
  */
public void displayOriginalSize() {
   setScaling( ORIGINAL_SIZE );
}
/** Display the image scaled to fit the panel; the
  * Sun BeanBox recognizes only methods without
  * parameters that return void
  */
public void displayScaledToFit() {
   setScaling( SCALED_TO_FIT );
}
```

Figure 8-20   ImageBean3: implements a scaling property to control the image display (continued)

```
/** Accessor for the filename property
 * @return The current image's filename
 */
public String getFileName() {
   return fileName;
}
/** Accessor for the fillColor property
 * @return The current fill color
 */
public Color getFillColor() {
   return fill;
}
/** The preferred size of the panel
 * @return The size of the current image
 */
public Dimension getPreferredSize() {
   return new Dimension( width, height );
}
/** How the image is drawn within the panel
 */
public int getScaling() {
   return scaling;
}
/** Method for monitoring the progress of the
 * loading of the current image
 */
public boolean imageUpdate( Image img,
                            int infoflags,
                            int x, int y,
                            int w, int h ) {
   if ( (infoflags & ImageObserver.ALLBITS) != 0 ) {
      int oldWidth = width;
      int oldHeight = height;
      width = img.getWidth( null );
      height = img.getHeight( null );
      if ( oldWidth != width
           || oldHeight != height ) {
         myListeners.firePropertyChange(
            "preferredSize",
            new Dimension( oldWidth, oldHeight ),
            new Dimension( width, height ) );
      }
      repaint();
      return false;
   } else {
      return true;
   }
}
```

Figure 8-20   ImageBean3: implements a scaling property to control the image display (continued)

```
    /** Set the image fill color to green; the Sun
      * BeanBox recognizes only methods without
      * parameters that return void
      */
    public void makeFillGreen() {
      setFillColor( Color.green );
    }
    /** Set the image fill color to red; the Sun
      * BeanBox recognizes only methods without
      * parameters that return void
      */
    public void makeFillRed() {
      setFillColor( Color.red );
    }
    /** Paint the fill color if the panel is bigger than
      * the image and the image will be displayed
      * original size; then draw the image according to
      * the selected scaling type
      * @param g the panel's graphics context
      */
    public void paintComponent( Graphics g ) {
      super.paintComponent( g );
      Dimension panelSize = getSize();
      Insets ins = getInsets();
      int actWidth = panelSize.width - ins.right
                         - ins.left - 1;
      int actHeight = panelSize.height - ins.top
                         - ins.bottom - 1;
      if ( scaling == ORIGINAL_SIZE &&
          ( panelSize.width > width ||
            panelSize.height > height ) ) {
        g.setColor( fill );
        g.fillRect( ins.left, ins.top,
                    actWidth, actHeight );
      }
      if ( image != null ) {
        if ( scaling == SCALED_TO_FIT ) {
          g.drawImage( image, ins.left, ins.top,
                       actWidth, actHeight,
                       fill, this );
        } else {
          g.drawImage( image, ins.left, ins.top, this );
        }
      }
    }
    /** Deserialization method called for the JavaBean;
      * this is necessary because Image objects can be
    * serialized and must be regenerated manually
```

Figure 8-20   ImageBean3: implements a scaling property to control the image display (continued)

```
    * @exception IOException if an error occurs
    *           reading the serialized JavaBean
    * @exception ClassNotFoundException if the
    *           serialized JavaBean can't be found
    */
private void readObject( ObjectInputStream ois )
        throws IOException, ClassNotFoundException {
    ois.defaultReadObject();
    image = getToolkit().getImage( fileName );
    repaint();
}
/** Mutator method for the fillColor property
  * @param c the new fill color value
  */
public void setFillColor( Color c ) {
    Color oldFill = fill;
    fill = c;
    myListeners.firePropertyChange( "fillColor",
                                    oldFill,
                                    fill );
    fireFillColorEvent( new FillColorEvent( this,
                        FillColorEvent.COLOR_CHANGE,
                        c ) );
    repaint();
}
/** Mutator method for the fileName property
  * @param fn the new image filename
  */
public void setFileName( String fn ) {
    String oldFileName = fileName;
    fileName = fn;
    image = getToolkit().getImage( fileName );
    myListeners.firePropertyChange( "fileName",
                                    oldFileName,
                                    fileName );
    repaint();
}
/** Mutator method for the image-scaling property
  * used to specify how the image should be drawn
  * within the panel
  * @param s the scaling type, either ORIGINAL_SIZE
  *           or SCALED_TO_FIT
  */
public void setScaling( int s ) {
    int oldScaling = scaling;
    scaling = s;
    myListeners.firePropertyChange( "scaling",
        new Integer( oldScaling ),
        new Integer( scaling ) );
}
```

Figure 8-20   ImageBean3: implements a scaling property to control the image display (continued)

```
    /** Add a listener interested in FillColorEvent
      * objects
      */
    public void
    addFillColorListener( FillColorListener l ) {
       fillColorListeners.addElement( l );
    }
    /** Add a listener interested in property change
      * events
      */
    public void addPropertyChangeListener(
       PropertyChangeListener l ) {
       myListeners.addPropertyChangeListener( l );
    }
    /** Remove a listener no longer interested in
      * FillColorEvent objects
      */
    public void removeFillColorListener(
       FillColorListener l ) {
       fillColorListeners.removeElement( l );
    }
    /** Remove a listener no longer interested in
      * property change events
      */
    public void
    removePropertyChangeListener(
       PropertyChangeListener l ) {
       myListeners.removePropertyChangeListener( l );
    }
}
```

Figure 8-20   ImageBean3: implements a scaling property to control the image
display (continued)

Breakdown of the `ImageBean3` Class

The `ImageBean3` class is a variation on the `ImageBean1` class that has a BeanInfo class.
The differences between this version and the previous version are highlighted in boldface.

```
public class ImageBean3 extends JPanel {
```

Three fields are added to the class. One is the field for holding the scaling, and the other
two are the constant values to be assigned to the scaling field.

```
private int scaling;
public static final int ORIGINAL_SIZE = 0;
public static final int SCALED_TO_FIT = 1;
```

Two methods are added for changing the scaling of the image. Because they return no value and take no input, they are very easy to connect to the events of other JavaBeans:

```
public void displayOriginalSize() {
   setScaling( ORIGINAL_SIZE );
}
public void displayScaledToFit() {
   setScaling( SCALED_TO_FIT );
}
```

An accessor method for the scaling property is then added:

```
public int getScaling() {
   return scaling;
}
```

The **paintComponent** method is changed to handle the choices of image scaling. If the scaling property has the value ORIGINAL_SIZE, the image is drawn as before. If the value is SCALED_TO_FIT, a different version of the **drawImage** method is used. This version takes the size that the image should become, which is the size of the panel after taking the panel's insets into account:

```
public void paintComponent( Graphics g ) {
   super.paintComponent( g );
   Dimension panelSize = getSize();
   Insets ins = getInsets();
   int actWidth = panelSize.width - ins.right
                     - ins.left - 1;
   int actHeight = panelSize.height - ins.top
                     - ins.bottom - 1;
   if ( scaling == ORIGINAL_SIZE &&
        ( panelSize.width > width ||
          panelSize.height > height ) ) {
      g.setColor( fill );
      g.fillRect( ins.left, ins.top,
                  actWidth, actHeight );
   }
   if ( image != null ) {
      if ( scaling == SCALED_TO_FIT ) {
         g.drawImage( image, ins.left, ins.top,
                      actWidth, actHeight,
                      fill, this );
      } else {
         g.drawImage( image, ins.left, ins.top, this );
      }
   }
}
```

8

A mutator method for the scaling type has been added:

```
public void setScaling( int s ) {
    int oldScaling = scaling;
    scaling = s;
    myListeners.firePropertyChange( "scaling",
        new Integer( oldScaling ),
        new Integer( scaling ) );
}
```

None of the other methods in the `ImageBean3` class are new or have been updated. However, this class uses two additional classes:

- The property editor class
- The bean information class

Property Editor Class for the `ImageBean3` Class

The scaling property of the `ImageBean3` class requires a customized editor, and the `ScalingEditor` class provides it. This simple property editor, shown in Figure 8-21, needs to present only a list of two choices for users. Therefore, `ScalingEditor` can be defined as a subclass of **PropertyEditorSupport** and can use most of the inherited method implementations.

```
package examples.beans;
import java.beans.*;
/** This class provides the editing support for the
  * scaling property of the ImageBean3 class
  */
public class ScalingEditor extends PropertyEditorSupport {
    /** Provide the names of the allowable values;
      * don't put spaces in these tags
      * for the Sun BeanBox, ensure that no
      * spaces appear in these tags
      * @return An array of strings containing the
      *         allowable values
      */
    public String[] getTags() {
      return new String[] { "original_size",
                            "scaled_to_fit" };
    }
    /** Convert a tag string into a tag name into a
      * value; the default is to set the value to
      * the ORIGINAL_SIZE value
      * @param s The tag string
      */
```

Figure 8-21   `ScalingEditor`: provides editing support for the scaling property of the `ImageBean3` class

```
    public void setAsText( String s ) {
       if ( s.equals( "scaled_to_fit" ) ) {
          setValue( new Integer(
                  ImageBean3.SCALED_TO_FIT) );
       } else {
          setValue( new Integer(
                  ImageBean3.ORIGINAL_SIZE) );
       }
    }
    /** For a given property value, return a string
     * that can be used for code generation; the
     * default value returned is the string for the
     * ORIGINAL_SIZE value
     * @return The string put into the generated code
     */
    public String getJavaInitializationString() {
       switch( ( (Number) getValue() ).intValue() ) {
          default:
          case ImageBean3.ORIGINAL_SIZE:
             return "examples.beans.ImageBean3."
                     +"ORIGINAL_SIZE";
          case ImageBean3.SCALED_TO_FIT:
             return "examples.beans.ImageBean3."
                     +"SCALED_TO_FIT";
       }
    }
}
```

Figure 8-21   `ScalingEditor`: provides editing support for the scaling property of the `ImageBean3` class (continued)

The `ScalingEditor` class overrides three methods of the **PropertyEditorSupport** class that relate to the names and values of the allowable choices. The `getTags` method returns the names of the value scaling for the property.

```
    public String[] getTags()
```

The **setAsText** method is overridden to convert the tag strings into the actual integer values they represent.

```
    public void setAsText( String s )
```

The **getJavaInitializationString** method returns a string in a form suitable for putting into a class definition. This method is used when a beanbox is generating a class definition and is preparing Java statements for inclusion in the class.

```
    public String getJavaInitializationString()
```

Information Class for the `ImageBean3` Class

To make the `ImageBean3` class usable as a bean, a BeanInfo class is required. The primary reason to create this class is to associate the `ScalingEditor` class with the scaling property of `ImageBean3`. Figure 8-22 is the complete source code for the `ImageBean3BeanInfo` class. Following the listing is a detailed breakdown of the code.

```java
package examples.beans;
import java.beans.*;
import java.lang.reflect.Method;
/** The class contains information about the ImageBean3
  * class in a format that is understood by JavaBean
  * builder programs like Sun's BeanBox
  */
public class ImageBean3BeanInfo extends SimpleBeanInfo {
    /** Create an array of PropertyDescriptor objects
      * representing each of the class's properties
      * @return The array of PropertyDescriptor objects
      */
    public PropertyDescriptor[] getPropertyDescriptors() {
      PropertyDescriptor[] pds = null;
      try {
        pds = new PropertyDescriptor[] {
          new PropertyDescriptor( "fillColor",
                                  ImageBean3.class ),
          new PropertyDescriptor( "fileName",
                                  ImageBean3.class ),
          new PropertyDescriptor( "scaling",
                                  ImageBean3.class ),
          new PropertyDescriptor( "preferredSize",
                                  ImageBean3.class,
                                  "getPreferredSize",
                                  null )
        };
        pds[0].setShortDescription(
          "The fill color around the image" );
        pds[1].setShortDescription(
          "The file containing the image" );
        pds[2].setShortDescription(
          "How the image should be drawn" );
        pds[3].setShortDescription(
          "The preferred size of the panel" );
        // all properties of this bean are bound
        for ( int i = 0; i < pds.length; i++ ) {
          pds[i].setBound( true );
        }
```

Figure 8-22   `ImageBean3BeanInfo`: contains information about the ImageBean3 class

```
            pds[2].setPropertyEditorClass(
                ScalingEditor.class );
        } catch( IntrospectionException ix ) {
            System.out.println( ix );
            return super.getPropertyDescriptors();
        }
        return pds;
    }
    /** Indicate that the fileName property is the
     * default property to be updated by returning
     * its index in the PropertyDescriptor array
     * obtained from the method
     * getPropertyDescriptors
     * @return The index of the fileName array
     *         element
     */
    public int getDefaultPropertyIndex() {
        return 1;   // the filename property index
    }
}
```

Figure 8-22   `ImageBean3BeanInfo:` contains information about the ImageBean3
class (continued)

Breakdown of the `ImageBean3BeanInfo` Class

The first method of the class, `getPropertyDescriptors`, returns an array of objects
in which each element describes a different property of the `ImageBean3` class:

```
public class ImageBean3BeanInfo extends SimpleBeanInfo {
    public PropertyDescriptor[] getPropertyDescriptors() {
```

The method begins by declaring the array and then initializing it using an anonymous array
that has the descriptor objects in it. The descriptor objects must be created inside a try block,
because their constructor may throw an **IntrospectionException** exception that can
be caught and handled. The minimum constructor arguments required are the name of the
property and the class to which the property belongs. These constructor arguments suffice
for all the properties except **preferredSize**. Because **preferredSize** is a read-only
property, additional arguments of the constructor are specified for the methods that read
and write **preferredSize**. The **null** value passed as the fourth parameter indicates that
the **preferredSize** property has no **set** method:

```
PropertyDescriptor[] pds = null;
    try {
        pds = new PropertyDescriptor[] {
            new PropertyDescriptor( "fillColor",
                                    ImageBean3.class ),
            new PropertyDescriptor( "fileName",
                                    ImageBean3.class ),
            new PropertyDescriptor( "scaling",
                                    ImageBean3.class ),
```

```
            new PropertyDescriptor( "preferredSize",
                                    ImageBean3.class,
                                    "getPreferredSize",
                                    null )
    };
```

The next group of statements sets the short descriptions for the properties. Not all bean-boxes make use of these short descriptions, but they can be helpful.

```
pds[0].setShortDescription(
    "The fill color around the image" );
pds[1].setShortDescription(
    "The file containing the image" );
pds[2].setShortDescription(
    "How the image should be drawn" );
pds[3].setShortDescription(
    "The preferred size of the panel" );
```

The for loop marks each property as a bound property.

```
for ( int i = 0; i < pds.length; i++ ) {
    pds[i].setBound( true );
}
```

The method setPropertyEditorClass makes the association between the scaling property and its editor class. In the pds array, the scaling property has the index value 2:

```
pds[2].setPropertyEditorClass(
    ScalingEditor.class );
```

The catch block is required to handle any errors that may occur, because the introspection process could not be completed for the JavaBean. This catch clause recovers by printing a message to the console and returning the default list of property descriptors, as determined by the superclass SimpleBeanInfo. If no errors occur, the array calculated in this method is returned:

```
    } catch( IntrospectionException ix ) {
        System.out.println( ix );
        return super.getPropertyDescriptors();
    }
    return pds;
```

The other method in this BeanInfo class is used to indicate the default property for the JavaBean. It does this by returning the index of a property in the array prepared by getPropertyDescriptors. The Sun BeanBox doesn't do anything special with the default property, but the capability to identify it is something that may be useful for other beanboxes. Returning a value of negative one (-1) indicates that there is no default. In this case, the default property is the filename for the image file:

```
public int getDefaultPropertyIndex() {
    return 1;    // the filename property index
}
```

To load the ImageBean3 into the BeanBox.

1. Add lines to the ImageBeans.manifest file in the folder into which you unpacked the examples.jar file, so that the manifest file lists the three image beans, as follows, with a blank line after the last entry:

```
Name: examples/beans/ImageBean1.class
Java-Bean: True

Name: examples/beans/ImageBean2.class
Java-Bean: True

Name: examples/beans/MagentaButton.class
Java-Bean: True

Name: examples/beans/ImageBean3.class
Java-Bean: True
```

2. Issue the following command, on one line, from the parent folder of the examples folder to create a .jar file named ImageBeans.jar:

```
jar cfm ImageBeans.jar ImageBeans.manifest
                 examples\beans\*.class
```

3. Copy the file **ImageBeans.jar** into the **jars** subfolder of the folder in which you installed the BDK.

4. Start the **BeanBox**. See that the ToolBox window now lists ImageBean3.

   The interesting feature of this bean is the scaling property and the customized property editor, ScalingEditor.

5. Drop an **ImageBean3** bean onto the BeanBox window, and make sure that the bean is selected.

6. You may have to resize the Properties window to see all of it. Click the **down arrow** beside the scaling property or on the scaling entry field. The drop-down menu that is shown in Figure 8-23 appears.

7. Select **scaled_to_fit**, and see the image in the bean expand to fill the dimensions of the bean. Select **original_size**, and the image is redrawn at the original size.

8

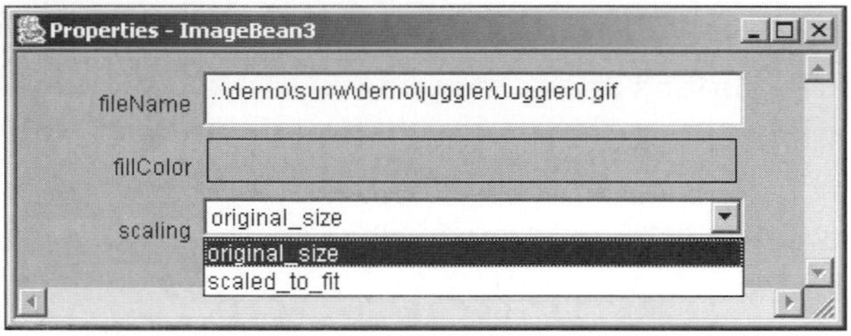

Figure 8-23   The scaling editor for `ImageBean3`

CHAPTER SUMMARY

- The JavaBeans component model is a framework for creating reusable Java classes. Classes that conform to the JavaBeans specification can be loaded into development tools called beanboxes, with which developers can create applications by constructing them from parts.

- A beanbox uses the Reflection API in the package **java.lang.reflect** to interrogate the beans that are loaded into it. If the Reflection API cannot provide all the information that a beanbox needs about a bean, you can supply an additional information class that implements the interface **BeanInfo**. In simple cases, you can extend the class **SimpleBeanInfo** rather than implement the interface.

- Beanboxes typically provide property editors for properties of types **String**, **Font**, and **Color**. You can provide customized editors for other kinds of properties by defining a class that extends **PropertyEditorSupport** or implements the **PropertyEditor** interface.

- If the property editor dialog box of the beanbox is not adequate, you can supply a customizer class for the bean. By using the BeanContext API, a JavaBean object dynamically queries its run-time environment to discover and use services offered by other JavaBeans.

- There is no common superclass that all JavaBean classes extend. Instead, defining a JavaBean is a matter of adhering to a set of programming conventions. The interface to a JavaBean consists of methods, properties, and events.

- A bean must implement the interface **java.io.Serializable**, because beanboxes use object serialization. A bean must have a constructor that has no arguments. You must make provisions to pass arguments, if necessary, to the superclass of a bean. The package **java.beans** provides the core classes and interfaces that support beans.

- Properties are the attributes of a bean, commonly implemented as the fields of a Java class. Properties may be single entities or indexed properties, which are arrays of values. Properties may also be bound or constrained.

□ ~~Bound properties can notify other beans when their value changes. Use the class~~ **PropertyChangeSupport** to implement support for bound properties.

□ Constrained properties are bound properties with the additional characteristic that other listeners can prevent a change in value from occurring. Use the class **VetoableChangeSupport** to implement support for constrained properties.

□ Event handling follows the same model as event handling for components in the Swing and AWT APIs. If a bean can generate an event **Y**, the class for the event is **YEvent**. A listener class **YListener** should handle **YEvent** objects. Changes to properties trigger events of **PropertyChangeEvent** objects. You can add custom events for other kinds of events.

REVIEW QUESTIONS

1. Which of the following represent a major category of the JavaBeans interface? Select all that apply.

   a. properties

   b. events

   c. menus

   d. methods

   e. streams

2. Which of the following describe a category of JavaBeans events? Select all that apply.

   a. restrained

   b. indexed

   c. bound

   d. controlled

   e. reversible

3. If a JavaBean has a property called **X** with type **T**, which of the following are possible mutator methods for that property in the absence of any other information? Select all that apply.

   a. `T isX( )`

   b. `void setXValue( T newValue )`

   c. `T getX( )`

   d. `void setX( T newValue )`

   e. `void putX( T newValue )`

4. Which class can be used as the basis for supporting bound properties in a JavaBean?

5. If a JavaBean has a property called X with type T, which of the following are possible accessor methods for that property in the absence of any other information? Select all that apply.

   a. `T isX( )`

   b. `void getXValue( T newValue )`

   c. `T getX( )`

   d. `void setX( T newValue )`

   e. `T getX( int index )`

6. For a JavaBean class named A, which of the following would be the name of its associated BeanInfo class? Select the best answer.

   a. `BeanInfo`

   b. `SimpleBeanInfo`

   c. `ABeanInfo`

   d. `AInfo`

   e. `ASimpleBeanInfo`

7. Which of the following are classes that can be used to describe features of a JavaBean? Select all that apply.

   a. `ParameterDescriptor`

   b. `IndexedPropertyDescriptor`

   c. `MethodDescriptor`

   d. `ConstructorDescriptor`

   e. `EventSetDescriptor`

8. What class can be used to provide a basic editor for a JavaBean property with values that must be chosen from a list?

9. Which interface must all JavaBeans implement? Select the best answer.

   a. `Runnable`

   b. `Beanable`

   c. `Cloneable`

   d. `Serializable`

   e. `PropertyChangeListener`

10. How does a listener object veto a proposed property change?

PROGRAMMING EXERCISES

Debugging

1. Correct all of the errors in the following JavaBean class to create a bean that draws a square for which the length of the sides is determined by a public property called `sideLength`.

```
package questions.c8;
import javax.swing.JPanel;
import java.awt.*;
public class Debug8_1 extends JPanel {
   private String sideLength = "10";
   private static final Point START
      = new Point( 20, 20 );
   void setSideLength( String sideLength ) {
      this.sideLength = sideLength;
   }
   String getSideLength() {
      return sideLength;
   }
   public Dimension getPreferredSize() {
      return new Dimension( 100, 100 );
   }
   public void paintComponent( Graphics g ) {
      super.paintComponent( g );
      int sl = Integer.parseInt( sideLength );
      g.drawRect( START.x, START.y, sl, sl );
   }
}
```

Create the manifest file `Debug8_1.manifest` and add to this new file the following entry:

```
Name: questions/c8/Debug8_1.class
Java-Bean: True
```

Then, execute the following command (entered on a single line) from the parent folder of the questions folder to create the `.jar` file:

```
jar cfm0 questions/c8/Debug8_1.jar
        questions/c8/Debug8_1.manifest
        questions/c8/Debug8_1.class
```

2. Correct all the errors in the following JavaBean class to create a bean that draws a circle of a specified radius:

```
package questions.c8;
import javax.swing.JPanel;
import java.awt.*;
public class Debug8_2 extends JPanel {
   private String radius = "25";
```

```
      private static final Point START
         = new Point( 20, 20 );
      public void radius( String radius ) {
         this.radius = radius;
      }
      public String radius() {
         return radius;
      }
      public Dimension getPreferredSize() {
         return new Dimension( 100, 100 );
      }
      public void paintComponent( Graphics g ) {
         super.paintComponent( g );
         int r = Integer.parseInt( radius );
         g.fillOval( START.x, START.y, r, r );
      }
   }
```

Create the manifest file `Debug8_2.manifest` and add to this new file the following entry:

```
Name: questions/c8/Debug8_2.class
Java-Bean: True
```

Then, execute the following command (entered on a single line) from the parent folder of the questions folder to create the `.jar` file:

```
jar cfm0 questions/c8/Debug8_2.jar
            questions/c8/Debug8_2.manifest
            questions/c8/Debug8_2.class
```

3. Correct all the errors in the following JavaBean class to create a bean that draws the given text and provides notification when the text changes:

```
package questions.c8;
import javax.swing.JPanel;
import java.awt.*;
import java.beans.*;
public class Debug8_3 extends JPanel {
   private String text = "Default text";
   private static final Point START
      = new Point( 20, 20 );
   private PropertyChangeSupport listeners
      = new PropertyChangeSupport( this );
   public void setDrawText( String text ) {
      this.text = text;
   }
   public String getDrawText() {
      return text;
   }
   public Dimension getPreferredSize() {
      return new Dimension( 100, 40 );
   }
```

```
          super.paintComponent( g );
          g.drawString( text, START.x, START.y );
      }
      public void addPropertyChangeListener(
                  PropertyChangeListener l ) {
          listeners.addPropertyChangeListener( l );
      }
      public void removePropertyChangeListener(
                  PropertyChangeListener l ) {
          listeners.removePropertyChangeListener( l );
      }
  }
```

Create the manifest file `Debug8_3.manifest` and add to this new file the following entry:

```
Name: questions/c8/Debug8_3.class
Java-Bean: True
```

Then, execute the following command (entered on a single line) from the parent folder of the questions folder to create the `.jar` file:

```
jar cfm0 questions/c8/Debug8_3.jar
         questions/c8/Debug8_3.manifest
         questions/c8/Debug8_3.class
```

4. Correct all the errors in the following JavaBean class to create a bean that draws ovals and provides vetoable notification when the height or width of the oval changes:

```
package questions.c8;
import javax.swing.JPanel;
import java.awt.*;
public class Debug8_4 extends JPanel {
   private String ovalHeight = "25";
   private String ovalWidth = "50";
   private static final Point START
      = new Point( 20, 20 );
   public void setOvalHeight( String ovalHeight ) {
      try {
         listeners.fireVetoableChange( "ovalHeight",
                                       this.ovalHeight,
                                       ovalHeight );
         this.ovalHeight = ovalHeight;
      } catch ( PropertyVetoException pve ) {
         // change was vetoed, nothing to do
      }
   }
   public String getOvalHeight() {
      return ovalHeight;
   }
```

```
         public void setOvalWidth( String ovalWidth ) {
            try {
               listeners.fireVetoableChange( "ovalWidth",
                                             this.ovalWidth,
                                             ovalWidth );
               this.ovalWidth = ovalWidth;
            } catch ( PropertyVetoException pve ) {
               // change was vetoed, nothing to do
            }
         }
         public String getOvalWidth() {
            return ovalWidth;
         }
         public Dimension getPreferredSize() {
            return new Dimension( 100, 100 );
         }
         public void paintComponent( Graphics g ) {
            super.paintComponent( g );
            int h = Integer.parseInt( ovalHeight );
            int w = Integer.parseInt( ovalWidth );
            g.fillOval( START.x, START.y, w, h );
         }
      }
```

Create the manifest file `Debug8_4.manifest` and add to this new file the following entry:

```
Name: questions/c8/Debug8_4.class
Java-Bean: True
```

Then, execute the following command (entered on a single line) from the parent folder of the questions folder to create the `.jar` file:

```
jar cfm0 questions/c8/Debug8_4.jar
          questions/c8/Debug8_4.manifest
          questions/c8/Debug8_4.class
```

5. Correct all the errors in the following JavaBean class and its associated BeanInfo and editor classes to create a bean that draws a rectangle with either sharp or rounded corners:

```
package questions.c8;
import javax.swing.JPanel;
import java.awt.*;
public class Debug8_5 extends JPanel {
   public static final int SHARP = 0;
   public static final int ROUNDED = 1;
   private String sideLength = "60";
   private int corners = SHARP;
   private static final Point START
```

```
                 = new Point( 20, 20 );
      private static final int ROUNDING = 20;
      public void setCorners( int corners ) {
         this.corners = corners;
      }
      public int getCorners() {
         return corners;
      }
      public Dimension getPreferredSize() {
         return new Dimension( 100, 100 );
      }
      public void paintComponent( Graphics g ) {
         super.paintComponent( g );
         int sl = Integer.parseInt( sideLength );
         if ( corners == SHARP ) {
            g.drawRect( START.x, START.y, sl, sl );
         } else {
            g.drawRoundRect( START.x, START.y, sl, sl,
                              ROUNDING, ROUNDING );
         }
      }
   }
}
package questions.c8;
import java.beans.*;
public class Debug8_5BeanInfo extends SimpleBeanInfo {
   public PropertyDescriptor[]
   getPropertyDescriptors()  {
      PropertyDescriptor[] pds = null;
      try {
         pds = new PropertyDescriptor[] {
            new PropertyDescriptor( "corners",
                                    Debug8_5.class ),
         };
         pds[0].setShortDescription(
            "The shape of the rectangle's corners" );
         pds[0].setBound( false );
      } catch( IntrospectionException ix ) {
         ix.printStackTrace();
         return super.getPropertyDescriptors();
      }
      return pds;
   }
}
package questions.c8;
import java.beans.*;
public class Debug8_5Editor
   extends PropertyEditorSupport {
   public String[] getTags() {
      return new String[] { "sharp", "rounded" };
   }
```

8

```
        public String getJavaInitializationString() {
            switch( ( ( Number ) getValue() ).intValue() ) {
                default:
                case Debug8_5.SHARP:
                    return "questions.c8.Debug8_5.SHARP";
                case Debug8_5.ROUNDED:
                    return "questions.c8.Debug8_5.ROUNDED";
            }
        }
    }
}
```

Create the manifest file `Debug8_5.manifest` and add to this new file the following entry:

```
Name: questions/c8/Debug8_5.class
Java-Bean: True
```

Then, execute the following command (entered on a single line) from the parent folder of the questions folder to create the `.jar` file:

```
jar cfm0 questions/c8/Debug8_5.jar
        questions/c8/Debug8_5.manifest
        questions/c8/Debug8_5*.class
```

Complete the Solution

1. Extract the file `X:\Data\questions\c8\Complete8_1.java` from the CD-ROM. Complete the `Complete8_1` JavaBean class by adding another property, messageFont, which defines the font used to display the message. Then, execute the following command (entered on a single line) from the parent folder of the questions folder to create the `.jar` file:

    ```
    jar cfm0 questions/c8/Complete8_1.jar
            questions/c8/Complete8_1.manifest
            questions/c8/Complete8_1*.class
    ```

2. Beginning with the JavaBean class shown in Exercise 1, change the message property so that it is a bound message that provides notification when it changes.

3. Extract the file `questions\c8\Complete8_3.java` from the file `question.jar` on the CD-ROM. Complete the `Complete8_3` JavaBean class that implements a progress bar by adding the methods required to make the current position and upper limit into properties that the user can customize. Then, execute the following command (entered on a single line) from the parent folder of the questions folder to create the `.jar` file:

    ```
    jar cfm0 questions/c8/Complete8_3.jar
            questions/c8/Complete8_3.manifest
            questions/c8/Complete8_3*.class
    ```

4. Beginning with the JavaBean class shown in Exercise 3, add the support needed to make the current position and upper limit into constrained properties.

~~3. Beginning with the JavaBean class shown in Exercise 3, add a corresponding~~
BeanInfo class that gives short descriptions of the properties, indicates that the
properties are constrained, and identifies the position property as the default property for customization.

Discovery

1. Create a JavaBean class called **Prompter** that displays a prompting message and
   provides an entry field where users can enter their response to the prompt. This
   bean should also include an OK button so users can indicate that they are finished
   entering their response.

2. Create a JavaBean class called **Counter** that counts upward from 0 to some limit.
   The increment and the interval between ticks should be properties of this bean,
   and the actual count should be a bound property. Try connecting this bean to the
   progress bar bean from the Complete the Solution exercises so that the count and
   the progress bar move in unison to the same upper limit.

3. Create a JavaBean class called **BarGraph** that draws a simple bar graph for the
   data given by the user as five separate bar height properties.

8

9

USING RELATIONAL DATABASES

> **In this chapter you will:**
>
> ♦ Discover what Java DataBase Connectivity means and what composes the JDBC API
>
> ♦ Learn some best practices for programming relational databases
>
> ♦ See what Java types map to SQL types or encapsulate database concepts
>
> ♦ Learn how to connect to relational databases through JDBC drivers
>
> ♦ Create and execute SQL statements using the `java.sql` package
>
> ♦ Perform advanced operations such as batch updates and updatable result sets
>
> ♦ Program for transactional integrity
>
> ♦ Consider the advantages of data sources, connection pooling, and distributed transactions as supported by the `javax.sql` package

INTRODUCTION

Database technology is almost as old as the computer industry. Relational databases have been the most popular repository of information for organizations of all types and sizes for decades, and most commercial programs depend heavily on data that resides in relational databases. Some successful relational database management (RDBM) systems are DB2 from IBM, Oracle, Informix Dynamic Server, Sybase, and Microsoft SQL Server. These RDBM systems predate Java but provide Java-callable APIs called *drivers*. Cloudscape is a pure Java database and is becoming popular in Java environments that require a small, standards-based relational database.

Any Java program can use a relational database. All it needs is access to an RDBM installation that provides a driver that conforms to the *Java Database Connectivity* (JDBC) standard. The JDBC specification is part of the J2SE platform. A JDBC driver is a set of classes that provide the bridge between a Java program running on the Java platform and an RDBM system that is usually running on a native operating system.

In case you have not used a relational database before, the CD-ROM that accompanies this book includes a primer "Relational Databases and Structured Query Language." You can find this tutorial on the CD in file `Primers\RDBandSQL.pdf`. SQL has been the industry-standard language for relational databases since the 1980s. Most RDBM systems support variations of and provide extensions to standard SQL. This chapter tries to use only standard SQL but, when necessary, as in the commands to create the sample databases, it uses SQL as supported by DB2.

This chapter discusses the two packages that make up the JDBC API, **java.sql** and **javax.sql**. Together these packages are called JDBC 3.0, the version of JDBC included in J2SE version 1.4. The **java.sql** package supports connecting to a database directly from Java code, manipulating data in relational databases by running SQL statements and stored procedures, and some more advanced features such as using transactions. The **javax.sql** package is used primarily the enterprise environment, where the JDBC driver is installed on an application server and providing connections to resources such as databases is the responsibility of the application server.

> The original Java platform included a set of classes that is now called the JDBC 1 API. These classes are still used, but the features of JDBC expanded with JDBC 2 and again with JDBC 3. Java 2, or version 1.2 of the SDK, added JDBC 2 and split JDBC support into a core API and optional API. The standard API was grouped into the package **java.sql**, and the optional features into **javax.sql**. JDBC 3.0 adds a few more features and specifies that both packages are included in the J2SE platform.

You can also use JDBC to access data in forms other than databases, including spreadsheets and flat files, but this chapter concentrates on using JDBC to access data stored in relational databases.

In commercial environments, performance, data integrity, and security are primary concerns in applications that access databases. Many tests have shown that spending 80 or 90% of execution time retrieving and storing data is very common. If a program is slow in execution, the greatest performance improvement is usually gained by reviewing the way the application accesses the database. For most companies, the integrity of the data in databases is a measure of the accuracy of the company's records, so programs should never leave data in a corrupt or inconsistent state, regardless of any run-time errors or exception conditions that occur. Similarly, programs should not allow unauthorized access to sensitive data.

Therefore, the study of database programming goes far beyond learning how to use the JDBC API to store and retrieve data. Database programming has major implications for application design, security, and transaction management. This chapter introduces some of the broader concerns that make a program suitable for use in environments where data must be accurate, current, and secure at all times. Often these are the same environments in which performance is a top priority.

BEST PRACTICES FOR PROGRAMMING FOR DATABASES

This section contains some rules of thumb for designing robust, scaleable programs that use databases.

Apply the Model-View-Persistence Design Pattern

Chapter 1 of this book introduced the concept of organizing classes in an application into separate layers for presentation (view), control, and model (business logic) in the section "Model-View-Controller Design Pattern." The fundamental idea is that the user interface or presentation of the data should be separated from processing in the business logic. In MVC, the model layer performs the business of the application. Only the model layer operates on the persistent data. *Persistent* data is information stored outside of all program components, typically in a database.

MVC provides a first degree of security of the data and usually produces an application that scales better to large numbers of users than a program with a monolithic structure. For example, tasks of the controller can include verifying that the requested action is valid in the current state of the application, and that the requester is allowed to perform the requested operation. In contrast, in a monolithic structure you may code each user interface control to perform an associated end-to-end operation including updating the database. Verification code then must be included in every control. Without a centralized controller, safeguards are scattered through the application and become hard to manage.

This same principle of layering applies between the business logic and database. Just as the controller sits between the view and model, a persistence broker layer acts as interface between the model and classes that call the JDBC API. Figure 9–1 shows a five-level design pattern that clearly separates the model from persistence.

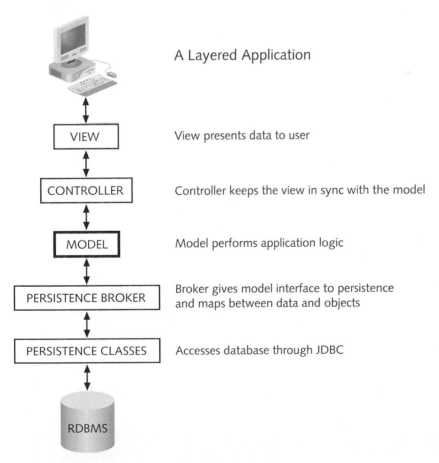

A Layered Application

VIEW — View presents data to user

CONTROLLER — Controller keeps the view in sync with the model

MODEL — Model performs application logic

PERSISTENCE BROKER — Broker gives model interface to persistence and maps between data and objects

PERSISTENCE CLASSES — Accesses database through JDBC

RDBMS

Figure 9-1 View-model-persistence separation

Model-persistence separation is partially achieved by the fact that databases are usually designed without regard to the Java classes or object models for any Java program. In business applications, the database is most often defined and used by other applications before development of a new application begins.

Model-persistence separation can also add a degree of security because the persistence layer, like the controller, can check that the requested operation is allowed in the current state of the application. What user name and password should be used to open the database connection? Rarely do you want to give all end users IDs and passwords for the database. More likely, the persistence layer uses an assigned identity and users acquire the right to access the database from the right to run parts of the application.

Creating layers of code between model and persistence is a best practice. For example, all JDBC calls and SQL should be contained in the persistence layer so that the model needs no knowledge of the database design. In contrast, the persistence layer must operate on specific databases and tables and know the type and name of each column of data. Unless the mapping of Java objects to database objects is very straightforward, you may need an intermediate layer that converts from the database structure to the objects used in the model. Measure your application design's need for a persistence layer by these criteria:

- Can the database be replaced by a different persistence solution in which the structure of the data storage is very different without changing the model layer logic?

- Are the classes that make up the core logic of the application designed independently of the user interface and of the database structure? See the next section for more discussion of object model-to-persistence mapping.

- Is the interface between the classes that perform business logic and the classes that store and retrieve data easily identifiable, and do all interactions between model and persistence layers flow through this interface?

Define a Mapping between Java Objects and Data Elements

Primer 9-1 on the CD that accompanies this book lists some of the differences between object-oriented modeling and relational database design that can pose challenges to Java programmers. Mostly the problems relate to relationships between tables or associations between objects. The issue may seem simple when the problem is small and the table definitions map closely onto Java classes, but some very ordinary situations can produce complex mappings. Figure 9-2 compares terms used in Java programming and database schema. The *schema* is the design of the database—its tables, columns, and relationships between them. Unfortunately, DB2 uses the same term as a qualifier for table names.

RDB Concept	OOAD Concept	Considerations
Entity relationship	Class associations	Entity relationships are foreign-key relationships between tables. One classic pitfall for novice database programmers is trying to reproduce foreign-key relationships as associations between classes. Try instead to model the real-world relationships that are represented by the foreign keys.
Table	Class	In simple situations, a table can map directly onto a class or JavaBean for which the main role is to hold and provide access to data. In many situations, a class has fields corresponding to columns in more than one table and does not contain fields for every column in a table.
Row	Instance	When a table maps onto a class, a row in the table maps onto an instance of the class.
Column	Instance variable	A column can map onto an instance variable of a class. The schema-to-object mapping can perform transformations such as type conversions and merging of data from multiple columns into one field in the class.
Unique key		A table can be defined with the constraint that the value of one column or a set of columns cannot be duplicated in another row. Java has no equivalent, so you must build this kind of rule into your business logic.
Primary key		Java has no simple equivalent for the primary key.
Foreign key	Object reference	Any Java class can contain a field for which the type is an object reference to another class. Primer 9-1 on the CD-ROM that accompanies this book explains how foreign keys also link rows in different tables, but using a nonobject-oriented paradigm.
Dependent table		A table that contains a foreign key is a dependent table. Constraints defined on the foreign key determine how the database manager enforces referential integrity. The JVM provides no equivalent services. For example, if you want to delete `OrderItem` objects when the customer cancels an order, you may have to write code to do so explicitly.
Parent table		In a database, the table whose field is used as a foreign key in another table is called the parent table. Unlike a Java class in which fields can hold object references to contained objects, there is nothing in the definition of a parent table that indicates there is a relationship with another table.

Figure 9-2   Database schema and object-oriented concepts

To illustrate the difference between foreign keys and Java object references, consider the many-to-many situation. For example, a student may take several courses and each course is attended by several students. Figure 9-3 is a possible database schema for the student–course relationship.

COURSECODE	COURSENAME	PROFESSOR	...
HIST105	Modern European History	Pavel Ivanov	
MATH233	Differential Equations	Joshua Newell	
ENG301	Middle English Prose	Pamela Markham	
...			

parent tables

primary keys

COURSECODE	STUDENTID
HIST105	32DW301
HIST105	23FGM73
ENG301	23FGM73
MATH233	22HYT32
...	

dependent table with 2 foreign keys

STUDENTID	STUDENTNAME	ADDRESS	...	...
32DW301	Mary Dawson	21 Wardon Road		
23FGM73	Ming XeYaun	3213 Cross Street		
22HYT32	Alain Dubois	775 Don Parkway		
...				

Figure 9-3 Possible database schema with a third table to represent many-to-many relationships

Contrast the database schema represented by Figure 9-3 with the partial class definitions shown in Figure 9-4.

```
public class Course {
   String courseName;
   String courseCode;
   String professor;
   ArrayList students;  // students is a collection of Student objects
   ...
}
public class Student {
   String StudentId;
   String StudentName;
   String address;
   ArrayList courses; // courses is a collection of Course objects
   ...
}
```

Figure 9-4 Many-to-many relationships in class definitions

The mapping of relationships becomes more complicated in object models that use inheritance. For example, some employees may be managers and all managers are employees. In Java, the implementation is obvious:

```
public class Manager extends Employee {
    ...
}
```

But how do you design the database schema? Three possible solutions are shown in Figure 9-5.

Single-table solution: EMPLOYEE

EMPNO	NAME	DEPT	ISMANAGER	EMAIL	PHONE	REPORTSTO	BUDGET	TARGET

nullable

Two-table solution: EMPLOYEE

EMPNO	NAME	DEPT	EMAIL	PHONE	REPORTSTO

Two-table solution: MANAGER

EMPNO	NAME	DEPT	EMAIL	PHONE	REPORTSTO	BUDGET	TARGET

Two-table solution with root-leaf inheritance: EMPLOYEE

EMPNO	NAME	DEPT	ISMANAGER	EMAIL	PHONE	REPORTSTO

foreign key

Two-table solution with root-leaf inheritance: MANAGER

EMPNO	BUDGET	TARGET

Figure 9-5 Database schema for inheritance

There is no one correct way to represent inheritance in entity relationships.

- A single-table solution is to add extra columns to the EMPLOYEE table for the manager-only fields. For regular employees, these columns contain null values, so this option makes inefficient use of space. You also need a discriminator column to indicate whether each employee is a manager.

- A two-table solution is to store managers in a separate table, MANAGER, that has the same columns as the EMPLOYEE table plus the manager-only fields. With this solution, you must read two tables to get basic information on all employees. Also, to promote an employee to management involves deleting the EMPLOYEE record and creating a MANAGER record.

- A two-table solution sometimes called *root-leaf inheritance* involves including managers in the EMPLOYEE table and defining a separate MANAGER table to hold only the extra management fields. A manager then has two records, probably with the same primary key, one in each table. You can optionally add a discriminator column to the EMPLOYEE table to indicate whether this employee is a manager. Here the disadvantage is that you must access records in two tables to build the record for one manager.

The key message here is that you cannot simply create a class for each table and add an instance variable to the class for each column in the table. Instead, build the object model to suit the needs of the model layer in your application. Then convert that data to and from database elements in your persistence layer.

Leverage the Power of the Database Manager

A good rule of thumb is to let the database do what it was designed to do and leave to Java those tasks the database cannot do. Many databases are defined to include some automatic integrity checks, such as the following:

- The primary key or identifier for a row must be unique. Let the database manager signal an error if a program tries to add a second row with a key identical to that of an existing row. For example, a second employee cannot be added with the same employee number as an existing employee.

- Use foreign key constraints to signal an error if a program tries to insert a row in a dependent table for which there is no row in the parent table. For example, you cannot insert an employee for a department that does not exist.

- Database designers can set rules of referential integrity to control what happens to rows in a dependent table when the associated row in the parent table is deleted or modified. For example, what happens to employees of a department when the department record is deleted? If the foreign key is defined with a constraint of *cascade delete*, the employee records are deleted automatically. Alternatively, the tables may be defined so that an attempt to delete the department causes an error if the department has employees. Another option tells the database manager to set the department field to null for the affected employees.

Almost always, letting the database enforce constraints is more efficient than doing so in Java code. If the database manager can provide functionality that you can also program in Java, the best approach is usually to take advantage of the database feature. In DB2, you can define *triggers* that are actions the database executes before or after any row in a table is altered. For example, if your human resource application assigns employee ID 1 to the first person hired, 2 to the second person, and so on, you can use a trigger to set the employee number automatically when a new employee is added to the database. Some sample programs in this chapter use this feature.

When you issue a command through JDBC that tries to break any of the constraints built into the database schema, the JDBC classes throw an exception, usually of type `java.sql.SQLException`. Your application should catch and handle all exceptions returned by the JDBC classes.

Design Your Application in Terms of Transactions

Often performing a business operation involves more than one database operation. A best programming practice is to design your code or application components to represent business operations rather than database operations. For example, an online shopping application must provide a feature to let customers submit their orders and buy the items they have added to their virtual shopping carts. Typically the application must issue several SQL queries, such as the following:

- Update the inventory record to reduce the number in stock by the number purchased.

- Update the customer account to bill for the purchased goods, or add a record of invoice information to a database used by the billing department.

- Record the customer order in a database for tracking.

- Add shipping information to a database used by the warehouse or shipping department.

In this example, the business operation is to process the order. If the customer cancels the order or if his credit check indicates an inability to pay, the store may refuse the order. In either case, it is not sufficient just to delete the order record. Changes to all databases involved—in this example, ORDERS, INVENTORY, BILLING, and SHIPPING— must be cancelled. If you delete the order and do not bill the customer, but still fail to return the items to the available inventory, your code fails to ensure *transactional integrity*.

The recommended approach to this problem is to start a transaction when starting to process the order, and stop the transaction when the order processing is complete. Think of a transaction as a logical unit of work containing all changes to persistent data during the process of completing a task and all that must be undone if the task fails at any point during processing. JDBC and many other software tools provide transactional capability. When a transaction completes successfully, you can commit changes, but if something goes wrong, you can roll back changes and stop processing. To *commit* is to send an instruction to the database to confirm updates and make them permanent. To *roll back* is to send an instruction to the database to cancel updates and revert to the previous data.

JDBC drivers give Java programmers access to the transactional capabilities of the database management software. The section "Coding Transactions" shows how to code a commit and rollback. Using the transactional processing feature of the database manager is far more efficient than trying to include undo logic in your code.

Transactional operations are easiest to develop and maintain if your program is structured so that program components represent the units of work that map to transactions, in terms not only of database writes but also of changes to the state of the application or system as a whole. For example, you can write a `processOrder` method for the online shopping example. The method may use many classes and call many other methods, but the key to transactional processing is that the method opens a transaction when it starts and ends immediately after closing the transaction. When closing the transaction, commit or roll back all changes made to the system.

The properties of transactional integrity have been formalized and are known as the ACID properties, after the first letter in each of four adjectives. The ACID properties are not wholly independent: they overlap. The goal is to create components that implement transactions with the following ACID properties:

- *Atomic*: A transaction is all or nothing. Either all changes made during transaction processing become permanent, or all changes are reversed. If the transaction is rolled back, the state of the system should be as though the transaction was never started.

- *Consistent*: Code that performs transactional processing should do the same thing, given the same input data and conditions, every time. It should never have unexpected side effects or vary due to temporary or external circumstances.

- *Isolated*: Each transaction must be independent of all other transactions. Two transactions active at the same time should have no impact on each other. You may have to define rules for what happens when two different processes concurrently read or update the same record in a database. Many database managers let you set isolation levels to control concurrent access to data.

- *Durable*: After a transaction has been committed, all changes made to the state of the system must be permanent. A committed transaction cannot be undone, except by subsequent operations that operate on the same data. For example, after the cost of an order has been added to a customer account balance, the new charge cannot disappear unless the customer returns the purchases in a separate transaction or clears the balance by paying the bill.

Consider Using Entity Enterprise JavaBeans

Building a robust persistence layer that performs database schema-to-object model mapping can be a complex task. In the IT industry, the chosen solution often does not involve coding to the JDBC API.

Large-scale applications often use Enterprise JavaBeans as a layer between a Java application and persistent data, especially when the application is distributed on different servers throughout the organization, and when transactional integrity and security are of high importance. EJBs are the subject of Chapter 14. For now, just be aware that Entity EJBs are J2EE-supported components designed to manipulate persistent data and often represent records in relational databases. Entity beans usually perform JDBC-based operations behind the scenes. The EJB developer creates methods that Java classes can call and designs the EJB as reusable application components. All database operations are encapsulated in the implementation of the EJB and hidden from the client program.

JDBC DRIVERS FOR RDBM SYSTEMS

9

To access a database, you need a suitable driver. Usually, drivers are supplied by the database vendor or third-party software developers. Drivers that conform to the J2SE specification are called JDBC drivers. Sun maintains a list of JDBC driver suppliers at the URL `http://industry.java.sun.com/products/jdbc/drivers`. Drivers come in two versions, JDBC 1.x and JDBC 2.x. JDBC 2 drivers also support JDBC 3, because the main difference between JDBC 2 and JDBC 3 is packaging. Before developing code, you should determine which JDBC version driver you are using. JDBC 1 drivers come in four types simply called types 1, 2, 3, and 4. JDBC 2 continues to recognize these types and adds additional drivers to support interface `javax.sql.datasource`. If your program uses only the package `java.sql`, use of the following four driver types:

- A *type 1 driver* is called the JDBC-ODBC bridge. ODBC provides a standard API for accessing SQL on Windows platforms and is based on the X/Open Call-Level Interface specification. The bridge translates from ODBC to JDBC and is therefore the least efficient of the four types.

- A *type 2 driver* provides a Java interface to vendor-specific APIs written in code that is native to the platform. Like ODBC, a type 2 driver is mostly implemented in native code, such as compiled C, and includes a set of Java classes that use Java Native Interface (JNI) to bridge between Java and the native code. JNI is briefly discussed in Appendix A of this book. The RDBM system or client-access software must reside on the same host as the client program. This is the most efficient driver. However, you cannot use it in a distributed environment unless all classes that operate on the database reside on the database host.

- A *type 3 driver* is like a type 2, except that the user accesses the database over a TCP/IP connection. Any program that does not reside on the same host as the database must use a type 3 or 4 driver.

- A *type 4 driver* is like a type 3 driver but contains only Java code. Therefore, a type 4 driver is called a pure Java driver. Only type 4 drivers are portable to any JVM. Other drivers are platform specific.

Choose the JDBC 1 driver for your RDBM that is likely to give the best performance. Generally, type 1 is the least preferable. Use type 2 if you know that the code layer accessing the database will always reside on the same host as the RDBM system, because it is faster. The examples in this chapter that do not use datasources use the DB2 type 2 driver. Datasources are introduced in the section "Using the `javax.sql` API."

Type 2, 3, and 4 drivers are packaged into jar or zip files. Add this file to your `CLASSPATH` environment variable so the JRE can find the JDBC driver classes when you need them. You can access databases that have only ODBC drivers using the ODBC-JDBC bridge, or type 1 driver. The ODBC-JDBC bridge is a database driver provided by Sun Microsystems in the package `sun.jdbc.objc.JdbcOdbcDriver`. It consists of a mixture of Java code and native code connected through JNI.

SQL TO JAVA TYPE MAPPINGS

When the value of a column in a row in a table is returned as a Java value, it is converted to a Java type. Figure 9-6 shows the default type conversions performed by JDBC. By far the most common type returned is `String`, for it represents most character types. Numeric types, such as `int` and `java.math.BigDecimal` used for fixed-point real numbers are also common, as are the date and time types. Not all RDBM systems support all the types listed in Figure 9-6, and some support additional types. For example, DB2 has `DECIMAL` but not `NUMERIC` type and adds the character type `GRAPHIC`.

SQL Type	Java Type	Comments
CHAR	`String`	
VARCHAR	`String`	
LONGVARCHAR	`String`	
NUMERIC	`java.math.BigDecimal`	
DECIMAL	`java.math.BigDecimal`	Decimal values are real numbers stored to fixed precision
BIT	`boolean`	
TINYINT	`byte`	
SMALLINT	`short`	

Figure 9-6   Default SQL to Java type mappings

SQL Type	Java Type	Comments
INTEGER	int	
BIGINT	long	
REAL	float	
DOUBLE	double	
BINARY	byte[]	
VARBINARY	byte[]	
LONGVARBINARY	byte[]	
DATALINK	java.net.URL	Datalinks are pointers to external files
BLOB	java.sql.Blob	Binary Large Objects can be any data including multimedia
CLOB	byte[]	Use Character Large Objects for text documents such as XML
DATE	java.sql.Date	java.sql.Date extends java.util.Date
TIME	java.sql.Time	java.sql.Time extends java.util.Date
TIMESTAMP	java.sql.TimeStamp	java.sql.TimeStamp extends java.util.Date
ARRAY *	java.sql.Array	An ARRAY is a collection of SQL data types
REF *	java.sql.Ref	A SQL REF is a reference to a SQL structure type
Structure types *	java.sql.Struct	SQL allows user-defined data structures in the database

Figure 9-6   Default SQL to Java type mappings (continued)

The types marked with an asterisk (*) in Figure 9-6 are user defined. Note that the **java.sql** package has three types for date and time. They all extend **java.util.Date**. The **Date** class in **java.sql** is mapped to the SQL DATE type, so take care to use **java.sql.Date** in JDBC programming. The SQL DATE type holds date, month, and year values. The SQL TIME type holds hours, minutes, and seconds. The SQL TIMESTAMP type can store dates accurately to nanoseconds and is therefore more accurate than the Java **Date** classes. For high precision, use **java.sql.TimeStamp**.

UNDERSTANDING THE DATABASE USED IN THIS CHAPTER

For demonstration, all example code in this chapter operates on the database of the hypothetical Near Hills Ski Club. The RDBM system is DB2, and you can install a version of DB2 that works with this database from the CD-ROM that accompanies this book. The database name is SKICLUB, and it is given a DB2 schema name also of SKICLUB.

The Near Hills Ski Club is also the example used for the Web application in Chapter 13. The ski club organizes trips to local ski resorts on every Tuesday, Wednesday, and Thursday in January and February. The database is initialized to give a snapshot of operation in the year 2004. Figure 9-7 is an entity-relationship diagram of the **SKICLUB** database.

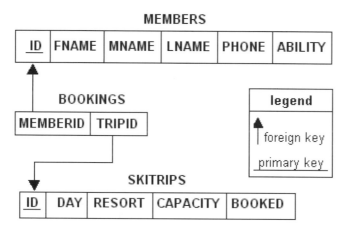

Figure 9-7   The **SKICLUB** database schema

From Figure 9-7 you can see that the **SKICLUB** database contains three tables:

- The **MEMBERS** table has a row for each member with primary key column **ID**. Other columns store the name, phone number, and skiing ability of a member. This table is created with a *trigger*: a command automatically executed by the database manager after a specified database operation. In this case, the trigger assigns a unique value to the **ID** field when an SQL statement inserts a new member and supplies an **ID** value of zero. An additional database constraint ensures that the combination of first name and last name is unique for each member.

- The **SKITRIPS** table has a row for each trip with primary key column **ID**. The other columns store the date, resort name, capacity (number of members that can attend), and the number of number of members already booked on the trip. To calculate the number of places available, subtract the number booked from the capacity. A capacity of zero indicated a cancelled trip.

- The **BOOKINGS** table resolves the many-to-many relationship between **MEMBERS** and **SKITRIPS**: One member can attend many trips and a trip can accommodate several members. Two constraints on this table enforce additional business rules: a member from cannot be deleted the **MEMBERS** table if that member has booked trips. If a trip is deleted from the **SKITRIPS** table, all bookings for that trip are automatically deleted.

DB2 command files to define and populate this database and to delete it are included with the code examples on the CD-ROM that accompanies this book. The **Readme.html** file on the CD-ROM that accompanies this book gives detailed instructions for installing

DB2 from the CD-ROM and creating the example database. If you are interested, you can find the SQL commands that define the SKICLUB database in file `X:\Data\ examples\SkiclubDB\NEWSKICLUBDB.sql`, where X is the drive letter of your CD-ROM.

USING THE `java.sql` API

This section explains how to use JDBC classes in the package `java.sql`. The example programs have a simple command-line interface to test the code and to emphasize that the persistence layer of an application should be separate from the model layer and at the opposite end of the layered architecture from the view or user interface.

Figure 9-8 lists the interfaces, and Figure 9-9 lists the classes, in the package `java.sql`. For a full description of the types not covered further in this chapter, refer to the J2SDK documentation or the help system that comes with your RDBMs.

Interface	Description
Array	Defines the Java mapping for the SQL type ARRAY
Blob	Defines the Java mapping for binary large objects or SQL BLOBs
CallableStatement	Provides the methods you call to execute stored procedures
Clob	Defines the Java mapping for character large objects or SQL CLOBs
Connection	Encapsulates a connection to the database or a database session
DatabaseMetaData	Describes the database as a whole
Driver	Defines the methods all database vendors must implement in their JDBC drivers
ParameterMetaData	Provides information about the parameters in prepared statements
PreparedStatement	Represents precompiled SQL statements
Ref	Used to reference SQL structured types stored in the database
ResultSet	A collection containing the results of a database query
ResultSetMetaData	Provides information about the types and properties of fields in ResultSet
Savepoint	Represents a point within a transaction to which operations can be rolled back
SQLData	Allows custom mappings from SQL user-defined types to Java types
SQLInput	An input stream containing values for an instance of a SQL structured or distinct type
SQLOutput	An output stream for writing attributes of a user-defined type to the database
Statement	Provides the methods you call to execute SQL statements
Struct	Defines the standard mapping of a SQL structured type

Figure 9-8   Interfaces defined in the `java.sql` package

Class	Description
Date	Wraps a millisecond value so that SQL can use an instance as a SQL DATE value
DriverManager	Gives you access to database drivers
DriverPropertyInfo	Contains the property information drivers need to make a connection
Time	Wraps a java.util.Date object so that SQL can use it as a SQL TIME value
Timestamp	Wraps a java.util.Date object so that SQL can use it as a SQL TIMESTAMP value
Types	Defines constants used to identify generic SQL types

Figure 9-9   Classes defined in the `java.sql` package

The SQL package also defines exception types **BatchUpdateException**, **DataTruncation**, **SQLException**, and **SQLWarning**. JDBC methods can throw these exceptions, and most can throw **SQLException** and **SQLWarning** exceptions. You should always provide a handler for these exceptions and provide some feedback to your users to say the operation could not be completed.

The following types are part of what was called JDBC 2 and introduced with version 1.2 of the J2SDK: **Array**, **Blob**, **Clob**, **Ref**, **SQLData**, **SQLInput**, **SQLOutput**, **Struct**, and **BatchUpdateException**. **ParameterMetaData** and **Savepoint** are new with version 1.4 in JDBC 3.

Creating and Executing SQL Statements

Accessing a database from Java programs involves establishing a connection to the database, then issuing queries expressed as SQL statements, and processing the results of those queries. This section gives an overview of the process, and following sections describe each step in detail. Java code that issues any dynamic SQL statement must work through the following standard steps:

1. Get a connection to the database by calling the **DriverManager. getConnection** method as described in the section "Establishing a Database Connection." A more advanced technique is to use a **javax.sql.DataSource** object, as described in the section "The DataSource Architecture."

2. Get a **Statement** object from the **Connection** object acquired in Step 1. Call the **Connection.createStatement** method to get an object in which you can execute a SELECT, UPDATE, INSERT, or DELETE statement, as described in the section "Issuing Dynamic SQL Statements."

3. Build the SQL statement in a string. The string contains the exact SQL you would type to a database command-line processor.

4. Call a method for the **Statement** object created in Step 2, passing the SQL command as its argument. The **Statement** interface provides different methods for different SQL statements.

5. Receive results as the return value of the method of the **Statement** interface.

6. Process the results as described in "Processing a **ResultSet**" and then either explicitly close the result object or let it be implicitly closed when you close the **Statement** object.

7. Implicitly or explicitly close the **Statement** object. Usually, you create a new **Statement** object for each dynamic SQL statement and then close the **Statement** object after you have processed the statement's results.

8. Implicitly or explicitly close the **Connection** object.

Establishing a Database Connection

Before you can connect to a database from a Java program, you must load the database driver into your JVM. Instead of instantiating an object of a class, use the class loader to load the driver classes. Usually, you do this by calling the **Class.forName** method. For example, the following line loads the DB2 type 2 driver supplied by IBM with the DB2 product:

```
Class.forName( "COM.ibm.db2.jdbc.app.DB2Driver" );
```

After the driver is loaded and before you can issue SQL statements, you must connect to the database. For this, you need an object of type **Connection**.

Interface

`java.sql.Connection`

Purpose

The **Connection** interface defines the behavior of the context within which you issue SQL statements and receive results.

Methods

■ **void close( )**

The **close** method releases the JDBC resources used by the connection. If you do not call this method explicitly, the resources are released by the JRE when the **Connection** object goes out of scope.

■ **boolean isClosed( )**

The **isClosed** method returns **true** if this connection is closed and **false** if it is open.

- **DatabaseMetaData getMetaData( )**

  The **getMetaData** method returns an object that contains information about the database.

- **int getTransactionIsolation( )**

  The **getTransactionIsolation** method returns a value that indicates which transaction isolation level is set for the connection. The isolation level determines how the database manager handles concurrent access to the database, and its value is one of the fields of this class, ordered from least to most restrictive: **TRANSACTION_READ_UNCOMMITTED**, **TRANSACTION_READ_COMMITTED**, **TRANSACTION_REPEATABLE_READ**, **TRANSACTION_SERIALIZABLE**, and **TRANSACTION_NONE**.

- **void Savepoint setSavepoint (String *name*)**
  void releaseSavepoint (Savepoint *savepoint*)

  The **setSavepoint** method identifies the current point in execution as a savepoint. A *savepoint* is a point to which transactional processing can be rolled back, as described in the section "Coding Transactions." The **releaseSavepoint** method removes the savepoint.

- **boolean getAutoCommit( )**
  void setAutoCommit(boolean *autoCommit*)

  Call the **setAutoCommit** method passing a value of **false** if you do not want changes to be committed to the database until you call the **commit** method. This gives you the opportunity to back out changes with the **rollback** method and is a good idea if a single transaction requires more than one database query. Call **setAutoCommit** passing **true** to turn on autoCommit mode. To find out the current setting, call **getAutoCommit**.

- **void commit ( )**
  void rollback ( )
  void rollback (Savepoint *savepoint*)

  The **commit** method makes any changes made since the last call to **commit** or **rollback** permanent. Call the **rollback** method to undo all changes since the last call to **commit** or **rollback**. These methods also release database locks held by the connection. If you set a savepoint, you can undo changes made since the last savepoint was set.

- **void createStatement( )**
  void createStatement(int *resultsetType*,
  **   int *resultSetConcurrency*)**

The **createStatement** method instantiates a **Statement** object to contain the SQL statement. Use the first argument to specify whether the **ResultSet** can be traversed backward as well as forward, is scrollable, and is sensitive to changes made by others. The second argument controls the concurrency mode. The arguments are described in the sections "Using Scrollable **ResultSets**" and "Processing a **ResultSet**."

- ```
  void prepareCall()
  void prepareCall(int resultsetType,
                   int resultSetConcurrency )
  ```

  The **prepareCall** method creates a **CallableStatement** object that you can use to call stored procedures. The **int** arguments are the same as those for the method **createStatement**.

- ```
  void prepareStatement()
  void prepareStatement(int resultsetType,
                        int resultSetConcurrency)
  ```

  The **prepareCall** method creates a **PreparedStatement** object for sending parameterized SQL queries. The **int** arguments are the same as those for the method **createStatement**.

Since JDBC 2, the preferred way to get a **Connection** object is to use a **javax.sql.DataSource** object. Using datasources is an advanced JDBC topic and requires an application server to supply the datasource. For now, use the **DriverManager** class and call its **getConnection** method. The great advantage of datasources is that your program automatically benefits from services performed by the application server such as connection pooling and centralized security for database connections. See the section "The DataSource Architecture" for an explanation of these services.

A connection from a **DataSource** object has the same type as one from a **DriverManager** object. Use a connection from a **DriverManager** object exactly like you use one from a **DataSource** object.

Class

java.sql.DriverManager

Purpose

The **DriverManager** class is a service class that manages JDBC 1 drivers. It also can explicitly load drivers on demand.

Methods

- `Connection getConnection( String url )`
  `Connection getConnection( String url, Properties info )`
  `Connection getConnection( String url, String user,`
  `                                      String password )`

  The **getConnection** method establishes a connection to the database at the given URL. The URL has the form *protocol:subprotocol:subname*. The protocol is **jdbc**, and possible subprotocols include **db2**, **oracle**, and **odbc**. For example, the URL for a local DB2 database called **MYSHOP** is **jdbc:db2:MYSHOP**. If the database is remote, the URL might look like **jdbc:db2://DB2SERVER:6789/MYSHOP** where **6789** is the port used by DB2. You can specify the user ID and password in a separate **Properties** object or as **String** arguments in overloaded versions of this method. If the connection fails, the method throws a **SQLException** exception.

The program in Figure 9-10 opens a connection to a database and prints information about the RDBM system.

```
package examples.jdbc;
import java.sql.*;
/**
 * Class to create connection to a database and
 * print some of the connection metadata
 */
public class DBconnect {
   /**
    * the connection object
    */
   static Connection connection = null;
   // select DB2 type 2 driver
   static final String dbDriver =
      "COM.ibm.db2.jdbc.app.DB2Driver";
   static final String dbUrl = "jdbc:DB2:SKICLUB";
   // use the SKICLUB database
   static final String dbName = "SKICLUB";
   // set dbUser to any user on your Windows OS
   static final String dbUser = "userid";
   // set dbPassword to Windows password for dbUser
   static final String dbPassword = "password";
   /**
    * method to open the connection
    */
   public Connection getConnection() {
      if ( connection != null )
         return connection;
```

Figure 9-10   A program that demonstrates connecting to a database

```
        try {
           connection = DriverManager.getConnection(
              dbUrl, dbUser, dbPassword );
        } catch( SQLException e ) {
           System.err.println(
              "Cannot connect to database: for DB2, "
                 + "check that DB2 is running and  "
                 + "the SKICLUB database exists.");
        }
        return connection;
     }
     /**
      * main method
      * @param not used
      */
     public static void main( String[] args ) {
        DBconnect dbdemo = new DBconnect();
        System.out.println(
           "Getting Database driver" );
        try {
           Class.forName( dbDriver );
        } catch( ClassNotFoundException e ) {
           System.err.println(
              "Cannot load database driver: for DB2, "
                 + "your classpath must include "
                 + "SQLLIB\\JAVA12\\DB2JAVA.ZIP." );
        }
        System.out.println(
           "Getting Database connection");
        Connection connection = dbdemo.getConnection();
        if (connection == null)
           System.exit(0);
        System.out.println("Database ready");
        try {
           // print info from the driver metadata
           DatabaseMetaData md =
              connection.getMetaData();
           System.out.println("Product name: "
              + md.getDatabaseProductName() );
           System.out.println( "Driver name: "
              + md.getDriverName() );
           // ...
           // close the connection when done
           connection.close();
           // general purpose collection handler
        } catch (Exception e) {
           System.err.println( e.getClass().getName()
              + ": " + e.getMessage() );
        }
     }
  }
```

Figure 9-10   A program that demonstrates connecting to a database (continued)

Note that a user ID and password are required and that the database manager checks whether a user is authorized to access the database. The database has been set up so that any user ID recognized on your Windows workstation is granted access to the database. If necessary, change the value assigned to **dbUser** and **dbPassword** before running this program. Also make sure the JDBC driver is on your classpath. For DB2 installed in the default install directory, add the following file to your classpath:

```
C:\program files\IBM\sqllib\java\db2java.zip
```

When you run this program from the command line, you see the following output:

```
Getting Database driver
Getting Database connection
Database ready
Product name: DB2/NT
Driver name: IBM DB2 JDBC 2.0 Type 2
```

Issuing Dynamic SQL Statements

The **Statement** interface encapsulates the behavior of dynamic SQL statements. The interface provides different execute methods for different SQL commands, and the string that contains the SQL command is passed as an argument to one of these methods. The results from a **SELECT** statement are returned in an object of type **java.sql.ResultSet**. The method that issues **INSERT**, **UPDATE**, and **DELETE** statements returns an integer value that indicates the number of rows affected.

A **Statement** object can have one open result at a time. If a result object exists when one of the execute methods is called, the existing result object is closed.

Interface

java.sql.Statement

Purpose

Use **Statement** objects to execute Dynamic SQL queries and obtain results. Call the **Connection.createStatement** method to create a **Statement** object.

Methods

- **void close( )**

  The **close** method explicitly releases the resources taken by the **Statement** object. If you do not call this method, the resources are released when the **Statement** object is automatically closed.

- **ResultSet executeQuery(String** *sql* **)**

  The **executeQuery** method executes statements that return a single result set. Use this method for **SELECT** statements. The method throws a **SQLException** exception if a database access error occurs.

- **ResultSet getResultSet( )**

The **getResultSet** method returns the results of the query as a **ResultSet** object. You should call this method only once after a statement has executed.

- **int executeUpdate(String _sql_)**

Call the **executeUpdate** method to execute INSERT, UPDATE, and DELETE statements. The return value is the number of rows in the database affected by the statement. The method throws a **SQLException** exception if a database access error occurs.

- **boolean execute(String _sql_)**

Call the **execute** method to execute statements that can return more than one **ResultSet** or integer count. Use this method in relatively unusual situations, such as when the SQL query is an unknown string or when stored procedures may be called. The return value is **true** when a **ResultSet** is produced and **false** when the result is an update count or there is no result. Call **getResultSet** and/or **getUpdateCount** to get the first result. Call **getMoreResults** to retrieve the next result. The method throws a **SQLException** exception if a database access error occurs.

- **int getUpdateCount( )**

The **getUpdateCount** method returns results of the query as an update count. If the query returns a **ResultSet** object, **getUpdateCount** returns –1. You should call this method only once after a statement has executed.

- **boolean getMoreResults( )**

The **getMoreResults** method moves to the next result available from the statement and implicitly closes the current **ResultSet** if there is one. The return value is **true** if the result is a **ResultSet** and **false** if there are no more results or the type is an update count. The method throws a **SQLException** exception if a database access error occurs.

- **void addBatch(String _sql_)**

Call the **addBatch** method to add a SQL statement to the list of commands to be executed in a batch update.

- **int[] executeBatch(String _sql_)**

The **executeBatch** method submits a batch of SQL statements for execution. If all run successfully, the method returns an array of update counts, one for each SQL statement. If one of the commands fails, the method throws a **BatchUpdateException** exception. In some circumstances the value of an element in the returned array can be **SUCCESS_NO_INFO** if the command was successful but the number of rows affected is unknown, or **EXECUTE_FAILED** if the command was not successful but following commands continue to execute.

9

- `int getQueryTimeout( )`
  `void setQueryTimeout( int seconds )`

  You can specify how long the driver can wait for a query to run by calling **setQueryTimeout**. The **getQueryTimeout** method returns the number of seconds the driver will wait for the statement to run.

- `int getMaxRows( )`
  `void setMaxRows( int max )`

  Call the **setMaxRows** method to specify that any **ResultSet** should be limited to the specified number of rows. Call **getMaxRows** to see what limit has been put on the number of rows returned.

- `int getMaxFieldSize( )`
  `void setMaxFieldSize( int max )`

  Call the **setMaxFieldSize** method to limit the number of bytes in any column to the specified number of bytes. Call **getMaxFieldSize** to see how many bytes a column may hold.

Before proceeding to the section that discusses result set processing, here are some methods that demonstrate how to execute **SELECT**, **INSERT**, **UPDATE**, and **DELETE** methods. These methods are extracted from the **DBdemo** class. The **DBdemo** class uses the same **getConnection** method as the **DBconnect** class in Figure 9-10.

The method in Figure 9-11 retrieves all the data in the **MEMBERS** table using a **SELECT** statement.

```
public ResultSet getAllMemberInfo() {
   ResultSet rs = null;
   try {
      Statement statement =
         getConnection().createStatement();
      String sql =
         "SELECT * FROM SKICLUB.MEMBERS";

      System.out.println( sql );
      statement.executeQuery( sql );
      rs = statement.getResultSet();
   } catch ( SQLException e ) {
      System.out.println(
         "SQLException " + e.getMessage());
   } finally {
      return rs;
   }
}
```

Figure 9-11   A method to issue a SQL **SELECT** statement

The method in Figure 9-12 adds a new member to the database using an **INSERT** statement.

```
    public void addMember( ClubMember member )
       throws SQLException, DBopException {
       int nrows = 0;
       Statement statement =
          getConnection().createStatement();
       String sql =
          "INSERT INTO SKICLUB.MEMBERS VALUES ("
             + member.getId()
             + ",'"
             + member.getFirstName()
             + "','"
             + member.getMiddleName()
             + "','"
             + member.getLastName()
             + "','"
             + member.getPhoneNumber()
             + "','"
             + member.getAbility()
             + "')";
       System.out.println( sql );
       nrows = statement.executeUpdate( sql );
       if ( nrows != 1 ) {
          throw new DBopException(
             "Instead of 1 row, "
                + nrows
                + " were inserted." );
       }
       return;
    }
```

Figure 9-12   A method to issue a SQL `INSERT` statement

In the **addMember** method, the value returned by **member.getId** is zero, thus asking the DB2 to assign the ID using the trigger set up when the table was created. The method issues the **INSERT** statement using the **Statement.executeUpdate** method. The method retrieves the values to insert into the columns of the new row from the object of type **ClubMember** that it receives as an argument. Note that each character literal must be enclosed in single quotes in a SQL statement. The code in Figure 9-12 encloses the single quotes in double quotes to build the Java **String**.

The **ClubMember** class represents a club member in the model layer of the application. It is also used as a helper class to pass information between the model and persistence layers. Using helper classes in this way can help you implement the model–persistence separation design pattern. The application thinks in terms of Java objects of type **ClubMember**. Because the mapping is simple, the persistence layer converts the data at the point of building the SQL statement. The exception type **DBopException** is defined as part of the application that hides exceptions thrown by the JDBC classes so that end users never receive raw DB2 error codes.

A successful insert operation is indicated by the absence of exceptions and the fact that exactly one row was inserted into the table.

The method in Figure 9-13 modifies a row in the MEMBERS table using an UPDATE statement.

```
public void updateMember( ClubMember member )
   throws SQLException, DBopException {
   int nrows = 0;
   Statement statement =
      getConnection().createStatement();
   String sql =
      "UPDATE SKICLUB.MEMBERS SET "
         + "FNAME = '"
         + member.getFirstName()
         + "',"
         + " MNAME = '"
         + member.getMiddleName()
         + "',"
         + " LNAME = '"
         + member.getLastName()
         + "',"
         + " PHONENUM = '"
         + member.getPhoneNumber()
         + "',"
         + " ABILITY = '"
         + member.getAbility()
         + "'"
         + " WHERE FNAME = '"
         + member.getFirstName()
         + "'"
         + " AND LNAME = '"
         + member.getLastName()
         + "'";
   System.out.println( sql );
   nrows = statement.executeUpdate( sql );
   if ( nrows != 1 ) {
      throw new DBopException(
         "Instead of 1 row, "
            + nrows
            + " were updated." );
   }
   return;
}
```

Figure 9-13   A method to issue a SQL UPDATE statement

Much like the addMember method, the updateMember method maps from fields of a ClubMember object to columns of the MEMBER table at the point of issuing a SQL statement. This method does not actually know which columns are changing and does not need to in this application design. The application updates the ClubMember object and calls this method to store the changes in the database.

If successful, the update affects only one row because a business rule implemented as a constraint in the database schema is that the combination of first name and last name of each club member be unique.

The method in Figure 9-14 removes a row from the MEMBERS table using a DELETE statement.

```java
public void deleteMember( ClubMember member )
    throws SQLException, DBopException {
    int nrows = 0;
    Statement statement =
        getConnection().createStatement();
    String sql =
        "DELETE FROM SKICLUB.MEMBERS"
            + " WHERE FNAME = '"
            + member.getFirstName()
            + "'"
            + " AND LNAME = '"
            + member.getLastName()
            + "'";
    System.out.println( sql );
    nrows = statement.executeUpdate( sql );
    if ( nrows != 1 ) {
        throw new DBopException(
            "Instead of 1 row, "
                + nrows
                + " were deleted." );
    }
    return;
}
```

Figure 9-14   A method to issue a SQL DELETE statement

Figure 9-15 is the **main** method in the DBdemo class. It tests the four methods in Figures 9-11 through 9-14 by calling each one in turn.

```java
public static void main( String[] args ) {
    DBdemo dbdemo = new DBdemo();
    System.out.println( "Getting Database driver" );
    try {
        Class.forName( dbDriver );
    } catch( ClassNotFoundException e ) {
        System.err.println(
            "Cannot load database driver: for DB2, "
            + "your classpath must include "
            + "SQLLIB\\JAVA12\\DB2JAVA.ZIP." );
    }
```

Figure 9-15   The **main** method in the DBdemo class

```
        System.out.println(
            "Getting Database connection");
        Connection connection = dbdemo.getConnection();
        if ( connection == null )
            System.exit( 0 );
            System.out.println( "Database ready" );
        try {
            dbdemo.getAllMemberInfo();
        // demonstration an INSERT Statement
            ClubMember member = new ClubMember();
            member.setFirstName( "Another" );
            member.setLastName( "Skier" );
            member.setPhoneNumber( "4167533234" );
            member.setAbility( "Expert" );
            dbdemo.addMember( member );
        // demonstrate an UPDATE Statement
            member.setMiddleName( "Good" );
            dbdemo.updateMember( member );
        // demonstrate an DELETE Statement
            dbdemo.deleteMember( member );
        // close the connection when done
            connection.close();
        // general exception handling
        } catch( Exception e ) {
            System.err.println(
                e.getClass().getName()
                    + ": "
                    + e.getMessage() );
        }
    }
}
```

Figure 9-15   The **main** method in the DBdemo class (continued)

The DBdemo program retrieves all the data from the MEMBERS table. Then it adds one row, modifies that row, and deletes it. If you run the program, the output shows the SQL commands that are issued, split to fit on the page:

```
Getting Database driver
Getting Database connection
Database ready
SELECT * FROM SKICLUB.MEMBERS
INSERT INTO SKICLUB.MEMBERS VALUES
    (0,'Another','null','Skier','4167533234','Expert')
UPDATE SKICLUB.MEMBERS SET FNAME = 'Another',
    MNAME = 'Good', LNAME = 'Skier',
    PHONENUM = '4167533234', ABILITY = 'Expert'
    WHERE FNAME = 'Another' AND LNAME = 'Skier'
DELETE FROM SKICLUB.MEMBERS WHERE
    FNAME = 'Another' AND LNAME = 'Skier'
```

Processing a ResultSet

Objects of type **ResultSet** encapsulate the data retrieved from the database. A **ResultSet** is a collection of rows. You must call methods defined in the **ResultSet** interface to move to a particular row and then call methods to get individual column values. All **ResultSet** objects have an associated cursor object that points to one row at a time, known as the *current row*. If the database is updatable, the cursor is pointing to the insert row. The *insert row* is a buffer in which you can build a record in preparation for inserting a new record in the database.

Interface

java.sql.ResultSet

Purpose

The methods that extract data from the database return **ResultSet** objects. The **ResultSet** interface defines a large number of methods. Not all of the methods that navigate through the **ResultSet** or manipulate column values from the current row are listed. The interface defines methods to get and update column values of all the types listed in Figure 9-6. Only the **get** and **update** methods for columns of **String** and **int** type are included here as examples.

The interface also defines several constants. Those listed here can be used as arguments of the **Connection.createStatement** method to determine whether the **ResultSet** is scrollable and whether its contents reflect changes made by concurrent access.

Fields

- **TYPE_FORWARD_ONLY**

  In a **ResultSet** object created with **TYPE_FORWARD_ONLY**, the cursor can move forward only. This is the default.

- **TYPE_SCROLL_INSENSITIVE**

  A **ResultSet** object created with **TYPE_SCROLL_INSENSITIVE** is scrollable but doesn't reflect changes to the database made by others.

- **TYPE_SCROLL_SENSITIVE**

  A **ResultSet** object created with **TYPE_SCROLL_SENSITIVE** is scrollable and reflects changes to the database made by others.

- **CONCUR_READ_ONLY**

  A **ResultSet** object created with **CONCUR_READ_ONLY** cannot be updated concurrently. This is the default.

- **CONCUR_UPDATABLE**

  A **ResultSet** object created with **CONCUR_UPDATABLE** can be updated concurrently. Not all database drivers support this mode.

Methods

- `boolean first( )`
  `boolean last( )`
  `boolean beforefirst( )`
  `boolean afterlast( )`
  `boolean next( )`
  `boolean previous( )`
  `boolean absolute( int row )`
  `boolean relative( int rows )`

  You can move to any row in a scrollable **ResultSet** by calling one of these methods. If the **ResultSet** is **TYPE_FORWARD_ONLY**, you can move only in a forward direction. The **relative** method moves forward or backward by the specified number of rows, and a negative value indicates a backward direction. The method **absolute** moves to the specified row number. The method throws **SQLException** if you ask for an improper move.

- `int getInt( String columnName )`
  `int getInt( int columnIndex )`

  Call the **getInt** method to get the value of the specified column of the current row. The column in the database must hold a type that maps onto a Java **int** variable. You can specify the name or the index of the column. The method throws **SQLException** if a database access error occurs.

- `String getString( String columnName )`
  `String getString( int columnIndex )`

  Call the **getString** method to get the value of the specified column of the current row. The column in the database must hold a type that maps onto a Java **String** object. You can specify the name or the index of the column. The method throws **SQLException** if a database access error occurs.

- `Xxx getXxx( String columnName )`
  `Xxx getXxx( int columnIndex )`

  Analogous to the methods for types **int** and **String**, methods for all supported types return the value of the specified column of the current row. The column in the database must hold a type that maps onto the type specified by **Xxx**. The method throws **SQLException** if a database access error occurs.

- `void updateXxx( String columnName, Xxx value )`
  `void updateXxx( int columnIndex, Xxx value )`
  `void updateInt( int columnIndex, int value )`
  `void updateString( int ColumnIndex, String value )`

  For every supported type, an **updateXxx** method sets the column specified in the first argument to the value specified in the second argument. The column in the database must hold a type that maps to the type specified by **Xxx**. These methods do not update the underlying database. Call **updateRow** or **insertRow** to write the change to the database. These methods throw **SQLException** if a database access error occurs.

- **void close( )**

  The **close** method explicitly releases the resources taken by the **ResultSet** object. If you do not call this method, the resources are automatically released when the **ResultSet** object is closed.

- **void deleteRow( )**

  The **deleteRow** method deletes the current row from this **ResultSet** object and the database. The method throws **SQLException** if the current row is the insert row.

- **void insertRow( )**

  The **insertRow** method inserts the contents of the insert row into this **ResultSet** object and the database. The method throws **SQLException** if the current row is not the insert row.

- **void updateRow( )**

  The **updateRow** method updates the database to match updates made to the current row in the **ResultSet** object. The method throws **SQLException** if a database access error occurs.

- **void refreshRow( )**

  The **refreshRow** method sets the values in the current row to the latest values set in the database. The method throws **SQLException** if the current row is an insert row.

- **void moveToInsertRow( )**
  void moveToCurrentRow( )

  Use the methods **moveToInsertRow** and **moveToCurrentRow** to switch between the insert row and the current row. The **moveToInsertRow** method records the position of the current row. The **moveToCurrentRow** method has no effect unless the cursor is on the insert row. These methods throw **SQLException** if the database is not updatable.

Column numbers start at 1 and reflect the order of columns in the database, so that column 1 is the first field in a record. If you refer to columns by name, supply the column name exactly as it appears in the database, except that the name is not case-sensitive. If you do not include column names in the statement that retrieved the **ResultSet**, you should identify the columns by number only. The safest approach is to read each column only once in a left-to-right order.

Figure 9-16 is a class that reads all the rows from the **SKITRIPS** table. It creates a **SkiTrip** object for each row and copies the fields from all the columns into the **SkiTrip** object. Then it prints the **SkiTrip** object on the console.

```
package examples.jdbc;
import java.sql.*;
/**
 * Class to show processing a ResultSet
 */
public class DisplaySkiTrips {
    private Connection connection = null;
    static final String dbDriver =
        "COM.ibm.db2.jdbc.app.DB2Driver";
    static {
        try {
            Class.forName( dbDriver );
        } catch ( ClassNotFoundException e ) {
            System.err.println(
                "Cannot load database driver");
            System.exit( 0 );
        }
    }
    /**
     * main method
     * @param not used
     */
    public static void main(String[] args) {
        try {
            Connection connection =
                new DBconnect().getConnection();
            if (connection == null) {
                System.out.println(
                    "unable to open connection to database");
                System.exit(0);
            }
            // retrieve all trips that are not cancelled
            // (capacity > 0)
            ResultSet rs = null;
            Statement statement =
                connection.createStatement();
            String sql =
                "SELECT * FROM SKICLUB.SKITRIPS"
                    + " WHERE CAPACITY > 0 ORDER BY RESORT";
            statement.executeQuery( sql );
            rs = statement.getResultSet();
            // and print each Ski Trip
            while ( rs.next() ) {
                SkiTrip trip = new SkiTrip();
                trip.setId( rs.getInt( "ID" ) );
                trip.setDay( rs.getDate( "DAY" ) );
                trip.setResort(
                    rs.getString( "RESORT" ).trim() );
                trip.setCapacity(
                    rs.getInt( "CAPACITY" ));
                trip.setBooked( rs.getInt( "BOOKED" ) );
```

Figure 9-16   A class that prints the result set returned by a SELECT statement

```
                System.out.println( trip );
            }
        } catch (Exception e) {
            System.err.println(
                e.getClass().getName()
                    + ": "
                    + e.getMessage());
        }
    }
}
```

Figure 9-16   A class that prints the result set returned by a SELECT statement (continued)

This program uses a static initializer block to load the JDBC driver and calls the **getConnection** method of the **DBconnect** class to get a connection object. Just to add interest, it issues a **SELECT** statement with **WHERE** and **ORDER BY** clauses. Another helper class, **SkiTrip**, represents a ski trip in Java. The **SkiTrip** class overrides the **toString** method for formatted display of trip attributes.

If you run the **DisplaySkiTrips** program, the output starts as follows. The full output is considerably longer, and the information for each trip appears on one line. Lines are split to fit the printed page.

```
Trip Number5 on Jan 14, 2004 to Alpine Grove
    capacity=6 booked=4
Trip Number 10 on Jan 27, 2004 to Alpine Grove
    capacity=6 booked=6
Trip Number 14 on Feb 4, 2004 to Alpine Grove
    capacity=6 booked=6
```

Using Scrollable `ResultSets`

The example in Figure 9-16 reads the **ResultSet** from first row to last and must do so because the **ResultSet** has the default type of **TYPE_FORWARD_ONLY**. To make this **ResultSet** navigable in both directions and not updatable, and then read it from the last row to the first, make the changes shown in bold in Figure 9-17 to the excerpt from the code in Figure 9-16.

```
           // retrieve all trips that are not cancelled
           //    (capacity > 0)
             ResultSet rs = null;
             Statement statement =
                connection. createStatement(
                ResultSet.TYPE_SCROLL_INSENSITIVE,
                  ResultSet.CONCUR_READ_ONLY );
             String sql =
                "SELECT * FROM SKICLUB.SKITRIPS"
                    + " WHERE CAPACITY > 0 ORDER BY RESORT";
             statement.executeQuery( sql );
             rs = statement.getResultSet();
             // and print each SKI TRIP
           rs.afterLast();
           while ( rs.previous() ) {
              // ...
           }
```

Figure 9-17 Code that uses a scrollable `ResultSet`

In the modified listing shown in Figure 9-17, the ability to scroll through the `ResultSet` in both directions is controlled by the first argument to the `createStatement` method. The three possible values are `TYPE_READ_ONLY`, `TYPE_SCROLL_INSENSITIVE`, and `TYPE_SCROLL_SENSITIVE`. The difference between the last two is that `TYPE_SCROLL_INSENSITIVE` ignores changes to the `ResultSet` made by other code when moving the cursor.

The second argument determines whether other code is allowed concurrent access and can modify the `ResultSet`. The possible values are `CONCUR_READ_ONLY` and `CONCUR_UPDATABLE`. With `CONCUR_UPDATABLE`, the `ResultSet` can change while you are processing it. The DB2 drivers do not allow `CONCUR_UPDATABLE`.

Scrollable `ResultSet` objects are one of the features that made JDBC 2 more flexible than JDBC 1. A scrollable `ResultSet` is one in which you can move backward as well as forward through a `ResultSet` by calling methods such as `previous`, `absolute`, and `relative`.

Using Precompiled SQL

If you issue the same statement repeatedly, altering only the literal values in the `WHERE` clause, consider precompiling the SQL statements. Do this to improve performance by not asking the database manager repeatedly to parse the same SQL statement and compile it. You can still formulate the statement at runtime, but you do so in two stages: first build a reusable template statement and then supply specific values each time you run it.

Basically the difference in syntax between a dynamic and precompiled SQL statement is that some or all of the literal values are replaced by question marks when the statement is compiled. The question marks are parameterized values in the template statement. Each time a statement executes, literal values replace the parameters. For example, here is a pre-compilable UPDATE statement to change the salary of an employee:

```
UPDATE EMPLOYEE SET SALARY = ? WHERE ID = ?
```

Before executing the statement, make sure that every parameter is assigned a value. Otherwise an exception occurs when you execute the statement.

Use a **PreparedStatement** object to encapsulate precompiled SQL.

Interface

java.sql.PreparedStatement

Purpose

Use **PreparedStatement** objects to execute precompiled SQL queries and obtain results. Call the **Connection.prepareStatement** method to create a **PreparedStatement** object. As with the **Connection.createStatement** method, you can set the scrolling and concurrency attributes of a **ResultSet** in the arguments of **createStatement**.

The **PreparedStatement** interface extends **Statement** so all the methods of **Statement** are available. Only those new to **PreparedStatement** are listed here:

Methods

- **void setInt(int *index*, int *value*)**
  void setString(int *index*, String *value*)
  void set*Xxx* (int *index*, *Xxx* *value*)

The **setString**, **setInt**, and other **set*Xxx*** methods assign the specified value to the parameter with the specified index in the statement. The type of the associated column must be consistent with the type of the value. The first parameter in the template statement has index 1, the second has index 2, and so on.

The following method adds new trips to the SKITRIPS table using precompiled SQL. The scenario is that the ski club decides to add Monday trips for the eight weeks of the ski season. Therefore, it issues the following template statement:

```
INSERT INTO SKICLUB.SKITRIPS

   ( ID, DAY, RESORT, CAPACITY, BOOKED ) VALUES ( ?, ?, ?, ?, 0 )
```

The new trips all start without bookings, so the final column is set to zero. The other columns are calculated between statement calls, as shown in Figure 9-18.

```
/**
 * method AddTripsDemo.addWeeklyTrips
 * inserts trip records in SKITRIPS table
 * @param Calendar sets the first date
 * @param capacity an array of openings
 * @param resort is an array of resort names
 */
static void addWeeklyTrips (
Calendar startDate,
int[] capacity,
String[] resort)
   throws SQLException {
// first get the highest trip ID so far
String sql =
   "SELECT max(ID) FROM SKICLUB.SKITRIPS";
Statement s = connection.createStatement();
System.out.println("Issuing: " + sql);
s.executeQuery(sql);
ResultSet rs = s.getResultSet();
rs.next();
int tripID = rs.getInt(1);
s.close();
// prepare the compiled statement
PreparedStatement ps =
   connection.prepareStatement(
      "INSERT INTO SKICLUB.SKITRIPS "
         + "( ID, DAY, RESORT, CAPACITY, BOOKED)"
         + "VALUES ( ?, ?, ?, ?, 0)");
// issue statement 8 times for 8 weeks
for (int i = 0; i < 8; i++) {
   // calculate field values
   ps.setInt(1, ++tripID);
   java.sql.Date sqldate =
      new java.sql.Date(
         startDate.getTimeInMillis());
   ps.setDate(2, sqldate);
   ps.setString(3, resort[i]);
   ps.setInt(4, capacity[i]);
   System.out.println(
      " issuing insert for values: "
         + tripID  + " "
         + sqldate  + "  "
         + resort[i] + " "
         + capacity[i]);
   ps.executeUpdate();
   startDate.add(Calendar.WEEK_OF_YEAR, 1);
}
System.out.println("done");
ps.close();
}
```

Figure 9-18   A method that uses precompiled SQL

~~The method in Figure 9-18 is taken from the example class~~ **examples.jdbc.** AddTripsDemo. The **main** method of the AddTripsDemo class is not listed; it opens the database connection, and loads values into the objects passed as arguments of addWeeklyTrips, and calls the method.

Using Stored Procedures

Database programmers often claim that the best performance is given by stored procedures. They are right, but the amount of time saved over dynamic and precompiled SQL varies greatly depending on the RDBM system. DB2 performs such extensive optimization on dynamic SQL that other factors, such as program design and whether you use connection pooling, have a far greater effect on performance.

Another factor is that stored procedures can be inflexible because they are not easy to extend or modify. Reusing existing components is a best practice in general, and calling stored procedures can lead to excellent application design. But stored procedures can impose design constraints, especially when a legacy application is being updated to use an object-oriented technology or to become a Web application. Often developers who have to integrate legacy stored procedures with object-oriented applications find that the stored procedure model business processes in a very different way from Java programs.

How to build a stored procedure varies from one RDBM system to another, and stored procedures are often not coded in Java. Therefore, creating stored procedures is not covered in this chapter. Look in the documentation from your database software vendor for instructions on adding stored procedures to your RDBM system. JDBC provides a common interface for calling stored procedures in the **CallableStatement** interface.

Unlike dynamic or precompiled SQL, stored procedures can produce more than one **ResultSet**. They can take input arguments, return output, or have input-output parameters. Methods for passing parameters are included in the **CallableStatement** interface. Use methods inherited from **PreparedStatement** to supply input parameters. Use additional methods to register output parameters before the statement is executed and then to retrieve the return values.

Interface

java.sql.CallableStatement

Purpose

Use **CallableStatement** objects to execute stored procedures and obtain results. Call the **Connection.prepareCall** method to create a **CallableStatement** object. The argument of **Connection.prepareCall** is a string holding a parameterized SQL statement in which question marks represent parameters. The **CallableStatement** interface extends **PreparedStatement**.

ResultSet object returns are always **TYPE_FORWARD_ONLY** and **CONCUR_READ_ONLY**.

Methods

- `void registerOutParameter( int index, int sqlType )`
  `void registerOutParameter( int index, int sqlType,`
  `                           int scale )`
  `void registerOutParameter( int index, int sqlType,`
  `                           String typeName )`
  `void registerOutParameter( String index, int sqlType)`
  `void registerOutParameter( String index, int sqlType,`
  `                           int scale )`
  `void registerOutParameter( String index, int sqlType,`
  `                           String typeName )`

Use `registerOutParameter` to register parameters before executing a stored procedure. The `index` argument specifies the ordinal position of the parameter in the calling statement. An `int` argument specifies the type of the output value as defined in the class `java.sql.sqlTypes`. The `scale` parameter is used where appropriate for the number of digits to the right of the decimal point. The `typeName` string is a fully qualified SQL structure type.

In the `Connection.prepareCall` method, specify the stored procedure with a string with one of these formats:

- `{ ?= call <procedure name> [ <arg1>, <arg2>, ... ] }`

  This form allows an output parameter. The parameter must be registered as an output parameter by calling one of the overloaded `registerOutParameter` methods on the `CallableStatement` object.

- `{ call  <procedure  name> [ <arg1>, <arg2>, ... ] }`

  This form returns no results.

To process the `ResultSet` objects, use methods inherited from the `Statement` class.

Updating the Database Using a `ResultSet`

So far in this chapter, the only use of a `ResultSet` object has been to hold data retrieved from the database. The `ResultSet` interface also includes methods for updating the database. For these methods to be usable, that statement that produces the `ResultSet` must be created with concurrency type `CONCUR_UPDATABLE`. Therefore, this feature is available only with RDBM systems that let the database be updated concurrently with being read.

To insert a row, follow these steps:

1. Call `moveToInsertRow` to position the cursor at the insert buffer maintained by all updatable `ResultSet` objects.

2. Call one of the `updateXxx` methods to update each column that you want to set.

3. Call `insertRow` to add the row to the database and clear the insert buffer.

To update an existing row, follow these steps:

1. Make sure the cursor is positioned at the row to be changed.

2. Call one of the **updateXxx** methods to update each column that you want to change.

3. Call **updateRow** to write the change to the database.

To delete an existing row, follow these steps:

1. Make sure the cursor is positioned at the row to be deleted.

2. Call **deleteRow** to remove the row from the database and the **ResultSet**.

3. The cursor may still be moved to a row that has been deleted. Method **rowDeleted** returns **true** if the current row is a deleted row.

The JDBC drivers for DB2 do not support updatable result sets.

CODING TRANSACTIONS

The **Connection** class controls the transactional properties of database operations. By default, connections are opened in autoCommit mode. *AutoCommit* means that the changes made by an **INSERT**, **UPDATE**, or **DELETE** statement immediately become permanent. The only way to undo a database operation in autoCommit mode is to issue another SQL command that negates the first. This is a very inefficient solution. For example, you can delete a newly inserted record. It is easy to imagine situations where formulating the undo SQL statement is very difficult. For example, how would you undo a command such as the following?

```
UPDATE MYCOM.EMPLOYEE SET SALARY = 20000 WHERE SALARY < 20000
```

The only way to perform this undo operation in autoCommit mode is to design your application to record every salary before issuing the **UPDATE** statement and then use a batch update to reinstate to the previous salaries.

Almost always, you need transactions to completely and accurately undo operations that affect more than one table. For example, if you use an online service to buy a ticket to attend a concert, the ticketing application typically updates one table to mark the seat as sold, a second to record billing information, and a third to record your mailing address. If you change your mind or fail to provide a valid credit card before the order processing is complete, the sale must be undone. Several tables or even separate databases maintained by the ticketing agency must revert to a prior state.

RDBM can perform the undo for you. Conceptually, you can tell RDBM to start a log of all changes to tables and databases. Think of the start of the log as the start of a transaction and the release of the log as the end of the transaction. The lifetime of the log demarks transaction boundaries. If you perform some operations and then tell the database manager to commit, the log is cleared and the database writes become permanent. If you perform some operations and then tell the database to roll back, the database manager reverses all operations recorded in the log and then clears the log. After a rollback, the database is in the exact state it was in before the transaction started.

This process is called *one-phase commit*. A *two-phase commit* is used in distributed transactions that involve more than one RDBM system or other enterprise information systems and is available only when you acquire connections from **DataSource** objects. Distributed transactions are discussed in the **javax.sql** section of this chapter.

The methods of the connection class that support one-phase commit are listed in Figure 9-19.

Method	Description
Connection.getAutoCommit	Returns a **boolean** parameter with value **true** in autoCommit mode or **false** otherwise.
Connection.setAutoCommit	Supplies a **boolean** parameter **false** to turn off autoCommit and enable transactional processing. If you do not call this method, the default mode is equivalent to **setAutoCommit(true);**
Connection.commit	When autoCommit is **false**, this method commits all database operations since the last commit or rollback and starts a new transaction.
Connection.rollback	When autoCommit is **false**, this method undoes or rolls back all database operations since the last commit or rollback and starts a new transaction. You can specify an optional rollback to a savepoint by specifying the savepoint as an argument.
Connection.setSavepoint	Sets a savepoint in the current transaction and returns the savepoint object. You can specify a name to create a named savepoint.
Connection.releaseSavepoint	Removes the specified savepoint from the current transaction.

Figure 9-19 Connection methods for transactions

Use the **java.sql.Savepoint** interface to set intermediate points in the duration of a transaction that you can roll back to. Without **Savepoint** objects, a transaction is an all-or-nothing commit or rollback. For example, your transaction may start with some operations that you will eventually commit or roll back, such as ordering an item online. Later in the transaction you try to pay for the item with a credit card. If the credit card is rejected, and you have no savepoint, you must roll back the whole transaction. If you set a savepoint just before the credit card transaction, you can roll back to the savepoint and then try a different payment option. Eventually you can commit or roll back the whole transaction, including the ski trip operation and the payment operation.

> The **Savepoint** interface is new with J2SDK version 1.4 and may not be supported by JDBC drivers that conform to earlier J2SDK versions.

The ski club application contains a good example of a situation in which transactions are necessary to maintain consistency across tables, and transactional logic cannot be expressed as constraints in the database schema. If a member quits the ski club, three tables may need to be updated:

- If the member had booked any trips, the number of occupied seats on each of those trips must be adjusted to show that a seat is now available for someone else to book. To do that, subtract 1 from the value of the field BOOKED of the table SKITRIPS for each trip the member had booked.

- All bookings made by the member must be removed from the BOOKINGS table.

- The member record must be deleted from the MEMBERS table.

The sample program in Figure 9-20 deletes a member from the ski club and wraps the three updates in one transaction. For demonstration purposes, it is a monolithic, command-line program. In a real application, the logic would be distributed among several classes, but it would then be hard to show in a single listing. For example, the deleteMember operation should be an operation of the ClubMember class and be responsible for starting and stopping the delete-member transaction. Only the Bookings class should be able to operate on bookings and should collaborate with the SkiTrips class, which in turn updates the number of members booked to go on a trip. The delete-member transaction should flow through all of these classes and be translated by the persistence layer into the JDBC calls you see in the listing shown in Figure 9-20.

```
package examples.jdbc;
import java.sql.*;
import java.io.*;
/**
 * Class to show JDBC transaction operations
 */
public class DeleteMember {
   private static Connection connection = null;
   static final String dbDriver =
      "COM.ibm.db2.jdbc.app.DB2Driver";
   static {
      try {
```

Figure 9-20   A class that demonstrates transaction rollback and commit

```
            Class.forName( dbDriver );
        } catch( ClassNotFoundException e ) {
            System.err.println(
                "Cannot load database driver" );
            System.exit( 0 );
        }
    }
    /**
     * method to find all trips booked by member
     * @param member ID
     */
    static String findTripsForMember( int memberID )
        throws SQLException {
        ResultSet rs = null;
        Statement statement =
            connection.createStatement();
        String sql =
            "SELECT TRIPID FROM SKICLUB.BOOKINGS"
                + " WHERE MEMBERID = "
                + memberID;
        System.out.println( "Issuing: " + sql );
        statement.executeQuery( sql );
        rs = statement.getResultSet();
        String trips = "ID = ";
        while ( rs.next() ) {
            trips += rs.getInt( "TRIPID" );
            trips += " OR ID = ";
        }
        if ( trips.equals( "ID = ") )
            return null;
        trips = trips.substring( 0, trips.length() - 9 );
        System.out.println( "TRIPS AFFECTED: " + trips );
        return trips;
    }
    /**
     * main method of delete member class
     * @param not used
     */
    public static void main( String[] args )
        throws IOException {
        Statement statement = null;
        BufferedReader br =
            new BufferedReader(
                new InputStreamReader( System.in ) );
        System.out.print(
            "Enter ID of Member to Delete: " );
        int memberID = Integer.parseInt( br.readLine() );
        int nrow = 0;
        String sql;
        try {
            connection = new DBconnect().getConnection();
            if ( connection == null ) {
```

Figure 9-20   A class that demonstrates transaction rollback and commit (continued)

```
                    System.out.println(
                       "unable to open connection" );
                    System.exit( 0 );
                 }
                 statement = connection.createStatement();
                 String trips =
                    findTripsForMember( memberID );
                 if (trips != null) {
                    // turn off autoCommit
                    connection.setAutoCommit( false );
                    System.out.println(
                       "Starting transaction" );
                    // Update BOOKED column in SKITRIPS TABLE
                    System.out.println(
                       "Preparing to delete member with ID "
                          + memberID );
                    System.out.println(
                       "Updating trips booked by member "
                          + memberID );
                    sql =
                       "UPDATE SKICLUB.SKITRIPS"
                       + " SET BOOKED = BOOKED-1"
                       + " WHERE "
                       + trips;
                    System.out.println( "Issuing: " + sql );
                    nrow = statement.executeUpdate( sql );
                    System.out.println(
                       nrow
                       + " row(s) updated in SKITRIPS" );
                    // remove records from BOOKINGS table
                    sql =
                       "DELETE FROM SKICLUB.BOOKINGS "
                       + "WHERE MEMBERID = "
                       + memberID;
                    System.out.println( "Issuing: " + sql );
                    nrow = statement.executeUpdate( sql );
                    System.out.println(
                       nrow
                       + " row(s) deleted from BOOKINGS" );
                 }
                 // remove the MEMBER
                 sql =
                    "DELETE FROM SKICLUB.MEMBERS"
                    + " WHERE ID = "
                    + memberID;
                 System.out.println( "Issuing: " + sql );
                 nrow = statement.executeUpdate( sql );
                 System.out.println(
                    nrow + " row(s) deleted from MEMBERS" );
                 // confirm
                 System.out.print(
                    "Type y to confirm delete member: " );
```

Figure 9-20   A class that demonstrates transaction rollback and commit (continued)

```
            if ( br.readLine().charAt( 0 ) == 'y' ) {
               connection.commit();
               System.out.println(
                  "Delete Member Committed" );
            } else {
               connection.rollback();
               System.out.println(
                  "Delete member rolled back");
            }
            statement.close();

        } catch (Exception e) {
            System.err.println(
                e.getClass().getName()
                    + ": " + e.getMessage() );
        }
    }
}
```

Figure 9-20 A class that demonstrates transaction rollback and commit (continued)

For convenience, the `DeleteMember` method loads the JDBC driver in a static initializer block class and uses the `getConnection` method of the `DBconnect` class. Another convenience is using the `findTripsForMember` method that builds the conditions for the `WHERE` clause used to update the `SKITRIPS` table. All the transactional operations occur in the **main** method. Note that the code performs updates first, and deletes next, and then asks the user to confirm the deletion. If the user enters a response starting with "y", all operations are committed. Otherwise the entire delete operation is cancelled, and the SQL statements are rolled back.

Transaction Isolation Levels

The isolation level controls the way the database manager behaves when two or more programs try to access the same database at the same time. Concurrent access during transactions can cause conflicts because the data involved has an indeterminate value while the transaction is active. For example, two applications can try to assign values to the same piece of data in concurrent transactions. What if one application has modified the database but not committed the changes when a second application tries a read? Should the second application see the original data or new values that may not be committed? What is the impact on an application if data it retrieves from the database changes unexpectedly in the middle of a transaction?

The isolation level is typically set when an application is bound to the database, but can be changed programmatically by calling **Connection.setTransactionLevel**, passing as an argument one of the isolation levels defined in the **Connection** class. Figure 9-21 lists these levels with the least restrictive first and most restrictive last.

Isolation Level	Details
TRANSACTION_NONE	This level cannot be set programmatically because it states that transactions are not supported.
TRANSACTION_READ_UNCOMMITTED	Allows reads of uncommitted values, known as *dirty reads*. The column values may change, and rows that satisfy the WHERE clause of the statement may appear or disappear during the transaction.
TRANSACTION_READ_COMMITTED	Allows only committed values to be read, but does not prevent a second application from updating values and committing the changes, including deleting or adding rows.
TRANSACTION_REPEATABLE_READ	Allows only committed values to be read and does not let the data read change during the transaction. However it does not prevent *phantom reads* caused by new rows that satisfy the WHERE clause of the statement from being inserted by another application.
TRANSACTION_SERIALIZABLE	Enforces repeatable read and prevents phantom reads by giving only one application access to the data at a time.

Figure 9-21   Transaction levels defined in the `Connection` class

When selecting an isolation level, you may have to choose between data reliability and performance. Serialized access is safest but can produce bottlenecks or have a severe impact on performance. You may have to analyze usage patterns, evaluate the impact of reading unstable data, or even find an acceptable compromise by trial and error. You must also consider what isolation levels are recognized by your RDBM system. The levels listed in Figure 9-21 are defined in the JDBC specification. Different database products define different isolation levels.

USING THE `javax.sql` API

This section introduces the JDBC types in the package `javax.sql`. The fundamental difference between `java.sql` and `javax.sql` is that the types in `javax.sql` are designed for use in an enterprise environment where application components are installed on application servers that provide the infrastructure for connecting to resources such as databases.

Standalone Java programs can also use the `javax.sql` types, but may have to perform some setup to access the services required by `javax.sql`.

All programs that use types defined in `javax.sql` continue to use many of the types in `java.sql` including `Connection`, `Statement`, `PreparedStatement`,

CallableStatement, and **ResultSet**. The package **javax.sql** does not replace the majority of basic JDBC classes; it gives you the following additional capabilities:

- You can acquire **Connection** objects from datasources instead of loading a JDBC driver and using the **java.sql.DriverManager** class. A datasource is defined outside your application, and you acquire a reference to it through a Java Naming and Directory (JNDI) service. The JNDI API is discussed in the section "JNDI" in Chapter 11.

- Through datasources, your program can take advantage of pooled connections and other services provided by the application server.

- You can manipulate tabular data through the **javax.sql.RowSet** interface. **RowSet** interfaces have the JavaBean properties described in Chapter 8 of this book, including support for JavaBean events.

The **javax.sql** package was included in J2SE with JDBC 3 and J2SDK 1.4. Previously it was available only in J2EE. JNDI was also a J2EE service, but moved into J2SE with version 1.3.

Figure 9-22 lists the interfaces, and Figure 9-23 lists the classes in the package **javax.sql**. Many of the **javax.sql** types are implemented by services provided by the application server and you do not use them directly in your code. For a full description of the types not covered further in this chapter, refer to the J2SDK documentation or the help system that comes with your application server.

Interface	Description
XAConnection	Instances of this class are connections that support distributed transactions. The class extends **PooledConnection**.
XADataSource	Instances of this class generate **XAConnection** objects, and typically are bound to a JNDI service.
DataSource	Instances of this class generate **Connection** objects. Use this class as an alternative to **DriverManager** when using JDBC drivers that support datasources but do not require distributed transactions.
PooledConnection	An instance of this class represents a physical connection to a datasource and is used by the service that manages connection pooling.
ConnectionPoolDataSource	Instances of this class generate **PooledConnection** objects.
ConnectionEventListener	Objects implementing this interface are notified about events related to pooled connections. Usually, this interface is used by an application server.

Figure 9-22   Interfaces defined in the **javax.sql** package

Interface	Description
RowSet	This interface extends **java.sql.ResultSet**, and classes that implement it conform to the JavaBean component model.
RowSetInternal	This interface helps **RowSet** objects use **RowSetReader** or **RowSetWriter** objects.
RowSetListener	Objects that want to be notified of events that affect **RowSet** implement this interface.
RowSetMetaData	These objects contain information about a **RowSet** object, such as column properties.
RowSetReader	Instances of this class are used by disconnected **RowSet** objects to populate themselves with data from the database.
RowSetWriter	Instances of this class are used by disconnected **RowSet** objects to update the database.

Figure 9-22   Interfaces defined in the `javax.sql` package (continued)

Class	Description
ConnectionEvent	Extends **java.util.EventObject** to represent a connection-related event such as closing a pooled connection or the occurrence of an error.
RowSetEvent	Extends **java.util.EventObject** to represent an event that occurs in a **RowSet** object.

Figure 9-23   Classes defined in the `javax.sql` package

The **RowSet** interface is new with J2SDK version 1.4. Not all JDBC drivers provide **RowSet** implementations, but any driver that claims to be J2SDK version 1.4-compliant should do so.

The `javax.sql` types implement an architecture in which the application components interact with services provided by J2EE-compliant application servers. An application server and RDBM system also cooperate through contacts defined in the J2EE specification to provide quality-of-service features for the Java components. *Quality-of-service* features include the following services that are desirable in commercial, large-scale, or mission-critical applications:

- Connection pooling

- Transaction management

- Security services, including checking the identity of users and what they are authorized to do

- Activity tracing and logging error, warning, and informational messages

These features contribute to the robustness of an application and to its scalability. Scalability is a measure of how the application performs as the number of users grows from a small number possibly in a controlled or test environment to perhaps hundreds or thousands of concurrent users. The current trend to Web-enable applications and provide convenient access over networks or the Internet is creating situations where the quality-of-service features become extremely important.

You can use **javax.sql** in the small scale, but must work in a more complex environment and learn about J2SE and J2EE services than you did using **java.sql**. For example, to use a datasource, you must also use JNDI.

The DataSource Architecture

In J2EE terms, a database is one of many kinds of resources that a program may use. Different kinds of enterprise information systems, EJBs, and other program components are resources too. The J2EE specification describes how resources are bound to a JNDI namespace. You can think of the JNDI namespace as a registry in which objects are stored and retrieved by name. The *binding* process conceptually adds an object that contains information about the resource to the JNDI internal storage and registers a name for it. The J2EE specification also describes how a program can access the resource by looking up its name in the JNDI server. Typically, a program that uses a datasource accesses the datasource from the JNDI service provided by an application server. Before the program runs, a server administrator must complete two tasks:

- Install the appropriate JDBC driver on the application server.
- Bind a JDBC resource to the JNDI service of the application server.

Often, both of these tasks are performed through the user interface of the application server.

An object of type **DataSource** is a factory for creating connections and contains all the information that the factory needs to open a connection, such as the name of the database, the database user ID, and the password for that user. Therefore, one impact of using a datasource is that your program no longer needs to hold this information. Another implication is that the database security of user identification can be delegated to the application server.

Interface

javax.sql.DataSource

Purpose

Using a datasource to open connections to a database is the preferred method to using the **java.sql.DriverManager** class in enterprise environments.

Methods

- **void getConnection( )**

  This method opens a connection to the database.

To open a connection, a program looks up the datasource by its JNDI name and receives an object of type **javax.sql.DataSource**. The program then calls **getConnection** on the **DataSource** object and receives an object of type **java.sql.Connection**. Now the program can use the API in the package **java.sql** to store and retrieve data from the database, as described earlier in this chapter.

Figure 9-24 is an excerpt of code that gets a connection from a datasource.

```
// refer to datasource by name
String dsName = "jdbc/skiclubds";
Connection con = null;
try {
    // use default WebSphere JNDI context
    javax.naming.Context ctx = new
        javax.naming.InitialContext();
    // retrieve named Object from JNDI and
    //     cast to datasource
    ds = (DataSource) ctx.lookup( dsName );
} catch ( NamingException ne ) {
    System.out.println(
        "datasource not found by name: "
        + dsName );
}
try {
    // open a connection on datasource
    con ds.getConnection();
} catch ( SQLException sqle ) {
    System.out.println(
        "Cannot open connection on datasource"
        + dsName );
}
```

Figure 9-24   Code to get a connection from a datasource

Depending on your JNDI service, you may have to supply arguments to the **javax.naming.InitialContext** constructor to locate the JNDI service. Note that the **java.sql.DriverManager** class is not used and the program does not need to know the type of the database driver. Indeed, one of the advantages of datasources is that you can change RDBM systems without changing your code, unless in the process you change your database schema or use nonstandard SQL in your application.

Database vendors usually supply separate JDBC drivers for use with datasources in addition to the drivers that are used with the **java.sql.DriverManager** class. For example, DB2 provides two such drivers:

- The class **COM.ibm.db2.jdbc.DB2ConnectionPoolDataSource** is suitable for most applications that use datasources. This driver supports connection pooling.

- If your program uses distributed transactions, use the DB2 driver class **COM.ibm.db2.jdbc.DB2XADataSource**. This driver also supports connection pooling.

Using a Datasource with WebSphere Application Server

IBM WebSphere Studio Application Developer (Application Developer) contains a full installation of IBM WebSphere Application Server as its internal unit test environment, so the easiest way to develop and test code that uses a datasource with WebSphere Application Server is to use Application Developer. The process has the following main steps:

- Install the datasource on the application server and bind it to the server's JNDI service.

- Make sure the server is running and that your program can access it over a TCP/IP connection.

- Create a Java application that uses the datasource. To access the JNDI service and runtime environment of the application server, the client application must have access to various jars containing classes implemented by the application server. If you know a lot about the run-time environment of your application server, you may be able to set up the client environment manually. However, the easiest way to build a client in Application Developer is to build it as a J2EE client application. See the section "J2EE Client Applications" in Chapter 14 to learn more about J2EE client applications.

- In your client code, look up the datasource by name and use it to get a **java.sql.Connection** object, as shown in Figure 9-24. Whether the connection object is an instance of **PooledConnection** or **XAConnection** depends upon the kind of JDBC 2 driver that is installed on the application server.

- Use the connection with the classes and interfaces defined in the **java.sql** package as described in the section "Using the **java.sql** API" of this chapter.

Tutorial 9-1 on the CD-ROM that accompanies this book shows you how to configure a datasource in the WebSphere test environment of Application Developer. Then it walks you through creating and testing a sample program that accesses the **SKICLUB** database with a connection provided by the datasource. You can find this tutorial on the CD in file **Tutorials\Tutorial9_1.pdf**.

CONNECTION POOLING

Database operations are costly. The first step in improving performance of programs that use databases is to minimize the number of database operations. The most costly kind of database operation is opening and closing connections. If your program frequently opens connections, uses them for a short time, and then closes them, consider using connection pooling to cut down the number of individual connections you open and then close.

A connection pool is a set of connections opened and maintained by an application server. When a program calls the **getConnection** method on a **DataSource** object, the server assigns one of the connections in the pool. The program can use the connection without being aware that it is a pooled connection. When the program closes the connection, the server returns it to the pool but does not close it. In this way, many programs or threads of a single program can share connections.

You can code your own connection pooling, but a far easier solution is to use datasources and the connection-pooling capabilities of an application server. When the server administrator sets up a datasource and binds it to the JNDI service, the administrator can usually set up a connection pool at the same time. A J2EE client application automatically uses the connection pool set up for the datasource it locates through JNDI lookup. The administrator sets parameters such as

- The minimum number of connections to keep in the pool

- How large the pool can grow

- How long to wait for a connection to become available when all connections are busy and the pool is at maximum size

- How long to let one program keep a connection without using it (unfortunately, the server cannot force programs to release connections, so a timeout mechanism is required)

- How long to let one program keep a connection even if it continues to use it

- The reap interval, or how often to check for connections that have timed out

Refer to Figure 9-5b in Tutorial 9-1 to see where the connection pool is configured in the WebSphere test environment. The test environment is an application server built into Application Developer. The production WebSphere Application Server has a similar dialog panel.

Changing the setting for these parameters can greatly affect the performance of applications.

A JDBC driver that supports connection pooling must provide a class that implements **javax.sql.ConnectionPoolDataSource**. For example, the DB2 driver class **COM.ibm.db2.jdbc.DB2ConnectionPoolDataSource** implements this interface.

For pooled connections, the database user ID and password are usually associated with the datasource and set when the datasource is configured in the application server. Security is enforced by controlling which users can run the application, not by assigning database IDs and passwords to users of your application.

Distributed Transactions

The transactions described earlier in this chapter are managed by the RDBM systems. This means that the commit and rollback instructions are forwarded to the database manager. These transactions are called local transactions because they are local to one RDBM system.

In enterprise-wide applications, business processes often involve more than one database, or a combination of databases and other enterprise information systems. For example, a retail company may keep customer and account records in a DB2 database, and inventory in an Oracle database. What happens if something goes wrong after the customer account and inventory databases are updated but before the order processing is complete? If the transaction was committed by only one of the two database managers before the problem occurred, data integrity has been compromised. To enclose a unit of work that uses more than one RDBM system or different types of resource managers, the application needs *distributed* or *global transactions*. A distributed transaction is managed not by one RDBM or resource manager, but by the application server. Its context is therefore global within an application and the unit of work is distributed over multiple resources.

J2EE-compliant application servers support the Java Transaction Architecture (JTA). JTA defines a standard interface between transaction managers of the resource management systems and the application server transaction manager. JTA is compatible with the Object Transaction Service (OTS) specified by the Object Management Group (OMG) and is therefore often called Java implementation of the industry-standard XA interface. Global transactions are transactions that conform to JTA or XA architecture and extend the commit and rollback processes to a distributed environment.

Global transactions require an additional step in the commit or rollback process in what is called *two-phase commit*. A two-phase commit works roughly as follows:

- Open a transaction.

- Update the various resources while performing application logic.

- Ask each resource manager whether it can commit by calling a prepare-to-commit method.

- If any resource manager cannot successfully prepare, call rollback on all resource managers.

- If all resource managers successfully prepare, call commit on all resource managers.

period between a successful prepare-to-commit step and the final commit.

A JDBC driver that supports global transactions must provide a class that implements **javax.sql.XADataSource**. For example, The DB2 driver class **COM.ibm.db2.jdbc.DB2XADataSource** implements this interface. An **XADataSource** object creates connections that implement **javax.sql.XAConnection**, which in turn extends **javax.sql.PooledConnection**.

To implement distributed transactions in your code, use the methods of the **javax.transaction.UserTransaction** interface. This interface is part of JTA but not part of JDBC, and therefore falls beyond the scope of this book. If you are writing applications that require global transactions, you probably should be using EJBs and fully leveraging the services of the application server.

CHAPTER SUMMARY

- ❑ The JDBC 3 classes are part of the J2SE version 1.4 platform. Before you can use them, you need a relational database management system (RDBMS) and a JDBC driver that usually comes with the RDBMS. The JDBC classes communicate with the database through the driver.

- ❑ JDBC is composed of two packages: **java.sql** and **javax.sql**. Use classes and interfaces in **java.sql** to issue SQL commands and process results. The **javax.sql** package adds the ability to work in an enterprise environment and use the services of a J2EE-compliant application server.

- ❑ When designing applications that access databases, you should extend the design pattern of model-view separation and design also for model-persistence separation. Create a persistence layer of types that encapsulates all code that requires knowledge of the details of the database. This layer should also map between entity relationships in the database schema and the Java object model.

- ❑ One way to get a connection is to use the **java.sql.DriverManager** class. Using a datasource is the preferred method, but requires a JNDI service and a J2EE-compliant application server that is configured, running, and available to your program.

- ❑ Call methods of the **java.sql.Statement** class to run dynamic SQL. Pass the SQL statement as a **String** to one of the following methods.

  - Call **executeQuery** to issue a **SELECT** command. Then use the **ResultSet** class to access the results.

  - Call **executeUpdate** to issue an **INSERT**, **UPDATE**, or **DELETE** command. The return value is the number of rows affected.

9

- ❐ Use the class **PreparedStatement** for precompiled SQL. Use the class **CallableStatement** for stored procedures.

- ❐ If your JDBC driver supports updatable result sets, you can update the database by updating the **ResultSet** object produced by calling **executeQuery**.

- ❐ Transactional processing is necessary to maintain data integrity when more than one SQL statement is required in one logical unit of work. The **java.sql.Connection** class supports transactional processing with methods **setAutoCommit**, **commit**, and **rollback**.

- ❐ Performance is a major concern in most database programs because database operations are inherently costly in terms of system resources. Two key ways to improve performance are:

  - Take advantage of features of the database. For example, define or use database constraints rather than write Java code to achieve the same effect.

  - Minimize database operations and use datasources to gain the advantage of connection pooling managed by the application server.

- ❐ Datasources can also support distributed transactions in which the application server manages units of work that span multiple RDBM systems and other enterprise resources.

REVIEW QUESTIONS

1. Which of the following are true of JDBC and RDBMS drivers? Select all that apply.

   a. Only a JDBC type 4 driver is entirely coded in Java.

   b. If the database has an ODBC driver but no JDBC driver, you can use the JDBC-ODBC bridge, also known as a type 1 driver.

   c. In addition to the ODBC-JDBC bridge, drivers for most popular databases are included in JDBC.

   d. The JDBC driver classes must be added to your classpath.

   e. You can use a method of the **DriverManager** class to load the driver classes into the JVM.

2. Which one of the following methods of the **java.sql.Statement** class do you call to execute a SQL **DELETE** statement? Select the best answer.

   a. **executeQuery**

   b. **executeDelete**

   c. **executeStatement**

   d. **executeUpdate**

   e. **execute**

3. When you change the database by changing a **ResultSet**? Select all that apply.

   a. always, but there is no guarantee when the changes are written to the underlying database

   b. only when the **ResultSet** is produced by a SQL UPDATE statement

   c. when the transaction isolation level on the connection allows uncommitted reads

   d. when the **ResultSet** is created with CONCUR_UPDATABLE

   e. when the **ResultSet** is created with TYPE_FORWARD_ONLY

4. What usually happens when the database cannot complete an operation that you request by calling a JDBC API? Select the best answer.

   a. The return value is **null** or 0, depending on the method you called.

   b. A **JDBCException** exception is thrown.

   c. A **SQLException** exception is thrown.

   d. An exception is thrown. The database driver determines the type of the exception object.

   e. Your program is terminated.

5. In the **SKICLUB** database used as an example in this chapter, the **BOOKINGS** table has foreign keys that reference the **MEMBERS** and **SKITRIPS** tables. Which of the following statements accurately describes the multiplicity of the relationship between the rows of the three tables? Select the best answer.

   a. MEMBERS to BOOKINGS is one-to-many. BOOKINGS to SKITRIPS is one-to-many. MEMBERS to SKITRIPS is many-to-many.

   b. MEMBERS to BOOKINGS is one-to-one. SKITRIPS to BOOKINGS is one-to-many. MEMBERS to SKITRIPS is one-to-one.

   c. MEMBERS to BOOKINGS is one-to-many. BOOKINGS to SKITRIPS is one-to-one. MEMBERS to SKITRIPS is one-to-many.

   d. MEMBERS to BOOKINGS is one-to-many. SKITRIPS to BOOKINGS is one-to-many. MEMBERS to SKITRIPS is many-to-many.

   e. MEMBERS to BOOKINGS is one-to-many, SKITRIPS to BOOKINGS is one-to-many. There is no relationship between MEMBERS and SKITRIPS because there is no foreign key connecting them.

9

6. What type do you use to call a stored procedure for a database? Select the best answer.

    a. `java.sql.Statement`

    b. `java.sql.PreparedStatement`

    c. `java.sql.CallableStatement`

    d. `javax.sql.StoredStatement`

    e. `java.sql.StoredProcedure`

7. Which of the following are valid constraints that the database manager can enforce? Select all that apply.

    a. Primary keys must be unique and cannot have value **NULL**.

    b. A foreign key with a non-**NULL** value cannot refer to a column with a **NULL** value in the parent table.

    c. When a field used as a foreign key is deleted from the parent table, the row(s) containing the foreign key is (are) deleted from the dependent table.

    d. Only authorized users can write to a table.

    e. A **ResultSet** for this table is updatable.

8. If you are processing a **ResultSet** object in which the third column is called DOB and has SQL type DATE, which of the following statements can you use? Select all that apply. (Assume **rs** is a valid object reference to the **ResultSet** object.)

    a. `java.util.TimeStamp dob = rs.getDate( 3);`

    b. `java.util.Date dob = rs.getDate(3);`

    c. `java.sql.Date dob = rs.getDate("DOB");`

    d. `java.sql.Time dob = rs.getTime("DOB");`

    e. `java.sql.Date dob = rs.getDate("3");`

9. Which of the following lists shows **java.sql.Statement** types in order from fastest to slowest when used to perform the same database operation? Select the best answer.

    a. `PreparedStatement`, `CallableStatement`, `Statement`

    b. `Statement`, `CallableStatement`, `PreparedStatement`

    c. `CallableStatement`, `PreparedStatement`, `Statement`

    d. `CallableStatement`, `Statement`, `PreparedStatement`

    e. `PreparedStatement`, `Statement`, `CallableStatement`

    f. `Statement`, `PreparedStatement`, `CallableStatement`

production, it grew slower and slower as more people started to use it. Which one of the following is most likely to give the greatest performance improvement, assuming that you have not already implemented it? Select the best answer.

a. Replace dynamic and precompiled SQL statements with stored procedures.

b. Use **StringBuffer** objects instead of instances of **String** when building SQL queries as strings in your code.

c. Use connection pooling, either through a datasource or by implementing your own.

d. Minimize queries involving joins.

e. Create all **ResultSet** objects to be TYPE_FORWARD_ONLY and CONCUR_READ_ONLY.

PROGRAMMING EXERCISES

The version of DB2 that comes with this book includes a sample database called SAMPLE. The Debugging and Complete the Solution exercises use this database. If you have not yet built the SAMPLE database, do so now:

1. From the Windows Start menu, select **Start**, **Programs**, **IBM DB2**, **Set up tools**, **First Steps**.

2. In the First Steps panel, select **Create Sample Database**.

3. Close the First Steps panel.

The user name with which you logged into Windows becomes the DB2 schema name for the SAMPLE database, and only that user is granted access to the SAMPLE database. For example, if you log into Windows as MADDOG, the full name of the EMPLOYEE table is MADDOG.EMPLOYEE.

If any user other than the creator of the SAMPLE database tries to access the database, the DB2 JDBC driver throws an exception of type **COM.ibm.db2.jdbc. DB2Exception**.

All classes for the Debugging and Complete the Solution exercises that use the SAMPLE database declare three class variables:

```
static private String id = "USERID";
static private String password = "PASSWORD";
static private String schema = "USERID";
```

Change these lines to use the user name and password of the Windows user who created the SAMPLE database.

For more information on installing DB2 and creating the SAMPLE database, including how to give all users access to the SAMPLE database, see the ReadMe.html document on the CD that accompanies this book.

9

To get the files required for the Debugging and Complete the Solution exercises, copy the folder \Data\questions\c9 from the CD that accompanies this book to the folder \Data\questions\c9 on your hard drive. Work in the folder that contains the folder `questions`. Make sure `questions` contains the folder `c9` and that `c9` contains the original Java source files.

Debugging

1. Extract the source for class `questions.c9.Debug9_1` from file `X:\Data\questions\c9\Debug9_1.java`, where `X` is the drive letter of your CD-ROM. Correct the source so that the class successfully connects to the `SAMPLE` database using the DB2 Type 3 driver, also know as the DB2 net driver. All the changes you must make are in the method `connectToSAMPLE`. The driver class name and URL in the main method are correct for the DB2 net driver.

2. Extract the source for class `questions.c9.Debug9_2` from file `X:\Data\questions\c9\Debug9_2.java`, where `X` is the drive letter of your CD-ROM. Correct the source so that the class successfully adds one record to the `DEPARTMENT` table using a dynamic SQL statement. To connect to the database, use the corrected version of method `connectToSAMPLE` from the `Debug9_1` class. All the changes you must make are in the method `addDepartment`.

3. Extract the source for class `questions.c9.Debug9_3` from file `X:\Data\questions\c9\Debug9_3.java`, where `X` is the drive letter of your CD-ROM. Correct the source so that the class successfully reads from the `EMP_ACT` table in the `SAMPLE` database and returns a **ResultSet** object. Change only the `readTable` method and do not make it less general than the original version. The first argument is the name of the table to read. The second argument determines whether the returned **ResultSet** object is scrollable.

4. Extract the source for class `questions.c9.Debug9_4` from file `X:\Data\questions\c9\Debug9_4.java`, where `X` is the drive letter of your CD-ROM. Correct the source so that the class successfully converts an arbitrary row from the `EMP_ACT` table in the `SAMPLE` database to an `EmployeeActivity` object and prints that object to the console. Use the `EmployeeActivity` class provided in the same package and the corrected `readTable` method from class `Debug9_3`. Change only the `getEmployeeActivityRecord` method.

5. Extract the source for class `questions.c9.Debug9_5` from file `X:\Data\questions\c9\Debug9_5.java`, where `X` is the drive letter of your CD-ROM. Correct the source so that the class successfully builds and executes precompiled SQL statements to retrieve records from the `EMPLOYEE` table in the `SAMPLE` database. Retrieve records for all employees who do a specified job. Change only the `getEmpByJob` method. Use the method **Statement.executeBatch** to insert all the new records in one database operation.

Complete the Solution

1. Using the **SKICLUB** database used as the example in this chapter, fill in the blanks to complete the precompiled SQL statement below so that it retrieves the members booked on any particular trip. Each returned record should contain the date of the trip and the first name, last name, and skiing ability of a member booked on the trip.

   ```
   SELECT _____

   FROM _____

   WHERE TRIPID = ?

   AND _____
   ```

2. Using the **SAMPLE** database, fill in the blanks to complete the dynamic SQL statement below so that it retrieves department numbers, department names, manager first names, and manager last names for all departments.

   ```
   SELECT _____

   FROM USERID.DEPARTMENT, USERID.EMPLOYEE

   WHERE _____
   ```

3. Extract the source for class **questions.c9.Complete9_3** from file **X:\Data\questions\c9\Complete9_3.java**, where **X** is the drive letter of your CD-ROM. Add statements to the class so that is successfully issues the **SELECT** statement from Complete the Solution Question 2 on the **SAMPLE** database.

4. The DB2 driver used by the **DeleteMember** class in the chapter does not support savepoints. If you have access to a database driver that can handle savepoints, add logic to the **DeleteMember** class to implement the following requirements:

   ❑ Insert a savepoint at the point where SQL statements to delete trip bookings have been issued, but not the statements to delete the member record.

   ❑ If, after all SQL statements have been issued, the user gives the instruction not to delete the member, roll back to the savepoint. Then ask whether to delete the trip bookings for the member.

   ❑ If the member gives instructions to keep the trip bookings, roll back the whole transaction.

   ❑ If the member gives instructions to delete the trip bookings but keep the member, commit the operations that have been completed up to the savepoint.

5. Extract the source for class **questions.c9.Complete9_5** from file **X:\Data\questions\c9\Complete9_5.java**, where **X** is the drive letter of your CD-ROM. Add statements to the **addManyMembers** method to perform a batch update that inserts a row into the **MEMBERS** table for every line of data read from the input file **\Data\questions\c9\members.txt**. Use the method **Statement.executeBatch** to insert all the new records in one database operation.

Discovery

1. Write a command-line application that the organizers of the SKICLUB database might use. Prompt the user for a user ID and password and use these values to get the connection to the database. (*Hint*: Use any Windows login user name and password.) Then prompt them to enter a trip ID in the range 1 to 24. Print a list of the members booked on that trip, in alphabetic order by last name. State each trip member's skiing ability.

2. Draw an Entity Relationship diagram in the style of Figure 9-3 or 9-7 to show the structure of a database you would design for an online shopping application. Indicate primary keys and foreign keys. Below the diagram, list for each table: column names, SQL types, and other column restraints such as NOT NULL. The shopping application is designed around five main classes listed below. There is no need actually to create the database.

Customer: Holds personal information such as name and address. A customer must have one account and may have multiple accounts.

Account: Every account has a unique identifier and an owner. Fields include current balance, credit rating, value of last statement, and date of last payment.

Order: An order is owned by an account. An order has a unique identifier and fields for account identifier, date opened, date closed, status, and total value. An order must have at least one ordered item and may have several items.

Item: An item that has been purchased and added to an order. Each item has a part number, picture (an image file), and quantity.

Inventory: A list of the items available for sale (simplified). Each item in inventory has a part number, description, unit cost, and number in stock.

3. Write a program with a Java GUI that displays the entire EMPLOYEE table from the SAMPLE database in a **JTable** object. Refer to Chapters 6 and 7 for details on programming a **JTable** object. No activity beyond displaying the data is required.

10

XML

In this chapter you will:

♦ Learn what XML is, where it came from, and why it is used in so many places

♦ Discover how to create your own XML files

♦ Look into what is contained within the Java API for XML Processing (JAXP)

♦ Investigate the Simple API for XML (SAX) and put it to use for parsing XML files

♦ Parse XML files using the Document Object Model (DOM) API and contrast its use with that of SAX

♦ Use the DOM API to construct an XML document in memory and then output it to a file

♦ Validate XML files using both the Document Type Definition (DTD) language and XML Schema

♦ See how to use Extensible Stylesheet Language Transformations (XSLT) and XPath expressions to transform XML file content into other forms such as HTML

INTRODUCTION

There's little doubt that if you are familiar with the Java platform you have heard about Extensible Markup Language (XML), because XML has become a foundation technology that seems to be everywhere in the software industry. XML is used in a whole host of applications including configuration files, data interchange, and business-to-business (B2B) electronic commerce because of its power to describe the structure of data in a straightforward format that is open and easy to process. Perhaps you are wondering where it came from and what is behind its apparent overnight success. If so, you may be surprised to discover that the roots of XML go back many years to something called Standard Generalized Markup Language (SGML), which became an international standard in 1986. But in between SGML and XML came another related language, HyperText Markup Language (HTML), which you are certainly aware of. HTML is the standard language for publishing on the World Wide Web. Its wide range of features reflect the needs of a very diverse and international community wishing to make information available on the Web. During 1999, in recognition of the popularity and importance of both languages, HTML and XML began the long, ongoing process of merging together. HTML 4 was recast in

XML, and the resulting XHTML 1.0 became a World Wide Web Consortium (W3C) Recommendation in January 2000. Work has continued since that time, producing new profiles of XHTML and planning for the future.

XML is a markup language just like its predecessors SGML and HTML, meaning that XML uses tags that are placed within the content of a document to identify (mark up) the components of a document. It is important to realize that a markup language doesn't specify how these components should be presented when the document is displayed or printed. Presentation details are left for stylesheets to define. For example, the markup language identifies which pieces of text are first-level headings and the stylesheet specifies that a first-level heading is centered, bold, and uses a 28 point Helvetica font. Let's go back to HTML for a moment because it so familiar. HTML requires authors to use tags to identify document components like those shown in Figure 10-1.

```
<html>
<body>
<h1>Heading Text Goes Here</h1>
<p>This is a paragraph with some <b>boldfaced</b> text as well as some text
that forms a list
<ul>
<li>First list item
<li>Second item
</ul>
</body>
</html>
```

Figure 10-1   A simple HTML example

The Web browsers take this content and transform it into something that is easy to read. The output from this simple HTML example is shown in Figure 10-2. XML looks like HTML because its tags are also enclosed in angle brackets, and it also uses backslash characters to denote end tags. But there is one important difference between the two: All HTML tags are predetermined and you cannot define your own. On the other hand, XML enables you to create any tags you might like to have. It is this capability that gives XML its name: the Extensible Markup Language.

Heading Text Goes Here

This is a paragraph with some **boldfaced** text as well as some text that forms a list

- First list item
- Second item

Figure 10-2   Output from the simple HTML example

up just about any kind of information. In that respect, XML is very much like a blank slate. However, to give programmers guidance and to have standard formats, many industries that have requirements to exchange information electronically have formed standards committees to define a set of XML tags that suit the needs of their industry and facilitate information sharing among competitors and suppliers. Despite this expressive power of XML, it is not difficult to create a simple XML document because the basics of XML can be learned quickly and anyone who is familiar with HTML immediately feels comfortable with XML.

No special editor applications or document processors are required to create or maintain an XML document. The plain-text nature of XML means that you can create and view XML files with the simplest of text-editor support. This makes XML files portable. Like character information support on the Java platform, XML is based upon Unicode to provide global data support. In the same way that Java delivers on the promise of portable programs, XML provides portable and extensible data support.

XML STRUCTURE

Like HTML, every XML tag begins with an open angle bracket, <, and closes with a close angle bracket, >. These same two symbols are also often referred to as the less-than and the greater-than symbols, respectively. Every tag is either an opening tag, or a closing tag. An XML element is the combination of an opening tag, a closing tag, and all the data in between. For example,

```
<tag1>sample text for the element</tag1>
```

is a complete XML element. Notice that the closing tag is the same as the opening tag, except that it contains a backslash character immediately following the open angle bracket. If an element is empty (contains no data), the opening and closing tags are collapsed like so:

```
<tag1/>
```

Here the presence of the backslash character immediately preceding the close angle bracket is the indication that it is an empty element.

The data that appears within an element can contain other tags. When it comes to nesting elements, the rule is that the nested element must be closed before its containing element is closed. To illustrate this rule, consider the following example of nesting tags that is allowed:

```
<tag1>Some text<tag2>more text</tag2></tag1>
```

as opposed to the following nesting structure that is invalid:

```
<tag1>Some text<tag2></tag1>more text</tag2>
```

10

The second nesting structure is invalid because the `tag2` element is still open when the `tag1` element that contains it is closed.

Using Attributes

Not all the data for an element must be placed between its opening and closing tags. XML allows a programmer to define any attributes for any opening tag. They are used to convey additional, specific information about the tags that contain them. Essentially, an attribute is a name-value pair in which the value is enclosed within quotes (either double or single quotes are allowed) and an equal sign is put between them. The attribute is placed within the angle brackets of the opening tag. For example, if a `tag1` element had `height` and `length` attributes, it could be coded as follows:

```
<tag1 height="12.1" length="7">sample text for the element</tag1>
```

It is worth noting that the same information could be conveyed using nested tags in place of the attributes. If this approach were taken, the XML would look like this:

```
<tag1><height>12.1</height><length>7</length>sample text for the
element</tag1>
```

Choosing between the two approaches is often a matter of personal style. As you can see, the approach that uses attributes is well suited for cases in which the values are compact and will not make the tag that contains them too long.

Using Namespaces

As many sets of elements and corresponding tags are defined, the potential for naming conflicts is considerable, especially for commonly used names. To handle such conflicts, XML provides for the definition of namespaces. A namespace is typically declared in the root element of the document (so that it can be used throughout the document) as an instance of the attribute `xmlns`. More than one namespace can be defined. For example, the following lines define the default namespace first and then the namespace called `xyz`. Both namespaces have an element called `tag1`. If you don't specify a namespace, it is assumed that the element is defined in the default namespace. However, if the name of a namespace is used as a prefix on a tag name (separated by a colon), the document parser searches for the element in that namespace, as shown in the following code:

```
<tagRoot xmlns="http://www.defaulttags.com/tags"
         xmlns:xyz="http://www.xyztags.com/tags">
<xyz:tag1>some text goes here</xyz:tag1>
<tag1>more sample text</tag1>
</tagRoot>
```

Inserting Comments

You can include comments in an XML document that someone viewing the document source file can read. These comments aren't considered part of the content of the document but provide helpful insight into what the programmer was thinking at the time he or she created the XML document. A comment element begins with the four-character sequence `<!--` and ends with the three-character sequence `-->`.

```
<!-- an example of a comment -->
```

Inserting Special Characters

Certain special characters, such as the open and close angle brackets, always trigger XML processing when they are encountered. If you ever find it necessary to include them in your document content, you must use special encoding. These special characters and their corresponding encodings are provided in Figure 10-3.

Character	Encoding
& (ampersand)	&amp;
' (apostrophe)	&apos;
> (close angle bracket)	&gt;
< (open angle bracket)	&lt;
" (quotation mark)	&quot;

Figure 10-3   Special XML characters and their encodings

XML documents that follow all of the rules noted so far are considered to be "well-formed" documents. However, a well-formed document isn't necessarily a valid document because there may be additional rules that, for example, require tags to be used in a prescribed sequence. There may also be mandatory tags or mandatory attributes that a document must include. Breaking any of these rules would mean that the document is invalid. This is similar in concept to a program that compiles successfully because it is syntactically correct but does not execute properly. Later in this chapter, in the section "Validating XML Documents Using DTD and XML Schema," you examine techniques to ensure that an XML document is not only well formed but also valid.

HTML, XHTML, and XML

Because much has been made of the similarities between HTML and XML, you may have wondered if HTML can be considered a special set of XML tags that is used for displaying documents in Web browsers. This is nearly true, but HTML documents are not necessarily well-formed XML documents. For example, not all HTML elements require a closing tag. The paragraph element that begins with `<p>` is one of the most

10

common examples that violate this rule. In HTML, no closing `</p>` tag is required, whereas XML requires one. In HTML, the names of the tags are case-insensitive, meaning that `<B>` and `<b>` are interpreted to mean the same thing. XML is case-sensitive, so `<B>` and `<b>` are different tags. In XML, the value of an attribute must be enclosed in quotes. HTML supports putting quotes around attribute values but does not require this unless there are spaces embedded in the value.

To bridge between HTML and XML, the World Wide Web Consortium (W3C) defined the design language known as XHTML. XHTML is defined such that any well-formed XHTML document is also a well-formed XML document.

XML EXAMPLE DOCUMENT

With a brief introduction to the structure of XML documents behind you, you can now examine a more meaningful example of an XML document. The document in Figure 10-4 is the simple beginning of a catalogue of the many species of known dinosaurs.

```
<?xml version="1.0" encoding="UTF-8"?>
<DinoList>
    <Dinosaur period="Late Cretaceous">
        <Name>Tyrannosaurus Rex</Name>
        <Group>Carnosaur</Group>
        <Range>
           <Region>Europe</Region>
           <Region>North America</Region>
        </Range>
        <PhysicalAttr>
           <Length unit="feet">39</Length>
           <Weight unit="tons">6</Weight>
        </PhysicalAttr>
    </Dinosaur>
    <Dinosaur period="Early Jurassic">
        <Name>Dilophosaurus</Name>
        <Group>Coelurosaur</Group>
        <Range>
           <Region>Asia</Region>
           <Region>North America</Region>
        </Range>
        <PhysicalAttr>
           <Height unit="metres">3</Height>
           <Length unit="metres">6</Length>
           <Weight unit="tons">2</Weight>
        </PhysicalAttr>
    </Dinosaur>
    <Dinosaur period="Late Jurassic">
        <Name>Stegosaurus</Name>
        <Group>Stegosaur</Group>
```

Figure 10-4   Excerpt from a catalogue of dinosaurs in XML format

```
        <Range>
           <Region>Europe</Region>
           <Region>Asia</Region>
           <Region>North America</Region>
        </Range>
        <PhysicalAttr>
           <Length unit="metres">9</Length>
           <Weight unit="kgs">3100</Weight>
        </PhysicalAttr>
     </Dinosaur>
  </DinoList>
```

Figure 10-4   Excerpt from a catalogue of dinosaurs in XML format (continued)

The top-level element for this document is the `<DinoList>` tag. Another way of saying this is to describe `<DinoList>` as the document's root element. A document should have only one root element.

You may be wondering about the first line of this document and its purpose within the document. This line is the document header and is a processing instruction, as identified by the opening two-character sequence of `<?` and closing two-character sequence `?>`.

```
<?xml version="1.0" encoding="UTF-8"?>
```

Its purpose is to identify the version of XML used within the document and to specify the character encoding for the document. UTF-8 encoding is the default for XML documents, but it certainly doesn't hurt to be explicit about it. The other tags used within the `dinosaurs.xml` file are described in Figure 10-5.

Tag Name	Description
`<DinoList>`	A collection of one or more `<Dinosaur>` tags.
`<Dinosaur>`	Contains the tags `<Name>`, `<Group>`, `<Range>`, and `<PhysicalAttr>` to provide a description of a particular species of dinosaur. It has one attribute, `period`, which identifies the geologic time period in which the dinosaur lived.
`<Name>`	Contains a character string with the name of the dinosaur species.
`<Group>`	Contains a character string with the name of the group of which this dinosaur species is a part.
`<Range>`	Contains one or more `<Region>` tags to identify the area over which this species ranged.
`<PhysicalAttr>`	Contains at least one of the `<Height>`, `<Length>`, and `<Weight>` tags and possibly all three.
`<Region>`	Contains a character string with the name of a region of the world in which a dinosaur species may live.

Figure 10-5   Tags used in the `dinosaur.xml` file

Tag Name	Description
`<Height>`	Contains a character string with the average height of the dinosaur species. It has one attribute, `unit`, which identifies the units for the height value.
`<Length>`	Contains a character string with the average length of the dinosaur species. It has one attribute, `unit`, which identifies the units for the length value.
`<Weight>`	Contains a character string with the average weight of the dinosaur species. It has one attribute, `unit`, which identifies the units for the weight value.

Figure 10-5   Tags used in the `dinosaur.xml` file (continued)

PARSING AN XML DOCUMENT WITH SAX

The Java API for XML Processing (JAXP) was added to the Java platform, Standard Edition, in version 1.4 and includes support for two methods to parse an input XML file. You begin by examining the Simple API for XML (SAX). A SAX parser processes the contents of an XML file sequentially and uses callback methods to indicate to the application when it encounters each item in the file. This is also known as event-based programming interface for parsing. Each time that the parser identifies a tag as it progresses sequentially through the file is considered to be an event. The type of tag that is identified determines which callback method that the parser will invoke, if any.

To use SAX, you must implement the interface `org.xml.sax.ContentHandler`. Typically you accomplish this by extending the `org.xml.sax.DefaultHandler` class because it provides default implementations for all of the callbacks in the SAX handler classes. Then you override the methods of the interface and specify which action will be taken as the various parts of the XML document are encountered.

Along with the parser implementation, it is necessary to define the Java classes in which the data from the parser will be stored as the document is processed. Although it is tedious, the most straightforward method is to define a class for each unique element in the document with `set` and `get` methods for each element that can nest within it. Having such a predictable structure makes it possible to use Java's Reflection API, discussed in Chapter 2, to store data in objects as the parser encounters elements. Figure 10-6 is the source code for the most significant of the classes that map to XML elements in the `dinosaurs.xml` file, the `Dinosaur` class. Because `Dinosaur` is a public class, it is found in a file called `Dinosaur.java`. The structure of packages mirrors the file system, so you will find this source code in the `X:\Data\examples\xml` directory on the CD-ROM. (Here `X:` is the drive letter of the CD-ROM.)

```
package examples.xml;
/**
 * Class that is used to represent the data found in
 * <Dinosaur> tags in the file dinosaurs.xml
 */
public class Dinosaur extends BaseElement {
   private String period;
   private Name name;
   private Group group;
   private PhysicalAttr physicalAttr;
   private Range range;

   public PhysicalAttr getPhysicalAttr() {
      return physicalAttr;
   }
   public Range getRange() {
      return range;
   }
   public Group getGroup() {
      return group;
   }
   public Name getName() {
      return name;
   }
   public String getPeriod() {
      return period;
   }
   public void setPhysicalAttr( PhysicalAttr pa ) {
      this.physicalAttr = pa;
   }
   public void setRange(Range range) {
      this.range = range;
   }
   public void setPeriod(String period) {
      this.period = period;
   }
   public void setGroup(Group group) {
      this.group = group;
   }
   public void setName(Name name) {
      this.name = name;
   }
   public void setAttributeValue( String name,
                                  String value ) {
      if ( name.equals( "period" ) ) {
         setPeriod( value );
            }
      }
```

Figure 10-6   Dinosaur: a class to represent the data found in <Dinosaur> tags

10

```
    public String toString() {
       return "(Name:" + name + ", Group:" + group
              + ", Period:" + period
              + ", Range:" + range
              + ", Physical attributes:" + physicalAttr
              + ")";
    }
}
```

Figure 10-6   `Dinosaur`: a class to represent the data found in `<Dinosaur>` tags
(continued)

For the `Dinosaur` class, a field in the class definition represents each element that is nested within it and a **String** object represents its one property. All but two methods of the class are involved with setting and getting the values of the nested elements. The `setAttributeValue` method overrides the method definition in the superclass, `BaseElement`, and ensures that only an attribute with the correct name is ever set. The `toString` method is a convenient method for outputting the contents of the element.

Because there really isn't much additional insight to be gained from them, the class definitions for `DinoList`, `Name`, `Group`, `Height`, `Length`, `Weight`, `PhysicalAttr`, `Range`, and `Region` are not provided here, but you can obtain them from the `X:\Data\examples\xml` directory on the CD-ROM. (Here `X:` is the drive letter of the CD-ROM.). All these classes that represent an element have a common ancestor in the `BaseElement` class. This class provides support for adding text to the element that most of the subclasses require. It also defines a method, `setAttributeValue`, for adding an attribute to the class. Note, however, that any element that has one or more attributes has to override this method and handle its attributes explicitly. The source for this class is provided in Figure 10-7.

```
package examples.xml;
import java.util.Properties;
/**
 * Common superclass for all classes that represent data
 * from tags in the file dinosaurs.xml
 */
public abstract class BaseElement {
   private StringBuffer text = new StringBuffer();
   public void setAttributeValue( String name,
                                  String value) {
      throw new Error( "No attributes defined for element"
                     + getClass() );
   }
```

Figure 10-7   `BaseElement`: the common superclass for all classes that represent data
from tags in the `dinosaur.xml` file

```
   public void addText( String s ) {
      text.append( s );
   }
   public String getText() {
      return text.toString();
   }
   public String toString() {
      return text.toString();
   }
}
```

Figure 10-7   `BaseElement`: the common superclass for all classes that represent data from tags in the `dinosaur.xml` file (continued)

The `BaseElement` class provides support for three common features of XML elements. The `setAttributeValue` method provides support for setting an attribute for the element. However, if an element does have one or more attributes, it has to override this method, otherwise an error occurs when an attempt is made to set an attribute's value. The methods `addText` and `getText` provide support for storing and retrieving the text contained within an element. In this example, the elements `<Name>`, `<Group>`, and `<Region>` require nothing more than this because they have no attributes and no other elements are nested within them.

Figure 10-8 is the complete source code for the class `SAXModelBuilder` found in the file called `SAXModelBuilder.java` in the `X:\Data\examples\xml` directory. (Here `X:` is the drive letter of the CD-ROM.) `SAXModelBuilder` is the class that supports the actual parsing of the XML input files. A discussion of the contents of the file follows.

```
package examples.xml;
import org.xml.sax.*;
import org.xml.sax.helpers.*;
import java.util.*;
import java.lang.reflect.*;
/**
 * Example SAX parser
 */
public class SAXModelBuilder extends DefaultHandler {
   Stack stack = new Stack();
   BaseElement element;
   /**
    * Method called when the opening tag of an element is
    * encountered
    */
   public void startElement( String namespace,
                             String localname,
                             String qname,
```

Figure 10-8   `SAXModelBuilder`: an example SAX parser

```
                                       Attributes attrs )
                                       throws SAXException {
      BaseElement element = null;
      try {
         Class c = Class.forName( "examples.xml."+qname );
         element = (BaseElement)c.newInstance();
         for (int i=0; i<attrs.getLength(); i++) {
            element.setAttributeValue( attrs.getQName(i),
                                       attrs.getValue(i) );
         }
         stack.push( element );
      } catch ( Exception e ) {
         System.err.println( e.toString() );
      }
   }
   /**
    * Method called when the closing tag of an element is
    * encountered
    */
   public void endElement( String namespace,
                           String localname,
                           String qname )
                           throws SAXException {
      element = (BaseElement)stack.pop();
      if ( !stack.empty() )
         try {
            setProperty( qname, stack.peek(), element );
         } catch ( Exception e ) {
            System.err.println( e.toString() );
         }
   }
   /**
    * Method called when data within an element is
    * encountered
    */
   public void characters( char[] ch, int start,
                           int len ) {
      String text = new String( ch, start, len );
      ((BaseElement)(stack.peek())).addText( text );
   }
   /**
    * Method to take the data from the parser and put it
    * into the appropriate object instance
    */
   void setProperty( String name, Object target,
                     Object value ) throws SAXException {
      Method method = null;
      try {
         method = target.getClass().getMethod(
                  "add"+name,
```

Figure 10-8   SAXModelBuilder: an example SAX parser (continued)

```
                        new Class[] { value.getClass() } );
        } catch ( NoSuchMethodException e ) {
           /* ignore, try another method name format */
        }
        if ( method == null ) try {
           method = target.getClass().getMethod(
                     "set"+name,
                     new Class[] { value.getClass() } );
        } catch ( NoSuchMethodException e ) { }
        try {
           method.invoke( target, new Object [] { value } );
        } catch ( Exception e ) {
           throw new SAXException( e.toString() );
        }
     }
     /**
      * Convenience method to return the root element of the
      * document
      */
     public BaseElement getModel() {
        return element;
     }
  }
```

Figure 10-8   `SAXModelBuilder:` an example SAX parser (continued)

The `startElement` method is called whenever a new element begins. The name of this element is passed to the method along with any attributes it may have. An object must be created to correspond with this element, and so the Reflection API is used to determine the appropriate class based on the element's name.

```
public void startElement( String namespace,
                          String localname,
                          String qname,
                          Attributes attrs )
                          throws SAXException {
   BaseElement element = null;
   try {
      Class c = Class.forName( "examples.xml."+qname );
      element = (BaseElement)c.newInstance();
```

After the object has been created, attributes are added to it using the `setAttributeValue` method from the base class. Now it can be pushed onto the **Stack** object to wait until the closing tag for the element is found.

```
      for (int i=0; i<attrs.getLength(); i++) {
         element.setAttributeValue( attrs.getQName(i),
                                    attrs.getValue(i) );
      }
```

10

```
        stack.push( element );
    } catch ( Exception e ) {
      System.err.println( e.toString() );
    }
  }
```

When the closing tag for an element is found, it can be popped off the stack. If the stack isn't empty, the last thing to be done with the element is to pass the element's object instance to set the associated property for the enclosing element. For example, when a <Group> element is closed, the object created to hold the <Group> text is passed to the Dinosaur object as input to the Dinosaur object's setGroup method.

```
public void endElement( String namespace,
                        String localname,
                         String qname )
                         throws SAXException {
    element = (BaseElement)stack.pop();
    if ( !stack.empty() )
       try {
          setProperty( qname, stack.peek(), element );
       } catch ( Exception e ) {
          System.err.println( e.toString() );
       }
  }
```

When the parser processes the text within an element, the characters method is called. This text needs to be added to the object on the top of the stack, so the stack is accessed without adding or deleting any objects in order to get a reference to the object on the top of the stack, and then the addText method is used to put the text into the element.

```
public void characters( char[] ch, int start,
                        int len ) {
    String text = new String( ch, start, len );
    ((BaseElement)(stack.peek())).addText( text );
  }
```

The method setProperty is a helper method that is not defined in the ContentHandler interface. It takes an element that has just ended and applies the Reflection API to call the appropriate method to set the property of the enclosing element with this object as the input data. For example, if a <Group> element has just ended, the method addGroup is tried; if that doesn't work, setGroup is attempted. If the methods of the class were created using the standard naming convention, one of these two methods will work.

```
void setProperty( String name, Object target,
                  Object value ) throws SAXException {
    Method method = null;
```

```
            method = target.getClass().getMethod(
                    "add"+name,
                    new Class[] { value.getClass() } );
        } catch ( NoSuchMethodException e ) {
            /* ignore, try another method name format */
        }
        if ( method == null ) try {
            method = target.getClass().getMethod(
                    "set"+name,
                    new Class[] { value.getClass() } );
        } catch ( NoSuchMethodException e ) { }
        try {
            method.invoke( target, new Object [] { value } );
        } catch ( Exception e ) {
            throw new SAXException( e.toString() );
        }
    }
}
```

The method getModel returns a reference to the last object pulled off the stack. This last object will be the root element.

```
    public BaseElement getModel() {
        return element;
    }
```

10

To test the SAX parser, a test program is required. Figure 10-9 contains the class TestModelBuilder that serves this purpose by testing the parser with the dinosaurs.xml file.

```
package examples.xml;
import org.xml.sax.*;
import org.xml.sax.helpers.*;
import javax.xml.parsers.*;
public class TestModelBuilder {
    public static void main( String[] args ) throws Exception {
        SAXParserFactory factory
            = SAXParserFactory.newInstance();
        SAXParser saxParser = factory.newSAXParser();
        XMLReader parser = saxParser.getXMLReader();
        SAXModelBuilder mb = new SAXModelBuilder();
        parser.setContentHandler( mb );
        parser.parse( new InputSource( "dinosaurs.xml" ) );
        DinoList dinoList = (DinoList)mb.getModel();
        System.out.println( "Dinosaurs = " + dinoList );
    }
}
```

Figure 10-9   TestModelBuilder: a program to test the SAX parser with the dinosaur.xml file

The **main** method of the `TestModelBuilder` class begins by creating a `factory` object, then using `factory` to create a SAX parser:

```
SAXParserFactory factory
  = SAXParserFactory.newInstance();
SAXParser saxParser = factory.newSAXParser();
XMLReader parser = saxParser.getXMLReader();
SAXModelBuilder mb = new SAXModelBuilder();
parser.setContentHandler( mb );
parser.parse( new InputSource( "dinosaurs.xml" ) );
DinoList dinoList = (DinoList)mb.getModel();
System.out.println( "Dinosaurs = " + dinoList );
```

Now all that's left to do is to call the parser against the input file, then retrieve the model. In the absence of something more useful to do with the model, the contents of the model are simply output to the console. The output from this file is a single line, the content of which is shown in Figure 10-10.

```
Dinosaurs = [(Name:Tyrannosaurus Rex, Group:Carnosaur, Period:Late
Cretaceous, Range:[Europe, North America], Physical
attributes:[Length:39feet,Weight:6tons]), (Name:Dilophosaurus,
Group:Coelurosaur, Period:Early Jurassic, Range:[Asia, North America],
Physical attributes:[Height:3metres,Length:6metres,Weight:2tons]),
(Name:Stegosaurus, Group:Stegosaur, Period:Late Jurassic, Range:[Europe,
Asia, North America], Physical attributes:[Length:9metres,Weight:3100kgs])]
```

Figure 10-10   Output of the `TestModelBuilder` program

PARSING AN XML DOCUMENT WITH DOM

The other method available for parsing XML files that comes with version 1.4 of the Standard Edition of the Java platform is the Document Object Model (DOM) API. DOM is significantly different from SAX, because the DOM parser begins by creating a hierarchical object model of the input XML document. This object model is then made available to the application for it to access the information it contains in a random access fashion. This allows an application to process only the data of interest and ignore the rest of the document. By not having to process every element of a document, the programmer using DOM is freed from having to define a complete set of classes that map to the elements in the document. DOM also makes it easy to revisit elements encountered earlier in the document.

All this is not to say that DOM should be preferred over the use of SAX in every case. The DOM API is memory intensive, and large XML documents may be better parsed using SAX, especially if only a fraction of the information from the document needs to be processed.

pass the XML file to the parser and you are returned an **org.w3c.dom.Document** object. This **Document** object contains all the information parsed from the file, and you call methods to extract individual elements or lists of elements from the object.

Figure 10-11 is the complete source code for the class **DOMParser** found in the file called **DOMParser.java** in the **X:\Data\examples\xml** directory on the CD-ROM. (Here **X:** is the drive letter of the CD-ROM.) This example illustrates how to scan through a DOM data structure to find a specific piece of information. This program retrieves the contents of the **<Group>** element for the dinosaur entry with the name "**Dilophosaurus**". The helper methods, **getFirstElement** and **getSimpleElementText**, are required because the DOM document structure isn't as intuitive to navigate as it could be. For example, obtaining the character string in the **<Group>** element is not as simple as making a single method call. Instead, the programmer must access another layer of child data structures below the **<Group>** element and then use the **instanceof** method to verify that what is found is truly character data. DOM was not developed specifically for use in Java programs, and so it does not take advantage of the Java platform's collection classes. This means that a programmer who is an expert in the structure and conventions of the Java collection classes must learn a new collection programming interface. A discussion of the contents of the file follows the figure.

10

```
package examples.xml;
import javax.xml.parsers.*;
import org.xml.sax.InputSource;
import org.w3c.dom.*;
/**
 * Class for testing the DOM method of parsing XML files
 */
public class DOMParser {
    public static void main( String [] args ) throws Exception {
        DocumentBuilderFactory factory
            = DocumentBuilderFactory.newInstance();
        DocumentBuilder parser
            = factory.newDocumentBuilder();
        Document document
            = parser.parse(
                new InputSource("dinosaurs.xml") );
        Element dinoList = document.getDocumentElement();
        NodeList dinosaurs
            = dinoList.getElementsByTagName("Dinosaur");
        Element currElement = null;
        String groupName = null;
        for( int i=0; i<dinosaurs.getLength(); i++ ) {
            currElement = (Element)dinosaurs.item(i);
            String nameValue
                = getSimpleElementText( currElement,
                                        "Name" );
```

Figure 10-11   **DOMParser:** an example of the DOM method of parsing XML files

```
            if ( nameValue.equals("Dilophosaurus") ) {
                groupName
                    = getSimpleElementText( currElement,
                                             "Group" );
            }
        }
        System.out.println( "Dilophosaurus group: "
                            + groupName );
    }
    /**
     * Method to return the first element of a specified
     * name from the given element
     */
    public static Element
    getFirstElement( Element element, String name ) {
        NodeList nl = element.getElementsByTagName( name );
        if ( nl.getLength() < 1 ) {
            throw new RuntimeException( "Element: "
                + element + " does not contain: " + name);
        }
        return (Element)nl.item(0);
    }
    /**
     * Method to return the text contained within an
     * element
     */
    public static String
    getSimpleElementText( Element node, String name ) {
        Element nameEl = getFirstElement( node, name );
        Node textNode = nameEl.getFirstChild();
        if ( textNode instanceof Text ) {
            return textNode.getNodeValue();
        } else {
            throw new RuntimeException( "No text in " + name);
        }
    }
}
```

Figure 10-11   `DOMParser`: an example of the DOM method of parsing XML files (continued)

When the `DOMParser` program is run, the output is a single line as follows:

```
Dilophosaurus group: Coelurosaur
```

As with the SAX example, the first step towards getting a parser is to create and set up the content handler for the parser, then parse the input source file into a document.

```
DocumentBuilderFactory factory
    = DocumentBuilderFactory.newInstance();
DocumentBuilder parser
    = factory.newDocumentBuilder();
```

```
                      = parser.parse(
                          new InputSource("dinosaurs.xml") );
```

Next, the root level document is extracted and the list of all the `<Dinosaur>` tags is extracted.

```
      Element dinoList = document.getDocumentElement();
      NodeList dinosaurs
          = dinoList.getElementsByTagName("Dinosaur");
```

Then the code iterates through the list of dinosaurs looking for a name that will match the text "`Dilophosaurus`". When it is found, it extracts the text from the associated `<Group>` tag and the extraction is complete.

```
      Element currElement = null;
      String groupName = null;
      for( int i=0; i<dinosaurs.getLength(); i++ ) {
          currElement = (Element)dinosaurs.item(i);
          String nameValue
              = getSimpleElementText( currElement,
                                        "Name" );
          if ( nameValue.equals("Dilophosaurus") ) {
              groupName
                  = getSimpleElementText( currElement,
                                            "Group" );
          }
      }
      System.out.println( "Dilophosaurus group: "
                            + groupName );
}
```

Parsing an XML Document with JDOM

DOM is a technology that is independent of programming language. Because DOM was not developed to take advantage of the power of the Java platform, it can be awkward to use and Java developers may find themselves wondering why features, such as the collection classes, that Java provides have been bypassed. If you feel the same way, you may want to use JDOM, available for download from `http://www.jdom.org`. The JDOM Project is the result of the efforts of a group of Java developers who saw an opportunity to create a Java-centric and Java-optimized API for manipulating XML. Some day this may be part of the Java platform, but for now you'll have to download it and install it separately. All the information that you need for doing this is available on the JDOM Web site.

10

GENERATING AN XML DOCUMENT WITH DOM

So far this chapter has focused on parsing an existing XML document, without worrying too much about how to generate an XML document in the first place. Of course you could take the brute force approach and print string after string of XML tags and text to a file output stream, but that would certainly be prone to errors. Fortunately, there is a better way: using DOM, which begins by creating the document in memory and then applying a simple transformation to direct it to an output stream.

It is worth noting that the techniques shown in this section for creating elements and attributes within a new document work equally well for modifying an existing XML document. For example, after parsing an existing XML document using DOM it is possible to add new elements, or remove and replace existing elements, and then output the updated XML document.

Figure 10-12 is the complete source code for the class `DOMPrinter` found in the file called `DOMPrinter.java` in the `X:\Data\examples\xml` directory on the CD-ROM. (Here `X:` is the drive letter of the CD-ROM.) This example illustrates how to create an empty DOM document in memory, add elements and attributes, transform it, and then direct the transformation output to the console. A discussion of the contents of the file follows.

```java
package examples.xml;
import java.io.FileOutputStream;
import javax.xml.parsers.*;
import javax.xml.transform.*;
import javax.xml.transform.dom.DOMSource;
import javax.xml.transform.stream.StreamResult;
import org.xml.sax.InputSource;
import org.w3c.dom.*;
/**
 * Class for demonstrating how to generate a simple
 * XML file using DOM
 */
public class DOMPrinter {
    public static void main( String [] args ) throws Exception {
        DocumentBuilderFactory factory
            = DocumentBuilderFactory.newInstance();
        DocumentBuilder builder
            = factory.newDocumentBuilder();
        DOMImplementation domImpl
            = builder.getDOMImplementation();
        Document document
            = domImpl.createDocument( null, "tagRoot",
                                      null );
```

Figure 10-12   `DOMPrinter:` class for demonstrating how to generate a simple XML file using DOM

```
        Element root = document.getDocumentElement();
        root.setAttribute( "testAttr", "testValue" );
        Element tag1Element
            = document.createElement( "tag1" );
        Text tag1Text
            = document.createTextNode( "sample text" );
        tag1Element.appendChild( tag1Text );
        root.appendChild( tag1Element );
        Element tag2Element
            = document.createElement( "tag2" );
        Text tag2Text
            = document.createTextNode( "more text" );
        tag2Element.appendChild( tag2Text );
        tag1Element.appendChild( tag2Element );
        Element tag3Element
            = document.createElement( "tag3" );
        root.appendChild( tag3Element );
        TransformerFactory tf
            = TransformerFactory.newInstance();
        Transformer transformer = tf.newTransformer();
        Source source = new DOMSource( document );
        FileOutputStream fos
            = new FileOutputStream( "tags.xml" );
        Result output = new StreamResult( fos );
        transformer.transform( source, output );
    }
}
```

Figure 10-12   DOMPrinter: class for demonstrating how to generate a simple XML
file using DOM (continued)

The output from running this example is written into the file **tags.xml**. The content
of this file is shown in Figure 10-13.

```
<?xml version="1.0" encoding="UTF-8"?>
<tagRoot testAttr="testValue"><tag1>sample text<tag2>more
text</tag2></tag1><tag3/></tagRoot>
```

Figure 10-13   Output from the DOMPrinter program in the file tags.xml

The method **main** for this example begins in a fashion similar to the DOM parser
example. But instead of using the DocumentBuilder object to create a document
based on parsing an existing file, a DOMImplementation object is obtained for the purpose of creating a DOM document.

```
DocumentBuilderFactory factory
    = DocumentBuilderFactory.newInstance();
DocumentBuilder builder
    = factory.newDocumentBuilder();
```

10

```
DOMImplementation domImpl
   = builder.getDOMImplementation();
```

The parameters for creating a document are a namespace Uniform Resource Identifier (URI), the name of the document's root element, and a document type object. For simplicity, the namespace and document type are omitted. The root element is called tagRoot.

```
Document document
   = domImpl.createDocument( null, "tagRoot",
                             null );
```

To begin adding content to the document, a reference to the root element is required. To demonstrate how attributes are handled, an example attribute is added to this element.

```
Element root = document.getDocumentElement();
root.setAttribute( "testAttr", "testValue" );
```

Next, the first element nested inside the root element, tag1, is created. This element has text, and the text is created as a child node of this element. Then the element and its child text node are added to the root.

```
Element tag1Element
   = document.createElement( "tag1" );
Text tag1Text
   = document.createTextNode( "sample text" );
tag1Element.appendChild( tag1Text );
root.appendChild( tag1Element );
```

Not all elements must be added directly to the root. The next element, tag2, is created in the same fashion as tag1 but is nested inside tag1, not the root.

```
Element tag2Element
   = document.createElement( "tag2" );
Text tag2Text
   = document.createTextNode( "more text" );
tag2Element.appendChild( tag2Text );
tag1Element.appendChild( tag2Element );
```

An element doesn't have to have any content. To illustrate this, tag3 is created without any attributes or text content. It is added as a child of the root element.

```
Element tag3Element
   = document.createElement( "tag3" );
root.appendChild( tag3Element );
```

You could go on adding elements for quite some time, but the basics of creating and adding elements are covered with these few example elements. Now it is time to output the contents of the document to a file. The process of going from the DOM document to a text file is a transformation, and so a **Transformer** document is first obtained.

```
TransformerFactory tf
    = TransformerFactory.newInstance();
Transformer transformer = tf.newTransformer();
```

A transformation requires a source and an output result target. In this case, the source content comes from the DOM document and the output target is a file output stream.

```
Source source = new DOMSource( document );
FileOutputStream fos
    = new FileOutputStream( "tags.xml" );
Result output = new StreamResult( fos );
```

Finally, the transformation is executed and the output file is created.

```
transformer.transform( source, output );
```

VALIDATING XML DOCUMENTS USING DTD AND XML SCHEMA

Earlier in this chapter, the rules for creating a well-formed XML document were discussed. This section investigates how to specify the rules for determining when a document can be considered valid. Although there are many approaches for doing this, this section focuses on just two of them: Document Type Definition (DTD) and XML Schema. At the current time, the DTD approach is the established method and XML Schema is the emerging technology for document validation. It is likely that XML Schema will eventually dominate, because it is more powerful and because it has an XML structure. However, the DTD approach is well entrenched and so it is useful to become familiar with both.

10

DTDs

When creating the rules for validating a document, you must focus on issues such as which elements are required and which are optional, whether an element can appear multiple times, which elements can be nested inside another, and which values are allowed for an element. A DTD is a text file that uses a formal syntax to lay out the rules that specify which tags and attributes are allowed in a document, in what order they must appear, and which are mandatory. Figure 10-14 is the DTD for the **dinosaurs.xml** file found in the file called **dinosaur.dtd** in the **X:\Data\examples\xml** directory on the CD-ROM. (Here **X:** is the drive letter of the CD-ROM.)

```
<?xml version='1.0' encoding="UTF-8"?>
<!ELEMENT DinoList (Dinosaur+)>
<!ELEMENT Dinosaur (Name,Group,Range,PhysicalAttr)>
<!ATTLIST Dinosaur period CDATA #IMPLIED>
<!ELEMENT Group (#PCDATA)>
<!ELEMENT Height (#PCDATA)>
<!ATTLIST Height unit CDATA #IMPLIED>
<!ELEMENT Length (#PCDATA)>
<!ATTLIST Length unit CDATA #IMPLIED>
<!ELEMENT Name (#PCDATA)>
<!ELEMENT PhysicalAttr (Height?,Length?,Weight?)>
<!ELEMENT Range (Region+)>
<!ELEMENT Region (#PCDATA)>
<!ELEMENT Weight (#PCDATA)>
<!ATTLIST Weight unit CDATA #IMPLIED>
```

Figure 10-14   Document Type Definition (DTD) for the `dinosaur.xml` file

The first line of the DTD that follows the usual processing instruction describes the `<DinoList>` element as one or more `<Dinosaur>` elements. If an asterisk were substituted for the plus sign, a `<DinoList>` element would be defined as zero or more `<Dinosaur>` elements. There is no `ATTLIST` statement for `<DinoList>`, so there will be no attributes allowed for `<DinoList>` elements.

```
<!ELEMENT DinoList (Dinosaur+)>
```

The following `ELEMENT` and `ATTLIST` statements describe the `<Dinosaur>` element as exactly one `<Name>`, `<Group>`, `<Range>`, and `<PhysicalAttr>` element—in that order. One attribute is defined, called `period`, and the value of this attribute will be a string because the symbol `CDATA` indicates that character data is expected.

```
<!ELEMENT Dinosaur (Name,Group,Range,PhysicalAttr)>
<!ATTLIST Dinosaur period CDATA #IMPLIED>
```

The following `ELEMENT` statement describes the `Group` element as a string. The `<Name>` and `<Region>` elements are similar to this. Here, `PCDATA` stands for parsed character data.

```
<!ELEMENT Group (#PCDATA)>
```

The following `ELEMENT` and `ATTLIST` statements describe the `<Height>` element as a string with an attribute called `unit`. The `<Length>` and `<Weight>` elements have the same statements.

```
<!ELEMENT Height (#PCDATA)>
<!ATTLIST Height unit CDATA #IMPLIED>
```

The following `ELEMENT` statement describes the `<PhysicalAttr>` element as a sequence of a `<Height>`, a `<Length>`, and a `<Weight>` element. The question mark

~~character (?) that follows each of these three elements indicates that they are all optional.~~ Regardless, if the elements are present they must be in the order specified.

```
<!ELEMENT PhysicalAttr (Height?,Length?,Weight?)>
```

The following `ELEMENT` statement describes the `<Range>` element as a sequence of one or more `<Region>` elements:

```
<!ELEMENT Range (Region+)>
```

To apply this DTD to the `dinosaurs.xml` file, it is necessary to make modifications to the header of the XML file to add the following line:

```
<!DOCTYPE DinoList SYSTEM "dinosaurs.dtd">
```

This statement identifies the element `<DinoList>` as the root element of the document and specifies that the file `dinosaur.dtd` from the local file system be associated with the XML document. All that is left to be done is to activate the validation feature when the parser is created and install an error handler. For the file `TestModelBuilder.java`, this means adding calls to the parser factory's `setValidating` method and the `XMLReader` object's `setErrorHandler` method. The updated class is located in the file `TestModelBuilderDTD.java`. Figure 10-15 shows the **main** method taken from the `TestModelBuilderDTD` class, with the additions highlighted in boldface.

10

```
public static void main( String[] args ) throws Exception {
   SAXParserFactory factory
      = SAXParserFactory.newInstance();
   factory.setValidating( true );
   SAXParser saxParser = factory.newSAXParser();
   XMLReader parser = saxParser.getXMLReader();
   SAXModelBuilder mb = new SAXModelBuilder();
   parser.setContentHandler( mb );
   parser.setErrorHandler( new ParserErrorHandler() );
   parser.parse( new InputSource( "dinosaurs.xml" ) );
   DinoList dinoList = (DinoList)mb.getModel();
   System.out.println( "Dinosaurs = " + dinoList );
}
```

Figure 10-15   **main** method of the `TestModelBuilderDTD` class

Similar changes to take advantage of the DTD are required in the file `DOMParser.java`. The updated class is located in the file `DOMParserDTD.java`. Figure 10-16 shows the updated **main** method taken from the `DOMParserDTD` class. The differences between this **main** method and the **main** method of the `DOMParser` class are highlighted in boldface.

```
public static void main( String [] args ) throws Exception {
    DocumentBuilderFactory factory
        = DocumentBuilderFactory.newInstance();
    factory.setValidating( true );
    DocumentBuilder parser
        = factory.newDocumentBuilder();
    parser.setErrorHandler( new ParserErrorHandler() );
    Document document
        = parser.parse(
            new InputSource("dinosaurs.xml") );
    Element dinoList = document.getDocumentElement();
    NodeList dinosaurs
        = dinoList.getElementsByTagName("Dinosaur");
    Element currElement = null;
    String groupName = null;
    for( int i=0; i<dinosaurs.getLength(); i++ ) {
        currElement = (Element)dinosaurs.item(i);
        String nameValue
            = getSimpleElementText( currElement,
                                    "Name" );
        if ( nameValue.equals("Dilophosaurus") ) {
            groupName
                = getSimpleElementText( currElement,
                                        "Group" );
        }
    }
    System.out.println( "Dilophosaurus group: "
                        + groupName );
}
```

Figure 10-16   `main` method of the `DOMParserDTD` class

The error handler objects that are installed in the methods shown in Figures 10-15 and 10-16 are instances of the class **ParserErrorHandler**, shown in Figure 10-17, that you define for handling error messages. This class implements the **org.xml.sax.ErrorHandler** interface. The complete source code for the class **ParserErrorHandler** is located in the file called **ParserErrorHandler.java** in the **X:\Data\examples\xml** directory on the CD-ROM. (Here **X:** is the drive letter of the CD-ROM.) This error handler is about as simple as it can be. All it does is log each error, and for the case of fatal errors, it also throws an exception. Of course you are free to do whatever you consider to be appropriate in the error handler. This is just the starting point.

```
package examples.xml;
import org.xml.sax.ErrorHandler;
import org.xml.sax.SAXException;
import org.xml.sax.SAXParseException;
```

Figure 10-17   `ParserErrorHandler`: class for handling errors that occur while using a SAX parser

```
/**
 * Class of objects for handling errors that occur while
 * using a SAX parser
 */
public class ParserErrorHandler implements ErrorHandler {
   /**
    * Handle parser warnings by logging only
    */
   public void warning(SAXParseException exception)
      throws SAXException {
      System.out.println( "Warning:" + exception );
   }
   /**
    * Handle parser errors by logging only
    */
   public void error(SAXParseException exception)
      throws SAXException {
      System.out.println( "Error:" + exception );
   }
   /**
    * Handle fatal parser errors by logging and throwing
    * the exception
    */
   public void fatalError(SAXParseException exception)
      throws SAXException {
      System.out.println( "Fatal Error:" + exception );
      throw exception;
   }
}
```

Figure 10-17   `ParserErrorHandler:` class for handling errors that occur while using a SAX parser (continued)

10

XML Schema

Using a DTD is not the only way to express the rules that apply to the structure and content of a valid XML document. Programmers can also use the XML Schema language to do this. Figure 10-18 is the XML Schema that also defines the structure of the `dinosaurs.xml` file, and the source for it is located in the file called `dinosaur.xsd` in the `X:\Data\examples\xml` directory on the CD-ROM. (Here `X:` is the drive letter of the CD-ROM.) As you can see, an XML Schema file is much more verbose than a DTD file. However, it is an XML file in its own right and, unlike a DTD file, can be processed by standard XML tools. It is much more expressive than a DTD, and this allows it to define arbitrary relationships between elements. For example, XML Schema allows fine control over the format and data types of tag and attribute values. Schemas can enforce specific rules about the content of tags and attributes and also rules about the number and sequence of nested elements that can appear in a specific location.

```
<?xml version="1.0" encoding="UTF-8"?>
<xsd:schema xmlns:xsd="http://www.w3.org/2001/XMLSchema">
    <xsd:element name="DinoList">
        <xsd:complexType>
            <xsd:sequence>
                <xsd:element maxOccurs="unbounded"
                 minOccurs="1" ref="Dinosaur"/>
            </xsd:sequence>
        </xsd:complexType>
    </xsd:element>
    <xsd:element name="Dinosaur">
        <xsd:complexType>
            <xsd:sequence>
                <xsd:element ref="Name"/>
                <xsd:element ref="Group"/>
                <xsd:element ref="Range"/>
                <xsd:element ref="PhysicalAttr"/>
            </xsd:sequence>
            <xsd:attribute name="period" type="xsd:string"
             use="optional"/>
        </xsd:complexType>
    </xsd:element>
    <xsd:element name="Group" type="xsd:string"/>
    <xsd:element name="Height">
        <xsd:complexType>
            <xsd:simpleContent>
                <xsd:extension base="xsd:string">
                    <xsd:attribute name="unit"
                     type="xsd:string" use="optional"/>
                </xsd:extension>
            </xsd:simpleContent>
        </xsd:complexType>
    </xsd:element>
    <xsd:element name="Length">
        <xsd:complexType>
            <xsd:simpleContent>
                <xsd:extension base="xsd:string">
                    <xsd:attribute name="unit"
                     type="xsd:string" use="optional"/>
                </xsd:extension>
            </xsd:simpleContent>
        </xsd:complexType>
    </xsd:element>
    <xsd:element name="Name" type="xsd:string"/>
    <xsd:element name="PhysicalAttr">
        <xsd:complexType>
            <xsd:sequence>
                <xsd:element maxOccurs="1" minOccurs="0"
                 ref="Height"/>
                <xsd:element maxOccurs="1" minOccurs="0"
                 ref="Length"/>
```

Figure 10-18   XML schema that defines the structure of the `dinosaur.xml` file

```
                    <xsd:element maxOccurs="1" minOccurs="0"
                        ref="Weight"/>
                </xsd:sequence>
            </xsd:complexType>
        </xsd:element>
        <xsd:element name="Range">
            <xsd:complexType>
                <xsd:sequence>
                    <xsd:element maxOccurs="unbounded"
                        minOccurs="1" ref="Region"/>
                </xsd:sequence>
            </xsd:complexType>
        </xsd:element>
        <xsd:element name="Region" type="xsd:string"/>
        <xsd:element name="Weight">
            <xsd:complexType>
                <xsd:simpleContent>
                    <xsd:extension base="xsd:string">
                        <xsd:attribute name="unit"
                            type="xsd:string" use="optional"/>
                    </xsd:extension>
                </xsd:simpleContent>
            </xsd:complexType>
        </xsd:element>
    </xsd:schema>
```

10

Figure 10-18   XML schema that defines the structure of the `dinosaur.xml` file
(continued)

Other than presenting the concepts behind XML Schema, we won't go into detail on
the syntax and usage of the technology. The use of XML Schema is mostly behind the
scenes and not something that you are likely to have to deal with. It is a standard put
forward by the W3C (World Wide Web Consortium), and so you can find additional
details by visiting the W3C Web site at `http://www.w3.org/XML/Schema`.

Transforming XML Using XSLT

The concept of using stylesheets to handle the presentation of data separately from the
structure of data was introduced earlier in this chapter. Up to this point, this chapter has
focused on the data in the XML documents without much regard for how it might be
presented to users. Now you take a look at a powerful technology for transforming XML
data into other forms, such as HTML, to be viewed using a browser. This same technique can be used to transform data for presentation in other places, such as the small
display of a mobile phone or a Personal Digital Assistant (PDA) using Wireless Markup
Language (WML) or some similar technology.

XSLT (Extensible Stylesheet Language Transformations) is a standard that is XML-based. This means that an XSLT stylesheet is an XML document with its own tag definitions. These tags are used to define a number of templates within the stylesheet that correspond to elements within the document. Each template specifies how an element that matches the template should be transformed. It can also specify how all the elements nested within it are transformed, but, for modularity's sake, a template will usually transfer control to another template for the nested element.

XPath

As XML documents are processed and transformed, a mechanism is required for referring to all of the element and attribute names and associated values. XPath provides a mechanism that is intuitive, simple, and compact. As a component of JAXP and a standard in its own right, XPath has much more detail to it than can be discussed here. This discussion focuses on the parts of XPath that are used to specify elements and attributes for use within an XSL stylesheet and identifies them as you encounter them.

Stylesheet Example

Figure 10-19 is the XSL stylesheet, `dinosaurs.xsl`, created for transforming the `dinosaurs.xml` file into a series of HTML tables, one for each dinosaur in the list. It is located in the `X:\Data\examples\xml` directory on the CD-ROM. (Here `X:` is the drive letter of the CD-ROM.) A discussion of the contents of the file follows.

```
<?xml version="1.0" encoding="UTF-8"?>
<xsl:stylesheet
 xmlns:xsl="http://www.w3.org/1999/XSL/Transform"
 version="1.0">
    <xsl:output method="html"/>
    <xsl:template match="/">
        <html><head><title>Dinosaurs!</title></head>
        <body><h1>Dinosaurs!</h1>
        <xsl:apply-templates select="DinoList/Dinosaur"/>
        </body></html>
    </xsl:template>

    <xsl:template match="Dinosaur">
        <h2><xsl:value-of select="Name"/></h2>
        <table border="1" width="400" cellpadding="5">
        <tr>
        <th>Period</th>
        <td><xsl:value-of select="@period"/></td>
        </tr>
        <tr>
        <th>Group</th>
```

Figure 10-19   XSL stylesheet for transforming the `dinosaur.xml` file into a series of HTML tables

```
        <td><xsl:value-of select="Group"/></td>
        </tr>
        <xsl:apply-templates select="Range"/>
        <xsl:apply-templates select="PhysicalAttr"/>
        </table>
</xsl:template>

<xsl:template match="Range">
    <tr>
    <th>Range</th>
    <td>
    <ul>
    <xsl:for-each select="Region">
        <li><xsl:value-of select="."/></li>
    </xsl:for-each>
    </ul>
    </td>
    </tr>
</xsl:template>

<xsl:template match="PhysicalAttr">
    <xsl:if test="Height">
        <tr>
        <th>Height</th>
        <td>
        <xsl:value-of select="Height"/>
        <xsl:text disable-output-escaping="yes">
         
        </xsl:text>
        <xsl:value-of select="Height/@unit"/>
        </td>
        </tr>
    </xsl:if>
    <xsl:if test="Length">
        <tr>
        <th>Length</th>
        <td>
        <xsl:value-of select="Length"/>
        <xsl:text disable-output-escaping="yes">
         
        </xsl:text>
        <xsl:value-of select="Length/@unit"/>
        </td>
        </tr>
    </xsl:if>
    <xsl:if test="Weight">
        <tr>
        <th>Weight</th>
        <td>
        <xsl:value-of select="Weight"/>
        <xsl:text disable-output-escaping="yes">
```

Figure 10-19   XSL stylesheet for transforming the `dinosaur.xml` file into a series of HTML tables (continued)

```
             
            </xsl:text>
            <xsl:value-of select="Weight/@unit"/>
            </td>
            </tr>
        </xsl:if>
    </xsl:template>
</xsl:stylesheet>
```

Figure 10-19   XSL stylesheet for transforming the `dinosaur.xml` file into a series of HTML tables (continued)

The header of the XSL stylesheet should look familiar. The first line is the same opening line of most XML documents. The second statement is the opening tag of the stylesheet (the root element) and defines the `xsl` namespace that will be used throughout the stylesheet. All the stylesheet tags are prefixed with `xsl`. The third statement of the header specifies that the output of this transformation will be HTML. Everything else that follows is a template for use in transforming elements into HTML.

```
<?xml version="1.0" encoding="UTF-8"?>
<xsl:stylesheet
  xmlns:xsl="http://www.w3.org/1999/XSL/Transform"
  version="1.0">
    <xsl:output method="html"/>
```

This first template matches the root element of the document and so is the starting point of the transformation. This is the place to put the HTML tags that open and close the document. After opening the `<body>` element and adding a heading, this template yields control by applying the templates for the `<Dinosaur>` elements. The value of the `select` attribute of the `xsl:apply-templates` tag is an XPath expression that references the `<Dinosaur>` elements that are nested within a `<DinoList>` element. This reference is relative to the current position within the document. To create a reference with an absolute path, the XPath expression must begin with a forward slash (/) character.

After all the elements that match the `select` attribute value have been processed, the flow of control returns to this template. Then the HTML tags to close the body and the entire document are output.

```
<xsl:template match="/">
    <html><head><title>Dinosaurs!</title></head>
    <body><h1>Dinosaurs!</h1>
    <xsl:apply-templates select="DinoList/Dinosaur"/>
    </body></html>
</xsl:template>
```

The template used to process a `<Dinosaur>` element creates an HTML table for each element under a second-level heading that contains the name of the dinosaur. The content of the heading and the table cells are drawn from the XML document using xsl:value-of tags. Here again, the value of the select attribute is an XPath expression. Note that an @ character in an XPath expression is used to specify an attribute name. Element names do not use an @ character.

As with the template that matches the root element, this template also applies templates for other elements. In this case, templates for <Range> and <PhysicalAttr> elements are applied. After they finish, the table is closed.

```
<xsl:template match="Dinosaur">
    <h2><xsl:value-of select="Name"/></h2>
    <table border="1" width="400" cellpadding="5">
    <tr>
    <th>Period</th>
    <td><xsl:value-of select="@period"/></td>
    </tr>
    <tr>
    <th>Group</th>
    <td><xsl:value-of select="Group"/></td>
    </tr>
    <xsl:apply-templates select="Range"/>
    <xsl:apply-templates select="PhysicalAttr"/>
    </table>
</xsl:template>
```

The template for <Range> elements must handle an unbounded number of nested <Region> elements. To accomplish this, this template uses an xsl:for-each element to loop through all the <Region> elements. The text content of each one is output as an item in an unnumbered list.

```
<xsl:template match="Range">
    <tr>
    <th>Range</th>
    <td>
    <ul>
    <xsl:for-each select="Region">
        <li><xsl:value-of select="."/></li>
    </xsl:for-each>
    </ul>
    </td>
    </tr>
</xsl:template>
```

The template for transforming a <PhysicalAttr> element does not require a loop, but it must handle the cases where the <Height>, <Length>, and <Weight> elements are present and the cases where they are not. Fortunately, the xsl:if element is suited for the job. The name of the element from the XML document is used as the value of the test attribute, and the result will be true only if the element exists. If it exists, the content of the element is output along with its unit attribute with a nonbreaking space in between. The nonbreaking space is output within an xsl:text element in order that the escaping of output can be disabled. The processing of any present `<Length>` or `<Weight>` elements is handled in the same ways as for the `<Height>` element.

```
<xsl:template match="PhysicalAttr">
    <xsl:if test="Height">
        <tr>
        <th>Height</th>
        <td>
        <xsl:value-of select="Height"/>
        <xsl:text disable-output-escaping="yes">
         
        </xsl:text>
        <xsl:value-of select="Height/@unit"/>
        </td>
        </tr>
    </xsl:if>
```

The Java program that will apply this transformation to turn the XML file into an HTML file is straightforward. Figure 10-20 is the complete source code for the class `XSLTransform` located in the file called `XSLTransform.java` in the `X:\Data\examples\xml` directory on the CD-ROM. (Here `X:` is the drive letter of the CD-ROM.)

A `Transformer` object is created using the stylesheet as input. The XML file is used as input to create the `StreamSource` object. The output `StreamResult` object is associated with the HTML file to be created. Calling the `transform` method of the `Transformer` object generates the HTML file. Allowing for differences in browser versions, the output should be similar to Figure 10-21. Note that only two of the three generated tables are visible in this figure.

```
package examples.xml;
import java.io.FileOutputStream;
import javax.xml.transform.*;
import javax.xml.transform.stream.*;

public class XSLTransform {
    public static void main( String[] args ) throws Exception {
        TransformerFactory factory
            = TransformerFactory.newInstance();
        Transformer transformer
            = factory.newTransformer(
                new StreamSource( "dinosaurs.xsl" ) );
        StreamSource xmlsource
            = new StreamSource( "dinosaurs.xml" );
```

Figure 10-20   XSLTransform: example program to apply the transformation to turn an XML file into an HTML file

```
      StreamResult output
         = new StreamResult(
            new FileOutputStream( "dinosaurs.html" ) );
      transformer.transform( xmlsource, output );
   }
}
```

Figure 10-20   `XSLTransform:` example program to apply the transformation to turn an XML file into an HTML file (continued)

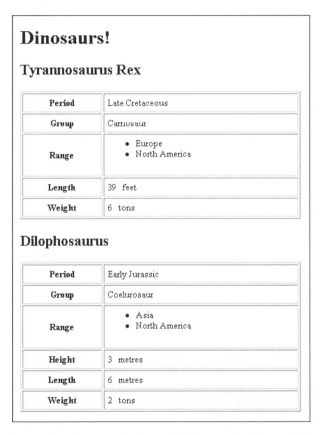

Figure 10-21   Output HTML file created by applying the XSL stylesheet

CHAPTER SUMMARY

❑ Using XML provides a way to create portable data to complement the portable programs that are created with the Java programming language. XML is a markup language with a structure that is similar to HTML, but with stricter rules and the ability for users to define their own tags.

◻ The Java platform, Standard Edition, added support for the Java API for XML Processing (JAXP) in version 1.4. This support included support for parsing documents using both SAX and DOM, and for transforming documents using XSLT.

◻ The difference between using SAX and DOM for parsing documents is that SAX processes the input XML document sequentially, whereas DOM begins by building a hierarchical model of the document that allows the programmer to access data in the model in a random order fashion.

◻ The DOM API can also be used to create an XML document in memory and then output the created document into a text file.

◻ Documents that follow the rules for correct XML syntax are considered to be well formed. However, there is much more to a document than simply having correct syntax.

◻ XML allows for developing files that specify how the elements within a document are to be used. Two approaches are worth noting. The use of a Document Type Definition (DTD) is the established technology.

◻ A more powerful, XML-based technology called XML Schema has been recently developed and will likely eventually replace the use of DTD files.

◻ The Extensible Stylesheet Language (XSL) supports the creation of stylesheets that can be used to define how an XML document can be transformed into something such as HTML that is readily viewable in a friendly format.

REVIEW QUESTIONS

1. Which of the following fragments are not well-formed XML? Select all that apply.

   a. `<tag1>text</tag1>`

   b. `<tag1/>`

   c. `<tag1 attr=value/>`

   d. `</tag1>`

   e. `<tag1>text<tag1/>`

2. Which of the following fragments are not well-formed XML? Select all that apply.

   a. `<tag1>text<tag2>more text</tag2></tag1>`

   b. `<tag1><tag2>more text</tag2>text</tag1>`

   c. `<tag1>text</tag1><tag2>more text</tag2>`

   d. `<tag1>text<tag2>more text</tag1></tag2>`

   e. `<tag1></tag1>text<tag2>more text</tag2>`

3. Which of the following fragments are not well-formed HTML? Select all that apply.

a. `<!-- add more data here if x &gt; y -->`

b. `<tag1>is the value > eleven?</tag1>`

c. `<!-- add more data here if x > y -->`

d. `<xyz:tag1>text<tag2>more text</tag2></xyz:tag1>`

e. `<xyz:tag1>text<xyz:tag2>more text</xyz:tag2></xyz:tag1>`

4. True or False: All valid HTML documents are also well-formed XML documents.

5. To use the SAX API it is necessary to define a class that implements which interface? Select the best answer.

a. `org.xml.sax.ParserHandler`

b. `org.xml.sax.DefaultHandler`

c. `org.xml.sax.ErrorHandler`

d. `org.xml.sax.SAXHandler`

e. `org.xml.sax.ContentHandler`

6. True or False: A significant advantage of the DOM API over the SAX API is that the DOM API uses the collection classes that are part of the Java platform to hold the data it parses.

7. Which of the following DTD statements defines an element with three required nested elements? Choose the best answer.

a. `<!ELEMENT Tag1 (Tag2?,Tag3?,Tag4?)>`

b. `<!ELEMENT Tag1+, Tag2+,Tag3+ (Tag4)>`

c. `<!ELEMENT Tag1 (Tag2*,Tag3*,Tag4?)>`

d. `<!ELEMENT Tag1 (Tag2+,Tag3+,Tag4?)>`

e. `<!ELEMENT Tag1 (Tag2,Tag+,Tag4+)>`

8. What technology that is part of JAXP defines the syntax for specifying elements of an XML document?

9. Which XSL tag can be used to output the value of the `name` attribute of the current element? Select the best answer.

a. `<xsl:value-of select="@name"/>`

b. `<xsl:text select="@name"/>`

c. `<xsl:text select="name"/>`

d. `<xsl:value-of select="name"/>`

e. `<xsl:value-of select="/@name"/>`

10. Which XSL tag can be used to output the value of the ID element nested within the current element? Select the best answer.

    a. `<xsl:text select="@ID"/>`

    b. `<xsl:value-of select="/ID"/>`

    c. `<xsl:value-of select="@ID"/>`

    d. `<xsl:text select="/ID"/>`

    e. `<xsl:value-of select="ID"/>`

11. What class of objects is used to apply the XSLT templates and create the output file?

PROGRAMMING EXERCISES

Debugging

1. Correct all the errors in the XML document in the file `debug10_1.xml` in the `X:\Data\questions\c10` directory on the CD-ROM. (Here `X:` is the drive letter of the CD-ROM.)

2. Correct all the errors in the DTD in the file `debug10_2.dtd` so that it can be used for the corrected XML document in the previous question. The file is in the `X:\Data\questions\c10` directory on the CD-ROM. (Here `X:` is the drive letter of the CD-ROM.)

3. Correct all the errors in the class `Debug10_3` to create a **main** method that will successfully parse the specified XML document. The class is in the file `Debug10_3.java` in the `X:\Data\questions\c10` directory on the CD-ROM. (Here `X:` is the drive letter of the CD-ROM.)

4. Correct all the errors in the class `Debug10_4` to create a **main** method that will successfully generate the specified XML document. The class is in the file `Debug10_4.java` in the `X:\Data\questions\c10` directory on the CD-ROM. (Here `X:` is the drive letter of the CD-ROM.)

5. Correct all the errors in the XSLT stylesheet in the file `debug10_5.xsl` so that it can be used with the corrected XML document `debug10_1.xml` from question 1 to generate an HTML file that can be viewed in a Web browser. The file is in the `X:\Data\questions\c10` directory on the CD-ROM. (Here `X:` is the drive letter of the CD-ROM.)

Complete the Solution

1. Extract the file `X:\Data\questions\c10\Complete10_1.xml` from the CD-ROM. (Here `X:` is the drive letter of the CD-ROM.) Complete the XML document by adding another property, `Major`, to each `Student` element. This new element requires an attribute to indicate whether the student's major is an honors or general program.

2. Extract the file `X:\Data\questions\c10\Complete10_2.java` from the CD-ROM. (Here `X:` is the drive letter of the CD-ROM.) Add a `startElement` method to the class so that it can be used as a SAX parser.

3. Extract the file `X:\Data\questions\c10\Complete10_3.java` from the CD-ROM. (Here `X:` is the drive letter of the CD-ROM.) Add the statements required so that the `main` method is able to output an XML document with a `StudentList` element and one representative `Student` element.

4. Extract the file `X:\Data\questions\c10\Complete10_4.java` from the CD-ROM. (Here `X:` is the drive letter of the CD-ROM.) Add the support needed to enable validation for the XML documents that the program parses.

5. Extract the file `X:\Data\questions\c10\Complete10_5.xsl` from the CD-ROM. (Here `X:` is the drive letter of the CD-ROM.) Add the missing templates so that the resulting stylesheet can be used to transform the `Complete10_1.xml` file into HTML for easy viewing.

10

Discovery

1. Define a set of XML elements that can be used to create an XML document that describes a person's music collection. Be as flexible as possible and take into account different music media such as CD, MP3, vinyl album, etc. Develop both a DTD and an XML Schema that are used to validate the music collection document.

2. Rework the example XSLT stylesheet for the `dinosaurs.xml` file so that all the dinosaur information contained in the document is presented in a single table instead of a series of separate tables.

11

NETWORK PROGRAMMING

In this chapter you will:

- Perform network I/O using the core classes in the package `java.net`
- Write programs that establish connections to URLs and perform stream I/O between URLs
- Read and write data to local and remote sites using TCP/IP sockets and datagram sockets
- Use Remote Method Invocation (RMI) to develop classes of objects that are accessible from a server
- Learn the steps involved in compiling and deploying an application that uses RMI
- Be introduced to the Java Naming and Directory Interface (JNDI)
- Discover the relationship between CORBA, RMI-IIOP, and the Java Interface Definition Language (IDL)

INTRODUCTION

Input and output (I/O) is not restricted to your workstation or the personal computer (PC) that hosts the Java platform. There is a high probability that you are connected to a network. If you are not on a local area network (LAN), you may have a dial-up connection to the Internet. For many programmers, the need to program for the Internet or Web-oriented HTML browsers is among the main reasons for learning the Java programming language. Unlike most other programming languages, the Java programming language is designed for use in just such an environment. The Java platform includes a package `java.net`, specifically so that you can make connections and perform I/O to and from other stations on the network.

A program can communicate with another program on the same host or on a different host. Often, the programs have a client-server relationship with each other. For example, if you are reading an HTML document in a Web browser, the system from which the document originates is the server, and your workstation is the client. When you are developing and locally testing applets written in the Java programming language, your workstation is both server and client.

You can perform network programming at different levels. For example, you can work with URLs and sockets. A socket is an abstraction of the end points of connections between processes or applications. The term *socket* originated in the UNIX environment, where it applied to communication between unrelated processes. Using the Java platform, you can set up connections and communicate over TCP/IP sockets. With a little more programming effort, you can send and receive packets of data using datagram sockets.

Most of the classes in **java.net** can be categorized by whether they support URLs, TCP/IP sockets, or datagram sockets. Some classes are used by all supported protocols. For example, instances of the **InetAddress** class represent Internet Protocol (IP) addresses. An IP address is a 32-bit or, more recently, a 128-bit binary value that identifies one host on the Internet. To be human-readable, an IP address can be represented as decimal numbers separated by dots, as in 63.208.157.52, or by a string, such as **http://www.course.com**.

WORKING WITH URLS

You are probably used to specifying URLs to your Web browser. As you know, URLs begin with a protocol specification, such as **http** (for HyperText Transfer Protocol) or **ftp** (for File Transfer Protocol), followed by a colon and two forward slashes (**://**) and the host name, along with optional file and port information.

The **java.net** package contains classes that are designed around URLs. The sample program in Figure 11-1 demonstrates two of these: **URL** and **URLConnection**. Use these classes for creating and manipulating URLs. You can get the file associated with a URL and process the contents in any manner in which you choose to program. Also, you can connect to the host of a URL and perform more complex operations.

The safest way to communicate with the host of a URL is through a **URLConnection** object. After you connect, you can request and receive information. However, a **URLConnection** object closes after one exchange, and you cannot sustain a long-running conversation. You must reestablish the link for every exchange. To create a connection that can stay open, you should use a TCP/IP socket.

Figure 11-1 is a simple program that connects to the home page for IBM Software.

```
package examples.network;
import java.net.*;
import java.util.Date;
/** An example class to demonstrate the use of URL
  * and URLConnection class objects
  */
```

Figure 11-1   TryURLObjects: a program demonstrating the use of the URL and URLConnection objects

```
public class TryURLObjects {
   /** The test method for the class
    * @param args not used
    */
   public static void main( String[] args ) {
      try {
         URL ibmsw = new URL( "http://www.ibm.com/software/" );
         URLConnection ibmswConn = ibmsw.openConnection();
         long lastMod = ibmswConn.getLastModified();
         if ( lastMod > 0 ) {
            Date lastModDate = new Date( lastMod );
            System.out.println( ibmsw
               + " was last modified " + lastModDate );
         } else {
            System.out.println( "Date that " + ibmsw
               + " was last modified is unknown" );
         }
         String contentType = ibmswConn.getContentType();
         System.out.println( ibmsw
            + " has content type " + contentType );
      }
      catch( Exception x ) {
         System.out.println( x );
      }
   }
}
```

Figure 11-1 `TryURLObjects`: a program demonstrating the use of the `URL` and
`URLConnection` objects (continued)

The output is of the following form:

```
Date that http://www.ibm.com/software/ was last modified is unknown
http://www.ibm.com/software/ has content type text/html
```

Notice how easy it is to construct a **URL** object by passing a string containing a URL
to the constructor. To open a connection, you call the method **openConnection** for
the **URL** object. This method creates and then returns a **URLConnection** object.

This program queries when the page was last modified by calling **getLastModified** for
the **URLConnection** object. A return value of zero means that the last modification date
is unknown. Assuming the returned value is nonzero, the program creates a **Date** object
and then prints the date in a readable format by taking advantage of the fact that the **Date**
class overrides the **Object.toString** method to display the date information contained
within the object in a format that is easy to understand. Next, the **getContentType**
method is used to determine the content type as defined in the content-type header field
contained within the page.

This simple program demonstrates how easy it is to set up a connection with systems that host URLs. You can perform many meaningful activities with URL connections. For example, using the methods shown in this sample, you could write an application to monitor when URLs on your site are updated. You also can send information to the URL, if the page has a form that has been set up in some other way to receive data.

This program is a rudimentary Web browser. All that is required to convert it to a usable, though limited, Web browser is logic to read the page, to interpret and display its contents, and to follow the hypertext links coded in the page.

URLs beginning with `http://` or `ftp://` are examples of specific proper subsets of a generic addressing technology called Uniform Resource Identifier (URI). In other words, every URL is a URI, but the opposite is not true. If a URI is not a URL, it falls into a third class called Uniform Resource Name (URN). A URN names a resource but doesn't contain the information necessary to locate the resource as a URL would do.

Because URI is a more inclusive term, it is has become commonly used in technical specifications in place of the term URL. In recognition of the rising use of the term, the Java platform, beginning with v1.4, has added the class **java.net.URI**. The URI class contains a method, **toURL**, which can be used to construct a URL object from a URI object to be compatible with older programs that only work with URL objects. If the URI is not a valid URL, either **IllegalArgumentException** or **MalformedURLException** is thrown.

WORKING WITH SOCKETS

Different programs can communicate through communications channels called sockets. You can use sockets to transfer data between unrelated processes that can be running on the same workstation or on different hosts on a network. The concept of sockets originated in UNIX environments but is now supported on a wide range of operating systems. The Java platform supports two types of sockets: TCP/IP and datagram, including multicast datagram.

TCP/IP Sockets

A TCP/IP socket is connection-oriented. When you create a socket, you create an endpoint for a connection between two processes. This is analogous to plugging a telephone into a suitable outlet in the wall. The system at the other end of the "conversation" must also be plugged into a suitable outlet, and the telephone company plays the role of the network by connecting the points. The programs at the two ends of the socket can write to and read from the socket. This is analogous to using a pipe to pass data between streams in a multithreaded program.

You can easily read and write to TCP/IP sockets using stream I/O. All you need to do is set up the socket by creating a **Socket** object, ask the socket for its input stream and

ple program in Figure 11-2 demonstrates this process.

The ease of use of TCP/IP sockets is one of the most appealing features of network programming in the Java programming language. Because sockets are connection-oriented, you can use them as two-way communications channels over a period of time. If you are sending more than a brief message—for example, if you are transferring a file—you can be sure that no parts of the transmission are lost and fail to reach the destination.

However, TCP/IP sockets impose an overhead that datagram sockets do not have. A connection requires setup time before and shutdown time after you transfer any data. Therefore, delivery of information is slower than with datagram sockets, but more reliable.

A sample program that creates a TCP/IP socket with a server side and a client side follows. In this case, the client and server reside on the same host. Nevertheless, they run as separate processes, just like client and server programs on different hosts. To identify its server, the client side uses a combination of a server-host name and a port number that makes up a unique identifier to the server. The server is not hard coded for a particular port because the socket is created with the port number as an argument of the socket constructor.

Figure 11-2 is the server class `AdditionServer`. A detailed breakdown of the class follows the code.

11

```java
package examples.network;
import java.io.*;
import java.net.*;
import java.util.StringTokenizer;
/** An example class that uses the server socket class
  */
public class AdditionServer {
   private int port;
   // This is not a reserved port number
   static final int DEFAULT_PORT = 8189;
   /** Constructor
     * @param port The port where the server
     *         will listen for requests
     */
   AdditionServer( int port ) {
      this.port = port;
   }
   /** The method that does the work for the class */
   public void run() {
      try {
         ServerSocket ss = new ServerSocket( port );
         Socket incoming = ss.accept();
         BufferedReader in;
```

Figure 11-2   `AdditionServer`: an example TCP/IP socket server program

```
            in = new BufferedReader( new InputStreamReader(
               incoming.getInputStream() ) );
            PrintWriter out = new PrintWriter(
               incoming.getOutputStream(), true );
            String str;
            while ( !( str = in.readLine() ).equals( "" ) ) {
               double result = 0;
               StringTokenizer st = new StringTokenizer( str );
               try {
                  while( st.hasMoreTokens() ) {
                     Double d = new Double( st.nextToken() );
                     result += d.doubleValue();
                  }
                  out.println( "The result is " + result );
               }
               catch( NumberFormatException nfe ) {
                  out.println( "Sorry, your list contains "
                              + "an invalid number" );
               }
            }
            incoming.close();
         }
         catch( IOException iox ) {
            System.out.println( iox );
            iox.printStackTrace();
         }
   }
   /** The test method for the class
     * @param args[0] Optional port number in place of
     *           the default
     */
   public static void main( String[] args ) {
      int port = DEFAULT_PORT;
      if ( args.length > 0 ) {
         port = Integer.parseInt( args[0] );
      }
      AdditionServer addServe = new AdditionServer( port );
      addServe.run();
   }
}
```

Figure 11-2   `AdditionServer`: an example TCP/IP socket server program (continued)

The following breakdown of the code does not follow the order of statements in the program listing, so that explanation can follow more closely the order in which statements are executed.

The constructor of an **AdditionServer** object, shown next, stores the port number that it receives as an argument:

```
public class AdditionServer {
   private int port;
```

```
static final int DEFAULT_PORT = 8189;
AdditionServer( int port ) {
    this.port = port;
}
```

The **main** method creates an **AdditionServer** object, **addServe**, using a port number that you can supply as a command-line argument or take from an arbitrarily chosen default.

The client and server must use the same port, and that port must not be used or reserved by another process. A convention on UNIX and some other operating systems is to reserve port numbers 0 to 1023 for system services. If you run the server and client in separate threads of one multithreaded program, the client thread can create the server thread object and pass the port number to the server constructor. Otherwise, the programmers of the client and server sides must agree on a port number to use.

The **main** method starts the server by calling the **run** method of this class:

```
public static void main( String[] args ) {
    int port = DEFAULT_PORT;
    if ( args.length > 0 ) {
        port = Integer.parseInt( args[0] );
    }
    AdditionServer addServe = new AdditionServer( port );
    addServe.run();
}
```

The **run** method does all the work of this server. It creates a **ServerSocket** object for the port and then calls the method **accept**. This is an important method defined by the **ServerSocket** class. The nature of a server is to listen passively to its port. The **accept** method puts the server into a wait state until input arrives, and then it returns a socket:

```
public void run() {
    try {
        ServerSocket ss = new ServerSocket( port );
        Socket incoming = ss.accept();
```

When the connection is established, the server asks the socket for its input stream by calling the method **getInputStream**. Notice that in the code that follows, you use buffered, character-oriented input by wrapping a **BufferedReader** object and an **InputStreamReader** object around the **InputStream** object returned by **getInputStream**. Similarly, on the output side, you ask the socket for its output stream and wrap a **PrintWriter** object around the **OutputStream** object returned. The second argument of the constructor for **PrintWriter** is a **boolean** value set to **true** when you want every call of **println** to flush the output buffer. Flushing the output buffer with each **println** call is useful for debugging, because any output will appear as soon as possible, but it does have a negative effect on the performance of the program.

```
BufferedReader in;
in = new BufferedReader( new InputStreamReader(
    incoming.getInputStream() ) );
```

11

```
PrintWriter out = new PrintWriter(
    incoming.getOutputStream(),true );
```

After setting up the streams, you can use ordinary stream I/O to and from the socket. This server only reads and adds numbers. It reads from the socket, one line at a time. An empty line indicates the end of the input. The method uses the classes **StringTokenizer** and **Double** to extract numbers from the input and convert them to type **double** so that it can add them. After handling the last token, the server writes the sum of the numbers to the output stream.

```
String str;
    while ( !( str = in.readLine() ).equals( "" ) ) {
        double result = 0;
        StringTokenizer st = new StringTokenizer( str );
        try {
            while( st.hasMoreTokens() ) {
                Double d = new Double( st.nextToken() );
                result += d.doubleValue();
            }
            out.println( "The result is " + result );
        }
```

Finally, the server closes the socket. The server also contains handlers for the two types of exceptions that may occur. It has nested try blocks with catch blocks for **NumberFormatException** and **IOException**:

```
        catch( NumberFormatException nfe ) {
            out.println ( "Sorry, your list contains "
                            + "an invalid number" );
        }
    }
    incoming.close();
}
catch( IOException iox ) {
    System.out.println( iox );
    iox.printStackTrace();
}
}
```

Figure 11-3 is the client-side class that goes with the server-side class in Figure 11-2. Again, the detailed breakdown follows the class.

```
package examples.network;
import java.io.*;
import java.net.*;
/** A client-side class that uses a TCP/IP socket
  */
```

Figure 11-3   AdditionClient: an example TCP/IP socket client program

```
public class AdditionClient {
   private InetAddress host;
   private int port;
   // This is not a reserved port number
   static final int DEFAULT_PORT = 8189;
   /** Constructor
     * @param host Internet address of the host
     *          where the server is located
     * @param port Port number on the host where
     *          the server is listening
     */
   public AdditionClient( InetAddress host, int port ) {
      this.host = host;
      this.port = port;
   }
   /** The method used to start a client object
     */
   public void run() {
      try {
         Socket client = new Socket( host, port );
         BufferedReader socketIn;
         socketIn
            = new BufferedReader(
               new InputStreamReader(
               client.getInputStream() ) );
         PrintWriter socketOut
            = new PrintWriter(
               client.getOutputStream(), true );
         String numbers = "1.2 3.4 5.6";
         System.out.println( "Adding the numbers "
                           + numbers + " together" );
         socketOut.println( numbers );
         System.out.println( socketIn.readLine() );
         socketOut.println ( "" );
      }
      catch( IOException iox ) {
         System.out.println( iox );
         iox.printStackTrace();
      }
   }
   /** The test method for the class
     * @param args[0] optional port number
     * @param args[1] optional host name
     */
   public static void main( String[] args ) {
      try {
         InetAddress host = InetAddress.getLocalHost();
         int port = DEFAULT_PORT;
         if ( args.length > 0 ) {
            port = Integer.parseInt( args[0] );
         }
```

Figure 11-3 `AdditionClient`: an example TCP/IP socket client program (continued)

```
            if ( args.length > 1 ) {
                host = InetAddress.getByName( args[1] );
            }
            AdditionClient addClient
                = new AdditionClient( host, port );
            addClient.run();
        }
        catch ( UnknownHostException uhx ) {
            System.out.println( uhx );
            uhx.printStackTrace();
        }
    }
}
```

Figure 11-3   `AdditionClient`: an example TCP/IP socket client program (continued)

The structure of the client class, `AdditionClient`, is complementary to that of the server. The constructor stores the host address, which is of type **InetAddress**, as well as the port number. The class **InetAddress** is defined in the **java.net** package to represent IP addresses:

```
public class AdditionClient {
    private InetAddress host;
    private int port;
    // This is not a reserved port number
    static final int DEFAULT_PORT = 8189;
    public AdditionClient( InetAddress host, int port ) {
        this.host = host;
        this.port = port;
    }
```

As on the server, let the port number be either a command-line parameter or a stored arbitrary default value. Here, the default value is `8189`.

Beginning with version 1.4 of the Java platform, 128-bit Internet addresses were supported as part of the overall support for Internet Protocol Version 6 (IPv6). To accomplish this, two new subclasses of **InetAddress** were introduced, **Inet4Address** and **Inet6Address**, to represent both the old and the new. However, **InetAddress** should continue to be used unless there is a need to know the exact addressing scheme.

The **main** method of the `AdditionClient` class gets the IP address for the server host by calling the method **InetAddress.getLocalHost** to serve as the default value. The user can override this default by specifying a different host address as the second command-line parameter. With these two pieces of information, the **main** method can create a client object, **addClient**, and then start the client by calling its **run** method:

```
public static void main( String[] args ) {
    try {
        InetAddress host = InetAddress.getLocalHost();
        int port = DEFAULT_PORT;
        if ( args.length > 0 ) {
            port = Integer.parseInt( args[0] );
        }
        if ( args.length > 1 ) {
            host = InetAddress.getByName( args[1] );
        }
        AdditionClient addClient
            = new AdditionClient( host, port );
        addClient.run();
    }
    catch ( UnknownHostException uhx ) {
        System.out.println( uhx );
        uhx.printStackTrace();
    }
}
```

Like the server, the client has its work performed by its **run** method. The first job of this method is to create the client end of the socket. Next, **run** sets up a **BufferedReader** object for input and a **PrintWriter** object for output, much like the server does, except that these objects are associated with the sides of the socket that are opposite those of the server end:

```
public void run() {
    try {
        Socket client = new Socket( host, port );
        BufferedReader socketIn;
        socketIn = new BufferedReader(
            new InputStreamReader(
            client.getInputStream() ) );
        PrintWriter socketOut = new PrintWriter(
            client.getOutputStream(), true );
```

The processing is simple: The client writes a textual representation of three numbers to the socket. Then, it reads whatever the server sends back and outputs that line to **System.out**:

```
String numbers = "1.2 3.4 5.6";
System.out.println( "Adding the numbers "
                    + numbers + " together" );
socketOut.println( numbers );
System.out.println( socketIn.readLine() );
socketOut.println( "" );
}
```

Like the server, the client catches **IOException** objects that can occur during any kind of stream I/O:

```
catch( IOException iox ) {
    System.out.println( iox );
    iox.printStackTrace();
}
}
```

For this application to work, TCP/IP must be installed and running on your system. A working Internet connection is proof that TCP/IP is running. You must start the server class in one window and then start the client in a different window.

To run this application:

1. Open two command-line windows. One will be used for the server program and the other for the client program.

2. If you are running from the CD-ROM that contains all sample programs, make the **X:\Data\examples\network** directory the current directory in both windows. (Here **X:** represents the drive letter of the CD-ROM.) If you haven't already done so, make the **X:\Data** directory part of your classpath by entering the following command in both windows:

   `SET CLASSPATH=X:\Data;%CLASSPATH%`

3. In one window, start the server by entering the following command, optionally adding a port number to the end of this command string. If you do not specify a port, 8189 is used.

   `java examples.network.AdditionServer [port]`

4. In the other window, start the client by entering the following command, optionally adding a port number to match the port on the server. If you do not specify a port, 8189 is used. You also can specify the host name of the system on which the server process is running. If you do not specify a host name, the local host name is used.

   `java examples.network.AdditionClient [port]`

   If you run and receive a message saying the connection is refused, it could be that another program on your computer is using the same port number. To work around this problem, try running the client again with a different port number. For example, try port 8190 if the default port number 8189 isn't working.

5. If you cannot open a connection successfully, stop the server by pressing **Ctrl+C** in the window in which you started the server.

   If the connection is successful, the output appears in the client window as follows:

   `Adding the numbers 1.2 3.4 5.6 together`
   `The result is 10.2`

   Then, both the client and server programs stop.

Datagram Sockets

Datagram sockets are not connection-oriented. Instead of establishing a two-way connection that is used to send many blocks of data back and forth, you send self-contained packets of data whenever necessary. Each packet contains information that identifies the network destination in addition to the content of your message. The class **DatagramPacket** represents these packets. The amount of data transmitted is less than that sent over a TCP/IP socket, because TCP/IP sockets transmit additional packets for connection setup and teardown. They also transmit checksum data to detect data corruption. (However, while a connection is open, datagram sockets give you no speed advantage.) On the other hand, delivery of datagram packets is not guaranteed. The intended recipient might miss a packet due to some network error or congestion, and neither the sender nor recipient may be aware of the loss. The User Datagram Protocol (UDP) used by these sockets makes no attempt to recover from lost or damaged packets.

Datagram sockets provide an alternative communications interface to TCP/IP sockets. For example, the Simple Network Management Protocol (SNMP) uses datagrams, and games played across a network often use datagrams. Use datagram sockets, rather than TCP/IP sockets, if your application meets the following criteria:

- You want to avoid the overhead of opening and closing connections.
- The nodes in the network periodically send relatively short messages to each other.
- Losing the occasional packet does not have serious repercussions.

Figure 11-4 is a sample program that uses datagrams for communication between the client and server. The classes **DatagramAdditionServer** and **DatagramAdditionClient** perform exactly the same functions as **AdditionServer** and **AdditionClient** did in the previous TCP/IP socket example, except that they use datagrams. The data being transferred between client and server has not changed. Because the only difference between the client-server examples is the transport mechanism, only the **run** methods of the two classes have changed.

Figure 11-4 shows the **run** method of the server class, **DatagramAdditionServer**. Only the **run** method is shown because the rest of the class is exactly the same as **AdditionServer**. A detailed breakdown of the method follows the code.

```
public void run() {
   try {
      DatagramSocket ss = new DatagramSocket( port );
      byte[] buffer = new byte[256];
      DatagramPacket inDgp = new DatagramPacket( buffer,
         buffer.length );
```

Figure 11-4   `DatagramAdditionServer: run` method of an example datagram socket server program

```
        String req, rsp;
        do {
           ss.receive( inDgp );
           InetAddress senderAddress = inDgp.getAddress();
           int senderPort = inDgp.getPort();
           req = new String( inDgp.getData(), 0,
                              inDgp.getLength() );
           if ( ! req.equals( "" ) ) {
              double result = 0;
              StringTokenizer st = new StringTokenizer( req );
              try {
                 while( st.hasMoreTokens() ) {
                    Double d = new Double( st.nextToken() );
                    result += d.doubleValue();
                 }
                 rsp = "The result is " + result;
              } catch( NumberFormatException nfe ) {
                 rsp = "Sorry, your list contains an "
                       + "invalid number";
              }
              DatagramPacket outDgp
                 = new DatagramPacket( rsp.getBytes(),
                                       rsp.length(),
                                       senderAddress,
                                       senderPort );
              ss.send( outDgp );
           }
        } while( ! req.equals( "" ) );
        ss.close();
     }
     catch( IOException iox ) {
        System.out.println( iox );
        iox.printStackTrace();
     }
}
```

Figure 11-4   `DatagramAdditionServer:` **run** method of an example datagram
socket server program (continued)

The **run** method of the server begins by creating a datagram socket on the prearranged
port number that is known by the client.

```
        DatagramSocket ss = new DatagramSocket( port );
```

In preparation for the arrival of the first request datagram, the server allocates a buffer
for the incoming requests and creates an incoming **DatagramPacket** object that will
use this buffer. This is necessary because **DatagramPacket** objects do not have buffers
of their own. The request and response will be handled as **String** objects, so the references **req** and **rsp** are declared for later use.

```
byte[] buffer = new byte[256];
DatagramPacket inDgp = new DatagramPacket( buffer,
    buffer.length );
String req, rsp;
```

A **do-while** loop begins the server's loop for receiving requests and returning responses. The first statement within the loop receives the incoming request datagram. The address and port of the client that sent the request are extracted and saved for later use. The request data is taken from the datagram and put into a **String** object for easier manipulation:

```
do {
    ss.receive( inDgp );
    InetAddress senderAddress = inDgp.getAddress();
    int senderPort = inDgp.getPort();
    req = new String( inDgp.getData(), 0,
                      inDgp.getLength() );
```

If a non-null request string is received, the processing of the request begins. The processing in this example is similar to the processing in the TCP/IP example, with the main difference being that the response string cannot be sent to the client by stream I/O, but instead is put into a **String** object for later transmission in a datagram:

```
if ( ! req.equals( "" ) ) {
    double result = 0;
    StringTokenizer st = new StringTokenizer( req );
    try {
        while( st.hasMoreTokens() ) {
            Double d = new Double( st.nextToken() );
            result += d.doubleValue();
        }
        rsp = "The result is " + result;
    } catch( NumberFormatException nfe ) {
        rsp = "Sorry, your list contains an "
            + "invalid number";
    }
```

11

After the response string is determined, an output **DatagramPacket** object is created, and the response, along with the client's address and port, is put into it. After the outgoing datagram is constructed, it is sent to the client using the same socket that was used to receive the original request:

```
DatagramPacket outDgp
    = new DatagramPacket( rsp.getBytes(),
                          rsp.length(),
                          senderAddress,
                          senderPort );
    ss.send( outDgp );
}
```

The server loop is terminated when a datagram containing an empty string is received. Then the datagram socket is closed and the server is finished.

```
    } while( ! req.equals( "" ) );
    ss.close();
```

Figure 11-5 is the **run** method of the client-side class, `DatagramAdditionClient`. Only the **run** method is shown because the rest of the class is exactly the same as `AdditionClient`. A detailed breakdown of the method follows the code.

```
public void run() {
   try {
      DatagramSocket client = new DatagramSocket();
      String numbers = "1.2 3.4 5.6";
      DatagramPacket outDgp = new DatagramPacket( numbers.getBytes(),
                              numbers.length(),
                              host, port );
      client.send( outDgp );
      System.out.println( "Adding the numbers "
                           + numbers + " together" );
      byte[] buffer = new byte[256];
      DatagramPacket inDgp
         = new DatagramPacket( buffer, buffer.length );
      client.receive( inDgp );
      String rsp = new String( inDgp.getData(), 0,
                           inDgp.getLength() );
      System.out.println( rsp );
      String quit = "";
      outDgp.setData( quit.getBytes() );
      outDgp.setLength( quit.length() );
      client.send( outDgp );
      client.close();
   }
   catch( IOException iox ) {
      System.out.println( iox );
      iox.printStackTrace();
   }
}
```

Figure 11-5   `DatagramAdditionClient: run` method of an example datagram
socket client program

The **run** method of the client begins by constructing the datagram socket needed for sending and receiving information. It does not specify a port number because a default

tion is put into each **DatagramPacket** object and is not kept with the datagram socket:

```
DatagramSocket client = new DatagramSocket();
```

The data to be sent to the server is defined in a **String** object. The **DatagramPacket** object to be used for sending the information is created and the data, in the form of a byte array, is put into the **DatagramPacket** object, along with the host address and port number:

```
String numbers = "1.2 3.4 5.6";
DatagramPacket outDgp = new DatagramPacket( numbers.getBytes(),
                                            numbers.length(),
                                            host, port );
```

The outgoing **DatagramPacket** object is sent, and a message is written to the console:

```
client.send( outDgp );
System.out.println( "Adding the numbers "
                    + numbers + " together" );
```

In preparation for receiving a response, a buffer is created for the response and the incoming **DatagramPacket** object is created with the buffer and its length as constructor parameters. The same socket that was used to send the request datagram is then used to receive the response datagram:

```
byte[] buffer = new byte[256];
DatagramPacket inDgp
   = new DatagramPacket( buffer, buffer.length );
client.receive( inDgp );
```

The response is extracted from the incoming datagram data and put into a **String** object. The response is then written to the console:

```
String rsp = new String( inDgp.getData(), 0,
                         inDgp.getLength() );
System.out.println( rsp );
```

To stop the server, the client puts the empty string and its length into the outgoing **DatagramPacket** object and sends it. It isn't necessary to set the host address and port because that is unchanged from the previous outgoing **DatagramPacket** object. After the final **DatagramPacket** object is sent, the socket is closed:

```
String quit = "";
outDgp.setData( quit.getBytes() );
outDgp.setLength( quit.length() );
client.send( outDgp );
client.close();
```

11

For this application to work, UDP must be installed and running on your system. Typically, a working Internet connection is proof that UDP is installed and running. You must start the server class in one window and then start the client in a different window.

To run this application

1. Open two command-line windows. One will be used for the server program and the other for the client program.

2. If you are running from the CD-ROM that contains all sample programs, make the **X:\Data\examples\network** directory the current directory in both windows. (Here **X:** represents the drive letter of the CD-ROM.) If you haven't already done so, make the **X:\Data** directory part of your classpath by entering the following command in both windows:

```
SET CLASSPATH= X:\Data;%CLASSPATH%
```

3. In one window, start the server by entering the following command with an optional port number. If you do not specify a port, 8189 is used.

```
java examples.network.DatagramAdditionServer [port]
```

4. In the other window, start the client by entering the following command on one line, optionally adding a port number to match the port on the server. If you do not specify a port, 8189 is used. You also can specify the host name of the system on which the server process is running. If you do not specify a host name, the local host name is used.

```
java examples.network.DatagramAdditionClient [port]
[localhost]
```

If you run and receive a message saying the connection is refused, it could be that another program on your computer is using the same port number. To work around this problem, try running the client again with a different port number. For example, try port 8190 if the default port number 8189 isn't working.

5. If you cannot open a connection successfully, stop the server by pressing **Ctrl+C** in the window in which you started the server.

If the connection is successful, the output appears in the client window as follows:

```
Adding the numbers 1.2 3.4 5.6 together
The result is 10.2
```

Then, both the client and server programs stop.

REMOTE METHOD INVOCATION

You will find that the techniques in the preceding sections that describe how to use URLs and sockets are very useful when you want to move data from one point to another. For example, socket programming easily solves the problem of copying the contents of a file from System A to System B. However, there will be occasions when an object that provides a particularly useful service has been created on another system and you will want to invoke the methods of this object directly. This problem is not easily solved with URL objects or sockets, though it can be done. To do so, you could create and install a server that runs on the other system, establish a TCP/IP connection to it, and then send and receive messages using a format that indicates the object, method, parameters, and return value for each invocation. After all of your hard work, you would have merely created a subset of the functionality already provided by Java Remote Invocation Method (RMI).

RMI is a technology that allows programmers to call directly the methods of Java objects that reside on other systems. The fact that you are using remote objects is nearly transparent to you as a programmer when you are developing your application. You must take one additional step to contact the local Object Request Broker (ORB) to locate the object within your network after your application starts, but after you do have the object reference, you use it just as you would use any other object reference.

What makes this an interesting aspect of application development is the fact that you do not have a reference to the object on the remote system itself. Instead, you have a reference to a stub object. A *stub object* is a local surrogate object for the remote object that is generated automatically by the RMI compiler provided with the Java platform SDK, `rmic` and returned by the local ORB in response to your request to locate the object. The stub object has all the same methods supported by the remote object, but, instead of executing the methods independently, it forwards the parameters to the remote object and passes back any return value for the method. The technique used to forward the parameters to the remote object is called *marshaling*, and it is done automatically for you by the RMI service. After marshaling, the parameters are serialized into a byte stream and sent to the remote system. As a result, only primitive types and reference types that implement the **Serializable** interface can be used as parameter types for remote methods.

On the remote system, a *skeleton object* receives this byte stream and uses a technique called *unmarshaling* to deserialize the contents of the parameter list. The skeleton object passes the parameters to the remote object, and the method is executed. If there is a return value, it is serialized and returned using the same process, but in reverse. Like stub objects, skeleton objects are created automatically by the RMI compiler. Figure 11-6 summarizes the execution flow of a remote method call.

11

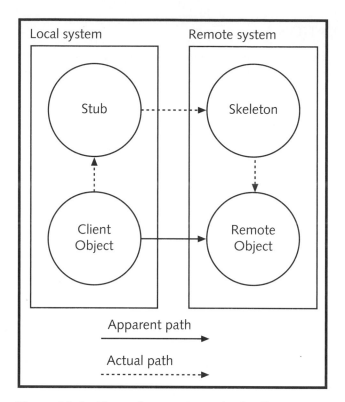

Figure 11-6 Flow of a remote method call

Developing a Remote Class of Objects

A class of objects that provides a particularly useful service that may be needed by programs on many different computers is an excellent candidate to be made available remotely to these programs. A class of objects that provides access to a central corporate personnel directory would be an example of such a class. To make such a class available remotely via RMI, begin by taking the public methods of the class that are needed to access the service and placing them into an interface definition. Unfortunately, static methods cannot be part of the interface, and neither can any fields. Only nonstatic methods are allowed. You define the interface just as you would any other Java interface definition, but with a couple of additional requirements: the interface must extend the interface **java.rmi.Remote**, and all methods in the interface must indicate that they might throw a **java.rmi.RemoteException** object. The **Remote** interface is a marker interface and defines no methods. Its purpose is to identify interfaces that are to be made available to clients. The **throws RemoteException** clause is needed for each method, because there are many things that could go wrong when invoking one of these remote methods—they are much more complex than a usual method invocation.

of objects to represent students enrolled at a college. Such a class could expose many potential methods to clients. For example, these methods would get the ID number for a student, retrieve and update the student's name, and retrieve and update the number of credits the student has accumulated. Following the preceding rules, a remote interface for the Student class would look like Figure 11-7.

```
package examples.network;
import java.rmi.Remote;
import java.rmi.RemoteException
/** A remote interface definition for a Student object
  */
  public interface Student extends Remote {
  public int getID() throws RemoteException;
  public void setName( String name ) throws RemoteException;
  public String getName() throws RemoteException;
  public int getCredits() throws RemoteException;
  public int addCredits( int credits ) throws RemoteException;
}
```

Figure 11-7   Remote interface for the Student class

This remote interface definition defines the interface that a client would use to manipulate the Student objects, but the job of defining the class that implements this interface remains to be done. You will locate this class of objects on the server and make them available to the client. However, the client will never access this class directly but will instead use the interface defined previously. The convention is to give this class the name of the interface with the characters Impl as a suffix. Using the interface in Figure 11-7 as an example, the corresponding class name would be StudentImpl. In this class, Impl is short for implementation because this class is an implementation of the interface.

In addition to implementing the Student interface, the StudentImpl class must also extend the class **java.rmi.server.RemoteObject**. The **RemoteObject** class is the superclass for all remote classes just as **Object** is the superclass for all classes. In particular, **RemoteObject** overrides the methods **equals, hashCode**, and **toString** to make sense for remote objects. But the **RemoteObject** class does not implement a particular remote behavior, instead leaving that for its subclasses. One such subclass, **java.rmi.server.UnicastRemoteObject**, implements a remote object that supports point-to-point active object references using TCP streams. Because this behavior is suitable for most cases, implementation classes extend **UnicastRemoteObject**, by convention. The StudentImpl class definition that follows this convention is shown in Figure 11-8.

```
package examples.network;
import java.rmi.RemoteException;
```

Figure 11-8   StudentImpl: a class that implements the Student remote interface

```
import java.rmi.server.UnicastRemoteObject;
/** An implementation of the Student interface as a remote object
 */
public class StudentImpl extends UnicastRemoteObject implements Student {
   private int ID;
   private String name;
   private int credits = 0;

   public StudentImpl( int ID, String name ) throws RemoteException {
      this.ID = ID;
      this.name = name;
   }
   public int getID() throws RemoteException {
      return ID;
   }
   public void setName( String name ) throws RemoteException {
      this.name = name;
   }
   public String getName() throws RemoteException {
      return name;
   }
   public int getCredits() throws RemoteException {
      return credits;
   }
   public int addCredits( int credits ) throws RemoteException {
      return ( this.credits += credits );
   }
}
```

Figure 11-8   `StudentImpl`: a class that implements the `Student` remote interface (continued)

After the implementation class has been defined and compiled successfully, you must create the stub and skeleton classes required by RMI. Fortunately, this is easy because the Java 2 SDK includes the RMI compiler utility `rmic` to automate this job. This compiler is located in the same directory as the Java compiler, `javac`, that you've used many times already. The `rmic` tool takes the name of the implementation class as input and generates the two `.class` files for the stub and skeleton. The names of these generated classes are the same as the implementation class, but with the suffixes `_Stub` and `_Skel`. For example, executing the command

    rmic examples.network.StudentImpl

creates the files `StudentImpl_Stub.class` and `StudentImpl_Skel.class` and causes them to contain the stub and skeleton classes, respectively.

Developing an RMI Server Class

You can use a combination of server and client program classes to put the remote class of objects to work. Essentially, the server program creates the remote objects and registers them with a naming service, and the client program looks for these objects using a naming service to obtain object references. The content of a server program class is shown in Figure 11-9, and a detailed breakdown of the class follows.

```
package examples.network;
import java.rmi.Naming;
import java.rmi.RMISecurityManager;
/** A server-side program that creates and registers
  * StudentImpl objects with the RMI registry for use
  * by clients
  */
public class StudentEnrollment {
   public static void main( String[] args ) {
      System.setProperty( "java.security.policy",
                          "RMISecurity.policy" );
      if ( System.getSecurityManager() == null ) {
         System.setSecurityManager( new RMISecurityManager() );
      }
      try {
         StudentImpl[] students = {
            new StudentImpl( 1001, "Maria Jones" ),
            new StudentImpl( 1002, "Patricia Hartswell" ),
            new StudentImpl( 1003, "Darius Smith" ),
            new StudentImpl( 1004, "Mary Bagshaw" ),
            new StudentImpl( 1005, "Iona Miller" )
         };
         for ( int i = 0; i < students.length; i++ ) {
            int id = students[i].getID();
            Naming.rebind( "Student" + id , students[i] );
         }
         System.out.println( "Student objects bound." );
      } catch ( Exception x ) {
         x.printStackTrace();
      }
   }
}
```

Figure 11-9   `StudentEnrollment`: an example RMI server class

```
grant {
  permission java.net.SocketPermission "*:1024-65535", "connect,accept";
};
```

Figure 11-10   `RMISecurity.policy`: a security policy for RMI programs

Consider the following line of code. Unlike the `Student` interface and the `StudentImpl` class, this server program class has neither interfaces that it must implement nor a prescribed superclass.

```
public class StudentEnrollment {
```

The server program class contains only a **main** method. This method creates the remote objects and registers them with a naming service. The class has no additional purpose, so no other methods exist. Because the server is opening up an interface to its objects and allowing programs on other systems to access them, there are security risks. It would be most unwise to make the objects available within a JVM that has no **SecurityManager** object installed, so the server program first checks to see if **SecurityManager** has been installed. In fact, the class loader used by RMI doesn't download any classes from remote locations unless you have installed **SecurityManager**.

The **SecurityManager** object used in the following code is an instance of the **java.rmi.RMISecurityManager** class. This class is an example of a security manager for applications that use downloaded code. This **SecurityManager** object enforces a security policy that is described in the file RMISecurity.policy and shown in Figure 11-10. The file RMISecurity.policy can be found in the X:\Data\examples\network directory. (Here X: represents the drive letter of the CD-ROM.) The one statement contained in this file gives the code loaded over the network the ability to listen and connect on sockets with port numbers between 1024 and 65535. Granting this permission is necessary for RMI to work successfully. For more details on the structure and content of security policy files such as this one, refer to the security section of Chapter 12. The first statement in the following block of code sets the property that contains the filename of the security policy:

```
System.setProperty( "java.security.policy",
                    "RMISecurity.policy" );
if ( System.getSecurityManager() == null ) {
    System.setSecurityManager( new RMISecurityManager() );
}
```

As shown next, the **StudentImpl** objects are created and loaded into an array for convenient access. In a more realistic program, this information would not be hard coded into the server program, but would be read from an existing file or a database. Chapter 9 describes how to access a relational database from Java programs.

```
StudentImpl[] students = {
    new StudentImpl( 1001, "Maria Jones" ),
    new StudentImpl( 1002, "Patricia Hartswell" ),
    new StudentImpl( 1003, "Darius Smith" ),
    new StudentImpl( 1004, "Mary Bagshaw" ),
    new StudentImpl( 1005, "Iona Miller" )
};
```

After the method creates the array of **StudentImpl** objects, the method uses a **for** loop to iterate through the list and register each object with the naming service. In a Java program, the naming service is represented by the class **java.rmi.Naming**. The method **rebind** takes two parameters—the name of the object as a string and a reference to the object—and binds the object reference using the given name.

In this chapter's program, the names being used to identify **StudentImpl** objects uniquely are a concatenation of the word **Student** and the student's ID number. For

client program must follow the same naming scheme to locate the student objects.

```
for ( int i = 0; i < students.length; i++ ) {
    int id = students[i].getID();
    Naming.rebind( "Student" + id , students[i] );
}
```

By default, the names are registered and available from a registry service on the local host. The registry service listens for requests from clients on port 1099. (The RMI registry uses port 1099 by default.) To specify a different host name or port number for the registry service, the name should be provided in the format //host:port/name.

Because it can take some time for the registry service to create and bind all the StudentImpl objects, the method uses the statement shown next to display an information message when the process completes. After this message appears on the host, you can safely run the client programs that remotely access the objects.

```
System.out.println( "Student objects bound." );
```

Developing an RMI Client Class

If the client program is an application or enabling class, it needs a **main** method to look up the remote objects using a naming service and to obtain references to the objects of interest. After the program obtains these references, it uses them just like any other object reference. Only the need to catch potential **RemoteException** objects indicates the program is working with remote objects. Figure 11-11 is the content of a client program class. A detailed breakdown of the class follows.

```
package examples.network;
import java.rmi.Naming;
import java.rmi.RMISecurityManager;
/** A client program that accesses and updates Student
  * objects on the server
  */
public class StudentClient {
    private static final String HOST_NAME = "localhost";
    public static void main( String[] args ) {
        System.setProperty( "java.security.policy",
                            "RMISecurity.policy" );
        if ( System.getSecurityManager() == null ) {
            System.setSecurityManager( new RMISecurityManager() );
        }
        try {
            Student s1001
                = (Student) Naming.lookup( "//" + HOST_NAME
                                + "/Student1001" );
```

Figure 11-11   StudentClient: an example RMI client class

```
        Student s1005
           = (Student) Naming.lookup( "//" + HOST_NAME
                                        + "/Student1005" );
        System.out.println( s1001.getName() );
        System.out.println( s1005.getName() );
        System.out.println( s1001.getCredits() );
        s1001.addCredits( 3 );
        s1001.setName( "Maria Goldman" );
        System.out.println( s1001.getName() );
        System.out.println( s1001.getCredits() );
      } catch ( Exception x ) {
        x.printStackTrace();
      }
   }
}
```

Figure 11-11   `StudentClient`: an example RMI client class (continued)

Consider the following code. The `StudentClient` class uses the remote objects but is not required to extend a particular superclass or implement any specified interfaces.

```
public class StudentClient {
```

When the program uses the naming service to look up the remote objects, a host name can be specified to indicate where to find the registry in which the objects have been bound. To make it easy to change the host name, this class contains a constant that holds the registry's host name, as the following code shows:

```
private static final String HOST_NAME = "localhost";
```

Because the client is opening and accepting stubs for remote objects, there are security risks. Just as for the server, the class loader used by RMI on the client will not download any classes from remote locations unless `SecurityManager` has been installed. The `SecurityManager` object used by the client is also an instance of the `java.rmi.RMISecurityManager` class.

```
public static void main( String[] args ) {
    System.setProperty( "java.security.policy",
                        "RMISecurity.policy" );
    if ( System.getSecurityManager() == null ) {
       System.setSecurityManager( new RMISecurityManager() );
    }
```

The calls to the naming service and the calls to the methods of the remote objects are enclosed in a try block so that any exceptions they may throw are caught. References to two remote objects are obtained using the **lookup** method of the **Naming** class. The input to the **lookup** method is a URL string of the form `//host:port/name`. `host` that indicates the system on which the registry for the remote objects is located, and `port` is the port number to which the registry is listening for requests. The default host is `localhost`, and the default port number is 1099. The **rmiregistry** program that comes with the java platform SDK uses this port number as well. The provided name must match the name to which the object was originally bound.

In the following example, the name is a concatenation of the word **Student** and the student number. The **lookup** method returns a reference of the type **Remote**. You should cast the return value to the expected object type before using the reference.

```
try {
   Student s1001
      = (Student) Naming.lookup( "//" + HOST_NAME
                                    + "/Student1001" );
   Student s1005
      = (Student) Naming.lookup( "//" + HOST_NAME
                                    + "/Student1005" );
```

Consider the following code. To see whether the client program obtained references to the objects that it expected, the client program calls three accessor methods and echoes the return values to the console, where you can see them.

```
System.out.println( s1001.getName() );
System.out.println( s1005.getName() );
System.out.println( s1001.getCredits() );
```

The next two remote method calls make changes to the remote objects. The inputs to these methods are serialized and sent to the remote system, where they are deserialized and used.

```
s1001.addCredits( 3 );
s1001.setName( "Maria Goldman" );
```

Finally, a check is made to see whether the changes of the preceding methods have actually occurred. The **main** method uses accessor methods to retrieve the values. The values are then echoed to the console.

```
System.out.println( s1001.getName() );
System.out.println( s1001.getCredits() );
```

Running the Server and Client Programs

You have reached the point where all classes have been defined, and the gratifying part of compiling and running the programs has now arrived.

To compile and run the files for the student remote object example

1. Copy the files from the directory **X:\Data\examples\network** on the CD-ROM to a directory for which you have read and write privileges. (Here **X:** represents the drive letter of the CD-ROM.) For the remainder of these steps, it will be assumed that the files have been copied to **C:\Data\ examples\network** and that the directory **C:\Data** has been added to the classpath environment variable.

2. Open a command-line window and make the directory **C:\Data\ examples\network** the current directory. Compile the file **Student. java** by using the following command:

```
javac Student.java
```

3. Compile the file **StudentImpl.java** by using the following command:

```
javac StudentImpl.java
```

4. Make the directory **C:\Data** the current directory. Create the stub and skeleton classes for the **examples.network.StudentImpl** class by using the following command:

```
rmic examples.network.StudentImpl
```

5. Make the directory **C:\Data\examples\network** the current directory again. Compile the file **StudentEnrollment.java** by using the following command:

```
javac StudentEnrollment.java
```

6. Compile the file **StudentClient.java** by using the following command:

```
javac StudentClient.java
```

7. Open a new command-line window and start the RMI registry program by typing:

```
rmiregistry
```

Unfortunately, no messages are displayed to indicate that the registry is running. The only indication you will get is that the window's title bar text changes to end with – **rmiregistry**.

8. Next, you start the server program, **StudentEnrollment**, that will construct and register the **StudentImpl** objects. In addition to supplying the class name to the JVM, you must supply the codebase from which the stub and skeleton files will be made available. The stub class files will be automatically downloaded to client programs from this location as needed. To start the server program, open a command-line window, make **C:\Data\examples\network** the current directory, and then enter the following command on one line, adding a space between the lines:

```
java –Djava.rmi.server.codebase=file:C:\Data
examples.network.StudentEnrollment
```

9. Wait until the message **Student objects bound.** appears in the window to indicate that the server has successfully constructed and registered the **StudentImpl** objects. Open another command-line window, make the directory **C:\Data\examples\network** the current directory, and start the client program, **StudentClient**, with the following command:

```
java examples.network.StudentClient
```

The program output will look like this:

```
Maria Jones
Iona Miller
0
Maria Goldman
3
```

10. The client program terminates after it runs, but the server and `rmiregistry` programs must be ended manually. To end the server program or the `rmiregistry` program, make the window in which the program is running the active window, and then press **Ctrl+C** to end the program.

JNDI

The `rmiregistry` program, which is supplied with the Java platform SDK, is a useful program and works well for small applications, such as the one described earlier in this chapter. However, the `rmiregistry` program does not scale well when applications become large and are spread across many host systems.

In anticipation of this problem, Sun developed the Java Naming and Directory Interface (JNDI). JNDI is not itself a naming or directory service, but is a unified interface to multiple naming and directory services that already exist for enterprise development. It gives Java programmers easy access to heterogeneous enterprise naming and directory services. Figure 11-12 lists the JNDI packages.

JNDI works in concert with J2EE technologies, such as Enterprise JavaBeans (EJBs), to organize and locate components in a distributed computing environment. As a result, JNDI is revisited in Chapter 14 from the perspective of EJB development and deployment.

 Beginning with version 1.3 of the Java platform, JNDI became a part of the Java 2 platform. Included in this support were class libraries and service providers for the Lightweight Directory Access Protocol (LDAP), the CORBA Object Services (COS) naming service, and the Java Remote Method Invocation (RMI) registry.

Package	Description
`javax.naming`	This package is the core of JNDI and defines the basic operations of binding names to objects and looking up objects for a given name.
`javax.naming.directory`	This package defines methods for making changes to directories such as examining and updating the attributes of a directory object.
`javax.naming.event`	This package defines classes and interfaces that support event notification in naming and directory services.

Figure 11-12   JNDI packages

11

Package	Description
`javax.naming.ldap`	This package defines classes and interfaces for supporting LDAP extended operations and controls.
`javax.naming.spi`	This package contains the server provider interface that is intended to be used by companies and organizations for integrating their existing naming and directory service products into JNDI.

Figure 11-12   JNDI packages (continued)

CORBA, RMI-IIOP, and IDL

Java RMI provides support that makes it easy to define and use remote objects, but it does have a drawback: It works only with remote objects that are developed using the Java programming language. Common Object Request Broker Architecture (CORBA) is a more generic architecture for defining and using remote objects. It allows for the mixing of objects developed using different programming languages, such as C++ and COBOL. A consortium of companies, known as the Object Management Group (OMG), developed the CORBA standard.

At a high level, CORBA and RMI are similar. The concepts of stubs, skeletons, and ORBs that you have already learned for RMI programming also apply to CORBA. One important difference between the two, however, is the way in which the ORBs communicate with each other. RMI ORBs use a protocol called Java Remote Method Protocol (JRMP), but CORBA ORBs use Internet Inter-ORB Protocol (IIOP), which is based on the standard TCP/IP protocol. Unfortunately, in the early days of RMI, this meant that RMI programmers could not communicate with CORBA clients.

But the good news is that support has been available on the Java platform since version 1.3 to allow RMI programmers to use CORBA's IIOP communications protocol to communicate with clients of any type, whether written entirely in the Java programming language or made up of components written in other CORBA-compliant languages. This RMI-IIOP technology enables the programming of CORBA servers and applications via the RMI API. The RMI API utilizes the Java CORBA ORB and IIOP, so you can write all of your code in Java and use the `rmic` compiler to generate the code necessary for connecting your applications via IIOP to others written in any CORBA-compliant language. RMI-IIOP provides interoperability with other CORBA objects implemented in various languages, but only if all the remote interfaces are originally defined as Java RMI interfaces. RMI-IIOP is of particular interest to programmers using Enterprise JavaBeans (EJBs), since EJBs use a remote object model that is RMI-based.

An important difference between CORBA and RMI is that the interfaces of CORBA objects are defined using a language called Interface Definition Language (IDL). To make

not originally defined as Java RMI interfaces but have been defined in CORBA IDL, the Java platform SDK provides a tool called `idlj` that generates the Java bindings (for example, interfaces and stub and skeleton classes) for the specified IDL file. The `idlj` tool is installed in the same place as the standard Java compiler, `javac`, and the `idlj` tool is also invoked from a command-line window.

 The `idlj` tool became available beginning with version 1.3 of the Java platform and replaced the original tool made available for this purpose, `idl2java`. The `idlj` tool includes features required to support RMI-IIOP.

A CORBA-compliant ORB is included in the SDK. You can use it for those cases where you choose to develop remote objects that can interact with objects created using programming languages other than Java.

The development process you follow with Java IDL is similar to the Java RMI development process that has been described in this chapter. The process begins by using IDL to define the interfaces that will be distributed and registered for use by CORBA client programs. The `idlj` tool generates the Java interface, and stub and skeleton classes. The implementation of the class is then defined and compiled, just as was done for Java RMI.

11

CHAPTER SUMMARY

- The Java platform includes core classes with which you can communicate with URLs and create TCP/IP and datagram sockets.

- Objects of the **URL** class hold the details of URLs, such as the protocol and host. To exchange information with a URL, you must create a **URLConnection** object. Do this by calling the method **openConnection** for a URL.

- For a connection that remains open, you can connect to a system on your network with a TCP/IP socket. A number of classes, including **Socket**, support TCP/IP sockets. To perform ordinary stream I/O to and from a TCP/IP socket, use the methods **Socket.getInputStream** and **Socket.getOutputStream**.

- You can use the **ServerSocket** class to create the server side of a TCP/IP socket. Datagram sockets are also useful. Some extra programming is required, but this may be worthwhile if you intermittently send short messages and do not need the reliability of a TCP/IP connection.

- Java RMI makes it possible to define and implement classes of objects that can be accessed remotely from client programs running on different systems within a network. Only the interfaces of these objects are exposed to the client programs.

❐ Classes of objects that implement remote interfaces are constructed on the server systems, and then they are bound to names that are registered with a naming service. Client programs look up these names using Object Request Brokers (ORBs) to obtain references to these remote objects.

❐ Stub classes act as local surrogates for remote objects to provide access to the remote objects. Stub classes communicate with skeleton classes on the server. Skeleton classes marshal and unmarshal parameters and return values between the stub and the remote object.

❐ Security is a concern when using RMI. RMI server and client programs must install a **SecurityManager** object to protect against unauthorized access.

❐ JNDI is not a naming and directory service, but it provides Java applications with a unified interface to multiple naming and directory services.

❐ RMI-IIOP provides interoperability with other CORBA objects implemented in various languages. RMI-IIOP is preferable to Java IDL for most purposes, in enabling a programmer to write CORBA-compliant interfaces directly in Java rather than in the OMG-specified IDL used with Java IDL.

REVIEW QUESTIONS

1. True or False: A **URLConnection** object closes after one read/write operation.

2. Which of the following classes can be passed as a parameter to the constructor of the **Socket** class? Select all that apply.

   a. **InetAddress**

   b. **URL**

   c. **URLConnection**

   d. **ServerSocket**

   e. **DatagramSocket**

3. True or False: TCP/IP sockets have input and output streams that can be used just like any other I/O streams.

4. True or False: Datagram sockets are connection-oriented and guarantee the delivery of all packets sent through them.

5. Examine the following code:

```
import java.io.*;
import java.net.*;
public class Quiz11_5 {
    public static void main( String[] args ) {
        Socket client = new Socket();
        BufferedReader socketIn;
```

```
              = new PrintWriter( client.getOutputStream(),
                                 true );
         socketOut.println( "Quiz question 11_5" );
         client.close();
      }
   }
```

Which of the following statements are true when the code is compiled and run? Select all that apply.

a. The compiler rejects the method `Quiz11_5.main` because of missing socket constructor parameters.

b. Compilation is successful, and the method `Quiz11_5.main` establishes a TCP/IP socket and sends one message before closing the socket.

c. Compilation is successful, and the method `Quiz11_5.main` establishes a datagram socket and sends one message before closing the socket.

d. The compiler rejects the method `Quiz11_5.main` because the possible `IOException` exception is not caught.

e. Compilation is successful, and the method `Quiz11_5.main` establishes a TCP/IP socket and receives one message before closing the socket.

6. Examine the following code:

```
import java.io.*;
import java.net.*;
public class Quiz11_6 {
    private static byte[] buffer;
    private static DatagramSocket ss;
    private static DatagramPacket inDgp;
    public static void main( String[] args ) {
        try {
            ss = new DatagramSocket( 9002 );
            inDgp = new DatagramPacket( buffer,
                                        buffer.length );
            ss.receive( inDgp );
            ss.close();
        }
        catch( IOException iox ) {
            System.out.println( iox );
            iox.printStackTrace();
        }
    }
}
```

11

Which of the following statements are true when the code is compiled and run? Select all that apply.

a. The compiler rejects the method `Quiz11_6.main` because of missing datagram socket constructor parameters.

b. Compilation is successful, and the method `Quiz11_6.main` establishes a datagram socket and receives one datagram before closing the socket.

c. Compilation is successful, and the method `Quiz11_6.main` establishes a TCP/IP socket and receives one datagram before closing the socket.

d. Compilation is successful, but the method `Quiz11_6.main` causes a `NullPointerException` exception because the field buffer does not refer to a `byte[]` object.

e. Compilation is successful, and the method `Quiz11_6.main` establishes a datagram socket and sends one datagram before closing the socket.

7. Which of the following are methods defined within the interface `java.rmi.Remote`? Select all that apply.

a. `public void remote()`

b. `public void rebind( String, Object )`

c. `public void bind( String, Object )`

d. `public void lookup( String )`

e. `public void remote() throws java.rmi.RemoteException`

8. True or False: The class loader used by RMI will not download any classes from remote locations if no `SecurityManager` object has been installed.

9. Examine the following command:

```
rmic questions.c11.EmployeeImpl java
```

Which of the following statements are true when the command is executed, assuming that the file `questions.c11.EmployeeImpl` has previously compiled successfully? Select all that apply.

a. The command completes successfully, and the file `EmployeeImpl_Stub.class` is generated.

b. The command completes successfully, and the file `Employee_Stub.class` is generated.

c. The command completes successfully, and the file `EmployeeImpl_Skel.class` is generated.

d. The command completes successfully, and the file `Employee_Skel.class` is generated.

e. The command does not complete successfully because the `.java` file extension is missing from the input parameter.

10. Which of the following are valid superclasses for a class of remote objects that are accessible by RMI? Select all that apply.

     a. `java.rmi.Naming`

     b. `java.rmi.server.RemoteObject`

     c. `java.rmi.RemoteException`

     d. `java.rmi.server.UnicastRemoteObject`

     e. `java.rmi.Remote`

11. True or False: RMI-IIOP provides interoperability with other CORBA objects implemented in various languages—but only if all the remote interfaces are originally defined using CORBA IDL.

PROGRAMMING EXERCISES

Debugging

1. Correct all the errors in the class `Debug11_1` so that it returns the type of content located at the specified URL. This class can be found in the file `Debug11_1.java` in the `X:\Data\questions\c11` directory on the CD-ROM. (Here `X:` is the drive letter of the CD-ROM.)

2. Correct all the errors in the class `Debug11_2` so that the **run** method successfully opens and then closes a server TCP/IP socket. This class can be found in the file `Debug11_2.java` in the `X:\Data\questions\c11` directory on the CD-ROM. (Here `X:` is the drive letter of the CD-ROM.)

3. Correct all the errors in the class `Debug11_3` so that the **run** method successfully opens a TCP/IP socket to the **host** and **port** values specified, and then writes a test message to the socket. This class can be found in the file `Debug11_3.java` in the `X:\Data\questions\c11` directory on the CD-ROM. (Here `X:` is the drive letter of the CD-ROM.)

4. Correct all the errors in the class `Debug11_4` so that the **run** method successfully opens a datagram socket to the **host** and **port** values specified, and then sends one datagram and receives one datagram. This class can be found in the file `Debug11_4.java` in the `X:\Data\questions\c11` directory on the CD-ROM. (Here `X:` is the drive letter of the CD-ROM.)

5. Correct all the errors in the `Employee` interface and the `EmployeeImpl` class so that the instances of `EmployeeImpl` class can be used successfully as remote objects accessible by RMI. The interface and class can be found in the files `Employee.java` and `EmployeeImpl.java`, respectively, in the `X:\Data\questions\c11` directory on the CD-ROM. (Here `X:` is the drive letter of the CD-ROM.)

11

Complete the Solution

1. Extract the file `X:\Data\questions\c11\Complete11_1.java` from the CD-ROM. (Here `X:` is the drive letter of the CD-ROM.) Complete the `Complete11_1` class definition by finishing the method `printPage`. This method should construct a `URL` object, get the input stream for the URL, and then wrap it in a `BufferedReader` object so that the contents of the URL can be read and printed to the console.

2. Extract the file `X:\Data\questions\c11\Complete11_2.java` from the CD-ROM. (Here `X:` is the drive letter of the CD-ROM.) Complete the `Complete11_2` class definition by finishing the method `waitForMessage`. This method should open a server TCP/IP socket for the port number specified and wait for a connection. When the connection is made, it should read a string from the connection, echo it to the console, and then close the socket.

3. Extract the file `X:\Data\questions\c11\Complete11_3.java` from the CD-ROM. (Here `X:` is the drive letter of the CD-ROM.) Complete the `Complete11_3` class definition by finishing the method `waitForDatagram`. This method should open a server datagram socket for the port number specified and wait for a datagram to arrive. When a datagram arrives, it should read a string from it, echo the string to the console, and then close the socket.

4. Extract the file `X:\Data\questions\c11\Complete11_4.java` from the CD-ROM. (Here `X:` is the drive letter of the CD-ROM.) Complete the `Complete11_4` class definition by adding code to the **main** function that will create in separate threads an instance of both the client and server classes. The **main** method should give the client enough time to send about 20 messages to the server, and then it should end.

5. Extract the files `X:\Data\questions\c11\RemoteEcho.java`, `X:\Data\questions\c11\RemoteEchoImpl.java`, `X:\Data\questions\c11\EchoServer.java`, and `X:\Data\questions\c11\EchoClient.java` from the CD-ROM. (Here `X:` is the drive letter of the CD-ROM.) Complete the class definitions by adding code to the **main** functions of the classes `EchoServer` and `EchoClient`. The **main** method of `EchoServer` should create an instance of `RemoteEchoImpl` and register it with the naming service. The **main** method of `EchoClient` should use the naming service to locate the `RemoteEchoImpl` object and obtain a reference to it of type `RemoteEcho`. The client should then use the **echo** method to send strings to the remote object that will be echoed to the console by the remote object.

Discovery

1. Create a class called URLMonitor that can be used to monitor a list of URLs for changes. Objects of this class will provide support to check the modification dates of a list of URLs and print a report of which URLs have changed since the last time they were checked. You will probably find it useful to serialize the Date objects collected by the objects to simplify the storing and retrieval of the information for later comparison. The URL list should be read from a file.

2. Create a pair of classes called ImmediateMessage and ImmediateMessageServer. Objects of the ImmediateMessageServer class should listen on a specified port for a connection from other systems, and then display the information received on the connection. Objects of the ImmediateMessage class will connect to these server objects and send a single message to be displayed at the server system.

3. Create a pair of classes called TemperatureServer and TemperatureClient. Objects of the TemperatureServer class contain a table of current temperatures for a number of cities around the world. They receive requests from TemperatureClient objects in the form of datagrams. Each datagram contains the name of a city that the server looks up in its table. The current temperature for the city is returned by the TemperatureServer object to the TemperatureClient object in a datagram. If the requested city cannot be found, an empty string is returned.

4. Take the Employee interface and EmployeeImpl class that you corrected in the debugging exercises previously and write a **main** method that creates and registers many EmployeeImpl objects as part of a HumanResources class. Then, write a client class that provides a GUI interface to update the name and salary of a remote employee object that is found based on a serial number that the user enters in a text field of the GUI.

11

12

SECURITY

INTRODUCTION

With the Java programming language, Sun developed a language and development platform that operated system-independent and, with the Internet in mind, secure. The Java Virtual Machine (JVM) can run code that originates on the local machine (typically, an application) or that is downloaded from the network (typically, an applet). By default, code executed from the local file system is trusted, and remote code is not trusted. You can accept default security policies or establish more fine-grained access controls.

This chapter focuses on two basic elements of security: first, how to verify the origin of a program and determine that it has not been altered, otherwise known as authentication. To understand how this is accomplished, you will investigate the concepts of cryptography that act as the foundation for the use of digital signatures and certificates. Second, you have to decide how to control what a program is allowed to do, otherwise known as access control. The Java platform has extensive support for creating fine-grained security policies and applying them to perform access control. The application of security policies can be based upon the origin of the program code being executed, the identity of the person who signed the program code, or the identity of the person running the program code.

CRYPTOGRAPHY

Cryptography is the science and study of secret writing. It involves the application of a cipher to transform cleartext into ciphertext, the process of which is called encryption. The reverse process of transforming ciphertext into cleartext is called decryption. To understand how things such as digital signatures and certificates work, it is important to know the basic concepts of cryptography. Fortunately, the Java Cryptography Extension (JCE) has been integrated into the Java 2 SDK, Standard Edition since v 1.4 and this means that Java programs can be used to illustrate these concepts.

Symmetric and Asymmetric Cryptographic Systems

A cryptosystem is made up of the following components: cleartext messages, ciphertext messages, keys, an enciphering transformation, and a deciphering transformation. Figure 12-1 illustrates these components and the flow through the system.

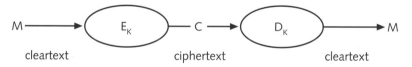

Figure 12-1   Components of a cryptosystem

Cryptosystems can be divided into two categories: symmetric or secret key cryptosystems, and asymmetric or public key cryptosystems. Until the mid 1970s, all cryptosystems were symmetric secret key cryptosystems. Secret key cryptosystems get their name from the fact that the same key is used to encrypt the cleartext and decrypt the ciphertext. Thus, the key must be kept secret, otherwise an attacker can use the key to decrypt the ciphertext and know the cleartext. The system illustrated in Figure 12-1 is considered a secret key cryptosystem if E_K and D_K are the same secret key used in the encryption and decryption processes. The symmetry of using the same key for both encryption and decryption is why these systems are also called symmetric key cryptosystems.

Secret key cryptosystems are typically very efficient, allowing for speedy encryption and decryption. Examples in use today are Data Encryption Standard (DES) and Triple DES. The drawback of these cryptosystems is that the sender and receiver must share the secret of the key. This leads to a key distribution problem whereby the secret keys must be transmitted separately and securely. During the Second World War, German naval forces used the famous Enigma machine to encrypt and decrypt messages they sent amongst themselves. But as powerful as the enciphering and deciphering transformations that were provided by the Enigma machine were, codebooks that contained the key to be used each still had to be distributed to all ships and submarines, and these were typically valid for a month or more because of the long stretches of time that a ship would spend at sea. Every time one of these codebooks was captured, Allied forces were able to decipher the German naval messages despite the power of the machine. The distribution and security of codebooks were the weak links in the cryptosystem.

A public key cryptosystem is one in which the key for encryption is not the same as the key for decryption. Although it is not impossible, it is computationally extremely difficult to determine the decryption key even if you know the encryption key, and the difficulty increases as the number of bits in the key increases. In such a system, every person can have his or her own pair of keys: one public and one private. Figure 12-2 illustrates the components of a public key cryptosystem. For Alice to send a secret message to Bob, she must obtain his public key, E_{Bob}, from a directory and use it to encrypt her message. Now the only person who will be able to decrypt the message is Bob, because only he has the matching private key that he keeps secret (D_{Bob}). The asymmetry of using different keys for encryption and decryption is why these systems are also called asymmetric key cryptosystems.

Although public key cryptosystems avoid the problem of having to distribute codebooks of secret keys, the transformations they use for encryption and decryption are more complex and not as efficient as in secret key cryptosystems. Examples in use today are Digital Signature Algorithm (DSA), Rivest-Shamir-Adleman (RSA), and Elliptic Curve DSA.

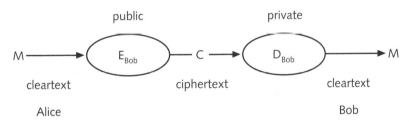

Figure 12-2   Components of a public key cryptosystem

Java Support for Cryptosystem Keys

Although the encryption and decryption transformations are certainly important, the focus in most cryptosystems is on the keys. This isn't really all that surprising, because the details of the transformations are usually public and so breaking a cipher becomes a matter of learning the key. The more possible key values there are, the harder it is to determine the key. This is why there is such a focus on the length of keys. For example, if a cryptosystem used keys that were 8 bits in length, there would be 256 possible key values. With such a small number of keys, it would not be hard simply to systematically try all key values until the ciphertext yielded its cleartext message. Fortunately, cryptosystems in use today have much larger key sizes: DES uses 56-bit keys resulting in

7.21×10^{16} possible keys, and Triple DES can use keys as long as 168 bits—that allows for 3.74×10^{50} possible keys!

The Java 2 SDK includes a program called `keytool` that you can use to generate a public key encryption key pair using either the DSA or RSA algorithms. By default, the key size is 1024 bits, but you can specify any multiple of 64 between 512 and 1024. The `keytool` program requires that each key pair be identified by an alias and be kept in a file known as a *keystore*. The `keytool` command in Figure 12-3 generates a 1024 bit key pair that uses RSA and is stored in the keystore file called `jpatkeystore.ks` under the alias `exampleRSApair`. However, before the process can be completed, the `keytool` program requires more information. Figure 12-3 shows the transcript of how the key pair was created. User input is shown in bold. Although the `keytool` command at the top of the figure appears on two lines, it must be entered as a single command.

```
keytool -genkey -keyalg RSA -alias exampleRSApair -storetype JCEKS -keystore
jpatkeystore.ks
Enter keystore password:  changeit
What is your first and last name?
  [Unknown]:  Wigglesworth McMillan
What is the name of your organizational unit?
  [Unknown]:  Java Programming Advanced Topics
What is the name of your organization?
  [Unknown]:  Course Technology
What is the name of your City or Locality?
  [Unknown]:  Toronto
What is the name of your State or Province?
  [Unknown]:  ON
What is the two-letter country code for this unit?
  [Unknown]:  CA
Is CN=Wigglesworth McMillan, OU=Java Programming Advanced Topics, O=Course
Technology, L=Toronto, ST=ON, C=CA correct?
  [no]:  y
Enter key password for <exampleRSApair>
        (RETURN if same as keystore password):  changeit
```

Figure 12-3   Key pair creation transcript

The additional information is used to create something called the *X.500 Distinguished Name* for the key pair. It includes information that should make the name unique across the Internet. The passwords that the tool requires control access to the keystore file and also to the individual key pairs within the keystore. In Figure 12-3, the keystore and key pair passwords are the same, but that isn't necessary.

A keystore is a secure location where keys and certificates are kept. The default implementation of a keystore provided by the Java platform SDK v 1.4 is referred to as JKS, but a more secure and more flexible keystore implementation is provided as part of the Java Cryptography Extension (JCE) that is bundled with SDK v 1.4 and is known as JCEKS. Examples in this chapter use the JCEKS keystore implementation. The contents of the keystore file are accessible to a Java program. Figure 12-4 contains a simple

program using the KeystoreAccess class that begins by creating an empty keystore, then
loads the contents of the keystore created by the **keytool** command from Figure 12-3.
It then retrieves the new key pair by its alias and confirms the algorithm used by the key
pair by using the **Key.getAlgorithm** method. Because **KeystoreAccess** is a public
class, it is found in a file called **KeystoreAccess.java**. The structure of packages mirrors the file system, so you will find this source code in the **X:\Data\examples**
security directory on the CD-ROM. (Here **X:** is the drive letter of the CD-ROM.)

```
package examples.security;
import java.io.*;
import java.security.Key;
import java.security.KeyStore;
/** An example class that accesses a key within a keystore
 */
public class KeystoreAccess {
   static final String KEYSTORE = "jpatkeystore.ks";
   static final String KEYALIAS = "exampleRSApair";
   static final String STOREPASSWD = "changeit";
   static final String ALIASPASSWD = "changeit";
   /** The test method for the class
     */
   public static void main( String[] args ) {
      try {
         KeyStore ks = KeyStore.getInstance( "JCEKS" );
         ks.load( new FileInputStream( KEYSTORE ),
               STOREPASSWD.toCharArray() );
         Key k = ks.getKey( KEYALIAS,
                        ALIASPASSWD.toCharArray() );
         System.out.println( "The algorithm for alias "
                     + KEYALIAS + " is "
                     + k.getAlgorithm() );
      }
      catch( Exception x ) {
         System.out.println( x );
         x.printStackTrace();
      }
   }
}
```

Figure 12-4   KeystoreAccess: an example class that accesses a key within a keystore

The output from the program in Figure 12-4 is:

```
The algorithm for alias exampleRSApair is RSA
```

Encrypting and Decrypting Stream I/O

An obvious application of cryptography is encrypting stream I/O data so that it is kept
private and can only be understood by those who have the key for decrypting it. To make

this straightforward, the classes **javax.crypto.CipherInputStream** and **javax.crypto.CipherOutputStream** were added to the Java SDK. These classes are filter streams that are subclasses of the classes **java.io.FilterInputStream** and **java.io.FilterOutputStream**, respectively. Figure 12-5 is the complete source code for the class **FileEncryption** found in the file called **FileEncryption.java**. The structure of packages mirrors the file system, so you will find this source code in the **X:\Data\examples\security** directory on the CD-ROM. (Here **X:** is the drive letter of the CD-ROM.) This example program is capable of either encrypting or decrypting the specified input file and directing the output to the output file. A command-line option indicates whether encryption or decryption is requested. A discussion of the contents of the file follows.

```java
package examples.security;
import java.io.*;
import javax.crypto.*;
import java.security.Key;
import java.security.KeyStore;
/** Class definition that handles the encryption and
  * decryption of files
  */
public class FileEncryption {
    static final String KEYSTORE = "jpatkeystore.ks";
    static final String KEYALIAS = "exampleDESkey";
    static final String STOREPASSWD = "changeit";
    static final String ALIASPASSWD = "changeit";
    /** Get the key for encrypting/decrypting the file
      * from the keystore; if it doesn't exist then
      * generate a key and save it for next time
      */
    private static Key getKey() {
      Key k = null;
      try {
        KeyStore ks = KeyStore.getInstance("JCEKS");
        ks.load( new FileInputStream( KEYSTORE ),
              STOREPASSWD.toCharArray() );
        if ( ks.isKeyEntry( KEYALIAS ) ) {
          k = ks.getKey( KEYALIAS,
                    ALIASPASSWD.toCharArray() );
        } else {
          KeyGenerator kg
             = KeyGenerator.getInstance( "DES" );
          k = kg.generateKey();
          ks.setKeyEntry( KEYALIAS, k,
                    ALIASPASSWD.toCharArray(),
                    null );
          ks.store( new FileOutputStream( KEYSTORE ),
                  STOREPASSWD.toCharArray() );
        }
```

Figure 12-5   FileEncryption: an example class that encrypts and decrypts file content

```
      } catch ( Exception x ) {
         System.out.println( x );
         x.printStackTrace();
      }
      return k;
   }
   /** Get the cipher needed for either encryption or
     * decryption
     * @param opMode specify either encrypt or decrypt mode
     */
   private static Cipher getCipher( int opMode ) {
      Cipher c = null;
      try {
         Key k = getKey();
         c = Cipher.getInstance( k.getAlgorithm() );
         c.init( opMode, k );
      } catch ( Exception x ) {
         System.out.println( x );
         x.printStackTrace();
      }
      return c;
   }
   /** Encrypt a file
     * @param clearFile the file to be encrypted
     * @param encrFile the encrypted output file
     */
   private static void encryptFile( String clearFile,
                                    String encrFile ) {
      try {
         FileInputStream fis
            = new FileInputStream( clearFile );
         FileOutputStream fos
            = new FileOutputStream( encrFile );
         Cipher c = getCipher( Cipher.ENCRYPT_MODE );
         CipherOutputStream cphout
            = new CipherOutputStream( fos, c );
         byte[] byteBuff = new byte[ 8196 ];
         int bytesRead = fis.read( byteBuff );
         while ( bytesRead != -1 ) {
            cphout.write( byteBuff, 0, bytesRead );
            bytesRead = fis.read( byteBuff );
         }
         cphout.close();
         fis.close();
         fos.close();
      }
      catch( IOException iox ) {
         System.out.println( iox );
      }
   }
```

Figure 12-5   `FileEncryption:` an example class that encrypts and decrypts file content
                  (continued)

```
  /** Decrypt a file
   * @param encrFile the file to be decrypted
   * @param clearFile the decrypted output file
   */
  private static void decryptFile( String encrFile,
                                      String clearFile ) {
    try {
       FileInputStream fis
          = new FileInputStream( encrFile );
       Cipher c = getCipher( Cipher.DECRYPT_MODE );
       CipherInputStream cphin
          = new CipherInputStream( fis, c );
       FileOutputStream fos
          = new FileOutputStream( clearFile );
       byte[] byteBuff = new byte[ 8196 ];
       int bytesRead = cphin.read( byteBuff );
       while ( bytesRead != -1 ) {
          fos.write( byteBuff, 0, bytesRead );
          bytesRead = cphin.read( byteBuff );
       }
       fis.close();
       fos.close();
       cphin.close();
    }
    catch( IOException iox ) {
       System.out.println( iox );
    }
  }
  /** Method used to display a message explaining how the
   * utility is to be used
   */
  private static void displayUsageMessage() {
    System.out.println( "Usage: "
                         + FileEncryption.class.getName()
                         + " { /e | /d }"
                         + " source_file target_file" );
  }
  /** Method used to encrypt or decrypt a file based on
   * the option specified
   * @param args[0] /e or /d option
   * @param args[1] source filename
   * @param args[2] target filename
   */
  public static void main( String[] args ) {
    if ( args.length < 2 ) {
       displayUsageMessage();
```

Figure 12-5   `FileEncryption`: an example class that encrypts and decrypts file content
            (continued)

```
    } else {
      if ( args[0].equalsIgnoreCase( "/e" ) ) {
        // encrypt the source file to the target file
        encryptFile( args[1], args[2] );
        System.out.println( args[1]
            + " successfully encrypted as " + args[2] );
      } else if ( args[0].equalsIgnoreCase( "/d" ) ) {
        // decrypt the source file to the target file
        decryptFile( args[1], args[2] );
        System.out.println( args[1]
            + " successfully decrypted as " + args[2] );
      } else {
        // unrecognized option
        displayUsageMessage();
      }
    }
  }
}
```

Figure 12-5   `FileEncryption`: an example class that encrypts and decrypts file content (continued)

The `getKey` method begins by creating a **KeyStore** object and initializing it with the contents of the file `jpatkeystore.ks`. If the required key alias, `exampleDESkey`, is present, it is retrieved.

```
private static Key getKey() {
   Key k = null;
   try {
      KeyStore ks = KeyStore.getInstance("JCEKS");
      ks.load( new FileInputStream( KEYSTORE ),
            STOREPASSWD.toCharArray() );
      if ( ks.isKeyEntry( KEYALIAS ) ) {
         k = ks.getKey( KEYALIAS,
                     ALIASPASSWD.toCharArray() );
```

If `exampleDESkey` is not present, then a key must be created. A **KeyGenerator** object for the DES algorithm generates the needed key:

```
      } else {
         KeyGenerator kg
            = KeyGenerator.getInstance( "DES" );
         k = kg.generateKey();
```

12

So that the correct key will be available for later decryption, the key is set in the **KeyStore** object and then the contents of the **KeyStore** object are stored back into the disk file:

```
    ks.setKeyEntry( KEYALIAS, k,
                    ALIASPASSWD.toCharArray(),
                    null );
    ks.store( new FileOutputStream( KEYSTORE ),
              STOREPASSWD.toCharArray() );
}
```

The method ends with the catch block for handling exceptions and the statement to return the **Key** object:

```
    } catch ( Exception x ) {
        System.out.println( x );
        x.printStackTrace();
    }
    return k;
}
```

It is the **Cipher** object that does the actual encryption or decryption of the data. After obtaining the secret key, a **Cipher** object is obtained that uses the same algorithm associated with the key:

```
private static Cipher getCipher( int opMode ) {
    Cipher c = null;
    try {
        Key k = getKey();
        c = Cipher.getInstance( k.getAlgorithm() );
```

Before a **Cipher** object can be used, it must be initialized. To do that, both the mode of the cipher (i.e., encryption or decryption) and the key that will be used must be specified. After the **Cipher** object has been successfully initialized, it can be returned:

```
        c.init( opMode, k );
    } catch ( Exception x ) {
        System.out.println( x );
        x.printStackTrace();
    }
    return c;
}
```

The encryptFile method begins by obtaining I/O streams for the input and output files:

```
private static void encryptFile( String clearFile,
                                 String encrFile ) {
    try {
        FileInputStream fis
            = new FileInputStream( clearFile );
        FileOutputStream fos
            = new FileOutputStream( encrFile );
```

`CipherOutputStream` object is created that is wrapped around the `FileOutputStream` object and initialized with the **Cipher** object:

```
Cipher c = getCipher( Cipher.ENCRYPT_MODE );
CipherOutputStream cphout
    = new CipherOutputStream( fos, c );
```

The data is copied from the input stream to the output stream using a loop. As the data is written to the output file, the **CipherOutputStream** object encrypts the information:

```
byte[] byteBuff = new byte[ 8196 ];
int bytesRead = fis.read( byteBuff );
while ( bytesRead != -1 ) {
    cphout.write( byteBuff, 0, bytesRead );
    bytesRead = fis.read( byteBuff );
}
```

After the entire file has been handled, the stream objects are closed and the method ends:

```
        cphout.close();
        fis.close();
        fos.close();
    }
    catch( IOException iox ) {
        System.out.println( iox );
    }
}
```

The `decryptFile` method is similar in structure to the `encryptFile` method. The most important difference is that a **CipherInputStream** object is created as a wrapper for the **FileInputStream** object, so that data is decrypted as it is read from the source file. Other than that, the two methods are nearly identical:

```
private static void decryptFile( String encrFile,
                                 String clearFile ) {
    try {
        FileInputStream fis
            = new FileInputStream( encrFile );
        Cipher c = getCipher( Cipher.DECRYPT_MODE );
        CipherInputStream cphin
            = new CipherInputStream( fis, c );
        FileOutputStream fos
            = new FileOutputStream( clearFile );
        byte[] byteBuff = new byte[ 8196 ];
        int bytesRead = cphin.read( byteBuff );
        while ( bytesRead != -1 ) {
            fos.write( byteBuff, 0, bytesRead );
            bytesRead = cphin.read( byteBuff );
        }
```

12

```
            fis.close( );
            fos.close( );
            cphin.close( );
        }
        catch( IOException iox ) {
            System.out.println( iox );
        }
    }
```

To test the program, begin by copying the file `X:\Data\examples\security\hamlet1.txt` from the CD-ROM to the current directory. Using the following command in a command-line window to encrypt the contents of `hamlet1.txt` and put the results of the operation into `hamlet1.enc`:

```
java examples.security.FileEncryption /e hamlet1.txt hamlet1.enc
```

the output will be

```
hamlet1.txt successfully encrypted as hamlet1.enc
```

The encrypted file, `hamlet1.enc`, can be decrypted by using the following command:

```
java examples.security.FileEncryption /d hamlet1.enc hamlet1.clr
```

The output will be

```
hamlet1.enc successfully decrypted as hamlet1.clr
```

If you compare the contents of the original `hamlet1.txt` file to the file `hamlet1.clr` that was the result of the decryption steps, you will find that the two files are identical.

Message Digests and Message Authentication Codes

Often it isn't necessary to hide the contents of a message from view. Sometimes all that is required is a way to verify that the message (i.e., program, data file, etc.) received has not been altered. For such cases, a message digest is the answer. You can think of a message digest as a fingerprint for a message. Running the entire message contents through a digest algorithm creates a small chunk of data called a digest value. This value is unique to the message. The algorithms for creating message digests are selected because they have the property that even a small change in the message will result in a digest value for the altered message that is markedly different from the digest value for the original message. These algorithms are also one-way functions, meaning that it is not possible to reconstruct a message from its digest value.

Used alone, including a message digest with a message is a useful technique for being able to detect when a message has been altered in transmission. However, it will not detect the case in which an attacker alters the message and includes a valid message digest for the altered message. To detect such an attack requires that the digest be encrypted. The recipient of the message will first decrypt the digest, then compare the decrypted digest with the expected digest value for the received message. If they are the same, the

These encrypted digest values are also known as message authentication codes, or simply MACs. MACs are discussed in more detail later in this section.

The two most commonly used algorithms for calculating a message digest are Message Digest 5 (MD5) and Secure Hash Algorithm 1 (SHA-1). The latter, developed by the National Institute of Standards & Technology (NIST) in the United States, is preferred because it produces a slightly longer digest value (160 bits). However, MD5 is typically faster than SHA-1. The corresponding algorithms for creating MACs are HmacMD5 and HmacSHA1.

Figure 12-6 contains the complete source code for the class `GenerateDigest` found in the file called `GenerateDigest.java` in the directory `X:\Data\security` from the CD-ROM. (Here `X:` is the drive letter of the CD-ROM.) This example program calculates a SHA-1 message digest for the file specified as an input to the program. A discussion of the contents of the file follows.

```java
package examples.security;
import java.io.FileInputStream;
import java.nio.ByteBuffer;
import java.nio.channels.FileChannel;
import java.security.MessageDigest;
import sun.misc.BASE64Encoder;
/** An example class that generates a message digest
  * for a file specified as an input parameter
  */
public class GenerateDigest {
   /** The test method for the class
     */
   public static void main( String[] args ) {
      if ( args.length >= 1 ) try {
         MessageDigest md
            = MessageDigest.getInstance( "SHA-1" );
         FileInputStream fis
            = new FileInputStream( args[0] );
         FileChannel fc = fis.getChannel();
         ByteBuffer bb
            = ByteBuffer.allocate( (int) fc.size() );
         fc.read( bb );
         byte[] result = md.digest( bb.array() );
         String b64Encoded
            = new BASE64Encoder().encodeBuffer( result );
         System.out.println( "The SHA-1 digest of "
                              + args[0] + " is "
                              + b64Encoded );
         fc.close();
         fis.close();
      }
```

Figure 12-6   `GenerateDigest`: an example class that generates a message digest

```
        catch( Exception x ) {
          System.out.println( x );
          x.printStackTrace();
        } else {
          System.out.println( "A file name is required." );
        }
      }
    }
```

Figure 12-6   GenerateDigest: an example class that generates a message digest
(continued)

The program begins by creating an empty digest that uses the SHA–1 digest algorithm:

```
MessageDigest md
  = MessageDigest.getInstance( "SHA-1" );
```

Then the contents of the specified file are read into a byte array:

```
FileInputStream fis
  = new FileInputStream( args[0] );
FileChannel fc = fis.getChannel();
ByteBuffer bb
  = ByteBuffer.allocate( (int) fc.size() );
fc.read( bb );
```

This byte array is provided as input to the digest, and the resulting digest value is created and converted to base 64 for output purposes. It is worth noting that the **BASE64Encoder** class is an unsupported, undocumented class provided by Sun in the Java SDK, and it would not be a good idea to build a program that depends heavily on this class because **BASE64Encoder** could be withdrawn by Sun without any warning. Regardless, it is a quick and convenient way to display raw byte data as ASCII characters so that you can get an idea of what is in the digest:

```
byte[] result = md.digest( bb.array() );
String b64Encoded
  = new BASE64Encoder().encodeBuffer( result );
System.out.println( "The SHA-1 digest of "
                    + args[0] + " is "
                    + b64Encoded );
```

To get an idea of the power of message digests, two versions of Shakespeare's famous "To be, or not to be" soliloquy from Hamlet are provided in the files **Hamlet1.txt** and **Hamlet2.txt** in the **X:\Data\examples\security** directory on the CD-ROM. (Here **X:** is the drive letter of the CD-ROM.) The only difference between the two files is a missing comma in **Hamlet2.txt** that you would be hard pressed to find by visually scanning the two files. Copy both of these files from the CD-ROM to the current directory so that they will be accessible to the program. Despite this minor difference between

by this example program:

```
The SHA-1 digest of Hamlet1.txt is LLS2WcLYm9QV1PicxCEzSmtm3no=
The SHA-1 digest of Hamlet2.txt is qjEKrcDzjmzwJ9jv8rnboDcfLMI=
```

MACs are typically used in secret key cryptosystems, and so a secret key is a required input to the creation of a MAC. Figure 12-7 is the complete source code for the class `GenerateMAC` found in the file called `GenerateMAC.java`. The structure of packages mirrors the file system, so you will find this source code in the `X:\Data\examples\security` directory on the CD-ROM. (Here `X:` is the drive letter of the CD-ROM.) This example program calculates an HmacSHA1 message authentication code for the file specified as an input to the program. A discussion of the contents of the file follows.

```java
package examples.security;
import java.io.FileInputStream;
import java.nio.ByteBuffer;
import java.nio.channels.FileChannel;
import java.security.SecureRandom;
import javax.crypto.Mac;
import javax.crypto.SecretKey;
import javax.crypto.spec.SecretKeySpec;
import sun.misc.BASE64Encoder;
/** An example class that generates a message
 * authentication code (MAC)
 */
public class GenerateMAC {
   /** The test method for the class
     */
   public static void main( String[] args ) {
      if ( args.length >= 1 ) try {
         String macAlg = "HmacSHA1";
         SecureRandom sr = new SecureRandom();
         byte[] keyData = new byte[20];
         sr.nextBytes( keyData );
         SecretKey sk
             = new SecretKeySpec( keyData, macAlg );
          Mac mac = Mac.getInstance( macAlg );
          mac.init( sk );
          FileInputStream fis
             = new FileInputStream( args[0] );
          FileChannel fc = fis.getChannel();
          ByteBuffer bb
             = ByteBuffer.allocate( (int) fc.size() );
          fc.read( bb );
          byte[] result = mac.doFinal( bb.array() );
```

Figure 12-7   `GenerateMAC`: an example class that generates a message authentication code

```
            String b64Encoded
               = new BASE64Encoder().encodeBuffer( result );
            System.out.println( "The " + macAlg + " MAC of "
                              + args[0] + " is "
                              + b64Encoded );
         fc.close();
         fis.close();
      }
      catch( Exception x ) {
         System.out.println( x );
         x.printStackTrace();
      } else {
         System.out.println( "A file name is required." );
      }
   }
}
```

Figure 12-7   GenerateMAC: an example class that generates a message authentication code (continued)

After verifying that it does have the required input parameter, the program begins by creating a secure random number generator to provide input data to create a secret key value:

```
String macAlg = "HmacSHA1";
SecureRandom sr = new SecureRandom();
byte[] keyData = new byte[20];
sr.nextBytes( keyData );
SecretKey sk
   = new SecretKeySpec( keyData, macAlg );
```

Now it is possible to go ahead and create the MAC object and initialize it with the secret key:

```
Mac mac = Mac.getInstance( macAlg );
mac.init( sk );
```

After reading the entire file into a buffer, calculating the MAC key isn't difficult to do. The entire operation is accomplished with a single statement:

```
byte[] result = mac.doFinal( bb.array() );
```

The value of the MAC is then output in base 64 and displayed for all to see:

```
String b64Encoded
   = new BASE64Encoder().encodeBuffer( result );
System.out.println( "The " + macAlg + " MAC of "
                  + args[0] + " is "
                  + b64Encoded );
```

Using the following command line to ... ...

```
java examples.security.GenerateMAC hamlet1.txt
```

one possible output will be

```
The HmacSHA1 MAC of hamlet1.txt is 92TcYl7oapcH3tNfxtn6Rdrucl4=
```

Digital Signatures

Digital signatures are used to verify the integrity and the authenticity of a message. The concept is similar to that of MACs, with the important difference being that MACs use secret key encryption and digital signatures use public key encryption. The process of producing a digital signature begins with the process for producing a message digest. Figure 12-8 illustrates this process. Suppose that Bob wants to send Alice a signed message. Bob will begin by creating the digest for his message, and then he will encrypt the digest with his private key that only he knows. When Alice receives the message she will decrypt the digest using Bob's public key (known by all), and then compare the decrypted digest, D_1, with the expected digest value she calculated from the received message, D_2. If they are the same, Alice can be confident that the received message is the original, unaltered message that could have only been sent by Bob.

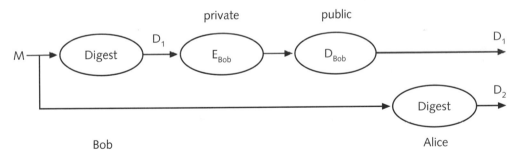

Figure 12-8   Digital signature usage

The program `SignAndStore` shown in Figure 12-9 demonstrates how a key can be used to generate a digital signature for the text file `hamlet1.txt`. The signature is stored in its own file, `hamlet1.txt.sig`, from which it can be extracted to verify the integrity of the `hamlet1.txt` file. A discussion of the contents of the file follows. The companion program, `ReadAndVerify`, in Figure 12-10 similarly calculates the digital signature for the file `hamlet1.txt` and then compares the signature that it has calculated against the signature stored in the file `hamlet1.txt.sig`. If they match, the reader can be assured that the file `hamlet1.txt` has not been changed since its digital signature was calculated.

```
package examples.security;
import java.io.*;
import java.nio.ByteBuffer;
import java.nio.channels.FileChannel;
import java.security.*;
/** An example class that accesses a key within a keystore and uses
  * the key to create a digital signature
  */
public class SignAndStore {
   static final String KEYSTORE = "jpatkeystore.ks";
   static final String KEYALIAS = "exampleRSApair";
   static final String STOREPASSWD = "changeit";
   static final String ALIASPASSWD = "changeit";
   /** The test method for the class
     */
   public static void main( String[] args ) {
      try {
         KeyStore ks = KeyStore.getInstance( "JCEKS" );
         ks.load( new FileInputStream( KEYSTORE ),
               STOREPASSWD.toCharArray() );
         Key k = ks.getKey( KEYALIAS, ALIASPASSWD.toCharArray() );
         Signature sig = Signature.getInstance( "SHA1withRSA" );
         sig.initSign( (PrivateKey) k );
         FileInputStream fis = new FileInputStream( "hamlet1.txt" );
         FileChannel fc = fis.getChannel();
         ByteBuffer bb = ByteBuffer.allocate( (int) fc.size() );
         fc.read( bb );
         sig.update( bb.array() );
         byte[] result = sig.sign();
         FileOutputStream fos = new FileOutputStream( "hamlet1.txt.sig" );
         fos.write( result );
         fc.close();
         fis.close();
         fos.close();
         System.out.println( "Signature generated successfully and saved" );
      }
      catch( Exception x ) {
         System.out.println( x );
         x.printStackTrace();
      }
   }
}
```

Figure 12-9   SignAndStore: a program that generates and stores a digital signature for a file

The program begins by creating a **KeyStore** object and loading it with the key and certificate information contained in the file **jpatkeystore.ks**. The key corresponding to the alias **exampleRSApair** is then retrieved for use as the key:

```
KeyStore ks = KeyStore.getInstance( "JCEKS" );
ks.load( new FileInputStream( KEYSTORE ),
    STOREPASSWD.toCharArray() );
Key k = ks.getKey( KEYALIAS, ALIASPASSWD.toCharArray() );
```

Next, an instance of the **Signature** class that will be a combination of the SHA-1 and RSA algorithms is obtained. The **Signature** object is initialized with the private key of the RSA key pair:

```
Signature sig = Signature.getInstance( "SHA1withRSA" );
sig.initSign( (PrivateKey) k );
```

Using the new I/O API described in Chapter 3, the entire contents of the **hamlet1.txt** file are read into a **ByteBuffer** object:

```
FileInputStream fis = new FileInputStream( "hamlet1.txt" );
FileChannel fc = fis.getChannel();
ByteBuffer bb = ByteBuffer.allocate( (int) fc.size() );
fc.read( bb );
```

The contents of the **ByteBuffer** object are then converted to an array and input to the **Signature** object to update the value of the signature. In this case, there is only a single buffer so the **update** method is invoked once. But if there were many buffers of data for this file, each one would have to be applied to the **Signature** object. After the entire contents of the file have been used to update the **Signature** object, the resulting digital signature is generated by invoking the **sign** method:

```
sig.update( bb.array() );
byte[] result = sig.sign();
```

The program ends by writing the contents of the signature to a file, then closing all the streams and displaying a message to inform the user of the positive outcome:

```
FileOutputStream fos = new FileOutputStream( "hamlet1.txt.sig" );
fos.write( result );
fc.close();
fis.close();
fos.close();
System.out.println( "Signature generated successfully and saved" );
```

The **ReadAndVerify** program in Figure 12-10 is a companion to the **SignAndStore** program (Figure 12-9). The **ReadAndVerify** program calculates the digital signature for the file **hamlet1.txt** and then compares the signature that it has calculated against the signature stored in the file **hamlet1.txt.sig**. If they match, the reader can be assured that the file **hamlet1.txt** has not been changed since its digital signature was calculated. A discussion of the contents of the file follows.

12

```
package examples.security;
import java.io.FileInputStream;
import java.nio.ByteBuffer;
import java.nio.channels.FileChannel;
import java.security.*;
import java.security.cert.Certificate;
/** An example class that accesses a key within a keystore in order
 * to verify a digital signature
 */
public class ReadAndVerify {
    static final String KEYSTORE = "jpatkeystore.ks";
    static final String KEYALIAS = "exampleRSApair";
    static final String STOREPASSWD = "changeit";
    static final String ALIASPASSWD = "changeit";
    /** The test method for the class
      */
    public static void main( String[] args ) {
        try {
            KeyStore ks = KeyStore.getInstance( "JCEKS" );
            ks.load( new FileInputStream( KEYSTORE ),
                    STOREPASSWD.toCharArray() );
            Certificate cert = ks.getCertificate( KEYALIAS );
            Signature sig = Signature.getInstance( "SHA1withRSA" );
            sig.initVerify( cert );
            FileInputStream fis = new FileInputStream( "hamlet1.txt" );
            FileChannel fc = fis.getChannel();
            ByteBuffer bb = ByteBuffer.allocate( (int) fc.size() );
            fc.read( bb );
            sig.update( bb.array() );
            FileInputStream fisSig = new FileInputStream( "hamlet1.txt.sig" );
            FileChannel fcSig = fisSig.getChannel();
            ByteBuffer bbSig = ByteBuffer.allocate( (int) fcSig.size() );
            fcSig.read( bbSig );
            boolean success = sig.verify( bbSig.array() );
            if ( success ) {
                System.out.println( "Signature verified" );
            } else {
                System.out.println( "Signature rejected" );
            }
            fc.close();
            fis.close();
            fcSig.close();
            fisSig.close();
        }
        catch( Exception x ) {
            System.out.println( x );
            x.printStackTrace();
        }
    }
}
```

Figure 12-10   ReadAndVerify: a program that verifies the digital signature of a file

The program begins by creating a **KeyStore** object and loading it with the key and certificate information contained in the file **jpatkeystore.ks**. The certificate for which the public key corresponds to the alias **exampleRSApair** is then retrieved:

```
KeyStore ks = KeyStore.getInstance( "JCEKS" );
ks.load( new FileInputStream( KEYSTORE ),
        STOREPASSWD.toCharArray() );
Certificate cert = ks.getCertificate( KEYALIAS );
```

Next, an instance of the **Signature** class that will be a combination of the SHA-1 and RSA algorithms is obtained. The **Signature** object is initialized for the purposes of verification with the certificate containing the public key of the RSA key pair:

```
Signature sig = Signature.getInstance( "SHA1withRSA" );
sig.initVerify( cert );
```

Using the new I/O API, the entire contents of the **hamlet1.txt** file are read into a **ByteBuffer** object:

```
FileInputStream fis = new FileInputStream( "hamlet1.txt" );
FileChannel fc = fis.getChannel();
ByteBuffer bb = ByteBuffer.allocate( (int) fc.size() );
fc.read( bb );
```

The contents of the **ByteBuffer** object are then converted to an array and input to the **Signature** object to update the value of the signature. In this case, there is only a single buffer so the update method is invoked once. But if there were many buffers of data for this file, each one would have to be applied to the **Signature** object:

```
sig.update( bb.array() );
```

The reference digital signature is kept on disk in the file **hamlet1.txt.sig**, and so it is read from disk into a **ByteBuffer** object for easy comparison:

```
FileInputStream fisSig = new FileInputStream( "hamlet1.txt.sig" );
FileChannel fcSig = fisSig.getChannel();
ByteBuffer bbSig = ByteBuffer.allocate( (int) fcSig.size() );
fcSig.read( bbSig );
```

After the original **Signature** object has been retrieved from the disk file, it is compared against what has just been calculated by the program by using the **verify** method. Then the appropriate message is displayed:

```
boolean success = sig.verify( bbSig.array() );
if ( success ) {
   System.out.println( "Signature verified" );
} else {
   System.out.println( "Signature rejected" );
}
```

12

Finally, all the input streams are closed before the program ends:

```
fc.close();
fis.close();
fcSig.close();
fisSig.close();
```

When you successfully run the `SignAndStore` program, you will see the output line

Signature generated successfully and saved

Next, run the `ReadAndVerify` program and, assuming the `hamlet1.txt` file and `hamlet1.txt.sig` file are unchanged, you will see the following output:

Signature verified

Try altering the `hamlet1.txt` file or the `hamlet1.txt.sig` file and then run `ReadAndVerify` again. This time the output you will see is

Signature rejected

Certificates

An important use of digital signatures is to create certificates to prove the authenticity of a piece of information such as a person's public key. On its own, a public key is just a sequence of numbers and there is nothing about it that connects it with the person to whom it belongs. You may be given a public key and told that it belongs to Alice, but you can't be sure that the key is really Alice's key.

Certificates solve this problem by having a trusted, well-known, readily verifiable source called a Certificate Authority (CA) issue a certificate containing the name of the person to whom the certificate is issued (the subject of the certificate) and the public key associated with the subject. The CA signs the certificate with its own digital signature. In this way the problem of verifying the public keys of countless people is simplified to the problem of verifying the digital signature of just a few CAs. Preloading the digital signatures of the CAs into software applications, such as browsers, typically solves this problem. To simplify the processing of certificates, standards have been developed to describe the file format of certificates. The most prevalent of these standards is the X.509 standard digital certificate format.

You can create your own certificate using the `keytool` utility provided with the SDK. Figure 12-11 shows the command-line session to create a certificate based on a key pair in a keystore file. User input is shown in bold. Although the `keytool` command at the top of the figure appears on two lines, it must be entered as a single command.

```
keytool -export -alias exampleRSApair -keystore jpatkeystore.ks -
storetype JCEKS -rfc -file exampleRSA.cer
Enter keystore password:  changeit
Certificate stored in file <exampleRSA.cer>
```

Figure 12-11   Certificate creation transcript

Normally you would submit the file created in Figure 12-9 to a CA for authentication and to have it signed by the CA. That could be time consuming and will likely cost you a few hundred dollars. So, for the purpose of demonstration, we'll just simply put the certificate directly into a file where trusted certificates are kept, called a *truststore*. Figure 12-12 shows the command-line session to create a certificate based on a key pair in a truststore file. User input is shown in bold. Although the `keytool` command at the top of the figure appears on two lines, it must be entered as a single command.

```
keytool -import -alias exampleRSAcert -file exampleRSA.cer -storetype JCEKS -
keystore jpattruststore.ks
Enter keystore password:  changeit
Owner: CN=Wigglesworth McMillan, OU=Java Programming Advanced Topics,
O=Course Technology, L=Toronto, ST=ON, C=CA
Issuer: CN=Wigglesworth McMillan, OU=Java Programming Advanced Topics,
O=Course Technology, L=Toronto, ST=ON, C=CA
Serial number: 3e3dfa96
Valid from: Mon Feb 03 00:13:58 EST 2003 until: Sun May 04 01:13:58 EDT 2003
Certificate fingerprints:
        MD5:  09:69:5E:89:8A:D6:D9:CA:43:E5:7A:94:D1:02:D0:48
        SHA1: 63:56:D0:FD:FC:45:84:A2:8A:01:3A:CF:55:22:95:DF:F7:DE:B5:AF
Trust this certificate? [no]:  y
Certificate was added to keystore
```

Figure 12-12   Transcript of storing a certificate in a truststore file

The contents of a truststore file are accessible to a Java program. Figure 12-13 contains a simple program that begins by creating an empty truststore, then loads the contents of the keystore created by the previous command. Finally, it retrieves the new key pair by its alias and confirms the certificate type used by the key pair.

The output from the program in Figure 12-13 is

```
The certificate type for alias exampleRSAcert is X.509
```

12

```
package examples.security;
import java.io.FileInputStream;
import java.security.cert.Certificate;
import java.security.KeyStore;
/** An example class that accesses a key within a keystore
  */
public class TruststoreAccess {
    static final String TRUSTSTORE = "jpattruststore.ks";
    static final String CERTALIAS = "exampleRSAcert";
    static final String STOREPASSWD = "changeit";
    /** The test method for the class
      */
    public static void main( String[] args ) {
        try {
            KeyStore ts = KeyStore.getInstance( "JCEKS" );
            ts.load( new FileInputStream( TRUSTSTORE ),
                       STOREPASSWD.toCharArray() );
            Certificate c = ts.getCertificate( CERTALIAS );
            System.out.println( "The certificate type for "
                               + "alias " + CERTALIAS
                               + " is " + c.getType() );
        }
        catch( Exception x ) {
            System.out.println( x );
            x.printStackTrace();
        }
    }
}
```

Figure 12-13 `TruststoreAccess:` an example class that accesses a certificate within a truststore

SECURE SOCKET LAYER (SSL)

The cryptosystem concepts presented so far in this chapter, such as private and public key cryptography, digests, MACs, digital signatures, and certificates, have many applications, but one of their most common applications is the securing of communications channels to protect them from eavesdropping. Although you have probably used the Secure Socket Layer (SSL) Internet technology every day, you probably never gave much thought to its underlying security implementation. SSL makes use of nearly every technology presented so far in this chapter. You use SSL within your Web browser when you are transmitting sensitive information, such as a credit card number, from your computer to the Web server. By convention, a URL that begins with `https:` instead of the usual `http:` will require an SSL connection.

Secure Socket Layer Handshake

SSL is a protocol that was developed by Netscape for transmitting private documents over the Internet on a secure communications channel. Transport Layer Security (TLS) is an associated Internet standard based on SSL that is an improvement over SSL. It is through something called the SSL handshake that the secure channel is established. The following list is a simplified summary of the steps involved in this handshake:

1. The client sends a message to the server requesting an SSL connection and providing a list of encryption and decryption algorithms (cipher suites) that it can support.

2. The server responds by sending its certificate containing its public key and by sending a recommendation of what cipher suite should be used based on the client's and the server's capabilities.

3. The client uses the received certificate to authenticate the server with a trusted CA. Assuming the server can be authenticated, the client encrypts a piece of data called the premaster secret using the server's public key and sends it to the server.

4. The server decrypts the premaster secret with its private key.

5. Both the client and the server generate the session key using the premaster secret as input to an algorithm defined by SSL. The session key is now a secret that the client and server share, and that no one else knows.

6. The client and server exchange messages acknowledging that the handshake is complete. All future messages in the session are encrypted with the secret key and include a MAC in order that any tampering with the data will be detected.

Note that the handshake begins using public key cryptography, but switches to symmetric secret key cryptography once the secret key has been established. This is done for reasons of performance, because encryption and decryption are much faster when using symmetric secret key cryptography as opposed to asymmetric public key cryptography. But public key cryptography plays a vital role in the steps to establish the secret key. And digital certificates play a vital role in authenticating the server so that the client can have confidence that the Web server it has contacted is, in fact, the Web server that it expected.

Java Secure Socket Extension

The Java Secure Socket Extension (JSSE) enables secure Internet communications by providing a framework and a 100% Pure Java implementation of the SSL and TLS protocols. Fortunately, the JSSE implementation follows the same implementation pattern used for standard TCP/IP sockets that was discussed in Chapter 11, and so it is not difficult to take a program written using standard sockets and convert it to use secure sockets. Figure 12-14 contains the same server socket programming example first presented in Chapter 11, except that it has been modified to use secure sockets. The differences are identified using a bold font.

12

```
package examples.security;
import java.io.*;
import java.net.*;
import javax.net.ssl.*;
import java.security.*;
import java.util.StringTokenizer;
/** An example class that uses the secure server socket class
  */
public class SecureAdditionServer {
   private int port;
   // This is not a reserved port number
   static final int DEFAULT_PORT = 8189;
   static final String KEYSTORE = "jpatkeystore.ks";
   static final String TRUSTSTORE = "jpattruststore.ks";
   static final String STOREPASSWD = "changeit";
   static final String ALIASPASSWD = "changeit";
   /** Constructor
     * @param port The port where the server
     *     will listen for requests
     */
   SecureAdditionServer( int port ) {
      this.port = port;
   }
   /** The method that does the work for the class */
   public void run() {
      try {
         KeyStore ks = KeyStore.getInstance( "JCEKS" );
         ks.load( new FileInputStream( KEYSTORE ),
                 STOREPASSWD.toCharArray() );
         KeyStore ts = KeyStore.getInstance( "JCEKS" );
         ts.load( new FileInputStream( TRUSTSTORE ),
                 STOREPASSWD.toCharArray() );
         KeyManagerFactory kmf
            = KeyManagerFactory.getInstance( "SunX509" );
         kmf.init( ks, ALIASPASSWD.toCharArray() );
         TrustManagerFactory tmf
            = TrustManagerFactory.getInstance( "SunX509" );
         tmf.init( ts );
         SSLContext sslContext
            = SSLContext.getInstance( "TLS" );
         sslContext.init( kmf.getKeyManagers(),
                       tmf.getTrustManagers(), null );
         SSLServerSocketFactory sslServerFactory
            = sslContext.getServerSocketFactory();
         SSLServerSocket sss
            = (SSLServerSocket)
              sslServerFactory.createServerSocket( port );
         sss.setEnabledCipherSuites(
            sss.getSupportedCipherSuites() );
```

Figure 12-14   SecureAdditionServer: example of the client side of a secure network connection

```
            SSLSocket incoming = (SSLSocket)sss.accept();
            BufferedReader in;
            in = new BufferedReader(
               new InputStreamReader(
               incoming.getInputStream() ) );
            PrintWriter out
               = new PrintWriter(
               incoming.getOutputStream(), true );
            String str;
            while ( !(str = in.readLine()).equals("") ) {
               double result = 0;
               StringTokenizer st
                  = new StringTokenizer( str );
               try {
                  while( st.hasMoreTokens() ) {
                     Double d = new Double( st.nextToken() );
                     result += d.doubleValue();
                  }
                  out.println( "The result is " + result );
               }
               catch( NumberFormatException nfe ) {
                  out.println( "Sorry, your list "
                           + "contains an "
                           + "invalid number" );
               }
            }
            incoming.close();
         }
      catch( Exception x ) {
         System.out.println( x );
         x.printStackTrace();
      }
   }
   /** The test method for the class
    * @param args[0] Optional port number in place of
    *         the default
    */
   public static void main( String[] args ) {
      int port = DEFAULT_PORT;
      if (args.length > 0 ) {
         port = Integer.parseInt( args[0] );
      }
      SecureAdditionServer addServe
         = new SecureAdditionServer( port );
      addServe.run();
   }
}
```

Figure 12-14   `SecureAdditionServer`: example of the client side of a secure network connection (continued)

12

The secure version of the client shown in Figure 12-14 begins with expected differences in terms of package name and import statements. Of course, the name of the class is also different. The secure version defines several string constants that will be used later in the program. These strings are the names of the keystore and truststore files, as well as the password for accessing these two files (both files have the same password in this example) and the password to access the particular entries of interest via their aliases:

```
static final String KEYSTORE = "jpatkeystore.ks";
static final String TRUSTSTORE = "jpattruststore.ks";
static final String STOREPASSWD = "changeit";
static final String ALIASPASSWD = "changeit";
```

The **run** method of the secure version begins with a large block of statements to set up security. The following statements create an empty **keystore** and an empty **truststore** objects and then load them with the contents of the program's keystore and truststore files:

```
KeyStore ks = KeyStore.getInstance( "JCEKS" );
ks.load( new FileInputStream( KEYSTORE ),
        STOREPASSWD.toCharArray() );
KeyStore ts = KeyStore.getInstance( "JCEKS" );
ts.load( new FileInputStream( TRUSTSTORE ),
        STOREPASSWD.toCharArray() );
```

The SSL connection will require access to encryption keys and certificates. For that reason, factory objects to create both **KeyManager** and **TrustManager** objects are created and then initialized with the **KeyStore** and **TrustStore** objects:

```
KeyManagerFactory kmf
    = KeyManagerFactory.getInstance( "SunX509" );
kmf.init( ks, ALIASPASSWD.toCharArray() );
TrustManagerFactory tmf
    = TrustManagerFactory.getInstance( "SunX509" );
tmf.init( ts );
```

With the groundwork in place with respect to the keys and certificates, an **SSLContext** object can be created. The input parameter, **TLS**, indicates that we want to use the Transport Layer Security standard. This is the most recent standard in the SSL family of standards. Once the **SSLContext** object is created, it is initialized with all the **KeyManager** and **TrustManager** objects that the factory objects support. The initialization method will also accept a third parameter, a random number used in the process of generating the secret key·that the SSL handshake will use. In this case the **null** reference is input, so the default random number seed will be used:

```
SSLContext sslContext
    = SSLContext.getInstance( "TLS" );
sslContext.init( kmf.getKeyManagers(),
        tmf.getTrustManagers(), null );
```

ate the factory object that will create the SSL server socket, because there is no public constructor for the **SSLServerSocket** class that you can call:

```
SSLServerSocketFactory sslServerFactory
    = sslContext.getServerSocketFactory();
```

Once a factory object is available, the **SSLServerSocket** object can be created to listen on the specified port. To provide for maximum flexibility when doing protocol negotiation with clients, all supported cipher suites are enabled and the **accept** method is invoked to begin listening for connections:

```
SSLServerSocket sss
    = (SSLServerSocket)
        sslServerFactory.createServerSocket( port );
sss.setEnabledCipherSuites(
        sss.getSupportedCipherSuites() );
SSLSocket incoming = (SSLSocket)sss.accept();
```

The catch block at the end of the **run** method has been altered to catch the more generic **Exception** class instead of the **IOException** class. This was required because the statements that work with keys and certificates and the statements to set up an SSL connection have the potential to throw a wide range of exception classes.

The last difference between the original server class and the secure server class is the statement in the **main** method that constructs the **SecureAdditionServer** object. However, the difference is due only to the difference in class names. The function is the same.

Figure 12-15 contains the same client socket programming example first presented in Chapter 11 except that it has been modified to use secure sockets. The differences are identified using a bold font.

```
package examples.security;
import java.io.*;
import java.net.*;
import java.security.KeyStore;
import javax.net.ssl.*;
/** A client-side class that uses a secure TCP/IP socket
  */
public class SecureAdditionClient {
    private InetAddress host;
    private int port;
    // This is not a reserved port number
    static final int DEFAULT_PORT = 8189;
    static final String KEYSTORE = "jpatkeystore.ks";
    static final String TRUSTSTORE = "jpattruststore.ks";
    static final String STOREPASSWD = "changeit";
    static final String ALIASPASSWD = "changeit";
```

Figure 12-15   `SecureAdditionClient:` example of the client side of a secure network connection

12

```
    /** Constructor
      * @param host Internet address of the host
      *        where the server is located
      * @param port Port number on the host where
      *        the server is listening
      */
    public SecureAdditionClient( InetAddress host, int port ) {
        this.host = host;
        this.port = port;
    }
    /** The method used to start a client object
      */
    public void run() {
        try {
            KeyStore ks = KeyStore.getInstance( "JCEKS" );
            ks.load( new FileInputStream( KEYSTORE ),
                    STOREPASSWD.toCharArray() );
            KeyStore ts = KeyStore.getInstance( "JCEKS" );
            ts.load( new FileInputStream( TRUSTSTORE ),
                    STOREPASSWD.toCharArray() );
            KeyManagerFactory kmf
                = KeyManagerFactory.getInstance( "SunX509" );
            kmf.init( ks, ALIASPASSWD.toCharArray() );
            TrustManagerFactory tmf
                = TrustManagerFactory.getInstance( "SunX509" );
            tmf.init( ts );
            SSLContext sslContext
                = SSLContext.getInstance( "TLS" );
            sslContext.init( kmf.getKeyManagers(),
                             tmf.getTrustManagers(), null );
            SSLSocketFactory sslFact
                = sslContext.getSocketFactory();
            SSLSocket client =
                (SSLSocket)sslFact.createSocket(host, port);
            client.setEnabledCipherSuites(
                client.getSupportedCipherSuites() );
            BufferedReader socketIn;
            socketIn
                = new BufferedReader(
                  new InputStreamReader(
                  client.getInputStream() ) );
            PrintWriter socketOut
                = new PrintWriter(
                  client.getOutputStream(), true );
            String numbers = "1.2 3.4 5.6";
            System.out.println( "Adding the numbers "
                                + numbers
                                + " together securely" );
            socketOut.println( numbers );
```

Figure 12-15 `SecureAdditionClient`: example of the client side of a secure
network connection (continued)

```
            System.out.println( socketIn.readLine() );
            socketOut.println ( "" );
        }
        catch( Exception x ) {
            System.out.println( x );
            x.printStackTrace();
        }
    }
    /** The test method for the class
     * @param args Optional port number
     *             and host name
     */
    public static void main( String[] args ) {
        try {
            InetAddress host = InetAddress.getLocalHost();
            int port = DEFAULT_PORT;
            if ( args.length > 0 ) {
                port = Integer.parseInt( args[0] );
            }
            if ( args.length > 1 ) {
                host = InetAddress.getByName( args[1] );
            }
            SecureAdditionClient addClient
                = new SecureAdditionClient( host, port );
            addClient.run();
        }
        catch ( UnknownHostException uhx ) {
            System.out.println( uhx );
            uhx.printStackTrace();
        }
    }
}
```

12

Figure 12-15   `SecureAdditionClient`: example of the client side of a secure
network connection (continued)

Although there are also many differences between the original client class and the secure
client class, most of these differences are the same changes that were made to the server
class and were already discussed. But there is one notable change that is unique to the
client. Instead of constructing a factory to create **SSLServerSocket** objects, the client
needs an **SSLSocketFactory** object instead:

```
SSLSocketFactory sslFact
    = sslContext.getSocketFactory();
```

With the factory object available, the required **SSLSocket** object is created to connect
with the specified host using the port identified. As with the **SSLServerSocket** object,
all the supported cipher suites are enabled for the client to maximize its flexibility when

negotiating with the server to agree upon the cipher suite that will be used for the secure connection:

```
SSLSocket client =
    (SSLSocket)sslFact.createSocket(host, port);
client.setEnabledCipherSuites(
    client.getSupportedCipherSuites() );
```

To run this server and client example that has been modified to use SSL, you must first successfully generate a key pair in the keystore file, as shown in Figure 12-3 (substitute your own information in place of the information shown). You must also successfully export a certificate from the keystore file, as shown in Figure 12-9, and then import that certificate into a truststore file, as shown in Figure 12-10. Once that is done, you can begin by running the server program and then running the client program. Run these two programs in two different command windows making sure that the current directory is the directory containing the keystore and truststore files. When the example runs successfully, you will see the following output lines:

```
Adding the numbers 1.2 3.4 5.6 together securely
The result is 10.2
```

SECURITY POLICY DEFINITION AND ENFORCEMENT

So far in this chapter you have examined cryptography and how it can be used to provide data privacy, ensure data integrity, and allow for user authentication. Now you turn to the different, but related, topic of defining and enforcing a security policy.

Security is a serious concern, because many Java programs (notably applets) are designed to be loaded from the Web. Because many of these programs originate from unknown host systems, the worry about viruses and other unwanted side effects is valid. The JVM puts many restrictions on applets, which severely limit their activity. During execution, it is a **SecurityManager** object that enforces security restrictions. Java applications that are executed from the local file system run in an environment that does not, by default, have a security manager installed. This means that a Java application, by default, has no restrictions on what it may do.

The **SecurityManager** class provides many methods with names that start with the word **check**. Each **check*xxx*** method corresponds to an action that can possibly be disallowed. For example, every time a user attempts to delete a file, the method **checkDelete** is called. You can set arguments that determine whether the method decides to allow the operation, or disallow it by throwing a **java.lang.SecurityException** object. Because different browsers implement the check methods differently, sometimes the same applet may execute without an error within one browser but trigger a security exception within another browser.

Permissions and Policy Files

With the release of the Java 2 platform, an object of the **java.security.Policy** class represents the security policy for all kinds of Java programs. The information used to build the **Policy** object is taken from a default, systemwide policy file and an optional user policy file. The default name for these files is **java.policy**. The default location of the systemwide file is the directory *java.home*\lib\security, where *java.home* is the directory in which the Java runtime is installed, as defined in the system property called **java.home**. Use the system property **user.home** in the directory *user.home*\lib\security to locate the user policy file.

The contents of the systemwide and user **java.policy** files include one or more of the grant entry statements in the form shown in Figure 12-16. The square brackets are not part of the statement syntax but are used to indicate which parts of the statement are optional. Italicized text represents values that are replaced by actual user information.

```
grant [signedBy "signer_names",] [codeBase "URL"] {
    permission permission_class_name
        "target_name", ["action"]
        [, signedBy "signer_names"];
}
```

Figure 12-16   Example grant entry statements

The **signedBy** and **codeBase** clauses of the statement identify the code to which the permissions listed inside the brace brackets { } apply. The **signedBy** clause is used to indicate that the permissions apply to code signed by the names inside the double quotes that follow. The Java 2 SDK provides a utility called **jarsigner** that you can use to sign a **.jar** file. The **codeBase** clause is used to indicate that the permissions apply to code from the URL specified inside the double quotes that follow. These can be used singly or together. If both are omitted, the permissions will apply to all code, regardless of origin and who may have signed it.

The contents of an example policy file, **examplePolicy**, are shown in Figure 12-17. Two grant statements are included: The first applies to code signed by ACME Software, and the second applies to code from the URL **www.mycompany.com**. The dash at the end of the URL indicates that the statement also applies to all files in all subdirectories. If an asterisk were used in place of the dash, it would apply to all files in the specified directory, but not to any subdirectories.

The Java 2 security model is a fine-grained model, because you can now specify the permissions that you grant. Figure 12-18 lists the available permission class names that can be used in a grant statement and describes the purpose for each class. Example target names are also given as well as any applicable actions. The Java 2 SDK provides a tool called **policytool** that you can use to help you create your own policy file.

```
grant signedBy "ACME Software" {
   permission java.io.FilePermission
      "c:\\autoexec.bat", "read";
   permission java.lang.RuntimePermission
      "queuePrintJob";
}
grant codeBase "http://www.mycompany.com/-" {
   permission java.util.PropertyPermission
      "java.*", "read";
   permission java.util.PropertyPermission
      "user.*", "write";
   permission java.lang.RuntimePermission
      "exitVM";
}
```

Figure 12-17   Example policy file

In the discussion of the Java Authentication and Authorization Service in the next section, you expand the usefulness of grant statements by seeing how it is possible to grant permission based on the identity of the user, not only based on the origin of the code or who signed the code.

Permission Type Class Name	Description
`java.security.AllPermission`	This permission implies all other permissions. It is granted to allow code the ability to run without any security restrictions, so it should be used cautiously.
`java.security.AudioPermission`	This permission is granted to allow access to the audio system resources, e.g., the ability to be able to do audio playback or audio recording.
`java.awt.AWTPermission`	This permission is granted to allow code special privileges with respect to GUI operations. Examples of targets for this type are `accessClipboard`, which allows information to be placed upon and taken from the AWT clipboard, and `showWindowWithoutWarningBanner`, which allows frame windows created by applets to appear without any warning message.

Figure 12-18   Policy file permission class names and descriptions

Permission Type Class Name	Description
`java.security.BasicPermission`	This abstract class is provided to access the superclass of permission classes that don't implement an action list and thus are binary in nature—either you have the permission or you don't, without qualification.
`java.security.DelegationPermission`	This permission is granted to allow specific actions that are related to the Kerberos authentication security system.
`java.io.FilePermission`	This permission is granted to allow code access to read and write files. Targets of this type are specific files, directories, or directory trees. Actions that can be controlled are read, write, execute, and delete.
`java.security.LoggingPermission`	This permission is granted to allow control of the logging configuration, for example working with logging filters or the logging level.
`java.net.NetPermission`	This permission is granted to allow code to perform certain network-related operations. Examples of targets for this type are **setDefaultAuthenticator**, which allows the ability to set the way authentication information is retrieved when a proxy or HTTP server asks for authentication, and **requestPasswordAuthentication**, which allows the ability to ask the authenticator for a password.
`java.security.Permission`	This is the abstract class for representing access to a system resource. It is the superclass of all other permission classes.
`java.util.PropertyPermission`	This permission is granted to allow code to access property values. Targets for this type are specific properties or groups of properties specified with a wildcard match. Actions that can be controlled are read and write.
`java.lang.ReflectPermission`	This permission is granted to allow code to query information about classes. An example target for this type is **suppressAccessChecks**, which allows the ability to find out about public, private, and protected fields and methods.

12

Figure 12-18   Policy file permission class names and descriptions (continued)

Permission Type Class Name	Description
java.lang.RuntimePermission	This permission is granted to allow code the ability to perform operations related to the functioning of the JVM. Example targets for this type are exitVM, which allows the ability to halt the JVM; loadLibrary, which allows the dynamic linking of a specified library; and queuePrintJob, which allows a print job request to be initiated.
java.security.SecurityPermission	This permission is granted to allow code to perform operations related to the enforcement of security policy. Example targets for this type are getPolicy, which allows the retrieval of the systemwide security policy, and setPolicy, which allows the setting of the systemwide security policy.
java.io.SerializablePermission	This permission is granted to allow code to perform operations related to serializing and deserializing objects. Example targets for this type are enableSubclassImplementation, which allows the default implementations of ObjectOutputStream and ObjectInputStream to be replaced with a user-defined subclass, and enableSubstitution, which allows one object to be substituted for another during a serialization or deserialization operation.
java.net.SocketPermission	This permission is granted to allow code to perform operations related to establishing connections to host systems. The targets for this type are port numbers or ranges of port numbers on specific host systems. Actions that can be controlled are accept, connect, listen, and resolve.
java.security.SQLPermission	This permission is granted to allow the setting of the logging stream related to SQL queries.
java.security.SSLPermission	This permission is granted to allow actions related to the Secure Socket Layer protocol.

Figure 12-18   Policy file permission class names and descriptions (continued)

JAVA AUTHENTICATION AND AUTHORIZATION SERVICE

From the beginning, the Java platform has emphasized security, but the methods initially used to provide security were based upon where the code originated. Simply put, code that came as an applet from a Web server was not trusted and was very restricted in what it could do, whereas code run from the local file system was trusted completely and ran without restrictions. Because it was understood that some Web sources should be trustworthy, the idea of signing code and then determining the restrictions based upon the identity of the signer was introduced. What was missing was the ability to impose restrictions based on the identity of the user who ran the code. The Java Authentication and Authorization Service (JAAS) provides a framework that enhances the Java 2 security architecture with such support.

Pluggable Authentication Modules

JAAS introduces the concept of a *pluggable authentication module* (PAM). It was recognized that methods for authenticating users vary by operating platform and will also evolve over time as, for example, advances in smart cards and biometrics make new approaches for authentication possible. Making it simple to plug in a new authentication module without disturbing the application motivated the design of PAMs. Figure 12-19 provides a high-level overview of the authentication flow when using a PAM. The steps are as follows:

1. The application creates a **javax.security.auth.login.LoginContext** object and provides a string that identifies an entry in the login configuration files and a reference to the application's callback handler to be used for authentication.

2. The application invokes the **login** method of the **LoginContext** object and then, based on the entry in the login configuration file, the requested PAM is invoked and provided with a reference to the application's callback handler object. More than one PAM will be invoked based on the contents of the entry in the login configuration file.

3. If the PAM needs to communicate with the application or with the user of the application, the PAM will call one or more of the methods of the **javax.security.auth.callback.CallbackHandler** interface. For example, the PAM may require that a user name and password be provided by the user and will use the **CallbackHandler** interface to have the application display a dialog box to prompt the user for this input.

4. Based on the results of all the PAMs involved, the overall results of the authentication process are reported to the user.

12

Application

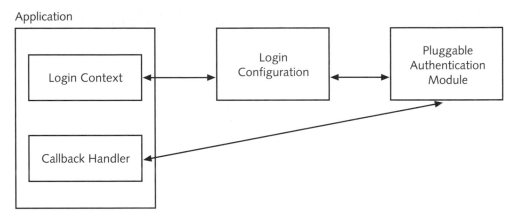

Figure 12-19   Authentication flow when using a Pluggable Authentication Module

JAAS also uses the classes `javax.security.auth.Subject` and `java.security.Principal` as they relate to the processes of authentication and authorization. A **Subject** object represents a collection of identity information about a single entity, such as a person. A **Principal** object represents one facet of a **Subject** object's identity. For example, a Social Security number, driver license number, credit card number, or computer system userid can identify a person. A **Principal** object would represent each of these pieces of identification, and the person who owns them all would be considered the **Subject.**

Figure 12-20 shows an example login configuration file. Each entry in the file begins with a name to identify the entry followed by a block delimited by brace brackets and terminated by a semicolon. Within each block is the list of the fully qualified class names of the PAMs to be invoked. PAMs are invoked in the order in which they are listed in this file. Each PAM class name is followed by a login control flag. Figure 12-21 lists the valid login control flags and their meanings.

```
AccessProperty {
   com.sun.security.auth.module.NTLoginModule required;
};

ProgramLogin {
   examples.security.UserLoginModule required;
};

MoreComplexApp {
   com.sun.security.auth.module.NTLoginModule required;
   com.sun.security.auth.module.JndiLoginModule optional;
};
```

Figure 12-20   Example login configuration file

Login Control Flag	Description
Required	This PAM is always called, and the user must pass its authentication test in order to be successfully authenticated.
Sufficient	If the user passes the test set out by this PAM, then only remaining PAMs with a Required login control flag will be called.
Requisite	If the user passes the test set out by this PAM, other modules will be called but it is not important they pass unless they are Required.
Optional	It Is not necessary for the user to pass this test. But if all the modules are marked as Optional, at least one must pass.

Figure 12-21   Login control flags used in login configuration files

A few login modules ship with the J2SDK now that JAAS is part of the Java platform. Exactly which modules are available to you depends upon the platform you are using. For the Windows version of the J2SDK, the following modules are available:

- **com.sun.security.auth.module.NTLoginModule** All information that this PAM collects comes from the operating system.

- **com.sun.security.auth.module.JndiLoginModule** This module allows you to authenticate a user using Java 1.2 and higher.

In addition to those modules that ship with the Java 2 SDK, you can develop your own login module that implements the **LoginModule** interface. Following is summary of this interface and its methods:

Interface

javax.security.auth.spi.LoginModule

Purpose

This interface defines the methods that are required to create a pluggable authentication module (PAM).

Methods

- **public void initialize(Subject *s*, CallbackHandler *cbh*, Map *sharedState*, Map *options*)**
  The **initialize** method is called after the **LoginModule** object is instantiated using the constructor with no arguments. The information required to set up the **LoginModule** object is passed through the **initialize** method. The first parameter identifies the subject to be authenticated, and the second parameter is a reference to the handler that should be used if the **LoginModule** object requires more information from the application that is requesting authentication. Note that this reference may be **null**.

The map passed as the third parameter can be used for instances of the class to share state information. The map containing options is typically used to pass values such a debug flag to indicate that the **LoginModule** object should output messages detailing the steps it takes.

- **public boolean login() throws LoginException**

  The **login** method is called as the first phase of authenticating a **Subject** object. If the authentication procedure used within this method succeeds, the method returns **true**, otherwise **false.**

- **public boolean commit() throws LoginException**

  The **commit** method is called as the second phase of authenticating a **Subject** object if the overall authentication has succeeded. The **commit** method is called so that the specific **Principal** object that was authenticated by this **LoginModule** object can be added to the **Subject** object.

- **public boolean abort() throws LoginException**

  The **abort** method is called as the second phase of authenticating a **Subject** object if the overall authentication has failed. The **abort** method is called so any actions taken by this **LoginModule** object can be reversed.

- **public boolean logout() throws LoginException**

  The **logout** method is used to log out a **Subject** object, typically by removing the **Subject** object's **Principal** objects that were previously authenticated by this **LoginModule** object.

Figure 12-22 provides an example of a pluggable login module class that implements the **LoginModule** interface. The authentication procedure implemented by this class is simply to verify that the user name and password obtained from the application using callback methods is found within the **Map** object referenced by a **static final** field, shared by all instances. A detailed discussion of notable code fragments from the class follows.

```
package examples.security;
import java.io.IOException;
import java.util.*;
import javax.security.auth.Subject;
import javax.security.auth.callback.*;
import javax.security.auth.login.LoginException;
import javax.security.auth.spi.LoginModule;
/** An example of a pluggable authentication (i.e., login)
  * module that does its own userid and password
  * verification using a static map
  */
```

Figure 12-22   `UserLoginModule`: an example of a pluggable authentication module (PAM)

```java
public class UserLoginModule implements LoginModule {
   private Subject subject;
   private CallbackHandler cbHandler;
   private UserPrincipal principal;
   private String userName;
   private boolean loginSuccessful = false;
   private static final Map user2pw;
   static {
      HashMap tempMap = new HashMap();
      tempMap.put( "Darius", new char[] { 'q','L','1' } );
      tempMap.put( "Iona", new char[] { 'q','t','2' } );
      user2pw = Collections.unmodifiableMap( tempMap );
   }
   /** Initialize the module with the provided input
     */
   public void initialize( Subject s, CallbackHandler cbh,
                           Map sharedState, Map opts) {
      subject = s;
      cbHandler = cbh;
   }
   /** Invoked when the user calls the login method of its
     * LoginContext object
     * @return boolean value indicating login success
     */
   public boolean login() throws LoginException {
      NameCallback ncb
         = new NameCallback( "User", "defaultUser" );
      PasswordCallback pcb
         = new PasswordCallback( "Password", false );
      try {
         if ( cbHandler == null ) {
            throw new LoginException();
         }
         cbHandler.handle( new Callback[] { ncb, pcb } );
         char[] storedPassword
            = (char[]) user2pw.get( ncb.getName() );
         String inputName = ncb.getName();
         char[] inputPassword = pcb.getPassword();
         if ( Arrays.equals( storedPassword,
                             pcb.getPassword() ) ) {
            userName = ncb.getName();
            loginSuccessful = true;
         } else {
            loginSuccessful = false;
         }
      } catch ( Exception x ) {
```

Figure 12-22 `UserLoginModule`: an example of a pluggable authentication module (PAM) (continued)

```
                loginSuccessful = false;
                System.err.println( x );
                throw new LoginException();
            }
            return loginSuccessful;
        }
        /** Invoked if the overall authentication succeeds for
          * the login context
          */
        public boolean commit() throws LoginException {
            if ( loginSuccessful ) {
                principal = new UserPrincipal( userName );
                if ( !subject.getPrincipals().contains( principal ) ) {
                    subject.getPrincipals().add( principal );
                }
            }
            return true;
        }
        /** Invoked if the overall authentication fails for
          * the login context
          */
        public boolean abort() throws LoginException {
            logout();
            return true;
        }
        /** Invoked by the login context to reverse a login
          */
        public boolean logout() throws LoginException {
            if ( principal != null ) {
                subject.getPrincipals().remove( principal );
            }
            principal = null;
            userName = null;
            loginSuccessful = false;
            return true;
        }
    }
```

Figure 12-22   `UserLoginModule`: an example of a pluggable authentication
module (PAM) (continued)

The **initialize** method simply saves the references provided to the **Subject** object
and the **CallbackHandler** object provided from the application. Neither the shared
state nor the options **Map** objects are used in this PAM:

```
public void initialize( Subject s, CallbackHandler cbh,
                        Map sharedState, Map opts) {
    subject = s;
    cbHandler = cbh;
}
```

The map that contains the user names and passwords is built in a static initialization block that will be invoked when the first instance of the **UserLoginModule** class is constructed. All instances of the class will use this same **Map object**. To discourage tampering, the reference to the **Map** object is **final**, and the **Map** object itself is transformed to a read-only **map** after all the entries are put into it. Of course this approach of putting the user names and passwords right in the program is naively simple. Such a table should actually be built using encrypted information that is stored in a file on disk somewhere:

```java
private static final Map user2pw;
static {
    HashMap tempMap = new HashMap();
    tempMap.put( "Darius", new char[] { 'q','t','1' } );
    tempMap.put( "Iona", new char[] { 'q','t','2' } );
    user2pw = Collections.unmodifiableMap( tempMap );
}
```

The **login** method begins by constructing instances of the two callback classes that it needs to obtain input from the user: a **NameCallback** object to get the user name and a **PasswordCallback** object to get the user's password. After verifying that the callback handler reference provided as input to the **initialize** method isn't **null**, the two callback objects are put into an array that is then passed to the callback handler. Each of the objects in the array will cause an action to be taken by the application, and the results are put into the callback objects:

```java
public boolean login() throws LoginException {
    NameCallback ncb
        = new NameCallback( "User", "defaultUser" );
    PasswordCallback pcb
        = new PasswordCallback( "Password", false );
    try {
        if ( cbHandler == null ) {
            throw new LoginException();
        }
        cbHandler.handle( new Callback[] { ncb, pcb } );
```

The password and the user name are extracted from the callback objects, and then the user name is used to retrieve a password from the **Map** object. If the password taken from the **Map** object matches the password provided through the callback object, phase one of the authentication is successful:

```java
char[] storedPassword
    = (char[]) user2pw.get( ncb.getName() );
String inputName = ncb.getName();
char[] inputPassword = pcb.getPassword();
if ( Arrays.equals( storedPassword,
                    pcb.getPassword() ) ) {
    userName = ncb.getName();
    loginSuccessful = true;
```

12

```
        } else {
            loginSuccessful = false;
        }
```

If the overall authentication is successful, the **commit** method is called. It is possible that the overall authentication succeeded even though the **login** method of this PAM failed, provided that this PAM was considered "optional" in the login configuration file. Because of this possibility, the **commit** method first checks to see whether the **login** method succeeded before adding the UserPrincipal object associated with this PAM to the **Subject** object. A second check is made to avoid adding the same **Principal** object to a **Subject** object twice. A listing of the UserPrincipal class is given in Figure 12-23. Unless an exception occurs, the **commit** method always succeeds:

```
public boolean commit() throws LoginException {
    if ( loginSuccessful ) {
        principal = new UserPrincipal( userName );
        if ( !subject.getPrincipals().contains( principal ) ) {
            subject.getPrincipals().add( principal );
        }
    }
    return true;
}
```

The **abort** method simply calls the **logout** method to clear the state of the UserLoginModule object. Unless an exception occurs, the **abort** method always succeeds:

```
public boolean abort() throws LoginException {
    logout();
    return true;
}
```

The **logout** method reverses any steps taken by either the **login** or **commit** methods by removing the UserPrincipal object from the **Subject** object's set of principals, clearing the user name, and setting the flag used to indicate a successful login to **false**. Unless an exception occurs, the **logout** method always succeeds:

```
public boolean logout() throws LoginException {
    if ( principal != null ) {
        subject.getPrincipals().remove( principal );
    }
    principal = null;
    userName = null;
    loginSuccessful = false;
    return true;
}
```

The UserPrincipal class, shown in Figure 12-23, is a class that implements the **Principal** interface in a simple fashion to act as a wrapper around the user name that was authenticated:

```
package examples.security;
import java.io.Serializable;
import java.security.Principal;
/** A basic class that implements the Principal interface
  */
public class UserPrincipal implements Principal,
                                        Serializable {
   private String name;
   /** Class constructor
     */
   public UserPrincipal( String name ) {
      this.name = name;
   }
   /** Retrieve the name for the Principal
    */
   public String getName() {
      return name;
   }
   /** Determine equality based on the value of the
     * Principal's name
     */
   public boolean equals( Object obj ) {
      if ( obj instanceof UserPrincipal ) {
         return ( (UserPrincipal) obj )
               . name.equals( this.name );
      } else {
            return false;
      }
   }
}
```

Figure 12-23   `UserPrincipal`: an example class that implements the `Principal` interface

To complete the total example, an application that uses the `UserLoginModule` PAM is needed. Figure 12-24 contains just such an example as the class `ProgramLogin`. It contains an inner class definition called `LoginCallbackHandler` that implements the **CallbackHandler** interface. The **handle** method of the `LoginCallbackHandler` object is the method invoked by the PAM's **login** method.

The `ProgramLogin` class displays a **JFrame** window that contains a menu bar with a single menu when it starts. That menu has only two items: Login and Exit. Selecting the Login menu item invokes the class's `loginAction` method and results in the user being prompted to provide a username and password. A message informs the user if the login was successful. A detailed discussion of notable code fragments from the class follows Figure 12-24.

```
package examples.security;
import java.awt.event.*;
import javax.swing.*;
import javax.security.auth.*;
import javax.security.auth.callback.*;
import javax.security.auth.login.*;
/** An example of a program that handles its own user login
  * using a CallbackHandler object
  */
public class ProgramLogin extends JFrame {
   class LoginCallbackHandler implements CallbackHandler {
      public void handle( Callback[] cb )
                     throws UnsupportedCallbackException {
         for ( int i=0; i<cb.length; i++ ) {
            if ( cb[i] instanceof NameCallback ) {
               NameCallback ncb = (NameCallback) cb[i];
               String inputName
                  = JOptionPane.showInputDialog(
                       ProgramLogin.this,
                       ncb.getPrompt(),
                       ncb.getDefaultName() );
               ncb.setName( inputName );
            } else if ( cb[i] instanceof PasswordCallback ) {
               PasswordCallback pcb
                  = (PasswordCallback) cb[i];
               String inputName
                  = JOptionPane.showInputDialog(
                       ProgramLogin.this,
                       pcb.getPrompt() );
               pcb.setPassword( inputName.toCharArray() );
            } else {
               throw new UnsupportedCallbackException( cb[i],
                              "LoginCallbackHandler" );
            }
         }
      }
   }
   /** Class constructor
     */
   public ProgramLogin( String titleText ) {
      super( titleText );
      setDefaultCloseOperation( JFrame.EXIT_ON_CLOSE );
      setJMenuBar( buildMenuBar() );
      setSize( 500, 400 );
      setVisible( true );
      System.setProperty(
           "java.security.auth.login.config",
           "login.conf" );
   }
```

Figure 12-24   `ProgramLogin`: an example class that authenticates a user using the `UserLoginModule` PAM

```
/** Log in to the program
  */
public void loginAction() {
   LoginContext lc = null;
   try {
      lc = new LoginContext( "ProgramLogin",
                        new LoginCallbackHandler() );
   } catch ( LoginException lx ) {
      lx.printStackTrace();
   }
   try {
      lc.login();
      JOptionPane.showMessageDialog( this,
                              "Login Success" );
   } catch( Exception x ) {
      JOptionPane.showMessageDialog( this,
                              "Login Failure" );
   }
}
/** Build the menu bar and menu
  */
public JMenuBar buildMenuBar() {
   JMenuBar menuBar = new JMenuBar();
   JMenu fileMenu = new JMenu( "File" );
   JMenuItem loginItem = new JMenuItem( "Login" );
   JMenuItem exitItem = new JMenuItem( "Exit" );
   loginItem.addActionListener(
      new ActionListener() {
         public void
         actionPerformed( ActionEvent event ) {
            loginAction();
         }
      }
   );
   exitItem.addActionListener(
      new ActionListener() {
         public void
         actionPerformed( ActionEvent event ) {
            dispose();
            System.exit( 0 );
         }
      }
   );
   menuBar.add( fileMenu );
   fileMenu.add( loginItem );
   fileMenu.add( exitItem );
   return menuBar;
}
```

12

Figure 12-24 `ProgramLogin`: an example class that authenticates a user using the `UserLoginModule` PAM (continued)

```
    /** Test method for the class
     */
    public static void main( String[] args ) {
            new ProgramLogin( "Program Controlled Login" );
    }
}
```

Figure 12-24　`ProgramLogin:` an example class that authenticates a user using the `UserLoginModule` PAM (continued)

A PAM is intentionally separated from the applications that it serves to insulate the applications from operating system dependencies and to make it possible to replace one PAM with another without requiring any change to the applications. But this separation makes it difficult for the PAM to integrate with an application when it comes to displaying windows and dialog boxes to obtain user feedback. To solve this problem, an application provides a **CallbackHandler** object to the PAM with a **handle** method that the PAM can call to request input.

For the `ProgramLogin` class, it is the nested inner class `LoginCallbackHandler` that implements the **CallbackHandler** interface and provides the required **handle** method. The **handle** method takes an array of **Callback** objects as input. Each object in the array represents a request from the PAM to the application for input, so the **handle** method iterates through the array, examining each object in the array to see if the request can be processed. If any unsupported **Callback** object is encountered, the method throws an **UnsupportedCallbackException** exception object:

```
class LoginCallbackHandler implements CallbackHandler {
    public void handle( Callback[] cb )
                    throws UnsupportedCallbackException {
        for ( int i=0; i<cb.length; i++ ) {
```

A number of classes that implement the **Callback** interface are already defined in the **javax.security.auth.callback** package. Each of these classes is intended to be used for communicating between a PAM and the application. These classes are listed in Figure 12-25.

Class Name	Purpose
ChoiceCallback	Display a list of choices and retrieve the selected choice(s)
ConfirmationCallback	Ask Yes/No, OK/Cancel, Yes/No/Cancel, or other similar confirmation questions
LanguageCallback	Retrieve the **Locale** object used for localizing text
NameCallback	Retrieve name information
PasswordCallback	Retrieve password information
TextInputCallback	Retrieve generic text information
TextOutputCallback	Display information messages, warning messages, and error messages

Figure 12-25   Classes in the **javax.security.auth.callback** package that implement the **Callback** interface

The **ProgramLogin** class can handle **NameCallback** and **PasswordCallback** requests. If the objects in the array passed into the **handle** method are instances of one of these two classes, they will be processed. Otherwise an **UnsupportedCallbackException** object is created and thrown. For objects that are instances of the **NameCallback** class, an input dialog box is displayed to prompt the user to enter a username. The prompt used and the initial value of the user name are extracted from the **NameCallback** object, and the input from the user is put into the **NameCallback** object where the PAM will be able to access it when the **handle** method completes:

```
if ( cb[i] instanceof NameCallback ) {
    NameCallback ncb = (NameCallback) cb[i];
    String inputName
        = JOptionPane.showInputDialog(
            ProgramLogin.this,
            ncb.getPrompt(),
            ncb.getDefaultName() );
    ncb.setName( inputName );
```

Allowing for differences in operating systems, the output that appears when prompting for a username should be similar to Figure 12-26. You will need to copy the **login.conf** file from the CD-ROM to the current directory before running the program.

12

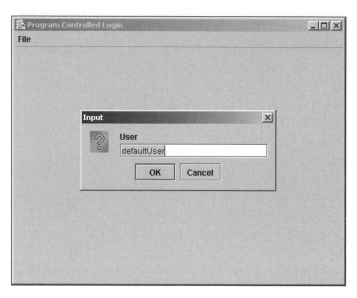

Figure 12-26   Output of the `ProgramLogin` class when prompting for a username

For objects that are instances of the **PasswordCallback** class, an input dialog box is displayed to prompt the user to enter a password. The prompt used is extracted from the **PasswordCallback** object, and the input from the user is put into the **PasswordCallback** object where the PAM will be able to access it when the **handle** method completes:

```
} else if ( cb[i] instanceof PasswordCallback ) {
   PasswordCallback pcb
      = (PasswordCallback) cb[i];
   String inputName
      = JOptionPane.showInputDialog(
           ProgramLogin.this,
           pcb.getPrompt() );
   pcb.setPassword( inputName.toCharArray() );
```

Allowing for differences in operating systems, the output that appears when prompting for a password should be similar to Figure 12-27.

For all other classes, an **UnsupportedCallbackException** object is created and thrown.

```
} else {
   throw new UnsupportedCallbackException( cb[i],
                      "LoginCallbackHandler" );
}
```

Figure 12-27   Output of the `ProgramLogin` class when prompting for a password

Allowing for differences in operating systems, the output that appears when a login is successful should be similar to Figure 12-28.

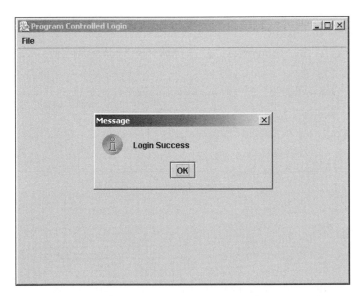

Figure 12-28   Output of the `ProgramLogin` class when a login is successful

Other than the `LoginCallbackHandler` nested inner class, there aren't all that many differences between `ProgramLogin` and any other application with a GUI. However, there are a couple code fragments that should be noted. First, in the class constructor, the value of the **java.security.auth.login.config** system property is assigned the name of the login configuration file used by the application:

```
System.setProperty(
    "java.security.auth.login.config",
    "login.conf" );
```

Second, in the `loginAction` method are the statements that actually invoke the login operation. The method begins by constructing a **LoginContext** object. It is the first parameter of this constructor where the tag of the entry in the login configuration file is provided. For this application, the tag is `"ProgramLogin"`. The second parameter of the **LoginContext** constructor is a reference to the application's **CallbackHandler** object, which, in this case, is an instance of the `LoginCallbackHandler` class:

```
public void loginAction() {
    LoginContext lc = null;
    try {
        lc = new LoginContext( "ProgramLogin",
                            new LoginCallbackHandler() );
    } catch ( LoginException lx ) {
        lx.printStackTrace();
    }
```

After the **LoginContext** object has been constructed, it is just a simple matter of calling the object's **login** method. If the **login** method completes with no exception being thrown, then it is successful:

```
    try {
        lc.login();
        JOptionPane.showMessageDialog( this,
                                "Login Success" );
    } catch( Exception x ) {
        JOptionPane.showMessageDialog( this,
                                "Login Failure" );
    }
}
```

Authorization

Once a **Subject** object has been authenticated through the use of a PAM, and has acquired one or more **Principal** objects, JAAS provides the capability to authorize a subject to perform specific operations. This is a more granular approach to security than the typical approach of allowing all users who are able to log in to a system successfully to have the same authority to perform actions.

To support this more granular approach, the syntax of policy files was enhanced to allow for granting permissions based on **Principal** objects. This is in addition to the previously supported methods of granting permission based on the origin of Java code or

Based on who signed the jar file in which an application is packaged. Figure 12-29 shows a policy file in which the first entry uses code location and the second entry uses **Principal** objects. Specifically, the second entry authorizes a **Subject** object that has **Principal** object of the class **com.sun.security.auth.NTUserPrincipal** with the value of **"wiggles"**.

```
grant codeBase "file:x:/Data/AccessProperty.jar" {
   permission java.util.PropertyPermission "java.security.auth.policy",
"write";
   permission java.util.PropertyPermission "java.security.auth.login.config",
"write";
   permission java.util.PropertyPermission "user.home", "read";
   permission java.util.PropertyPermission "java.home", "read";
   permission javax.security.auth.AuthPermission "createLoginContext";
   permission javax.security.auth.AuthPermission "doAs";
   permission javax.security.auth.AuthPermission "doAsPrivileged";
};

grant Principal com.sun.security.auth.NTUserPrincipal "wiggles" {
   permission java.util.PropertyPermission "user.home", "read";
};
```

Figure 12-29   Policy file that demonstrates authorization based on a
Principal object

Within an application, you use the **doAs** method of the **Subject** class to indicate that a particular **Subject** object is performing a particular action. The **SecurityManager** object will then verify that the specified **Subject** object has sufficient authorization to perform the action. If not, an exception object is thrown. The **AccessProperty** class in Figure 12-30 is an example of how an application can use this authorization by **Principal** object authorization. The **AccessAction** class in Figure 12-31 is an example of a class that encapsulates an action to be performed with privileges.

The **AccessProperty** class uses the same login configuration file shown in Figure 12-20, but specifies the tag name **AccessProperty** when creating its **LoginContext** object so it will use the **com.sun.security.auth.module.NTLoginModule** PAM. This module requires no interaction with the user because it takes all its information from the user's environment. For that reason, the **handle** method of the **NullCallbackHandler** class used by the application simply throws an **UnsupportedCallbackException** exception object if it receives any **Callback** objects. Further detailed discussion of the content of the class follows the figure.

12

```
package examples.security;
import java.util.*;
import java.security.Principal;
import javax.security.auth.*;
import javax.security.auth.callback.*;
import javax.security.auth.login.*;
/** An example class to demonstrate how to use a system
  * login module to obtain a login context and then use
  * that context to allow access to controlled actions
  */
public class AccessProperty {
   /** Class to handle callbacks from a login module
     */
   static class NullCallbackHandler implements CallbackHandler {
      /** No callbacks are supported
        */
      public void handle( Callback[] cb )
                    throws UnsupportedCallbackException {
         if ( cb.length > 0 ) {
            throw new UnsupportedCallbackException( cb[0],
                                "NullCallbackHandler" );
         }
      }
   }
   /** Test method for the class
     * @param args not used
     */
   public static void main( String[] args ) {
      System.setProperty( "java.security.policy", "policy" );
      System.setSecurityManager( new SecurityManager() );
      System.setProperty( "java.security.auth.login.config",
                          "login.conf" );
      LoginContext lc = null;
      try {
         lc = new LoginContext( "AccessProperty",
                                new NullCallbackHandler() );
      } catch ( LoginException lx ) {
         lx.printStackTrace();
      }
      try {
         lc.login();
      } catch( LoginException x ) {
         System.out.println( "Login failed: " + x );
      }
      Subject subject = lc.getSubject();
      Class pc = null;
```

Figure 12-30   `AccessProperty`: an example class that uses authorization by **`Principal`** object

```
      try {
        pc = Class.forName(
                "com.sun.security.auth.NTUserPrincipal");
      } catch ( ClassNotFoundException x ) {
        System.err.println( x );
      }
      Set principalSet = subject.getPrincipals( pc );
      Iterator i = principalSet.iterator();
      Principal p = (Principal) i.next();
      String userName = p.getName();
      Object o
        = Subject.doAs( subject, new AccessAction() );
      System.out.println( "User " + userName
                          + " accessed the value " + o  );
   }
}
```

Figure 12-30   `AccessProperty`: an example class that uses authorization by `Principal` object (continued)

```
package examples.security;
import java.security.PrivilegedAction;
/** An example class the encapsulates an action to be
 * performed with privileges enabled
 */
public class AccessAction implements PrivilegedAction {
   /** Action to be performed with privileges enabled
    */
   public Object run() {
      return System.getProperty( "user.home" );
   }
}
```

Figure 12-31   `AccessAction`: an example class that implements the `PrivilegedAction` interface

The program begins by setting the **java.security.policy** property with the name of the file containing the security policy it will use—in this case the file is simply called **policy**—and then creating and installing a **SecurityManager** object. It is important that these two steps be done in this order, because the security manager will not allow the **java.security.policy** property to be set after the security manager is installed with the default policy settings:

```
System.setProperty( "java.security.policy", "policy" );
System.setSecurityManager( new SecurityManager() );
```

The name of the login configuration file, **login.conf**, is assigned to the **java.security.auth.login.config** property, and then a **LoginContext** object is constructed passing the tag for the entry in the login configuration file to be used and reference to the callback handler. Calling the **login** method will cause the **NTLoginModule** PAM to extract information about the current user from the user's environment:

```
System.setProperty( "java.security.auth.login.config",
                    "login.conf" );
LoginContext lc = null;
try {
   lc = new LoginContext( "AccessProperty",
                          new NullCallbackHandler() );
} catch ( LoginException lx ) {
   lx.printStackTrace();
}
try {
   lc.login();
} catch( LoginException x ) {
   System.out.println( "Login failed: " + x );
}
```

After a successful login, the **Subject** object can be obtained. This object may potentially have many **Principal** objects associated with it. This program is interested only in finding the **Principal** object of the class **NTUserPrincipal** in order to find out the name of the current system user for debugging purposes. To obtain this **Principal** object, it is necessary to extract the set of all **Principal** objects of the class **NTUserPrincipal**. There should only be one of them, and it can be obtained by using an **Iterator** object:

```
Subject subject = lc.getSubject();
Class pc = null;
try {
   pc = Class.forName(
            "com.sun.security.auth.NTUserPrincipal");
} catch ( ClassNotFoundException x ) {
   System.err.println( x );
}
Set principalSet = subject.getPrincipals( pc );
Iterator i = principalSet.iterator();
Principal p = (Principal) i.next();
String userName = p.getName();
```

Using the **Subject** object obtained from the **LoginContext** object, an instance of the **AccessAction** class is constructed and then performed with privileges given to the particular **Subject** object. If the **Subject** object has sufficient authority to perform this action, it will complete normally, otherwise an **AccessControlException** exception is thrown:

```
Object o
   = Subject.doAs( subject, new AccessAction() );
System.out.println( "User " + userName
                    + " accessed the value " + o  );
```

security to the directory `C:\Data\examples\security` and copy the file `X:\Data\AccessProperty.jar` to the `C:\Data` directory. (Here `X:` is the drive letter for the CD-ROM.) Edit the file `C:\Data\examples\security\policy` and change `"MyUserID"` to the match your Windows user ID. Make `C:\Data\examples\security` the current directory and specify that the file `AccessProperty.jar` be added to the beginning of the class path by using the following command:

```
set classpath=C:\Data\AccessProperty.jar;%classpath%
```

Allowing for differences in the name of the user and the user's home directory, the output from this program will be similar to the following:

```
User wiggles accessed the value C:\Documents and Settings\wiggles
```

CHAPTER SUMMARY

- ❑ Cryptosystem concepts, such as secret and public key cryptography, are the foundations upon which digital signatures and certificates are based.

- ❑ A cryptosystem is made up of the following components: cleartext messages, ciphertext messages, keys, an enciphering transformation, and a deciphering transformation that can be divided into one of two categories: symmetric or secret key cryptosystems and asymmetric or public key cryptosystems.

- ❑ The Java SDK provides classes and tools for creating and managing secret and public keys.

- ❑ Encryption and decryption of stream I/O is accomplished using the classes `javax.crytpo.CipherInputStream` and `javax.crypto.CipherOutputStream`.

- ❑ Message digests can be considered a fingerprint for a message, and encrypted digest values are also known as message authentication codes, or simply MACs.

- ❑ Digital signatures are used to verify both the integrity and the authenticity of a message. The process of producing a digital signature begins with the process for producing a message digest followed by the encryption of the digest with the sender's private key.

- ❑ Certificates help solve the problem of securely transmitting public keys by having a trusted, well-known, readily verifiable source called a Certificate Authority (CA) issue a certificate containing the name of the person to whom the certificate is issued (the subject of the certificate) and the public key associated with the subject.

- ❑ SSL is a protocol that was developed by Netscape for transmitting private documents over the Internet on a secure communications channel. Transport Layer Security (TLS) is an associated Internet standard based on SSL that is an improvement on SSL. It is through something called the SSL handshake that the secure channel is established.

12

❐ The Java Secure Socket Extension (JSSE) enables secure Internet communications by providing a framework and a 100% Pure Java implementation of the SSL and TLS protocols.

❐ Java applications that are executed from the local file system run in an environment that does not, by default, have a security manager installed. This means that a Java application, by default, has no restrictions on what it may do.

❐ The information used to build the **Policy** object is taken from a default, systemwide policy file and an optional user policy file.

❐ The contents of the systemwide and user **java.policy** files are one or more grant entry statements.

❐ The Java 2 security model is a fine-grained model because you can exactly specify the permissions that you grant. The Java 2 SDK provides a tool called **policytool** that you can use to help you create your own policy file.

❐ The Java Authentication and Authorization Service (JAAS) provides a framework that enhances the Java 2 security architecture with support for determining the restrictions based upon the identity of the signer.

❐ JAAS introduces the concept of a pluggable authentication module (PAM), recognizing that methods for authenticating users vary by operating platform and will also evolve over time as advances in smart cards and biometrics make new approaches for authentication possible. These advances make it simple to plug in a new authentication module without disturbing the application.

❐ Once a **Subject** object has been authenticated through the use of a PAM, JAAS provides the capability to authorize the subject to perform specific operations. This is a more granular approach to security than the typical approach of allowing all users who are able to log in to a system successfully to have the same authority to perform actions.

REVIEW QUESTIONS

1. True or False: Symmetric key cryptography is another name for public key cryptography.

2. What is the name of the utility provided in the Java 2 SDK that is used to generate key pairs?

3. Which of the following is a commonly used algorithm for calculating a message digest? Choose the best answer.

   a. HmacMD5

   b. MD5

   c. SHA-1

   d. HMacSHA1

   e. RSA

4. True or False: A digital certificate is signed by a CA and includes both the owner's name and the owner's private key.

5. What is the name of the class from which factory objects for generating `SSLServerSocket` objects are created?

    a. `SSLContext`

    b. `SocketFactory`

    c. `ClientFactory`

    d. `SSLSocketFactory`

    e. `SSLServerSocket`

6. Which of the following is not a policy file permission? Choose the best answer.

    a. `java.security.AllPermission`

    b. `java.io.FilePermission`

    c. `java.net.SocketPermission`

    d. `java.security.SQLPermission`

    e. `java.lang.ReflectPermission`

7. Which of the following statements would *not* be a valid entry in a policy file? Choose the best answer.

    a.
```
AccessProperty {
        com.sun.security.auth.module.NTLoginModule required;
};
```

    b.
```
MoreComplexApp {
        com.sun.security.auth.module.NTLoginModule required;
        com.sun.security.auth.module.JndiLoginModule optional;
};
```

    c.
```
grant signedBy "ACME Software" {
        permission java.io.FilePermission
            "c:\\autoexec.bat";
        permission java.lang.RuntimePermission
            "queuePrintJob";
}
```

    d.
```
grant codeBase "http://www.mycompany.com/-" {
        permission java.util.PropertyPermission
            "java.*", "read";
        permission java.util.PropertyPermission
            "user.*", "write";
        permission java.lang.RuntimePermission
            "exitVM";
}
```

8. True or False: A **Principal** object can contain credentials from more than one **Subject** object.

12

9. Which of the following is not a login control flag?

    a. Required

    b. Sufficient

    c. Requisite

    d. Prerequisite

    e. Optional

10. Which PAM callback method is used to display information messages, warning messages, and error messages? Choose the best answer.

    a. `TestInputCallback`

    b. `ConfirmationCallback`

    c. `LanguageCallback`

    d. `TextOutputCallback`

    e. `NameCallback`

Programming Exercises

Debugging

1. Correct all the errors in the class `Debug12_1` to create a **main** method that will access the keys successfully. The class is in the file `Debug12_1.java` in the `X:\Data\questions\c12` directory on the CD-ROM. (Here `X:` is the drive letter of the CD-ROM.)

2. Correct all the errors in the class `Debug12_2` to create a **main** method that will generate and display a valid SHA-1 message digest. The class is in the file `Debug12_2.java` in the `X:\Data\questions\c12` directory on the CD-ROM. (Here `X:` is the drive letter of the CD-ROM.)

3. Correct all the errors in the class `Debug12_3` to create a **main** method that can be used to generate and store a digital signature for a file. The class is in the file `Debug12_3.java` in the `X:\Data\questions\c12` directory on the CD-ROM. (Here `X:` is the drive letter of the CD-ROM.)

4. Change the file `policy` so that it contains an entry that will allow the NT user "guest" to modify the `java.home` system property. The file is in the `X:\Data\questions\c12` directory on the CD-ROM. (Here `X:` is the drive letter of the CD-ROM.)

5. Correct all the errors in the class `Debug12_5` to create a class that can be used as a principal for simple text user names. The class is in the file `Debug12_5.java` in the `X:\Data\questions\c12` directory on the CD-ROM. (Here `X:` is the drive letter of the CD-ROM.)

Complete the Solution

1. Extract the file **X:\Data\questions\c12\Complete12_1.java** from the CD-ROM. (Here **X:** is the drive letter of the CD-ROM.) Complete the **main** method so the resulting class is able to access certificates in a truststore successfully.

2. Extract the file **X:\Data\questions\c12\Complete12_2.java** from the CD-ROM. (Here **X:** is the drive letter of the CD-ROM.) Complete the **main** method so that the resulting class will generate a message authentication code using the HmacSHA1 algorithm for the file specified as a command-line argument.

3. Extract the file **X:\Data\questions\c12\Complete12_3.java** from the CD-ROM. (Here **X:** is the drive letter of the CD-ROM.) Complete the **main** method so that the resulting class is able to retrieve and verify a stored digital signature for the file specified as input. Test your program using a digital signature generated by the example program **SignAndStore.java**.

4. Extract the file **X:\Data\questions\c12\Complete12_4.java** from the CD-ROM. (Here **X:** is the drive letter of the CD-ROM.) Complete the **run** method of the class so that it can be used to start an **SSLServerSocket** object that listens for incoming connections on a specified port.

5. Extract the file **X:\Data\questions\c12\Complete12_5.java** from the CD-ROM. (Here **X:** is the drive letter of the CD-ROM.) Complete the **handle** method of the nested **LoginCallbackHandler** method so that the method will be able to display error and information messages that the PAM may generate.

Discovery

1. Create a password management class called **PasswordManager** that maintains a file containing a mapping of user names to passwords. The important feature of this class is that it does not store passwords in cleartext, but instead generates a message digest based on the password and stores that in the map. In this way, it is not possible to gain access to the file and read the passwords. However, it is still possible to verify the correct password for a user because the correct password will generate the same message digest that is stored in the map. In addition to being able to verify passwords, the **PasswordManager** class should also allow users to change their passwords securely.

2. Create a file viewer, **SecureFileViewer**, which, in addition to the usual "Open" and "Save" menu items, also provides "Secure Open" and "Secure Save" menu items that decrypt and encrypt files, respectively.

12

13

BUILDING WEB APPLICATIONS

In this chapter you will:

- Review the way the Web works and the non-Java technology that participates in Web applications
- Learn how J2EE packages Web applications
- Program dynamic Web content in servlets
- Become familiar with the Servlet API
- Provide continuity as the user navigates through your Web application
- Learn how to generate dynamic Web content in JavaServer Pages
- Design Web applications based on servlets and JavaServer Pages
- Use the JavaServer Page tags and Servlet API
- Apply design patterns and frameworks to Web applications
- Discuss design issues related to Web applications

INTRODUCTION

The Internet and the Java platform have matured together. In the early 1990s, the Internet was a worldwide forum designed primarily to facilitate the free exchange of information. Now it is an infrastructure supporting e-commerce and the essential IT activities of many organizations. The first use of Web sites was to distribute information. For example, companies advertised their services and public institutions made documents available as Web pages. Now, many kinds of organizations must exploit the Web and Web-based technologies to function in the Information Age and interact with their partners and customers. Business-to-business (B2B) and business-to-customer (B2C) operations have become traditional uses of the Internet. There is a high chance you have used free and commercial services available over the Web: You may have done research, bought books or other merchandise, ordered tickets, made reservations, checked your bank account, paid bills, filed your income tax return, played games, chatted with friends, and switched to doing many other activities online that only a few years ago would have required a visit to the appropriate institution.

The Web and related technology are changing rapidly. Web-aware software technology is providing many opportunities to the IT industry and evolving to meet the demands for new solutions. What you learn in this chapter was leading edge in 1999. But now it is a common way of using the Web and definitely material every Java programmer should know. This chapter describes Web applications and refers to them by the familiar short form of *Web app*. Mainly, it teaches how to build servlets and JavaServer Pages (JSPs).

Servlets and *JSPs* are the components that form the bridge between Web pages and Java application code. What is the difference between a Web app and a Web site? This chapter explains the following key differences:

- All content in Web sites is fixed when the site is installed. Certain options and multimedia elements may give the impression that a site is dynamic; however, all files served to the Web browser are constant. In other words, a Web site changes only when the files that compose it are updated by the site developer. In a Web site, all application processing occurs on the client side—usually when applets or JavaScript run in the browser's Java Runtime Environment (JRE). In contrast, Web apps provide server-side application processing. In a Web app, the Web browser provides a Web-based interface to an application that runs on a server. Therefore, Web apps have far greater potential for performing meaningful work and building Web content that is truly dynamic.

- Both Web apps and Web sites are accessed through a Web browser that retrieves and displays files served by a Web server. However, a Web app requires an application server in addition to the Web server to host the server-side application.

When the Java platform diversified into J2SE, J2EE, and J2ME in 1999, the APIs and tools that supported server-side Java for the Web became part of the enterprise edition of the Java platform. The J2EE specification formalized the definition of a Web app. This chapter covers the key elements of Java-based Web apps. It discusses how the Internet technologies of HyperText Markup Language (HTML) and HyperText Transfer Protocol (HTTP) relate to servlets and JSPs. It explains how Web and application servers support the generation of dynamic content on the server side, so that end users on the client side see information that is not only generated at runtime, but also specific to their individual requests. This chapter introduces the concepts of J2EE that are required for Web apps.

Prior to J2EE, servlets and JSPs were supported by a separate Sun product called the Java Server Web Development Kit (JSWDK). The JSWDK became available in August 1999 as a free downloadable from the Sun Web site. It included a rudimentary application server that was adequate for experimenting with JSPs and servlets. Several commercial application servers have supported servlets and JSPs since the servlet-based architecture for Web apps was first proposed. During the first few years, the servlet and JSP specifications changed rapidly. The J2EE specification clarifies many issues for which initial solutions were awkward or incomplete, such as how to package and install a Web app and how to provide security.

J2EE version 1.3 includes Java Servlet Specification version 2.3 and JavaServer Pages Specification version 1.2. Security services are now required by J2EE and supported by J2EE-compliant application servers. But an extensive discussion of security is beyond the reach of this chapter. The portion of the J2EE specification devoted to Enterprise

JavaBeans (EJBs) and enterprise applications is much larger than the pure Web apps. Enterprise JavaBeans and more J2EE features are introduced in Chapter 14. However, many of the features of J2EE are beyond the scope of this book. J2EE services are listed with brief descriptions in Appendix A. Appendix A also gives an overview of Web services, the emerging next-generation solution for some forms of Web-based commercial infrastructure.

Java has become the de facto industry-standard programming language for server-side coding in Web apps on non-Microsoft platforms. Whereas Microsoft supports Visual Basic controls and Active Server Page (ASP) technology on a .NET platform, the Java community runs servlets written in Java and JSPs on J2EE-compliant application servers. In both Microsoft and Java approaches

- Web browsers present the user interface and run on the client side.

- Server and client sides communicate over TCP/IP connections using the HTTP or HyperText Transfer Protocol Secure (HTTPS) protocols.

- Client-side scripting in languages such as JavaScript is allowed.

- HTML and, more recently, Extended HyperText Markup Language (XHTML) are tagging languages that turn text documents into pages that Web browsers can display.

A primer associated with this chapter gives a brief overview of HTML and XHTML for those who are not already familiar with these technologies. However, it cannot give a full description of these markup languages.

This chapter focuses on server-side coding. Therefore, it does not describe applets or JavaScript. Applets and JavaScript run in a context provided by the Web browser and usually enrich the user interface rather than provide the core functionality of the application. In other words, applets, JavaScript, and HTML typically make up the view layer of a Web app. This chapter explains how servlets and supporting classes make up the controller layer in the Model View Controller (MVC) design pattern. This chapter explains how servlets and supporting classes make up the controller layer and how the model layer need not even be aware that the application has a Web-based user interface.

THE TECHNOLOGY OF THE WEB

Web apps are composed of a blend of Web and Java technologies. This section looks at the underlying technology that provides the infrastructure for Web apps: Web and application servers, HTTP and HTTPS, URLs, HTML, and XHTML.

Web apps are different from the kinds of programs described in Chapter 11. In the section "Network Programming" Chapter 11 explained how Java programs can communicate with each other over networks and how you can build pure-Java distributed applications using socket programming or Remote Method Invocation (RMI). Those applications access native features, such as sockets, through the Java API and the JRE. The term *native* refers to the hardware and software platform on which the Java platform is installed. Building a distributed pure-Java application is relatively hard work, because your application is responsible for the communications layer, security, and all related issues. It is much easier to take advantage of the now pervasive Web infrastructure and build Web apps. A great advantage of building Web apps over network programming is that you reuse the standard and proven technologies developed for the Web.

A pure Java application needs one or more JREs provided by the Java platform. A Web app also requires a Web server and an application server on the server side and a Web browser on the client side. Information flows between client and server using HTTP or HTTPS protocols. The client sends an HTTP request, and the server returns an HTTP response. The response usually contains an HTML or XHTML document that the Web browser displays.

Web Servers and Application Servers

Web browsers communicate with Web servers. The main job of a Web server is to satisfy requests from Web browsers. Usually, the Web server retrieves a Web page, image, or other Web resource from its file system and serves the contents of the file to the browser. To support a Web app, there must be cooperation between the Web server and an application server.

All application servers include a Web server plug-in that extends the functionality of the Web server. The Web server *plug-in* is code that replaces some parts of the Web server when the application server is installed or updated. After the plug-in is installed, the Web server recognizes requests directed to Web apps and forwards them to the application server. The application server returns the response in a form that the Web server can serve to the browser. Figure 13-1 illustrates this situation. The Web and application servers may reside on the same host, or may be separated. The communication protocol between the plug-in and the application server depends upon the application server; it may be HTTP/HTTPS or a proprietary protocol.

Figure 13-1 shows that both the Web server and application server can store and return static Web content, such as HTML pages and images. The application server can also run Java code to build Web content at runtime, access databases, and use other resources available to the application server's JRE.

A wide range of Web and application servers support the architecture shown in Figure 13-1. Two successful commercial Web servers are Internet Information Server (IIS) from Microsoft, and Netscape Enterprise Server. The most popular Web server, Apache, is free. Apache forms the basis for many commercial servers including IBM HTTP Server (IHS). You can download the Apache Web server from `http://www.apache.org`. Apache Tomcat is an application server that supports servlets and JSPs and is downloadable from `http://jakarta.apache.org`.

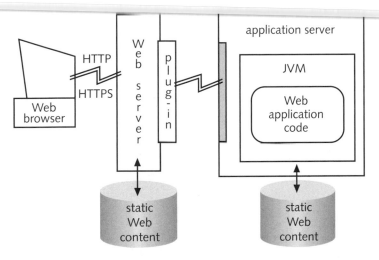

Figure 13-1   The relationships between Web browsers, Web servers, and application servers

The Apache Web server and Tomcat are adequate for this chapter. However, Tomcat is not a J2EE-compliant application server because it does not support Enterprise JavaBeans. This book uses WebSphere Studio Application Developer from IBM, and all examples run on the version of WebSphere Application Server built into Application Developer. Tomcat and IHS are also included in Application Developer.

Some of the many other J2EE-compatible application servers are WebLogic from BEA, IPlanet from Sun Microsystems, Borland Enterprise Server, and Macromedia JRun.

The HTTP and HTTPS Protocols

HTTP is the communication protocol over which Web browsers and servers communicate. HTTP operates over the TCP/IP protocol. In TCP/IP, an open connection between the client and server sides allows the two-way flow of data.

In HTTP, user input is called the request, and the server output is called the response. The request and response consist of headers followed by a body. Typically, request headers contain information about the client, and response headers contain instructions for the browser or meta-information about the body. The protocol specification specifies which headers are allowed in requests and responses. Typically, the body of a response is a Web page to be displayed by the browser.

HTTPS is a variant of HTTP that adds security provided by the Secure Socket Layer (SSL). SSL is a software layer between TCP/IP and HTTP. Many of the early worries about security of data that flows between client and server in a Web app are eased by the high degree of confidentiality assured through the HTTPS protocol. For more details, see the section "Secure Socket Layer" in Chapter 12.

HTTP is a stateless request-response protocol. In other words, the client sends a request, and the server responds. The states of the client and server are not altered by the exchange, and no record of the request is kept, except possibly as a URL in the Web browser's history list. Statelessness raises the question of how to provide some continuity in a conversation that consists of several request-response exchanges. One of the challenges of designing an effective Web app is allowing for a natural flow from Web page to Web page as users navigate through the Web-based user interface of the application. Techniques for recording and recalling what clients did on previous pages are discussed throughout this chapter and are the focus of the section "Storing Data in HTTP Sessions."

On the Web, the most common HTTP request is to get a resource, such as a Web page. The server responds by finding the resource in its file system and sending it back to the client. The Web page is an HTML document, and it becomes the body of an HTTP response.

HTTP requests have a method, an optional number of headers, and then a body. Figure 13-2 lists some methods. `GET` and `POST` are the HTTP methods of interest in this chapter. Headers give control information, such as the document's Multipurpose Internet Mail Extension (MIME) type. HTTP allows for a number of MIME types, including `text/HTML` for HTML text files and `image/gif` for images in the `.gif` format. HTTP responses have a status line, headers, and a body.

HTTP Request	Purpose
DELETE	Deletes a resource
GET	Requests a resource
POST	Transmits information, usually data entered in an HTML form
PUT	Stores a resource
OPTIONS	Requests information about communication options or requirements associated with a resource
TRACE	Echoes the request back to the client for testing

Figure 13-2   HTTP request methods

Uniform Resource Locators, Identifiers, and Names

You may be familiar with *Uniform Resource Locators* (URLs) from surfing the Internet. Essentially a URL is the unique address of a resource in a Web app or a Web site. To see a page, you specify its URL to a Web browser by typing it or clicking a link in a page you are currently viewing. The three related terms, URL, *Universal Resource Identifier* (URI), and *Universal Resource Name* (URN), are discussed after this breakdown of the full address of a resource on the Web.

Syntax

`protocol://domainName[:port]/resourceName`

Dissection

- *Protocol* is usually HTTP or HTTPS. Another protocol you may be familiar with is the File Transfer Protocol (FTP). The protocol is not case-sensitive.

- *DomainName* identifies the server and may be a name or a TCP/IP address. It specifies a domain rather than host name, because one physical host can serve several domains. In simple cases, the host name is the same as the domain name. For the examples in this chapter, one workstation hosts the client and server, so the host name for the examples is the name of your workstation or the common alias `localhost`.

- *Port* identifies the TCP/IP socket at which the server listens for requests. Port numbers may be arbitrary, but some are reserved for specific software or protocols. By default, the port used by the Internet for HTTP is 80, and for HTTPS it is 443. Therefore, all messages arriving at port 80 are routed to the Web server. Messages arriving at port 443 must be decoded first. Often you do not see the port number because the default is assumed.

- *ResourceName* is a URN that identifies a specific resource, such as a Web page, servlet, or other file in a Web app or site. Typically the URN is a filename, including a path relative to a folder called the *context root* that contains all resources in the Web app or site. However, actual filenames and paths are often hidden by aliases set up in the server.

Code Example

```
http: //localhost:9080/SkiClub/register.html
```

Code Dissection

This is the URL for a page in the sample Web app provided with this book. The test server built into IBM WebSphere Studio Application Developer uses port 9080 by default to avoid conflict with other servers that may be running on your system. The context root of this application is `SkiClub`; the URN of the particular page is `register.html`. If you do not supply a URN, `index.html` is usually assumed.

For historical reasons, there is much confusion over the exact meanings of the terms URL, Universal Resource Identifier (URI), and Universal Resource Name (URN). Often the term URI is used interchangeably with URL. To paraphrase current definitions specified by the World Wide Web consortium at `http://www.w3c.org`:

- *URI* is the generic term for the string that contains the address of a Web resource. For example, the URI for the registration page of the SkiClub Web app is `http://localhost:9080/SkiClub/register.html`.

- *URL* is an informal term for addresses that begin with the protocol followed by the name of the domain or host. For example, the URL for the SkiClub Web app is `http://localhost:9080/SkiClub/`.

- *URN* is the location of the resource within the local host or domain. For example, the URN for the registration page of the SkiClub Web app is `SkiClub/register.html`.

Referring to the full address of a resource as its URL is common practice, but this term is being dropped from technical documents. To distinguish the URL from the URN, consider that if a Web site or Web app moves from one host to another, its URL must change to include the new host name; however, the URN of each resource is a relative path within the host's file system and is not affected. To confuse the issue further, actual host names are usually hidden by aliases, and the URLs can move from one physical host to another. The simple story is that you may refer to an address of a Web site or Web app informally by its URL or more precisely by its URI. The address of a resource without the protocol and host name is a URN.

HTML and XHTML Documents

Web pages are documents that contain a mixture of text and tags that tell the Web browser how to display the text, insert graphics, link to other URLs, and perform other operations, such as execute JavaScript functions. HTML is the tagging language understood by Web browsers and is the traditional language of the Web. You should be familiar with HTML version 4 before reading this chapter. If you do not know HTML and XHTML, read the primer "HTML and XHTML" on the CD-ROM that accompanies this book.

The section "HTML, XHMTL, and XML" in Chapter 10 of this book also briefly introduces XHTML. XHTML is now the preferred language for creating Web pages, because it combines the well-established tags of HTML with the strict syntax and formal grammar of XML. The "HTML and XHTML" primer gives instructions for converting a document from HTML to XHTML, and Debugging Exercise 1 at the end of this chapter gives you an opportunity to perform and then test such a conversion.

Will Web browsers become XML capable? In a sense, some now are. Internet Explorer can display XML documents. However, it simply highlights the XML tags and makes no attempt to interpret them. You should try to code all Web pages as XHTML documents. It is possible that in the future Web browsers may insist on XHTML and no longer allow the loose grammar of HTML. Also XHTML files are valid XML documents and can be transformed using stylesheets. For example, an already popular transformation is from XML to Wireless Markup Language (WML) for hand-held devices that can display Web pages.

J2EE Web Application Packaging

To build and run Web apps, you must understand some of the packaging requirements of J2EE. With this knowledge and some familiarity with an Integrated Development Environment (IDE), you can write your own servlets and JSPs and complete the end-of-chapter exercises for this chapter. You can use Application Developer or the IDE of your choice.

The J2EE specification describes in detail how files that make up J2EE enterprise applications and Web apps must be organized and packaged. Chapter 14 discusses enterprise application packing in enterprise archive (ear) files. Web applications must be packaged in Web archive (war) files. *Ear* and *war* files are archives similar to jar files, in that they are essentially zip files that contain other files and can optionally be condensed. You can open a jar, war, or ear file with WinZip, but usually need a tool to build these files according to J2EE standards.

Here are some rules and conventions for organizing files in a war file:

- Include all Web resources, such as HTML, XHTML, and JSP files.

- By convention, put .`gif`, .`jpg`, and other image files into a subfolder called `images`.

- Put executable Java code into a subfolder called `WEB-INF\classes`. Within `classes`, follow the usual rules for matching class, interface, and package names with file and folder names.

- Put any jar files upon which your Web app depends (excluding the core J2SDK API) in the folder `lib`.

- Add the `web.xml` file to the folder `WEB-INF`. This important file is the deployment descriptor for the Web app and is described following this list.

- Like any jar file, your war file can have a manifest file called `MANIFEST.MF`. Put this file and any other metadata files describing your Web app in the folder `META-INF`.

- The war file may contain additional files including application server-specific files.

- If you include a Java source, gather the .`java` files into a folder called `WEB-INF\source`.

13

To facilitate deployment to an application server, you usually place a war file inside an ear file, even if you have only a Web app and no enclosing enterprise application. Think of the ear file as a zip file that contains other zips. (Note that most application servers can provide a default ear file if asked to install just a war file.)

The J2EE specification mandates that each archive must have a deployment descriptor. *Deployment descriptors* are XML files that describe your Web app for the application server and request run-time services from the application server. For example, the `web.xml` file may state that the *welcome file* or first page of your Web app is `index.html`.

Deployment descriptors support one of the goals of the J2EE specification: Developers can add features to their applications declaratively—not by coding and calling APIs, but by specifying characteristics in deployment descriptors. For example, you can add security settings before installation to the production environment. The responsibility for providing the relevant service then falls to the application server.

You can create deployment descriptors with a text editor and edit them manually, but doing so is error prone and requires detailed knowledge of J2EE packaging. For greater productivity, take advantage of IDEs that build deployment descriptors automatically and update them as you add files to your application.

SERVLETS

Servlets are essential features of Web apps. A *servlet* is a server-side Java program that runs in response to an HTTP request. The role of a servlet is to accept requests from the client, invoke the appropriate application logic to fulfill the request, and return the results to the client. A servlet can be small and do a specific task. But the real power of servlets comes from their ability to act as controllers in a Web app built to the MVC design pattern. MVC is introduced in the "Model View Controller Design Pattern" section of Chapter 1. This section provides more detail about applying MVC to Web apps.

Servlets provide the interface between Web pages displayed on a Web browser and Java components that run on the application server. Each servlet is an entry point into a Web app or an enterprise application running a J2EE-compliant application server. Thus servlets are far more than the server-side equivalent of applets.

In a typical servlet-based application, the client side performs minimal processing and is called a *thin client*. In contrast, a client page in which applets do considerable work is called a *fat* or *thick client*. A thin client needs only a Web browser that can display the chosen level of HTML. Servlets can even support limited clients, such as PDAs and hand-held devices with minimal display and local processing capabilities. Of course servlet-based applications can also include client-side processing. The key is that client-side processing should be limited to enhancing the look and feel of Web pages or reducing line traffic by performing light validation of user input. For example, if your Web app sells tickets, it is appropriate to use JavaScript or an applet to display the seating plan in a secondary window or to check that the customer supplied an all-digit credit-card number. But checking which seats are available on a selected day's performance and performing a credit check are server-side activities.

The following types of processing should occur on the server side:

- Accessing databases or resources that reside on the server side.
- Manipulating any data that is best kept behind the company firewall.
- Performing operations that make up the business processes of the application. For example, in the ticket selling application, marking a seat as sold and billing the customer are business processes.

- Performing any operations that require services of the app̲l̲i̲c̲a̲t̲i̲o̲n̲ ̲s̲e̲r̲v̲e̲r̲ such as transactional processing, security management, calling EJBs, and the EJBs themselves.

- Communicating with distributed components in the application other than the client's Web browser. For example, if several subsystems communicate through messaging software, all messaging activities should occur within the context provided by the application server.

The activities in the preceding list make up the model layer of the MVC design pattern. The server side should not be monolithic. It should have at least the model layer and the controller layer, and the servlets should make up the controller layer. For example, neither applets running on the Web browser nor servlets should be accessing databases.

Figure 13-3 shows the flow of a Web app. A discussion of its points follows the figure.

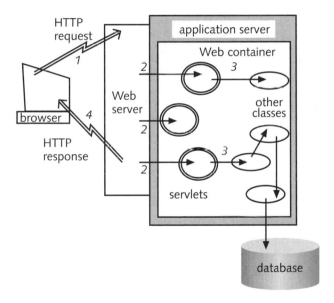

Figure 13-3   How a Web app processes HTTP requests

Here is what happens at the numbered points in the diagram:

1. The client issues an HTTP request, and the URI includes the URN of a servlet. The user could have entered the URI in the browser's navigation bar or clicked a link in a Web page.

2. The Web server receives the request and forwards it to the application server. Servlets are loaded into a Web container. A *Web container* is the context provided by the application server within which the Web app runs. The application server provides the JRE. Some application servers give each Web app a separate container to ensure that different Web apps cannot interfere with each other. The

application server calls a method of the servlet class and passes information from the HTTP request as an argument.

3. The servlet gets user input from the HTTP request. It should verify that the request is allowed and that the input is acceptable given the current state of the application. Then the servlet usually calls classes from the model layer to do the actual work.

4. The Web server returns the HTTP response to the client. The body of the response is the HTML created by the servlet.

From the browser's point of view, the Web server receives an ordinary HTTP request and returns an ordinary HTTP response.

If you have developed Web sites for several years, you may see a similarity between servlets and Common Gateway Interface (CGI) programs. CGI was an early solution to the problem of how to allow server-side processing for Web sites. CGI programs could be written in any language. Building search engines in Perl was a common application of CGI. In CGI technology, Web servers activated native code and forwarded parameters that the client appended to the request URL. The CGI programs ran as standalone applications but wrote HTML to an output stream known to the Web server. The Web server redirected the output back to the Web client. Servlet technology is superior to CGI in many ways: Applications scale better to handle large numbers of users; security options are greatly expanded, and parameter passing uses a more elegant and less limited mechanism. When Java technology became available, many programmers used servlets as replacements for CGI.

Named and Anonymous Servlets

Users can call servlets by requesting their URIs from the Web browser. A user supplies a URI in which the context root is followed by /servlet/, any folders in the path under WEB-INF/classes, and then the fully qualified class name. For example, the URI to access an application with the context root MyApp and call the servlet class com.myco.myapp.servlets.MyServlet is

        http://hostname/MyApp/servlet/com.myco.myapp.servlets.MyServlet

The full URI may be a lot to type and may contain more information about your file systems and program structure than you want to make public. If you provide short names for your servlets, users can call the servlet using the short name without knowing the real class name. For example, calling the MyServlet class can be shortened to

        http://hostname/MyApp/MyServlet

How do you set up a short name for a servlet? Use the deployment descriptor in web.xml. The servlet is registered in this file and mapped to the short name by including stanzas such as the following:

```
<servlet>
        <servlet-name>MyServlet</servlet-name>
        <servlet-class>com.myco.myapp.servlets.MyServlet</servlet-class>
</servlet>
<servlet-mapping>
        <servlet-name>MyServlet</servlet-name>
        <url-pattern>/MyServlet</url-pattern>
</servlet-mapping>
```

When a servlet is assigned a name in the deployment descriptor, it is called a *named servlet*. To call a named servlet, the URN includes only the context root of the Web app and the name mapped to the servlet.

You do not have to create named servlets. A servlet not listed in the Web deployment descriptor is an *anonymous servlet*. To use an anonymous servlet, the client must know where the servlet class is stored and its full class name.

Using named servlets is preferable for the following reasons:

- A named servlet hides implementation details, such as file and folder names, Java package structure, and actual class names, from the servlet's clients.

- When you install the application on an application server, you can disable the process called the invoker servlet. The invoker servlet finds anonymous servlets. When it is disabled, clients can call only named servlets.

- When you install the application on an application server, you can attach security restraints to named servlets. Anonymous servlets are not known to the server and therefore bypass server security.

If you want to protect your servlets from unauthorized use, make all servlets named servlets, disable anonymous servlets, and apply security settings to your Web app. Setting up security is usually a task that the application server administrator completes when the Web app is installed on a production environment.

THE SERVLET API

The Servlet API is included in two packages: **javax.servlet** and **javax.servlet.http**. The first package is intended to be generic and the second specific to the HTTP and HTTPS protocols. The original intention to support other protocols has not yet been realized.

Servlets are Java classes that extend **javax.servlet.http.HttpServlet**. Servlets perform their role in Web apps by calling the Servlet API. The classes and interfaces provided by the Servlet API are shown in Figure 13-4. In addition, two exception classes—**ServletException** and **UnavailableException**—are defined in **javax.servlet**.

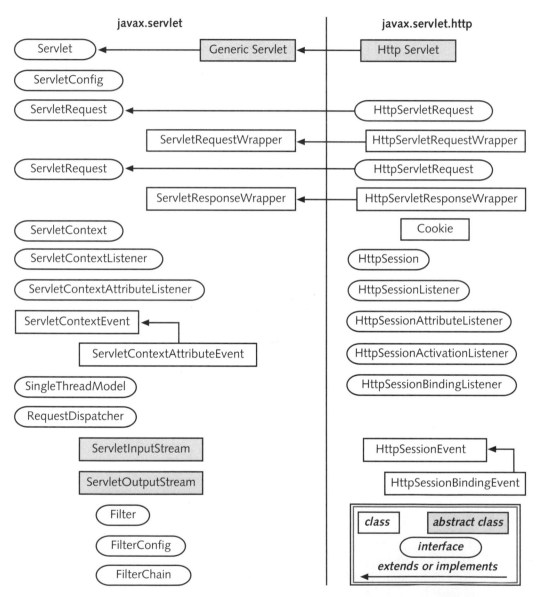

Figure 13-4   The Servlet API version 2.3

The most commonly used interfaces and classes are briefly described in Figure 13-5.

Type	Description
`HttpServlet`	Superclass of all servlets
`HttpServletRequest`	Object used to pass information from the HTTP request to the servlet
`HttpservletRequest Wrapper`	Wrapper class that can be subclassed to customize the request to a servlet
`HttpServletResponse`	Object used by the servlet to return HTTP headers and body to the client
`HttpservletResponse Wrapper`	Wrapper class that can be subclassed to customize the response from a servlet
`HttpSession`	Provides a mechanism for sharing data between servlets visited by one user during a browser session
`Cookie`	Holds data to be stored on the client browser for continuity between browser sessions
`HttpSessionBindingEvent`	Notification that an object is bound to or unbound from the session
`HttpSessionBinding Listener`	Object that is notified of a session binding event
`SessionConfig`	Passes initialization parameters from the container to the servlet
`SessionContext`	Allows for communication between the servlet and the container
`RequestDispatcher`	Wraps a resource, such as a servlet or JSP, and is most often used to redirect HTTP requests and responses
`ServletInputStream`	A binary input stream for reading data from the client request
`ServletOutputStream`	A binary output stream for writing binary data to the client
`SingleThreadModel`	Causes a servlet that implements this interface to run only in single-threaded mode
`Filter`	Preprocesses the request or response, or postprocesses the response from a servlet or Web resource
`FilterConfig`	Used by the servlet container to pass initialization information to a filter
`FilterChain`	Used to call the next filter in a chain of filters

Figure 13-5   Most commonly used types in the Servlet API

All the listener interfaces listed in Figure 13–5 extend **java.util.EventListener**. The event types extend **java.util.EventObject**. **ServletInputStream** extends **java.io**. **InputStream.ServletOutputStream** extends **java.io.OutputStream**.

13

Understanding the Lifespan of a Servlet

The J2EE specification mandates that Web apps run in Web containers. A *container* is a J2EE concept and essentially means the JRE and context within which programs run. J2EE defines different kinds of containers. For example, the container for applets is the JRE and applet context provided by a Web browser. J2EE-compliant application servers provide Web containers. Web containers must support passing requests and responses to the HTTP and HTTPS protocols and provide additional services, such as enforcing security.

A J2EE-compliant application server loads servlets and other classes that belong to a Web app into a Web container. The life of a servlet typically starts when the server administrator starts the Web app. Some servers let administrators identify servlets to be loaded automatically when the Web app starts and servlets to be loaded when they are first called. Typically, a servlet remains loaded until the server administrator stops the Web app or terminates the server. Some servers automatically unload a servlet and reload it if they detect a new version of the class. Except for such hot fixes, the lifespan of a servlet is usually the same as the lifespan of the Web app that contains it.

The **Servlet** interface defines a method to initialize a servlet when it is loaded and a method that is called when the servlet is unloaded.

Interface

javax.servlet.Servlet

Purpose

The **Servlet** interface declares methods that control the lifecycle of a servlet.

Methods

- **void init(ServletConfig** *config* **)**

  The **init** method initializes a servlet and puts it into service. Initialization parameter names and values are specified by the deployment descriptor of the Web app and accessed through the **ServletConfig** object. Call **ServletConfig.getInitParameterNames** to get an **Enumeration** of parameter names, and call **ServletConfig.getInitParameter()** to get the value of each parameter. If the servlet cannot be loaded, the method throws an exception of type **ServletException**.

- **void service(ServletRequest** *request,* **ServletResponse** *response* **)**

  The **service** method performs the work of the servlet. This is the method that the server uses when the client submits a request.

- **ServletConfig getServletConfig()**

  The **getServletConfig** method gives access to the initialization and startup parameters, including the **ServletContext** object.

- **String getServletInfo()**

  The **getServletInfo** method returns a **String** object that typically includes the name of the author, version number, copyright, and the like.

- **void destroy()**

  The **destroy** method unloads the servlet as soon as all active threads end or after a timeout period.

The **GenericServlet** and **HttpServlet** classes provide implementations of the **Servlet** methods. The most frequently used methods are introduced here:

- At load time, the **init** method runs. Use **init**—not the constructor—to perform any initialization required when the servlet is loaded. Often, the implementation provided by **HttpServlet** is adequate, but you can override the **init** method. For example, to record the time when the servlet became available for use, implement an **init** method that stores the current time.

- In response to a client request, the server calls the **service** method. Therefore, **service** is analogous to the **start** method of a thread or applet. The **HttpServlet** class overrides **service** with an implementation that looks at the HTTP request and then calls **doGet**, **doPost**, **doPut**, **doDelete**, or **doTrace** accordingly. **HttpServlet** also supplies empty implementations of the **doXxx** methods. When you extend **HttpServlet**, you have a choice of overriding **service** or the **doXxx** methods of interest.

- You can override the **destroy** method to perform specialized cleanup, such as releasing resources opened by **init**. Usually, the **destroy** method provided by **HttpServlet** is adequate.

13

Writing Servlets to Receive Requests and Send Responses

Most servlets that supply a Web page to a client implement the **doGet** method or the **service** method. Most servlets that accept input from an HTML form implement the **doPost** method, as described in the next section. Servlets implement at least one of these three methods. For example, you could write a **doGet** method that sends a form to the user and a **doPost** method that processes the user input to that form.

To understand how these three methods relate to each other and to HTTP requests and responses, you must become familiar with the **HttpServlet** class and the **HttpServletRequest** and **HttpServletResponse** interfaces in the **javax.servlet.http** package, as well as the classes and interfaces they extend in the **javax.servlet** package.

The abstract class **GenericServlet** implements the methods in the **Servlet** interface and adds more methods.

Class

`javax.servlet.GenericServlet`

Purpose

The **GenericServlet** class provides a blueprint for servlets that are not specific to any protocol. Future subclasses of **GenericServlet** may support other protocols.

Methods

- `String getInitParameter( String name )`

  The **getInitParameter** method returns a **String** object containing the named initialization parameter.

- `Enumeration getInitParameterNames()`

  Use this method to get the names of the initialization parameters. It returns a collection of **String** objects. Then, you can call **getInitParameter** to find the value of a specific initialization parameter.

- `ServletConfig getServletConfig()`

  The **getServletConfig** method returns the **ServletConfig** object for the servlet.

- `ServletContext getServletContext()`

  The **getServletContext** method returns the **ServletContext** object for the servlet. You can use this convenient method instead of calling **getServletConfig** and then **getServletContext** on the **ServletConfig** object.

- `void log( String message )`
  `void log( String message, Throwable t )`

  The **log** methods write a message to the servlet log file. The one-argument form writes the servlet name and a servlet message. The two-argument form writes a system exception message.

In practice, all servlets extend the abstract class **HttpServlet**. Most of the methods added by this class are called by the container to handle HTTP requests.

Class

- `javax.servlet.http.HttpServlet`

Purpose

Extend the abstract class **HttpServlet** to create a servlet for use with the HTTP protocol.

Methods

- `void doDelete ( HttpServletRequest request,`
  `              HttpServletResponse response )`
  `void doGet    ( HttpServletRequest request,`
  `              HttpServletResponse response )`
  `void doOptions( HttpServletRequest request,`
  `              HttpServletResponse response )`
  `void doPost   ( HttpServletRequest request,`
  `              HttpServletResponse response )`
  `void doPut    ( HttpServletRequest request,`
  `              HttpServletResponse response )`
  `void doTrace  ( HttpServletRequest request,`
  `              HttpServletResponse response )`

  Override the **doXxx** methods to handle the HTTP request **Xxx**. Usually, an **HttpServlet** object has a **doGet** or **doPost** method, or both. The other **doXxx** methods are less frequently used, and the default implementations are often adequate. All of these methods can throw an exception of type **ServletException** or **IOException**.

- `void service( HttpServletRequest request,`
  `            HttpServletResponse response )`

  `void service( ServletRequest request,`
  `            ServletResponse response )`

  The **HttpServlet** class overrides and overloads the **service** method. The arguments of the overloaded version supply the servlet with information about the HTTP request and response. The implementation provided calls one of the **doXxx** methods according to the method in the HTTP request. Overriding this method is a valid alternative to overriding the **doXxx** methods. Usually, you do not override the method with arguments of type **ServletRequest** and **ServletResponse**.

- `long getLastModified( HttpServiceRequest request )`

  The **getLastModified** method returns the time the **HttpServletRequest** object was last modified, measured in milliseconds since January 1, 1970 GMT.

13

A request object is essential for receiving information from the client. The server passes an **HttpRequest** object to the servlet. This object can hold data provided by the user, such as entries into an HTML form, as well as information about the request itself. The request object implements the **HttpServletRequest** interface. The **HttpServletRequest** interface extends the **ServletRequest** interface.

Interface

`javax.servlet.ServletRequest`

Purpose

The **ServletRequest** interface provides access to the servlet context and defines several methods that give information about the request.

Methods

- **Object getAttribute(String** *name* **)**
  Enumeration getAttributeNames()
  setAttribute(String *name*, **Object** *attribute* **)**
  removeAttribute(String *name* **)**

  Attributes are objects associated with the request and can be set by either the container or by servlets. For example, you can store JavaBeans to make them available to other servlets and JSPs. The container uses attributes to pass information not available through other APIs. Attributes and their values are stored as name-value pairs. Call **setAttribute** to add an attribute to the context. Call **getAttributeNames** to get the names of stored attributes. Then you can call **getAttribute** to retrieve a named attribute.

- **Locale getLocale()**
  Enumeration getLocales()

  The client may supply a locale or set of locales in order of preference based on the HTTP **Accept-Language** header. Use this information to customize servlet output to the client's preferred cultural environment. Locales are described in the section "Introducing Locales" of Chapter 4.

- **String getCharacterEncoding()**
  int getContentLength()
  String getContentType()

  These methods may be useful if you must read the request directly. The **getContentLength** method returns the number of bytes in the request. The **getContentType** method returns the MIME type. The **getCharacterEncoding** method returns the name of the request's character-encoding scheme. For example, you may need to know whether the client uses single-byte Latin-1 characters or 16-bit Unicode. For more information on character encoding, see the section on Unicode in Appendix A.

- **ServletInputStream getInputStream()**
  BufferedReader getReader()

  The **getInputStream** method returns binary data from the body of the request as a **ServletInputStream** object. The **getReader** method returns the body of the request as a **BufferedReader** object.

- Enumeration getParameterNames()
  String[] getParameterValues(String *name*)
  String getParameter(String *name*)
  Map getParameterMap()

Use these methods to get information from the body of the request. Typically, you use them in a **doPost** method to read the information a user has entered into an HTML form. Call **getParameterNames** to get an array containing the names of all the parameters. Parameter names usually match the names of input elements on forms. For example, an input field called **"AGE"** on an HTML form is associated with HTTP request parameter **"AGE"**. After calling **getParameterNames**, you can call **getParameterValues**, supplying the name of a parameter that may have more than one value, or **getParameter**, supplying the name of a parameter that can have only one value. For example, to get the value for the parameter **"AGE"**, use a statement like

```
int age =Integer.parseInt( getParameter ("AGE") );
```

The **getParameterMap** method returns all the parameters as a collection of type **java.util.Map**.

- String getScheme()
  String getServerName()
  String getServerPort()
  Boolean isSecure()
  String getRemoteAddr

These and other methods return a wealth of information about the nature and origin of the request. For example, **getScheme** can tell you whether the protocol is HTTP or HTTPS. You can use **getScheme**, **getServerName**, and **getServerPort** to build up the full URL for the client programmatically. (Note that these methods cannot correct for redirection by a proxy server, and often the safest approach is to use relative URLs whenever possible.) The method **isSecure** indicates whether the request used a secure channel, such as HTTPS. Call **getRemoteAddr** to get the client's IP address.

13

Interface

javax.servlet.http.HttpServletRequest

Purpose

The **HttpServletRequest** interface extends **ServletRequest** and adds many methods that supply information specific to an HTTP request.

Methods

- `String getAuthType()`

  The **getAuthType** method indicates the authentication scheme used by the server. It returns `"BASIC"` for basic authentication, `"SSL"` for Secure Socket Layer, and **null** when there is no user authentication between the Web server and the Web browser.

- `Cookie[] getCookies()`

  The **getCookies** method returns an array containing all the cookies sent by the browser.

- `Enumeration getHeaderNames()`
  `String getHeader( String name )`
  `long getDateHeader( String name )`
  `int getIntHeader( String name )`

  Use these methods to get fields from the HTTP headers. Each field is a name-value pair. The **getHeaderNames** method returns a collection of the header names. You can call it first and then call **getHeader**, **getDateHeader**, or **getIntHeader** to get the value for a named field. Dates are given in milliseconds since January 1, 1970 GMT.

- `String getMethod()`

  The **getMethod** method returns the name of the HTTP method with which the request was made, which is usually GET or POST.

- `String getRemoteUser()`

  If the user logged in using HTTP authentication, you can call **getRemoteUser** to get the user's name.

- `HttpSession getSession()`
  `HttpSession getSession( boolean create )`

  Use a session object to store information that relates to any individual client. The session resides on the server but is identified by an ID supplied with the HTTP request. Different servlets can access the same session by calling the **getSession** method. If you do not provide an argument or set the **boolean** argument to **true** and no session exists, a new session is created. If you do not want to start a new session, supply the **boolean** argument with the value **false**.

- `boolean isRequestedSessionIdFromCookie()`
  `boolean isRequestedSessionIdFromURL()`
  `boolean isRequestedSessionIdValid()`

  The server may get a session ID from a cookie or URL rewriting or because you created a new session by calling **getSession**. Use the first two of these methods if you need to know the source of the session ID and the last to check whether the session context has a session with the ID for the requested session.

You create subclasses of the wrapper classes **ServletRequestWrapper** and **HttpServletRequestWrapper** only if you want to adapt the request passed to a servlet. The wrapper classes are provided as a convenience. They provide default implementations of all methods that inherit the behavior of the wrapped request objects.

To send a response back to the client, servlets must use the HTTP response object that the **doXxx** and service methods receive as an input argument. The response object implements the **HttpServletResponse** interface. The **HttpServletResponse** interface extends the **ServletResponse** interface.

Interface

javax.servlet.ServletResponse

Purpose

The **ServletResponse** interface defines methods that help the servlet return a response to a client.

Methods

- **String getCharacterEncoding()**

  The **getCharacterEncoding** method returns the name of the character encoding of the body of the response.

- **ServletOutputStream getOutputStream()**

  Call the **getOutputStream** method to get a binary output stream if the servlet returns binary data.

- **PrintWriter getWriter()**

  Call the **getWriter** method to get a character output stream if the servlet writes character data.

- **void setContentLength(int** *length* **)**

  The **setContentLength** method sets the length of the content the server returns to the client.

- **void setContentType(String** *type* **)**

  The **setContentType** method sets the type of the response. Specify a MIME type and optionally include the type of character encoding. For example, a Web document in the Latin-1 character set may be specified as **text/html charset=ISO-8859-1.**

- **void setLocale(Locale** *locale* **)**
  locale getLocale()

13

Use these methods to set and query the locale for the response. **Locale** objects encapsulate cultural environments, including the character size of the content type. Locales are described in Chapter 4. You should consider making your servlet output locale-sensitive if your Web app is available internationally.

- ```
  int getBufferSize()
  void setBufferSize( int size )
  boolean isCommitted()
  void flushBuffer()
  void resetBuffer()
  void reset()
  ```

These methods operate on the output buffer that contains the response returned by the servlet. The larger the buffer, the more of the response that can be built before it is transmitted to the client. A smaller buffer requires less memory. When the headers and status codes have been written, the response is committed. Call **flushBuffer** to force the server to send the contents of the buffer. Flushing the buffer commits the response. Until the response is committed, you can call **reset** to clear the buffer or **resetBuffer** to clear the buffer contents, but not headers and status codes.

Interface

javax.servlet.http.HttpServletResponse

Purpose

The **HttpServletResponse** interface defines many constants as well as the methods listed here.

Fields

- **SC_OK**

- A large number of static fields hold integer values that indicate the status codes for HTTP requests. The field **SC_OK** has the value **200**, which is the code for success.

Methods

- **void addCookie(Cookie** *cookie* **)**

  Call the **addCookie** method to return a cookie to the client in the response. If you add a cookie that already exists in the response, you replace the old cookie and effectively change its value.

- **boolean containsHeader(String** *name* **)**

  The **containsHeader** method checks whether the response header has a field with the specified name. Use the **setHeader**, **setDateHeader**, or **setIntHeader** methods to add fields to the header.
  ```

- String encodeURL(String url)
  String encodeRedirectURL(String url)

  These methods encode a URL when encoding is required. If the client does not accept cookies, you can encode session-tracking information into the URL. This technique is called URL rewriting and adds the session ID to the supplied URL. If the URL is to be the destination of a redirect, use the **encodeRedirectURL** method.

- void sendError(int statusCode, String message)
  void sendError(int statusCode)

  The **sendError** method sends an error response to the client. You can use a version with two arguments to supply a message as well as a status code.

- void sendRedirect(String location)

  The **sendRedirect** method redirects the client to the specified location. Specify the location as an absolute URL.

- void setHeader(String name, String value)
  void setDateHeader(String name, long date)
  void setIntHeader(String name, int value)

  HTTP headers can contain fields. Each field is a name-value pair. Use one of these methods to add a field to the header. Specify the date in milliseconds since January 1, 1970 GMT. If a header already contains the named field, its value is overwritten.

- void setStatus(int statusCode)

  The **setStatus** method sets the status code for the response.

13

You create subclasses of the wrapper classes **ServletResponseWrapper** and **HttpServletResponseWrapper** only if you want to adapt the response from a servlet. The wrapper classes are provided as a convenience. They provide default implementations of all methods that inherit the behavior of the wrapped request objects.

Your First Servlet

Now that you've seen some of the Servlet API classes and interfaces, take a look at a simple servlet. The first example prints the current date and time. You can find the source for this in the Data\examples\servlets\TodayServlet.java file on the CD-ROM that accompanies this book. An explanation of the servlet and instructions for building and running it in Application Developer follow Figure 13-6.

```
package examples.servlets;
import java.io.*;
import java.util.Date;
import javax.servlet.*;
import javax.servlet.http.*;
public class TodayServlet extends HttpServlet {
    public void doGet( HttpServletRequest request,
                       HttpServletResponse response )
        throws IOException, ServletException {
        response.setContentType("text/HTML");
        response.setHeader("Pragma", "no cache");
        response.setHeader("Expires", "-1");
        PrintWriter out = response.getWriter();
        out.println("<HTML>");
        out.println("<head>");
        out.println("<title>Today</title>");
        out.println("</head>");
        out.println("<body>");
        out.println("<h1>The current date and Time is:</h1>");
        Date today = new Date();
        out.println("<p>" + today + "</p>");
        out.println("</body>");
        out.println("</HTML>");
        out.flush();
    }
}
```

Figure 13-6   Listing of the Today servlet

The output of this servlet is an HTML page similar to Figure 13-7.

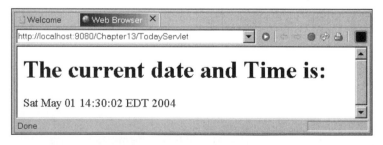

Figure 13-7   Output of the Today servlet

Most servlet classes invoked by an HTML **GET** request are similar in structure to the Today servlet. However, they can have additional methods and do different processing in the **doGet** method. The following paragraphs provide a detailed breakdown of the code.

Like any class, the source of the Today servlet starts with a package statement and import statements. All servlets should import the packages **javax.servlet** and **javax. servlet.http** to have access to the classes that support servlets. The **java.io** package is also required. This servlet uses the **java.util.Date** class:

```
package examples.servlets;
import java.io.*;
import javax.servlet.*;
import javax.servlet.http.*;
import java.util.Date;
```

Servlets that use the HTTP protocol extend the class **javax.servlet. http.HttpServlet**. This servlet prepares the response to an HTTP **GET** method. **GET** methods are forwarded to the **doGet** method of the **HttpServlet** class. The application server encapsulates the request in an instance of **HttpServletRequest** and also gives the servlet an **HttpServletResponse** object to use when building the HTML output. Of course, things can go wrong. Any I/O can cause an exception, so the **doGet** method must list the exception class **IOException** in its throws clause. Similarly, the servlet mechanism may encounter an unexpected condition, and the **doGet** method must include the exception class **ServletException** in its throws clause:

```
public class TodayServlet extends HttpServlet {
    public void doGet(HttpServletRequest request,
                    HttpServletResponse response)
        throws IOException, ServletException {
```

The first step in preparing an HTML response is to set the MIME type for the contents of the response to tell the browser what kind of document is coming:

```
response.setContentType( "text/HTML" );
```

13

Web browsers can keep a copy of all pages that you access in a local cache or history folder. They do this to speed repeat retrieval time: If you go to the same URI more than once, the browser can retrieve the page from its cache and save connection and download time. However, browser caching does not allow for dynamic content and is generally undesirable for Web apps. The next two lines tell the browser not to store the current page by adding headers to the HTTP response. Including them is optional; if you omit them, the servlet still works. However, if the users run the servlet, move to another page, and then return by clicking the browser's Back button, the old time still shows. When the page is not stored locally, the browser must retrieve it from the server every time and dynamic content is updated.

Unfortunately the command not to cache varies from browser to browser. Users can disable caching or clear the history folder using their browser tools, but a Web app should not depend upon such user actions. It is better for the HTML page to tell the browser that this specific page is not to be stored. Most browsers understand **META** or **PRAGMA** tags inserted into the **HEAD** section of the HTML document, but these tags are browser-specific. Use the **setHeader** method to add headers to a response HTML document.

The two **setHeader** calls in Figure 13-6 are for Netscape Navigator and Internet Explorer, respectively. The first tells certain versions of Netscape Navigator not to cache this page. The second sets the expiration date of the page for Internet Explorer to **-1**, indicating immediate expiry so the page is not entered into the history folder:

```
response.setHeader("Pragma", "no cache");
response.setHeader("Expires", "-1");
```

 Try to test your Web app with all possible browsers that users of your Web app may use. Turning off caching can be problematic: Point releases of Internet Explorer version 5 did not properly handle the META tag <META HTTP-EQUIV="Expires" CONTENT="-1">. There is no guarantee that the setHeader calls shown in Figure 13-6 will have the desired effect.

A servlet needs a character output stream to send the HTML output to. Most servlets call the **getWriter** method to acquire a reference to the **PrintWriter** object from the **HttpServletResponse** object.

```
PrintWriter out = response.getWriter();
```

The contents of the HTML page are written with ordinary stream output. The **PrintWriter** class implements the same methods as **PrintStream**, including **print** and **println**. The servlet must create a complete HTML document:

```
out.println( "<HTML>" );
out.println( "<head>" );
out.println( "<title>Today</title>" );
out.println( "</head>" );
out.println( "<body>" );
out.println(
    "<h1>The current date and Time is:</h1>" );
```

The next two lines create the dynamic content in this Web page. Just to show that you can mix any valid Java statements with the statements that create output, the **Date** object **today** is instantiated in a separate statement from the method call that inserts the date as a string into the HTML. You can call other methods and do as much processing as you want.

```
Date today = new Date();
out.println( "<p>" + today + "</p>" );
```

The final lines output the tags to end the HTML document and then make sure all characters are flushed from the output stream. Calling **flush** is optional but always a good idea at the end of a servlet:

```
        out.println( "</body>" );
        out.println( "</HTML>" );
        out.flush();
    }
}
```

Running the Samples for This Chapter

To run a Web app or even a single servlet, you need a Web server and application server. Both are included in IBM WebSphere Studio Application Developer (Application Developer) in addition to an Integrated Development Environment (IDE) for Web developers. Complete Tutorial 13-1, "Building and Running the Today Servlet," on the CD-ROM to build the Today servlet from scratch and test it in Application Developer. Tutorial 13-2 describes how to import the completed sample programs for this chapter into Application Developer from J2EE-compliant ear and war files included on the CD ROM.

Most of the examples in this chapter are from the Web site of a hypothetical ski club that runs mid-week day trips to local ski resorts. Members can register or join the club online, and registered members can log in. To register, a person must supply his or her name, skiing ability, and some other personal details. After registering, members can update their personal details. Members can also book ski trips and cancel trips they have booked. For simplicity, billing and payment is not included in the functionality of the Web site. Also, all trip dates are treated as though in the future. Figure 13-8 is a stylized site map of the SkiClub Web app showing most, but not all, links.

Before proceeding with this chapter, you should run the SkiClub Web app and become familiar with it as a user would. Then you can look into how the Web app is built.

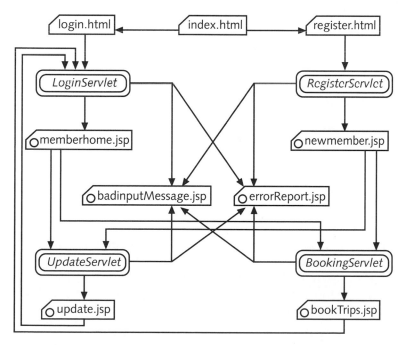

Figure 13-8   Some components of the SkiClub Web app

Writing Servlets to Process HTML Forms

Usually, the dynamic content in an HTML page produced by a servlet is based on input from the client. For example, the user may be adding items to a shopping cart, selecting items from a menu, or entering data. The Web app first gives the user an opportunity to supply input using an HTML form. Typically, the user completes the form and clicks its Submit button. This triggers an HTTP `POST` method and a request that contains data extracted from the form. A servlet processes the form and sends a dynamically generated response to give appropriate feedback to the user.

The SkiClub Web site includes several forms. One of the simplest is the login form. Clicking the Log in link from the Near Hills Ski Club welcome page (`index.html`) displays the page shown in Figure 13-9.

Figure 13-9 The SkiClub login form

Figure 13-10 shows the HTML code the SkiClub Web app produces to create the login form. Notice that the form contains two tables. The first table arranges the input fields beside labels, and the second table contains a submit button labeled Log in and a reset button labeled Clear. Most of the tagging deals with the layout and look of the tables. The lines specific to the login form are in bold font.

```
<HTML>
  <HEAD>
    <META HTTP-EQUIV="Content-Type" CONTENT="text/html" >
```

Figure 13-10 HTML source of the SkiClub login form

```
          <TITLE>Log In</TITLE>
      </HEAD>
      <BODY  BGCOLOR="#FFFFFF" LINK="#0000FF"
                        VLINK="#990099" 0>
<CENTER>
   <IMG  SRC="images/SkiClub.gif"
      ALT="Near Hills Ski Club " >
</CENTER>
<h3>Members, please log in</H3>
<p>The information you enter here must exactly match
   our records. Enter your last name and the ID you
   were assigned when you registered. <em>Your ID is
   your password.</em> If you are not a member,
   please return to
      <a href="/SkiClub/index.html">
         Near Hills Ski Club home page</a>
</p>
<CENTER>
<FORM METHOD=POST ACTION="/SkiClub/LoginServlet" >
   <TABLE BORDER=0 BGCOLOR="#DDDDFF" CELLPADDING=10 >
      <TR>
         <TD><strong>Last name</strong></TD>
         <TD>
            <INPUT TYPE="text" NAME="LNAME" VALUE="" SIZE=30
               MAXLENGTH=30 ></TD>
      </TR><TR>
         <TD><strong>ID</strong></TD>
         <TD>
            <INPUT TYPE="password" NAME="ID" VALUE="" SIZE=5
               MAXLENGTH=5 ></TD>
      </TR>
   </TABLE>
   <TABLE BORDER=0 CELLSPACING=20 >
      <TR>
         <TD><INPUT TYPE="submit" VALUE="  Log in   "></TD>
         <TD><INPUT TYPE="reset"  VALUE="  Clear    "></TD>
      </TR>
   </TABLE>
</FORM>
</CENTER>
   <p>Please wait after pressing
      <strong>Log in</strong> while we retrieve your
      record from the database.
   </p>
</BODY>
</HTML>
```

Figure 13-10   HTML source of the SkiClub login form (continued)

Figure 13-11 shows part of the source of the servlet that processes the login form. This servlet class has an empty **init** method and the three methods shown:

- **doPost** processes the login form. A breakdown follows the listing.

- **getMemberData** extracts user input from the form. A breakdown follows the listing.

- **confirmLogin** forwards the user to a confirmation page. This method is explained in the section "Storing Data in HTTP Sessions."

```
public class LoginServlet
    extends javax.servlet.http.HttpServlet {
    public void doPost(HttpServletRequest req, HttpServletResponse resp)
            throws ServletException, IOException {
        HttpSession session = req.getSession(false);
        if ( session != null ) {
            session.invalidate();
        }
        ClubMember skier = null;
        try {
            skier = getMemberData(req);
            confirmLogin( req, resp, skier );
        } catch( BadDataException e ) {
            req.setAttribute( "message", e.getMessage() );
            RequestDispatcher rd = getServletContext().
                getRequestDispatcher( "/badinputMessage.jsp" );
            rd.forward( req, resp );
        } catch( Exception e ) {
            getServletContext().
                setAttribute( "exception", e );
         RequestDispatcher rd = getServletContext().
            getRequestDispatcher( "/errorReport.jsp" );
            rd.forward( req, resp );
    }
        return;
    }
    private ClubMember
        getMemberData( HttpServletRequest req )
        throws DBopException, SQLException,
            BadDataException {
        int id;
        String lastName = req.getParameter( "LNAME" );
        if ( lastName.length() == 0 ) {
            throw new BadDataException(
                "Last Name Required" );
        }
        String sid = req.getParameter( "ID" );
        try {
            id = Integer.parseInt( sid );
        } catch( NumberFormatException e ) {
            throw new BadDataException(
                "ID must be an integer" );
        }
```

Figure 13-11   Source of the login servlet

```
        ClubMember skier = SkiClubDB.getMemberByID( id );
        if ( skier == null ) {
            throw new BadDataException(
               "The ID " + id + " is not correct." );
        }
        if ( ! ( skier.getLastName().equals( lastName ) ) )
        {
            throw new BadDataException(
                "Last name does not match records." );
        }
        return skier;
    }
    public void confirmLogin( HttpServletRequest req,
        HttpServletResponse res, ClubMember skier )
        throws IOException, ServletException
    {
        try {
            HttpSession session = req.getSession( true );
            session.setAttribute( "member", skier );
            RequestDispatcher rd = getServletContext().
                getRequestDispatcher( "/memberHome.jsp");
            rd.forward( req, res );
        } catch ( Exception e ) {
            req.setAttribute( "exception", e );
            RequestDispatcher rd = getServletContext().
            getRequestDispatcher( "/errorReport.jsp" );
            rd.forward( req, res );
        }
    }
}
```

Figure 13-11   Source of the login servlet (continued)

The **doPost** method is called when the user clicks the Log in button on the form. As with all the **doXxx** methods, the application server passes the request and response objects to the servlet. Like all **doXxx** methods, **doPost** must allow for I/O exceptions and servlet exceptions:

```
public void doPost( HttpServletRequest req,
        HttpServletResponse resp)
        throws ServletException, IOException {
```

The next four lines relate to the API that is discussed in the section "Storing Data in HTTP Sessions." For now, accept that they make sure the user is starting a new session with the SkiClub Web site. In case the member returned to the login page using the browser's Back button or using a bookmark stored in the browser, these lines clear any stored data so that the member can start again or someone else can log in.

```
HttpSession session = req.getSession( false );
if ( session != null ) {
    session.invalidate();
}
```

The rest of the **doPost** method makes little use of the Servlet API. It creates an object of type ClubMember to encapsulate the data about a member of the club. Then, it delegates the task of reading the input parameters and validating the user input to the method getMemberData. If the input is good, the getMemberData method returns a ClubMember object called skier. Then, the **doPost** method calls a confirmLogin method to generate and send a confirmation page. You will see the confirmLogin method in the discussions of sessions and cookies.

```
ClubMember skier = null;
try {
    skier = getMemberData( req );
    confirmLogin( req, resp, skier );
```

The getMemberData method signals errors by throwing exceptions. If it detects improper user input, it throws an exception of type BadDataException. The class BadDataException extends **java.lang.Exception**. If BadDataException or another exception occurs, the catch clauses handle it by forwarding the request to standardized error pages encoded as JSPs. JSPs and the way servlets pass information to JSPs are discussed in the section "JavaServer Pages" later in this chapter. The **forward** method is covered in the next section.

```
} catch( BadDataException e ) {
    req.setAttribute( "message", e.getMessage() );
  RequestDispatcher rd = getServletContext().
    getRequestDispatcher( "/badinputMessage.jsp" );
  rd.forward( req, resp );
} catch( Exception e ) {
  getServletContext().
        setAttribute( "exception", e );
 RequestDispatcher rd = getServletContext().
   getRequestDispatcher( "/errorReport.jsp" );
  rd.forward( req, resp );
return;
}
}
```

The method getMemberData processes the **HttpRequest** object from the submitted form. It creates and throws a BadDataException exception if it cannot accept the user input and also allows for a problem accessing the database. The core JDBC classes can throw exceptions of type **SQLException**. A **DBopException** exception is created and thrown by the classes in the **SkiClub** package that issue database queries for this application:

```
private ClubMember
    getMemberData( HttpServletRequest req )
    throws DBopException, SQLException,
        BadDataException {
```

Because the developer of the servlet knows the names of input controls in the HTML form, the easiest way to get the string the user typed into the last name field is to call getParameter, passing the parameter name "LNAME". In a large Web development project, good communication or naming conventions between the HTML author and the servlet programmer are essential.

```
int id;
String lastName = req.getParameter( "LNAME" );
```

Next, the getMemberData method makes sure the user did enter a last name and throws an exception if the input string is empty:

```
if ( lastName.length() == 0 ) {
   throw new BadDataException(
      "Last Name Required" );
}
```

Similarly, the getMemberData method retrieves the value the user entered in the ID input control and checks that it is an integer value. Each member is assigned a unique ID on joining the ski club. When they return to the Web site, members must log in by supplying their last names and using their IDs as a password.

```
String sid = req.getParameter( "ID" );
try {
   id = Integer.parseInt( sid );
} catch( NumberFormatException e ) {
   throw new BadDataException(
      "ID must be an integer" );
}
```

In this case, the ID plays double duty as the password and the primary key of the member's record on the database. The getMemberByID method of the class SkiClubDB retrieves a skier record from the database and returns an object containing the information stored about the member. If there is no record with the specified ID in the database, getMemberData throws an exception of type BadDataException. The method also throws the exception if the user supplies a valid ID but the wrong last name.

```
ClubMember skier = SkiClubDB.getMemberByID( id );
if ( skier == null ) {
   throw new BadDataException(
      "The ID " + id + " is not correct." );
}
if ( ! ( skier.getLastName().equals( lastName ) ) )
{
    throw new BadDataException(
       "Last name does not match records." );
}
```

If the name and ID match, the login is successful, and the getMemberData method returns the ClubMember object called skier that contains this member's personal data.

```
   return skier;
}
```

13

Note that this form of login is different from securing a Web app from unauthorized access. Anyone can access the Web app and join the club. The SkiClub Web app uses its own database table of members to validate existing members without calling on security services of the application server.

Options for Producing HTTP Responses

A servlet can send only one HTTP response to an HTTP request. If it does not respond, the browser eventually signals a time out on the request. Typically a servlet produces one complete HTTP page, but it may not build that page itself. The servlet can delegate the task of building the response to another Web resource, typically a JSP, or the servlet can choose between alternative responses. Often, you want to send an error page instead of the standard output, or you may want to transfer your user to different parts of your Web app. For example, if a form lets the user select one of several possible actions, the servlet that processes the form can forward the request to one of a set of servlets, each of which supports one of the possible actions. In the SkiClub Web app, the login servlet either sends the user to the member home page or responds with an error page, as you saw in the previous section. The three options for producing a response page from a servlet are covered here:

- *Output the HTML response page:* TodayServlet is an example of the output-the-HTML-response-page approach. You can provide alternative outputs by using if statements to write different HTML content. Coding HTML in Java print statements is clumsy and takes no advantage of a high function or what-you-see-is-what-you-get (WYSIWYG) HTML editor.

 When servlet technology was new, writing **doGet** and **doPost** methods that wrote HTML was the only option. Now that JSP technology has matured, developers avoid coding HTML in servlets unless the ratio of static to dynamic content is small.

- *Forward the request to another resource in the Web app:* The role of the servlet may be simply to route the incoming request to the appropriate resource in the Web app. The destination resource is usually a static HTML page, a JSP, or another servlet. Your servlet can ask the Web container to transfer the request. Do this by obtaining a request dispatcher object from the servlet context and then transferring the HTTP request and response objects through the request dispatcher. First, use the inherited method **GenericServlet.getServletContext** to access the Web container, and then call **ServletContext.getRequestDispatcher** specifying the new destination. Finally, use the method **RequestDispatcher.forward** to transfer the request and response. For example, when the login servlet in the SkiClub Web app admits a member to the Web site, it sends the member to the member home page with the following lines:

```
RequestDispatcher rd = getServletContext().
    getRequestDispatcher(
    "/SkiClub/MemberHome.jsp" );
rd.forward( req, res );
```

In this case, the destination is a JSP. When getting the RequestDispatcher object, specify an address relative to the context root of your Web app.

- *Redirect the request to another URI:* You also can pass the HTTP request to any resource that is available on the network. For example, you can send the user directly to another Web app or Web site. In this case, the transfer cannot be completed within the Web container. Instead, the response must be returned to the Web browser with instructions to send the current request to another URI. Do that by calling the **sendRedirect** method on the current **HttpServletResponse** object in a statement, such as

```
response.sendRedirect(
    "http://domain/someWeb/somePage.html" );
```

The URI specified in the argument of **sendRedirect** is returned to the Web browser. If you specify a relative address within your Web app, the Web container translates the URN into a complete URI. Then the Web server returns a response to the Web browser that instructs the browser to send the current request to the URL specified in the response. The browser does so immediately without informing the user. The user ultimately receives a response from the new URI and need not be aware that the original request was redirected.

How do you decide whether to use **RequestDispatcher.forward** or **HttpServletResponse.sendRedirect**? To transfer to a different Web app or Web site you must use **sendRedirect**. There is an overhead that cannot be avoided, in that there must be four network transmissions before the user sees any output: the original request from the browser to your URI, the redirect response back to the browser, the original request from the browser to new URI, the response from new URI to browser. Within one Web app, you can use either technique, and using **RequestDispatcher** has some advantages:

- Less network activity occurs because the transfer occurs within the application server.
- Within the same Web app, you can pass information to the destination of the **RequestDispatcher** object.

On the other hand, using a **RequestDispatcher** object gives the application server additional work to do, and using **HttpServletResponse.sendRedirect** instead of **RequestDispatcher.forward** can help performance if the application server is overloaded.

Servlet Filtering

The Servlet API has been mostly stable since version 2 of the Servlet API. Filtering is the most significant addition of version 2.3. Filters are classes that can transform the content of an HTTP request before a servlet receives it or an HTTP response after the servlet returns it. For example, you can write a filter to transform or encrypt the content of a request, log the activity, or cache information contained in the request. You can chain filters to perform a set of operations in a fixed order. Another use of filters is to wrap the request and response in subclasses of **HttpServletRequest** and

HttpServletResponse for a servlet that is customized for specialized types of requests or responses.

The interfaces **Filter**, **FilterChain**, and **FilterConfig** in the **java.servlet** packages make up the filtering API. To create a filter, define a class that implements the **Filter** interface. Implement the **doFilter** method to do the work. The Web container passes three arguments to this method: **ServletRequest**, **ServletResponse**, and **FilterChain**. The **FilterChain** argument is used to determine whether the filter is one in a chain and then invoke the next filter or the servlet. Use the **FilterConfig** object to perform initialization.

The developer must register filters by adding stanzas to the Web deployment descriptor. Then the application server has the responsibility of calling the first filter in the chain.

THE USER EXPERIENCE: BUILDING A WEB APP WITH CONTINUITY

One challenge of building a Web app is maintaining continuity as the user visits different HTML pages, servlets, and other resources. The HTTP protocol is stateless, so every request and response is a complete, independent transaction. However, the desired user experience is often an extended conversation between the user and the application. For example, in a shopping site, customers usually visit several pages and can add several purchases to a single virtual shopping cart. When they decide to confirm their orders, customers expect the site to remember the contents of the shopping cart.

Designing the user experience is the art of creating a unified look and feel and natural flow from page to page, at the same time allowing for the various paths clients may take through your site. The larger topic of Web design is beyond the scope of this book. Fortunately, the Servlet API provides a simple mechanism for supporting your design by letting you save information on the server side so it can be shared by servlets and JSPs. The Servlet API also lets you store information on the client side to provide some continuity between browser sessions.

Storing Data in HTTP Sessions

The key concept for maintaining user state in a Web app is the session. A *session* is a place to store state information for a specific client, so that the information is available to different servlets. A session is associated with one client's browser session and spans many HTTP requests. Typically, you start a session when a client first reaches your site. The end of a session is not as easy to pinpoint, but the important task is to maintain the session as long as the customer is active at the site. You can delegate the task of terminating a session to the Web administrator. Typically, the Web administrator configures the server to discard sessions based on a time interval since the last activity.

To the servlet programmer, a session is an **HttpSession** object provided by the server and accessible through the **HttpServletRequest** object. You can access or create a session for a client by calling the **HttpServletRequest.getSession** method. This method is overloaded to have one optional argument of type **boolean**. If you call the no-argument version or supply a value of **true**, the server gives you the session for this client, if there is one, and creates a new session object otherwise. Specify **false** to get an existing session without giving the server permission to create a new one. If called with **false** when no session exists, **getSession** returns **null**.

An **HttpSession** object contains a collection of name-value pairs. The name is an identifier of type **String** and the value has type **Object**. When you add objects to the session, you supply the object reference and a name as a **String** object. To retrieve the object, ask for it by name. One very important proviso: The objects in a session must be serializable. You may want to review the discussion of object serialization in Chapter 3. Usually, you save information that your servlet knows and that might be useful to other servlets in the **HttpSession** object. The section "Places to Store State Data on the Server Side" describes the options for storing state data. After the state is stored in a session, servlets run by the same client can then get the information from the **HttpSession** object.

Interface

javax.servlet.http.HttpSession

Purpose

The **HttpSession** interface defines the methods a servlet can use to manipulate a session object for the purpose of maintaining state information that spans a series of HTTP requests and responses.

Methods

- **long getCreationTime()**

  long getLastAccessedTime()

  long getMaxInactiveInterval()

  void setMaxInactiveInterval(int *interval* **)**

  The first two of these methods tell you when the session was created or last used, in milliseconds, since January 1, 1970. You can programmatically control how long the server must keep an inactive session using the **get** and **set** methods for the maximum inactive interval, in seconds.

- **String getId()**

  The **getId** method returns the identifier assigned to this session. The return value is a unique value generated by the server.

- **String[] getAttributeNames()**

  Object getAttribute(String *name* **)**

  void putAttribute(String *name*, **Object** *value***)**

  Object removeAttribute(String *name* **)**

13

You can add any serializable object to a session by calling **putAttribute** and retrieve a stored object by calling **getAttribute**. To get an array of all stored attribute names, call **getAttributeNames**. You also can remove objects from the session.

- **void invalidate()**

  You do not have to wait for a session to time out and be destroyed by the server. Instead, you can tell the server to invalidate a session by calling **invalidate**.

- **boolean isNew()**

  If you need to know whether the client has just joined the session, call **isNew**. Until the session ID has been sent to the client and returned in a subsequent request, the session is new.

The methods **getAttribute**, **putAttribute**, **getAttributeNames**, and **removeAttribute** were added to the Servlet API in version 2.2. Use these methods instead of the deprecated **putValue**, **getValue**, **getValueNames**, and **removeValue** methods. This change makes the interface to the session objects consistent with the interface to scopes in which you can store state information for a Web app.

Take another look at the login servlet from the SkiClub Web app and the listing in Figure 13-11. In the intended user experience, a member visits the login page only once. However, a member may log in, acquire a session object, and then return to the login page using the browser's Back button. Or, a member may return to the Web app before the previous session times out. Therefore, the login servlet must take steps to ensure that every login starts a fresh conversation with the client. The **doPost** method first checks for an existing session and invalidates the session if it finds one:

```
HttpSession session = req.getSession( false );
if ( session != null ) {
   session.invalidate();
}
```

After the member is authenticated, the **doPost** method instantiates an **HttpSession** object and adds information about the member to the session. The member data is encapsulated in a **ClubMember** object with identifier **skier**. Figure 13-11 shows that the method **confirmLogin**, called by **doPost**, sends confirmation to the member:

```
public void confirmLogin( HttpServletRequest req,
   HttpServletResponse res, ClubMember skier )
   throws IOException, ServletException
{
   try {
      HttpSession session = req.getSession( true );
      session.setAttribute( "member", skier );
```

```
RequestDispatcher rd = getServletContext().
    getRequestDispatcher( "/memberHome.jsp" );
rd.forward( req, res );
} catch ( Exception e ) {
    req.setAttribute( "exception", e );
    RequestDispatcher rd = getServletContext().
        getRequestDispatcher( "/errorReport.jsp" );
    rd.forward( req, res );
    }
}
```

What happens if you lose a session in the middle of a conversation? Sessions are invalidated when the server determines that it has timed out or a servlet calls the method **Session.invalidate**. You can never predict whether you will lose a session before the client returns to your site. Therefore, you should design all conversations so that each request-response could be the last exchange in the conversation. For example, before returning the HTTP response, complete or roll back all transactions initiated by the servlet to ensure that the database is left in a consistent state.

Adding an object to a session binds the object to the session. Conversely, removing an object from the session unbinds it. When the session is invalidated, all its objects are unbound. The Servlet API provides an event and listener mechanism in the **HttpSessionBindingEvent** class and the **HttpSessionBindingListener** interface for monitoring the binding and unbinding of objects to and from sessions. Usually, you need to use this mechanism only when you need to provide a recovery mechanism for the loss of a session or when objects that servlets may add to a session must track how they are used.

You can make objects sensitive to binding events by defining the class that the objects instantiate to implement **HttpSessionBindingListener**. Provide implementations for the two methods defined in this interface: **valueBound** and **valueUnBound**. The session context generates **HttpSessionBindingEvent** objects when an object is added to or removed from the session and notifies the object by calling **valueBound** or **valueUnBound**, passing the **HttpSessionBindingEvent** object as the argument of the method.

How do sessions provide continuity during stateless HTTP request-and-response sequences? Do the Web server and Web browser pass the **HttpSession** object back and forth? The answer is an emphatic "no." Sessions reside on the server. Instead, an identifying key passes between server and client using a Web technology that predates Java: cookies. If the client has a session, the server automatically adds a cookie containing the session ID to the response generated by the servlet. The mechanism is secure, because no client-specific data is sent except the session ID, and that is a computer-generated identifier with no meaning to human readers. When subsequent servlets ask the server for the **HttpSession** object for this client, the server uses the cookie to identify and supply the correct session. Note that the server is responsible for keeping track of which session belongs to which client.

13

Version 2.3 of the Servlet API adds additional listeners and events that are not described in detail here. The new types are interfaces: `SessionContextListener`, `SessionContextAttributeListener`, `HttpSessionAttributeListener`, `HttpSessionActivation Listener`, and classes `SessionContextEvent`, `SessionContext AttributeEvent`, and `HttpSessionEvent`. Create listeners that implement these interfaces to monitor other events relating to sessions and the session context.

Places to Store State Data on the Server Side

A servlet can store data in and retrieve it from four different scopes. In this context, a *scope* is a storage area that the Web container makes available to servlets and JSPs:

- *Session scope* is the `HttpSession` object. It is specific to the client or, more specifically, to the Web browser session. Storing state data in a session is described in the previous section, and is the most popular place to store state data.

- *Request scope* is the `HttpRequest` object. It can hold data for the duration of one HTTP request–response cycle. Typically you store information in the request before forwarding the request to another servlet or JSP, for the purpose of passing information to the destination of the `RequestDispatcher.` `forward` method. Do this rather than clutter the session with transitory information that is not required after the current request is completed. For example, the SkiClub Web app contains JSPs that report errors. Various classes in the Web app are programmed to throw a `BadDataException` exception upon detecting invalid user input. The login servlet catches this exception and forwards the request to a JSP. But first the servlet stores the exception message in the request object. Here is the catch block:

```
catch( BadDataException e ) {
  req.setAttribute( "message", e.getMessage() );
  RequestDispatcher rd = getServletContext().
    getRequestDispatcher(  "/badinputMessage.jsp" );
  rd.forward( req, resp );
}
```

The JSP retrieves the exception message and displays it. The message is deleted with the response when the HTTP response is sent.

- *Application scope* refers to the servlet context and provides a global storage area for the Web app. Data stored in the servlet context is available to all servlets and to all threads on which the servlets are running. Therefore, you should put only information that is not specific to one client into the context. Here is another snippet of code taken from the login servlet of the SkiClub Web app. Here, `exception` indicates an unspecific error that may affect the operation of the Web app:

```
catch( Exception e ) {
  getServletContext().setAttribute( "exception", e );
```

```
            getRequestDispatcher( "/errorReport.jsp" );
        rd.forward( req, resp );

    }
```

Data stored in the servlet context remains until it is overwritten or explicitly deleted, or until the Web app terminates.

- *Page scope* is the scope of the current page being built. This scope is more relevant in JSPs than in servlets, but is the least frequently used.

You may notice that fields of the servlet classes are not suggested as places to store information. Generally you avoid using fields of the servlet classes. The reason relates to multithreading and is explained in the section "Program Servlets for Multithreading."

Scalability is a factor to consider when deciding where to store state data. Sessions reside in the memory of the JRE. Consider the impact of many large sessions occupying memory. The total size of all sessions can limit scalability of your Web app. Therefore, you should look for alternative places to store state data. Even consider using files or databases for long-lasting data.

Many application servers have an internal algorithm for swapping sessions in and out of memory and sometimes write them to a database. That is the reason all objects you add to **HttpSession** objects should be serializable.

Providing Continuity with Cookies

Sessions provide state data only as long as the client is actively navigating through your Web site. If you want to store information so that it is available any time the client returns to your site, use cookies. *Cookies* are data objects stored on the client side of a Web app and passed back and forth between the Web browser and the server.

A cookie is a name-value pair. Both the name and value must be strings. Cookies are sent to the client in the header of the HTTP response. Browsers store cookies locally and tag each cookie with the domain name or IP address that sent the cookie. Every time the browser sends a request, it includes all cookies stored for that domain in the header of the HTTP request. In other words, if several servlets in your Web app add cookies, each servlet can retrieve all the cookies created by all the servlets. But no other site ever gets the cookies that originated from your Web app. You can specify how long a browser should retain a cookie by calling **Cookie.setMaxAge** and specifying the number of seconds after which the cookie will expire.

Cookies provide a handy way to store information, such as customer preferences. For example, your welcome servlet can interrogate the cookie and then redirect the request to a page written in the client's preferred language. Such a cookie could look like **"language"="Français"**. Always bear in mind that the content of a cookie may not be secure and that cookies are limited in size.

13

You program cookies explicitly. To send a cookie, call the **HttpServletResponse. addCookie** method supplying a **Cookie** object. To receive cookies, call the method **HttpServletRequest.getCookies**. This method has no arguments but returns an array of **Cookie** objects.

Class

javax.servlet.http.Cookie

Purpose

Instances of the **Cookie** class represent the objects known to Web browsers and servers as cookies. The class provides a number of methods that give information about the cookie as a whole as well as the methods listed here to get and set the name, value, comment, or lifetime of a cookie.

Constructor

- **Cookie(String** *name*, **String** *value* **)**

  The **Cookie** class has no default constructor. You must supply a name and a value when you create the cookie.

Methods

- **String getComment()**

  void setComment(String *value* **)**

  You can attach a descriptive comment to a cookie. The **getComment** method returns the comment for a cookie or **null** if it has no comment. The **setComment** method adds a comment or changes an existing comment.

- **String getName()**

  The **getName** method returns the name of this cookie. Note that you can change the value, but not the name, of a cookie.

- **String getValue()**

  void setValue(String *value* **)**

  The **getValue** method returns the value of a cookie, and the **setValue** method assigns a value to an existing cookie.

- **int getMaxAge()**

  void setMaxAge(int *expiry* **)**

  The **setMaxAge** method tells the browser how long to keep a cookie. A negative number means that the cookie lives only as long as the browser runs. A positive number is the number of seconds the browser must keep the cookie. Specify a positive number to make the cookie persistent on the client machine for the specified

~~time An input value f ... ll ... l .. k ..... the cookie immediately. The~~
getMaxAge method returns the positive or negative age assigned to a cookie. It never returns zero because such a cookie must have been deleted.

Web browsers have supported cookies for several years. The cookie mechanism was originally used by CGI programs. The developers of the Servlet API incorporated the de facto industry standard for cookies into the servlet specification.

In the SkiClub Web app, new members join the club by running the **RegisterServlet** class. This servlet is similar in structure to the **LoginServlet** class except that it requires more data from the input form and adds a new member to the database. Then the **doPost** method calls the **confirmRegistration** method to redirect the request to a JSP. The **confirmRegistration** method adds a cookie to the HTTP response to indicate that this member is new to the club, with the following code:

```
public void confirmRegistration(
    HttpServletRequest req, HttpServletResponse resp,
    ClubMember skier )
    throws IOException
{
    //...
        resp.addCookie(
            new Cookie( "NewMember", "yes" ) );
//...
    }
}
Cookie[] cookies = req.getCookies();
req.setAttribute("new", "no");
for (int i = 0; i < cookies.length; i++) {
    if (cookies[i].getName().equals("NewMember")
      && cookies[i].getValue().equals("yes")) {
      resp.addCookie(new Cookie("NewMember", "no"));
      req.setAttribute("new", "yes");
      break;
    }
}
```

The cookie named **NewMember** is used by the servlet that lets members book ski trips. The first time a member books trips, descriptive sentences appear above the booking form. After you have seen them once, these sentences do not appear again. The following lines control whether the extra sentences are output:

```
Cookie[] cookies = req.getCookies();
for( int i = 0; i < cookies.length; i ++ ) {
    if( cookies[i].getName().equals("NewMember")
        && cookies[i].getValue().equals("yes") ) {
      resp.addCookie(
      new Cookie( "NewMember", "no" ) );
// ...
    break;
```

13

To see what the descriptive sentences say, go to the SkiClub Web app, register, and then select to book ski trips. Note that the descriptive sentences appear only the first time you run `BookingServlet`, regardless of whether you first book trips during your initial visit to the SkiClub Web app or during a subsequent visit. Add the `NewMember` cookie again; this time with the value "no," which overrides the value "yes."

You can put any information you want into a cookie, but you should never include sensitive information. People with expertise and tools have little trouble intercepting and decoding HTTP requests and responses. As a result, some Web users are uncomfortable with cookies. Fortunately, most commercial Web apps use cookies appropriately and use the HTTPS protocol to encrypt requests and responses. On the whole, cookies are now safe, and it is reasonable to insist that users allow them.

URL Rewriting

Most browsers let users disable cookies, and you may have to make provisions for users who turn off cookies. There is an alternative way to send the cookie: *URL rewriting*, which appends the cookie data to the URL. The data appears to be a string of random characters because it is encrypted. But the information is not secure, because the encryption algorithm is simple and publicly known. Before each of your servlets returns the response to the client, ask the server to encode the session ID and other cookies by calling `HttpServletResponse.encodeURL` or `HttpServletResponse.encodeRedirectURL`. Pass the URL as a `String` object in the argument and receive the encoded URL as the returned `String` object. Both methods check whether the client supports cookies and returns the unaltered URL if rewriting is not necessary. Use `encodeRedirectURL` when you are redirecting the request and response to another resource and `encodeURL` when replying directly to the client. You should use URL rewriting only as a fallback for users who do not allow cookies.

 The older versions of the URL encoding API are still available, but are deprecated. You should call `encodeURL` instead of `encodeUrl` and `encodeRedirectURL` instead of `encodeRedirectUrl`.

Storing Information in Hidden Fields of HTML Forms

One final place to consider storing data is in the HTML pages, in hidden fields of HTML forms. *Hidden fields* are like ordinary `INPUT` fields except that they are not displayed and therefore cannot be modified by the user. Make a field hidden by declaring their type to be `HIDDEN`, as in

```
<input type="hidden" name="formID" value="TA45"/>
```

Hidden fields are submitted in the HTTP request just like other `INPUT` fields, so the servlet that processes the form data also receives the hidden values. You can use these fields to contain information that the servlet needs but the user should not see. If you build the form dynamically in your Web app, you can use hidden fields as a client-side storage area and an alternative to the server-side sessions. However, hidden fields are not secure and their values appear as unencoded strings in the source of the HTML page. Therefore, do not use hidden fields for sensitive information.

You may be able to reduce the amount of data stored in the server-side session object by storing information that requires no security in hidden fields. For example, rather than recording user activities in the client's **HttpSession** object and providing server-side logic to figure out where the user is in the Web app, you can include an identifier for each form or HTML document in a hidden field. Then each form can effectively tell the servlet where the user is.

JAVASERVER PAGES

A *JSP* is Web resource with embedded Java code. It usually takes the form of an HTML or XHMTL document that includes ordinary HTML tags and some additional JSP-specific tags. Unlike the Java code in an applet, for which the Java classes are downloaded and run in a Web browser, the Java code in a JSP is preprocessed on the server side. The application server converts the entire page to HTML and resolves all dynamic content before sending the page to the client browser.

To call a JSP, a client requests its URL from a Web browser, much like requesting any HTML page, except that the file extension is `.jsp` instead of `.htm` or `.html`. Like other Web resources, the URL of a JSP can be entered directly by the user, by the `href` value of an HTML hyperlink, by the action of an HTML `FORM` tag, or by the destination of a forward or redirect from a servlet.

A JSP serves the same purpose as a servlet: to produce HTML pages with dynamic content. Everything you can do with a servlet, you can do with a JSP. Everything you can do with a JSP, you can do with a servlet. Why, then, would you use JSPs? They help solve the following problems that are inherent to servlets:

- Calling Java print methods to output HTML is clumsy. Instead of using WYSIWYG HTML editors, you must write large volumes of tedious code. The resulting HTML is hard to manage and maintain. For example, it takes a programmer to change the wording of static text in an HTML document output by a servlet. A JSP is written in HTML, so you can use your favorite HTML authoring tools to create at least the static portions of the page.

- Developing a large Web site requires a team of people with a variety of skills. Programmers, graphic designers, HTML authors, user-interface designers, and others may be involved. When programmers write servlets, they start doing the jobs of HTML authors and all the others who have a hand in designing Web pages. This may be a misuse of human resources and prove to be an expensive way to produce content for a Web site. Using a JSP gives the job of designing and authoring Web pages back to the people whose primary skill is in Web development rather than programming.

- Using JSPs and servlets together can provide a much cleaner implementation of the MVC design pattern than using servlets or just JSPs alone. The section "Implementing MVC with Servlets and JSPs" explains this further.

13

Because JSPs are converted to HTML, they do not provide a way to enhance the user interface by adding GUI controls, multimedia, and the like. JSPs do not replace applets or JavaScript. You can continue to embed applets and JavaScript in the HTML portions of a JSP.

A file that contains a JSP must have the extension `.jsp` and be packaged with the HTML documents in the Web app. All J2EE-compliant application servers support JSPs, and version 1.3 of the J2EE specification includes version 1.2 of the JSP specification. Use JSPs to write your dynamic content in HTML, XHMTL, or XML documents rather than in Java classes.

Implementing MVC with Servlets and JSPs

You can design Web apps using only servlets or only JSPs. However, when servlets or JSPs receive HTTP requests and direct the operation of the Web app, they are performing the job of the controller in MVC; yet when they generate HTML or XHTML, they are participating in the view. Thus, a strongly recommended approach is to separate view and controller roles by using servlets to receive user input and JSPs to build the HTML or XHTML response.

Figure 13-12 shows how the servlets and JSPs interact. A description of the flow follows the diagram. Compare this diagram to Figure 13-3.

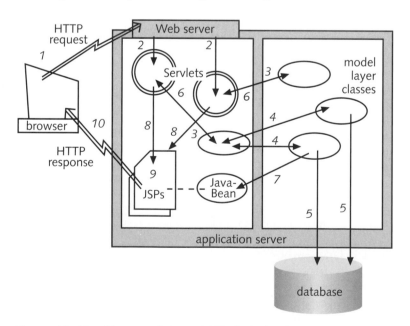

Figure 13-12   How servlets and JSPs help implement MVC

1. The client issues an HTTP request, and the URL includes the URI of a servlet, exactly as in Figure 13-3.

2. The Web server receives the request and forwards it to the application server.

3. The servlet extracts user input from the HTTP request. As controller, it is responsible for ensuring that the request is allowed and that the input is acceptable. Then the servlet calls classes from the model layer to do the actual work. In a small Web app, all the classes may reside in the Web container. In a larger application, model layer classes can be EJBs and reside in a separate container. The application server handles communication between containers.

4. The model layer classes can call each other.

5. The model layer classes can access database-management software or other enterprise information systems.

6. Sometimes, model layer classes can return results to the servlet. The servlet can store the results in the session, request, or application scope. Then the JSP can retrieve them as described in the section "Java Coding in JSPs."

7. Alternatively, the model layer classes can build JavaBeans that contain the results. The section "JSP Tags for JavaBeans" explains how JSPs access the prepared beans.

8. The servlet forwards the request to the JSP, using the same API as it would to forward to another servlet or any URI.

9. Execution of the JSP inserts the dynamic content into the HTML document, and the output is written to a stream that is available to the Web server.

10. The Web server returns an HTTP response containing the resulting HTML to the client browser.

13

JSP TAGS AND API

The classes and interfaces required by JSPs are included the package **javax. servlet.jsp**. You do not use the types defined in this package directly; the application server uses them to process JSPs.

You can write JSPs as HTML or XHTML documents or as XML documents. This chapter covers the HTML format first. When written as HTML or XHMTL documents, the JSP can contain snippets of Java code enclosed in the tags listed in Figure 13-13. Figure 13-14 is an example of such a JSP.

Most enclosed Java code takes the form of a scriptlet or an expression. A *scriptlet* contains one or more complete Java statements or blocks of code. An *expression* is a Java expression of any type. For a scriptlet to add to the resulting HTML output, it must contain explicit calls to methods, such as **print** or **println**, and provide the output as a **String** argument, just like the code in a servlet. In contrast, the string representation of the value of an expression is automatically added to the HTML output.

The ultimate goal of the evolving JSP specification is to provide tags that let you replace all Java code with constructs that conform to JSP syntax, so that JSPs can be created by authors who do not know any Java. The sections "JSP Tags for JavaBeans," "Custom Tags in JSPs," and "Building Robust Web Apps" introduce techniques you can use to eliminate scriptlets and expressions from your JSPs. But your first JSPs are likely to create dynamic content by including scriptlets and expressions.

> Prior to version 1.2 of the JSP specification, support for JSPs as XML documents was optional for application servers, and the HTML or XHTML format is still more commonly used. A number of tags and features have been added to the JSP specification since the original version. Many of these tags have only the XML syntax but can be used in the HTML form of JSP. In general, new tags have contributed to the goal of eliminating Java code from JSP pages. Such tags provide HTML-like constructs that represent Java coding or ways of invoking Java code that is stored outside the JSP.

JSPs as HTML or XHTML Documents

You can use JSP tags as extensions to the set of HTML tags. The HTML form of JSP tags starts with **<%** and ends with **%>**. They are summarized in Figure 13-13.

JSP Element	Description	Examples
`<%-- comment --%>`	Hidden Comment container ignores the contents and they do not appear in the JSP output.	`<%-- seen only in the JSP --%>`

`<%@ page`
`language="java"`
`import="package,`
`   class, …"`
`session="true │ false"`
`buffer="none │ Nkb"`
`isThreadSafe=`
`   "true │ false"`
`errorpage="URN"`
` isErrorPage=`
`   "true │ false"`
`contentType="mimeType"`
`pageEncoding="charSet"`
`%>`
	Page Directive defines attributes of the page, including scripting language, superclass, imports, whether to use the HttpSession object, page to redirect to in case of error, whether this is an error page, and the like.	`<%@ page import= "java.util.*" %>`
		`<%@ page lang="java"`
		`      session="true" %>`

`<%@ include file="URN"` `%>`	Include Directive replaced by text or code from the specified file.	`<%@ include file="banner.html" %>`

Figure 13-13   JSP tags that conform to HTML or XHTML syntax

JSP Element	Description	Examples
`<%@ taglib uri="urn" prefix ="prefix" %>`	Taglib Directive declares a library of custom tags to extend the set of JSP tags. Use the XML form `<tagprefix:name>` to call a custom tag.	`<%@taglib uri="myTagLibrary" prefix= "mtl" %> …` `<mtl:start loop count="6" />`
`<%! … %>`	Declaration declares variables and methods for use in this JSP. You can also declare variables in scriptlets.	`<%! Double intRate=2.32 ; %>` `<%! skier = new ClubMember(); %>`
`<%= … %>`	Expression inserts the value of the Java expression into the page.	`<%= ( a*a + b*b ) / c*c %>` `<%= new Date() %>`

`<% … %>`	Scriptlet executes the enclosed Java code.	`<% // items holds data`
		`for ( int m=0; m< items.length;`
		`        m++ ) {`
		`    out.println( "Item: " +`
		`        items[m].getName( ) );`
		`}`
		`%>`

Figure 13-13 JSP tags that conform to HTML or XHTML syntax (continued)

13

Here is a JSP page that gives exactly the same output as the Today servlet shown in Figures 13-6 and 13-7. The JSP tagging is shown in bold.

```
<?xml version="1.0" encoding="ISO-8859-1" ?>
<!DOCTYPE html PUBLIC "-//W3C//DTD XHTML 1.1//EN"
"http://www.w3.org/TR/xhtml11/DTD/xhtml11.dtd">
<html>
  <head>
    <meta http-equiv="Pragma" CONTENT="no-cache" />
    <meta http-equiv="expires" CONTENT="-1" />
    <title>Today</title>
  </head>
  <%@ page import="java.util.*" %>
  <body >
     <H1> The current date and time is:</h1>
     <p> <%= new Date() %>
```

Figure 13-14 A JSP to print the current date and time

```
        <%--  the expression above could be written as:
              <% out.println( new Date() ) ;   %>
        --%>
        </p>
    </body>
</html>
```

Figure 13-14   A JSP to print the current date and time (continued)

Next is a breakdown of this JSP.

The following file conforms to XHTML. The first lines containing the `<?xml ... ?>` and `DOCTYPE...xhtml111.dtd>`" tags specify the version of XHTML used.

```
<?xml version="1.0" encoding="ISO-8859-1" ?>
<!DOCTYPE html PUBLIC "-//W3C//DTD XHTML 1.1//EN"
    r"http://www.w3.org/TR/xhtml11/DTD/xhtml11.dtd">
```

All ordinary HTML tags are added to the output unchanged. The `<meta>` tags turn off page caching in the Web browser so that if the user revisits the JSP, the date and time are recalculated.

The following page directive makes all types in the **java.util** package available to scriptlets and expressions in the JSP:

```
<%@ page import="java.util.*" %>
```

The expression `new Date()` is evaluated; the resulting value is cast to type **String** using the **toString** method of the **java.util.Date** class, and the result is added to the output. The expression must be a valid Java expression, and any variables referenced in it must be assigned values before the expression is evaluated:

```
<%= new Date() %>
```

The following is a comment that is trimmed off when the JSP is processed and does not appear in the resulting HTML, even as a comment. The comment includes a scriptlet that produces identical output to the expression `<%= new Date() %>`.

```
<%--  the expression above could be written as:
      <% out.println( new Date() ) ;   %>
--%>
```

For a convincing argument for using JSPs instead of servlets, compare this listing to the Today servlet.

See Tutorial 13-1, "Building and Running the Today Servlet," on the CD-ROM for instructions on importing the Today JSPs into Application Developer and running them. When running it on a WebSphere Test Environment server, the URL for this JSP is `http://localhost:9080/Today/todayJSP.jsp`.

JSPs as XML Documents

Why write JSPs as XML documents? When you do, the developers must understand both XML and HTML. A WYSIWYG editor for HTML may be useable for XHTML and the tags in Figure 13-15, but may not be useful for XML. The resulting documents are marginally longer and look more complex than the equivalent HTML or XHTML versions. XML syntax is described in Chapter 10.

The upside stems from the fact that XML is rapidly being adopted as a standard for information storage and interchange throughout the IT industry. If you adopt XML standards, you can take advantage of the rapidly growing body of XML-based tools to assist in JSP development. For example, you can parse the JSPs using XML validators and manipulate their source programmatically using APIs, such as those described in Chapter 10.

Consider a JSP as a collection of components. Some components contain pure HTML elements, such as paragraphs, lists, and links. Others are dynamically generated output. In many applications, JSPs may be constructed by combining standard components that a company develops and stores in a library. Tools that manage the library or build documents by combining components can be based on utilities that process XML. There is a demand for productivity tools for building Web apps. Eliminating manual authoring of HTML and JSP documents can save companies money and development time and ensure that pages meet standards. Expect future tools that generate JSPs to use the XML form.

The tags that conform to the XML style syntax are summarized in Figure 13-15. There are equivalents for most the HTML tags, and some additional tags. The tags that operate on JavaBeans use custom tags defined in a tag library, or forward the request to another URL can use both HTML- and XML-based JSPs.

13

JSP Element	Description	Examples

`<jsp:root>` … `</jsp:root>`	Root element as required by XML: Attributes identify JSP namespaces, any tag libraries used in the JSP, the version, and other optional elements.	`jsp:root xmlns:jsp=`
		`  "http://java.sun.com/JSP/Page"`
		`  xmlns:tablibPrefix="mtl"`
		`  version="1.2">`
		`  ...`
		`</jsp:root>`

`<jsp:directive.page`
`attribute="value" />`
	Page Directive: Defines attributes of the page, and allows the same attribute list as `<%@ page … %>` in HTML syntax.	`<jsp:directive.page`
		`  import= "java.util.*"  />`
		`<jsp:directive.page lang="java`
		`  session="true" />`

Figure 13-15   JSP tags that conform to XML syntax

JSP Element	Description	Examples
`<jsp:directive.include file="URN" />`	Include Directive: Replaced by text or code from the specified file.	`<jsp:directive.include` `  file="banner.html" />`
`<jsp:text> … </jsp:text>`	Enclosed characters are passed as is to output.	`<jsp:text> <p>Hello</p></jsp:text>`

`<jsp:declaration> …`
`    </jsp:declaration>`
	Declaration: Declares variables and methods for use in this JSP.	`<jsp:declaration>`
		`  Double intRate=2.32 ;`
		`</jsp:declaration>`
		`<jsp:declaration>`
		`  skier = new ClubMember();`
		`</jsp:declaration>`

`<jsp:expression> …`
`    </jsp:expression>`
	Expression: Inserts the value of the Java expression into the page.	`<jsp:expression> (a*a + b*b)/c*c`
		`</jsp:expression>`
		`<jsp:expression>  new Date()`
		`</jsp:expression>`

`<jsp:scriptlet> …`
`    </jsp:scriptlet>`
	Scriptlet: Executes the enclosed Java code.	`<jsp:scriptlet>`
		`// items is declared & holds data`
		`for ( int m=0; m< items.length;`
		`  m++ ) {`
		`  out.println( "Item: " +`
		`    items[m].getName( ) );`
		`}`
		`</jsp:scriptlet>`

`< tagPrefix:customtag attribute=value  … />`	Runs a custom tag and optionally inserts output to the current location in the JSP.	`<mtl:start loop count="6" />`
`<jsp:forward page="URN" />`	Forwards to the specified page.	`<jsp:forward` `  page="confirmOrder.jsp:" />`

`<jsp:plugin`
`    type="bean | applet"`
`  …`
`/>`
	Triggers invocation of a bean or applet in the specified plug-in. Parameters are name-value pairs specified in `<jsp:params>` tags.	`<jsp:plugin type="applet"`
		`  code="MyAppletCode"`
		`  width="200" height="150" />`

`<jsp:usebean id="instance" scope="page | request | session | application" type="className"`	Finds a bean in the specified scope or instantiates an instance of a bean class.	`<jsp:usebean id="member"`
		`  class="ClubMember"`
		`  scope="session" />`

`<jsp:getProperty name="bean" property="field" />`	Inserts the value of an attribute of a bean into the HTML.	`<jsp:getProperty name="member"` `  property="firstName" />`

Figure 13-15   JSP tags that conform to XML syntax (continued)

JSP Element	Description	Examples

`<jsp:getProperty`
`name="bean"`
`property="field"`
`value="value" />`
	Sets the value of an attribute of a bean.	`<jsp:setProperty name="member"`
		`    property="firstName"`
		`    value="Mary" />`

Figure 13-15 JSP tags that conform to XML syntax (continued)

Figure 13-16 is the Today JSP from Figure 13-14 written as an XML document. The XML JSP tags are in bold.

```
<jsp:root xmlns:jsp="http://java.sun.com/JSP/Page" version="1.2">
  <jsp:directive.page language="java"
                    import="java.util.Date"
                    contentType="text/html; charset=ISO-8859-1"
                    pageEncoding="ISO-8859-1" />
  <jsp:text>
    <![CDATA[ <?xml version="1.0" encoding="ISO-8859-1" ?> ]]>
  </jsp:text>
  <jsp:text>
    <![CDATA[ <!DOCTYPE html PUBLIC "-//W3C//DTD XHTML 1.1//EN"
                "http://www.w3.org/TR/xhtml11/DTD/xhtml11.dtd"> ]]>
  </jsp:text>
  <html xmlns="http://www.w3.org/1999/xhtml">
    <head>
       <META HTTP-EQUIV="Pragma" CONTENT="no-cache" />
       <META HTTP-EQUIV="Expires" CONTENT="-1" />
       <title>Today</title>
    </head>
    <body>
        <h1>The current date and time is:</h1>
        <p>
         <jsp:expression> new Date() </jsp:expression>
        </p>
    </body>
  </html>
</jsp:root>
```

Figure 13-16 An XML JSP to print the current date and time

There is no equivalent of the `<jsp:root>` element in the HTML. Unlike XML, HTML and XHTML documents do not require a single root element. The xmlns attribute in the root element specifies the XML schema that defines the JSP tags. In this example, the `<jsp:text>` tags are required to enclose the XML and DOCTYPE declarations so that the JSP page compiler can pass them on unaltered. When running on a WebSphere Test Environment server, the URL for this JSP is

`http://localhost:9080/Today/todayXML.jsp.`

How the Server Processes JSPs

When the application server receives a request for a JSP, it checks to determine whether the JSP is already loaded and, if not, it calls a process called the *page compilation*. To help picture the page compilation process, consider that a servlet is written in Java but contains snippets of HTML. A JSP is written in HTML or XML and contains snippets of Java. You can think of a JSP as a servlet turned inside out. The page compiler converts the JSP into a servlet conceptually by turning it inside out again.

The page compiler creates a servlet class. It adds import statements and the like according to the directives in the JSP. It generates a **service** method from the body of the JSP source. Simple HTML or text enclosed in **<jsp:text>** tags becomes character data written to the servlet output stream. Java scriptlets, expressions, and declarations are left alone, except that the surrounding tags are stripped off so they become Java source code. Statements that output HTML, scriptlets, and expressions are added to the **service** method in the order that corresponding elements appear in the JSP. In short, page compilation translates a JSP to the Java source of the servlet class that includes a **service** method. The container then compiles the class into bytecode and runs the resulting servlet.

By default, a JSP is compiled when it is first called. If you change the **.jsp** file between calls, the server reads the source page and compiles, loads, and runs it again. After it is loaded, the JSP remains loaded in the Web container on the server until its source is changed again, the JSP is destroyed, or the server process stops. Therefore, the overhead of page compilation usually happens only the first time the JSP is used. Some application servers can preload and precompile JSPs when the Web application is loaded so that any delay caused by page compilation occurs when the application is started rather than when the first user accesses the JSP.

Java Coding in JSPs

In the Today JSP you saw how expressions and scriptlets can contain snippets of Java code. Java code always runs in the context of the class and method that contains it. For example, you can declare local variables, refer to instance or class fields, and use the arguments of the method. You have seen that JSP directives and declarations produce Java code elements that are part of a servlet class definition placed outside the **service** method, such as import statements and method declarations. How do expressions and scriptlets refer to fields of the servlet class generated from the JSP and to arguments of the method within which they reside? The JSP specification identifies a number of implicit identifiers for this purpose.

Predefined Variables in JSPs

Page compilation converts the body of the JSP into the body of a **service** method. In a servlet, the **doGet**, **doPost**, and **service** methods receive the HTTP request and response object... arguments and access the servlet context by calling methods on those arguments. JSP expressions and scriptlets are given predefined variables representing the HTTP request and response and servlet context. The objects listed in Figure 13-17 are implicitly available to JSPs.

JSP variable	Type	Description
request	javax.servlet.http.HttpServletRequest	The HTTP request originally sent to the server
response	javax.servlet.http.HttpServletResponse	The HTTP response to the request
pageContext	javax.servlet.jsp.PageContext	An object encapsulating the context for this page
session	javax.servlet.http.HttpSession	The session object associated with the client
application	javax.servlet.ServletContext	The object returned by getServletConfig(). getContext()
out	javax.servlet.jsp.JspWriter	An object that writes to the response output stream
config	javax.servlet.ServletConfig	The ServletConfig object for this JSP
page	java.lang.Object	The this object reference in this JSP

Figure 13-17   Implicit objects in JSPs

In a Web app that uses servlets and JSPs, the typical flow of an HTTP request and response is as follows:

1. The servlet receives the HTTP request and performs precondition testing.

2. If the request is GET, the servlet forwards the request to a JSP that may display a form.

3. If the request is POST, the servlet retrieves the user input from the request and forwards it to model layer classes for processing.

4. When the processing by the model layer classes is complete, the servlet redirects or forwards the request to the JSP.

5. The JSP produces the output.

One way the servlet can pass information to the JSP is by storing it in the application, session, or request scopes. The listing in Figure 13-11 shows how the login and registration servlets in the SkiClub Web app store member information in the session scope, and exception information in the application and request scopes. The registration servlet also adds the member information to the SkiClub database and then forwards it to `memberHome.jsp` to display the page shown in Figure 13-19. The JSP can call the **getAttribute** method on the variables **application**, **session**, or **request** to access objects stored there. The forth scope, **pageContext**, is limited to the JSP page. The lines from `Newmember.jsp` in the SkiClub Web app shown in Figure 13-18 retrieve member information from the session scope and display it.

```
<h3>Thank-you for joining us
  <%= ( ( ClubMember ) session.
      getAttribute( "member" ) ).getFirstName() %>,
</h3>
<p>You have been assigned an ID. For identification
   purposes, you will be asked to log in whenever
   you return to this site. Please make note of the
   following information because you must supply
   it exactly as shown here to log in.</p>
<CENTER>
<TABLE BORDER=0 BGCOLOR="#DDDDFF" CELLPADDING=10 >
<TR>
<TD><strong>Last name</strong></TD>
<TD>
  <%= ( ( ClubMember ) session.
    getAttribute( "member" ) ).getLastName() %>
</TD>
</TR><TR>
<TD><strong>ID</strong><br\></TD>
<TD>
  <%= ( ( ClubMember ) session.
      getAttribute( "member" ) ).getId() %>
</TD>
</TR>
</CENTER>
</TABLE>
```

Figure 13-18   Part of a JSP expression that retrieves data from the session scope

Figure 13-19   The page that displays when a new member joins the ski club

JSP Tags for JavaBeans

Writing the Java snippets for the JSP expressions in Figure 13-18 requires a sound understanding of the Java language and may be demanding for HTML authors. There are tags you can use to eliminate such Java expressions from your JSP. You can insert a `<jsp:usebean>` tag to access a JavaBean by instantiating it or retrieving it from the specified scope. When you have a bean, you can use `<jsp:getProperty>` and `<jsp:setProperty>` to get and set the values of fields.

These three tags conform to the XML syntax, but can also be used in HTML- or XHTML-based JSPs. Figure 13-20 gives a summary of their usage.

13

JSP Tag	Purpose

`<jsp:useBean`
    `class= "classname"`
    `id="name"`
 	
   `■ scope="page"`
 	
   `■ scope="request"`
 	
   `■ scope="session"`
 	
   `■ scope="application"`
 	
 `/>`
	Instantiates or returns an object of the class named with the `class` attribute. The identifier of the object reference is specified by the `id` attribute. The `scope` attribute specifies that the object has one of the following scopes:
	 ■ `page`—The object is local to this JSP page. This is the default.
	 ■ `request`—The object is obtained by calling the method
	 `request.getAttribute( name )`
	 and lives as long as the session is valid.
	 ■ `session`—The object may be obtained by calling the method
	 `session.getAttribute( name )`
	 and is discarded when the request is completed.
	 ■ `application`—The object may be obtained by calling the method
	 `application.getAttribute( name )` and is discarded when the server reclaims the servlet's context.

`<jsp:setProperty`
 	
   `■ name="beanName"`
    `property="propertyName"`
    `value="expression"`
   `■ name="beanName"`
    `property="propertyName"`
    `param="parameterName"`
   `■ name="beanName"`
    `property="propertyName"`
   `■ name="beanName"`
    `property="*"`
 `/>`
	Sets the value of a property of the named bean in one of four ways:
	 ■ Specify the property name and supply a value attribute of the tag. The value must be a Java expression of an appropriate type.
	 ■ Specify the property name and a parameter of the request. The value of the parameter is assigned to the property.
	 ■ If you omit both the value and parameter attributes from the tag, the value of the parameter with the same name as the property is assigned to the property.
	 ■ To read all parameters into properties with matching names, specify * as the property name.

`<jsp:getProperty`
 `name="beanName"`
 `property="propertyName"`
 `/>`
	Returns the value of the named property of the named bean.

Figure 13-20   JSP tags for JavaBeans

When processing a `<jsp:useBean>` tag, the server first looks for an existing object in the specified scope. If there is no such object, the server calls the default constructor of the class to instantiate an object. Make sure that classes you use this way have no-argument constructors. The `<jsp:setProperty>` and `<jsp:getProperty>` tags call the `get` and `set` methods of the fields of the JavaBean. Make sure all fields of classes that you use

this may b ... j ... and ... methods. See Chapter 8 for a full description of the JavaBeans specification. The beans used by JSPs do not have to conform to every part of the JavaBean specification but must at least provide a no-argument constructor and getter and setter methods for properties that the JSPs use.

This practice of using JavaBeans to pass results of a request back to the JSP enforces MVC conformance between the servlet and JSP rather elegantly. The JSP retrieves results by accessing a bean created by the model layer classes, as shown in Steps 7 and 9 of Figure 13-12. The servlet can invoke the model layer classes and then redirect to the JSP without processing the results produced by the model layer beyond storing a bean in an appropriate scope.

If you use JSPs only to produce output, you are unlikely to use the `<jsp: setProperty>` tag. In an all-JSP solution, the `<setProperty>` tag can load a JavaBean with input data, typically the values entered into an HTML form.

Figure 13-21 shows the form that is displayed in the SkiClub Web app when members select to update their member profiles. When this form appears, its fields are populated from state data held in the **HttpSession** object before the HTML is sent to the browser.

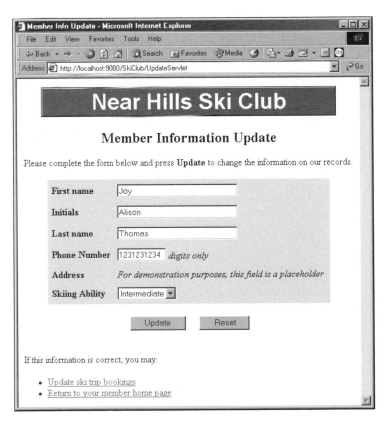

Figure 13-21   The update form in the SkiClub Web app

Figure 13-22 shows the source of the JSP that creates this form. The JSP tags are in bold.

```
<HEAD>
<META NAME="Pragma" CONTENT="no-cache">
<META NAME="Expires" CONTENT="-1">
<TITLE>Member Info Update</TITLE>
</HEAD>
<BODY BGCOLOR="#FFFFFF" LINK="#0000FF" VLINK="#990099" >
<jsp:useBean id="member" class="com.nearhills.ClubMember"
   scope="session" />
<CENTER>
<IMG  SRC="images/SkiClub.gif"
   ALT="Near Hills Ski Club " >
<h2>Member Information Update</H2>

<p>Please complete the form below and press
   <strong>Update</strong> to change
   the information on our records.
</p>
<FORM METHOD=POST ACTION="/SkiClub/UpdateServlet">
<TABLE BORDER=0 BGCOLOR="#DDDDFF" CELLPADDING=5>
<TR>
<TD><strong>First name</strong></TD>
<TD><INPUT TYPE="text" NAME="FNAME"
    VALUE="<jsp:getProperty name="member" property="firstName" />"
     SIZE=30 MAXLENGTH=30 /> </TD>
</TR>
<TR>
<TD><strong>Initials</strong></TD>
<TD><INPUT TYPE="text" NAME="MNAME"
    VALUE="<jsp:getProperty name="member" property="middleName" />"
     SIZE=30 MAXLENGTH=30 /> </TD>
</TR>
<TR>
<TD><strong>Last name</strong></TD>
<TD><INPUT TYPE="text" NAME="LNAME"
    VALUE="<jsp:getProperty name="member" property="lastName" />"
     SIZE=30 MAXLENGTH=30 /> </TD>
</TR>
<TR>
<TD><strong>Phone Number</strong></TD>
<TD><INPUT TYPE="text" NAME="PHONE"
    VALUE="<jsp:getProperty name="member" property="phoneNumber" />"
     SIZE=10 MAXLENGTH=10 />
     <em>digits only</em>
</TD>
</TR>
<TR>
<TD><strong>Address</strong></TD>
<TD><em>For demonstration purposes,
     this field is a placeholder</em></TD>
```

Figure 13-22   The welcome page of the SkiClub Web app

```
</TR>
<TR>
<TD><strong>Skiing Ability</strong></TD>
<TD>
<SELECT NAME ="ABILITY">
   <OPTION VALUE="Novice"
       <%= member.getAbility().equals("Novice") ?
           " SELECTED " : "" %>
    > Novice </OPTION>
   <OPTION VALUE="Intermediate"
       <%= member.getAbility().equals("Intermediate") ?
           " SELECTED " : "" %>
   > Intermediate </OPTION> ":
   <OPTION VALUE="Advanced"
       <%= member.getAbility().equals("Advanced") ?
           " SELECTED " : "" %>
   > Advanced </OPTION> ":
   <OPTION VALUE="Expert"
       <%= member.getAbility().equals("Expert") ?
           " SELECTED " : "" %>
   > Expert </OPTION>
</SELECT>
</TD>
</TR>
</TABLE>
<TABLE BORDER=0 CELLSPACING=20 >
<TR>
<TD><INPUT TYPE="submit" VALUE="   Update    "></TD>
<TD><INPUT TYPE="reset"  VALUE="     Reset   " ></TD>
</TR>
</TABLE>
</FORM>
</CENTER>
<p>If this information is correct, you may:
<ul>
<li><a href="/SkiClub/BookingServlet">
   Update ski trip bookings</a></li>
<li><a href="./memberHome.jsp">
   Return to your member home page</a></li>
</ul>
</BODY>
</HTML>
```

Figure 13-22   The welcome page of the SkiClub Web app (continued)

Note that the **<jsp:useBean>** and **<jsp:getProperty>** tags replace all Java code from the JSP except the conditional expression that determined which of the Ability options to set as the default for the HTML **<SELECT>** tag. Clearly there cannot be standard tags for everything and sometimes you must code in Java.

13

Custom Tags in JSPs

The next step in removing Java code from a JSP is to create custom tags. This book can do no more than introduce custom tags so that you recognize them when you encounter JSPs that use them. The JSP specification lets you define your own tags, build Java classes that implement them, and then use the tags in your JSPs. You can use custom tags to generate output and provide constructs, such as loops and conditional execution. Custom tags can have attributes, and you use the attributes to pass arguments to the methods that implement the custom tags.

Custom tags are grouped into libraries, and each library has a unique prefix. For example, if you create tags `sayHello`, `Sing`, and `Dance` and gather them in a library with the prefix `perform`, to use the tags in the JSP, you would include the prefix in the tag, as shown here:

```
<perform:sayHello name="World" />
```

The tags associated with custom tags in HTML-based JSPs are

- Declare a tag library with a directive that specifies the location of the descriptor file for the tag library and the prefix that identifies tags in the JSP page:`<%@ taglib uri="urn" prefix="prefix" %>`

- Use the tags in XML-compatible format: `<prefix:tag attribute="value" … />`

- In XML-based JSPs, the tag library is listed as a namespace in the `<jsp:root>` element and tags are used as in HTML-based JSPs: `<jsp:root … xmlns:prefix="urn" … />`

You may define your own tag libraries, but the emerging trend is to use predefined libraries. Sun Microsystems released the JavaServer Pages Standard Tag Library (JSTL) in 2003. You can find out more at `http://java.sun.com/products/jsp/jstl/index.html`. The Jakarta Taglibs is a free implementation of the JSTL, downloadable from `http://jakarta.apache.org/taglibs/`.

For every tag library, there is a descriptor file identified by the `uri` attribute of the `taglib` directive. The descriptor is an XML file, and it contains elements describing every tag in the library. This descriptor file has the extension `.tld`. It must be included in the war file of the Web app and reside in the folder `WEB-INF\tld`.

Every tag in a taglib has a handler class. Tag handlers implement one of the interfaces—`Tag`, `BodyTag`, or `IterationTag`—defined in the package `javax.servlet.jsp.tagext`. These interfaces define methods including an initializer for the tag handler, a `doStartTag` method, and a `doEndTag` method. These methods can produce output that appears in the resulting HTML or perform some other action, such as forwarding it to another Web resource. The classes must be included in the war file and reside in folder `WEB-INF\classes`.

FRAMEWORKS FOR BUILDING WEB APPLICATIONS

The way Web apps are developed in professional development environments is changing with the emergence of frameworks for building Web apps. Writing HTML and JSP pages with a WYSIWYG editor and coding servlets individually is a good way to start. However this approach leads to repetitious work that can be automated. For example, building an HTML form, a JSP to populate the form with data from the client's session object, and a servlet to extract and verify the user input on the form are common tasks. Frameworks are productivity aids for creating resources that are common requirements in Web apps. Moreover, frameworks can incorporate best practices for Web app design so that the Web apps they produce are extensible, easy to maintain, and lend themselves to being made secure.

The popular framework, Structs, is an open-source product of the Apache Jakarta project. Structs supports the MVC design pattern for Web apps described in this chapter and adds refinements—most notably an architecture based on a central controller servlet—that are beyond the scope of this chapter to describe. Struts includes extensive tag libraries and classes you can extend when building servlets. The Web apps it produces facilitate internationalization by separating textual elements from code. Structs is usually adopted by developers who have considerable experience building Web apps. The Apache Jakarta project also supports the frameworks Turbine and Expresso that provide basic services for Web builders. For more information, see `http://jakarta.apache.org`.

BUILDING ROBUST WEB APPS

There are additional factors that you should take into consideration when you start to build a servlet-driven Web app. Some factors relate to programming techniques, and others are design principles.

Program Servlets for Multithreading

When an application server loads a servlet, it instantiates one instance of the servlet class. By default, the container creates a new thread whenever a client sends a request to the servlet and runs the **doGet**, **doPost**, or **service** method on a separate thread for each client. Therefore, only one instance of the servlet exists, but several different threads may be sharing the servlet code at any particular time. As a result, servlets should be designed for multithreaded use.

Be sure you understand the multithreading concepts explained in Chapter 5, and then program your servlets to be thread-safe. You do not have to provide a **run** method, because that method is provided by the server-generated **Thread** object and is the method that calls your servlet. The **wait**, **notify**, and **notifyAll** methods generally are not relevant, because the different client threads should not be aware of each other, and interthread communication is not an issue. The important issue is thread safety of variables. You do not want the threads to interfere with each other by altering variables used by one another.

Generally, you can achieve thread safety by following some guidelines:

- Do not use fields of the servlet class as working storage. The threads share the same instance variables. Therefore, all active clients share instance variables much like they share class variables of the servlet class.

- Use **HttpSession** objects rather than fields to store state data. Each client has a separate session, so session data is thread-safe.

- Local variables are thread-safe because the JRE maintains a separate stack frame for each thread.

- Declare methods that should run for only one client at a time to be synchronized. For example, the method **ClubMember.store** in the SkiClub Web app is synchronized. This method is called by the registration ID, and then asks the database for the last ID used and adds one. If this method were not synchronized, two members might simultaneously receive the same ID.

If you must use instance variables, or for some reason cannot make your servlets thread-safe, declare the servlet to implement the **SingleThreadModel** interface. The application server creates a separate instance of a **SingleThreadModel** servlet for every client. The resulting overhead may degrade the performance and limit the ability of your Web app to scale up to large numbers of concurrent users. So you should use the **SingleThreadModel** only when necessary.

The **SingleThreadModel** interface has not been popular and will be deprecated in future versions of J2EE.

Use Applets Judiciously

One of the desirable results of creating dynamic content on the server side is that overhead on the client is reduced. Download time is less if you do not have to send applets and supporting jar files to the client JRE, and demands on the client's processor are decreased. If you eliminate client-side processing completely, the user does not even need a Java-enabled browser!

Applets or JavaScript can still play a key role in your Web app, and there is no suggestion that they are inherently undesirable. Some kinds of processing must be done on the client. Animation and any display effects that cannot be coded in HTML fall into this category. Sometimes, adding a little fat to clients saves transmission time and aggravation. Using JavaScript to perform input validation that does not require database lookup can improve performance. For example, if you make sure that a telephone number is all digits and do similar first-pass checking before submitting a form, you can eliminate a sequence of HTTP requests and responses.

A servlet can emit an HTML document that includes any valid HTML, including `<OBJECT>` and `<SCRIPT>` tags. `<OBJECT>` tags run applets. `<SCRIPT>` tags run JavaScript. Of course, an applet called in an HTML page generated by a servlet can do anything applets in any Web page can do, including opening a TCP/IP connection to perform two-way communication with the server and use RMI.

As a rule of thumb, do not write applets and JavaScript that undermine conformance of your application to the MVC design pattern. Operations of the model layer, such as updating the database, should not be performed by an applet.

Prior to HTML 4, `<APPLET>` tags ran applets. As of HTML 4, `<OBJECT>` tags are preferred and `<APPLET>` is deprecated. When Java first appeared, applets were extremely popular. However, their usage has declined dramatically as JavaScript is proving a more efficient approach to client-side coding. In general, applets are justified now only in very specialized situations, such as when Swing controls are required.

Allow for Unexpected User Navigation

You may design a Web app that is easy to navigate and lets users reach only pages that are appropriate from any particular page, only to be undermined by the user using features of the browser to bypass your designed flow. One such feature is the Back button. Consider what happens when a shopper in a virtual store visits the shirt department and puts a shirt in the shopping cart. Then the shopper visits the shoe department and adds a pair of shoes to the shopping cart. If the shopper then clicks the Back button to look for another shirt, do the shoes disappear from the shopping cart?

You cannot prevent the user from remembering a URL or adding it to a list of bookmarks or favorite addresses. At a later time, the user may try to go directly to a servlet or JSP that should run only in the middle of a scenario. Here are some approaches for dealing with these problems:

- Turn off caching for all pages and responses that include dynamic content. When the user uses the Back button or a bookmark to go to a page that is not in the browser history record, the browser must request the page from its URL. If the page is the response to an HTTP **GET** request, the browser requests the page again. If the page is the response to an HTTP **POST** request, the browser cannot retrieve the form input data to submit **POST** again and prints a message saying the page cannot be displayed. This behavior may not be ideal, but it is better than displaying an outdated page.

- Build precondition checks that ensure that the user has reached a servlet or JSP through a route that your Web app allows. For example, if the user does not have a valid session, your servlet can forward the request to the login or welcome page of your Web application.

13

Be Prepared for Users who Double-Click

A user who does not see an immediate response to a request may submit the request again before the server side completes the operation. The user may be unsure whether the first request was sent, or may simply click more than once by mistake. A second or third click does not automatically stop processing started on the server side, but it does tell the browser to display only the response to the last request. Consider an online banking application. If the user submits a form to withdraw $100 from a bank account but clicks twice before seeing the response page, should the user see the bank balance reduced by $100 or $200? How does the Web app decide whether the second click is a mistake or a request to withdraw for a second time?

There are a number of ways to deal with this problem. A client-side solution is to use JavaScript to disable the submit button after the first click. A server-side solution is to program the servlet to record the start and stop of processing as session state data. Then as requests arrive, the servlet can check whether a previous request is still being processed and reject requests that arrive before the last response has been sent.

Use URNs for Internal Addresses

Avoid using full addresses (URLs or URIs) when one resource in your Web app refers to another resource in the same Web app. Use relative addresses or URNs in hypertext links from one HTML or JSP page to another, as the destination a servlet passes to the `RequestDispatcher` object, in the `ACTION` attribute of HTML `FORM` tags, and all other places where you supply addresses. Within a Web app, you can specify an address relative to the context root by starting the address with a slash (/) as in `/login.html` rather than `http://localhost/skiclub/login.html`. As a result, switching between the HTTP and HTTPS protocols or changing the port number does not affect your Web app, and links are not broken if the Web app is moved to a different host or domain name.

Make all servlets named servlets, as described in the section "Named and Anonymous Servlets." As a result, you can change the names of packages and servlet classes without breaking links. Using named servlets can also help you add security to your Web app.

CHAPTER SUMMARY

❒ Java Web applications leverage the infrastructure of the Web. The user uses an ordinary Web browser. The browser communicates with a Web server using the HTTP or HTTPS protocol. HTTPS adds the Secure Socket Layer (SSL) protocol for increased security. The pages displayed on the client side are ordinary HTML or XHTML documents served by a Web server. In a Web application, the content of these pages can be dynamically created at runtime by Java components that run on the server side.

❑ J2EE gives a formal definition for a web application. A web application runs on an application server that plugs into a Web server. The application server provides a JRE and supplies services to a Web container. The container provides the context within which servlets and JSPs run.

❑ To be deployed on an application server, a J2EE Web app must be packaged in a Web archive (war file) that in turn is usually packaged in an enterprise application archive (ear file). The ear and war files also contain deployment descriptors, which are XML files containing deployment information required by the application server. Security and other services are requested declaratively in the deployment descriptors.

❑ The server-side components that form the bridge between HTML and Java code are servlets and JavaServer Pages (JSPs).

❑ A recommended design model for Web apps conforms to the MVC design pattern as follows:

- The view layer consists of static HTML pages and JSP documents.

- The controller layer consists of servlets that receive HTTP requests.

- The model layer consists of classes and other components that perform the core functionality of the application.

❑ Using servlets to receive HTTP requests and JSPs to prepare HTTP responses can help increase MVC conformance and clarify the roles of HTML authors and Java programmers on the development team.

❑ To develop Web apps, you should use an IDE that has productivity tools for building servlets and JSPs and packaging Web apps as required by J2EE.

❑ Servlet classes extend **javax.servlet.http.HttpServlet**.

❑ By default, only one instance of a servlet runs in the server's JRE. The servlet creates a new thread for every HTTP request to that servlet.

❑ The application server passes the HTTP request and the HTTP response to servlet methods as Java objects of type **HttpServletRequest** and **HttpServletResponse**. The server calls the servlet's **service** or **doGet** method when the client issues an HTTP **GET** request, and the servlet's **doPost** method when the client issues an HTTP **POST** method. Use **POST** to submit user input from an HTML form.

❑ A **doPost** method can call the **getParameterNames**, **getParameterValues**, and **getParameter** methods on the request object to access user input.

❑ HTTP requests and responses are stateless. You can provide continuity as the client moves about a Web app by creating an **HttpSession** object to store state information. Session objects are stored on the server, and the server uses cookies or URL rewriting to send the session ID to the client. Subsequent servlets and JSPs can then get the session from the HTTP request.

13

❑ There are four scopes for passing data between servlets and JSPs:

- Data stored in the session scope is specific to one client.

- Data stored in the application scope is global to the Web app.

- The lifetime of data stored in the request scope is the duration of one HTTP request-response cycle.

- Data stored in the page scope is accessible only in the current page.

❑ You can also use **Cookie** objects to store data on the client side from one browser session to the next.

❑ Servlets can forward requests to other Web resources in the same Web app using the **RequestDispatcher** object. Use the **HttpServletResponse.sendRedirect** method to tell the browser to reroute the request to another URL.

❑ JSPs are HTML, XHTML, or XML documents that contain snippets of Java code. They run on the server side, and the Java code creates the dynamic elements in the resulting HTML page. Use XML syntax when you want to use XML tools to maintain your JSPs.

❑ From the run-time perspective, servlets and JSPs can be used interchangeably. The Web container converts a JSP into a servlet using the page compile process.

❑ JSPs that conform to HTML or XHTML syntax have four types of tags that start with **<%** and end with **%>**:

- Java directives are enclosed in **<%@ … %>** tags. Use directives to import packages and set other parameters of the page as a whole.

- Java declarations are enclosed in **<%! … %>** tags. Declarations define methods and variables used by Java code in the JSP.

- Expressions are enclosed in **<%= … %>** tags. Each Java expression is evaluated, and its string representation of the value is inserted into the resulting HTML in place of the expression tag.

- Scriptlets are enclosed in **<% … %>** tags. Scriptlets contain one or more complete Java statements or blocks of code. They are executed where they appear in the JSP page.

❑ Java code in JSPs can use a number of predefined variables including **out**, **session**, **request**, **response**, and **application**.

❑ You should try to minimize the amount of Java code in JSPs. The **<jsp:useBean />**, **<jsp:getProperty/>**, and **<jsp:setProperty>** tags give you an HTML syntax for using JavaBeans to pass data to other components in the Web app.

❑ You can define your own custom tags. Custom tags can help remove all Java code from JSPs. A number of custom tag libraries and frameworks for building Web apps are available.

REVIEW QUESTIONS

1. Which of the following statements are accurate? Select all that apply.

   a. Web servers provide the JRE in which servlets run.

   b. Servlets can be written in Java or JavaScript.

   c. The Servlet API is included in the J2SE platform.

   d. Servlets and the classes they call must be packaged in jar files for deployment.

   e. A Web page created by a servlet can contain an applet or JavaScript.

2. A class that extends `HttpServlet` can override which of the following methods? Select all that apply.

   a. `doGet`

   b. `doPost`

   c. `getSession`

   d. `doPut`

   e. `service`

3. Which of the following insert "hello" in the HTML page generated from the containing JSP? Select all that apply.

   a. `<jsp:exp> "hello" </jsp:exp>`

   b. `<%= "hello" %>`

   c. `<%! out="hello" %>`

   d. `<jsp:scriptlet>out.print( "hello"); </jsp:scriptlet>`

   e. `<% out.println( "hello" ) %>`

4. Which of the following variables can you use in expressions and scriptlets in a JSP without explicitly declaring them? Select all that apply.

   a. `session`

   b. `exception`

   c. `context`

   d. `request`

   e. `buffer`

5. How can you make sure only one client at a time runs a method in your servlet? Select all that apply.

   a. Specify in the deployment descriptor that the servlet is single threaded.

   b. Declare the servlet class to implement `SingleThreadModel`.

   c. Begin the servlet class definition with the keyword `synchronized`.

   d. Begin the method definition with the keyword `synchronized`.

   e. Do nothing; the server lets only one client at a time run a servlet.

13

6. A restaurant has a Web app for booking tables, but does not store customer data in any persistent medium. Which is the most appropriate place to record customer preferences, such as smoking or non-smoking?

   a. in the session object for this customer

   b. in the request scope

   c. in the application scope

   d. in a cookie

   e. in an instance field of the servlet

7. To which of the following does the `RequestDispatcher` object let the servlet or JSP forward an HTTP request? Select the best answer.

   a. another servlet or JSP or HTML page in the same Web app

   b. Java classes that perform the business logic to complete the user's request

   c. the security services of the application server

   d. any valid URI on the network

   e. another Web server or application server

8. Which of the following sets of lines in a JSP retrieve the field "`age`" from a JavaBean of type `com.xyz.Person`? Assume that a servlet prepared the bean. Select all that apply.

   a.
   ```
   <%@ page import="com.xyz.*" %>
   <jsp:useBean id="somebody" class=" Person" scope="request">
     <jsp.getProperty value="somebody.age" />
   ```

   b.
   ```
   <%@ page import="com.xyz.Person" %>
   <jsp:useBean id="somebody" class="Person" >
   <jsp.getProperty name="somebody" property="age" />
   ```

   c.
   ```
   <jsp:useBean id="person" class="com.xyz.Person" scope="request">
   <jsp.getProperty id="person" property="age" />
   ```

   d.
   ```
   <%@ page import="com.xyz.Person" %>
       <jsp:useBean id="person" class="Person" scope="request">
   <jsp.getProperty name="person" property="age" />
   ```

   e.
   ```
   <jsp:useBean  name="somebody" class="com.xyz.Person"
   scope="request" />
   <jsp.getProperty name="somebody" type="int" value="age" />
   ```

9. Which two of the following tasks are involved in initializing a servlet?

   a. specifying initialization parameters and value in the deployment descriptor of the Web app

   b. inserting initialization code in the constructor for the servlet class

......ding the inherited **service** method to ensure that initialization is complete before calling **doPost** or **doGet**

   d. overriding the inherited **init** method

   e. storing the initialization parameters and values as strings in a properties file

10. In which of the following circumstances does a session object become no longer useable by servlets and JSPs? Select all that apply.

   a. when the HTTP request is returned to the Web browser

   b. when the session times out or is invalidated by the application server

   c. when the user directs the Web browser to a URL that is outside the Web application

   d. when code called by a servlet or JSP calls **HttpSession.invalidate**

   e. after an **HttpSessionEvent** class instance occurs

PROGRAMMING EXERCISES

Files for all exercises are included in the **Chapter13.war** Web app in the **Data\questions\c13** folder on the CD-ROM. To build your solutions in Application Developer, create Web projects to hold your work. Use Tutorial 13-1 as a guideline for how to create a new Web project and how to add servlets, HTML pages, and JSPs to a Web project. Then you can import the files or cut and paste the contents into files you first create in Application Developer.

Debugging

13

1. Extract the file **Debug13_1.html** from **X:\Data\questions\c13\Debug13_1.html** where **X** is the drive letter of your CD-ROM. The file contains an HTML 4 document that most Web browsers can display. Convert it to a well-formed and valid XHTML version 1.0 document. Follow the link included in the document to access an XHTML validator provided by the World Wide Web Consortium to verify your solution.

   Hint: Add the following lines to the start of the file:

```
<?xml version="1.0" encoding="ISO-8859-1" ?>
<!DOCTYPE html
    PUBLIC "-//W3C//DTD XHTML 1.0 Strict//EN"
    "http://www.w3.org/TR/xhtml1/DTD/xhtml1-strict.dtd">
```

To build the answer for Debugging Exercises 2, 3, and 4, build a Web app called **StockQuote** and package it in a war file called **StockQuote.war**.

2. Extract the file **Debug13_2.html** from X:\Data\questions\c13\Debug13_2.html where **X** is the drive letter of your CD-ROM. The file is the first part of a three-part debugging project. The answers to Debugging

Chapter 13   Building Web Applications

Exercises 2, 3, and 4 together make a small, complete stock quote Web app. The user enters a stock symbol and receives back a value (actually a random number). If the symbol is not three characters starting with a letter, it is considered invalid and the user receives an error page. Correct all the errors in the file `Debug13_2.html` so that it calls the servlet class `questions.c13.Debug13_3` when the user clicks the Get Quote button.

3. Extract the source for servlet class `questions.c13.Debug13_3` from the file `X:\Data\questions\c13\Debug13_3.java` where `X` is the drive letter of your CD-ROM. The servlet is the second part of the three-part debugging project begun in Debugging Exercise 2. Correct all errors in the servlet so that it processes the parameter received from the form in `Debug13_2.html`. The servlet tries to build a `StockQuote` object for the given stock symbol and, if successful, stores the object in the request scope. Then the servlet forwards the request to either `questions.c13.Debug13_4.jsp` or `questions.c13.ErrorPage.jsp` to generate a response.

   This Web app uses the class `c13.questions.StockQuote` that you can extract from the file `X:\Data\questions\c13\StockQuote.java` and the JSP page `ErrorPage.jsp` that you can extract from the file `X:\Data\questions\c13\ErrorPage.jsp`. The `StockQuote` class and `ErrorPage` JSP contain no errors.

4. Extract the source for JSP `Debug13_4.jsp` from the file `X:\Data\questions\c13\Debug13_4.jsp` where `X` is the drive letter of your CD-ROM. The JSP is the third part of a three-part debugging project begun in Debugging Exercises 2 and 3. Correct all errors in the JSP so that it generates the correct HTML page when called from the servlet class `Debug13_2`:

   To build the answer for Debugging Exercise 5, build a Web app called `Debug13_5` and package it in a war file called `Debug13_5.war`.

5. Extract the HTML document `Debug13_5.html` from the file `X:\Data\questions\c13\Debug13_5.html` where `X` is the drive letter of your CD-ROM. Extract the source for servlet class `questions.c13.Debug13_5` from the file `X:\Data\questions\c13\Debug13_5.java`. Extract the JSP `ErrorPage.jsp` from the file `X:\Data\questions\c13\ErrorPage.jsp`. Extract the source of the `TodayServlet` class from the file `X:\Data\examples\servlets\TodayServlet.java`.

   Add all these files to the Web app you build to answer this question. The HTML document has no errors and contains a form that calls the servlet. The `Debug13_5` servlet uses the JSP and the Today servlet. The JSP contains no errors. Fix the servlet so that it sends the user to the URL `www.w3c.org` when the user clicks the `w3c.org` button in the form and runs the Today servlet when the user clicks the Today button in the form.

   There is a trick: You have to add a **doPost** method to the `TodayServlet` class that calls the `TodayServlet.doGet` method.

Complete the Solution

1. Extract the source code for servlet class **Complete13_1** from the file **X:\Data\ questions\c13\Complete13_1.java** where **X** is the drive letter of your CD-ROM. Build a Web app that contains this servlet. Insert code as indicated by comments. The **doGet** method is complete and outputs a change-password form. For test purposes, an initial password is set to **password**. The **doPost** method must check the three input fields. Did the user enter in the correct old password, supply a new password that contains five to eight characters, and type the new password identically twice? The **doPost** method then either changes the password and outputs a confirmation page or outputs a page that gives the reason for not changing the password.

2. The **doGet** method of **Complete13_1** outputs a static form. Convert the form to an XHTML page and delete the **doGet** method from the **Complete13_1** servlet. Call the new page **Complete13_2.html** and add it to the Web app. To make sure the document is valid XHTML version 1.1, add the following declarations to the top of the document, and then go to the same validation service you used in Debugging Exercise 1, **http://validator.w3.org**:

```
<?xml version="1.0" encoding="ISO-8859-1" ?>
<!DOCTYPE html PUBLIC "-//W3C//DTD XHTML 1.1//EN"
          "http://www.w3.org/TR/xhtml11/DTD/xhtml11.dtd">
<html xmlns="http://www.w3.org/1999/xhtml">
```

3. Extract the source code for servlet class **Complete13_3** from the file **X:\Data\ questions\c13\Complete13_3.java** where **X** is the drive letter of your CD-ROM. Complete the definition of the servlet: Insert code as indicated by comments so that this servlet prints information about the HTTP request that it receives.

4. Extract the source code for servlet class **Complete13_4** from the file **X:\Data\ questions\c13\Complete13_4.java** where **X** is the drive letter of your CD-ROM. Complete the definition of the servlet: Insert code as indicated by comments so that this servlet first lists all the cookies stored in the HTTP request, then adds a cookie to the request, and finally invites you to run the servlet again. For each new cookie, set the name to a letter randomly chosen from the alphabet. Set the value so that the first cookie has the value "A", the second has the value "B", and so on through the alphabet. For example, the cookies listed after three repeats may be:

Cookie	Value
R	A
T	B
B	C

Adding cookie:

E	D

When you test, repeat until you use the same cookie name twice. Then you can verify that creating a cookie with the same name as an existing cookie changes the value of the cookie.

13

Discovery

1. Write a simple chat room servlet. One servlet class can have a **doGet** and **doPost** method. The **doGet** method displays all messages entered by previous clients, followed by a form for the user to enter, sign, and submit a new message. The **doPost** method adds the new message and client's signature to the list of messages and then redirects the server to the **doGet** method of this servlet. When you test, use some imagination and pretend other clients are adding messages and reading yours. There is no need to make the messages persistent. The chat room can start with an empty list of messages every time the servlet is loaded into the server.

2. Write a simple temperature conversion Web app. It must contain three components:

   ❑ An input HTML page that contains an HTML form. On this form the user enters a number of degrees, selects an action to convert from Celsius to Fahrenheit or from Fahrenheit to Celsius, and then clicks a submit button to do the conversion.

   ❑ A servlet that processes the form and stores a JavaBean with the temperature information in the request scope.

   ❑ A JSP that prints out a message such as "22 degrees Celsius is approximately equal to 71.6 Fahrenheit" or "32 degrees Fahrenheit is approximately equal to 0.0 Celsius" and provides a link back to the input form.

14

ENTERPRISE JAVABEANS

In this chapter you will:

- ◆ Explore an enterprise application's needs for secure distributed access, scalability with high performance, robustness, data persistence with transactional integrity, and management of distributed and often disparate resources

- ◆ Discover how the EJB framework provides the quality of services enterprise applications require

- ◆ Learn how stateful and stateless session EJBs provide components that perform business logic

- ◆ Learn how to program an EJB client

- ◆ Discuss exception handling in EJBs and EJB clients

- ◆ Learn how entity beans represent persistent data in Java objects

- ◆ Discuss mapping fields of entity beans to elements in databases using container-managed persistence (CMP) and bean-managed persistence

- ◆ Learn how to use container-managed relationships and EJB query language with container-managed persistence

- ◆ Learn what Java Message Service is and learn how message-driven beans consume asynchronous messages

- ◆ Discuss transactional properties of EJBs

- ◆ Discuss elements of application security that relate to EJBs

- ◆ Consider some best practices for designing applications that use EJBs

INTRODUCTION

This chapter introduces the subject that occupies the largest portion of the J2EE specification, Enterprise JavaBeans (EJBs). This is one of the most complex topics for Java programmers to master, and you should not attempt it until you have a sound basis in the Java language. You should also have some experience developing J2EE Web applications or have completed Chapter 13.

This chapter cannot cover EJBs in depth because the topic is large, but it does introduce the key concepts. The goal is to give you an understanding of what EJBs are and when using them makes sense. The nature of EJBs is such that they are rarely appropriate for the sort of programs one person or a very small team of developers can create, unless that program is a prototype or proof-of-concept for a larger software system. EJBs are usually used in applications built by large development teams and are often designed to be reusable components that can be used concurrently by multiple applications.

Five tutorials associated with this chapter guide you through creating some simple EJBs and testing them in small programs, even though such use of EJBs is not typical. Much of the chapter concentrates on the advantages and quality-of-service features that EJBs can bring to enterprise applications. Think in terms of mission-critical operations that are central to the IT infrastructure of large companies and organizations. This chapter should help you understand the role EJBs play in enterprise applications. It discusses application design to show you where EJBs fit in the architecture of large programs.

Even if you do not develop EJBs early in your professional Java programming career, you may be called upon to create components that are clients of EJBs. For example, the processing engine behind a Web application may be a set of EJBs, and servlets or helper classes for the servlets may be EJB clients. Therefore, this chapter gives detailed coverage to programming EJB clients.

ENTERPRISE PROGRAMMING

The scope of the enterprise edition of the Java 2 platform extends beyond writing Java programs that connect to non-Java resources or that communicate over a network: It defines an environment and framework through which disparate and distributed elements in large IT systems can interoperate. The EJB specification is a description of this environment and the framework for building distributed objects that implement a standard interface.

The non-Java elements in an IT system can include databases, programs in other languages, messaging middleware, or enterprise information systems (EIS). Messaging middleware is introduced in the section "Message Driven Beans." The term *EIS* is a catch-all for a variety of legacy and traditional IT systems including nonrelational databases, such as IBM IMS, mainframe transaction processing systems, most notably IBM CICS, and enterprise resource management (ERP) systems, of which SAP, JD Edwards, and PeopleSoft are examples.

The section "J2EE Platform Services" in Appendix A gives a brief overview of the J2EE Connector Architecture (J2C) for connecting to non-Java resources listed in the previous paragraph. In addition to many APIs, J2EE provides the services required by mission-critical applications that form the backbone of an organization's IT infrastructure. Here are some examples of requirements enterprise applications place on software services:

- *Distributed systems* are software systems that reside on several physical hosts, and the components must interoperate over a network that may be a local area network (LAN) or the Internet. Heterogeneous systems consist of software that runs on different hardware and software platforms. The distribution of functionality between the different servers may be far from optimal for historical and other reasons, such as when companies merge or purchase other companies.

Computer-based distributed systems are not always separated geographically. Within one location, there are advantages in distributed software environments. Performance can be greatly improved by eliminating bottlenecks and replacing one server with several servers and some front-end software that balances the load between them. Failover is a technique for achieving high availability, or as near to 100 percent up-time as possible. *Failover* means duplicating software and services on multiple physical platforms so that the system can continue to run, perhaps with reduced performance, even if one or more hardware components fail. The advantages of distributed architectures include high performance, high availability, and the flexibility to include non-J2EE and legacy components.

- *Scalability* refers to the ability of a system to continue to give high performance as the number of users increases. Consider the classical downfall of many Web applications: After passing all tests of correctness and performing well in test environments, they can grind to a halt in production because thousands of Internet users access the Web application at one time. The problem may not be the capacity of the Web server or application server. For example, when many clients can access databases and other back-end systems indirectly through a Web interface, components that have performed well for decades may become bottlenecks after legacy applications are Web-enabled. To a large extent, distributed architectures can help scalability by spreading the load. A key factor in scalability is the ability of many users to access the system concurrently. For example, multithreading can improve scalability by letting several clients run the same code at one time rather than queuing clients for serialized access. In contrast to the form of multithreading discussed in Chapter 5, the concurrent access required in enterprise applications typically extends to all parts of the system and is generally not something that developers of individual components should control.

- *Persistence* refers to any data that outlives any software component. Usually, but not always, persistent data refers to information stored in databases. The validity of any IT system is clearly tied to the integrity of persistent data. When many components, possibly residing in different subsystems, read and update the same persistent data, there is plenty of scope for data integrity to be compromised. Often, irresolvable conflicts exist between the demand for performance, achieved through concurrent access, and the need for data integrity. In real IT situations, a compromise is often the only resolution.

- *Resource management* is required whenever the system makes high demands on databases and other resources. For example, opening and releasing connections can be expensive operations. In enterprise applications, resource management typically includes connection pooling. *Connection pooling* means keeping a set of connections open so that different software components can be given an open connection for short-term exclusive use. When the component releases the connection, it is returned to the pool but not closed. Of

14

course connection pooling has security implications, because the connections are kept open and the connection pool bypasses the user authentication built into the resource management system.

- *Security* is usually of critical importance in enterprise applications. There are many aspects of security, and solutions apply at many levels in an enterprise application. For example, encrypting data for transmission and attaching digital certifications to verify a sender's identity are part of the responsibility of the communication software. Firewalls can protect local area networks or individual machines from being accessed from unrecognized locations. Web and application servers can assign aliases to elements of Web applications to hide their true names and locations in the file system. Application servers can ensure that only authenticated users (those who have passed password or certificate checks) may access an enterprise application. However, the enterprise application should then be concerned with what the user is authorized to do. For example, in an online banking application, can the user retrieve account information, open new accounts, and alter the interest rate on savings accounts? Does every online banking customer have an ID and password for the bank's database, or does access to the database come with access to the application?

- *Transactional integrity* is often the quality that most concerns developers of enterprise applications. Transactional processing is introduced in Chapter 9 with the discussion of using the JDBC API to commit or roll back database operations. Transactions are logical units of work, with the property that all changes of state made during an activity are either *committed* (made permanent) when the activity completes successfully or *rolled back* (not just reversed, but undone to revert to the state before the activity started) completely if anything goes wrong. Transactional processing is not restricted to database operations, because an enterprise application may touch a variety of distributed components and enterprise information systems. For example, when a customer of an online banking operation transfers funds from a checking account to a credit card, the following actions occur:

  - A debit operation is performed on the checking account and recorded in a transaction log.

  - Perhaps a service charge is calculated, logged, and then applied to the account.

  - Some notification message is sent to the credit card agency.

What if the credit card agency is temporarily unable to receive messages? How can the debit from the checking account, the entries in the account transaction log, and service charge be undone automatically if the attempt to connect to the credit card agency fails? The answer is to wrap the entire transfer operation in one transaction. Now the question becomes, "which element in the system manages the transaction and coordinates the actions of all components that participate in the transaction?" Transactions may need to be rolled back due to conditions detected by application logic, such as a bad-credit-rating or item out of ~~stock condition~~, ~~or problems~~ detected by the system, such as connection fail-ures or temporarily unavailable components. You cannot anticipate all possible problems, but you can wrap all critical operations in transactions. Designing applications so that the start and stop points of logical units of work map onto transaction boundaries is a respon-sibility of software architects and developers.

In this chapter, you learn how many of the concerns listed here can be delegated to the context within which components run. EJBs do not automatically solve all these chal-lenges, but EJBs provide a framework for building components that leverage the services of the J2EE platform. This chapter introduces the rich set of services available to J2EE enterprise applications and describes how you can declare which services you want to apply to specific components.

WHAT ARE EJBS?

Enterprise JavaBeans (EJBs) are server-side software components that conform to the J2EE architecture for development and deployment of distributed systems. The J2EE architec-ture defines a standard component model and sets specifications for application servers that support this model. J2EE-compliant application servers must provide a run-time environment for the EJBs: an *EJB container*. The role of the container is described in the section "EJB Containers and Services."

EJBs come in three basic kinds, and detailed descriptions follow this section of this chap-ter. To introduce them briefly, the three types are listed here:

- *Session beans* can perform any kind of processing. Use them to encapsulate activities performed by an application. For example, a session bean can do a calculation, make a reservation, return a quote, process an order, or construct a document.

- *Entity beans* represent persistent data. Use them like a persistence broker layer between the working of your application and databases. Think of entity beans as the Java representation of objects for which state is maintained in rows and columns of database tables.

- *Message-driven beans (MDB)* have a specialized purpose and are used with messaging software.

The EJB specification has undergone some major revisions since EJBs were first introduced in the Java 2 platform. In the first version, 1.0, application server support for only session beans was mandatory, but most application servers supported session and entity beans. In version 1.1, session and entity beans support was a requirement for J2EE-compliance of all application servers. Version 1.3 of J2EE included support for messaging middleware and the EJB 2.0 specification. MDBs are new with version 2.0. Version 1.4 of the J2EE specifi-cation is in final draft at the time of this writing and includes version 2.1 of the EJB specification. EJB 2.1 expands the role of MDB.

14

Developers frequently refer to individual EJBs as "beans," so the first possible misconception to avoid is that EJBs are in any way related to JavaBeans. The only common elements are their names and the fact that JavaBeans and Enterprise JavaBeans are component models. JavaBeans are essentially ordinary Java classes written to conform to a strict set of coding standards. JavaBeans are portable and distributable because, like any classes, they can be loaded into any standard JRE. In contrast, each EJB consists of a set of classes and interfaces that must implement a specific API and must interact in a standard way with the J2EE context within which they run. EJBs are portable and distributable because the EJB framework includes the infrastructure to support distributed objects.

The goal of the EJB specification is to remove the burden of coding the infrastructure that supports secure, robust, scalable, high-performance applications from the developer. The idea is to delegate the complex and difficult level of software often called "plumbing" to the container. The developer can declare certain characteristics of a bean and leave the enforcing of the characteristics up to the container. For example, if the developer declares that only certain kinds of users can run specific methods, the container denies access to users who do not fit the authorization criteria. The developer concentrates on coding the business logic and adds methods to the EJB that the clients can call.

A fundamental principle in the architecture of EJBs is that clients never instantiate or call the beans directly. EJBs do not have accessible constructors; the EJB containers control the lifecycle of beans and make references available to clients. Every method call from client to an EJB passes through the EJB container, giving the container an opportunity to call upon its security service, transaction manager, and other services. As a result, the EJB developer must define at least one class and two interfaces to build an EJB. The types that make up an EJB are described in more detail with the description of each kind of bean, but the main ones are listed here:

- The *bean class* is the actual EJB class. You implement business logic in methods here.

- A *home interface* provides methods though which the client calls lifecycle methods, such as **create**, to request access to an instance and **remove** to eliminate an instance of the EJB. The J2EE specification allows only certain lifecycle methods.

- A *local or remote interface* defines the business methods that clients can call on the EJB. EJB developers make non-lifecycle methods available to clients by adding them to this interface. This interface is analogous to the remote interface you define for Remote Method Invocation (RMI) and extends **java.rmi.Remote** for clients that do not reside in the same Java Virtual Machine (JVM) as the EJB. You may want to review the section "Remote Method Invocation" in Chapter 11, because remote clients use RMI to call methods on EJBs. However, the EJB framework builds the RMI infrastructure and you do not code EJBs for RMI.

Version 2.0 of the EJB specification defines four interfaces, two for use by any EJB clients, and two for use only by co-located clients. A *co-located* client is an EJB that calls methods on another EJB that resides in the same JVM. For simplicity, this overview discusses all clients as though they are remote. The section "Local and Remote Clients" gives a more complete picture. Prior to version 2.0, the EJB specification assumed that all clients were remote and all clients used the interfaces designed for remote access. Some application servers, including WebSphere Application Server, optimized calls from local clients, but for application servers that did not optimize, the remote method call protocol imposed an unnecessary overhead on method calls between co-located EJBs.

EJB method calls are more flexible than RMI, because the EJB infrastructure combines RMI with the J2EE Java Naming and Directory Interface (JNDI) service for locating EJBs and the industry standard line protocol Internet Inter-Orb Protocol (IIOP) for network communication. IIOP was developed as part of the Common Object Request Broker Architecture (CORBA) to be a flexible, language-neutral protocol for distributed object communication. CORBA is a standard of the Object Management Group (OMG); you can find out more about all OMG standards at `http://www.omg.com`. The protocol for EJB method calls is called RMI over IIOP (RMI/IIOP).

Developers do not declare characteristics of EJBs by calling APIs. Instead, they build an XML file called the *deployment descriptor*, adding stanzas (sets of XML tags) that identify the EJB, name its implementing class and interfaces, specify which services and level of service are required from the EJB container, and so on. EJBs are packaged in jar files, and the deployment descriptor must be included in each EJB jar. Specifying the bean's characteristics outside of code has many advantages. For example, the functionality of the bean can be developed and tested with minimal regard to issues like security. Security and other settings can be added later. Indeed, one EJB can be deployed in many different applications and require different levels of service in each. For example, in one application, the `transferFunds` method can be available to bank managers only, but in another, it can be available to all bank account owners.

One of the many enhancements to the EJB specification introduced in version 1.1 was formatting the deployment descriptors as XML files and publishing the DTD for EJB deployment descriptors. Prior to version 1.1, deployment descriptors were in a unique format strongly resembling properties files. XML is discussed in Chapter 10 and properties files in Chapter 4.

The EJBs belong to the model layer in any application. You may want to review the overview of the J2EE architecture in the section "Java 2 Enterprise Edition" of Chapter 1 and look again at Figure 13-3 in the "Servlets" section of Chapter 13. Session beans or sets of session beans should represent business operations or core application activities. Entity beans should be placed between application code and persistent storage systems, such as a relational database. The relationship between J2EE containers is shown in Figure 14-1. When writing an EJB, you should not be concerned with the user interface or how the

14

user navigates from one activity to another. Such functionality is enclosed in the EJB and may be used in different business activities at different times, and even in different applications.

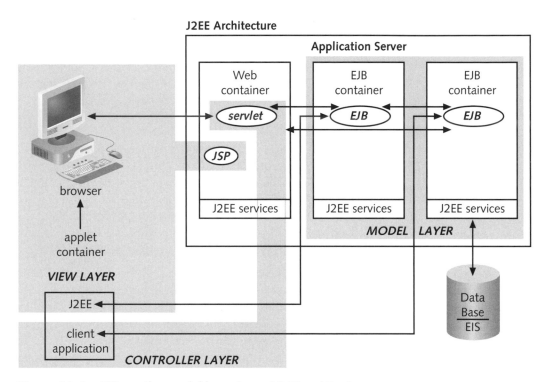

Figure 14-1   EJBs as the model layer in an MVC architecture

EJB Containers and Services

J2EE-compliant application servers provide EJB containers that include JREs and an extensive set of services. EJB containers provide the run-time environment in which the resulting beans run. The EJB specification is largely written for application server vendors. In addition to specifying the APIs that must be available to EJB developers, the J2EE and EJB specifications define contacts between the developer and the EJB container, between the EJB container and the application server, and between the application server and various resources that provide J2EE-compliant drivers or resource adapters. The role of the EJB container is to provide all the APIs included by the J2EE specification and the following:

- *The distribution infrastructure and a naming service to help client code locate and access EJBs.* The container manages the lifecycle of EJBs. It can create bean instances to meet client demand and pool instances for reuse by different clients. An EJB container manages its own memory, but more is involved than running constructors and garbage collection because EJBs can hold state and represent persistent data.

- *The ability to place EJBs in a scalable architecture. The host application* server provides the capability to add servers for high performance and replicate containers across multiple servers for failover. In this sense, the EJB container is a distributable component in an application server configuration.

- *Support for concurrent access.* Many clients, even clients using different applications, can use your EJBs at the same time. You are not expected or even allowed to code for multithreading in EJBs. Instead, let the container handle the allocation of EJB instances to multiple clients wanting to use the same EJB at the same time.

- *Resource management, including connection pooling.* The J2EE specification establishes standard interfaces between the application server and non-Java systems. For example, relational databases provide JDBC drivers, and EIS systems can provide resource adapters.

- *Security services in addition to the secure environment that can be configured for applications loaded into the application server.* Classes can call the Java Authentication and Authorization Service (JAAS) API to control security programmatically.

- *Transaction managers that interact with JDBC drivers and resource adapters.* Transaction management services are available to classes through the Java Transaction (JTA) API.

J2EE Enterprise Application Packaging and Deployment

You first encountered J2EE packaging in Chapter 13, where you saw that the files that make up Web applications must be gathered for deployment in Web archive (war) files, and that war files are usually contained in enterprise application archive (ear) files for installation into application servers. Figure 14-2 shows the structure of an ear file. You can see that a war file is one module in the ear file. EJB jars and client application jars are used when enterprise applications contain EJBs.

The files that compose EJBs are packaged in jar files. Several EJBs may be combined in one jar file. To deploy EJBs, combine one or more or EJBs that are destined to reside on the same EJB container in one EJB jar file. An *EJB jar* is similar to an ordinary jar except that it must contain a deployment descriptor file. One application may have several EJB modules, so an ear can contain several EJB jars. In the production environment, EJBs used by one enterprise application may be loaded into one EJB container or distributed over several EJB containers. EJB containers used by one application may reside on one application server or different servers connected by a network.

Unlike war files, EJB jars cannot be deployed on their own. EJB jars must be contained in an ear file, which can contain a war if the enterprise application has a Web user interface. It may also contain a client application jar if the user interface is a standalone Java application. Client application jars are explained in the section "J2EE Client Applications." Your user interface can be a Web application or a Java application with a Java GUI or even a command-line interface. The ear deployment descriptor lists all the modules contained in the enterprise application.

14

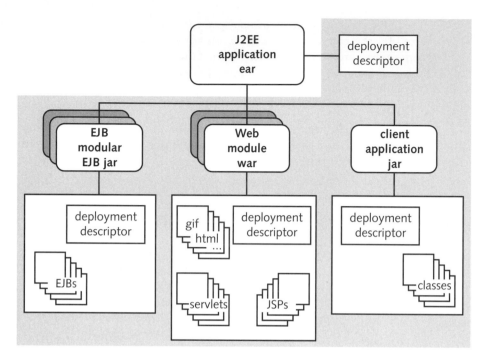

Figure 14-2   J2EE packaging into archive files

When an enterprise application is installed on an application server, it contains more types than the class and interfaces written by the EJB developer. Additional code is required to form the bridge between the elements built by the EJB developer—the bean class, its client interfaces, and the deployment descriptor—and the services of the EJB container in the application server. Deploy code consists of classes generated according to the services requested and characteristics specified in the EJB deployment descriptors. The EJB developer is not responsible for building the deploy code. It is usually generated when the ear is built in the development environment or installed on an application server.

J2EE Defined Roles

The J2EE specification defines roles that companies and individuals may play in the building and managing of an enterprise application. It may help to review these roles with regard to EJBs. The six identified roles are listed here:

- The *J2EE product provider* supplies the implementation of the J2EE platform. For example, if you run your applications on IBM WebSphere Application Server, the J2EE product provider is IBM.

- The *application component provider* is the developer or team that creates the software components, including the EJBs. The target audience for this chapter is programmers who may become component providers by building EJBs or Web components, such as servlets or other classes that are clients of EJBs.

- The *application assembler* is the p... ...mbines components and deployment descriptors into applications. Application assemblers may modify the deployment descriptor for EJBs to levels of service specific to the application. For example, the application assembler may determine transactional requirements for the EJBs. Often the distinction between an application assembler and component provider is very subtle, and these roles tend to merge when one person builds some components and reuses others.

- The *deployer* takes the assembled application and installs it into the production environment. The deployer may override the setting in the EJB deployment descriptors to suit the configuration of the application server. The deployer may set security levels, resolve references to names of resources installed in the application server, and determine the final location of components on different servers in a distributed configuration.

- The *system administrator* configures and runs the application server and has responsibility for day-to-day operation of the server. Generally the system administrator's responsibilities toward installed enterprise applications include troubleshooting and gathering statistics on performance and usage.

- The *tool provider* is the set of software vendors who create the development IDE or handy utilities used in the development and deployment process.

Of course every company has its own distribution of tasks, and often roles are shared or one person performs several roles. However, the J2EE defined roles shed light on the nature of J2EE components. A theme to note is the separation of component provider, application assembler, and deployer. Only the EJB developer writes Java code in EJBs. The developer prepares a preliminary deployment descriptor, but there is lots of scope for the component to be customized when the deployment descriptor is modified by the application assembler and then by the deployer. A second theme to note is that J2EE product and tool providers are considered partners with developers and designers in the building and running of enterprise applications.

EJB Development Environments

To write EJBs, do you need to understand the entire EJB specification and know XML so you can write deployment descriptors? The answer to this question is related to which tools you use to build your EJBs. You can code EJBs and write the deployment descriptors manually, but to do so, you must know many details and write lots of code required by the J2EE specification. The only practical alternative is to use a development environment that has tools specifically designed for building EJBs.

Just as the goal of the J2EE architecture is to simplify the task of developing EJBs by delegating infrastructure concerns to the container, the EJB specification helps tool builders identify steps in the development process that can be automated and delegated to EJB development environments. Such environments generate skeleton code with all the required methods and interfaces, so you can fill in the business logic and direct tools

14

to generate deployable classes. These tools also build the deployment descriptors as you build the beans and then provide editors with helpful GUIs for tailoring deployment descriptors after a bean is built and tested.

Building and Running the EJB Samples

The examples in this chapter were built with IBM WebSphere Studio Application Developer version 5. You first saw Application Developer in Chapter 1 and used it extensively in Chapter 13, but only in this chapter do you start to explore some of its more powerful features. Application Developer makes EJB development surprisingly easy and comes close to automating deployment if the target production server is WebSphere Application Sever. With Application Developer, you can build and export *installed* ears (ear files that contain server-specific deploy code) for WebSphere Application Server and *installable* ears (ear files that contain the information the application server needs to generate deploy code) for other J2EE-compliant application servers.

At appropriate places, this chapter suggests that you complete tutorials to build and test the EJB samples used. The tutorials are included as printable pdf files in the `Tutorials` folder on the CD-ROM that accompanies this book:

- *Tutorial 14-1*: Building a Stateless Session EJB with Application Developer
- *Tutorial 14-2*: Testing an EJB with Application Developer
- *Tutorial 14-3*: Building a J2EE Application Client with Application Developer
- *Tutorial 14-4*: Building a CMP Entity Bean with Application Developer

You can import the completed samples into Application Developer instead of building them from scratch by completing the following tutorial:

- *Tutorial 14-5*: Importing and Exporting EJB Samples with Application Developer

You must decide whether to import the complete sample EJBs or build them from scratch. You cannot do both unless you change the names of all your Application Developer projects. Completing Tutorial 14-5 and then following the instructions in the other tutorials produces name conflicts.

The samples are contained in one enterprise application and packaged in the file `Chapter14.ear` located on the CD in the folder `Data\examples\Chapter14.ear`. You can import this ear into the EJB development environment of your choice, or simply open it with an unzip utility and inspect its contents.

Session EJBs

Now that you understand where EJBs stand in the development process and in the architecture of enterprise application, you can learn what is involved in creating EJBs. All

EJBs implement the interface **javax.ejb.Enterprise Bean**. This discussion starts with the most general purpose type of EJB, the stateless session EJB.

Stateless Session EJBs

Session beans can perform almost any activity, so you can define them to perform almost any of the tasks done by some part of your IT operations. The EJB container controls the lifecycle of session beans. A session bean becomes active when a client sends a request to use it, and all active session beans are associated with a particular client. As its name implies, a stateless session bean stores no information specific to a client from one usage to the next. The rule is that all information required to complete the tasks performed by the bean must be passed as parameters or obtained by methods of the bean as they run.

Because clients can be remote, parameters of EJB methods must be primitive types or serializable objects. Object serialization is covered in Chapter 3 of this book.

The application server may keep a pool of session bean instances available rather than create an instance for each client request and destroy it when it is done. Then any instance may be used by different clients, and one client may use different instances of the same session bean at different times. This is possible because, between method calls, no state information is stored in a stateless session bean.

All session beans must implement the interface **javax.ejb.SessionBean**. Methods defined in the interface are *call-back methods* (methods used by the container and never called directly by the client) that control the lifecycle of the bean. The container may call one of these methods to fulfill a request from the client or for internal purposes, such as memory management.

Interface

javax.ejb.SessionBean

Purpose

This interface contains a set of methods that notify a bean of an impending change in state.

Methods

- **void ejbActivate()**

  The method **ejbActivate** is called when the bean is made active or available for use. In a session bean, there is no need to override this method.

- **void ejbPassivate()**

  The **ejbPassivate** method is called when the bean is about to be swapped out of memory and become unavailable for use. In a stateless session bean, there is no need to override this method.

14

- `void ejbRemove()`

  The `ejbRemove` method effectively deletes the EJB instance.

- `void setSessionContext( SessionContext context )`

  The `setSessionContext` method provides an interface between the bean and the container. `SessionContext` is a subtype of `EJBContext` and inherits methods to provide the bean with information about its security identity and transaction status. A session bean can obtain its object reference from its context.

In addition to implementing `javax.ejb.SessionBean`, a session bean must provide one method the client uses to access a bean instance. This method must have the following signature:

```
void ejbCreate() throws javax.ejb.CreateException;
```

A `create` method in the home interface with the following signature must be associated with the `ejbCreate` method:

```
clientInterface create() throws javax.ejb.CreateException;
```

The return type is the type of the client interface containing business methods of this EJB. Note the naming convention used here: When the bean class has a method beginning with `ejb`, the client interfaces can have a corresponding method with the same name minus the `ejb` prefix.

Here is an overview of the steps required to create a stateless session EJB:

1. Define a class that extends the **SessionBean** interface. For a stateless session bean, default or empty implementations of the four methods are adequate. Add the `ejbCreate` method to the bean class.

2. Then create a home interface that has methods associated with the methods in the **SessionBean** interface. The methods in the home interface have the same name as the methods in the class with the prefix `ejb` dropped. For example, when the client calls **create**, the EJB container calls `ejbCreate`.

3. Add business methods to the session bean class and write implementations of those methods.

4. Add a remote interface and include all the business methods that can be called by remote clients.

5. Write the deployment descriptor.

See the section "Local and Remote Clients" for a more precise definition of the interfaces you can give to EJBs.

The best way to get a feel for building an EJB is to do it. At this point you should complete Tutorial 14-1, "Building a Stateless Session EJB with Application Developer." In this tutorial, you build a stateless session bean called the `BMICalculator`. Regardless of whether you build the `BMICalculator` bean by ~~~~~~~~~ Tutorial 14-1 or import it by completing Tutorial 14-5, you can run it in the test environment of Application Developer. You should also complete Tutorial 14-2, "Testing an EJB with Application Developer."

Stateful Session EJBs

The session beans you have seen so far are stateless objects: Each method performs a self-contained class and stores no information in fields for use by methods called later. Different clients, in any order, can call methods of a stateless session bean, and the container assigns bean instances to clients accordingly. However, sometimes you want to store information between method calls and ensure that the same client receives the same session bean on the first and subsequent method calls. For this purpose, use stateful session beans.

For example, if your EJB is building a financial portfolio for a client, you can provide methods that let the client specify income, investments, debts, and predictable expenses. Other methods may determine financial goals and the level of acceptable risk. You can include these methods in a stateful session bean that builds state data describing the client. Additional methods may suggest investment strategies based on the state data and market indicators. Another example is a shopping application. Your EJB could have a method to create an order for a customer, another method to add an item to the order, and a third method to submit the order when the customer purchases the goods.

Instances of a stateful session bean are tied to one client. The EJB container ensures that the client who originally accessed a bean instance by calling **create** on the home interface has exclusive use of that instance, until the client closes the session by calling **remove** or the bean times out. The container cannot pool instances as it does with stateless session beans, so stateful session beans can impact the application's scalability and performance.

Where to Store State in an Enterprise Application

Some important design issues are raised by the matter of whether to use stateful session beans and where to store state in an enterprise application. First, consider the nature of the state data:

- *Conversational state* is information that must be retained as long as the client is actively interacting with the application. In a Web app, conversational state should live as long as the client continues to return to the Web app and end when the client explicitly logs out, or is inactive until some timeout limit is reached. Information held in stateful session beans should be conversational state.

- *Transactional state* is data that must be permanently recorded when the client activity ends. Transactional state consists of persistent data that is usually stored in databases. Use entity beans to act upon persistent data. In general, holding transactional data in a stateful session bean is not appropriate.

After you have determined that the state is conversational, you should decide where it is best in your application to store state. For example, in Web applications, you can use `javax.servlet.http.HttpSession` objects. See the section "Storing Data in HTTP Sessions" in Chapter 13 for more details. Using an `HttpSession` object has the effect of moving state from the model layer to the controller layer of the MVC design pattern. Doing that may make sense, for example, if the state affects the navigability of the Web app; in such a case, the servlets that make up the controller should have access to it. Non–Web clients should also have a controller layer in the MVC design pattern, and you can always store state in helper classes with instances for each user.

The purpose of this section is not to discourage the use of stateful session beans, but to make you think carefully about whether using them is consistent with the design of your application. State can be stored in a stateful session bean or with the EJB client and passed as arguments to methods of a stateless session bean. Where the state is stored greatly affects the relationship of the EJB and its client and can determine which actually drives the flow of control in your application. In general, make sure that including state data in a stateful session bean reflects the responsibilities of the reusable component the EJB is modeling.

Developing Stateful Session Beans

Building a stateful session bean is much like building a stateless session bean, except the EJB developer has the following extra options and responsibilities:

- Use instance fields of the bean class to store state, just as you do with any ordinary class.

- Mark the bean as stateful in the deployment descriptor.

- Provide at least one `ejbCreate` method. A stateful session bean can have more than one overloaded `ejbCreate` method. Its home interface must have corresponding `create` methods. You can initialize the bean state by passing values as arguments to a `create` method.

- Ensure that the state data is always available when the methods of the EJB are in a ready-to-execute state. Methods are not always ready, because the EJB container can swap EJB instances out of memory to manage the amount of available memory in its JRE. The swap-out process is called *passivation*. Swapping a bean instance back in is called *activation*. The EJB developer may have to supply implementations of `ejbActivate` and `ejbPassivate` methods in the bean. If the bean state consists entirely of serializable data, the default `ejbActivate` and `ejbPassivate` methods are sufficient. But if the state includes transient data and objects, such as connectors to EIS systems or databases, the EJB developer must provide implementations of `ejbPassivate` and `ejbActivate` to save and then restore nonserializable state elements. The container automatically calls these methods.

EJB Clients

Any Java classes can call methods of EJBs. When the calling classes are servlets, they usually belong to a Web app that is a module in the same enterprise application as the EJBs; the Web app is a client of the EJB module(s). EJBs can call methods on instances of other EJBs, so EJB clients may be other EJBs. When one EJB calls methods of another, the EJBs do not have to be packaged in the same EJB jar or deployed to the same EJB container. However, you usually package EJBs that are tightly coupled into the same jar. Like any classes, sets of EJBs are *tightly coupled* when many method calls link them, when they are closely related typically by inheritance, or when they are highly dependent on each other.

 The J2EE version 2.0 specification requires that EJB containers also recognize clients that conform to the CORBA component architecture so EJBs can interoperate with non-Java distributed objects.

Local and Remote Clients

Because EJBs and their clients may be located in different JVMs and on different hosts, calling methods on EJBs using remote method invocation adds considerable overhead and can impact application performance. The amount of impact depends on whether the application server recognizes when a client resides in the same container and optimizes to eliminate the overhead of remote method invocation. To improve application performance, the EJB 2.0 specification adds interfaces to all entity and session beans specifically for use by co-located clients. Thus, there are four rather than two interfaces that you can define for a session or entity bean. These are listed in Figure 14-3 with the full definition of the interfaces they must extend.

Interface	Client Location	EJB Interface (Methods Relating to Primary Keys Are for Entity Beans Only)
| Home | Remote or local | ```java
public interface javax.ejb.EJBHome
        extends java.rmi.Remote
{
    public abstract HomeHandle getHomeHandle()
        throws java.rmi.RemoteException;
    public abstract EJBMetaData getEJBMetaData()
        throws java.rmi.RemoteException;
    public abstract void remove ( Handle handle )
        throws java.rmi.RemoteException,
                java.ejb.RemoveException;
    public abstract void remove ( Object primaryKey )
        throws java.rmi.RemoteException,
                java.ejb.RemoveException;
}
``` |

Figure 14-3   Methods in the client interfaces of an EJB

14
```

Interface	Client Location	EJB Interface (Methods Relating to Primary Keys Are for Entity Beans Only)
| LocalHome | Local only | ```
public interface javax.ejb.EJBLocalHome
{
    public abstract void remove ( Object primaryKey )
        throws RemoveException, EJBException;
}
``` |
| Remote | Remote or local | ```
public interface javax.ejb.EJBObject
        extends java.rmi.Remote
{
    public abstract EJBHome getEJBHome()
        throws java.rmi.RemoteException;
    public abstract Handle getHandle()
        throws java.rmi.RemoteException;
    public abstract void Object getPrimaryKey()
        throws java.rmi.RemoteException;
    public abstract boolean isIdentical( EJBObject obj )
        throws java.rmi.RemoteException;
    public abstract void remove()
        throws java.rmi.RemoteException,
                java.ejb.RemoveException;
}
``` |
| Local | Local only | ```
public interface javax.ejb.EJBLocalObject
{
    public abstract EJBLocalHome getEJBLocalHome()
        throws javax.ejb.EJBException;
    public abstract void Object getPrimaryKey()
        throws javax.ejb.EJBException;
    public abstract boolean isIdentical( EJBObject obj )
        throws javax.ejb.EJBException;
    public abstract void remove()
        throws javax.ejb.EJBException,
                javax.ejb.RemoveException;
}
``` |

Figure 14-3   Methods in the client interfaces of an EJB (continued)

As you can see, the nomenclature of EJBs and their interfaces can be confusing. Subtypes of **EJBObject** and **EJBLocalObject** are the remote client interfaces and local interfaces that contain the business-logic method that the remote and local clients, respectively, can call on the bean instance. These types serve as proxies for the actual bean. Clients use them like object references, but a *proxy* is really an indirect reference supplied by the EJB container because only the container can access a bean instance. In contrast, **Home** and **LocalHome** are the indirect references through which remote and local clients, respectively, operate on the entire bean class.
```

Prior to version 2.0 of the EJB specification session and entity beans had only home and remote interfaces. For compatibility, all clients can still use the home and remote interfaces, regardless of whether they are co-located with the target bean. Only local clients can use the local home and local interfaces. An EJB can have home and remote interfaces, local home and local interfaces, or all four interfaces. Some design considerations concern which interfaces to build:

- On application servers that do not optimize local EJB method calls, using the local home and local interfaces can provide considerable performance improvement.

- When a client uses the local home and local interfaces, it must reside in the same JVM as the EJB. This limits the distribution options for application deployers and may therefore have a potential impact on performance and scalability of client applications.

Consider using local home and local interfaces only when the client and target are EJBs and are always used together.

Note that when clients call methods on the remote interface, the method call uses RMI and all arguments are passed by value. When clients call methods on the local interface, an ordinary Java method call occurs and the usual rules of call by reference apply. Take care if you convert existing EJBs to use the local home and local interfaces when they previously used the home and remote interfaces. Unexpected side effects may indicate that the target EJB altered attributes of objects passed as arguments. When the method call was remote, the changes were lost. But when the method call is local, the changes to arguments of reference types are retained after the method returns.

Writing EJB Clients

The client's first task is to locate the EJB. The J2EE specification states that EJBs are assigned names and these names are bound to a naming service that supports the Java Naming and Directory Interface (JNDI). Usually the JNDI service provided by the application server is used. See Chapter 11 for an introduction to JNDI. The JNDI name is recorded in the deployment descriptor for the EJB. This name is bound to the namespace when the enterprise application is installed in the application server.

The client starts by accessing the JNDI namespace, by instantiating an object of type **javax.naming.InitialContext**. After the client has a JNDI context, it looks up the name by using the JNDI API, and receives an object of type **Object**, so the client must cast it to the home interface type of the bean. For a session bean, the client calls a **create** method to get the remote or local interface. Finally the client can call business methods on the remote or local interface.

Figure 14-4 shows code for a Java client of the BMI calculator EJB you build in Tutorial 14-1. This client is a Java application and uses the home and remote interfaces to access the EJB. Similar code could appear in a servlet or a class that is called by a servlet and would reside in Web container, or in another EJB.

14

If the client class is a command-line program, output to **System.out** is sufficient. A real application that uses EJBs is likely to have a more sophisticated GUI. However, the way the client uses the values returned by the EJB and passes those values to the view layer for presentation is not the concern here. A breakdown of the code follows the figure.

```
package examples.ejbs.clients;
import java.rmi.RemoteException;
import javax.rmi.PortableRemoteObject;
import javax.naming.InitialContext;
import javax.naming.NamingException;
import javax.ejb.CreateException;
import examples.ejbs.BMICalculator;
import examples.ejbs.BMICalculatorHome;
import examples.ejbs.exceptions.InvalidInputException;
public class TestBMICalculator {
public static void main( String [] args ) {
   BMICalculator bmi = null;
   try {
   //  Explicitly set up JNDI context for WebSphere
   //  *  Hashtable env = new Hashtable();
   //  *  env.put( Context.INITIAL_CONTEXT_FACTORY,
   //  *     "com.ibm.websphere.naming." +
   //  *                  "WsnInitialContextFactory" );
   //  *  env.put(Context.PROVIDER_URL,
   //  *     "corbaloc:iiop:localhost:2809" );
   //  * InitialContext ctx = new InitialContext( env );
   // Alternatively use the default initial context
      InitialContext ctx = new InitialContext();
   //
      Object o = ctx.lookup(
         "ejb/BMICalculatorHome" );
      BMICalculatorHome bmiH =
         ( BMICalculatorHome ) PortableRemoteObject.
            narrow( o,
            examples.ejbs.BMICalculatorHome.class);
      bmi = bmiH.create();
   } catch ( NamingException ne ) {
      System.out.println(
        "Cannot locate EJB by name" );
   } catch ( RemoteException ce ) {
      System.out.println(
        "Cannot create EJB instance" );
   } catch ( CreateException ce ) {
      System.out.println(
        "Cannot create EJB instance" );
   }
```

Figure 14-4   Client code for an EJB

```
    if ( bmi == null ) {  ...  ...  ( 0 );
    try {
        System.out.println(
           "Get BMI for 2 Meters and 100 Kilograms" );
        System.out.println( bmi.BMImetric( 2.0, 100.0 ) );
        System.out.println(
           "Get BMI for 2 Meters and -50 Kilograms" );
        System.out.println( bmi.BMImetric( 2.0, -50.0 ) );
    } catch ( RemoteException re ) {
        System.out.println(
           "Can't call method on EJB" );
    } catch ( InvalidInputException ie ) {
        System.out.println( ie.getMessage() );
    }
}
}
```

Figure 14-4   Client code for an EJB (continued)

In this case, the code is in a **main** method of a test program, but you can use similar code in any method of an EJB client class. Before the client can look up the name, it must access the context of the JNDI namespace. The exact code to do that may vary for different JNDI service providers. You may have to supply the type of factory object that builds the JNDI context for the client, the URL of the service provider, and other properties. The lines in comments set properties for the default JNDI context for WebSphere Application Server and are equivalent to using the default constructor with the WebSphere JNDI server.

```
try {
//   Explicitly set up JNDI context for WebSphere
//   *   Hashtable env = new Hashtable();
//   *   env.put( Context.INITIAL_CONTEXT_FACTORY,
//   *       "com.ibm.websphere.naming."
//   *       + "WsnInitialContextFactory" );
//   *   env.put( Context.PROVIDER_URL,
//   *       "corbaloc:iiop:localhost:2809" );
//   * InitialContext ctx = new InitialContext( env );
// Alternatively use the default initial context
    InitialContext ctx = new InitialContext();
//
```

The argument of the JNDI lookup can be any name bound to the JNDI namespace. In this case, `"ejb/BMICalculator"` is the name assigned in the EJB's deployment descriptor. When the client resides in a J2EE container, the name can be a subcontext of **java:com/env**. For example, an EJB can look up another EJB using a name that is local to the enterprise application with a JNDI method call similar to `ctx.lookup("java:com/env/ejb/BMICalculatorHome")`. Names of this format are local to the application and can help reduce naming conflicts.

```
Object o = ctx.lookup(
    "ejb/BMICalculatorHome");
```

The **narrow** method performs what is conceptually a cast from the type **Object** to the type **BMICalculatorHome**. Often a simple cast works, but using **PortableRemoteObject** is recommended to make sure the client always works with the IIOP communications protocol:

```
BMICalculatorHome bmiH =
    ( BMICalculatorHome ) PortableRemoteObject.
        narrow( o,
        examples.ejbs.BMICalculatorHome.class );
```

When the client has the EJB home, it uses a **create** method to get a handle to the remote interface. In this application, a no-argument **create** is sufficient. The **create** method returns the remote interface that the client can use exactly like an object reference to the EJB. The reference actually points to a proxy object that resides on the client side and manages all argument and return value serialization and network communications for the client:

```
    bmi = bmiH.create();
  // handle naming, create, and remote exceptions
}
 if ( bmi == null ) System.exit( 0 );
 try {
    System.out.println(
        "Get BMI for 2 Meters and 100 Kilograms" );
    System.out.println( bmi.BMImetric( 2.0, 100.0 ) );
  // handle remote and application exceptions
  }
```

Exceptions of type **NamingException** can occur when building the JNDI context and during the JNDI lookup. The **create** method can throw an exception of type **CreateException**. **RemoteException** exceptions can also occur in the **create** method of a **Home** interface and when any method of the remote interface is called. Methods of the remote interface can also throw user-defined exceptions, such as **InvalidInputException**:

```
} catch ( NamingException ne ) {
      System.out.println(
        "Cannot locate EJB by name" );
   } catch ( RemoteException ce ) {
      System.out.println(
        "Cannot create EJB instance" );
   } catch ( CreateException ce ) {
      System.out.println(
        "Cannot create EJB instance" );
   }
```

The output produced by running this client is

```
Requesting BMI for 2 Meters and 100 Kilograms
25.0
Requesting BMI for 2 Meters and -50 Kilograms
weight must be a positive number
```

Figure 14-14 in the section "Message Driven Beans" is a listing of a method in an EJB that calls another EJB using the local client interface.

Handling Exceptions in EJB Clients

You may want to review the basics of exception handling before reading this section. Recall that the exceptions you detect in try blocks and handle in catch clauses are instances of the class **Exception** or subclasses of **Exception**. The class **RuntimeException** extends **Exception** to represent exceptions you can catch but which are not specific to application logic. Exceptions that are **Exception** objects but not **RuntimeException** objects are *checked exceptions*. You should define checked exceptions for conditions specific to your application. For example, you may define a class **ItemOutOfStockException** for an online shopping application or class **InsufficientFundsException** for a banking application. If a checked exception might occur while your method is executing, you must do one of the following:

- Catch and handle the exception.

- List the exception in the throws clause of the method.

The exception-handling mechanism extends to EJBs and EJB clients. The EJB container passes exceptions that occur in the EJB, but are not caught, back to the client. Exceptions that your business logic can anticipate and possibly recover from are called *application-level exceptions*. You should define exception classes to encapsulate these conditions in EJBs just as you do in ordinary classes. The exception classes themselves are ordinary classes that extend **Exception**. As with all checked exceptions, if the exception is not handled in the EJB method, it must be listed in the method's throws clause. Also, the exception classes must be packaged in the EJB jar and with the client code so that both the EJB and client can work with instances of the exceptions.

Of course, exceptions that do not relate to application logic can occur. A condition that only the EJB container can detect, such as a problem instantiating a bean or connecting to a database for an entity bean, results in a *system-level exception*. The **EJBException** class extends **RuntimeException**, so it is appropriate for system-level exceptions. The **RemoteException** class extends **Exception** and is therefore a checked exception. The container throws exceptions of type **RemoteException** when the client is remote and of type **EJBException** when the client is local.

You must not list **RemoteException** in the throws clause of a method in your EJB bean class. List **RemoteException** only in the throws clause of the equivalent method in the remote interface. The result may seem like a conundrum in situations where your bean method catches a **RemoteException** exception because it called a method on another EJB. The solution is to rethrow **EJBException**. You may list **EJBException** in the throws clause of the bean method.

It is important to use application-level exceptions as much as possible. Do not use **EJBException** as a catch-all for all exceptions for two reasons:

- System exceptions inform the client only that something went wrong. In contrast, application-level exceptions can be very specific and can give the client all the information necessary to recover.

- The EJB container handles system and application exceptions differently. This difference relates to transactional processing and is explained toward the end of this section.

Five types of application-level exceptions are defined and used by the method of the home and local home client interfaces:

- **javax.ejb.RemoveException**
- **javax.ejb.CreateException**
- **javax.ejb.FinderException** for entity beans only
- **javax.ejb.DuplicateKeyException** for entity beans only
- **javax.ejb.ObjectNotFoundException** for entity beans only

Other exceptions thrown by methods of the client interfaces or the container are listed in Figure 14-3. Even though **RemoteException** is not a subclass of **RunTimeException**, instances of **RemoteException** are treated as system-level exceptions by the EJB container. The EJB specification mandates that the EJB container treats exceptions of types **RemoteException** and **EJBException** the same way.

The type **javax.ejb.EJBException** was introduced in EJB specification 1.1. Prior to the EJB 2.0 specification, all clients were remote and EJBs returned a **java.rmi.RemoteException** exception to all clients to indicate a system-level exception. Throwing a **RemoteException** exception in a bean method is still supported by J2EE-compliant application servers, but it is a deprecated practice.

The difference between system-level exceptions and application-level exceptions is in the way the EJB container handles the exception before passing it back to the client:

- EJB containers take no action on an application-level exception except to pass the exception directly to the client. The application code and client are responsible for recovery. If a transaction is active, the EJB container leaves it active, so the application code must decide whether to ask for a transaction rollback or to complete any remaining operations so the transaction can be committed. The client can base the decision on the condition encapsulated in the exception.

- EJB containers act on system-level exceptions before passing them back to the client. The container logs the exception so the application server administrator has a record in the server log files. If a transaction is active and being managed by the container, the container rolls the transaction back. To the client, the result is as though none of the operations since the start of the transaction occurred. The container also discards the bean instance because it is no longer operational. The client cannot continue to use the bean.

To understand the relationship between exceptions and transactions further, see the section "EJB Transactional Characteristics."

J2EE Client Applications

EJB client applications differ, depending upon the environment in which they run:

- A servlet or other element in a Web app runs in a Web container provided by the application server. Otherwise, Web clients access EJBs using the RMI/IIOP protocol and must use the home and remote interfaces.

- When one EJB is the client of another, the client and target EJBs run in EJB containers. If they run in the same container or containers in the same JVM, the client EJB can use the local home and local interface, and the method call is an ordinary Java method call. If the EJBs are in different JVMs, the client must use the home and remote interface, and the method call uses the RMI/IIOP protocol.

- Clients can also be standalone Java applications. They may be ordinary J2EE programs or classes that run in J2EE client applications. They access EJBs using the RMI/IIOP protocol and must use the home and remote interfaces.

What is the difference between ordinary J2SE clients and J2EE application clients? Both contain a **main** method and run in a JRE. Both can do considerable processing on the client side, including providing a Java GUI, and therefore can be fat clients. But if you try to call an EJB from an ordinary Java application, you may have trouble setting the classpath or may have difficulties with different versions of class loaders on the client and server side. The first symptoms of trouble are usually baffling exceptions that occur at runtime.

A J2EE client application runs in a lightweight server container and therefore gives the client access to services of the server. If you build your client as a J2EE client, you do not have to add jars supplied by your application server to your classpath. Using a J2EE client can also simplify JNDI lookup by providing the initial context of the server container and making a server API, such as the security API, available to the client.

A J2EE client application can be packaged in the ear file with the Web and EJB modules file that make up the enterprise application. Then the application client is packaged in a jar file and has a deployment descriptor. If you name the main class of the client application in the manifest file of the jar, you can run the client application from the jar.

14

The client application deployment descriptor lists, among other things, all EJB references for the client application. Each *EJB reference* entry declares that the client uses an EJB and specifies the name the client code uses for JNDI lookup and the types of EJB client interfaces. Figure 14-5 is a listing of the client deployment descriptor when you complete Tutorial 14-3 to build a client for the **BMICalculator** bean.

```
<?xml version="1.0" encoding="UTF-8"?>
<!DOCTYPE application-client PUBLIC
    "-//Sun Microsystems, Inc.//DTD J2EE Application Client 1.3//EN"
    "http://java.sun.com/dtd/application-client_1_3.dtd">
<application-client id="Application-client_ID">
   <display-name>Chapter14Client</display-name>
   <ejb-ref id="EjbRef_1046043564778">
     <description></description>
     <ejb-ref-name>ejb/BMICalculator</ejb-ref-name>
     <ejb-ref-type>Session</ejb-ref-type>
     <home>examples.ejbs.BMICalculatorHome</home>
     <remote>examples.ejbs.BMICalculator</remote>
     <ejb-link>Chapter14EJB.jar#BMICalculator</ejb-link>
   </ejb-ref>
</application-client>
```

Figure 14-5   Deployment descriptor for a J2EE client application

You should now complete Tutorial 14-3, "Building a J2EE Client Application with Application Developer," to build a client for the **BMICalculator** bean that you created and tested in the previous tutorials. If you imported the samples by following Tutorial 14-5, you can skip to Step 15 in the tutorial and run the client application that you imported.

ENTITY EJBs

Entity beans represent persistent data. Use entity beans as the interface between Java components and relational or object-oriented databases. Any database management software that supplies JDBC drivers is appropriate. See Chapter 9 for more details on JDBC drivers. Usually, entity beans are used to access relational databases.

You can think of an entity bean as representing a row in a table in a database. The actual mapping can be far more flexible. An entity bean does not have to contain a field for every column in the table and can contain the following:

- Fields for columns that reside in more than one table

- Fields that are composed of multiple columns in the tables

- Fields with values transformed from those in the tables; the simplest transformation is a type conversion

For simplicity, this discussion refers to entity beans as though each bean maps onto one row in one database table.

Many applications can access the ~~~ ~~~~~~ in a database, and the same is true of entity beans. Session bean instances are associated with clients, but entity bean instances are associated with data records in persistent storage. Many clients, even clients from different applications, can access the same entity bean, just as many different applications can use the same database. You should think of an entity bean as the bridge between your application and external resources that manage persistent data.

Because you can do almost any kind of processing in session beans, you can code to the JDBC API and build your persistence layer in session beans. However, a much better approach is to use session beans only for business logic and build your persistence layer out of entity beans. Define session beans for all operations that are interesting to the business logic. Let the session beans be clients of the entity beans. The result is a clear distinction between the model and persistence layers of your application. To reduce the resulting method-call overhead, you may be able to co-locate the session beans with the entity beans that they use. Some architects believe all entity beans should have only the local home and local interfaces and always be accessed though session beans that reside in the same container.

In the original EJB specification, version 1.0, it was optional for EJB containers to support entity beans. Therefore, the first EJB developers often wrapped their database operations in session beans. Although you may encounter such code, and it is allowed by the current EJB specification, using JDBC code in session beans is generally not a best practice.

Sometimes, the distinction between business logic and data manipulation can be subtle. Consider a banking application. If bank accounts are stored in a database table, one account may be represented by an instance of an entity bean called **BankAccount**. How should deposit and withdraw operations be implemented? Because deposit and withdraw are closely tied to the bank account objects, they can be implemented as methods of the **BankAccount** entity bean. However, more may be involved than modifying the bank balance. Perhaps the activity is logged to appear on a monthly statement. Are service charges applied? There may be business rules such as that when a client tries to withdraw a larger amount from one account than its current balance, money to cover the account is automatically transferred from other accounts that the client owns. In a situation like this, it is better to add **deposit** and **withdraw** methods to a session bean and let that session bean be a client to all **BankAccount** and other entity beans involved in the banking operation.

One field in each entity bean must be designated as the *primary key* of the bean. Usually this field maps onto a primary key field in the database table. Every instance of the EJB must have a unique primary key value. The primary key must have a reference type, so each entity bean has an associated primary key class. Very often, the primary key class is a wrapper for a primary type, such as **int**. The container uses the primary key to locate the data when a client requests an entity bean and creates only one bean to represent that data in a Java object.

14

Like session EJBs, entity beans have home and remote interfaces, local home and local interfaces, or both. The home and local home interfaces can have **create** methods and must have at least one finder method. Call a **create** method to insert a new row into the database. Call a *finder* method to retrieve a row that is already stored. A **create** or finder method returns the remote or local interface of a bean instance.

The one mandatory finder method is **findByPrimaryKey**. This method has one argument with the type of the primary key field. The **findByPrimaryKey** method performs a SQL query analogous to the SQL statement:

```
SELECT * FROM TABLE
WHERE primaryKeyField = argumentOfFindermethod
```

You can define more finder methods, called *custom finders*. Each custom finder performs the equivalent of a SQL **SELECT** statement with a customized **WHERE** clause. You can add any finders that are useful for your application. For example, you can define a custom finder for the **BankAccount** entity bean to find all bank accounts with a balance over a parameterized amount as method **findAccountsWithBalanceOver(double amount)**. Finder methods must start with the prefix **find** and are added to the home or local home interface of the bean. If the finder method can retrieve more than one row, its return type is a collection in which each element is a remote or local interface of a bean instance.

To an entity bean, methods that set the values of fields are considered logic. For example, if the **BankAccount** entity bean has a field called **balance**, the remote or local interfaces have the methods **getBalance** and **setBalance**.

All entity beans implement the interface **javax.ejb.EntityBean**. This interface defines callback methods that affect the lifecycle of the bean.

Interface

javax.ejb.EntityBean extends javax.ejb.EnterpriseBean

Purpose

This interface contains a set of methods that notify a bean of an impending change in state. These are lifecycle methods called by the container and never by the client.

Methods

- **void ejbActivate()**

  The method **ejbActivate** is called when the bean is made active or available for use.

- **void ejbPassivate()**

  The method **ejbPassivate** is called when the bean is about to be swapped out of memory and become unavailable for use.

- **void ejbLoad()**

  The method **ejbLoad** is called to load data values from the database into the bean fields.

- **void ejbStore()**

  The method **ejbStore** is called to write data values from fields of the bean into the database.

- **void ejbRemove()**

  The **ejbRemove** method effectively deletes the EJB instance.

- **void setEntityContext(EntityContext *context*)**

  The **setEntityContext** method provides an interface between the bean and the container. **EntityContext** is a subtype of **EJBContext** and inherits methods to provide the bean with information about its security identity and transaction status. An entity bean can obtain its object reference and primary key from its context.

- **void unsetEntityContext(EntityContext *context*)**

  The **unsetEntityContext** method disassociates the bean instance from the context of its container.

In addition to implementing **javax.ejb.EntityBean**, an entity bean must have the method **findByPrimaryKey** and zero or more **ejbCreate** methods. For every **ejbCreate** method, there must be an **ejbPostCreate** method. The **ejbPostCreate** method is called after the new row is inserted into the table to provide an opportunity to reflect relationships between tables and other processing necessary before the bean is made available to clients.

Whether the EJB developer must supply implementations of the methods of the **EntityBean** interface depends upon how the EJB fields are mapped to the database.

14

EJB to Database Schema Mapping

A very large part of designing entity beans is determining the mapping between the fields in the bean to the columns in the database tables. There are three approaches, based on whether the database already exists or you are designing an application from scratch:

- *Top-down* mapping is possible when a new database is required and Java developers are allowed to create databases. Top-down design starts with EJBs and derives a database schema from the EJB object model. This may be a pleasing approach for Java developers, but may not produce a database design that optimizes for performance.

- *Bottom-up* mapping occurs when you have a database and can design your EJBs to match the tables and columns defined in the database schema. This is a tempting solution for data-oriented designers, but may produce a set of EJBs that are awkward for the Java application.

- *Meet-in-the-middle* mapping is the most common solution in practice. Independently design the database schema (or use an existing one) and the object model for your EJBs. Achieve a mapping by applying transformation and conversion functions between the fields of the database and the fields of the beans.

In all cases, the mapping can be straightforward or complex. See the section "Define a Mapping between Java Objects and Data Elements" of Chapter 9 to review some of the issues.

The next major decision is whether to code the mappings and JDBC calls explicitly, or delegate the task to the EJB container. Here, you should be largely influenced by the complexity of the mappings and the capabilities of your application server and developer tools. The EJB specification allows two approaches:

- *Container Managed Persistence (CMP)* involves declaring the mapping between the deployment descriptor and delegating all code generation to the container.

- *Bean Managed Persistence (BMP)* is a do-it-yourself solution in which you implement all methods that operate on the database using the JDBC API.

Often, the demands for high performance are in direct conflict with demand for developer productivity. CMP can be very quick to develop but inefficient at runtime. Usually, BMP is required to achieve satisfactory performance unless the mapping is straightforward. However, CMP is excellent for prototyping and learning about EJBs.

Container Managed Persistence

In CMP, the container is responsible for saving state, including ensuring that values stored in the bean are synchronized with data stored in the database. The developer declares CMP bean fields in the deployment descriptor and sets up the mappings the container uses to find the values in the database. An advantage in this approach is that the bean contains no direct references to the database, tables, or column names. If you change databases or alter the database schema, you modify the deployment descriptors but not the bean itself. Thus, a CMP entity bean can be written independently of the final persistence resource manager.

If you look at the contents of a CMP entity bean class, such as Figure 14-6, you see that the fields are not defined in the class and that the **get** and **set** methods for the fields are abstract. In other words, a CMP entity bean is built as an abstract class. A concrete bean class with fields and concrete **get** and **set** methods is generated as part of the deploy code. The EJB 2.0 specification introduces this *abstract persistence model*. The benefit is that you can write code that refers to fields of the bean class and does not depend on the database schema. This chapter discusses only the EJB 2.0 specification and EJB 2.0 CMP.

Figure 14-6 shows what the bean class for a CMP entity bean looks like, except that exception handling is omitted to simplify the listing.

```
public abstract class BankDes
        implements EntityBean {
    public Integer ejbCreate( Integer id ) {
        setId( id ) ; return null; }
    public void ejbPostCreate( Integer id ) { }
    public abstract Integer getId();
    public abstract void setId( Integer id );
    public abstract double getBalance();
    public abstract void setBalance( double amount );
    public abstract String getOwner();
    public abstract void setOwner( String owner );
    public void setEntityContext( EntityContext ectx ) {};
    public void unsetEntityContext() {};
    public void ejbLoad() {};
    public void ejbStore() {};
    public void ejbActivate() {};
    public void ejbPassivate() {};
    public void ejbRemove() {};
}
```

Figure 14-6   A possible CMP entity bean class definition

Notice that the **FindByPrimaryKey** method is not included in Figure 14-6. The container generates that method in one of the concrete deploy classes. The concrete implementation of a CMP entity bean has the name **Persistence.xxx**, where **xxx** is the name of the entity bean. For example, the container generates the class **Persistence_BankAccountBean** from the **BankAccountBean** class and its deployment descriptor.

 The persistence model for CMP changed radically between the EJB 1.1 and EJB 2.0 specifications. The J2EE specification states that EJB containers must support both the EJB 1.1 CMP and the EJB 2.0 CMP. This is necessary to support the large body of existing EJBs. The deployment descriptor of an EJB jar lists all the EJBs in the jar and for each entity bean, specifies whether it uses the 2.0 or 1.1 persistence model. An enterprise application can contain a mixture of 1.1 and 2.0 entity beans.

In the EJB 1.1 specification, the CMP entity bean class is a concrete class. It includes finder methods, and the query strings in finder methods are SQL statements. Thus, 1.1 CMP beans are tied to the database schema because they refer to actual database field and table names.

As with session EJBs, Application Developer makes building entity beans deceptively easy. Tutorial 14-4, "Building a CMP Entity Bean with Application Developer," walks you through the steps. Complete Tutorial 14-4 now.

Container Managed Relationships

A common problem in managing persistent data is how to handle relationships. For an example, consider financial institutions with which customers may have accounts and

14

that maintain a relational database with a CUSTOMER table and an ACCOUNTS table. The primer "Relational Databases and Structured Query Language" on the CD-ROM explains that the relational database must use a foreign key to model the customer-account relationship. How do you model this relationship with CMP entity beans? If you define independent CMP Customer and Account EJBs, no joins are required but the relationship is lost. Combining the account and customer data into one CMP EJB works, but has a negative impact on performance: A database join operation is required every time the bean is accessed even when only customer or account fields are involved.

The traditional solution is to use BMP and implement the relationship in your code. The abstract persistence model of EJB 2.0 provides an elegant CMP solution: Declare a Container Managed Relationship (CMR) between the beans in the EJB deployment descriptor and leave the rest up to the container. The implementation of CMR is usually more efficient than CMP mappings that involve joins.

CMR is available only with the EJB 2.0 persistence model. CMR is new with the EJB 2.0 specification and was introduced at the same time as the abstract persistence model. Some application servers offered extensions to the EJB 1.1 specification that gave a capability similar to CMR. For example, WebSphere Application Server supports IBM extensions, called associations, between version 1.1 EJBs. Because of CMR and other radical changes in the CMP persistence model, migrating existing EJBs to the 2.0 specification is not a trivial task. It is quite likely that both 1.1 and 2.0 persistence models will be supported for some time.

Only EJBs that reside in the same JVM can participate in a CMR relationship, because the implementation code depends upon local home and local interfaces. Generally that is not a limiting factor because EJBs used in relationships are usually tightly coupled by the business logic. The performance gain in being co-located helps offset the more frequent method calls between the EJBs. Often there is a net performance gain because you can create fine-grained EJB objects rather than coarse-grained objects that link all fields involved in a relationship. For example, you can declare a CMR relationship between fine-grained CMP entity beans Customer and Account. Without CMR, you must create a single coarse-grained Customer bean that includes customer and account information.

One CMR restriction is that you can't provide **set** and **get** methods for relationship fields in the EJB's remote interface. If account is a relationship field in the Customer EJB, you cannot add getAccount and setAccount methods to the remote interface of the Customer EJB because the account field is a reference to a local interface. However, you can get around the restriction by adding methods to the remote interface of the Customer bean. For example, write a getCustomerAccount method that calls **get** methods on the account local interface, builds a simple CustomerAccount JavaBean that contains a copy of all data stored in the account bean, and returns the CustomerAccount object.

A very nice feature of CMR is the ability to delegate the responsibility to maintain referential integrity to the container. Referential integrity applies in a "customer-account" relationship when a business rule states that no account can exist without a customer. If you want the container to delete all accounts for a customer automatically when that customer is deleted, add a **`<cascade delete/>`** tag to the definition of the account that has the customer role in the deployment descriptor.

Figure 14-7 is an excerpt from a deployment descriptor that defines a customer-has-accounts relationship between **Customer** and **Account** beans. The XML tag values are shown in bold.

```
<relationships>
 <ejb-relation>
  <description>Customer has accounts</description>
  <ejb-relation-name>
   Customer-Account
  </ejb-relation-name>
  <ejb-relationship-role
          id="EJBRelationshipRole_1048369151634">
   <ejb-relationship-role-name>
    From many Accounts to one Customer
   </ejb-relationship-role-name>
   <multiplicity>Many</multiplicity>
   <cascade-delete />
   <relationship-role-source>
    <ejb-name>Account</ejb-name>
   </relationship-role-source>
   <cmr-field>
    <cmr-field-name>Customer</cmr-field-name>
   </cmr-field>
  </ejb-relationship-role>
  <ejb-relationship-role
          id="EJBRelationshipRole_1048369322790">
   <ejb-relationship-role-name>
    From Customer to collection of Accounts
   </ejb-relationship-role-name>
   <multiplicity>One</multiplicity>
   <relationship-role-source>
    <ejb-name>Customer</ejb-name>
   </relationship-role-source>
   <cmr-field>
    <cmr-field-name>Accounts</cmr-field-name>
    <cmr-field-type>
     java.util.Collection
    </cmr-field-type>
   </cmr-field>
  </ejb-relationship-role>
 </ejb-relation>
</relationships>
```

Figure 14-7   A CMR relationship defined in a deployment descriptor

14

The relationship defined by the deployment descriptor has the following characteristics:

- The **Account** bean has a field named **customer** and the **Customer** bean has a field named **accounts**, so the relationship is navigable in both directions. You can also define unidirectional relationships.

- One customer may have many accounts. The **<multiplicity>** tags set up the relationship from **Account** to **Customer** as many to one. Therefore, the **Customer.getAccount** method returns a **Collection** object in which each element is an **AccountLocal** reference.

- One account is owned by only one customer. Therefore the **Account. getCustomer** method returns a **CustomerLocal** reference.

EJB Query Language

Enterprise JavaBean Query Language (EJB QL) was introduced in the EJB 2.0 specification to support the abstract persistence model. EJB QL is a language for expressing the equivalent of SQL **SELECT** statements for CMP beans. For example, use EJB QL to define custom finder methods, to navigate relationships, and to retrieve data in methods that you do not expose in the remote or local interface as finders. Just as the container generates the mapping from bean fields to database columns, it also translates from EJB QL to SQL.

The grammar and syntax of EJB QL is based on SQL **SELECT** statements. Most of the keywords, such as **SELECT**, **FROM**, and **WHERE**, are taken from SQL, and you construct queries much like you do in SQL. However, in EJB QL, you select objects or attributes from classes rather than rows and columns from tables. EJB QL does have different operators and constructs from SQL that this chapter cannot describe in detail. Figure 14-8 compares equivalent EJB QL and SQL statements.

EJB QL	SQL
SELECT OBJECT (e) FROM Employee e	SELECT * FROM EMPLOYEE
SELECT OBJECT(si) FROM StockItem AS si WHERE si.price BETWEEN 10 and 100	SELECT * FROM STOCKITEM WERE STOCKITEM.PRICE >= 10 AND STOCKTIEM.PRICE <=100
SELECT DISTINCT w.lastname FROM Winners w WHERE w.lastname LIKE 'Mac%'	SELECT DISTINCT LASTNAME FROM WINNERS WHERE WINNERS.LASTNAME LIKE 'Mac%'

Figure 14-8   Comparing EJB QL and SQL statements

The **AS** clause in EJB QL is optional, but can be helpful because it explicitly shows the assigned variable's name. In SQL and EJB QL, a **SELECT** statement can return objects (whole rows) or specific attributes (columns) extracted from the data. In both languages, a **SELECT** statement can return a single object or multiple objects. In EJB QL, the result is a single bean, or an instance of **java.util.Collection** when the query retrieves several objects. When you use SQL with JDBC, the type of the result is always **java.sql.ResultSet**.

Several shortcomings of FIB QL are removed in version 1.4 of the J2EE specification. Support for an ORDER BY clause and SQL-like functions, such as MAX, COUNT, and SUM, are added to EJB QL. Many application servers support these enhancements in version 1.3 as proprietary extensions to standard EJB QL.

The EJB QL statements for finder methods contain WHERE clauses that depend on method arguments. To parameterize the EJB QL query, use ?1 to represent the first argument, ?2 to represent the second argument, and so on. For example, the custom finder to select a person based on name could be

```
SELECT OBJECT(p) FROM People WHERE p.firstname = ?1 and p.
lastname = ?2
```

You do not write Java code that contains EJB QL, even as the contents of a **String** object. Use EJB QL in deployment descriptors. For example, to add a custom finder method **findSkiTripsByResort** to the **SkiClubInfo** EJB in Tutorial 14-4, add the query stanza in Figure 14-9 to the deployment descriptor of the EJB jar.

```
<entity>
  <ejb-name>SkiClubInfo</ejb-name>
  <!-- ... lines deleted -->
  <query>
    <query-method>
      <method-name>findSkiTripsByResort</method-name>
      <method-params>
        <method-param>java.lang.String</method-param>
      </method-params>
    </query-method>
    <ejb-ql>SELECT OBJECT(t) FROM SKITRIPS AS t
          WHERE t.Resort = ?1
    </ejb-ql>
  </query>
</entity>
```

Figure 14-9   Using EJB QL to define a custom finder method

Bean Managed Persistence

Instead of choosing CMP, where the application server generates most of the code to handle persistence, you can choose BMP and write the code that accesses the database. When you create a BMP entity bean, you still can depend on the EJB container and application server to support connection pooling, transaction management, security, and other services. But in BMP, you code the EJB-to-database mapping and persistence layer logic. Typically, you use the JDBC API in the entity beans to issue SQL queries on the database. Use JDBC exactly as described in Chapter 9.

In contrast to a CMP bean class, a BMP bean class is a concrete class. The fields are declared in the bean class, and the `getter` and `setter` methods are not abstract. For example, the `BankAccount` bean listed in Figure 14-6 is coded as shown in Figure 14-10.

```
public class BankAccountBean implements EntityBean {
   private javax.ejb.EntityContext entityCtx
   private Integer id;
   private double balance
   private String owner;
   public void setEntityContext( EntityContext ectx ) {
      entityContext = ectx; }
   public void unsetEntityContext() {
      entityContext = null; }
   public javax.ejb.EntityContext getEntityContext() {
     return entityCtx; }
   public void ejbLoad() {
      // get primary key from entity context
      // use JDBC to get data from database
      // set field values from the results
   }
   public void ejbStore(){
      // use JDBC to store field values to database
   }
   public void ejbActivate(){
      // code to reinstate transient fields
      // after passivation
   }
   public void ejbPassivate(){
      // code to store transient fields before
      // passivation to allow activation
   }
   public void ejbRemove()
      throws javax.ejb.RemoveException {
      // code to delete the row from the database
   }
   public Integer ejbFindByPrimaryKey(Integer primaryKey)
                throws javax.ejb.FinderException {
      // use JDBC to get data from database
      // set field values from the results
   }
   public Integer ejbCreate( Integer id )
       throws javax.ejb.CreateException {   // code to insert a row in the database
      // code to insert a row in the database
   }
  public void ejbPostCreate( Integer id )
     throws javax.ejb.CreateException {
     // code required to execute after insertion
  }
 public Integer getId() {
    return id; }
```

Figure 14-10   A possible BMP entity bean class definition

```
          void setId( Integer id )}
      this.id = id; }
   public abstract double getBalance() {
      return balance; }
   public void setBalance( double amount )
      balance = amount; }
   public String getOwner() {
      return owner; }
   public abstract void setOwner( String owner ) {
      this.owner = owner; }
}
```

Figure 14-10   A possible BMP entity bean class definition (continued)

Note that there is a lot of code to write for BMP beans. In addition to implementing **create**, **postCreate**, **remove**, and finder methods, you are responsible for the following methods:

- The **ejbActivate** and **ejbPassivate** methods are necessary because the EJB container may swap beans out of memory to conserve space. As with a stateful session bean, you must ensure that the state of a BMP bean is correctly reinstated when the bean is activated. The default **ejbPassivate** and **ejbActivate** methods are adequate for serializable fields, but you may have to write code to store and reinstate transient fields.

- The **ejbLoad** and **ejbStore** methods set the bean's fields from database values and update the database from field values. These two methods keep the bean and database synchronized.

The EJB 2.0 specification describes the sequence and circumstances in which these methods are called, so you have all the information you need to write the persistence logic.

The most compelling reason for choosing BMP is to gain acceptable performance as the application scales to support large numbers of concurrent users. The reality is that BMP is required by the majority of large, heavily used applications because of the following performance problems with CMP:

- EJB containers tend to call **ejbLoad** and **ejbStore** methods every time the bean is accessed, regardless of whether any data needs to be stored or refreshed. Because you write **ejbLoad** and **ejbStore** methods in BMP entity beans, you can fine-tune when they actually access the database.

- The code generated for CMPs that require joins, with the exception of joins for CMR relationships, is usually inefficient. Consider using BMP when you have EJBs that map to more than one table.

- Sometimes CMP cannot generate the required code. It cannot cope with complex or arbitrary SQL statements.

14

- CMP maps only onto databases with JDBC drivers; for other persistent media, you can use BMP and access storage using an API other than JDBC. For example, you can create BMP beans that persist data to XML documents in your file system.

CMP is excellent for prototyping, and you can use it in production if performance is adequate. Most application servers have extensions to the EJB standard or perform optimizations to improve CMP performance, and exploiting CMR may help. However, be prepared to use BMP to achieve high performance and scalability.

MESSAGE-DRIVEN BEANS

One of the main enhancements to the J2EE version 1.3 platform is integration with messaging middleware, also known as message-oriented middleware (MOM). This enhancement in J2EE has three main elements:

- Message-driven beans (MDB) in the EJB 2.0 specification

- The Java Message Service (JMS) specification, a Java architecture and API for messaging. This chapter cannot cover the JMS API apart from what is used by MDB; the primer "Messaging Middleware and the Java Message Service" provides an overview of JMS.

- The requirement that J2EE-compliant application servers provide an IMS messaging service

The fundamental characteristics of messaging middleware are asynchronous send and receive of messages and guaranteed delivery. For additional information on these concepts and on message-oriented middleware, read the primer "Messaging Middleware and the Java Message Service" in the file `Primers\Messaging.pdf` on the CD-ROM that accompanies this book. It explains the traditional role of messaging middleware, and the impact of asynchronous messaging on software design and provides an overview of the JMS architecture.

Messaging is likely to be used increasingly by Java applications because its benefits are compatible with J2EE architectural goals. J2EE messaging provides a standard interface between application components and allows for loose coupling between those components. With J2EE version 1.3, you can do messaging without purchasing any additional software beyond a J2EE-compliant application server.

MDBs have a specific purpose: They receive messages from a JMS messaging service. An MDB is a message consumer that solves the problem of programming for asynchronous receive. Essentially, you delegate that task to the application server. The MDB is an entry point into your application and is activated by the EJB container when a message arrives. You add code to an MDB to extract the body from a message and pass it to your application for processing.

The J2EE intention is that MDBs be used in programs that implement messaging using the J2EE messaging service and JMS API. Use MDBs also if your application uses an external messaging system, such as WebSphere MQ, and your application server is configured to support that messaging system as a resource. When you program messaging in Java, use the JMS API. The message producers for external messaging software can be any clients that the message-oriented middleware supports. Thus, messaging is one way to connect Java applications to the non-Java system.

Figure 14-11 compares the analogous elements of messaging with database manipulation.

Resource Type	J2EE Messaging Service	Relational Database
EJB type	MDB	Entity (CMP or BMP)
Java API	JMS	JDBC
Connection	Listener port for a JMS destination: queue or topic	Database connection from a datasource

Figure 14-11   Comparing relational database and messaging systems

As with all EJBs, you declare many of the characteristics of an MDB in a deployment descriptor rather than set them in lines of code. The deployment descriptor specifies the name and class of the MDB and the destination, as shown in the example listed in Figure 14-12.

```
<ejb-jar id="ejb-jar_ID">
 <display-name>OrderMarketEJB</display-name>
 <enterprise-beans>
  <message-driven id="MessageDriven_1046745579823">
   <ejb-name>OrderMDB</ejb-name>
   <ejb-class>
     com.ibm.ordering.ejb.OrderMDBBean
   </ejb-class>
   <transaction-type>Container</transaction-type>
   <message-driven-destination>
    <destination-type>javax.jms.Queue</destination-type>
   </message-driven-destination>
  </message-driven>
 </enterprise-beans>
</ejb-jar>
```

Figure 14-12   A deployment descriptor that includes one MDB

Unlike session and entity beans, an MDB does not have a client interface because the job of an MDB is to initiate processing in response to an external event. No client or user interface is required. For example, suppose a user purchases goods online and the online shopping program uses JMS to send a message containing a delivery order to the warehouse. Later, the warehouse returns a message saying the delivery is scheduled. The online shopping

14

program updates the order record in persistent storage. Perhaps the user interface of the online shopping program has an option to show the status of an order. The MDB is involved only in the step that receives the message from the warehouse. Figure 14-13 is a diagram of such a situation: The JMS message producer and consumer on the left could be the shopping Web application and on the right could be a warehouse application containing an MDB and session beans activated when a delivery order arrives. Either a simple Java class or a session bean can call the JMS API to become a message producer. The message consumer on the left could be another MDB or a class that uses the JMS API to wait for the response.

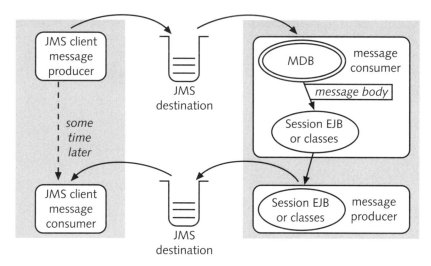

Figure 14-13   A possible scenario that uses MDBs

To create an MDB, you must build the bean class, but no home or local home and no remote or local interfaces. The MDB class must implement `javax.ejb.MessageDrivenBean` and `javax.jms.MessageListener`.

Interface

`javax.ejb.MessageDrivenBean`

Purpose

This interface contains the callback method for an MDB.

Methods

- `void ejbRemove()`

    The `ejbRemove` method effectively deletes the EJB instance.

- void setMessageDrivenContext(MessageDrivenContext context)

  The setMessageDrivenContext method provides an interface between the bean and the container. **MessageDrivenContext** extends **EJBContext** and inherits the method to provide the bean with information about its security identity and transaction status.

An MDB must also provide a **create** method with no arguments:

        void ejbCreate();

Usually, the only method that you must override is the only method in the **javax.jms. MessageListener** interface.

Interface

javax.jms.MessageListener

Purpose

This interface is the method called by the EJB container to consume a message.

Methods

- void onMessage(javax.jms.Message *msg*)

  The container provides an incoming message to the **onMessage** method as an argument of type **Message**. The argument is an instance of a class that implements one of the interfaces that extend **Message**: **BytesMessage**, **MapMessage**, **ObjectMessage**, **StreamMessage**, or **TextMessage**.

14

A good practice is to put minimal processing into the **onMessage** method. Call the JMS API to extract any header fields of interest and determine the type of the message. Then pass that message to another component, such as a stateless session bean, to perform the processing. Figure 14-14 shows a simple **onMessage** method that passes a text message to a co-located stateless session bean.

Caution

The role of MDB will expand in future versions of J2EE. J2EE version 1.4 extends MDB to support kinds of messaging services other than JMS services. Future extensions to the J2EE connector architecture (J2C), described in Appendix A, will make it possible for EIS systems to send messages to Java enterprise applications through MDB.

```
public void onMessage( javax.jms.Message msg ) {
   String textStr = "";
   try {
      TextMessage txt = ( TextMessage ) msg;
      textStr = txt.getText();
      System.out.println( textStr );
   } catch( ClassCastException cce ) {
      System.out.println( "Message of wrong type" );
   } catch( JMSException jmse ) {
      System.out.println( "Cannot extract text" );
   }
   try {
      InitialContext ctx = new InitialContext();
      TextProcessorLocalHome tplh  =
         ( TextProcessorLocalHome ) ctx.lookup(
         "java:comp/env/ejb/TextProcessor" );
      TextProcessor tp = tplh.create();
      tp.process( textStr );
   } catch( NamingException ne ) {
       System.out.println(
         "Cannot find TextProcessorLocalHome" );
   } catch( CreateException ce ) {
      System.out.println(
         "Cannot create TextProcessor" );
   } catch( EJBException ee ) {
      System.out.println(
         "Cannot process text" )
   }
}
```

Figure 14-14   An MDB **onMessage** method that calls a stateless session EJB

EJB Transactional Characteristics

One of the most powerful features of EJB containers is the support they provide for transactions. Before reading this section, you should understand what a transaction is and may benefit from reviewing the section of Chapter 9, "Design Your Application in Terms of Transactions." Briefly, the goal of transactional processing is to ensure that any state that outlives execution of any part of the application is always consistent with the state of the business being modeled. Transactional state refers not only to information in databases but also to the state of other enterprise resources. For example, messages on JMS destination are included in transactional state. Transactional state does not include conversational state, or information temporarily remembered to provide continuity in an interaction with a user. For example, in an online shopping application, the conversational state may keep track of a customer's movements through the virtual store, while the transactional state may include the database entries recording the customer's purchase order.

First, you add transactional management to your application by identifying logical units of work. Then you design methods so that calling the method corresponds to the start of a logical unit of work and the method returns when the logical unit of work is complete. For example, purchasing an item can be a logical unit of work and the task of a method.

The EJB specification gives you options for defining transactions:

- *Container managed transactions (CMT)*: You can declare transactional characteristics of methods in session beans, entity beans, and MDBs in the deployment descriptor. Then you can leave transaction management to the EJB container. In general, EJB containers provide efficient and robust transaction managers, and you should use this option whenever possible. This section of this chapter discusses only CMT in detail.

- *Bean managed transactions (BMT)*: For session beans and MDBs, you can elect to include code to begin, commit, and roll back transactions in your methods. Use JNDI lookup to acquire an object of type `javax.transaction`. `UserTransaction` and manipulate it by calling methods on the `UserTransaction` object such as `begin`, `commit`, `rollback`, and `getStatus`. You cannot use BMT for entity beans. For entity beans, JDBC drivers have a system-level interface with the application server through which the EJB container and database-management software coordinate transaction management. Allowing BMT for entity beans would bypass the EJB container's role and compromise transaction management.

- *Client demarked transactions*: The J2EE specification lets EJB clients create `UserTransaction` objects and use them to manage the transaction context within which EJB methods run. However, this approach is not recommended because it gives the client inappropriate responsibilities and the power to undermine the intended transactional characteristics of the EJBs.

The trick with transactions is identifying their boundaries—when they should start and stop. In CMT, the container can automatically start a transaction when the method is called and commit the transaction when the method returns successfully. If the method terminates prematurely due to a system-level exception, the container can roll back the transaction. A recommended technique is to introduce a layer of stateless session beans with methods that map onto logical units of work in the business activities your application performs.

Chapter 9 of this book explained the effect of transaction commit and rollback on a database. For messaging software, committing a message-send operation makes the message in a JMS destination available for a consumer to read. When a transaction that sends a message rolls back, it removes the message from the JMS destination before the consumer can read it. When a transaction that consumes a message is rolled back, the message is returned to the JMS destination. There are three points to note about transactions in MDB:

- The producer and consumer of the same message cannot take part in the same transaction. No transactional context covers the time messages sit in

JMS destinations. For a message producer, the transaction ends with the message stored in the JMS destination. For a message consumer, the transaction starts when the message is received from the JMS destination.

- If the MDB **onMessage** method runs in a transaction, the container starts the transaction and then calls the **onMessage** method. All methods called by **onMessage** can be contained in the same transaction, including producing a reply message.

- Take care if the reason an MDB transaction rolled back is related to the data in the message. When the message returns to the queue, it becomes available for redelivery. To prevent an endless loop in which the same message is consumed but rolled back onto the queue, include a stanza in the deployment descriptor to limit the number of tries at consuming any one message. Then the container can discard the message after the specified number of read attempts and record the fact in a log that is available to the server administrator.

EJB Transaction Levels

What happens when one EJB method calls another EJB method? If they both are transactional, which method's call and return maps onto the start and end of the transaction? The answer is that a transaction is not a simple on/off switch. There are six transactional levels, listed in Figure 14-15, and the level determines whether and how transactions are propagated down the call stack.

Transactional Level	Description
Required	Set the transactional level to **Required** to specify that the method must run in a transaction. If the method is called within the context of an existing transaction, that transactional context is used by this method. If there is no existing transaction, the container starts a new one.
RequiresNew	Set the transactional level to **RequiresNew** to specify that the method must run in a transaction and that the transaction must start with this method. An existing transactional context must not be used. J2EE does not support nested transactions, so the existing transaction is suspended. The container starts a new transaction and either commits it or rolls it back before control returns to the calling method. Then the suspended transaction resumes.
Mandatory	Set the transactional level to **Mandatory** to specify that the method must run in the transactional context of the calling method. If there is no existing transactional context, the container throws an exception of type **javax.transaction.TransactionRequiredException**.
Supports	Set the transactional level to **Supports** to specify that the method can run in the transactional context of the calling method if it is called from within a transaction. The method can run without a transaction if no transaction is active when it is called.

Figure 14-15 Declarable transactional levels of EJBs

Transactional Level	Description
NotSupported	Set the transactional level to **NotSupported** to specify that the method does not run in a transactional context. If the calling method has a transactional context, the existing transaction is suspended and resumes when the current method ends.
Never	Set the transactional level to **Never** to specify that the method must not run in a transactional context. If the calling method has a transactional context, the container throws a system-level exception.

Figure 14-15   Declarable transactional levels of EJBs (continued)

Here is a stanza from a deployment descriptor that sets the transaction attribute for all methods in an EJB named `PurchaseItem` to **Required**:

```
<container-transaction>
   <method>
      <ejb-name>PurchaseItem</ejb-name>
      <method-name>*<method-name>
   </method>
   <trans-attribute>Required</trans-attribute>
</container-transaction>
```

All six transactional levels are allowed on session beans. For CMP entity beans, you can use only **Required**, **RequiresNew**, or **Mandatory**. For MDB, only **Required** and **NotSupported** are allowed.

Consider a couple of examples:

- If you want to enforce the rule that entity beans are available only in a transactional context and that clients can access them only through session beans, you can set the transactional level of the entity beans to **Mandatory** and the transactional level of the session beans that call them to **Required**.

- If you have a session bean that processes messages forwarded to it by several MDBs, you can allow the processing to be transactional on some calls but not transactional on others by setting the session bean transaction level to **Supports**. Then the transactional level of the calling MDB determines whether a transaction is propagated from the MDB's **onMessage** method to the session bean. Set the transactional level of **onMessage** to **Required** to run in a transaction or **NotSupported** for nontransactional processing.

Transactions and Exceptions

The EJB container rolls back an active transaction if a system-level exception occurs, but not if an application-level exception occurs. In CMT, EJBs are not allowed to start and stop transactions, so what does an EJB do if it catches an application-level exception and determines that further processing in the current transaction is futile? It is not sufficient to catch the exception and return. The calling method may continue processing, unaware of the caught and handled exception.

The best that a CMT EJB can do when you want to cancel the current transaction is request that the container roll back the transaction. It does this by calling the method **setRollbackOnly** on its **EJBContext** object. Then the container rolls back the transaction when it ends, instead of committing it. Meanwhile EJB methods on the call stack regain control when the method that called **setRollbackOnly** returns and may continue to do work that will be undone by the transaction rollback. These methods can call the method **getRollbackOnly** on the **EJBContext** object. The **getRollbackOnly** method returns **true** if the transaction has been marked for rollback. The EJB may be coded to execute statements only when **getRollbackOnly** returns **false**.

Local and Global Transactions

One of the most powerful features of EJB containers is their ability to commit or roll back transactions that involve more than one resource manager.

Local transactions are adequate when EJBs use only one resource manager, such as a database or messaging service. In local transactions, the transaction manager that comes with the resource software performs transaction commit and rollback. The term *local* refers to the fact that the transaction management is local to the resource.

In contrast, *global* transaction management is common to all participating resources. The resource managers must let the application server coordinate commits or rollbacks using a process called *two-phase commit*. Two-phase commit for relational databases is described in Chapter 9 in the section "Distributed Transactions." A *distributed transaction* is a global transaction and is not restricted to RDBM systems. Any resource manager that has a driver or resource adapter that supports the Java Transaction Service (JTS) can participate in global transactions.

For an example of a global transaction, assume an MDB consumes a message from a JMS destination and can call other EJBs that write data from the message into a database. The message read and database write can occur in one global transaction. If the database fails and the transaction must be rolled back, the message returns to the queue and the database is unchanged so all operations within the scope of the transaction are undone.

Global transactions do not totally eliminate the possibility of inconsistent state. One resource management system could fail between the prepare-to-commit and commit steps of two-phase commit, but the likelihood of such a condition is low.

Security is often of paramount importance in enterprise applications, but of little concern to developers. Fortunately this situation is not only acceptable but consistent with the J2EE architecture.

There are many aspects of security, and some fall outside the responsibility of EJB builders. Generally you can assume that if your EJB has been called, the user has passed security checks for access to the enterprise application.

However, selective access to the functionality of EJBs is an aspect of security that EJB developers must consider. For example, an online shopping application may let registered customers buy items. But only employees can query the quantity of an item in stock, and only managers can order new stock.

Role-Based Security

The J2EE security model is based on the concept of *roles*. For example, customer, employee, and manager are roles you can assign to individuals or groups of users. You can give each role access privileges to components in your application. For example, if Thomas is an employee and an employee can query the quantity of an item in stock, Thomas can query the quantity of an item in stock. However, Thomas cannot order new stock unless he is a manager. In the relationships Thomas-to-employee and employee-to-query, the role employee gives Thomas the authority to issue the query.

The main security element of application design is identifying the roles to be recognized by the application, and determining which roles have access to which EJB methods. Role-based security can be applied to entire EJBs or to individual methods. EJB developers are not responsible for user *authentication* (verifying the user's identity by performing a password or certificate check), or *authorization* (mapping the user to a role); those tasks are performed by the application server or server administrator. The EJB developer or application developer deals only with security roles.

The concept of passing security roles down the call stack as EJB methods call other EJB methods is called *delegation*. An EJB can accept the delegated role, but does not have to. For example, it may make more sense for an EJB to access a database or other resource with some reserved identity than to grant database access roles set up for end users. For any EJB method, you can specify one of the two following options:

- Run with the privileges of an adopted security role.
- Run with the role delegated from the caller.

As with persistence mapping and transaction management, you can delegate security to the EJB container and application server, or program it. Using the security service of the container is recommended.

14

To add security declaratively to an EJB method, you add a stanza's deployment descriptor for the EJB jar. A complete list of options and syntax of the security tags is beyond the scope of this chapter, but the following is a short list of tags that declare the security options:

- The `<security-role>` tag defines a logical security role for this application module.

- The `<method-permission>` tag sets a permission for EJB methods. The security role, EJB, and method(s) are specified within the tag. Only clients in the specified role can run the method(s). If you supply the method name with an asterisk (*), the role applies to all methods.

- Within a `<method-permission>` tag, specify `<unchecked>` instead of a role name to turn off role checking for EJB method(s). Then any client can run the specified method(s).

- Within the EJB declaration in the deployment descriptor, insert a `<security-identity>` tag that includes `<use-caller-identity/>` to specify that the EJB method(s) adopt the caller's identity and run in the caller's role. Include `<run-as>` to specify that the EJB method(s) adopt a role specified in the `<run-as>` tag.

- The `<security-role-ref>` tag maps application-specific roles to the global roles known to the application server. This tag introduces another layer of indirection and flexibility: There is a mapping from the user to the global role and then from the global role to the application-specific role.

If you choose to program security, your EJB methods can call two methods of the **EJBContext** interface:

- `isCallerInRole( String roleName )` returns **true** if the caller of the EJB is in the role specified by *roleName*.

- `getCallerPrincipal()` returns an object of type **java.security. Principal** that encapsulates security information about the client.

With programmatic security, you must declare the role you refer to in the deployment descriptor with a `<security-role-ref>` tag. There should be little reason to resort to programmatic security.

The role-based security model has one shortcoming: You cannot selectively grant access to specific instances of EJBs. You can control which roles can call which methods of the **BankAccount** bean, but you cannot use role-based security to ensure that users access only instances of **BankAccount** representing accounts that they own. Your application logic must enforce that business rule.

BEST PRACTICES FOR DESIGNING EJB-BASED APPLICATIONS

Best practices for designing EJB-based applications is a large topic. Clearly the first best practice is to make sure that EJBs are appropriate. Use EJBs when the need for enterprise-level services described at the start of this chapter in the section "Enterprise Programming" justifies the inherent overhead of EJBs.

Some generally accepted best practices for more detailed EJB design are listed here:

- Design EJBs as reusable components. Do not build in assumptions that tie them to one application.

- As much as possible, minimize coupling, or dependencies, between beans. Consider co-locating tightly coupled beans and using local interfaces for interactions among them.

- If the mapping from entity bean to database is simple or uses relationships, use CMP and CMR to develop robust code quickly. Use BMP entity beans for high performance when arbitrary joins or complex SQL queries are involved.

- Do not let non-EJB clients directly access entity beans. Create a layer of session beans that access entity beans. You can enforce this design by giving the entity beans only local client interfaces so only co-located session beans can access them. The session beans then become a session façade layer between application logic and the persistence layer provided by the entity beans.

- Build a session bean to represent each business operation. Finding the right level of granularity can be more of an art than a science, but you can use transaction boundaries as excellent guidelines. If your methods map onto logical units of work, you can easily set transactional requirements in the deployment descriptor.

- Minimize the number of method calls over a remote interface. Rather than call a series of methods to set several individual values, build an object that contains all required information and pass it as a single argument.

- Avoid stateful session beans. They add complexity and hamper scalability because the developer and container must ensure integrity of their states. Often the conversational state can be stored elsewhere and your session beans can be stateless session beans. If you use stateful session beans, be sure to call **remove** on the home interface as soon as you are finished with them.

- The most expensive part of using an EJB can be the JNDI lookup of the home interface. The client code uses the same bean repeatedly; cache the home interfaces returned by JNDI lookup by storing it where the client can extract it for reuse.

- Unless you have a good reason to do otherwise, let the EJB container manage transactions and security. The container usually performs these services efficiently, and programming for a comparable level of transaction and security support can be difficult.

14

CHAPTER SUMMARY

❑ EJBs are distributable server-side components that run in EJB containers provided by J2EE-compliant application servers.

❑ The EJB specification is one of many specifications that make up the Java 2 enterprise platform (J2EE). EJBs are always packaged in J2EE enterprise applications.

❑ EJBs bring considerable overhead and are thus usually used in large-scale or mission-critical enterprise applications where services, most notably transactions and security, of the EJB container and application server are required.

❑ Session EJBs can do general purpose processing. They are associated with the client that calls them. Stateful session EJBs retain conversational state between method calls and are used by only one client. Stateless session beans can be shared among clients.

❑ Entity beans represent persistent data, usually extracted from relational databases. All entity bean instances have a unique primary key.

❑ Entity beans can be designed for container-managed persistence (CMP) or bean-managed persistence (BMP). In CMP, you declare the mapping of fields in the bean to columns in database tables and let the container do the rest. BMP is a do-it-yourself option.

❑ You can model relationships in CMP entity beans using container-managed relationships (CMR).

❑ EJB QL is a SQL-like language for writing database queries in terms of CMP bean classes and fields.

❑ EJBs have a pair of interfaces—LocalHome and Local—used by clients that reside in the same JVM, and a different pair of client interfaces—Home and Remote—that all clients can use. A remote EJB call uses the RMI over IIOP (RMI/IIOP) communication protocol.

❑ EJB clients locate bean instances by looking up the name in a JNDI server. The lookup returns a Home or LocalHome interface, and the client gets the Remote or Local interface by calling a method on the home. Clients call business methods on the remote or local interface.

❑ Clients can access instances of EJBs by calling the **create** method on the Home or LocalHome interfaces. For an entity bean, the **create** method inserts new records into the database; the method **findByPrimaryKey** or a custom finder returns bean instances that represent existing data.

❑ Define and use application-level exception classes to encapsulate anticipated problem conditions. The EJB container returns these exceptions to the client without rolling back an active transaction.

~~Message-driven beans (MDB)~~ are consumers of messages from JMS service providers. They are entry points into an enterprise application and do not have clients.

❑ All EJBs can run in a transactional context. You can program transactions or use the transaction manager built into the EJB container.

❑ Container managed transactions can be local (one-phase commit) or global (two-phase commit). Global transactions can span multiple persistence resources.

❑ The transaction level set on each method controls whether transactions are propagated down the call stack.

❑ Security is also programmable, but is usually left to the EJB container.

❑ There are a number of Web-recognized design patterns and best practices for EJBs. One of the most popular is to create a façade of session beans in front of all entity beans.

REVIEW QUESTIONS

1. Which of the following types of EJBs can have both local and remote client interfaces? Select all that apply.

    a. stateless session beans

    b. stateful session beans

    c. CMP entity beans

    d. BMP entity beans

    e. message-driven beans

2. Can the code in EJB methods spawn threads? Select the best answer.

    a. Yes, for stateless session beans only.

    b. No, because the container manages concurrent use.

    c. No, because all client access to EJBs is automatically synchronized.

    d. Yes, for MDBs only.

    e. No, except that entity beans can create and start threads when the database isolation level is set to serializable.

3. Which of the following characteristics of entity EJBs are declared in the deployment descriptor? Select all that apply.

    a. the type of fields in a CMP entity bean

    b. the type of fields in a BMP entity bean

    c. the type of the database driver

    d. the name of the database, tables, and columns used by the EJBs

    e. whether transactions are subject to one-phase or two-phase commit

14

4. Which of the following are good reasons for including EJBs in your application design? Select all that apply.

   a. because clients of your components may be a mixture of Web applications, Java applications, and other types of programs

   b. for transactional integrity of all database operations

   c. to fine tune code to optimize for high performance

   d. to leverage application server support for failover and scalability

   e. because your application components may be dispersed over a network

5. What is the effect when the following **main** method in an EJB client runs? (Assume **Trader** is a stateless session EJB loaded that is running on an application server, that its method **buyStock** is used correctly in this code, and unqualified names are resolved by import statements.)

```
public static void main(String[] args) {
   try {
      TraderHome tradeHome;
      Trader trade;
      Context initialContext = new InitialContext();
      TraderHome tradeHome = initialContext.lookup(
         "ejb/TraderHome" );
      trade = traderHome.create();
      if ( trade.buyStock( "PRQ", 3 ) ) {
         System.out.println( "trade successful" );
      } else {
         System.out.println( "trade not completed" );
      }
   } catch ( NamingException nameEx ) {
      nameEx.printStackTrace();
   } catch ( CreateException createEx ) {
      createEx.printStackTrace();
   } catch( RemoteException remoteEx ) {
      remoteEx.printStackTrace();
   }
}
```

   a. Compilation reports an error because the catch statement for the **RemoteException** exception is not reachable.

   b. The code compiles and runs, and the output is either **transaction successful** or **trade not completed**.

   c. The code compiles but throws a **NamingException** exception because the argument of lookup should be **"java:comp/env/ejb/TraderHome"**.

   d. The compilation reports an error that it cannot convert from **Object** to **TraderHome**.

   e. Compilation reports an error because you cannot perform JNDI lookup on a default instance of **InitialContext** created with a default constructor.

6. Which of the following are optional in an ear? Select all that apply.

   a. a deployment descriptor

   b. one or more EJB jar files

   c. a war file

   d. a client application jar file

   e. source for all executable classes

7. Which of the following statements describe good design practices for EJBs? Select all that apply.

   a. Build value objects to use as arguments and return types to reduce remote method calls.

   b. Use BMP for finer-grained transaction boundaries than CMP allows.

   c. Use CMR for efficient fine-grained related objects.

   d. Make your JSPs clients of MDBs.

   e. Create a layer of session beans between entity beans and non-EJB clients.

   f. Create a layer of session beans that model business operations.

   g. Program security using the JAAS API for greater efficiency than delegating to the server.

   h. If EJB A calls method b on EJB B, set the transaction on B.b to RequiresNew to nest the transactions.

   i. When the client is a Web application, use a stateful session bean to hold conversational state rather than an HttpSession object.

   j. When two EJBs are highly co-dependent, co-locate them and provide local interfaces for efficient local method calls.

8. Fill in the code as indicated by comments in the following method from an EJB that calls a method on another EJB using the local client interfaces:

```
public void createAccount(String accountId) {
   InitialContext context;
   AccountLocalHome AccountHome;
   AccountLocal account;
   String beanName = "java:comp/env/ejb/Account";
   try {
      // insert lines here to access Account entity bean
      // Primary key is a string holding accountId
      // insert a new Account record into database
   }
   catch ( /* insert exception type */ e ) {
      throw new AccountOpeningException(
         "Cannot open account" );
   }
```

14

```
        catch ( /* insert exception type */ e )
            throw new AccountOpeningException(
                "Cannot open account" );
        }
        account.setLimit( 1000.00 );
        account.setOwner( "Joy McAlison" );
        }
```

9. Consider the following scenario:

A column in a database table named PRICE has value 150 and is accessed by a method b of entity bean B. Method b has transaction level **RequiresNew**. Session bean A has method a with transaction level **Required**.

1) The client calls method a.

2) Method a calls method b. The method sets the value of PRICE to 200 and returns.

3) A system-level exception occurs before a completes. Method a catches the exception and handles it by printing a message.

4) Method a completes.

What is the final value of the column price?

a. 150

b. 200

c. null

d. uncertain—it depends upon the isolation level of the database table and row

10. If EJB A calls EJB B, and B is an entity bean that uses a database, which of the following must be specified in the deployment descriptor? Select all that apply.

a. the name of EJB A for JNDI lookup

b. the name of EJB B for JNDI lookup

c. the names of the methods in the remote or local interface of B that A calls

d. the names of the methods in the remote interface of A that the client application can call

e. the JNDI name of the datasource used by B

f. the name of the EJB reference in A to B

g. the names of the fields in B that map onto columns in the database

h. the role for principals that can call the methods of A

PROGRAMMING EXERCISES

Discovery

1. Study the SkiClub example Web app used in Chapter 13. It has virtually no model layer and uses the SkiClubDB class to perform all database operations. Redesign

1. ......uu application to have the same functionality as the example Web app, but build a model layer as a set of EJBs. The `SkiClubDB` class should be completely replaced by entity beans with a session bean façade. For the exercise, you are not expected to build a working enterprise application. Produce a design that uses the supplied user interface and the `MEMBERS`, `BOOKINGS`, and `SKITRIPS` tables in the `SKICLUB` database. Create a document that lists

   ❑ The name and type (session or entity) of each EJB with a one-sentence description of its purpose.

   ❑ The fields and methods in each client interface of each EJB.

   ❑ What servlets or other classes are clients of which EJBs (a diagram may show this best)

   ❑ Any helper classes that call EJBs, are passed as arguments, or are used as return types, such as `ClubMember`

2. If you have a suitable development environment, build and test a stateless session EJB that provides quotes for stocks. The EJB should have one method, `getQuote`, that takes as input the stock symbol as a string and returns a currency value formatted as a string. Because you do not have access to real stock prices, base the return values on random numbers in the range $0.00 to $200.00. For business logic, check that the input symbol contains exactly three characters and starts with a letter. If the input is not valid based on these criteria, throw an exception of type `InvalidStockSymbol`. Create a client application and test with a variety of stock symbols, including at least one invalid stock symbol.

   Optional extension:

   Because the quotes given are random numbers, the quote for one symbol may fluctuate wildly from one quote to the next. Write a variation or the EJB that is a stateful session bean. This bean stores as state data the symbol input on each call of `getQuote` and the last value quoted for that stock. If the client asks for the same symbol a second or subsequent time, generate a new value that is within 10 percent of the last value quoted.

3. Use Application Developer or your IDE of choice to build a CMP entity bean that accesses the `MEMBERS` table in the `SKICLUB` database. This database is used in Chapter 9 and 13, and the files for building the database are included in the examples for those chapters. Write and test that a client can call to

   ❑ Retrieve a club member by ID

   ❑ Update any fields of a member except ID

   ❑ Insert a new member

14

A

JAVA- AND WEB-RELATED TECHNOLOGY

In this chapter you will:

♦ Learn about the Unicode character-encoding scheme of the Java platform

♦ Discover the role of native methods in the Java Native Interface for calling non-Java code

♦ See what services and APIs are provided by the J2EE platform

♦ Be introduced to an emerging paradigm for conducting business over the Web: Web services

♦ Consider some open-source products built upon Java technology: the Apache Jakarta project, Jini, and JUnit

♦ Learn what CORBA is and how it relates to the Java platform

---

The goal of this appendix is to fill some gaps in the coverage of J2SE, list the APIs and services of J2EE, and look at some emerging technologies that build upon Java and the Web. It also introduces a non–Java standard that has greatly influenced the J2EE architecture: CORBA. The discussions are brief and in many instances can only define terms and present the high–level concepts. Many of these technologies are evolving rapidly, and this appendix reflects the state of the art in the middle of 2003.

FEATURES OF THE J2SE PLATFORM

This section overviews two features in J2SE not described in the body of this book: Unicode and the Java Native Interface (JNI).

Unicode

Character-encoding schemes define the mapping from printable characters to unique binary representations. For example, your computer's operating system probably represents "X" in eight bits as `0101 1000`. Unicode is a multibyte character-encoding standard maintained by the Unicode Consortium, which is an organization of major computer software and hardware vendors, research institutions, and interested individuals that operates in cooperation with the International Standards Organization (ISO). The Unicode home URL is `http://www.unicode.org`.

All operating systems and programming languages require a character-encoding scheme and apply various terms such as *code page* to available mappings. The most commonly used character set in the Western world is informally known as Latin-1 and is an 8-bit representation allowing 256 unique characters. The first 128 Latin-1 characters are the ASCII 7-bit characters. Other names for Latin-1 are Unicode Transformation Format (UTF)-8, ISO8859-1, and CP1252 on Windows platforms.

The Java platform is designed for world-wide use. Therefore, it employs a Unicode representation for characters. Unicode characters can take different forms, and Java uses the *canonical form* or UTF-16. In this scheme, one character occupies two bytes, but characters that map onto values above `FFFF` Hex are represented by a two-character escape sequence. In UTF-32, all characters occupy four bytes. As a result, Java internal characters and character-oriented I/O streams can support more than 25 scripts and the principal written languages of the world, including Arabic, Chinese (simplified and traditional characters), Cyrillic (Russian), Greek, Hindi, Japanese, Korean, and many more. (Java byte-oriented I/O streams use UTF-8.)

Like all standards, Unicode evolves as new scripts and characters are added. For example, in 1999 the currency symbol of European Economic Community, € for the Euro, was mapped to hexadecimal value `20ac`.

Even though the Java platform supports Unicode, your computer operating system, keyboard, and display may not. Therefore, the Java language provides an escape sequence notation for Unicode characters: Use \u*dddd* where *d* is a hexadecimal digit. For example, to declare a variable of type `char` to represent the Euro, use

```
char euro = '\u20ac'
```

If you have a file produced by an operating system or software in some encoding scheme other than Latin-1, you can use the `native2ascii` utility supplied with the J2SDK to convert the file to Latin-1. For details see the J2SDK tools documentation. Version 1.4 of the J2SDK added the **java.nio.charset** package to the core API. Classes in this package provide encoders and decoders between character sets.

The Java Native Interface

Sometimes you want to link Java programs to code that resides outside the JRE and is written in a language other than Java, perhaps to integrate your Java application with existing code written in C or C++. You may also want to link to code that accesses a system-specific facility not accessible through the JRE, even though doing so builds a dependence on the native platform into your application. The Java native interface (JNI) is a mechanism for calling code that resides outside the JRE and is based on the Java language feature of *native methods*, which are wrappers for, or interfaces to, code that runs outside the JRE. A native method is declared with the keyword **native**, and has no body, as in

```
static native int doSomething( int arg1, String arg2 );
```

When your programs use JNI indirectly, for example by calling methods of a JDBC type 1, 2, or 3 driver, the JNI aspect has no impact on your code. To use JNI directly, you must write a native method. Here are simplified steps for creating and running a native method that can call a dynamic link library (DLL) of C language functions:

1. Define a class that contains the native method. Add a static initialization block in which you call the method **System.LoadLibrary** to load the DLL. The code may look like the following class:

```
public class NativeExample {
    /**
     * method doSomething is a wrapper for the C function
     * @param int
     * @param String
     * @return The return code is an int
     */
    static native int doSomething( int arg1, String arg2 );
    /**
     * main method tests the native method by passing
     * the command line arguments to the native method
     * @param first arg is a number
     * @param second arg is a string
     */
    public static void main( String [] args ) {
        if ( args.length < 2 ) {
            System.out.println(
                "usage: NativeExample int String" );
            System.exit( 0 );
        }
        int i = Integer.parseInt( args[0] );
        String s = args[1];
        int rc = doSomething( i, s );
        System.out.println(
            "The native method returned " + rc );
    }
```

A

```
/**
 * static initializer block to load FunctionLib.dll
 */
static {
   System.loadLibrary( "FunctionLib" );
}
}
```

2. Compile the class with the **java** command as usual.

```
java NativeExample.java
```

3. Run the **javah** tool that comes with the J2SDK on the class. Specify the option **-jni** to create a C header file containing the required function prototypes.

```
javah -jni NativeExample
```

4. Create a C source file that includes the header produced by the **javah** tool and provides an implementation of the method.

5. Create a DLL from the C source and header files provided by the J2SDK to resolve symbols in the JNI interface. Look for the file **jni.h** and system-specific headers in the subfolder **include** within the **install** folder of the J2SDK. These header files map the C primitive types to C types. For example, a Java argument of type **int** maps to JNI type **jint** and a C **typedef** statement in the JNI header maps **jint** onto a C signed 32-bit integer.

6. Test your Java class:

```
java NativeExample 5 Hello
```

Of course, the full story is more complicated:

- Native methods can throw exceptions. You should explicitly check for exceptions after the JNI call.

- You can pass objects of reference type as arguments of native methods.

- Non-Java code can call methods on Java classes.

See the J2SDK documentation and the tutorial at `http://java.sun.com/docs/books/tutorial/native1.1/` for more details.

J2EE PLATFORM SERVICES

This section lists J2EE services and related APIs that Java programmers can use. Several of these J2EE features are not mentioned in the body of this book:

- *Java Database Connectivity* (JDBC) API is included in J2SE, but the services in the package **javax.sql** depend upon a J2EE-compliant application server. JDBC is the subject of Chapter 9, "Using Relational Databases."

- *Java Transaction Service* (JTS) is the java implementation of Object Transaction Service (OTS), an industry standard for distributed transactions. OTS is introduced in the "CORBA" section of this appendix. The Java Transaction API gives programmers access to this service. See the section "Distributed Transactions" in Chapter 9 for more details.

- *Java Naming and Directory Service* (JNDI) plays two roles in J2EE. One role, that of providing a namespace to which resources can be bound so that Java applications can access resources by name, is introduced in the section "JNDI" of Chapter 11. Chapter 9 explains how Java applications use JNDI to access datasources, and Chapter 14 explains how EJB clients use JNDI to access EJBs.

  The second role of JNDI, to provide a standard way to operate on a directory service, is not covered in the book. A directory service is a hierarchical persistent storage media and is often used to store usernames and passwords, or information about system resources, such as printers. Some general-purpose directory services are Novell Directory Services (NDS), Network Information Services (NIS), Active Directory Services (ADS), and Windows NT Domains. The Lightweight Directory Access Protocol (LDAP), an industry standard, is now the most popular way for JNDI services to access directory services.

- *Java Message Service* (JMS) is an architecture and API for using a messaging service from Java classes. It is new to version 1.3 of J2EE along with Message Driven Beans and support for messaging in J2EE-compliant application servers. For background information on messaging software and an overview of JMS, see the primer "Messaging Middleware and the Java Message Service" in the file \Primers\Messaging.pdf on the CD-ROM that accompanies this book.

- *J2EE Connector Architecture* (J2C) is often called JCA, though that acronym stands for the unrelated Java Cryptography Architecture. J2C is a framework to which Enterprise Information Systems (EIS) resource adapters comply. Resource adapters give Java programs access to legacy databases such as IBM IMS, online transaction processing software such as IBM CICS, and enterprise resource-planning systems such as SAP, JD Edwards, and PeopleSoft. J2C is designed as a common architecture for EIS systems with different natures.

  The resource adapters play a role analogous to that of JDBC drivers for relational databases: They support a standard Java API through which clients of EIS systems can access resources managed by the EIS. The J2C architecture also has some common features with the interface to messaging software: resource adapters provide connection factory objects that build the connections clients use to access resources. EIS systems with very different natures can conform to the J2C architecture, because each EIS provides one or more customized connection factories. J2C defines the framework upon which EIS vendors build resource adapter and specifies the interface between the EIS system and the application server on which the resource adapter is installed. Some, but not all, J2C resource adapters support JTS and therefore can participate in distributed transactions.

A

Version 1.4 of the J2EE specification extends J2C to allow bidirectional communication so EIS systems can initiate work. For example, an EIS can be an EJB client. A new multithreading capability lets resource adapters submit requests for work that the application server manages and runs on a background thread.

- *Java API for XML Parsing* (JAXP) provides an API for parsing, building, and transforming XML documents as described in Chapter 11.

- *Java Mail* is an API for building and sending e-mail from Java classes. The mail APIs are gathered into the packages `javax.mail` and `javax.mail.internet`.

- *Java Activation Framework* (JAF) is used by Java Mail and some other services. You are unlikely to use this API directly.

- *Java Authentication and Authorization Service* (JAAS) provides an API for programmatic access to user authentication and authorization mechanisms of the application server, as described in Chapter 12 in the section "Java Authentication and Authorization Service."

- *RMI-IIOP* is the communication protocol used between J2EE containers. Web containers are introduced in the "Servlets" section of Chapter 13. EJB containers are introduced in the section "What Are EJBs" in Chapter 14. IIOP is CORBA standard communication protocol and is introduced in the "CORBA" section of this appendix. RMI is a pure Java mechanism for Remote Method Invocation described in Chapter 11. Thus, method calls between J2EE containers involve a Java-specific mechanism for passing arguments and returning results or exceptions over an industry-standard line protocol.

- *JavaIDL* provides a way for Java clients to call methods on CORBA objects. See the "CORBA" section of this appendix for more details.

- *Java Management Extensions* (JMX) is a framework for network and application management. Version 1.4 of the J2EE specification introduces the J2EE Management specification, giving developers and tool vendors a standard way of interacting with managed resources. Some application servers, including WebSphere Application Server, already use JavaBean classes, called *MBeans*, based on the JMX framework to manage J2EE containers and provide administrative services. The trend is for more application server vendors to adopt the JMX. The benefit may be more commonality in the administrative interface to different application servers and therefore easier migration from one server product to another. However, the adoption of JMX does not undermine competition between application servers: The J2EE specification leaves plenty of scope for vendors to design J2EE-compliant application servers with different internal architectures and implementations.

TECHNOLOGY THAT BUILDS UPON JAVA AND THE WEB

This section gives an overview of some technologies that have great potential and for which J2EE and the Web provide the foundation.

Web Services

Web services may be the next generation of e-business and the natural successor to Web apps as defined by J2EE. Web services are self-contained business processes that interact with each other using XML and Web standards. A Web service is self-describing, because the definition of a Web service is also a description of how to use it. The service-oriented architecture comprises a cooperating set of technologies for making services available for others to use over the Web and for locating and then using services made available by others.

For example, consider the travel agent who books trips for business travelers. The agent can reserve the flights, a hotel room, and a rental car over the Internet just as any individual can, but can improve business by automating the process. If the airlines, hotel chains, and car-rental companies make reservation services available over the Web and provide interfaces so that these services can be called programmatically, the travel agent can run programs that act as clients, or *consumers*, of the services. The travel agent can build a library of services.

The next problem is how to select from competing services for a particular travel request: for example, to find the cheapest rental car. An enterprising travel agent can create a new service that compares rates by calling several car-rental services. As well as using the new find-cheapest-car service, the travel agent can publish it so that business travelers can find it and become travel agency customers. Thus, the travel agent becomes a service *provider* as well as a service consumer.

The possibilities for Web services are limitless and particularly appealing in business-to-business (B2B) and business-to-customer (B2C) contexts. The basis of Web service technology is a set of XML-based industry standards and universal access to the Internet. Essentially the Web services technology is the set of standard interfaces between the provider, the consumer, and the *broker* through which providers and consumers find each other.

Figure A-1 shows the relationships between the three roles and XML standards most fundamental to Web services:

- The service consumer makes a remote method call on the service provided by the service provider. The format for sending input data to the service and receiving result data is Simple Object Access Protocol (SOAP), an XML format for transmitting messages. In Web services, SOAP identifies the business process that implements the service and carries input and output to and from that process.

A

- The service provider creates a description of the service and instructions for accessing it in Web Services Definition Language (WSDL), an XML format for the file that the service provider makes available to potential consumers, either by giving it directly to them or by publishing the WSDL to a service broker.

- The service consumer can go to a registry and use the Universal Description, Discovery, and Integration (UDDI) interface to find a service by name, by provider's business identity, or by one of many standard classification topologies, such as North American Industry Classification System (NAICS), Standard Industrial Classification (SIG), and GeoWeb Geographic Classification (GGC). UDDI is an XML application for navigating registries of services.

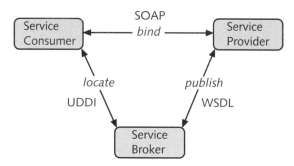

Figure A-1   The Web services architecture

The key point is that the service always resides on a host belonging to the service provider, and the consumer needs only the WSDL file to use the service. The service implementation is hidden, and the clients know only how to create the SOAP message to call it. The consumer builds the SOAP message according to the specification in the WSDL file and binds it to a URL and protocol specified in the WSDL file. WSDL files are split into two parts: One describes the service and its interface; the other gives the binding information for making the call. Usually the protocol of a Web service call is SOAP over HTTP.

The consumer may acquire the WSDL file in a number of ways. The original concept is that independent service brokers maintain registries and consumers use UDDI as the interface for exploring the registry. The registry entries include pointers to the WSDL files for services so consumers can download the WSDL files. Publishers provide the WSDL files to the broker and use UDDI to register their business and business services with the registry.

Alternatives to UDDI registries are emerging, and one of the most promising is based on Web Service Invocation Language (WSIL). The concern about UDDI relates to the dependency upon independent registries. The alternatives are based on direct communication between consumer and provider, or search engines that find services on the Web rather than in a registry.

The set of standards and APIs for web services is evolving and expanding rapidly. New XML applications and infrastructure technology, such as reliable HTTP (HTTPR), are helping resolve issues related to security and reliability. Currently, most commercial Web services are at the proof-of-concept stage, used in-house only, or provide nonsensitive information such as weather reports or stock market quotations.

The next stage is the integration of Web services into processes that link several services, allow for human interaction at specific points, and can encapsulate long-running business activities. Business Process Execution Language (BPEL) or BPEL for Web Services (BPEL4WS) is an XML application for defining business processes that consume and provide multiple services. BPEL depends upon an infrastructure for structuring business flows among activities, ensuring dependability, and the coordinating of the services' outcomes. Web services cannot support transactions with commit and rollback as RDBM systems do, so *compensation pairs* consisting of a service and a compensating service that perform the equivalent undo activities are required.

Interestingly, Web services technology is developed jointly by two traditional competitors in the marketplace: the Java community and Microsoft. The Web Services Interoperability Organization (`http://www.WS-I.com`) is dedicated to ensuring interoperability between the Java- and .NET-based services and to encouraging adoption of Web services technology by the IT industry.

One of the most prominent changes coming in version 1.4 of the J2EE platform is the integration of Web services. The 1.4 J2EE specification mandates that application servers support the WS-I Basic Profile, a specification that ensures interoperability between different implementations of Web services. For Web services developers, the J2EE specification includes

- Java API for XML Remote Procedure Calls (JAX-RPC) for implementing Web services as SOAP over HTTP remote procedure calls

- SOAP with Attachments API for Java (SAAJ) for producing and consuming SOAP messages that have attachments in Multipurpose Internet Mail Extensions (MIME) format

- Java API for XML Registries (JAXR) for interacting with services registries and UDDI servers

Starting in J2EE version 1.4, developers have a standard way of looking up and invoking Web services. The Java Community Process is working on the larger design with Java Specification Request (JSR) 109, entitled "Implementing Enterprise Web Services."

The Apache Jakarta Project

The Apache Software Foundation is a membership-based nonprofit organization that supports the building of open-source projects for the Java platform. Open-source software includes source code so that all technology is exposed and developers can reuse it, adapt it, and build upon it. For example, the IBM HTTP Server product is the Apache Web server with some small extensions.

The Jakarta Project (`http://jakarta.apache.org`) creates and maintains open-source products and makes them available to the public at no charge. The list of Jakarta products is long, but includes the following:

- The Tomcat Web server that supports the latest specifications for servlets and JSPs
- A collection of custom tag libraries for JSPs
- Structs, a framework for building Web applications based on servlets and JSPs and that conform to the Model-View-Controller design pattern
- Other templates and frameworks for building Web applications
- APIs for analyzing `.class` files, text processing, program testing, and much more

Jini

Jini is an open architecture for building network-centric services developed by Sun Microsystems in 1999. The Jini community (`http://www.jini.org`) is building a flexible network architecture that is independent of underlying communications protocols and is highly adaptive to change. Developers using Java technology can use Jini to integrate networked components, applications, and services. The goal of Jini is to provide an infrastructure to support scalable, robust, and secure enterprise services. The goal of the related Jiro project is to provide open-source services for the Jini community. *JavaSpaces* is a technology for sharing Java objects so that Java-based applications and resources can read, write, create, and persistently store objects. JavaSpaces are usually used with Jini.

JUnit and Agile Programming

JUnit is a framework for testing Java classes. Developed by leaders in the Agile programming methodology, JUnit is a unit-test tool that facilitates the building and frequent running of suites of test classes and regression tests. JUnit tools are included in IBM WebSphere Studio Application Developer and can be integrated with other Java development tools, including JBuilder by Borland. JUnit is an open-source project. You can download JUnit from `http://www.junit.org`.

Agile programming is a revolutionary approach to application development with the goal of building applications efficiently and rapidly. It proposes small teams of developers and an informal project-management process that facilitates responsiveness to changing requirements and circumstances. See Agile's manifesto for guidelines on applying the Agile methodology. The manifesto and more information on Agile programming are available at `http://www.agilealliance.com`.

CORBA

This section introduces an industry standard that, rather than being based on Java technology, predates the Java platform and in many ways is a precursor to J2EE: the Common Object Request Broker Architecture (CORBA). CORBA is a standard of the Object Management Group (OMG), an international consortium of software vendors. OMG was founded in 1989 to promote object-oriented technologies. At that time, object-oriented languages were beginning to gain acceptance. Smalltalk was well established, and C++ was relatively new. OMG recognized the need for standardized distributed architecture before J2EE or even Java existed, and in response, produced CORBA.

Taking a look at CORBA is worthwhile, because some of its elements are adopted by J2EE and others have greatly influenced the J2EE architecture. This discussion does not imply that J2EE replaces CORBA. CORBA continues to evolve and is currently at version CORBA 3. The J2EE 1.3 specification added a requirement that EJBs interoperate with CORBA distributed objects, so if anything, J2EE support for CORBA is increasing.

Like J2EE, CORBA is an open specification for an n-tier distributed architecture. Any software vendor could create a product that implements the CORBA specification. One of the more successful products was IBM Component Broker, which has now merged with WebSphere Application Server. CORBA is an ambitious architecture: It is independent of programming languages, operating systems, and hardware platforms. As a result, most products that implement CORBA are complex and application of CORBA is mainly restricted to large and sophisticated development teams.

Some of the key components of CORBA are listed here:

- The *Object Request Broker* (ORB) is the focal point of CORBA. An ORB is a self-running autonomous process. All program objects are associated with an ORB, and several ORBs participate in a distributed architecture. Each ORB can control the lifecycle of objects that it manages. The ORB also constructs method calls from messages received in IDL. It can bind method calls dynamically using the dynamic invocation interface (DII) when the client locates the server through the CORBA naming service. When the client server is fixed by the client code, the ORB can use the static invocation interface (SII).

- *Interface Definition Language* (IDL) is the contract between objects. It looks similar to a programming language except that its specialized purpose is to describe information required to call a method or service and return the result or exception produced. The complication is that IDL is language neutral and mappings are required from IDL to the specific programming languages of client and server objects. For example, IDL, unlike Java, supports multiple inheritance.

- *Internet Inter-Orb Protocol* (IIOP) is the protocol for communication between ORBs. General Inter-Orb Protocol (GIOP) is a collection of message requests an ORB can make over the network. IIOP maps GIOP to TCP/IP so that ORBs can operate over the Internet.

A

Figure A-2 shows at a high level the elements involved in a CORBA remote method call. In this context, the caller is the client object requesting a service of a server object. A stub object receives the call information from the client and passes the information to the ORB. The ORB communicates with the server's ORB, where a skeleton object receives the call information and passes it to the server. The *stub* and *skeleton* are analogous to the stub and skeleton of Java RMI, and both are generated from the IDL that defines the service.

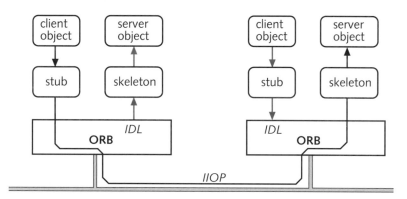

Figure A-2   A CORBA remote method call

CORBA defines many services that ORBs provide for client and server objects. Many CORBA services are analogous to services provided by J2EE containers. For example, ORBs handle concurrency when two clients access the same object at the same time, just as EJB containers manage concurrent access of EJBs. Two of the most notable CORBA services are listed here:

- The *CORBA naming service* is a registry of objects. Clients use it to find objects by name and bind dynamically to the ORB on which the objects reside. It serves the same function in CORBA that JNDI does in J2EE.

- *Object Transaction Service* (OTS) is the CORBA transaction service. It conforms to the Distributed Processing Model (DPM) and XA interface developed by X/Open. XA is also implemented by the two-phase commit model for distributed transactions in Java.

J2EE-compliant application servers can use CORBA services to implement the services required by the J2EE specification. For example, the JNDI service in WebSphere Application Developer is a CORBA naming service.

Index